Rural Economy and
Country Life
in the Medieval West

Rural Economy and Country Life in the Medieval West

by Georges Duby

Translated by Cynthia Postan

UNIVERSITY OF SOUTH CAROLINA PRESS
Columbia SC 29208

© EDWARD ARNOLD (PUBLISHERS) LTD. 1968

Authorized translation from the French
L'Économie Rurale et la Vie des Campagnes dans l'Occident Médiéval

Published by
Aubier, Éditions Montaigne

First Published 1962

Published in Great Britain by Edward Arnold (Publishers) Ltd.

Published in the United States of America by
The University of South Carolina Press, Columbia, S.C., 1968

Library of Congress Catalog Card Number: 68-20530

First Paperback Edition, 1976

Second Printing, 1981

ISBN: 0-87249-347-4

Contents

Contents

Contents

Documents

Contents

Maps

Preface to the French Edition

In the history of the world no civilization appeared to be more completely rural than that of the Middle Ages. We first see it taking shape as the urban scaffolding which the Romans for a while erected amongst the encompassing fields, pastures and woods, was slowly dismantled and at length collapsed. When medieval civilization came to its final fulfilment urban society and culture in all its aspects was utterly absorbed into the life of the countryside. But eventually, as its towns and burgesses gained strength, freed themselves from their rustic yoke and came to dominate the country around them, the medieval world itself expired. If so, it may seem paradoxical that we should know so much about medieval monks and priests and be so familiar with medieval warriors and merchants and yet remain so much in the dark about the countryside itself, and particularly its economic life.

Of course, the medieval peasant had no history. It is not that the framework of his life was, as Spengler presented it, rigid and untouched by the movements which affected the world of court, church and city. It is obvious that the rural framework was also drawn into the movements, although more slowly and with long delays. But if the changes are at first sight so hard to discern, the fault lies with the sources through which we can learn about them. The sources are both uncommunicative and scarce; and as most of them originated outside the rural scene, the picture they present is distorted and blurred. It is therefore no wonder that, deprived of the tools with which to tackle the story of the countryside, the historian should gropingly turn his attention to cloisters, courts, workshops, studios, and urban centres of trade, and that the countryside's past, so badly illuminated by the archives, should still remain unexamined by the enquiring historian.

It is true that nowadays history is not written from documents alone. The history of the medieval peasant and of his lord has to rely more than any other on those relics of the past which complement written sources. It requires the detailed assistance of auxiliary research by the archeologist and the geographer and even the botanist and the soil chemist. It is not possible to refer to the archeology of everyday things without regretting that its study should have been so much neglected in Western Europe. But we must remember that in France, at least, geographers may have contributed to our knowledge of rural life at the time of Charlamagne and St Louis more than have historians in the strict sense of the word. Be that as it may, the relative shortcomings of the documents have meant that progress in medieval agrarian history must depend largely on research conducted, so to speak, at ground level. A researcher must begin by an area covered by a sufficient number of documents; proceed to a searching scrutiny of the landscape as it is today, and the natural conditions which govern peasant activity, climatic features and soil fertility; tramp the countryside and gradually acquire a familiarity and intimacy with it until those hitherto unnoticed features which were so often deeply implanted upon it by the toil of an earlier generation are at last revealed beneath the outward appearance; then tackle the medieval documents and systematically despoil them; reconstruct from them a society with all its ramifications and attempt to isolate the relationships which bound hamlet and village to market town and peasant household to the lord's residence. These methods have the obvious advantage that they draw together all the threads from which are spun landscape, nature and man, and relate all the social groups who, be they local or distant, combined to exploit the soil. For, in the crucial phases of all worthwhile research, it is always necessary to come back to regional studies such as these.

*   *   *

This book is, in fact, written in quite another spirit, with the deliberate aim of a wider synthesis. Its primary objective is to bring together the results of the more fruitful local researches and to try to distil from them lessons from a wider range. It attempts also to escape from the national straitjacket which has for so long imprisoned historical research in Europe and which often keeps it still, willingly or unwillingly, captive. It is now thirty years since Marc Bloch published his great book in which, by the constant use of the comparative method he managed to demonstrate in such a masterly fashion the original character of French rural history.[1]

We owe to this study the lively interest in agrarian history which was then awakened in France and has never since slackened. It is indeed regrettable that similar studies should not exist for other Western countries too. Nevertheless, for those who wish to understand the economy of the medieval countryside and its deeper workings, the actual frontiers of European states are of no significance. On the contrary, they obstruct the real historical perspective. It has to be admitted that attitudes, spawned in the nineteenth century from political divisions, from the particular arrangement of repositories of archives, from different traditions of universities and of learning, and,

[1] May I express here my gratitude to the Marc Bloch Association and to Robert Mandrou, director of the Sixième Section of the École Pratique des Hautes Études, who have given me permission to consult the notes collected by Marc Bloch in the preparation of this book?

above all else, from the influence of a few pioneering scholars who blazed their own trails and thereby led their disciples into divergent paths, have created differences, often purely artificial, in the pictures which various countries now have of their own rural past. These differences have to be erased so that others may become visible, and for this purpose our horizons must be widened. But if we wish to mark out the real boundaries which invest the agrarian practices and the rural economy of the Middle Ages, we must first destroy the arbitrary frontiers. It was only his command of the heights of provincial history that enabled Marc Bloch to sketch out the broad lines of a historical geography of the French countryside. It is our task now to lengthen our sights and to extend our field of observation still further.

It is only to be expected that this wider view will reveal to us not merely the favoured regions already well covered by historical research, but also the contrasting backward sectors. This means that it will suggest new explorations and prepare new itineraries for the scholar. It will also give medievalists in various countries an opportunity to modify their plans for research by reference to results obtained elsewhere and to the methods used in their attainment. To show French research workers how their English colleagues have succeeded in throwing light on the topographical, economic, and demographic aspects of the thirteenth-century manor and to draw their attention to the way in which German historians have recently tackled the study of village lands in the Middle Ages, the retreat of cultivation and the economic changes of which this was the expression, is surely to direct their curiosity and their efforts into channels not hitherto explored in their own country. While conversely, their own excellent work on the colonization of the wastes, and on the lords' exploitation of their powers over men could encourage historians outside France to look again at these problems. The hope of stimulating new individual studies and of thereby gaining knowledge more than justifies this essay in synthesis.

*   *   *

That some of the countries of Western Christianity forming part of medieval civilization are omitted may well cause surprise. My lack of knowledge of the Slav languages and my consequent difficulty in coming to sufficiently intimate terms with the scientific literature of those countries has forced me to exclude Poland and Bohemia, though not without very real regret. But we can at least record that special circumstances have here for the last fifteen years encouraged rapid progress in archeological activities devoted not only to artistic remains, but also to humbler objects. The unusual circumstances are not only the scarcity of written documents, but also a patriotic urge to uncover the very foundations of national origins. The Marxist approach has also encouraged detailed examination of the material conditions of everyday life and the factors of production. Incidentally these studies could provide useful models for those French historians who are interested in the organization of villages, their houses, lands and tools. A whole book could well be devoted to such developments.

The language barrier has also prevented me from including Scandinavia. And here I may point out that the different agrarian systems on the fringes of Western civilisation in the Middle Ages, and the structure of rural life built upon them, has produced peculiarities which go some way to explain why my study has not included Scotland, or the islands of the extreme West, or some Celtic enclaves on the European mainland itself. As for the two Mediterranean peninsulas, Spain and Italy, it is well known that their natural aptitudes, the vicissitudes of history and the economic and social climate which they experienced, placed them in a world totally unlike that of the western countries subjected, to a greater or lesser degree, to Carolingian rule. It seems preferable to consider separately the as yet unfinished outline of their rural societies, at least in the preliminary stages.

There remains France, England and the Empire – a vast enough field in all conscience. To encompass it in one sweep, to combine and compare the principal studies devoted to the economic development of areas so remote from each other and so diverse, demands a tremendous effort, and I am fully aware of the temerity of such a task. It is not easy to free oneself, as one must for such an enterprise, from previous experience and from the myopic habits of vision acquired in examining in detail certain smaller regions which have to be integrated without distortion into the whole. The reader should therefore not be surprised to find in these pages more numerous and more detailed references to peasants and lords in France, and especially in those provinces whose history is familiar to me, i.e. Burgundy, Ile de France and Provence. This is the view of medieval Europe of a Frenchman writing first and foremost for French readers. This is said to forestall criticisms which the imperfections of this essay may justify. The reader will easily discover some local results misinterpreted, some others placed in the wrong perspective and many regional studies not given the full attention which they deserve.

I must add that this area of historical research has seemed to me served by studies which are often still too superficial and too few in number for me to dare to attempt more than an indication of the points of departure for future enquiry. This is why the chronological framework against which my enterprise is set may fit the realities of economic growth less well than it does the present state of documentation, or the current controversies, or the phases into which it is customary to divide the general history of European civilization. It is neatly divided into three sections, one for the Carolingian period, one for the eleventh, twelfth and thirteenth centuries, and one corresponding to the troubled period between 1330 and the beginning of the fifteenth century. A convenient framework this may be, but it can only be provisional – as indeed are all the conclusions of a book which calls on each page for corrections and further advances and whose very purpose is to provoke and to instigate them. I should like it to be considered as the master plan of a vast undertaking, useful for new discovery, but which will be rendered out of date as work progresses. The nature of this undertaking entails a very large bibliographical guide (it will be seen that this, too, accords a privileged place to French research) and many documents, maps, pictures and, especially, original texts, most of which are briefly commented upon. It has seemed, indeed, that direct contact with the materials of a history which is still in the course of construction could provoke ideas, raise questions and invite new answers. The pages which follow need generous margins to provide space for corrections and additions. This book can therefore be best likened to that essential foundation of rural economic history, the manorial inventory: barely will it be completed before its text will be scored through with erasures and corrections. If it is soon replaced by those who use it, it will have achieved its aim.

Plateau de Valensole, July 1961

Preface to the English Edition

This book was written in 1961. It was even then incomplete and recent accretions to historical research have placed in question some of its conclusions. But it appears still too early to put forward a new edition and the text printed here reproduces in its entirety that of the first French edition. However, thanks to three individuals, it has been possible to include certain amendments. Cynthia Postan, who has undertaken the translation, has provided me with the opportunity to remove some errors and obscurities. M. M. Postan, whose studies had already helped me while I was composing this book, has offered me his friendly criticisms. Lastly, Rodney Hilton has reread these pages in English and his suggestions have been invaluable. This is a suitable place to express my gratitude for their help.

October 1966

BOOK I

IX and X Centuries

BOOK I

IX and X Centuries

Introduction

The story of the countryside in western Europe gets suddenly flooded with light in the reign of Charlemagne. Before that time written documents were rare and unrevealing and could throw no more than a few feeble rays into the all-but impenetrable darkness. We have, it is true, one silent witness whose testimony is constantly before our eyes and must not be ignored. I mean, of course, the face of the countryside itself upon which the life of the peasants in the very early Middle Ages left indelible marks visible even today in the topography and vegetation, the pattern of field and path, the external appearance of the village and even in the very houses themselves. But for historical knowledge to be precise and well founded these visible traces of the past must be combined with what we can learn from documents. Only the latter can give us the time sequence we need to keep our generalizations from being too vague. We cannot get the history of rural life into focus without some chronological landmarks: its rhythm is so leisurely that it is essential to chart its rise and fall in detail. Before the year 800 the surviving documents are too few to allow even the broadest outlines to appear. But after that date all is different.

A number of historically significant documents appear in quick succession during what we may call the Carolingian renaissance: the period in the history of the Frankish lands when deliberate efforts were made to give new vigour to the church and the state, from which it was hardly distinguishable, by breathing into them new life, by recreating scholarly institutions and by restoring administrative practices based on the regular use of the written word. The documents also became more durable, for they were all written on that indestructible substance, parchment. Many of these documents have been preserved and their evidence forms the foundation of what we now know of this period and of the conduct of rural life.

However, their number must not be exaggerated: in all there are not

3

more than a few dozen. Furthermore, they were all drawn up either at the court of the King or in the religious communities closest to him, which severely restricts the area they cover. Indeed, outside the Empire there is nothing to dissipate the prevailing obscurity: of the Anglo-Saxon countryside we know no more than what we can glean – and that is very little – from collections of laws and the very few charters which guaranteed the King his rights. Even within the Empire itself huge areas were devoid of all written record. Amongst these were all the southern half of Gaul, incompletely controlled by the Frankish kings and little affected by the revival of letters. Bavaria and the Lombard countries, where the cultural traditions inherited from Roman antiquity remained to some extent alive, were more favoured. However, the region to which the greatest number, as well as the most explicit, of the documents refer was situated between the Rhine and the Loire. It is this region alone that is illuminated at all clearly by the documents. Yet even there we can observe no more than certain limited aspects of rural life, since the evidence relates mostly to the management of the larger landed estates. A very great deal remains uncertain and many questions must remain for ever unanswered.

There is but little hope of further important discoveries of documentary evidence for this period. The archives have given up all their secrets, and new interpretations of texts can hardly be expected to yield much. My task in the section dealing with this early period will therefore be a comparatively simple one. It will be to describe briefly the state of existing knowledge, to make some reflections upon it, and here and there to suggest some hypotheses; to indicate where research could perhaps be pushed a little further and to point out the few problems in which neighbouring disciplines might be able to carry forward the lessons of the documents. These then are the intentions of the following pages.

CHAPTER I

Land and Labour

I. SETTLEMENT OF THE SOIL. SYSTEMS OF PRODUCTION AND ORGANIZATION OF THE VILLAGE LANDS

One fact is outstanding: in the civilization of the ninth and tenth centuries the rural way of life was universal. Entire countries, like England and almost all the Germanic lands, were absolutely without towns. Elsewhere some towns existed: such as the few ancient Roman cities in the south which had not suffered complete dilapidation, or the new townships on trade routes which were making their appearance along the rivers leading to the northern seas. But except for some in Lombardy, these 'towns' appear as minute centres of population, each numbering at most a few hundred permanent inhabitants and deeply immersed in the life of the surrounding countryside. Indeed they could hardly be distinguished from it. Vineyards encircled them; fields penetrated their walls; they were full of cattle, barns and farm labourers. All their inhabitants from the very richest, bishops and even the king himself, to the few specialists, Jewish or Christian, who conducted long-distance trade, remained first and foremost countrymen whose whole life was dominated by the rhythm of the agricultural seasons, who depended for their existence on the produce of the soil, and who drew directly from it their entire worldly wealth. The historian of this period does not need therefore to consider the problem, so pressing in succeeding times, of the relationship between town and country.

Another thing is also certain. It was a countryside created by man around a few fixed points of settlement. Western Europe was peopled by a stable peasantry rooted in its environment. Not that we should picture it as totally immobile. There was still room in rural life for nomadic movements. In high summer cartage and pastoral activities took many peasants to distant places, while others were occupied in gathering the wild products of the woodland, in hunting, in raiding their neighbours, and in some other acti-

---

N.B The detailed subdivisions of the bibliographical section have already indicated the extent of the printed material which supports the different parts of the account which follows, and will enable the reader to carry his interest further. Footnotes to the text give precise references and the figure which follows the author's name is the number given to the work in the bibliography.

vities that were necessary to acquire vital food supplies for survival. Other members of the rural population regularly participated in warlike adventures. However, most of these were only seasonal or part-time nomads. They spent most of their days on land which housed their families and formed part of organized village territories. They give the impression of belonging to villages.

Indeed the countryman's life was very rarely conducted in solitude. Dwelling houses appear to have been close together and very seldom isolated. Clusters of houses were usual. Some historians and geographers (particularly in France where history and geography live together harmoniously to their mutual profit) anxious to draw from the remote past an explanation of the agrarian structure of today, have been able here and there to uncover in early medieval sources different types of settlement, some large villages, others more modest hamlets, contrasting types which doubtless reflected soil conditions as much as different social habits.[1] Déléage's exhaustive work on Burgundian sources shows the pitfalls inherent in these researches, but it also shows the fruitfulness of the ideas.[2] This is one of those fields of study where by drawing on the most varied range of observations it is sometimes possible to illuminate the laconic information provided by the documents. It would be worthwhile to carry these methods still further. But in the present state of researches it merely appears that the village, whatever its size or shape, provided the normal background of human existence. In Saxon England, for instance, the village served as the basis for the levying and collection of taxes. Around these fixed points was laid out the pattern of the cultivated land, and particularly the network of trackways and paths, which appear in the landscape of today as the most tenacious relic of our ancient heritage, the reality which provides the starting point for archeological study of the village territory.

In western Europe, pioneer excavations are under way which will one day help us to know better what medieval rural dwellings were like. Already evidence exists which leads us to believe that, except in the Mediterranean coastal lands where building was in stone, men's habitations in the early, and even the not-so-early, Middle Ages were huts of wattle and daub, short-lived and destructible; even at the beginning of the thirteenth century an English peasant was found guilty of having destroyed the house of his neighbour by merely sawing through the central beam.[3]

However, villages did not change their location readily, and for this there were two reasons. Firstly, because the land on which the village stood was subject to a particular legal status, different from that of the surrounding land,

---

[1] Juillard, 66   [2] Déléage, 218
[3] *Earliest Lincolnshire Assize Rolls, 1202-1209* (ed. E. Stenton), p. 108

and enjoying customary privileges which made its boundaries unalterable.[4] Legal historians have shown that the village was made up of contiguous parcels of land which most Carolingian documents describe by the word *mansus*, and which the peasant dialects of the earliest Middle Ages called variously *meix, Hof, masure, toft*. . . . We understand by this an enclosure, solidly rooted to its site by a permanent barrier such as a palisade or a living hedge, carefully maintained, a protected asylum to which the entry was forbidden and the violation of which was punished by severe penalties: an island of refuge where the occupant was assumed to be the master and at whose threshold communal servitude and the demands of chiefs and lords stopped short. These enclosures provided a haven for possessions, cattle, stocks of food, and sleeping men, protected them against natural and supernatural dangers, and taken together, constituted the kernel of the village, and expressed in terms of land and territory the essence of a society of which the family was the nucleus. Furthermore, it is probable that occupation of such a *manse* carried with it a place in the village community with collective rights over the surrounding fields. By the same token newcomers remained dwellers in a secondary zone of habitations outside the enclosures. Could not these individuals have been the people whom inventories of the ninth century listed as *hôtes*, i.e. 'guests', whose presence was tolerated but who were never wholly integrated into the village group and who did not participate in all their rights?

This strict legal framework, which prevented colonization from taking place by dispersion, also acted as a considerable brake on the removal of the actual dwelling place. Its stability also depended on another factor of an economic nature. The soil which lay nearest to the house and to the stable was especially rich and fertile. By proximity alone the site of peasant settlement fertilized itself: household waste and the domestic animals were sufficient to establish around the dwelling, precisely because it was immovable, a permanent condition of fertility. Moreover, this land, because it was so conveniently placed, could be repeatedly dug over. In no other spot could the natural state of the earth be so profoundly modified to meet the needs of man; the constant manuring and digging created there an artificial soil and raised on it a specialized and particular plant life. Thus each domestic fence enclosed and protected a vegetable garden, an 'allotment' or toft, in other words a continually cultivated plot, where the ground was never left to rest, and where in carefully protected conditions grew tender plants, the herbs and roots of the daily diet, hemp and the vine. These plots were undoubtedly most productive and the atmosphere of garden care which they cast over their surroundings did much to anchor the village to its site.

[4] Saint-Jacob, 173; Bader, 512

Beyond the encircling hedges, nature was also subject to a certain, even if a not very rigorous, discipline, Without the need to tame her, men could win from nature a large part of their subsistence. River, marsh, forest and thicket offered to whoever could take advantage of them, fish, game, honey and many other edible substances in generous measure. It is worth our while examining closely documents of the Carolingian and more recent periods for every clue which will allow us to gauge the part which hunting, fishing and gathering wild foods played in the countryman's activities. We are encouraged to believe that he was as skilled in the use of the hunting spear, the net and the warrener's stick as he was with the plough. In 1180 when Alexander Neckham, an English teacher in the schools of Paris, wrote his treatise *Du Nom des Outils*, he listed nets, lines, and snares for trapping hares and deer amongst the ordinary tools of the peasant household. It is certain that the thinly growing forest of the early Middle Ages, with its numerous clearings, and its varied vegetation ranging from thick woodland to grassy glades, formed an essential background to the domestic economy. Apart from the livelihood that it bestowed generously on foodgatherer and hunter, it furnished the larger domestic animals with their chief sources of nourishment. Sheep and cows grazed there and war- and farm-horses were let loose in it. But above all else the woods were the domain of pigs. In Germania September was known as 'the month of the woods' for then the acorns ripened.[5] Indeed over vast stretches of northern Europe in the ninth century bacon was an essential ingredient in the household economy. Herds of swine yielding both meat and lard formed everywhere the mainstay of every farming system, large and small: in the Salic Law no fewer than sixteen articles were concerned with the theft of pigs. In fact agrarian archeology leads us to suppose that many villages and especially those in the north-west and north-east, in England, Frisia and Saxony, possessed no cultivated lands, apart from the 'tofts'. And in the eleventh century we know of communities in the English fenlands, on the Wash and in the flooded valley of the Saône which lived solely by fishing.[6]

However, because of man's customary eating habits the cultivation of the small plots around the dwelling houses and the quest for the gifts of nature were nearly everywhere allied to the efforts to farm more extensively. We know very little about the food of early medieval man in western Europe outside the monastic communities. Here is an excellent and urgent subject for research upon which further progress of the history of rural economy may well depend. It is clear that at this period not only were men unable to feed themselves on what they found by chance, but they were driven to grow

[5] Timm, 570, p. 51
[6] A village of this kind paid the church at Ely a rent of 27,150 eels. Darby, 47, p. 202.

what custom decreed they should consume. R. Dion has shown how the expansion of winegrowing in Gaul was a direct consequence of the social habits of the nobles, with whom it was a point of honour to drink and to offer their guests none but the best wine. But on a much humbler level also the whole system of agricultural production was organized to fulfil the social requirements which determined eating habits.

References in documents (but we ought, also, as the Poles, for example, have done, to look at the archeological evidence) reveal the universal acceptance of bread as a basic foodstuff, even in the least civilized regions of the Christian world. To prove this here are two quotations, chosen from many others. An edict made in 844 by Charles the Bald in favour of the clergy of Septimania sets out that the bishop could at each stage of his pastoral progress requisition 10 chickens, 50 eggs and 5 sucking pigs – but before all else, 50 loaves: Again, according to a passage in the laws of King Ine an Anglo-Saxon village had to deliver 10 sheep, 10 geese, 20 chickens, 10 cheeses, 10 measures of honey, 5 salmon and 100 eels for royal consumption, but first of all 300 round loaves.[7] It is true these goods were to feed a bishop and a king, and, in a world where social status was primarily expressed in the quality of the food, it would be unwise to assume that bread occupied an equivalent position in the diet of the common people. But everything leads us to suppose that the latter, except perhaps in the northern countries which remained wild and therefore relied on a forest and pastoral existence, consumed even more cereals than the rich. Indeed, all the documents indicate that peas, vetches, beans – the leguminous plants – together with 'herbs' and 'roots', the ancestors of our garden vegetables (the hermits were praised for restricting their diet to these) and of course meat, a most desirable item of consumption from which the clergy ostentatiously abstained, comprised only the *companaticum*, the accompaniment to bread. It was the latter that was the mainstay of existence.

It is reasonably clear that bread was not baked solely from wheat, rye or spelt, but also from other, lesser, cereals, such as barley and even oats, which was eaten as much by humans as by animals. What is less easy to distinguish is in what measure these food grains were consumed in the form of porridge (*bouillie*) or brewed into ale, the commonest beverage throughout north-western Europe. Ale had often the consistency of thick soup and so could be counted perhaps more as a food than a drink. Eleventh-century peasants had to grow cereals even when climatic conditions were not favourable. As arable fields had to be laid out around the villages, the least exposed and most easily worked sites had to be cleared for the purpose, in close proximity to habitations and in the midst of woods and pastures.

[7] Stenton, 232, p. 285

Here and there, in places where the climate allowed grapes to ripen, a few vines were planted for the masters on the most suitable and permanently enclosed plots. Meadows were confined to damper ground, and the hay, together with the grass and rushes which could be gathered in the marshes, provided winter fodder for the cattle. Nevertheless neither vines nor meadows covered more than a very limited part of the cultivated area since the cereal crop was the really important one, and almost the whole of the area given over to agricultural activity was reserved for its culture. These fields had also to be protected against the depredations of animals, both domestic and wild. They can thus be visualized as separated from the uncultivated lands, which were open to pasture, by enclosures which in the country of the Franks seemed generally to have been temporary. In spring as soon as the new grass began to push up and the corn to sprout these mobile barriers made of wooden stakes (the Salic Law laid down penalties for those who stole or burnt them) were erected and signs were put up forbidding shepherds to let their animals stray there. For a season therefore these strips seemed, like the cultivated 'tofts' of the village, to be the territory of individual owners. But after the harvest, signs and fences were removed, and the strips returned for a time to pastoral use, and were reincorporated into the larger areas where access to animals was free.[8] To a greater or lesser extent then, according to the quantity of bread men were used to eating, the arable appeared as a limited and temporary extension of the cultivated 'toft' area and thus private property, at the expense of the wild area which was left to collective use.

Can we ever hope, even in the best documented regions, to plot the portion of village lands occupied by the arable fields? The vocabulary of manorial inventories which P. de Saint-Jacob has examined does not appear capable of revealing much in this respect.[9] The 'agronometric' method proposed by L. Champier would perhaps be more fruitful, especially if certain western village lands described by the more communicative Carolingian documents dealing with estate administration were examined with the help of soil scientists (*pédologues*), botanists and students of rural place-names. What we know now suggests that this area was small everywhere and that a large space was being left to natural vegetation, the forest and pasture, whose presence 'had helped to form this combination of agriculture and animal

[8] On enclosures and signs (*Wiffa*), see *Lex Baiuwariorum* X.15, 16; on the common land (*vaine pâture*) and the need to erect hedges, see *M.G.H. Capitularia Regum Francorum*, I.20, 17. Permanent enclosures sometimes marked the boundaries of the large cleared areas, of which only part was cultivated each year and surrounded at that time by temporary fences. Schröder-Lembke, 231.

[9] Saint-Jacob, 258, pp. 425 *et seq.*; L. Champier, 'Proto-histoire et géographie agraire, Essai de datation des plus anciens terroirs d'Europe occidentale', in *Rhodania*, 1959

husbandry which was the principal feature'[10] of rural economy in the west. It is probable that in many regions natural conditions, recent colonization and perhaps a tardy adoption of a cereal diet, gave pastoral activities a clear preponderance in this combination. This was probably the case over the larger part of England where animals made up the true wealth of peasant and lord alike, particularly in the Highlands and downland regions of Wiltshire, Somerset and the Cotswolds. It was also the case in the woodlands of north-western Germany where a pastoral system predominated and where arable hardly existed. However, the general rule seems to have been an indissoluble marriage between the two.[11] Ploughland and pasture, *ager* and *saltus*, *Allmende* (woods and pastures open to the collective use of the village) and *Gewannen* (the ploughed lands), *gagnage* and *communs*. This union indeed appears constant and fundamental throughout the Middle Ages. What we might describe as three concentric zones formed the picture which the author of *Annales Cameracenses* preserved of his childhood village at the end of the twelfth century – the village enclosures, the *coûtures*, that is the arable, and finally surrounding all, a broad uncultivated belt.[12] These were the three zones in which the effects of man's labour became less and less visible as the distance from the inhabited centre grew greater, but which were of equal importance to him as a means of subsistence.

2. HOW MANY MEN WERE THERE?

We shall have to resign ourselves never to know exactly how many men existed in the framework of these natural conditions which they could so imperfectly utilize. It must be admitted at the start that all attempts at an estimate, however approximate, are impossible. No figure, no matter how crude, can be advanced or sustained. However much we may endeavour to observe and interpret the economy of these early days, any researches are bound to run immediately into the most serious difficulties through their inability to contribute the most essential information about one of the factors – population.

According to the opinion currently held by historians, Carolingian Europe was very lightly populated. This impression is based on England of the late eleventh century, for which time it is possible, with the help of that extraordinary document, the Domesday Book, to make a rough count of heads. The population which we can discern with its aid is far from dense, and nothing leads us to think that it was any denser in the ninth century. We can presume that the northern fringes of Christianity, like Saxony and central

[10] Vidal de la Blache, 'Les genres de vie et la géographie humaine', in *Annales de Géographie*, 1911
[11] Timm, 570   [12] M. G. H., S.S., XVI, 511-512

Germany, as close to barbarism as was the England of that time, were no more heavily occupied. But what of Aquitaine? Or Burgundy? Or the lands between the Loire and the Rhine?

Of the latter region, which is better illuminated by documents, we can glean some information. Inventories and descriptions of estates put together by the more careful and intelligent administrators who felt the need for a precise evaluation of the manpower at their disposal, provide a little demographic material. They list holdings subject to labour services and describe their tenants' families. This kind of information, for instance, is given in the most famous and best constructed of these inventories, the *Polyptyque* made for the estates of the abbey of St Germain-des-Prés in Paris in the time of Abbot Irminon at the beginning of the ninth century. Now, the impression which these partial censuses give is not at all one of decline or even of stagnation of numbers. They give depth and movement to an otherwise static demographic picture for the population they describe appears to be both dense and vigorous.

Two illustrations of what can be found in documents of this kind may encourage their closer study. In eight villages owned by the abbey of St Germain-des-Prés around Paris the Carolingian surveyors (who left out of account the considerable household staffs of the manorial houses) counted 4,100 peasants. In the eighteenth century, at a time when proximity to a great city presented exceptionally favourable demographic conditions, 5,700 souls were counted in the same localities. The second example comes from the Midi of the tenth century. In the year 913 a record of resettlement in a valley in the Catalan Pyrenees around the monastery of San Juan de las Abadessas mentions 160 peasant households and 156 separate individuals living on some 50 square kilometres; and this was in a region not especially fertile, although being on the frontiers of Islam it held perhaps an exceptional number of refugees.[13] From these two cases we can see that land could in certain conditions be very heavily occupied.

Sometimes too heavily occupied. An overpopulation which appears to have been the result of recent growth is proved by other indications, in particular overcrowding on the farming units which contemporary documents call *manses*. These fiscal units, which ought to have corresponded to the needs of a single peasant family, appear in very many inventories of the ninth and tenth centuries to have been in fact occupied by a group of households. In the Ardennes, that is to say on a much less fertile soil than the Parisian heartlands, Villance, a village belonging to the abbey of Prüm, was described in a *polyptyque* drawn up in 892-893. It mentions 116 families as being established on 35 whole *manses*; 88 of them were crowded on to 22 *manses* and 15

13 F. Udina Martorel, *El archivo condal de Barcelona en los siglos IX-X*, pp. 160-162

families occupied five others; no more than five *manses* supported two families each and only three *manses* one family each. According to the evidence of most manorial surveys the Carolingian *manse* was overpopulated.[14] This disparity between the number of farming and taxable units on the one hand and the number of households on the other leads us to believe that rural population was increasing naturally in some regions. Figures in some inventories allow the rate of increase to be estimated.

More than a century ago, B. Guérard attempted to interpret the demographic material contained in the *polyptyque* of Irminon. This document enumerates 2,088 households and 10,026 individuals, which gives an average of slightly more than four persons to each family, the number of children being 5,316 and of parents 4,710.[15] Thus, there appears to be a positive rate of increase. More recently A. Déléage has continued the enquiry by counting the serfs mentioned in Burgundian documents of the tenth century. He counts 34 unmarried persons and 135 households, only seven of which had no children. The documents give us a glimpse of the composition of 80 families; 20 have one child, 22 have two children, 16 have three, and so on, giving an average of nearly three children per household. In all 304 adults and 384 children. With this proportion the population would increase by one-eighth every generation.[16] In fact, of course, these two historians have treated the numerical evidence in a very rudimentary way, and it should be added that the figures in the documents of that period reflected real conditions very imperfectly. We do not know whether the compilers of inventories registered accurately all newly born infants, whose expectation of life was very uncertain. And did they bother to record anybody else besides the active persons able to be of use to their masters? Doubtless the criteria for inclusion varied from one inventory to another. Whatever they were, however, and even making the most stringent qualifications when interpreting the sources, they show incontestably that in certain villages there were peasant families with a high fertility rate.

It is true that fertility is not the only factor of growth, and to be quite sure that the natural rate of increase was not actually at a very low level, we ought to know more about the mobility of rural population, the propensity to emigrate, the structure of the family, and in particular the marriage rate, all

[14] Perrin, 200, and 254

[15] *Polyptyque de l'abbé d'Irminon*, I, *Prolegomènes*, p. 897

[16] Déléage, 216, p. 576; D. Herlihy, 226, proposes the use of another index of the demographic growth and progressive overpopulation of villages in southern France and Italy. This is the multiplication of land transactions; the enlargement of the family divides the farming units, encourages their survey, exchange and sale and raises the fluidity of land ownership. This method deserves attention, but the documentary material used in this article appears too dispersed and discontinuous for the general trend in the graphs which accompany it to be altogether convincing.

of which are completely lacking. Nevertheless the crude figures of the surveyors, when compared with the obviously overcrowded farming units, must invite the conclusion that almost all the landed properties described by the administrators of the great imperial churches supported a very heavy population during Carolingian times.

It would nevertheless be very rash to treat as the normal average the demographic conditions revealed by certain passages in the *polyptyques*, and to attribute similar densities to the whole of the west or even the region between Loire and Rhine, or to calculate, as F. Lot did once, general densities from these local ones.[17] Attentive reading of the more precise inventories covering widely differing areas – indeed a comparison in the same *polyptyque* of Irminon of the estates in the Paris region with others, more isolated and in wilder parts of the country, which the abbey owned in the remote districts of Perche – show that in fact the reserves of manpower on the rural manors in different parts of the country were very unequal. The documentary evidence shows that some were much more sparsely inhabited than others, and enables us to visualize throughout the west an occupation of the soil distinguished by abrupt contrasts. Vast tracts probably remained completely deserted, elsewhere the pattern of inhabited places was scattered and discontinuous. Some villages again possessed as many inhabitants as in modern times. On the other hand it appears that the villages themselves were distinctly fewer in number, were irregularly clustered on the easily worked lands, and separated from each other by empty zones. The least unsubstantial hypothesis would be that of overpopulated islands, where biological increase stimulated by agrarian prosperity pushed men to the verge of scarcity, contrasted with ocean-like stretches of country where farming was well-nigh impossible.

This picture of sporadic settlement, which seems reasonable enough, also corresponds with what we can guess about the system of production and its special need for areas around the cultivated clearings left free for pasture and hunting. The absolute necessity to safeguard this surrounding wilderness doubtless explains why the settled area never seemed to expand. Despite what probably was a natural tendency towards an increasing population, the instances of expanding agrarian settlement were apparently extremely rare. In all the contemporary documents, of which many served as primers for manorial management or aimed at increasing the lord's profits, allusions to assarting, to felled trees, to ploughed wastes, are very seldom encountered (except in the Pyrenees, on the frontiers of Islam, where the Carolingians regularly received Christian refugees and settled them on new lands,[18] or

[17] F. Lot, 'Conjectures démographiques sur la France au IXe siècle', in *Le Moyen Age*, 1921   [18] Dupont, 222

perhaps in certain areas of the new country, Germania, which was still emerging from near savagery). Here and there – and one might expect the compilers of the *polyptyques* to be ready to note such occurrences – some new fields appeared on the edges of the clearings,[19] but we may guess that they were both small and exceptional, and that this timid advance was often matched elsewhere by the inexorable offensive of the forest.

What little the written evidence can teach us agrees convincingly with the studies which have been made on the sites occupied by man and particularly the researches of French geographers which are still going on.[20] Only archeological excavation of inhabited places, and estimation of the age of human settlements and measurement of the cultivated areas by means of a study of place-names can tell us what in those obscure periods was the population of the vast regions for which all documentary record is lacking. The present state of these researches shows that light, easily worked soils, which could be dug without too much effort, from which surface water drained readily, and on which the natural vegetation did not grow too thickly, were the only ones to be continuously cultivated and to be thus capable of supporting permanent settlements. The fortunate regions where such soils predominated were probably able to support a rural population at a level which was not very much lower than that of the eighteenth century. On the other hand, heavy lands, sticky and wet, which required elaborate drainage, were most frequently left in their virgin state, and it is unlikely that many men dwelt on such soils. In England the arable was on the light alluvial soils in the valleys, whereas the thick clay which surrounded them was almost wholly covered by meadows and woods. In Flanders the discontinuous nature of the overlying clay caused gaps in human settlement; on the estates of St Bavo of Ghent agricultural activity, unable to expand on the more difficult lands, remained limited.[21]

Village communities thus found themselves hemmed in with no way of absorbing the increase in their birth rate. Periodic waves of mortality, such as those caused by military activity and, increasingly in the second half of the ninth and in the tenth centuries, raids of invaders,[22] rather than any systematic clearing of the wastes and the resulting hiving off of colonists, relieved demographic pressure at intervals. Such a situation suggests a peasantry poorly equipped with efficient tools and incapable for this reason of taming the encircling wilderness.

[19] Assarts are mentioned in *Capitu aria Regum Francorum* I.77, c. 19; I.277, c. 12
[20] See in particular R. Dion, 53. Pedological observations can be of the greatest assistance to agrarian historians on this point.
[21] Darby, 47, pp. 129 *et seq.*; Verhulst, 233
[22] After the Norsemen passed through Villance in the Ardennes, 15 *manses* were left uninhabited.

3. THE TOOLS

The question of tools belongs to a domain whose exploration is essential to those who wish to understand the mechanism of production. Unfortunately, as far as the Carolingian period is concerned, this domain remains largely unexplored. Marc Bloch at one time undertook a preliminary reconnaissance for France, which proved very rewarding and opened up several lines of approach. But it cannot be said that he has had any successors. Nevertheless a thoroughgoing investigation into agricultural technique is a most pressing task, for only in this way can we appreciate the basic conditions which underlie the economy, we might almost say, of the whole of western civilization. Here we have one of the fields which deserve to be given priority, even if it may prove as difficult and disappointing as that of demography. Our present ignorance is due to the fact that documentary sources say very little about tools, and they must be combed carefully for what little they do say. To begin with, let us briefly summarize what we know about the position on those royal and ecclesiastical properties in the Carolingian provinces which were both well managed and situated and were therefore most likely to be in the forefront of technical usage.

The milling machinery with which these manors were equipped is fairly well known. In fact the inventories furnish definite information on this point, which attracted Marc Bloch's special attention.[23] Installing a water mill was certainly a costly and delicate matter. Constructing the mill race, and transporting, fashioning and setting in place the millstones meant a substantial investment and the maintenance of the driving machinery also required regular expenditure. Even so, such contrivances were by no means unusual on great estates in the ninth century and it appears that the number of water-driven mills was rapidly increasing around Paris: of the 59 mills recorded in the *polyptyque* of St Germain-des-Prés, eight had just been constructed and two recently renovated by Abbot Irminon. It is interesting to note, too, that Abbot Adalard of Corbie, seeking ways to strengthen the economy of his monastery, was greatly interested in the possibilities of mills.[24] Indeed skilled administrators who could lay hands on the means to build them, knew well how profitable mills could be.

We need not consider the vast amount of time previously wasted by domestic servants grinding grain by hand. Mills driven by running water released these servants for other useful tasks, but their masters were more likely to be interested in the higher income which resulted from making the estate mills available to the local peasant farms in return for payment. The profits from such services helped considerably to swell estate revenues. The

[23] Gille, 110   [24] Document No. 15, p. 378

description of one royal manor in northern Gaul, Annapes, has been preserved: as much grain was brought to the manorial granges from its five mills and brewery as was harvested on the entire arable area of the estate.[25] At Villemeux, millers in the service of St Germain-des-Prés delivered to the lord as much bread grain every year as all the wheat sown on the lord's fields. The importance of these dues (which incidentally provides another and convincing proof of the predominance of bread in the popular diet in certain regions) underlines the success of mechanical installations and shows that, in spite of taxes and the pre-emption on their own harvest, peasants found it to their advantage to make use of the manorial mills. A mill wheel turned by a jet of water could release throughout the neighbourhood, in peasant hut as well as in lordly mansion, a great deal of manpower. Time freed in this way could be occupied in productive work on the land and was a far from negligible factor in economic growth.

It is clear, however, that mills were not distributed uniformly even in those highly developed and privileged sectors of the rural economy which are described by our sources. The surviving fragment of Irminon's *polyptyque* records 22 estates, but only eight of them possessed mills. Hand-operated mills, voracious of time and effort, were thus still extensively used: on the manors of the abbey of St Bertin, where several water mills had already been built, dues in the form of flour were regularly exacted from tenants, as in the days, probably quite recent, when all the breadmaking processes were domestic tasks. And still as late as the beginning of the tenth century, the cartulary of this monastery presented the construction of a mill as worthy of great admiration. Undoubtedly progress in this direction was timid and slow.[26]

The quality and efficiency of agricultural tools are harder to deduce, since for this we need a precise description of the tools themselves. Alas, for this the historian will find in his sources no more than a few relevant words. Here is one such passage in the *polyptyque* of St Maur-des-Fossés. It says that six oxen led by tenants owing labour services drew one ploughing 'engine' on the great fields of the estate.[27] Whichever way this sentence is turned it tells us hardly anything. It is true the number of animals harnessed suggests that the machine was a powerful one and capable of usefully breaking up the ground. But we still need to know the effective strength of the animals, which may have been poor creatures emaciated from winter fasting, and unfit to do the March ploughing. Further, we know nothing of how the animals were harnessed or whether their full strength was drawn on. And the main question whether a primitive plough (*araire*) or a more elaborate one (*charrue*) was referred to remains unanswered.

[25] Document No. 2, p. 363   [26] *Cartulaire de Saint-Bertin* (ed. Guérard)
[27] *Polyptyque de l'abbé d'Irminon* (ed. Guérard), II, Appendices, p. 285

The *araire* was fitted with a symmetrically shaped share and it threw the earth on both sides, more or less, according to whether it had 'ears' attached to the share or not. Its advantage was that it was light and could be easily handled and assembled by the ploughman, who had no difficulty in fitting together the interlocking wooden pieces strengthened, if need be, with a strip of metal whose point had been hardened in the fire. The *araire* was thus suited to regions where agricultural technique was at an elementary level, where the plough team of animals was a feeble one, where metal was little used and specialized artisans were lacking. On the other hand it broke up only the surface of the ground, and moved it without turning it over. To prepare a field adequately with such an instrument it was necessary in addition to dig it deeply with a spade from time to time, perhaps every twelve, six, or even as often as four years. Considerable manual labour had thus to be used to supplement the work of the plough animals. The implement which can properly be called the *charrue*, was fitted with an asymmetrical share and a mouldboard, and it offered a marked advantage over the *araire* in economy of manpower. In handling it the ploughman managed in one operation to turn the ground sufficiently both to aerate it and to reconstitute its elements of fertility. Periodic hand digging was no longer necessary. Besides, the *charrue* could deal with heavy soils which the lighter *araire* could not cultivate, and thus make it possible to extend the potentially cultivable area. Against this, it required a much greater effort to drag and hence a more powerful team of beasts. And finally it was a complicated machine, more costly, and not one to be put together by anybody.[28] These considerations show how valuable it would be for our attempts to estimate the Carolingian peasants' output to know which of these two ploughs were used. But this is quite impossible in the present state of knowledge and probably will remain so for ever.

A study of the names given to the *charrue* and the *araire* in Germanic and Slavonic dialects reveals that at that moment between the fifth and the tenth centuries when the Hungarian invasions came to disrupt the Slavonic world, the *charrue* was well enough known in central Europe to possess its own special name.[29] Thus in the European countryside these two tools existed side by side in Carolingian times. But how can their respective spread be measured in the areas illuminated by written sources, where, in any case, only the largest and best-equipped properties are described? In the Statutes of Abbot Adalard of Corbie the plough is known as *aratrum*, and in Irminon's

---

[28] Faucher, 106

[29] Haudricourt, 117. F. Sach *'Radlo'* and *'Pluh'* in the *Czechoslovak Countryside*, I, *The oldest Tools* (in Czech), Prague, 1961, the most recent study, places the transition from symmetric to asymmetric share in Moravia between the seventh and the ninth centuries.

polyptyque as *carruca*. But does this verbal distinction signify a real difference in the construction of the tool, or only the different education of the clerks, one of whom used a classical Latin word and the other a popular one? The latter word, it should be noted, expresses the idea of a cart (*carruca* signifies primarily a vehicle: the word had still this sense in a passage of the laws of the Alamans which punishes by a fine of three sous the breaking of the front wheels of a vehicle thus named). It could therefore mean a machine fitted with a wheeled front portion. Such an appendage could certainly prove a useful improvement since it provided a kind of lever which allowed the ploughman to control the depth of the ridge by pressing more or less heavily on the handles: the wheeled front section also provided a means by which an inclined share could throw up a ridge which was more efficient on wet soil than flat ploughing. But what constituted the real plough (*charrue*), the real progress, the release of manpower, the possibility of cultivating heavy soils, was the mouldboard. Were the *aratrum* and the *carruca* of the ninth-century documents fitted with one or not? In order to appreciate the exact meaning of these names we must be able to compare them with archeological remains, and these simply do not exist. Iconographical evidence, so attractive at first sight, is deceptive. The art of those days was not deliberately realistic and was based on the stiff conventions of a school style, and we cannot be sure that the illustrator always reproduced what he saw and not an object copied from a decorator's model. An illumination of this kind from an Anglo-Saxon Ms. of the tenth century shows a wheeled plough with a double stanchion and a large mouldboard drawn by two coupled pairs of oxen.[30] But we would still like to know where and by whom such a tool, an obviously efficient one, could have been commonly employed. Scanty documentation need not dissuade us of course from continuing the enquiry. It is by no means impossible that archeological examination of ploughed lands pursued together with a careful re-reading of pages of the *polyptyques* which describe labour services of hand and plough may penetrate the shadows and especially those that conceal the continued existence of spade-work.[31] I believe the use of the spade to have been considerable even on the model properties of the abbeys in the Paris basin. Many manual labourers must indeed have come to work on the lords' demesnes, particularly on those central parcels of cultivated land, the best and closest to the manorial farmyard. So great were the labour demands for the cultivation of the most productive fields and so garden-like was the appearance which the cultivation of cereals presented as a result, that we are led to suppose that ploughs drawn by animals must have remained relatively inefficient.

However, even if we know next to nothing of the shape of the tools, it is

[30] Leser, 122, fig. 42   [31] Saint-Jacob, 258

not by any means impossible to know the way in which some of them were made. Up to the present little attention has been paid to the indications, albeit few and brief, which illuminate this aspect of the history of technique. Nevertheless, some inventories of the large estates record metal tools which were an extremely important part of the equipment of the farm. Thus in chapter 42 of the capitulary *De Villis*, the guide for the conduct of the royal manors, these objects are divided into utensils for the hearth – firedogs, pot-hooks, cauldrons – and tools. The latter, indeed – axes, hatchets, augers and billhooks – appear to be intended not for fieldwork, but for woodwork, either carpentry or joinery. The parts of the statutes of the abbey of Corbie which are concerned with the kitchen garden confirm this. A few tools are mentioned in them – six hoes, two spades, two sickles, one scythe – but the essential items were gouges, hatchets and billhooks. As for the inventory of the royal estate of Annapes and its dependencies, it lists, after the utensils for kitchen and hearth, a few garden tools, iron spades, hoes, scythes and sickles, but in astonishingly limited numbers. The labourers on the enormous property of Annapes, which supported more than 200 cattle, disposed of no more than two scythes, two sickles and two spades if we count iron tools alone. And here, too, the essential tools were intended to fashion wood. For the rest of the work it was *ustensilia lignea ad ministrandum sufficienter* – tools enough, but wooden ones – and they were not worth counting.[32] Such evidence suggests that on the largest estates of this sort, apart from the cutting blades for scything grass and corn or for chopping down trees, all other agricultural tools and specially those for tilling the soil, were normally made of wood. Each estate possessed no more than a small workshop provided with iron tools intended only for the manufacture or repair of other tools.

This hypothesis could, I think, be verified by a close study of the position in rural society occupied by the *faber*, the specialized iron worker, the blacksmith. All the Carolingian documents place him on an equal footing with the goldsmith and picture him as the maker of unusual and precious equipment.[33] He is hardly ever to be found in the inventories of rural estates. No forge, nor blacksmith, nor rent in iron is to be found in *polyptyques* of the abbeys of Montiérender and Prüm, whose landed property was situated in the heart of regions celebrated in medieval times for their metallurgical skills.[34] At Annapes the compilers of the inventories noted the absence of those *ministeriales ferrari* which the capitulary *De Villis* used to want counted so

[32] Document No. 2, p. 363

[33] In particular in the editions of barbarian, *Lex Burgundionum*, XXI.2; X.2, 3; *Lex Salica*, XXXV.6

[34] *Actes du Colloque international: Le fer à travers les Ages* (Annales de l'Est, memoire No. 16), Nancy, 1956

carefully. In the whole of Corbie there was but one single workshop to which all the stewards sent their equipment to be repaired. A significant fact is that it was placed under the supervision of the chamberlain, the official charged with purchases, money transactions and the handling of precious non-metallic objects which had been bought. But the ploughs used in the great kitchen gardens of the abbey were not made there, the stewards of the rural estates, who organized peasant labour had to provide them. The fact that these ploughing implements could be fashioned in the houses of the peasants was proof that they contained no more than a small quantity of iron. One only of the St Germain-des-Prés estates described in Irminon's *polyptyque* possessed forges, and that was Boissy-en-Drouais, which specialized in iron production. Occupants of servile tenures there were required to render an annual rent in iron bars. Further it should be noticed that those operating the workshops had to deliver not ploughshares, but axes and lances: not ploughing tools but military tools like those *fossoirs*, picks used in farmwork, which were exacted from a group of tenants of St Germain at La Celle-les-Bordes.[35] It is the same in all the regions about which we have information (except perhaps Lombardy where the *ferrarii* appeared much more frequently in manorial inventories, and where on the estates of Bobbio, San Giulia de Brescia and Nonantola[36] many village tenures supported regular rents in iron, and more precisely in ploughshares), the impression remains everywhere the same, that very little metal was used for peasant implements.

Was the undoubted technical progress to which the diffusion of the water mill bears witness accompanied in Europe of the ninth and tenth centuries by the spread of ploughs with wheeled foreparts, by improvements in harness, and by the adoption of a more efficient ploughshare? This important problem of technique cannot be resolved, but it is reasonable to assume that even in the most favoured sectors of rural life, those of the great farming complexes described by inventories, men used feeble wooden implements. They found themselves ill-equipped to come to grips with nature and worked with their bare hands for a great part of the time. The primitive technical equipment obviously restricted narrowly the individual's productive capacity. And this observation agrees completely with the impression gained from land settlement. Villages teemed with people whose efforts were needed to work the soil on the home fields, but they were situated in clearings separated by stretches of wild country because agricultural tools were not robust enough to overcome the obstacles of heavy, wet and thickly wooded land. Areas of natural vegetation adjoining the villages were of course actually necessary because the cultivation of cereals was so demanding of manpower that each rural community had to supplement its means of

[35] Perrin, 255   [36] *Historiae Patriae Monumenta*, XIII. Nos. 419 and 422

livelihood by making the most of the products of the wastelands – animal husbandry, hunting and foodgathering.

4. AGRICULTURAL PRACTICES

These limited portions of the village lands suitable for grain growing and therefore providing the village's main food supply, the *culturae*, or *coûtures* to use the old word which remains embedded in place-names in many parts of the French countryside, or 'furlongs' to use the English term, were not given over wholly to food production every year. Unlike the cultivated 'tofts' whose soil, manured by the household waste and stable dung, could be cultivated without interruption, the fields demanded a periodic rest if fertility was not to be lost. Every spring a section of the arable was not sown; it remained open, unenclosed, available for pasture, in the same way as the wild area of wastes and commons. For an understanding of the productivity of the land and the manner in which it was able to support human life, we need to know the rhythm of the resting periods. What was the place of the fallow and what the place of spring-sown corn, oats and leguminous crops? How much land was devoted to autumn-sown corn, that is the bread grains – wheat, rye and spelt (the most widely grown grain in the Rhineland and north-west France), and lastly barley, which was in those days often a winter-sown crop? Although even for the region between Rhine and Loire, best served by our sources, we cannot know with any certainty how the cycle of crop rotation was organized, the documents permit us to deduce some important information.

1. The description of harvest and sowing and, more often, that of dues in the form of grain exacted from peasant tenants proved that the fields of peasants as well as lords very frequently produced spring as well as winter corn and especially oats.

2. The arrangement of the ploughing services exacted from manorial dependants in the agricultural calendar shows that the cycle of ploughing was often divided into two sowing 'seasons', one in the winter (*ad hibernaticum*), and the other in the summer or the spring (*ad aestivum, ad tremissum*).

3. Ploughing units on the great properties appear often in groups of three; for instance, in nearly half the estates of the abbey of St Germain-des-Prés described in Irminon's *polyptyque*, the compilers record three, six or nine manorial fields. This arrangement leads us to think that cultivation was organized on a ternary rhythm. But it must be added that one and only one document, the *polyptyque* of the abbey of St Amand, shows conclusively a distribution of the manorial fields in three equal portions, occu-

pied successively by winter crop, spring crop and fallow.[37] By this arrangement, a third portion was prepared in May by a preliminary ploughing,
and was turned over again by the plough in November before sowing;
the following year after harvest the same fields were left throughout autumn
and winter for the animals to graze on, and were then ploughed in Lent
and sown with spring grain, after which they rested for a year. Thus at
least a third of the agricultural area produced nothing,[38] while another
third produced bread grains and the last third the ingredients of porridge
and soup.

I do not consider, however, that these indications are sufficient for us to
conclude without further consideration that a regular three-year rotation was
general, or even widespread. What argues against any such conclusion is that
none of our examples is in southern Europe where climatic conditions, and
above all early spring droughts, made March sowings somewhat hazardous,
and also that our documents describe none but the great monastic or royal
farms which were run in an unusually rational and even scientific manner.
In the general movement of *renovatio* which inspired the Carolingian intellectuals, with its emphasis on classical antiquity, and of which the use of
writing and the compilation of the *polyptyques* are the signs, administrators of
church lands might easily have been tempted to subject the fields in their care
to the orderly and rational methods recommended by Roman agriculturists.
We might take Vandalbert of Prüm's poem of the months for a literal re-
presentation of the calendar of agricultural activities in use in the Rhineland;
but it is soon evident that it is a pastiche of Virgil. How far was agricultural
practice of the monasteries influenced by the intellectual theories of antiquity? Here is the proper occasion to draw the attention of historians of
literature to the assistance they can render their colleagues who study rural
history. We should like to know whether there is evidence of the existence
of copies of Cato, Varro and Columella in the libraries of those times, for it
is not too wild a guess that improvements in agrarian technique on the progressive ecclesiastical estates were stimulated by a reading of the Roman
agriculturists, and among them not only the Elder Pliny or Cornelius Celsus
who recommended more extensive cultivation, aiming at reduced outgoings
even at the cost of lower output, but also those like Columella who, on the
contrary, preached an intensification of agricultural activity.[39] The origin of

[37] *Polyptyque de l'abbé Irminon* (ed. Guérard), II, p. 925

[38] There were thus three ploughings, two before the winter sowing and one before
the spring sowing. This is what is meant in the *polyptyque* of Irminon by the following
phrase: the *mansus arat ad tres sationes.*

[39] J. Kolendo, 'La moissonneuse antique en Gaule romaine', in *Annales E.S.C.*, 1960,
who quotes M. E. Sergenko, 'Two types of rural economy in Italy of the 1st Century of
our era' (in Russian), in *Bulletin of the Academy of Sciences of the U.S.S.R.; Class of Social
Sciences*, 1935.

one of the most profound impulses towards expansion of medieval agriculture may perhaps be traced to the study of these sources by contemporary scholars and administrators.

Nevertheless the influence of Roman example did not at that time extend to all the estates of the king and the church, even in the arrangement of the rotation of crops. Indeed there are many signs in our sources to show that the arable could sometimes be very unequally divided between winter cornfields, spring cornfields and fallow. On the four royal estates attached to the administrative headquarters of Annapes, barley was sown in the autumn (sowing was completed in fact by the time the inventory was compiled, as was customary in winter): spring corn came to no more than a fifth of the harvest at Cysoing, and a ninth at Annapes; Vitry and Somain produced none at all.[40] But here is a contrary example: land measuring more than ten acres, owned by the abbot of St Pierre-du Mont-Blandin at Ghent, was never sown with any seed other than oats, and thus produced a crop only once in every three years.[41] It is therefore safest to conjecture that there was considerable variation in the crop rotation in use. Man was forced to bow to the natural capacity of the soil because he was poorly prepared to alter it. We can imagine an infinite variety of systems in use ranging all the way from the strict three-course rotation to temporary cultivation based on burning where bits and pieces of land on the outer fringes of the village enclave would be tilled after the undergrowth had been burned, and continued to be cropped for years until fertility was exhausted. It is also probable that oats and other spring grains were often a supplementary crop taken from the fallow, and that such a system, even when the regular ploughings in winter and early spring (*trémois*) were adhered to, frequently lasted more than one year on the largest part of the available arable. It must be added that seed corn was sown very thinly; the most favourably situated lands of St Amand and St Germain-des-Prés were usually allowed four *muids* of wheat per *bonnier*, that is barely two hectolitres per hectare (or about 26 bushels per acre), and the level was even lower, perhaps less than a half, on less favoured lands. The agricultural practice of those early days demanded not only plentiful manpower, but wide open spaces.

The insistent demands for long fallow periods, and the need to scatter the seed thinly arose at least partly because of mediocre ploughing implements which could not turn the ground over properly, but they were also due to the virtual absence of manure. It is true that animal husbandry was always

[40] Grierson, 247
[41] Ganshof, 241. G. Schröder-Lembke's study, 231, on the agrarian organization of the furlongs on the great Carolingian estates establishes that a great variety of rotational cycles could be in use on them.

complementary to agriculture and the draught oxen whose task was to plough the fields could also fertilize them with their dung. In reality the combination of arable with pasture was not close enough to enable animal manure to make much impression. Men who were so inadequately equipped with tools were forced to devote all their energies to producing their own food, and cattle had to take second place. A little fodder was harvested, but barely enough to keep those few beasts which had not been slaughtered in the autumn alive during the lean winter months when nature's offerings failed. But for the rest of the year the herds grazed alone in the open air on the land which was not enclosed. They must also have ranged over the fallow fields and in doing so deposited their manure on them; but the deposit was quite insufficient to maintain fertility. Scarce fodder meant restricted periods of stall-feeding, and the limited quantities of stable manure thus available were almost wholly devoured by the cultivated 'tofts' in the inner fertile belt of the village territory. No wonder areas of fallow had to be huge. And we can appreciate afresh the need of each family to dispose of as large a space for subsistence as possible which had to cover, besides pasture, an arable area much more extensive than the portion actually in use each year. Even so, despite the long resting periods, output remained extremely low.

*   *   *

Throughout this book we shall find ourselves coming up against the fundamental problem of output without being able to solve it. Together with the paucity of demographic data and details about agricultural implements, the obscurity in which the productivity of the fields is shrouded raises a most obstinate barrier to our exact understanding of the agrarian economy of the medieval era. In Carolingian times it is even harder to penetrate the shadows, for the available details are even more exiguous. One document only for northern Gaul provides some figures. The surveyors who visited the royal estates attached to Annapes in the winter recorded both the quantity of the previous harvest and the amount which had just been subtracted for the sowing – they certified that the remainder was actually in the barns at the time of their visit. These figures are very baffling. Here are those for the estate of Annapes, for which the inventory gives the most complete details. It is not possible to compare seed with harvest for oats, peas or beans since the spring sowings had not been made. But of the 1,320 *muids* of spelt harvested 720 had to be returned to the land as seed; of 100 *muids* of wheat, 60; of 1,800 *muids* of barley, 1,100; and finally the new sowing absorbed the whole of the rye harvest, that is, 98 *muids*. The available surplus of the harvest did not therefore appear that year to exceed 46 per cent for spelt, 40 per cent for wheat, 38 per cent for barley, that is an output of 1·8, 1·7 and 1·6 to one respectively. There appeared to be no surplus for rye. The fragmentary evidence given for other estates agrees; an output of 2:1 for spelt and of 1·6:1 for rye at Cysoing; for barley 2·2:1 at Vitry, 1·5:1 at Cysoing, 2:1 at Somain.[42] Taken altogether the consumable surplus is revealed as markedly less, in the year of the inventory, than the quantity which had to be reserved for sowing. Could output really have been at such a derisory level?

The text, however, is categorical. It prevents us from assuming that, apart from seed corn, grain had already been taken away between harvest time and the visit of the compilers of the inventory for domestic consumption or for despatch outside the estate. Could we suppose that the text known from a single copy of the Carolingian period had been corrupted in transcription? More than likely it was transcribed, as a model for future inventories, by clerks who were only interested in the formula used and the layout of the manuscript; perhaps they did not copy all the figures or perhaps they made mistakes or introduced imaginary figures amongst those they copied. But the only reasonable hypothesis to explain the astonishingly low figures for output is to assume that the inventory was compiled after an exceptionally bad harvest. In fact, when it was drawn up grain harvested the previous year was still stored in the barns of these estates in quantities much greater than the insignificant surplus of the current year. The surveyors found at Annapes 1,081 *muids* of old spelt, as against 600 of new, and 1,200 *muids* of old barley, as against 700 of new. These important savings prove that the output of seed was clearly much higher the previous year. We can deduce from this unique document that the productivity of the fields varied enormously from one season to another and further that it could be devastatingly low.

We must not, of course, generalize from one set of figures obtained from a single source. But it is possible to find elsewhere some other traces of output, somewhat higher than that which can be derived from the Annapes inventory, but even so representing a low yield and a derisory rate of profit when compared with the value of the capital in land and seed corn. One significant fact is that compilers who visited the farms (*cours*) of the abbey of San Giulia of Brescia in 905–906 to compile a *polyptyque* found there reserves of grain in the barns which were barely higher and sometimes lower than the quantity needed for sowing. Thus at Prozano where the fields could take 300 *muids* of seed corn, the stocks in the estate barn amounted to only 360 *muids* of which 140 were of millet (*mil*). At Canella 90 *muids* were needed for sowing and 51 were in the barns; at Temulina 32 and 37.[43] Another relevant fact is that on

[42] Grierson, 247. Slicher van Bath, 31, p. 66, does not seem to interpret correctly the figures in the text.

[43] *Historiae Patriae Monumenta*, XIII, co. 707–710

the estate run by the abbey of St Germain-des-Prés at Maisons in the specially
fertile countryside of the Ile de France 650 *muids* were sown in the autumn
on the lord's furlongs. Every year the tenants of 34 *manses* had to thresh in the
barns 12 *muids* of corn each and carry them to the monastery. If we assume
that the labour services were roughly adjusted to the normal need for manpower, we might conclude that the manorial administrators did not expect,
even allowing for the quantities the domestic servants threshed and kept
back for their own consumption, a surplus very much greater than 400
muids for a sowing of 650. The proportion works out again at 1·6:1.[44]

These elusive details allow at any rate one firm conclusion. Carried out
with rudimentary equipment and in a generally unfavourable climate,[45] the
cultivation of cereal crops was at the mercy of the caprices of the weather.
Even on the best equipped farms an excessively wet spring or summer could
render the heavy toil in the fields totally unproductive. Despite an enormous
expenditure of manpower and the disproportionate size of the village lands
country folk could be racked with hunger. Obviously their main preoccupation was to survive through spring and early summer, that period of
backbreaking toil. When the scraps of food remaining to them after the demands of their masters had been exhausted, the yearly nightmare of hand-to-
mouth existence began, and the pangs of hunger had to be stilled by de-
vouring garden herbs and forest berries and by begging bread at the gates of
the rich. At such moments the threat of starvation overshadowed the whole
village world.

[44] *Polyptyque de l'abbé d'Irminon* (ed. Guérard), II.271-272
[45] Le Roy Ladurie, 70

CHAPTER II

Wealth and Society.
The Manorial Economy

The threat of famine did not hang equally over everyone. Some ate as much as they wanted. The burden of want and of daily toil was not shared by all. We now have to allot producers and consumers their place in society, to show what rank they and the classes to which they belonged occupied and to discuss how labour and profits were shared between the different social groups.

I. THE FRAMEWORK OF THE FAMILY

The most elementary social group was the family; around it was built the organization of the village and of its lands, as well as the division of labour and the consumption of goods. We have already shown how profound was the imprint of the family on the rural scene. The enclosure round the dwelling house sheltered and protected a group of persons related by blood: they were fed by the produce of the fields attached to it, and the whole complex formed the basis of the agrarian system of the time. In fact all men at that period, not only scholars and writers, were deeply imbued with the idea of a typical farming unit related to the abilities and needs of the family.

One word was used to express this concept in the Latin texts of the countries where the Carolingian civilization flourished from the seventh century onwards. It was the word *mansus*. The term *mansus* did not appear, however, to have been used in the peripheral provinces such as Maine or the extreme south of Gaul, and it did not spread to Brabant in the North until the end of the eighth century, or to Provence and Italy in the south till the ninth.[1] This word in its narrow sense meant the place in the village inhabited by the family, the site of the hearth, but it was extended to apply to the whole of the farming entity of which the homestead was the centre. The *mansus* was thus supported by the *appendicia* spread over the village possessions, including dependencies lying close at hand in the belt of cultivated tofts as well as fields dispersed amongst the furlongs. It even included the right to share collectively in the exploitation of the waste lands.[2] The word *huba*, used

[1] Latouche, 227; Ganshof, 244 and 245   [2] Saint-Jacob, 173

28

in the eastern regions where Germanic dialects were spoken, expressed the same meaning. England, too, had its equivalent – the 'hide'.

For many years historians have sought to define the true legal and social significance of the *manse* in the Carolingian period. The question remains a complicated one, and research has not yet dispelled all the difficulties. They will, however, be much simplified if we disregard the purely legal aspects and consider only the economic significance of the institution.

It should be realized in the first place that the abstract idea of the *mansus, huba* or hide, was familiar to contemporary men. The notion appeared to be closely linked with that of the family. Semantically equivalent notions appear in many documents of the time. For the Venerable Bede the hide was 'the land of the family'; in the records of Germania the *huba* was 'the place of residence of a family', or more simply the *familia*.[3] Furthermore these words were related to the simplest and most concrete measure of agricultural labour. The hide and the *huba* were 'ploughlands' (*terres d'une charrue*). By this were understood the parcels of the family landholding dispersed over the arable which were assumed to be equal in the aggregate to the area a plough team could cultivate in one year. This was the equivalent of 120 acres or 120 'dayworks', since an acre and a daywork represented (with variations allowing for soil conditions) the daily task of a plough team. The *manse* was conceived as a multiple of these dayworks. In the mind of the medieval peasant there existed a close natural relationship between the family group, the enclosure round the homestead and the three ploughing 'seasons' of forty days each.[4] Custom indeed for long perpetuated the use of the words *manse* or hide as a measure of area. Even in 1216 the Duke of Limburg gave land and a wood 'the length of a *manse* and the width of half a *manse*' to the abbey of Val Dieu. The following year the same abbey received 'a *manse* of land containing 12 *bonniers*'.[5]

In addition kings and overlords made practical use of the *mansus-huba-hide* as a convenient unit upon which to levy and collect taxes. Indeed, this probably was the principal function of the *manse* and its equivalents at that time. It was only to be expected that in a society based on the family, dues and taxes should be levied on the permanent, well-defined, easily-counted courtyards where the harvests were stored and the family lived, rather than on an individual who was hard to distinguish from the family group of which he formed part, or even on the fields whose number and extent, as well as their exact position in the village arable, probably changed according

[3] Déléage, 218, pp. 306-340
[4] 'In the Italian dialect the amount of land two oxen could plough in one year was called a *manse*.' *Close ordinaire et décrétales de Grégoire IX*, III.39, 10.
[5] *Cartulaire de l'abbaye cistercienne de Val-Dieu* (ed. Ruwet), Nos. 10 and 12

to the rotation of the crops, or the progress of slash-and-burn cultivation. The *manse* seemed destined to be both the frame into which agricultural production and family life fitted naturally, and the main channel through which flowed the two-way traffic of labour services and wealth associated with the exercise of power and the existence of the manor. The customary *manse* representing a unit of agricultural measurement, and the fiscal *manse* serving as a basis for the imposition of taxes and labour services, were two notions deeply assimilated into the collective consciousness. They are also important as reflections of the way in which the society of that period saw itself. Nevertheless the picture which these two notions give of one family living on each *manse*, and of each family endowed with a uniform allotment of ploughland, is very far from the one which the text of Carolingian *polyptyques* reveals.

★   ★   ★

The light thrown by the *polyptyques* curiously distorts the realities of country life. There are three principal reasons for this. The first is that the inventories describe only those peasant farms which are subject to the authority and economic power of a lord. Other independent farms certainly existed, but without additional evidence we shall never know their number, situation or structure. Secondly, there is nothing to prove that the entries in the *polyptyques*, upon which the charges incumbent on the holders were based, in fact coincided with the true division of land ownership in the village territory. For in order to simplify the work of tax collection the manorial officials who compiled the inventories probably used out of date and uncorrected lists. After all a *polyptyque* was not a census: it did not list *all* the parcels of ground in the village, but only those relating to the manor. How can we know whether one particular peasant who held his *manse* and some of the fields attached to it from the lord did not possess at the same time other pieces of land which were part of his farm and helped to feed his household? Having expressed these doubts, we must, however, admit that without the documents drawn up by the great estates we should know nothing whatsoever about the *manses* or the rural families who farmed them. These documents have fortunately been subjected to minute examination and consequently we are in the midst of the best explored territory of rural history. Thanks to this happy state of affairs our knowledge can be briefly summarized as follows.

1. According to all the evidence there was no exact correlation inside the Carolingian manors between the area of the arable attached to the *manse* and the amount of work a plough could do. Two examples from inventories can be quoted to illustrate this. At Poperinghe the abbey of St Bertin

possessed 47 *manses*. 10 of them had each attached to them 30 hectares of fields; 10 others 25 hectares, 19 more 19, and the rest only 17.[6] Again, four villages in the Paris region owned by the abbey of St Germain-des-Prés possessed *manses*. In one of them the *manses* contained an average of 4·35 hectares of ploughland, in another 6·10, in a third 8, in a fourth 9·65. It must be emphasized that these are only averages which mask considerable differences between individual farms. Indeed some *manses* disposed of attached ploughlands of 15 hectares, while others had no more than 20 ares.[7] Thus the first thing to note is that the useful area of the *manses* could vary between wide limits.

2. We must also consider whether these inequalities in some way correspond to the legal hierarchy of peasant tenancies. In some *polyptyques*, for example, the *manses* best provided with land are often those described as 'free' *manses*, while others are known as 'servile' *manses*. Since tenants of the latter owed their lord only manual labour services it may be thought that in general they possessed neither draught animals nor ploughs, and furthermore that they were more frequently required to work away from their own land. For these two reasons because they had to cultivate their own ground with a hoe and because they could not devote so much of their time to their own farm, the allotment of fields attached to their own dwellings could be expected to be smaller. It can thus be seen that the unequal division of ploughlands between *manses* on the manor was partly caused by the existence in peasant society of two economic and legal classes. The owners of a plough team who possessed greater freedom to dispose of their own time were better provided for than the manual workers whose masters controlled their activities more closely. Germanic custom reflected these social realities and recognized a theoretical free *manse* containing sixty dayworks, which was twice as many as on a theoretical servile *manse*.

3. Nevertheless there was also inequality within the different legal categories. Thus on the Parisian possessions of St Germain-des-Prés some free *manses* farmed ten times as much land as others and amongst the servile *manses* the disproportion was sometimes as much as 45 to one. Such a wide disparity in the land available on family farms must have resulted from a long process of change. Purchases, sales, divisions, exchanges, secret or with the lord's consent, could all have produced in the course of generations inequalities in the patrimony which were later embalmed in the *polyptyques*. To support this hypothesis we can see that in Belgium, where settlement, village organization and the institution of the manor were more recent, the *manses* were much more uniform in size in the ninth century.[8] One is led

[6] Ganshof, 242   [7] Perrin, 254
[8] F. Ganshof, *La Belgique carolingienne* (coll. Notre Passé), Brussels, 1958, p. 11

to believe that, in certain provinces at least, inside the manor, and even more outside, peasant landownership enjoyed a relative degree of mobility. Probably parcels of land were easily detached from one *manse* and as easily attached to another. In this way some households became richer and others poorer.[9] It is an important point. We should add finally that peasant migrations and the settling of new families in the village would sometimes accentuate the difference in the size of the plots. On certain village lands described by inventories we come across references to *appendaria, cabannariae* and *hospitia*, all holdings much smaller than the *manse*; these were patches of ground allocated to immigrants who were not integrated into the village community and who were not permitted to share in the use of the common lands.

4. Finally manorial documents show that the number of tenant families did not agree with the number of *manses* and that many of the latter were occupied not by one family, but by many. It could happen that this over-population resulted in a partition of the inhabited enclosure itself. In some *polyptyques*, particularly that of the abbey of Prüm, some *quarts de manses* are recorded.[10] But most frequently the lord maintained intact the unit of tax collection without bothering about the way in which the occupying families divided the dues, the area of the enclosure, or the attached fields between themselves. At Verrières near Paris, only one-fifth of the manses were occupied by a single family; half were occupied by two families, and a third by three.[11]

Thus preserved by the existence of hedges, by agrarian custom and by a rigid system of tax collection, the outward form of the *manse* survived as a mere desiccated tissue which bore no relation to the living organism, the family itself. Attention has already been drawn to the accumulation of households on certain parcels of land because of the glimpse it gives us of demographic trends. But if this unregulated distribution of settlement is compared with the unequal portions of arable allocated to each *manse* it can be seen that the *manses* best provided with arable were not necessarily those which supported the most human beings. The distortions in the economy resulting from the random division of the arable area were often aggravated still further, with the effect that there was no longer any relation between the capacity and needs of the family group, the amount of land they were able to cultivate, the food that their labour could produce or the demands made upon them by the lord.

This then is the real connection, or should we say lack of connection, between the *manse* and the family which emerges from the descriptions of the manor. It would be all the more useful to know the internal composition of

[9] Document No. 9, p. 372   [10] Perrin, 256   [11] Perrin, 254

the peasant family group. To what degree of relationship did individuals share a communal life under the same roof and around the same fireside? How many persons, including servants, made up the household? For the *familia*, of course, comprised not only relatives but all those who lived in the house, and the *polyptyque* of Prüm shows that peasant tenants owned their own slaves, who performed for them the tasks of forced labour.[12] Our information on all these points is quite inadequate. And the deficiency is all the more regrettable, because if we do not know whether the family group was large or small, or how many persons lived in the house, we are not in a position to estimate its productive capacity or its consumption of food, and thus to fit it into the economic setting of manorial charges and the exchange of commodities. The documents provide us with a little information which is capable of being interpreted and which is worth collecting carefully for that reason alone. The more detailed inventories, like Irminon's *polyptyque* which actually counts the inhabitants of the *manses*, reveal a picture of families which were generally small in size and based on a single married couple: father, mother and children. The ties did not seem to include more distant relatives, and married children were accustomed to set themselves up under their own roof. But this evidence refers only to the social milieu of tenant peasants, whose condition encouraged the speedy breaking of family ties. These ties were sometimes maintained for a longer period amongst the independent peasantry. Thus Irminon's *polyptyque* describes a large *manse* of about 68 acres of arable land, which had recently been offered as a gift to St Germain-des-Prés but which remained occupied and farmed by the descendants of the donor. Before the gift the family group had lived an independent existence. This household consisted of twenty persons, two married brothers, one with three children and the other with five, their sister and her six children and an unmarried sister.[13] The composition of the family thus also varied widely. The family, which after all was the lowest group capable of economic co-operation, was very unequally placed as regards the numbers it had to support, the amount of labour it could command and the physical resources at its disposal.

2. THE GREAT LANDED ESTATES

Some tenants of the manor were rich and some were poor, but all tilled the land of a master who was far wealthier than they. It was for the benefit of this landed aristocracy[14] that the documents which illuminate the rural scene for us were put together; and they are solely concerned with their possessions.

[12] Perrin, 256   [13] Document No. 20, p. 383
[14] Reference should again be made to the excellent analysis of the social structure presented by Boutruche, 155.

The picture they reflect is that of a highly stratified society, in which power was vested in a small group of people who controlled from above the activities of the vast mass of country folk. It is true that there existed between tenants and lords a class of modest farmers who succeeded in preserving at least some of their economic independence. A few lines back I drew attention to a peasant family numbering twenty souls whose existence is known to us by accident because their forebear had recently presented his land to a great monastery. Before this act of charity the family's possessions had been free from any overlordship. From other sources, and particularly from those which recorded service in the royal army, we catch glimpses of the existence and vitality of this class of peasants who farmed their own *manses*. It was more than likely that what enriched the great abbeys of south Germania in the ninth century were donations from such small farmers, each gift a modest one but commensurate with the donor's means.[15] But however they were assembled it cannot be denied that very large accretions of *manses* and waste were concentrated in the hands of the ruling princes, the great ecclesiastical establishments and a few wealthy families. Enormous landed estates thus came into existence. The part of the temporal property of St Bertin which was devoted to the support of the monks in the ninth century consisted of 25,000 acres, and the area of the lay estate of Leeuw St Pierre in Brabant was reckoned to be more than 45,000 acres[16] in extent.

Of all the forms which rural activity took at that time, these great estates were the first – and indeed very nearly the only – ones to be clearly revealed by written evidence. These carefully ordered institutions, run for the profit of their owners, were called in the scholarly parlance of the time *villae*, the same word which had been used in classical Latin texts. Those situated in the region of Carolingian civilization between Loire and Rhine, or in Lombardy, which can be more satisfactorily observed, belonged to the great monasteries. Inventories and descriptions have enabled historians to trace the characteristics of this economic organization which it is convenient to call 'the manorial system'. As it has been the subject of many studies, often very detailed, we shall not need to linger long over it.

*   *   *

The aspects of the system revealed by the most famous of the documents, the first to be described by scholars and represented by them as the 'classical' type, are the two, complementary, halves of the *villa*. One of these was farmed by direct management. French historians have been accustomed to call this part *la réserve*, but when medieval lords and peasants spoke of it, they used the word *le domaine* – the demesne – and I, too, shall use the same word.

[15] Document No. 19, p. 383   [16] Ganshof, *La Belgique carolingienne*, p. 106

The second half of the *villa* was composed of tenancies; small holdings let out on lease.

A demesne bore the same appearance as a *manse*, for it was after all the *manse* of the master, *mansus indominicatus*. But it was an outsize *manse*, because it corresponded to a specially numerous, productive and demanding 'household' or *familia*. Even so, its structure was no different from that of other *manses*. At the centre was an enclosure, the courtyard, the space surrounded by a solid palisade, enclosing as well as the orchard and kitchen garden a collection of buildings which amounted to a hamlet. Here is a description of Annapes, which belonged to the king. Around a well-built stone palace containing three halls on the ground floor and eleven rooms upstairs stood a cluster of wooden buildings, a cowhouse, three stables, kitchen, bakehouse and 17 huts to shelter the servants and store the food.[17] As for the *appendicia*, attached to the central plot, there were extensive stretches of arable and meadow, as many vineyards as possible, and finally huge tracts of waste. The farm of Somain, near Annapes, had attached to it fields measuring 625 acres, meadow measuring 110 acres and 1,970 acres of woods and pasture. Other 'farms' were not always so well provided for; the one belonging to the abbey of St Pierre-du-Mont-Blandin at Ghent possessed less than 250 acres.[18]

However, generally speaking, the *mansus indominicatus* was equal in size to several dozen peasant *manses* held as tenancies. And the picture most frequently given by the evidence is of a number of tenanted *manses* supporting the one farmed by the master. The area of arable possessed by the tenanted *manses* varied very greatly in size, as we have seen, but was always less than the quantity of land which theoretically corresponded to the physical capacity of a peasant family. Those holdings called 'free' were on the average endowed with attached fields larger in extent than the 'servile' holdings – but the status of the *manse* was not always the same as the personal status of its tenant.

* * *

The primary function of the great demesnes was to allow a few men to live in idleness, abundance and the exercise of power. They maintained a narrow circle of the magnates in a magnificent way of life. In a society still primitive, and at a time when food supplies were limited, the 'man of power' showed himself first of all as the man who could always eat as much as he wished. He was also open handed, the man who provided others with food, and the yardstick of his prestige was the number of men whom he fed, and the size of his 'household'. Around the great lay and religious leaders congregated vast retinues of relatives, friends, people receiving patronage

[17] Document No. 2, p. 363   [18] Grierson, 247; Ganshof, 241

(the latter were known officially at the court of Charlemagne as *les nourris*), guests welcomed with liberality who would spread tales of the greatness of a house, and a host of servants, amongst whom would be found those artists in metal, woodcarving and weaving who could fashion weapons, jewellery and ornaments, and thereby enhance the luxurious setting appropriate to the exalted rank of the ruler. This way of life assumed housekeeping on a gigantic scale; barns and cellars filled to overflowing; well-tended and fruitful gardens, trellises and vineyards; the cultivation of fields of almost limitless extent to provide sufficient grain in spite of low yields; and lastly the existence of enormous forests and wastes to harbour game and give pasture to the riding and warhorses which were the mark of the aristocrat. The springs of wealth had to be inexhaustible. It was the privilege of the noble at all times to avoid any appearance of shortage. He had to be prodigal in the midst of famine, but, as harvests fluctuated from year to year, his steward, anxious never to find himself in short supply, naturally tried to increase output, especially of corn.

It is important, however, not to attribute an incipient profit motive to the anxiety of masters and their agents to develop their resources and enlarge their revenues. They had no wish to accumulate goods as such: their desire was merely, without anxiety for the morrow, to have something always in hand to provide for the 'family' and if need be to increase the number of their dependants. In those days personal devotion and service was a virtue upon which great store was set. Our sources mostly reveal the principles of estate management laid down by the heads of religious houses and these 'intellectuals' were very probably more conscious of the need to provide for the future. Their main preoccupation, however, was to specify the exact extent of their requirements in terms of agricultural output. This certainly appears to have been the object of the 'statutes' compiled by Abbot Adalard for the monastery of Corbie; they specified in minute detail the quality of bread, the weight of the loaves, the provenance of the flour from which they were to be made, how many different recipients there were and what the ration of each was to be.[19] An exact knowledge of what was required thus preceded and regulated the apportionment of supplies from different demesnes according to their capacity to produce. The tours of the surveyors and the preparation of inventories were intended to improve this apportionment as well as to find out whether extra brothers could be supported and more alms given away, thus increasing the number of mouths which would have to be fed. Behind the long-term plans which were concerned with consumption rather than production lay the fact that the *villa* was the provider and must not be found wanting in the hour of need.

[19] Document No. 16, p. 379

3. FARMING THE DEMESNE

Scholars have in recent years constructed economic 'models' of what they choose to call the classic demesne system (*le régime domanial classique*), based on the evidence of the few authoritative documents, and in this ideal system the *villa* is shown as a centre for the direct exploitation of the land: a widely spread centre, it is true, because agricultural yields were so low. At the beginning of the tenth century the monastery of San Giulia of Brescia consumed 6,600 *muids* of grain per annum. To assure themselves of this quantity the monks had to sow 9,000 *muids*.[20] So rudimentary was agricultural technique that a single aristocratic family needed for its support a vast arable area, usually the extensive *appendicia* of several *villae*. Consequently the chief problem which faced estate managers was that of manpower.

*   *   *

The solution of this problem was much simplified by the existence of slavery. At that period the whole of western Europe practised slavery, and probably nowhere more actively than on the less advanced fringes closer to pagan lands, such as England and Germania. In any case there were very large numbers of men and women described in Latin texts by the classical names of *servus*, *ancilla*, or the collective noun of neuter gender, *mancipium*. Their legal condition, only slightly ameliorated by a Christian environment, was the same as that of Roman or heathen slaves. Their marriages were recognized, they could save small sums of money and acquire land. But their bodies were entirely at the lord's disposal and could be bought and sold: they, together with their offspring and their possessions, formed part of the equipment of the household. Their duty to obey was unlimited and their labour was without reward. Many were set up by their masters on *manses* where they could raise families and make a living, and these enjoyed a degree of freedom. But many more lived and worked in the lord's house where their position was the same as that of the farm animals. They were fed and looked after as became objects of capital value, and they worked at the lord's will. It may be that household slaves were more numerous than other slaves, and there is some evidence to show that some peasants employed them in their homes. The man of modest means who managed the demesne of the monks of St Bertin at Poperinghe had four slaves in his service; his neighbour who managed a *manse* of 62 acres of arable at Moringhem kept a dozen slaves for his own personal use.[21] In the houses of the nobles

---

[20] Luzzatto, 165
[21] *Polyptyque de l'abbé Irminon* (ed. Guérard), II, Appendices, p. 400. The tenants of the abbey of Prüm put their *mancipia* at the disposal of the lord for the labour services of haymaking and harvest. Perrin, 256.

and the headquarters of the *villae*, there were of course hordes of them. Our documents seldom mention the farm personnel as such. Slaves working with their hands (*servi manuales*), from whom these workers were drawn, and the *mancipia non casata* – the slaves who had no habitation in which to lead a separate family life but who were lodged in outhouses in the courtyard, and were also known as 'prebendaries', since their master gave them food – all these were lumped together in a capitulary of 806 with household movables which were not always listed in inventories.[22] Personnel of this character existed everywhere and agricultural production everywhere depended primarily on them. On a demesne *manse* of about 50 acres which had just been presented to St Germain-des-Prés when the *polyptyque* of Irminon was drawn up the work was done by three *mancipia*.[23] And 22 household slaves worked on the 200 acres of demesne arable on the *villa* of Ingolstadt presented by Louis the Pious to the abbey of Niederalteich. On the Lombardy possessions of the abbey of San Giulia of Brescia there were in the years 905-906 between eight and forty-nine slaves in each household.[24]

The support of these servants was not an insurmountable problem. On estates where there were mills, the profits of multure were often sufficient to maintain the servile *familia*.[25] Nor must it be thought that recruitment of domestics was difficult. It is true that the spread of Christianity somewhat hindered the slave traffic,[26] but the market remained well supplied. Furthermore, some of the servants were married (as was the case with two of the *homines manuales* who worked in the household on one of the abbey of Farfa's *villae*) and many had legitimate or illegitimate children.[27] It was probably not thought profitable to bring these children up in the master's household, since it would have meant feeding them until they were old enough to work. On the other hand it is more than likely that the lord's personal servants, both male and female, were the offspring of the slaves who had been settled on the servile *manses*. The latter could have been nurseries for rearing young domestic servants, and perhaps this was one of their chief economic functions.

There was one overwhelming reason, nevertheless, why masters did not leave all the fieldwork in the hands of their household staff. This was because the work itself was unequally spread over the agricultural calendar. Unlike

---

[22] Carolingian law distinguished between slaves who were not housed separately, who were classed with 'movables', and those who *jam casati sunt*, who constituted the 'immovable inheritance', *Capitularia regum Francorum*, I.129. In 804 certain Italians made over to their creditors all their goods *excepto mobilio, servos et ancillas manuales*. *Registrum Farfense*, No. 175.

[23] *Polyptyque de l'abbé Irminon* (ed. Guérard), II. 123

[24] Luzzatto, 165   [25] Document No. 2, p. 363

[26] Latouche, 227, p. 188   [27] Luzzatto, 227

animal husbandry or viticulture, cereal-growing alternates long seasons of inactivity with feverish periods when fieldworkers are needed in extraordinary numbers, Ploughing, harvesting and making hay to feed the draught animals in winter had to be accomplished with great speed in uncertain weather, and were times of frantic activity. To have enough personal servants to fulfil all the needs of the moment would have meant maintaining them in virtual idleness throughout the rest of the year. The food they ate would have been wasted and would have reduced the already restricted yield of agriculture. As a consequence the delicately poised economy of the demesne would have been disturbed. A far better solution was to supplement the small domestic labour force required to perform the daily tasks with the seasonal appointment of some hired labourers.

Economic conditions of the time did not absolutely preclude the possibility of wage labour. At Corbie the official in charge of cultivating the garden employed helpers for digging the borders, for planting and for weeding. Every year he was given towards the upkeep of these dayworkers 100 loaves, one *muid* of peas and beans and one of barley beer (which proves that these workers by the day were paid with meals), but 60 *deniers* were set aside as well 'to take on men'.[28] But even so the monetary medium lacked flexibility, and money wages remained exceptional. It was much more convenient to reward the temporary farmworkers of the demesne with a plot of land and to settle them upon a *manse*. The productive effort of these men and their families was thus divided. One part was left to provide themselves and their families with a living from their own plot of land. But the other had to remain at the disposal of the landlord. Here then was another economic function of the satellite holdings of the demesne.

*   *   *

In return for their endowment the peasant 'households' owed to the 'household' of their master various dues the nature of which was usually the same for each category of *manses* on the *villa* and also on other *villae* belonging to the same landowner. There were to begin with the various dues which had to be taken to the lord's hall on certain days of the year. The amounts were fixed, a few pieces of money, some chickens, eggs, one or two small animals such as sheep or pigs. These payments can be taken either as payments for the use of the woods and wastes of the lord, or as taxes of public origin. Some of them were the relics of the charges formerly imposed on peasants for supplies to the royal armies. It was the duty of the landlord to collect these, and in time he appropriated them for himself. These different dues were never heavy and the profit of the recipient was minimal. Their impact on the

[28] *Statuts d'Adelard*, II.1 (*Polyptyque de l'abbé Irminon* (ed. Guérard), II)

economy of the *villa* cannot have affected the real struggle for existence, the toil connected with garnering the main food supply, but was more a marginal matter of backyard poultry and small surplus items of diet. They formed only a superficial charge on the tenants' own farm production; and to the lord, as well, these odd amounts of food and small sums of money were trifling matters which contributed little if anything to his standard of living.

On the other hand the labour services imposed on the holdings were the essential economic link between them and the demesne and formed the very nexus of the demesne system. The manpower available on each satellite farm unit was, as we have seen, greater than that required to cultivate its fields. And this surplus manpower had to go to the demesne. It might take the form of periodic deliveries of objects upon which labour had been expended: thus, each *manse* might have to prepare a load of firewood, or a certain number of stakes, beams or planks, or perhaps some of those simple tools which could be constructed by any unskilled person. On servile holdings the women would weave cloth for the demesne. But the main tasks were agricultural, and they took three distinct but often interconnected forms.

1. The *manse* could in the first place be charged with a definite task. It could be responsible, for instance, for erecting in springtime a certain length of temporary fencing to protect the crops and the hay. More usually it was given the responsibility for an entire season's cultivation of a given plot of land, the *ansange*, taken from the demesne arable; activities which began with preliminary ploughing and continued right until storing of the grain in the lord's barn. In this way, every year some parcels of the demesne arable which needed cultivating were temporarily detached from the rest and were joined to the *appendicia* of the peasant *manses*. They rounded off the latter and absorbed the underemployed productive effort of the tenant population.

2. Other obligations were more exacting, since they left the workers less freedom. To perform them they were periodically taken away from the family group and put to join a team of workers on the lands attached to the demesne. These demands – the *corvées* in the real sense of the term, since the word means 'demand' or 'requisition' – only affected one labour unit in each *manse*, a worker either by hand or with a draught animal, i.e. a man or a plough team. If a *manse* was occupied by several families, or if the tenants themselves owned servants, as was fairly frequent, the service would be much lightened. Sometimes the *manse* owed a fixed number of days either at certain seasons, or else each week, and sometimes the man subject to the *corvée* assisted in a definite task until it was completed. In certain cases it was really manual labour (*manoperae*), for the man in question would come in the morning to the lord's hall to join the farm servants and await his orders whilst

his implements and plough team were left behind at the *manse*. Another kind of forced labour was specially assigned to certain tasks. The work of the women from the servile *manses* in the demesne workshops was of such a kind, and so were the errands and cartage requiring the use of cart and draught animals, which were usually the responsibility of the better-equipped, so-called 'free' *manses*.

3. Tasks referred to in the inventories as 'nights' were the third kind of work which might be required. These placed the tenant at the service of the lord for several days at a stretch without the certainty of returning home each evening. This enabled him to be employed at a distance or to be sent away on a mission, and it is clear that these obligations of an indeterminate nature provided the demesne with a reserve of immediately available and reliable labour in cases of unforeseen need.

These different tasks were often combined. But for the free *manse* they were usually lighter, more limited, and of less degrading nature. The free *manses* were generally occupied by peasants of free status, whose ancestors had often been independent, but who, because they were poor or weak, had allowed their lands to become part of the economic system of the *villa* in exchange for help and protection. But even where rural migration, mixed marriages and the alienation of land had obliterated the connection between the 'freedom' of the tenancy and the free status of the tenants, the holdings were of sufficient size to support the larger domestic animals. To be able to provide oxen or a horse, and thus to take part in ploughing, cartage and contacts with the outside world, was probably their most valuable contribution to the demesne activities; they could supply ploughmen, drivers and horsemen, rather than unskilled labourers. On the other hand, it is easy to believe that when landlords created servile *manses* to house some of their domestic serfs in order to be rid of responsibility for their maintenance and to let them bring up their own children, they did not for one moment relax their right to command obedience or to use them at their will. They had to do manual labour because they did not usually possess draught animals. It was they who guarded the headquarters of the demesne at night, did the laundry, dipped and sheared sheep, while their wives and daughters worked in the demesne workshops. Servile *manses* were also burdened with the weekly labour services of undefined nature. In Germania they had usually to put a man at the disposal of the lord for three days a week; or in other words each *manse* had to provide one half-time servant throughout the year. This explains their smaller allocation of arable land than that of the free *manses*. Their holders were forced to work away from home for longer and could thus devote less time to their own farms, but on the other hand, when performing forced labour in the demesne they ate in the refectory, and their consumption of food at home was accordingly reduced.[29]

Since the profit to be derived from a tenancy did not correspond to the services which it owed, the tenancy was not exactly a wage. The letting out of the *manses* ought primarily to be thought of as a way of relieving the demesne management of the necessity to provide the servants with board and lodging. The demesne could in this way have an abundant source of labour at its disposal. It has been calculated that the 800 dependent families of the abbey of San Giulia of Brescia at the beginning of the tenth century owed service to their masters amounting to 60,000 working days.[30] The lord, here as elsewhere, wanted to dip into a bottomless well, to be permanently able to command instant service in the event of unforeseen need. But in normal times it is unlikely that all the labour services owing were actually called upon.

This then was the manorial system. The surplus productive effort of the peasant families was appropriated by the lord, to whose rule they were subject, for the purpose of farming his lands. But since human labour could by itself produce so little, this surplus was also limited. And because of this, the demesne needed a large number of satellite *manses*.

4. THE DESTINATION OF THE DEMESNE PROFITS

The picture of the Carolingian *villa* as a closed community intended to operate entirely on its own resources is one which needs considerable modification. The individual *villa* actually fitted into a much larger economic system, because the nobles usually owned several demesnes. From this three consequences followed.

1. In the plan laid down for the fulfilment of the lord's needs the deliveries expected from the different demesnes were sometimes specialized because of differing natural conditions. This was particularly the case with such a highly prized commodity as wine. Wine was the beverage of the nobility. It graced the tables of the wealthy and it was the choicest gift to bestow on friends; great men boasted of the quality of the wine from their *clos* and basked in the honour which it shed on them. The plots on which vineyards were to be planted were selected with great care and this was the cause of much landgrabbing. The abbeys of northern Gaul and the powerful rulers of Germania strove to acquire lands in the Paris basin and the Rhine valley, where the climate favoured the ripening of the grape.

---

[29] An intermediate category can also be distinguished in some *polyptyques*, that of 'lidiles', *manses* which correspond to the social condition of freedmen
[30] Luzzatto, 229

2. Such a lord and his retinue resided in the fine house built for his occupation on the demesne at rare intervals only, for he owned several other houses which he visited in turn. When the time came for his visit beds and stables were made ready, bread baked and meat roasted. For a while the lord and his followers consumed the accumulated stores of food built up in anticipation of their arrival. But they were always on the move travelling from one demesne to the next, and aristocratic existence was a constant succession of migrations throughout the year. All this presented a problem of management, for in his long absences the lord had to have a representative on whose shoulders rested the entire demesne organization. The direction of the servants, the requisitioning of those chosen to give labour service, the safe custody of the stocks of provisions, all fell upon him. His responsibility was heavy, and he wielded great power, for when he was alone he could command and punish as he pleased. But his employer endeavoured to hold him in check; the capitulary *De Villis* is no more than a collection of instructions to the *villici*, the superintendants of the royal demesnes.[31]

3. Lastly, the many centres of production answerable to the same master needed contacts, and, to a certain extent, transport. When a demesne specialized in a certain crop the lord could not consume it all on the spot at one time; it had to be despatched to him wherever he was. This was the case with wine: every year at the time of the vintage a monk of St Bertin would visit the vineyard which the abbey owned near Cologne and would return with a convoy of casks.[32] Other transport had to be organized when the lord after one of his periods of residence sent to fetch something that he lacked.[33] Sending goods in this way became a larger and a much more regular affair when the manorial 'family' did not move from place to place and assembled all their provisions from distant demesnes. Monasteries were immobile institutions of this kind. The abbey of Corbie kept 140 servants whose special concern was to bring food supplies to the community of monks. The rivers and trackways of the wild and wooded countryside were constantly traversed by caravans and messengers. The methods of communication, too, were still very primitive. For errands and heavy transport horses and oxen in great numbers had to be mobilized, and men were needed to drive the carts, row the boats and carry the packs. Some of the labour services imposed on demesne tenants were devoted to this work, and, except at times of great pressure, a certain number of personnel were always occupied away from the demesne. This required a heavy expenditure of manpower.

[31] Document No. 1, p. 361
[32] Dion, 105, p. 419; H. van Werveke, 'Comment les établissements religieux belges, se procuraient-ils du vin au Haut Moyen Age?', in *Revue belge de philologie et d'histoire*, 1923
[33] Document No. 17, p. 381

In this way much effort was wasted. But the same relentless assembling of the necessities of life from the most remote possessions, as well as the incessant journeyings of the manorial 'households' are proof that the lords set before themselves the ideal of supplying all their needs from their own property, and that they believed that 'it should not be necessary to seek for, or to buy anything from outside'.[34] This ideal of self-sufficiency could never really be achieved. Some exchange between the group of demesnes constituting the feudal patrimony and the outside world had to take place. Besides, the internal structure of the demesne economy implied a certain freedom, mainly on account of the satellite peasant farms.

For one thing the topography of the *villa* encouraged relations with neighbouring centres of production. It seems certain that the area covered by the *villa* was very rarely identical with the village or its lands. It extended over several clearings without occupying any one completely. The furlongs of the demesne, the *manses* of the holdings, and their adjoining parcels of land thus lay side by side with fields and enclosures which did not belong to the lord. The tenants used the waste in common with other peasants who were their neighbours. This contiguity was almost certainly the occasion for the exchange of services. The stewards of the demesnes were more than likely to recruit the few dayworkers whom they engaged for wages from amongst the neighbours. It must also be supposed, as I have said before, that some tenants possessed, apart from their holdings which were in any case far too small to feed their families, other plots, either totally independent or else attached to another manor. The economic community made up of demesne workers was consequently not always an exclusive nor a completely closed one. Some peasants who were partly integrated into it were at the same time participating in other groups with a different interest, either in teams of another demesne, or simply in the village community.

Furthermore it must not be forgotten that money, that is coined 'pennies', small coins of 'black silver', played its part in the relationship of lord and peasant. In fact the most insignificant infractions of the peace or customary usage were punished by a pecuniary fine. To meet these debts the humblest tenant might from time to time have to disburse a few pieces of money. They also had to pay in money certain annual obligations. Except in the provinces on the fringes of the Carolingian world, such as Bavaria, the landowners levied each year some cash from the *manses*, or allowed the tenants to commute some deliveries in kind or some labour services. The documents of Bobbio, Lucca and San Giulia de Brescia show that money payments were

---

[34] *Capitularia de Villis*, c. 42

specially frequent on Italian manors. The institution of such periodic payments implies that those who farmed holdings regularly sold a portion of their own output or their labour.

Indeed the existence of very many weekly markets can be traced in the countryside and in the smallest villages. Many grew up in the ninth and tenth centuries. They were not part of the internal machinery of the demesne set up to deal only with transactions between tenants. They served the purpose of external relations, and the capitulary *De Villis* warns stewards against the attractions which the fairs offer to demesne labourers, who waste their time there in idleness, and perhaps dispose of the fruits of petty thieving. Thus, a natural rhythm of buying and selling existed: regular, even though restricted. The uneven output of agriculture from year to year and the constant passing of travellers along the tracks which led through the villages would offer small producers an occasion to exchange for money a few of the products of their garden or farmyard. Aware of such small profits, the lord would wish to take his share of them; in demanding dues in coin he benefited by the commercial activities of his dependants whilst at the same time stimulating them.

Furthermore he encouraged his administrators to engage more directly in commerce, and the demesne took as much part in trade as the villagers did, if not more. The Porter of Corbie regularly purchased wood[35]: the managers of the royal demesnes as regularly bought seed corn, because they had been advised, if they wished to increase yields, never to sow the seed which they themselves had just produced. Above all, equally regularly, a large part of the demesne output was drained away from home, some, at least, free of charge as gifts and relief which well repaid the lord in devotion and gratitude.

Every lordly household (more particularly the religious ones, and those of the rulers who were anxious to promote their own reputation) distributed alms to the destitute, and this periodic giving away of the demesne surplus to the least favoured social groups, and the sustenance which paupers derived from it, constituted an economic activity which it would be unwise to ignore. For instance, we know that 400 poor people received their daily allowance at the doors of the monastery of St Riquier. Certainly charity and gifts were more frequent than trade at that period.

But part also of the demesne profits was normally exchanged for money payment. On the demesnes farthest removed from the parent abbeys the monks arranged for heavy goods to be sold so as to avoid carrying them over long distances.[36] But the lords sold goods also, because they needed more

[35] *Polyptyque de l'abbé Irminon* (ed. Guérard), II, appendices, p. 370
[36] *Ibid.*, pp. 334-335

money than the insignificant amounts their tenants could supply in order to satisfy some of their needs. When the abbot of Ferrières ordered wine and grain to be sold he was thinking of the need to renew his monks' wardrobe.[37] Every year on Palm Sunday the administrators of the royal demesne brought 'the money drawn from the crops'[38] to the palace of Charlemagne. In this way, trading activities spread effectively beyond the confines of the village, and the flow of demesne surpluses carried commerce along the riverways and routes on which traffic was least difficult to distant horizons.

Cereals certainly formed the object of long-distance traffic. Einhard refers to 'merchants of the city of Mainz who were in the habit of buying wheat in the upper reaches and bringing it down to the city on the Main'.[39] But without doubt the most frequent and regular commercial operations concerned high quality wine. The north-west of Europe was incapable of producing it, and the magnates of those countries were prepared to pay dearly to obtain it. As a direct result of this demand vineyards sprang up in the Carolingian era along the banks of the Loire (Alcuin honoured Bishop Theodulph of Orleans with the title 'father of the vines') and the Rhine (if Ermold the Black is to be believed, it was the Frisians who built up the prosperity of the Vosges in coming to purchase the wine harvest). Above all they spread out over the basin of the Seine.[40] At the fair on 9th October the abbot of St Denis sold to the Saxons, the Frisians and the merchants of Rouen, who carried it away to England, enormous quantities of new wine produced on his demesnes.[41]

Everything leads us to believe that it was the excess production of the great demesnes which in the ninth century underpinned the growth of trade, the development along the rivers of the *portus* and the merchant communities, and the activities of the small group of specialists in exchange, the only men in whom the spirit of pure gain had been kindled. For this period which saw small purchases at subsistence level on the village market, also encouraged speculation, which was made profitable by the wide variations in production, overpopulation, permanent poverty and the threat of scarcity each spring. In 794 a capitulary attempted to fix the retail price of cereals. Another in 806 condemned 'those who, at harvest and vintage time, bought corn and wine without need, but with cupidity as their motive, for example buying one *muid* for two *deniers* and keeping it until they could resell it for six *deniers* or more'. A regulation of 809 refers to cultivators and lords who, driven by necessity, 'sell wine and corn before the harvest, and thus become im-

---

[37] Loup de Ferrières, Lettres (ed. Levillain), I.117
[38] Document No. 1, p. 361
[39] *Histoire de la translation des saints Marcelin et Pierre*, 39 (*Pat. Lat.*, CIV, col. 560)
[40] Dion, 105, p. 211   [41] Doerhaerd, 219

poverished'.[42] In such an economic climate, the demesne was not as isolated as it might appear from a too hasty reading of inventories. It had dealings with other demesnes, as well as with surrounding peasant farmers, and it lay in the midst of a world of movement.

5. DIFFERENCES IN MANORIAL STRUCTURE

The demesne was caught up and transformed by this movement, and the light shed by the sources enables us to distinguish some of the changes that took place. To begin with the changes were those of form, for the *villa* was generally part of an inheritance which was itself subject to change. Where the fortune belonged to a lay family the demesne underwent a division between heirs in each generation.[43] And even when the head of the family was very wealthy and the patrimony was made up of many *villae*, a natural anxiety to allot equal portions to heirs of the same standing often led to each demesne being cut up into 'shares'. Separated one from another, these shares tended to form economically independent units. Gifts, which were so important in the social relationships of the period, provided another dislocating factor. To begin with there was the generosity of the princes who were in large measure responsible for establishing the economic fortunes of the great families. There were their gifts to friends and to those whose services they wished to reward or whose devotion they wished to secure; there were also gifts to churches, for alms were in those days regarded as the most laudable form of piety. Such acts of generosity often amputated fragments of a *villa* by taking away from it one or more dependent *manses*, or even a part of the arable of the demesne. In this way demesne groups were constantly being broken up.

But, as frequently, others were built up again. In certain peripheral provinces, the formation of new *villae* followed in the wake of land settlement. It can be seen quite clearly in Flanders and Brabant where written documents and agrarian archeology both show that numerous demesnes were created in the ninth century on cleared wasteland newly opened up.[44] In regions slowly emerging from savagery the founding of large demesnes also accompanied the emergence of a less primitive social order. Thus in the part of Germania conquered by the Carolingians and Christianity, the installation of counts, and above all the foundation of Christian institutions, bishoprics and monasteries, helped to multiply the *villae* and to stimulate diffusion of the manorial system.

Evidence of the growth of demesne groups throughout the west is to be found in some church documents and particularly in the 'books of donations'

---

[42] *Capitularia Regum Francorum*, I.74, 132, 152; Latouche, 227, pp. 180 *et seq.*
[43] Document No. 18, p. 382   [44] Verhulst, 208 and 233

many of which were put together in the German abbeys.[45] The alms of greater and lesser men came year after year to enrich the inheritance of their religious patrons. The gifts normally included slaves but above all else, landed possessions of every value and size. If the donor was a magnate a gift could sometimes be a whole *villa* ready to take its place in the constellation of demesnes already supporting the monastery. But most of the gifts were trifling and dispersed: a *manse* or two in one village, a few acres in another. These scattered plots could be unified little by little and could provide the exchange of services which composed the heart of the demesne system. The integrating process, however, was slow. On some of the manors of St Germain-des-Prés, such as Corbon and Villemeux, when the *polyptyque* of Irminon was compiled, it was still imperfect.[46] Almost all the *manses* recently acquired by gift remained economically independent farms; forced labour had not been imposed on them, and they did not therefore participate in the general operations of the estate. The lord obtained their assistance in providing for his household in the simplest possible way, that is by demanding from them a portion of their own harvest each year. Here, recourse to share-cropping (*métayage*), a farming process fundamentally different from the 'classic' demesne system, was perhaps transitory and gradually prepared the way for the establishment of labour dues. But in any case, the historian should be on guard against the impression of immobility which a reading of the inventories might give. The state of affairs which these describe was in reality fluid and marked only a brief moment in a continual evolution.

*   *   *

The modifications to which the form of the *villa* was subjected, its disintegration and reassembly through partition and gift, were constantly throwing the 'manorial system' itself into a state of crisis, and disrupting the links between the demesne and its holdings. The essential balance between the labour needs of the demesne, the number of *manses* and the amount of labour services imposed on them, was constantly disturbed. If a lord were to break his connection with a holding, acquire a field or extend his arable by clearing the waste, he ran the risk of a shortage of labour. On the other hand if he were to part with a portion of the demesne, or add new *manses* to which labour services were attached, he had labour available for which there was no longer sufficient employment.

But lack of balance in the supply and demand for labour appears to have been partly connected with changes of a more profound nature. Technical developments could result in long term modifications. In so far as improve-

---

[45] Document No. 19, p. 383
[46] Document No. 6, p. 369; No. 20, p. 383

ments were introduced – for instance, by increasing arable or adding to its fertility by marling the land – they encouraged the lords to extend the demands for labour. Conversely, the taming of natural forces, the increase in the productivity of labour, and better technical equipment allowed the most disagreeable labour tasks, such as those which before the installation of water mills forced the occupants of servile *manses* to grind corn by hand, to fall into disuse.

Another factor was the instability of the manorial population. From time to time it suffered from accidental calamities; famines, epidemics and the disastrous forays of pillagers decimated the ranks. But at the same time natural demographic pressure, slow but continuous, tended to increase the number of households in the enclosure of the manse. In actual fact all the Carolingian inventories enumerate, sometimes even side by side, both overcrowded and deserted *manses (absi)*. The manpower which the tenants could put at the disposal of the lord shows in this way considerable variation, to which the manorial system had to adapt itself. In the *villa* of Villance in the Ardennes, when the description in the *polyptyque* of the abbey of Prüm, was drawn up in 893 after the Normans had passed through the land, several *manses* deserted since the invasion remained unoccupied. Thus they no longer provided labour, but actually increased demands for manpower, because servants or forced labour had to be employed on their arable temporarily joined to the demesne. On the other hand, on neighbouring farms peasants proliferated. Probably acceding to the demands of the families themselves, the lord had permitted the splitting up of *manses*. There were at Villance 11 half manses and 20 quarter manses, but two-thirds of the 35 *manses* which remained intact were each occupied by four farming families. The administrators had taken advantage of this overpopulation to increase their demands. The labour services of the divided *manses* had been made heavier; while in the undivided *manses* each occupying family was required to pay the whole of the rent due in cash.[47]

Lastly, the flexibility of economic conditions must be taken into consideration. Little by little trade in the produce of the soil introduced differences in wealth into the heart of peasant society, placing rich and poor side by side. Some tenants were thus tempted to sell, without their lords' knowledge, plots of land attached to their *manse*, upsetting the balance between the charges bearing on the taxpaying unit and the latter's power to bear them. An edict of Charles the Bald vainly attempted to bring such practices to an end on the royal demesnes, where some tenants were refusing to fulfil their obligations because their *manse* had lost almost all its appendages.[48] Finally in regions where the flow of exchange had penetrated farthest, the development

---

[47] Perrin, 200, p. 640   [48] Document No. 9, p. 372

of trade and a greater familiarity with the use of money, in peasant as well as lordly households, helped to base the economic relations between holdings and demesne at least partly on money payments.

*   *   *

Adjustments were therefore constantly necessary. Unfortunately the stories of individual *villae* are obscure even in the areas best illuminated by the *polyptyques*. The inventories which were regularly kept up to date and which would give successive pictures of changing conditions in the same demesne group are extremely rare. But we can guess that an inside story of this sort, concerned with the relationship between peasant and steward, would reveal a complex tangle of demands abandoned and renewed, of refusals and resistances. Concerned above all else to stabilize revenues upon which to base rates of consumption, administrators were continually forced to adapt their arrangements. We may assume that one of the functions of the *polyptyques* was to try to fix definitively the number of tenancies and the charges on them. They were also intended to prevent any particular service which had been temporarily renounced from being thereafter lost. We have a glimpse of the conflict between the monks of Cormery and their tenants in the village of Antoigné from the judgment of King Pépin of Aquitaine in 828. The tenants had refused to render their dues which 'for a long time' no one had demanded of them. But the advocate and the provost of the abbey were able to produce before the tribunal an ancient 'description' upon which at some past date these obligations had been inscribed on the oath of the dependants: they won their case.[49] On the other hand other documents prove that peasants could successfully oppose in the public courts the 'innovations' of their lord. In 905 the Church of Saint Ambrose in Milan had to surrender the labour services it had demanded from its dependants at Lemonta.[50] How many more country folk were able similarly to find support outside the village community against the encroachments of their lords? Our evidence is silent about other peasant victories: the rents and labour services lost through forgetfulness or through failure of managers to overcome the passive resistance of the tenants, or to extract anything from the destitute. But whatever happened, even on demesnes where inventories were drawn up, the development of the manorial system was not substantially hindered. The periodic overhaul of the *polyptyques* and the corrections which were necessary from time to time are proof of this.

Besides, the system described by the most ancient of these inquests appears to have been already time-worn and considerably modified. So

---

[49] *Recueil des actes de Pépin Iᵉʳ et de Pépin II, rois d'Aquitaine* (ed. Levillain)
[50] Leicht, 164, pp. 83 *et seq.*

much is clear from Irminon's *polyptyque*: in accordance with demographic movements and economic and social changes which had probably been going on for generations, there no longer existed on the *villae* around Paris the slightest correlation between the status of the tenant and that of his holding, between the number of tenancies and the number of peasant households, or between the services due from the labourers and the size of the plot which was allocated to them. By comparing the state of affairs at different periods on manors not too distant from each other in regions where some evidence is available, it is possible to trace the general direction of these changes.

*   *   *

The first, as well as the most obvious and general change, was that the distinction between the free and the servile *manse* gradually fell into disuse, and that all the units of habitation and taxation on the manor came to be treated in the same way. Peasant mobility which can be assumed, overpopulation on the *manse*, discrepancies between the condition of the tenant and the status of his tenure, probably facilitated this assimilation. It was also a simplification well suited to a bucolic society not likely to appreciate abstract legal distinctions.

There were other changes, even though they do not appear so marked in every province. In the most primitive regions, like Germania, it seems that in the ninth century charges on holdings, and labour services in particular, were becoming heavier. The laws of the Bavarians and the Alamans, drawn up in the first half of the eighth century, show that the servile *manse* normally owed no more than three days work as *corvée* each week. On certain manors, the subject of a description in the following century, holdings in the same category were also required to give help in ploughing the lords' fields similar to that which was formerly due from individual *manses* of free men.[51] This trend, as we can see, also brought the different categories of *manses* closer together and eventually confused them. But it was probably also explained by the internal growth of the demesne economy, and by the increase of agriculture at the expense of animal husbandry or even more primitive activities which forced the lord to add to his ploughing personnel: in short by the general progress of material civilization.

In the provinces which were by contrast more developed, it seems as if we can likewise distinguish in the course of the tenth century an increase in the number of cash dues amongst the charges imposed upon the tenants. Thus money dues occupied a much larger place on one Burgundian manor than they did in the *villae* of the abbey of Prüm in the Ardennes, inventoried some years earlier.[52] These money dues appear to have been demanded in

[51] Documents No. 3, p. 364, and No. 8, p. 371
[52] Document No. 10, p. 373

place of former liveries of animals or labour services, cartage of wood or look-out service. Peasants and lords, by common consent, seem to have chosen to make greater use of money. The substitution of money dues for labour services and dues in kind can be seen even more clearly in northern Italy in the second half of the ninth and in the tenth century. Here the phenomenon can be connected with the growth of trade and with the rise of rural markets which took place in the valley of the Po at this period.[53]

It should be noted that money dues were absolutely unknown at that time on many Bavarian manors. Very considerable discrepancies in the economic development of the various provinces of the west therefore existed. These regional contrasts, together with conditions which here and there accelerated or slowed down the development or growth of an estate, oblige us to modify the theory of the 'classic' demesne system and to substitute for it a more realistic picture which puts the main emphasis on the great diversities in the economic structure of the great landed properties in Carolingian times. In comparison with the Paris region, whose sources, so magnificently interpreted by B. Guérard more than a century ago, allowed the model of the manorial system to be constructed, very wide divergencies appear only a short distance westwards and still within the patrimony of St Germain-des-Prés. On the lands of this abbey at Villemeux and Boissy near Dreux, for instance, the proportion of fields integrated into the demesne and reserved for the use of the lord was much less than around Paris (11·5 per cent in the manor of Villemeux against 35·7 per cent at Palaiseau). Furthermore, possessions were much more dispersed and this reduced considerably the economic link between the large number of demesne furlongs and the holdings. Amongst the latter, many indeed owed no labour services at all and their occupants only appeared at the manorial hall to pay their dues.

The *polyptyques* of Germania describe even more widely scattered possessions. So dispersed were the lands that the 'hall' often appeared to have been no more than a centre for the receipt of dues. No more than a dozen *manses* were to be found close to the demesne[54] and servile *manses* predominated: the manors of the abbey of Lorsch included no others. While in the western parts of the Carolingian empire a large proportion of the 'free' peasantry was subjected to the strict economic domination of the great demesne, it appears that in Germany the farming of aristocratic lands remained self-sufficient and was much less closely connected with neighbouring peasantry. Private labour, prebendary slaves, fed in the household or

---

[53] Luzzatto, 229. In the tenth century, the tenants of San Giulia of Brescia had to take silk to the royal market of Brescia and, for every 10 *livres* sold, to pay the lord 50 souls (Lopez, in 6, pp. 279 *et seq.*).
[54] Document No. 11, p. 374

housed on a few holdings, performed the essential tasks. The demesne economy appears here to have been less public, more domestic and less invasive in nature and this was due to the firm existence of slavery in the outlying areas of Christian civilization, to the fairly recent establishment of manorial institutions, and, more likely still, to the existence of vigorous communities of peasants living in conditions of freedom. In any case it was unusual for the latter to assist in cultivating the estate.

The inventories of northern Italy show a different structure again. As in Germania, large teams of prebendary or household slaves (*masnad*) worked in the 'hall'. They had the help of some families of *servi*, housed on holdings and liable to service without limit (*angaria*). But the most of the tenants – there were 300 of them on the lands of the abbey of Bobbio in the midninth century – were *libellarii*, i.e. freemen, often owners of allods elsewhere, but who had received a grant of land by a written contract for a long term, at least 29 years. This agreement concluded with the landlord carried on an ancient tradition: it sometimes imposed a certain amount of labour service; this was limited, however, to a few weeks in the year. But most of the tenants remained exempt from any collaboration in demesne labour. Their association with the economy of the manorial 'hall' assumed another form. They had to deliver to the lord's granaries a certain proportion of their own harvest; a third of their grain and half their wine on the lands of San Giulia of Brescia: a tenth part of the grain and flax, and a quarter or a third of the wine on the lands of the Church at Ravenna.[55] This system differed even more widely from the classical demesne system. It was really domestic agriculture based on slavery on the German model, juxtaposed with a system of land management based on temporary leases and share-cropping. In addition the active state of exchange and the greater use of money tended rapidly to reduce the obligations of the tenants. By the end of the tenth century the tenants of the episcopal chapter of Lucca owed hardly any labour service or rents or kind; they paid nearly all in cash.[56]

But in considering the manors of Germania and Lombardy, and even those more westerly manors of St Germain-des-Prés, one cannot avoid a feeling of doubt. Is it really safe when making what is admittedly a hypothetical reconstruction of the rural economy of the Carolingian period to accord such a key position to labour services linking holdings with demesnes? Or to make the labour connection between peasant and lordly households the essence of the demesne system? In many regions such a system of farming appears to have been, if not exactly unknown, then at least very unusual. Little can be said about England, which was still veiled in shadows. Anglo-Saxon documents allow glimpses of a far from powerful aristocracy, a king

[55] Leicht, 164, p. 64; Luzzatto, 229   [56] Endres, 239

and his retinue supported by fixed liveries of food brought periodically from the villages, a custom of granting land, seed, or a team to peasant families in exchange for personal service, and no more.[57] But what of Flanders, Brabant and the borders of Frisia on the edges of Carolingian civilization? In 893, on the lands owned by the abbey of Prüm at Arnhem, the *manses* had each to deliver 26 *deniers*, two *muids* of rye, four cartloads of wood, a hen, five eggs, and two pigs worth five *deniers*; owing only four weeks labour services each year, two in May and two in the autumn, they cannot really be said to have been associated with the farming activities of the demesne.[58] As for the 75 acres of ploughland and the 45 acres of meadow which formed the demesne of the abbey of St Pierre of Ghent, the work was entirely performed by a small team of domestic serfs, 29 menservants, 10 farm girls and three herdswomen; the tenants of the 25 dependent *manses* owed no agricultural service at all.[59] Holdings on the five *villae* to the north-east of Ghent belonging to the Abbey of St Bavo, created by recent clearance, remote from the demesne headquarters and mainly devoted to animal husbandry, made no contribution to the cultivation of the demesne furlongs.[60] What is most striking here is the complete separation between the demesne, run entirely by the *familia*, and the holdings which produced rent. In western Gaul (Maine, where the word *mansus* was never used, and where the concentration of land in very large farming units appeared to be the exception)[61] and in southern Gaul, where admittedly documents are very rare and hard to interpret (in Auvergne for instance, where we cannot see any *corvées* uniting *manses* or *appendariae* to the *indominicatum*),[62] a similar separation was probably more frequent than not.

6. THE GREAT ESTATE AND THE PEASANT ECONOMY

This conclusion brings in its train another problem, perhaps the most important of all, although not one to which it is possible to find a convincing solution. Though less extensive and all-pervasive than appears from our evidence, which is very patchy and comes solely from records of landed proprietors, the great estate could not fail to make its influence felt on neighbouring farms. But to what extent did it do so? Did it govern the economic relations of the households and families around it? Or did these organize themselves spontaneously into communities of neighbours?

We can do little more than suggest hypothetical answers to these questions. For instance in some localities around the abbey of St Gall in the ninth century, and in certain areas in Lombardy or the Mâconnais in the tenth

[57] Stenton, 232, pp. 276 *et seq.*   [58] Sloet, 205. No. 66
[59] Ganshof, *La Belgique carolingienne*, p. 105   [60] Verhulst, 208
[61] Latouche, 227, pp. 226-228   [62] Fournier, 240

century, certain unusually communicative records reveal a number of allods, that is to say family holdings of varying size completely separate from all manorial ties. Around the huge manorial complexes of the kind described by the *polyptyques* flourished small autonomous farms comprising no more land than a satellite *manse* of a great estate. Certain written records, especially those instituting dowries in favour of wives, allow us to measure the size of these properties. Above all, everywhere where conditions for research are favourable the evidence bears witness to the presence of peasants of modest estate who managed their properties in complete independence with the help of their children and a few serfs. Some village territories were totally integrated in the manor and in these cases the lord's estate, occupying the site of an ancient Roman *villa*, dominated the whole of a clearing. But in most of the villages there were to be found side by side, growing or disintegrating, many farms whose economic life was totally independent. At Varanges, a little hamlet next door to Cluny, forty-seven separate landowners were counted in the second half of the tenth century; and there must have been others whom we do not know about. Some of them tried laboriously to increase their possessions. Such were David and Dominique, husband and wife, who for 28 sous acquired one by one in small purchases at well spaced out intervals eleven small parcels of land, amounting altogether to about an acre. Because they were childless and all they possessed passed into the hands of the church after their death, the slow accumulation of lands for which they saved has been recorded.[63] But how many more country folk were there like them who profited from their neighbours' embarrassments and invested in this way the money they had earned in the village market?

Such small farmers whose *manses* were intermingled in the village enclave must have found themselves bound together by many ties into a community which did not coincide with the group for whom the manorial 'hall' was the focal point. It was mainly agrarian interest that held them together. The documents are extremely uncommunicative on this point, but the annual movement of ploughlands and sowing between the different parts of the cultivated area, the allocation of grazing on stubble and fallow, and the erection of enclosures on certain dates presuppose a collective discipline, as does the communal possession of the grazing grounds, the *terres des Francs* which in the tenth century was current in all the villages of Mâconnais. As a matter of principle the free inhabitants felt themselves allied in the face of the public power of the king and his representatives. Every so often they came together in the neighbouring village, the seat of the Hundred, or of the *viguerie* in the Midi, to prosecute the small lawsuits which could not be settled amicably.[64] They subscribed together to offer hospitality to the en-

---

[63] Déléage, 218, p. 244   [64] Bosl, 516, p. 244

voys of king, count or bishop, or their agents, to respond to military requisitions and to victual the companies formed by the wealthier individuals at the start of expeditions of war. Finally, the parish church formed a rallying point for the villagers. By the ninth or at latest the tenth century, the last links in the chain of rural churches were complete.[65] Whether the imprint of Christianity, religious sentiment, or the echo of the sacraments had penetrated deeply into the hearts of men or not, the House of God was a weekly meeting place; it was also the resting ground of their forefathers, the scene of moving ceremonies, and the place where serfs received their freedom and contracts were concluded. Moreover, the belfry was the strongpoint of the village and provided a haven in times of danger where treasure, cattle and stocks of food could be stored in safety.

It is obvious that all these links must have given rise to economic relationships. The delicate equilibrium between arable, stockraising and wild foodgathering rested on collective constraints which bound the heads of houses together. Fines and taxes levied in the name of the king diverted to the rulers a part of the productive effort of the village. In addition the church, like the 'hall' of the lord, was the centre for levying dues. The priest in charge had his own *manse* which had to sustain him, but on feast days his parishioners would bring to the church offerings which were strictly laid down; bread, eggs, the Easter lamb, wax for the lamps. Little by little the custom grew of consecrating the tenth part of the harvest to God. The history of the establishment of the tithes, so important for an appreciation of the movement of goods at peasant level, remains to be written.[66] We have to ask ourselves whether these parochial and public services to church and state together were not the sole obligations of an economic nature for a considerable number of peasants.

There are, however, too many other indications of the enormous power which the feudal landowners enjoyed. They force us to admit that even peasants who were not tenants felt in some way the influence of the lord's estate and the master-*manse*, whether the latter was situated in the village proper or on its outskirts. This pressure certainly made itself felt even if the economic bond between the demesne and the holdings was less tight than one might guess from the testimony of some records, and even though the great patrimonies were fewer, more dispersed and offered more space for small autonomous agricultural undertakings to flourish. Thus every country church was exploited by a 'patron' and tithes went to fill the barns of a lord. In *polyptyques* the parish church appears amongst those units of the demesne which brought in external revenues. They were classed alongside mills, breweries and bakehouses. All such installations at the disposal of the neighbouring peasants, who were often obliged to use them, allowed the lord to

[65] Document No. 21, p. 384   [66] *Les dîmes en Forez*, 194

tap the profits of small local farms, including those which were not tenancies of his demesne. We should remember also the help which he gave his less fortunate neighbours and the employment he offered them in his garden and orchard at different seasons. As for the agricultural community at large, since the best fields and much of the wastes belonged to the great estates, how could it be independent of the wishes and interests of the lord?

But above all the lord was almost always a man in authority. Landed wealth was thus closely associated with the exercise of power and the giving of orders. Many great demesnes in fact belonged to the custodians of royal power, to the sovereign, and to his representatives, the counts and great men such as bishops and lawyers, who in the Carolingian world wielded that authority which the kings through the concession of the privilege of immunity, had granted to the great monasteries. Besides, in an enclosed society where travel was so difficult and public institutions so inefficient, the private individual who owned the best lands and the great woods of the clearing could with impunity extend *de facto* authority over his poorer neighbours. His authority spread far beyond his household, the serfs of his 'family' or his own tenants. The 'magnate', as he is called in the documents, played the part of protector and conciliator; and people turned to him to settle differences. He was the only one who could punish real crime on the spot. In time of peril and famine he was the sole source of help because he could arm his men-servants for common defence, and because his barns were the last to be emptied when grain ran short. Immigrants besought him to welcome them as settlers or 'guests' on the land, so as to obtain the right to build their cabins next to the *manses*. Lastly he was often charged with the raising of royal taxes, the organization of transport and the collection of liveries of hay and meat for the army. All these functions earned him gratitude, service and gifts. And in face of his demands and encroachments to whom could his neighbours turn for effective support?

About this actual domination our documents are all but silent. This is why the question I have raised about the true relationship between the demesne economy and its environment must remain unanswered. The amalgam of generosity and coercion, the habits in which they were rooted, the 'custom' which the commissioners hesitated to record because it did not seem to them sufficiently legitimate, but which none the less controlled the life of the manorial farming complex behind the rigid facade of our texts, also supported an entire network of services demanded and rendered, charges, exchanges of goods and labour, which bound the smaller farms closely to the greater. Perhaps in some of the marginal provinces which remained very backward and where the distribution of land was less unequal, such as Frisia, Saxony, and northern England, a strong independent peasantry escaped the manorial grip for a while longer. But everywhere else in this poverty-stricken society, where men worked themselves to the bone for their wretched crops, the mere presence of the great estate and the power it conferred on the lord and his steward combined to drain away for the use of the lords and their parasites the miserable surpluses won from minute patches of ground by the grim privation of peasant households. The extravagance of an aristocracy totally dominated by a love of luxury and a desire for conspicuous display speedily disposed of these surpluses. The idea of investment did not occur to wealthy men unless there was a prospect of gain to allow of even greater expenditure. The result was that such meagre capital as was formed in the ninth and tenth centuries through the peasants' toil ended as jewellery and precious ornaments in the treasure houses of churches and princes, or passed into the hands of the few professional merchants seated at the crossroads of the Lombard trade routes. The residue of capital which could in this period have served to improve the tools of production, or to increase the fertility of the soil, or the efficiency of men's labour, was so insignificant that it can be ignored.

BOOK II

XI-XIII Centuries

BOOK II

XI-XIII Centuries

The Rhythm and Limits of Expansion

The ninth century is a period when the rural history of western Europe is exceptionally clear. But thereafter the shadows lengthen. Written evidence becomes scarcer and, what is more, less informative, for the tentative beginnings of an intellectual renaissance attempted by the upper ranks of clergy largely collapsed. From the eleventh to the twelfth century social relations were once again founded on spoken words, acts and ceremonies rather than on written documents. And even in ecclesiastical institutions, where the semblance of a scholarly culture survived and perhaps grew, parchment was very little used in the management of rural estates. In his relations with his stewards and with the peasants on his holdings, the lord relied on memory which was refreshed by periodic meetings and 'avowals'. The rights and duties of each individual were laid down and maintained with some flexibility by custom and ancient usage and were kept alive by the collective memory of the community, the villagers and the manorial tenants. Furthermore the cartularies drawn up in monasteries and bishoprics at this time contained no more than deeds of acquisition or exchange, the documents of lawsuits, notes registering favourable verdicts, and titles guaranteeing possession. These admittedly provide abundant information about the history of landownership, but it is exceptional to find in them fragments of accounts, or lists of rents, or administrative documents which record the mechanics of the economy. Hardly any figures or valuations of any sort are to be found. It seems as though the feeling for numerical accuracy and the desire to count and estimate quantities and values were noticeably weakened.

However, in the second half of the twelfth century, records rapidly become more abundant and explicit. The administrative structure begins to change and to become more sophisticated. A group of specialists in administration emerges, whose particular technical expertise is based on the written word and reckoning, and who are occupied in registering, counting, valuing

61

and surveying.[1] It is through them that the light comes. The thirteenth century, and particularly its second half, is brilliantly illuminated, but the dark age before it is disabling. It interrupts our view and masks the connections between the types of economy described by the Carolingian *polyptyques* and those which come into the light of day at the close of the twelfth century. Economic development does not proceed at a regular speed but by fits and starts and short-term changes. We know, for instance, that in other better-known fields the years 1075-1120 were marked by singularly rapid progress. Were these years equally decisive for the relationship between peasants, lords and merchants, and for improvements in the means of production? The gaps in documentary material in the eleventh century and the early twelfth century prevent us from plotting exactly the amplitude and direction of many of these changes.

Furthermore our knowledge is patchy and the resulting areas of light and shade cause breaks in chronology which have nothing to do with the major turning points in economic development. And to describe the facts of the ninth, the eleventh and twelfth centuries and the period which begins in 1180 in different chapters would undoubtedly give too much importance to the periods which are relatively well documented.

*   *   *

If our records are unevenly distributed in time, they are perhaps even more so in space. Regional variations spring partly from the fact that archives have not everywhere been well preserved, or suffered to the same degree from war, revolution and neglect. However, the uneven distribution which today afflicts the surviving documentary evidence was already partly apparent in medieval times since it reflects differences in the forms of expression. In some regions recourse to the written word was widespread and administration benefited from a precocious technique. This was the case in the French Midi where it was already customary in rural societies before the end of the twelfth century to draw up contracts in the presence of a notary. In Italy the practice was even commoner and in the eleventh century written documents were much less scarce there than anywhere else. But in this respect England was better served than any other country, albeit for political rather than cultural reasons. This small compact kingdom was towards the end of the eleventh century briskly taken in hand and investigated by teams of competent scribes and accountants. By 1086 they had drawn up for the king an exceptionally comprehensive general survey. The Domesday Book is fully the equal in numerical detail to the most carefully compiled Carolingian *polyptyque*. But the inquest was here enlarged to encompass the whole kingdom. In

[1] De Smet, 282

one stroke the veils were stripped for ever from the English countryside.

A great many of the contrasts on the map of western Europe due to the amount of available information are further accentuated by the state and direction of historical research which has not everywhere been pushed to the same limits. In certain countries which are underdeveloped from the point of view of historical studies, muniment rooms and libraries have not yet yielded up all their secrets. In addition we must remember that history has in the last half-century been imprisoned in a national straitjacket, and was not free to pursue the same path in every European country. In England, already favoured by the quality and abundance of its sources, the medieval countryside has been actively studied by those who wished to apply the advances and theories of contemporary economics to the interpretation of the past, with the result that north of the Channel more work has been done than anywhere else. In France and Germany, probably as a result of the peculiar balance of university studies, attention has been concentrated less on economic conditions than on the occupation of the soil – the early appearance of *Siedlungsforschung*, as well as the vitality of the French school of human geography in the first thirty years of the twentieth century is due to this orientation – and also on the legal and political aspects of rural life. Medievalists in Italy have been mesmerized by their urban history.

Such an uneven advance and such manifold preoccupations risk distorting still further the perspective and accentuating inordinately the importance of, for instance, clearings in Germany and France compared with other regions, or the relationship of town and country in Italy, or laying excessive emphasis on the manorial economy in England where administrative records and manorial accounts are so abundant. It is, therefore, one of the aims of this book to moderate the artificiality of these contrasts, and to try to encompass in a single broad sweep what generations of historians have seen only piecemeal. It is a hazardous and perhaps even a premature undertaking, and the immensity of the field should never be forgotten. Composed of village communities still very isolated from each other, the peasant world was full of diversity and the differences were probably far more subtle than our sources reveal. All these considerations prevent us from taking the wide view of local and random observations. Any attempt to reconstruct the whole edifice of medieval country life on such insecure and scattered foundations might appear an enterprise so foolhardy as wholly to discourage us.

But despite their imperfect distribution, the documents do give an impression of a general and continuous growth of the rural economy, which went on expanding with a varying rhythm right up to about 1330. Without prolonged prosperity in the countryside the expansion of western civilization as a whole during the eleventh, twelfth, and thirteenth centuries would be incomprehensible. Should this long-term movement be linked with the tentative growth suggested by some Carolingian documents, with the early improvement of implements marked by the slow diffusion of water mills, with the gradual introduction of the manor into the backward countries of Germany, the penetration of monetary media and the speeding up of exchanges which can be discerned in certain advanced areas like Lombardy? Our knowledge is too exiguous and imperfect for us to be able to measure exactly the speed of progress in the Carolingian period. We cannot tell whether the retreats imposed here and there at the end of the ninth and in the tenth century by the Norse, Saracen or Hungarian invasions were sufficiently deep and lasting to arrest the movement completely. Nor can we know whether progress was maintained long enough to join and support the broad forward thrust which we know to have taken place about 1050. We are forced to limit ourselves to what is certain. As in Carolingian times, all our knowledge centres on manorial institutions, for most of what we know of medieval economy is set against this background; and in the chapters which follow our most accurate observations will be concerned with it. To begin with we shall try to analyze the economic growth and to establish its principal stages in the three centuries during which it continued. This is a very arduous task since the material is local, discontinuous, spread over immense areas and very long periods, and without any landmarks, and this prevents us from grasping all the links between output, trade and consumption of the products of the earth.

CHAPTER I

The Extension of the Arable

Man's food supply dominates the rural economy, and it probably never did so more insistently than in times when the means of existence were as precarious as they remained throughout the period now to be described. It is unfortunate that the dietary history of the medieval world remains wholly unexplored,[1] and if I present here a few isolated facts it is with the hope of instigating without further delay a thorough study of the whole subject.

At the present moment there is nothing upon which to base a valid comparison between the diet of the contemporaries of Charlemagne and those of Saint Louis. However, there is some indication that it changed in the course of the thirteenth century. We notice that for all social classes the *companagium*, the 'accompaniment to bread', became more varied and abundant. Here as an example are two rules for the inmates of leper houses in Champagne. One in the twelfth century gives each leper a weekly ration of three loaves, a pie and a measure of peas; the other, drawn up in 1325, lays down that the sick are to be given, apart from bread, oil, salt and onions, meat on three days a week and eggs or herrings on the other days. In 1244 in the community of Marœil-en-Artois, a canon's allowance was four eggs in the morning, three eggs in the evening and salt meat or three herrings.[2] Is it then true that the consumption of meat, butter and cheese, especially in north-western Europe, increased greatly in the thirteenth century? If so, how can this increase be measured? It is at least certain that at the end of the thirteenth century most men were not content with cereals alone. In 1289 at Ferring, a dependent manor of the English abbey of Battle, the men on carting services expected to be given with their rye bread and ale, cheese in the morning and meat or fish at midday. In 1300-1305 eggs, meat and plenty of wine were bought for the labourers erecting the belfry of the church of Bonlieu-en-Forez, as well as rye bread and beans for soup.[3] All the Norman inventories of about 1300

[1] We must wait for the enquiry opened in 1961 in *Annales E.S.C.* on the material conditions of life and biological behaviour gradually to illuminate the subject.

[2] The documents referring to Champagne are cited by P. Jonin, *Les personnages féminins dans les romans français de Tristan au XIIᵉ siècle*, Gap. 1958, p. 127; *La chronique et les chartes de l'abbaye de Marœil* (ed. Bertin).

[3] Bennett, 149, p. 235; E. Perroy, 'Note complémentaire sur les comptes de construction du clocher de Bonlieu', in *Bull. de la Diana*, 1959

mention peas, bacon, salt, herrings, poultry, cheese and enormous quantities of eggs as food for those performing labour services and their foremen. In one house of the Hospitallers the actual expenditure in 1338 on the *companagium* was two and a half times the value of the grain consumed; and in the same year at Jumièges in Normandy 740 livres were devoted to the purchase of bread grain and no less than 1,780 livres to the purchase of other victuals.[4]

This gradual widening of the diet which points to a growing prosperity and improvement of the material conditions of existence is an important factor in the economic progress of the countryside and merits serious study. An attempt should be made to learn its exact timing and spread at different social levels. In fact it could not have occurred without a change in the activity of the farm labourer, an enlargement of new areas of production, or a stimulus to the currents of exchange whose importance we shall analyze below. Nevertheless it appears that this improvement in diet was limited. At the beginning of the fourteenth century all victuals with the exception of bread grain were treated as secondary. They were served only for the pleasures of eating, and for the love of luxury: in fact the part they played in consumption varied markedly with the social standing of the consumer. Thus in a commandery of Hospitallers they were worth half as much for a ploughman as for a knight hospitaller and a third as much as for the head of the house.[5] Status was expressed by the amount of the superfluous items of food consumed as well as by the quality of clothing worn.

But deep down in men's hearts bread was still thought of as the staff of life. This fundamental attitude is clear in documents of the eleventh to the twelfth centuries, rules governing religious communities, the constitution of life pensions and domestic accounts. It seems clear that baking was the most important food trade in a town and many speculators got rich by taking over the running of a mill or a bakery in a growing market town. Even in the fifteenth century bread was still the principal foodstuff in the most highly developed urban centres.[6] It can even be questioned whether in many regions where primitive dietary habits were slowly being superseded bread did not occupy a larger place than in the eleventh century. Detailed research will one day perhaps give us the answer to this question. It is, however, certain that throughout the period rural workers were required primarily to produce cereal crops, and it is for this reason that the rural economy of the eleventh to the thirteenth centuries was before all else marked by growth in cereal production.

[4] L. Delisle, *Etude sur la condition de la classe agricole en Normandie*, Paris, 1851, pp. 189 *et seq.*; Archives des Bouches-du-Rhône, H. (O.M.), 115; Laporte, 459

[5] Duby, 445

[6] One citizen of Genoa had to buy nearly 19 tons of grain to provision his household of ten persons for three and a half years. Heers, 700, p. 42.

The expansion of cereal cultivation appears to have been very complex and caused changes throughout the agricultural system. It implied modifications to technical equipment and changes in the relationship between manpower, the area farmed and methods of work. It is true that many aspects of this development have escaped historical record, and we must resign ourselves to the fact that only some of them will ever be more than partially revealed. Let us begin with what we know most about, the extension of the arable. The argument, although incomplete, will follow our actual knowledge of the mechanics of production and the cycle of ploughing, seedtime and harvest, of implements and agricultural practice and of yields. Afterwards the little that we know about the numbers of men alive, the factor that we have already admitted to be fundamental to all changes in human society, will be discussed.

I. THE ADVANCE OF THE ARABLE

According to our evidence villages were overpopulated in Carolingian times, grain production was insufficient and poverty constant. Nevertheless, except in Germania and Flanders, records show few efforts to create new fields outside the light and easily worked soils. Was this apparent reluctance due to dislike of the solitary life of a settler? Or rather to insufficient equipment and the limitations of technique and tools? It seems that population growth was actually obstructed by man's impotence to enlarge the agrarian living space from which he could have augmented his subsistence. On the other hand obvious signs of an expanding rural economy from the tenth century onwards can be seen in otherwise laconic documents from the multiplication of terms such as 'assarts' or 'open country' which call to mind newly conquered land. In fact the new era opens with the progress of cultivation at the expense of pasture, dunes, forests, marshes and sea. For historians of all countries, but especially Frenchmen and Germans, the age of medieval rural prosperity is the age of land reclamation. All the same, this great movement of expanding exploitation which changed the face of the medieval world and upon which so much else depended remains very little known.

We must not exaggerate its extent. Without a doubt in some countries it completely transformed the way of life, but it seems as if other countries were only superficially affected. The urgency of research in this field is clear, but to what records can we turn for information?

* * *

It is probable that the most reliable evidence would be revealed by vegetable residues. Some soils, and particularly peat, have under certain climatic conditions preserved for centuries in a fossilized state the pollen grains given

67

off by surrounding plants. These successive layers of deposits can nowadays be dated and analyzed, and in this way the changing proportions of pollen from trees, undergrowth and cultivated plants through the ages can be measured. Such facts are the only ones which reflect the continuous evolution of the rural scene and make it possible to draw an uninterrupted curve. Botanical remains have for long been the subject of minute examination in certain countries, and particularly Germany. It is to be hoped that, allowing for different pedological conditions, similar enquiries can be undertaken in other European countries. It would also be desirable to plot more exactly the chronology of data obtained in this way, which is at present regrettably vague. But we shall very likely have to wait for many years upon the skill of the botanists before the body of evidence disclosed by this technique becomes sufficiently copious and well distributed.

In the meantime a mass of details which catch an observant eye in the existing landscape claim the historian's immediate attention. Village- and place-names, the appearance of the outskirts of present-day woodlands, the ground plan of inhabited places, the layout of fields, the composition of the natural vegetation which today covers commons and pastures, provide plenty of clues which can, if recognized, throw light on agricultural settlement. These details have the advantage of being very abundant and are naturally closely interconnected. The chief drawback is that they cannot be dated with any certainty.

We are forced therefore to fall back on written records. Some of these were drawn up in the course of reclamations, which they either prepared or sanctioned. This is specially the case with charters of settlement intended to attract settlers, or contracts by which lords bound themselves together to open up virgin ground for cultivation. These are clearly the most rewarding of all the different kinds of document. But they only reveal the most spectacular side of the great forward movement of arable land and are relatively few in number. To consider only these, or even to grant them excessive importance, would lead us to restrict this major event of European rural history within too narrow frontiers. In reality progress took place over a much wider area. This is why a careful examination of all contemporary documents is essential. There is otherwise the risk that clues may be hidden away in documents which appear to have nothing whatever to do with reclamation. The lives of saints and chronicles of wars, for instance, can reveal their share of place-names which are lost today. Some charters of gift or inheritance describe, often in the most minute detail, the appearance of the forest and the clearings which gradually penetrated into it. They all swarm with allusions to *hôtes*, that is to say pioneer settlers, to their crop-sharing payments (*champarts*) or their 'tasks' (*tâches*), that is to say typical payments due from recently reclaimed lands, and to *novales*, tithes levied from newly broken-up parts of the estate lands. The harvest of evidence is likely to be abundant, but in many areas it still awaits the reaper.

Finally, it must be realized that written sources may never bring to light more than a very small portion of reclamations. Consequently the most profitable approach will probably be to work in the regions where there are enough sources known to be both reliable and well dated, and to collate these with the evidence which emerges from observation of the actual countryside.[7] It might be possible in this way to isolate certain regional topographical and place-name types and to date them acceptably. We could then interpret with greater assurance the ancient features of the countryside revealed by maps and aerial photographs.

*   *   *

The primary aim of research is to ascertain more exactly the duration of the movement of reclamation, and especially the date of its commencement. At what moment did assarts begin to multiply and to spread in different regions? The poverty of sources before the twelfth century makes it impossible to answer this question so far as many provinces are concerned. In the documents relating to southern Burgundy the signs to which I have already drawn attention lead us to think that the assault on the forests on the clay soils of the banks of the Saône and on the Beaujolais hills began in the second half of the tenth century. About 1100 the draining of the marshes created in Flanders by a recent invasion of the sea began by the building here and there of small dykes, and religious communities possessed at that period polders which were already parcelled out and partially inhabited. On the other hand, references to recent assarts in Domesday Book are very rare, even though certain facts to which the commissioners drew attention, such as the reduction of herds of swine on certain manors between 1066 and 1086, could well be interpreted as indicating the retreat of woodlands.[8]

In any event, evidence of this kind becomes much commoner in all written texts from the twelfth century onwards. In the present state of studies, therefore, the following is the most convincing hypothesis. Pioneering activity which had remained timid, discontinuous and locally dispersed throughout two centuries became more intense and co-ordinated around 1150.

The increased intensity of effort after that time is clearly reflected in

---

[7] Document No. 45, p. 400. E. Juillard, 66, proposes also, in order to note the stages of the occupation of the soil, to classify plots of village lands according to their length.

[8] J. Dhondt, in *Revue belge de philologie et d'histoire*, 1941: Lentacker, 228; Darby, 47, p. 181

documents, especially in England, northern France, Germania and the plain of the Po. Attempts to tame the river waters of the Lombard plain and to irrigate the surrounding hills entered on a decisive phase. The great urban communities of northern Italy undertook the agrarian organization of the *contado* which they controlled. In 1186 the magistrates of Verona had just divided up between 180 settler households who were ready to occupy the *villafranca*, the huge territory opened to cultivation by the construction of a drainage canal. A few years earlier Henry Plantagenet, count of Anjou, ordered the consolidation and extension of the embankments of the Loire in order to protect the assarted villages of the lower valley from floods, and established along these *turcies*, or river walls, settlers whose duty it was to keep them in good repair.[9] It was the period when reclamation assumed a resolutely aggressive air in the Paris basin, an exceptionally well recorded region, which was perhaps more transformed than any other by the spread of cereal cultivation. The pollen analysis conducted at Roten Moor on the plateau of the Rhön[10] shows that beech tree pollen in the peat soil had declined regularly since the ninth century. This indicates that in the new parts of Germania the forest had been retreating since the days of Charlemagne. The decrease in woodland plants was exactly matched by the increase in cereals, proof of continual agricultural growth from Carolingian times onwards. But the share of cereal pollen in the vegetable residues grew rapidly between 1100 and 1150 which was the decisive period of agrarian conquest. The same technique permits us also to date to the twelfth century the great advance in cereal cultivation in the marshlands of Mecklenburgh.[11] We may conclude that all the evidence so far assembled agrees that the culminating period of reclamation occurred in the twelfth century.

*   *   *

Monks were not the chief architects of the movement of reclamation as has for so long been believed. The Cluniacs and Benedictines of the old school lived like great lords, that is to say, they led a life of ease. They depended on donations of land fully organized and staffed with the necessary working personnel, i.e. of *manses* 'clothed', as the phrase went, with men and beasts. They did not take the trouble to reclaim the waste themselves.[12] At the end of the eleventh century new religious orders, expressing greater con-

---

[9] Sereni 84, pp. 76-78; Dion, *Histoire des levées de la Loire*, Paris, 1961, p. 123
[10] Document No. 35, p. 391   [11] Abel, 585, pp. 45 *et seq.*
[12] This encourages us to ask whether reclamations in the ninth and tenth centuries were not more widespread than they appear in the documents of the period which almost all originate from monasteries of this type. This brings us up against one of the main difficulties of historical research: are not the changes revealed illusory, and do they not merely reflect the provenance of the documentary material rather than reality?

cern for ascetic values, decided to settle in the solitude of the wilderness; at the same time they restored the dignity of manual labour. At Grandmont and at Cîteaux teams of *conversi*, lay brethren, uneducated monks of peasant origin, performed the heavy tasks. We can guess that they undertook reclamation. Nevertheless, wherever detailed research has been carried out it has shown that these new monasteries were set up in clearings already prepared to a greater or less extent; furthermore these religious communities were devoted to rearing livestock and thus were little concerned with extending their fields. And lastly these new style abbeys, by the very care with which they protected their own 'wilderness', were more likely than not to preserve their forest retreats against the incursions of reclamation which would otherwise have obliterated them.[13] In actual fact the only holy men who effectively helped with their own hands to wage the assault against the wastes, who felled trees and ploughed up new arable, were the hermits who at that time lived in great numbers on the fringes of the European forests. The history of the life of these hermits has not yet been written; if it were we could estimate better what was the share of these solitary men, so apparently ill-equipped to wrestle with rude nature. Together with hunters, charcoal burners and men who lived for a time in the forest to make iron or collect wax, they blazed the first trails of reclamation, which were pushed forward in a more general way by the combined enterprise of lords and peasants. Reclamation thus appears to have been the result of a double initiative. As might be expected, peasants provided the manpower: they were numerous and many of them were near starvation level and in search of a plot of ground upon which to grow food. But it was also necessary for the lords who were masters of the wastes to consent to their transformation into arable: not an easy decision that, since by so doing they surrendered the advantages of marshland and thicket, and above all sacrificed hunting, their chief pastime. To admit the settlers into the woods and to allow their edges to be pushed back reduced the space within which wild animals could roam and browse. It is well known for how long the royal forest privileges in England obstructed the advance of cultivation. The monks of Cluny had to beg the count of Chalons to destroy his hedges and his deer park so that their peasants could continue clearing the land, and they had to offer him substantial compensation.[14]

The cultivated area could not spread openly and without restraint until the lords had discovered the advantages of agrarian exploitation, and until they had become accustomed to new ways of levying dues. When did they finally persuade themselves that it was profitable to levy *tâches* and *champart*, that is to say to pre-empt a share of the sheaves harvested from the one-time

[13] For the site of Cîteaux itself, see Roupnel, 27, p. 129
[14] Duby, 261, p. 302

scrub and copse? Put in another way, when did they begin to think in terms of interest and to be won over by the idea of profit? Because of the decisive part which the lords played, reclamation reflects a profound change in the psychological attitude of the aristocracy. It has repeatedly been said that the knights of the Ile de France had no thought of gain or of increasing revenue from the land, but in the days of Philip Augustus and Saint Louis they denied themselves some part of the pleasures of the chase in order to fill their granaries.

It would be worth while exploring in detail the motivation behind the first reclamations. Who was responsible, lay or ecclesiastical landlords? What part was played by owners of tithes who were the first beneficiaries from the enlargement of the cultivated area?[15] And ought we not to place the lords' agents at the head of the list of instigators of the movement, because they strove to attract new cultivators in order to enhance their own reputations and profit? We ought to find some answer to these questions in the documents drawn up in the central part of the Paris basin at the end of the twelfth and the beginning of the thirteenth century. But we also need to date more exactly the first attempts of lords and their agents. I should be tempted to distinguish two successive phases. One where the lords simply tolerated or permitted, not always with a good grace, the earliest conquests. Then a second phase followed when they themselves took charge of the assault, either by extending the arable part of their own demesnes, or by looking for new colonists. Could we not propose as a working hypothesis the idea that the speeding up of the reclamation movement in the first half of the twelfth century corresponded to a change in the attitude of owners of the waste?

2. THE ENLARGEMENT OF THE ANCIENT VILLAGE TERRITORIES

For the most part the new fields probably lay on the fringes of the ancient arable furlongs of the village and were won from the girdle of waste and pasture by a straightforward and progressive enlargement of the clearing. This was the easiest and the most discreet way of reclaiming land, and we can guess that it was often carried out secretly without the lords' knowledge. For this reason it has left little mark in our archives and is hard to distinguish. In order to trace this early method of agrarian expansion we have to collect various scattered clues, to explore the ground on the outskirts of still wooded areas and also to interpret minor place-names, that is names of fields or localities which in modern surveys call to mind either the act of reclamation itself (*assarts, artigue vieille, les plans*) or the natural vegetation from which the ploughland was won (*les brosses, les vernes*).

[15] Lamprecht, 20

Some manuscripts, however, bear direct witness to a furtive extension of the village lands. Some manors have left a series of inventories or continuous accounts in which we can see the number of fields liable to dues on certain village lands increasing. Thus in the villages which the bishop of Ely and the abbot of Ramsey possessed on the edge of the Fens, the total of rents was considerably raised between the twelfth century and the end of the thirteenth by the establishment of new holdings on ground brought in at the expense of the marsh.[16] More explicit details are given in the records of some lawsuits. Sometimes the village community had to bring settlers to justice in order to defend the collective grazing grounds. The records of the public courts of England preserve many traces of such complaints. It could also happen that the community supported its members in their quest for assarts against the private owners of forest and wasteland. Other conflicts again brought those farming the newly cultivated parts, whether lord or peasant, up against those who claimed from them tithes levied on newly broken up land.[17] But it must be admitted that most of this written evidence dates from the thirteenth century, a time when woods and pastures were becoming rarer, and infinitely more valuable, and for that reason were bitterly defended by those who enjoyed their use. At that time the movement of expansion was reaching its close. At its height it almost escapes our notice.

We can, however, observe that the enlargement of the ancient village territories could sometimes spring from a collective action which brought all the villagers together under the leadership of the lord; this was probably so in a few English villages where a new 'field' was added in the thirteenth century to the two old parts of the village lands.[18] Sometimes also the lord stimulated peasants' own efforts by settling new families in the village: Suger did this and boasted of having added 20 *livres* annually to the income of a manor near the abbey of St Denis by settling 80 new *hôtes* 'on new lands next door to it'.[19] Drainage and water control also often necessitated discipline, mutual aid and a pooling of effort, and these implied intervention on the part of the lord.

However, it remained exceptional. Fields created in the neighbourhood of old arable, in the outer zone of the village lands (the 'outfield' of the English countryside, the *terre gaste* of the Provençal manors) on a site traditionally subject only to temporary 'slash and burn' were probably mostly occupied separately by isolated pioneers. This fact comes out clearly in villages bordering the forest of Bragny-en-Chalonnais, in the depths of which the Cistercian

---

[16] Miller, 198, pp. 95 *et seq.*; Raftis, 201, pp. 74 *et seq.*
[17] Documents Nos. 43, p. 398; 44, p. 339; 49, p. 404
[18] Document No. 66, p. 417
[19] Suger, *Liber de rebus in administratione sua gestis* (ed. Lecoy de la Marche), I, p. 158

abbey of La Ferté was founded and whose history in the twelfth century is well known. As one left the territory of the village and went in the direction of the woods one entered the area where the plots of land and assarts bore the name of the peasant who was the first to cut down the trees and undergrowth. The fact that allods of small men, which were rather unusual near the village, multiplied on the recently reclaimed lands must also be noted. The country folk here claimed the sole possession of the fields they had won from the great princely forest, probably surreptitiously by deceiving the foresters. We can easily imagine that such individual reclamations had generally increased small peasant properties on the poorly supervised fringes of the woodlands in the eleventh and twelfth centuries.[20]

★   ★   ★

Thus the belt of uncultivated land was nibbled away piecemeal. In the idle winter days a few enclosures were here and there erected at the edges of heathland, or in woodlands, which were in any case rather scattered at that period. The plots of land thus protected and set aside for the use of the peasants who had burned the brushwood and rooted out the tree stumps, at first carried grass. Most frequently a hay field covered the assart for several years.[21] Then when the land was at last well drained, it was ploughed and sown with grain. Dispersed enclosures of this kind penetrated and divided woods and pastures. For some time they formed an intermediate zone between the wilderness and the farmlands, which Wolfram von Eschenbach describes in *Parzival*: it seemed to Gauvain who had for long been riding through the woods that 'little by little the forest thinned out, here a tongue of woodland and there a field so narrow that there was scarce room to raise a tent, then looking ahead he saw the cultivated fields . . . .'[22] But occupied plots increased in density and eventually joined up forming new and coherent groups of ploughed fields. The fences between the individual plots were retained for a few more seasons, then they were taken down; and the village lands received the addition of another 'open field' indistinguishable from the older ones, except by its name or perhaps the less regular pattern of its strips.

At the end of such a progressive movement, slow but insidious, the gain was often considerable. Here are some figures extracted from English manorial archives. In the second half of the twelfth century 30 peasants held 350 acres of assarts on the manor of Cranfield belonging to Ramsey Abbey; the plots

[20] Duby, 261, p. 305; Boutruche, 184, pp. 76 *et seq.*; Genicot, 189, p. 63
[21] In the woods of Favières near Paris in 1208: 'If one who has rights in the said wood makes a meadow. . . . If it should happen that he transforms the meadow into arable . . .' (Archives nationales, S.117, 530).
[22] VIII, verses 18 and 15

ploughed by dependants of the neighbouring manor of Holme covered 458½ acres at the end of the twelfth century and 605½ acres one hundred years later.[23] It often happened that in this way the woods and uncultivated ground for the use of livestock were pushed far away from the village. Sometimes the distance alone and the feeling that they lost too much time and exhausted their oxen by ploughing fields too far away from their *manse* were sufficient to stop the reclaimers. But often, also, where the villages were not far from each other and where they were separated only by a thin screen of trees and pasture the latter was destroyed and the village lands joined up. Landmarks and boundary stones, fruit trees and crosses planted at the road side henceforth marked the limits between parish lands in the midst of open country.

This commonest form of reclamation was without doubt also the earliest. It was sometimes completed well before the thirteenth century. In 1214 the peasants of Origgio near Milan still left uncultivated 45 per cent of the village lands; in 1320 no more than 16 per cent remained in that state.[24] It seems as if many European countries in the Middle Ages never knew any other method of extending cultivation. In Périgord, for example, all the communal lands of today were gradually added in successive rings around an ancient gallo-roman demesne which had become the site of the village.[25] Almost all England appears to have been the same, since according to the descriptions of the Domesday Book the wild spaces were already unusual and hamlets very close to each other.[26] Nevertheless, in some areas reclamation wore a different aspect: men founded new villages in the midst of uncultivated wastes.

3. THE NEW VILLAGES

Some parts of the country in the early Middle Ages were thickly settled with villages and were in striking contrast with other parts which were almost uninhabited. While in 1086 the southern half of Warwickshire was already fully colonized, woodland still covered almost the whole of the northern part of the county. Another area of vivid contrast was to be found in the eastern part of Brie which up till the twelfth century interposed a wild tract of forest between Champagne, covered with inhabited sites since before Roman times, and the Ile de France, where in the course of centuries men had been able to cut down the woods on the light and well drained soils, to extirpate trees from the farmlands and little by little to unite these clearings into a large tract of open country.[27] The outskirts of the densely overgrown wastes, where heavy and waterlogged soils had hitherto prevented the in-

---

[23] Raftis, 201, pp. 72-74   [24] Romeo, 481   [25] Fénelon, 55
[26] Darby, 47, map on p. 131; Lennard, 268, pp. 3 et seq.
[27] Harley, 300; Brunet, 44, pp. 307 et seq.; Hubert, 309

cursions of cultivators, were slightly reduced as villages on their borders expanded their lands. But the inhabitants of the latter could not usefully extend their reclamations more than a short distance.

Some wildernesses had been colonized much more deeply by pioneers. Turning their backs on the hamlets of their forefathers, these men established their homesteads on virgin land and began their fight against trees in the Paris basin, western France and the Garonne region, the river waters of the Loire valley and Lombardy, the marshes of northern and eastern Germania, and the sea itself in the Low Countries.

It appears that these rootless people, who were described as *aubains* or *hôtes*, used to act together in their adventurous tasks, and to fight their battles as a team. As a result they created not so much scattered habitations as new village enclaves, parishes and villages, each with their own group of *manses*, in short a social organization similar to the one they had left behind them. Sometimes they came together spontaneously. Thus, peasants who advanced from neighbouring areas along the forest rides in the middle of the eleventh century and built their cabins side by side at La Charmée or La Chapelle, deep in the Burgundian forest of Bragny, apparently came together on their own initiative. The same thing happened to the *aubains* from the Ile de France, whom the count of Champagne permitted nearly one hundred years later to settle in the forest of Jouy. Thus, some villages came into being spontaneously. Their birth can sometimes be observed through chance references in documents, as when the bishop was begged to upgrade an oratory into a parish church, or when the lord accepted a limitation on his hunting rights.[28]

It is, however, permissible to regard most of the *villeneuves* as being created by a deliberate act of the lord who prepared its advent. The founders were either holders of the king's authority, the king himself, counts, castellans, the great religious foundations, or, in northern Italy, the urban communities acting as manorial lords. The wild unoccupied spaces belonged almost without exception to the highest nobility, and the attitude of the latter towards these open spaces underwent a change: they now decided to organize their colonization.

This choice was frequently dictated by political considerations. It might be a question of securing the safety of a road by settling the forests through which it passed, or else of asserting control over the frontiers of a principality by establishing strong peasant communities obliged to perform armed service in wooded and deserted marches which had hitherto formed a protective ring round it. It was in this way that the *sauvetés* (sanctuaries) of the eleventh and twelfth centuries in the basin of the Garonne dotted the pilgrimage

[28] Duby, 261, p. 302; R. Bautier, 'Les foires de Champagne', in *Recueils de la Société Jean-Bodin, La Foire*, p. 110; Document No. 44, p. 399

routes of St James of Compostella with inhabited places, and that the *bastides* of the thirteenth century flanked the frontiers with strong military posts.[29] The profit motive also played its part. The new village would form a centre of taxation where the bishop could levy tithes and the prince customary dues, market rights, *tailles*, and fines for infringements of the law. In this connection it would be interesting to measure the relative share of land dues and public taxes in the charges imposed on settlers by the lords. In fact the founders of *villeneuves*, as holders of the power to command, apparently sought to increase not so much the number of their tenants as of those subject to taxation and to the law. They were less intent on creating landed estates than on increasing the profitability and the exploitation of some exclusive right. We can even ask whether these activities of the nobility did not coincide with the birth and development of an efficient tax system and the growth and consolidation of the type of lordship which derived its main revenues from privileges and monopolies. Chronological comparisons would be revealing on this point. Enlargement of clearings and extension of arable around the old villages benefited some peasants and small landlords, as well as owners of tithes; this kind of reclamation multiplied small allods and raised the yields of rents, money dues and tithes. On the other hand, settlement of the forest and marshland wastes and the siting of new villages profited chiefly the magnates, that is the members of the topmost rung of the political aristocracy. After all, the creation of *villeneuves* furnished territorial lords, from the most modest lords of the manor right up to the king himself, with a remedy against those insistent financial embarrassments which they all began to feel in the second half of the twelfth century. And it is easy to see that colonizing enterprises conducted on a large scale very efficiently promoted the growth of some feudal principalities, such as for example those of the count of Flanders or the bishops of north-western Germania.[30]

*   *   *

The problem for the lords was how to attract new inhabitants to a part of the country which had always been thought of as inimical to man. It was first of all necessary – and this was why the initiative could only come from

[29] Higounet, 302; even in the fifteenth century the bailiff, mayor and magistrates of Herstal in the Ardennes handed over three *bonniers* of woodland to a lay brother of the abbey of Valdieu to reclaim them and build there a hospice for the use of travellers, because it was 'a perilous and unsafe place, where there were murderers, robbers and wicked people'; *Cartulaire de l'abbaye cistercienne de Valdieu* (ed. Ruwet), No. 190 (1337). The kings of Germania encouraged settlement in the woods which belonged to them to reinforce the class of free peasants upon whose support they relied; Bosl, 489.

[30] Documents No. 36, p. 391; No. 39, p. 395; Van der Linden, 328. Could not the rarity of *villeneuves* in England be connected with the limited extension of private seigneurial power?

holders of public authority – for the authority to confer public jurisdiction on places chosen as future sites of human habitation, and to grant them privileges which might tempt immigrants. In the eleventh and twelfth centuries crosses were erected to mark the limits of a *sauveté* or a *bourg*, i.e. an area protected by God's peace, inside which violence was forbidden and safety was ensured. At a later period a charter was drawn up in advance limiting the lord's demands and specifying the favourable treatment which the colonists would enjoy. Sometimes the spot opened up to settlement was situated near to an overcrowded village where the poorest peasants or younger sons speedily became aware of the promised advantages. The transfer was then easily carried out. This was what happened for instance at Bonlieu in Beauce in 1225: men from the neighbouring land of Grigneville accepted the invitation of the nuns of Yères and quickly erected their huts on the *hostises* which were offered to them.[31]

On the other hand where the country was wilder and the sites to be settled isolated, or where the soil was too unpromising to attract local people, or required the collaboration of drainage experts, the whole undertaking became much more complicated. Considerable effort was required to recruit men, to move their households, provide them with essential equipment, feed them during the early months of settlement, help them to construct their *manses* and organize them for collective work. The lord, who was often a great prince, hesitated to take upon himself the whole responsibility for publicity, raising capital and arranging the distribution of land. He looked round for associates and drew up written contracts with them. This is why we are much bettter informed about the riskier and more delicate colonizing ventures than we are about the spontaneous and unrecorded growth of most village territories.

The associate was often a contractor in a minor position, socially very inferior to the lord, and he was able to give his undivided attention to the business in which his interest was engaged. Officials and servants belonging to the manorial *familia* (*ministeriales*) are often found performing this function. Sometimes when a religious house was concerned in the colonizing venture, one of the brothers or a canon was given woods to colonize and a personal share in the future profits.[32] But often a younger member of a knightly family also found in this kind of task an opportunity to create a small individual manor which augmented his share in the inheritance and allowed him to escape from the paternal roof, to marry and to live up to his rank in society. A knight called Odo whom the monks of St Avit of Orleans put in charge of settling and cultivating their land at Cercottes in 1207 was a man of this type; he was able to collect charges on all the produce but had to

[31] Archives Nationales, LL.1599 B, p. 143   [32] Document No. 42, p. 398

pay an annual rent of only two *muids* of wheat.[33] This co-operative system
has been thoroughly studied in the colonized lands of eastern Germany.
From about the middle of the twelfth century onwards, we can observe on
the middle reaches of the Elbe an increasing number of *locatores*, clerical or
lay members of a princely household, and sometimes townsfolk who were
anxious to put a little money capital to work in some landed enterprise. A
portion of the waste which could be parcelled out into a prearranged number
of farms was assigned to them. It was up to them to mark out the plots, to
find and establish the settlers. For their trouble they received a large allotment of land and a share of the manorial rights levied in the village which
they had helped to found.[34]

But frequently the lord of the 'wilderness' went into partnership with
another lord in one of those contracts called in France *pariage*. According to
these agreements each party contracted to contribute a share. One provided
the uncultivated land and the exclusive rights (*bans*) over it. The other contributed the influence or the connections which permitted recruitment or
the money with which to instal men. Profits from the undertaking, and
especially the product of the exclusive monopolies (*taxes banales*), were then
equally divided.[35] We know of partnerships of this kind uniting a religious
house and a lay lord. Since churchmen alone kept their archives in order this
information is yet another instance of knowledge due to surviving documents.

In fact priests and monks were often asked to join in because they owned
reserves of cash capital. Religious institutions were equally well placed
through the network of their congregations and daughter houses to publicize
their undertakings in distant parts of the country where overpopulation
existed. Sometimes they owned the land, and in such a case they would
negotiate with the prince to modify the territorial law and to grant the
franchises which would attract the flow of immigrants. Often monks and
canons, giving up direct exploitation themselves, wished to parcel out a
'grange' or an isolated forest demesne and convert it into a village. The
Premonstratensians made an agreement of this nature with the count of
Champagne in 1220 in connection with the grange of Septfontaines, and
many *bastides* in Aquitaine were founded in the same way. At other times the
lord of the forest himself sought a *pariage* with a group of monks who were
good 'recruiting sergeants' and had plenty of money to dispose of. This is
what Bouchard de Meung did when he entered into a contract with the
Hospitallers of Orleans in 1160 with the intention of colonizing his Bonneville woods; he contributed *droit foncier* and *droit banal* over the future village

---

[33] *Cartulaire de Saint-Avit d'Orleans*, No. 50
[34] Documents No. 38, p. 394; No. 39, p. 395   [35] Document No. 37, p. 393

lands to the partnership; he expected in return that the Hospitallers would find colonists and would develop sixty acres.[36]

Villages created in this way provided in their turn the leaven for further colonization. The village lands around them slowly spread as they had done in the older hamlets. In this piecemeal way the wild and lonely parts of western Europe little by little disintegrated and disappeared. We can recognize peasant settlements formed in this period by the names which they still carry today: they are the *villeneuves*, the *neuvilles*, the *abergements*, and in German-speaking parts the many settlements which bear a place-name composed of a man's name and the suffix *-berg*, *-feld*, *-dorf*, *-rode*, or *-reuth*. Often these villages show a peculiar structure. Aerial photography reveals in many an English hamlet the strictly regular plots which each pioneer household received in those early days.[37] Many villages carved out of the forest grew in ribbon fashion along the axis of the road, and the assault on the woodlands took the form of long strips of arable on both sides, each of them attached to the house and enclosure at the roadside.

★   ★   ★

These last paragraphs are full of allusions to the contribution of outside capital. This had been quite unnecessary for the enlargement of an existing village clearing; the gradual movement of reclamation had been accomplished by transferring to the reclaimable fringes small amounts of man-power, the natural increments of peasant population available during the off season, and combining it with small improvements in agricultural implements. By contrast, to build a new village an entrepreneur needed money. The second phase of reclamation was thus initiated by the speculative appetite of the lords, who took a conscious decision to dip into their treasure chests in order to add to the numbers of their subjects and through them to increase the yield of the taxes which they claimed. This was a turning point in the history of the medieval countryside. A portion of the slowly accumulated wealth of the aristocracy came into circulation by direct investment in cereal production. The date of this decisive moment in agricultural growth deserves to be pinpointed more exactly.

To date the movement a careful sifting of the known facts is necessary; place-names and topographical evidence are not by themselves sufficient. We can guess that it started early in certain provinces. In the Mâconnais all the new villages already existed before 1060, and the *sauvetés* of the Toulouse region were founded about 1100. In Normandy 11 *bourgs* appeared before 1066, 32 more before the end of the eleventh century, 46 in the twelfth cen-

---

[36] Higounet, 308; Document No. 37, p. 393; Archives Nationales, 8, 5010¹, fol. 43ᵛ
[37] Beresford, 40, p. 97

tury and 47 in the years after 1200. Between 1150 and 1225 a whole group of *villeneuves* was added to the ribbon villages in the forest of Briard which were established in the eleventh and twelfth centuries.[38] A map of all new villages whose creation is certified by a written deed mentioning the date of their foundation and covering the whole of Europe would be invaluable. It would be certain to reveal a number of regional discrepancies; it would show a series of waves of growth; and it would also lay bare some gaps, such as in southern Burgundy where neither charters of settlement nor manorial foundations exist. Such a cartographic venture is not impossible and it would furnish political, ecclesiastical and cultural historians, as well as their economic history colleagues, with a tool of exceptional value.

We can guess that the movement continued in the fourteenth century to the outermost northern and eastern limits of the Germanic lands, and that it was still active in the middle of the thirteenth century in Aquitaine where strategic considerations appear once more to have been important. Nevertheless, almost everywhere and particularly in the Paris basin, one of the most favoured areas for *villeneuves*, it was definitely checked by 1230-1240. After the first third of the thirteenth century agricultural reclamation continued in districts where the distribution of village communities remained scattered. But for the most part the pioneers no longer lived in groups. They ventured forth alone and erected their homesteads far apart in the middle of the ground which they won from the wastes.

4. THE SETTLEMENT OF THE INTERVENING SPACES

Isolated dwellings between hamlets and villages certainly existed in the early Middle Ages. But they were for the most part temporary and mobile shelters occupied by woodland folk, such as hermits, hunters or the many swineherds who lived in the forests, particularly in England.[39] Some solitary cultivators also existed in frankish Gaul. The mountains of Auvergne in the tenth century were dotted with isolated houses, and some farms in Brie, remote from villages, appeared to have grown up on gallo-Roman agricultural sites.[40] This kind of dispersed settlement probably spread slightly at the end of the eleventh century and in the twelfth in the areas recently opened to cultivation, and many of them had a religious origin. The growth of road traffic caused many religious shelters and hospices to be erected in the wilder parts of the route. Offshoots of hermit orders such as the Carthusians, were hived off into the depth of the forests. Regular canons and Cistercians established 'granges' and the older monasteries such as Cluny and St Denis followed

[38] Duby, 261, p. 302; Ourliac, 320; Boussard, 279; Brunet, 44
[39] Document No. 23, p. 385; Lennard, 268, pp. 14-15
[40] Fel, 54; Brunet, 44, p. 441

suit. These large farms were all set up on the outskirts of the anciently occupied lands and some of them even settled on former village sites whose inhabitants went to live elsewhere after having made over to the monks their rights over the land.[41] But in some cases the new habitations in remote places were created by the initiative of a few pioneering peasants who chose not to associate closely with each other.

Sometimes in fact the enclosure of the arable enforced dispersal. Sometimes the colonists established predominantly pastoral farms, and the necessity of remaining close to the pasture lands required them to build 'vaccaries' or sheepfolds at some distance from each other. This type of settlement became common in the lands won from the sea, where the new fields were for years primarily devoted to animal husbandry while waiting for the salt to be leached out of the soil. At the end of the twelfth century houses in the Flemish polders or on the river banks of Lincolnshire were built on roads or on dykes, but were separated from each other by the surrounding tracts of enclosed pasture or marshland belonging to a single tenant. Basically they were 'ribbon villages' but they were so far apart that the social community was completely broken up.[42]

It would be unwise to generalize from observations which are still far too fragmentary. It seems, however, as if isolated rural habitations increased greatly in the thirteenth century, and especially just before and after the year 1225. Many separate dwellings founded at that time were built by the lords and formed the centre of large farms comparable in extent to the monastic granges established in the previous century. I have discovered a tendency in the Mâconnais of the thirteenth century for knights to remove their houses from the village centre close to the church (probably on the original site of a Roman *villa*) where they had been sited since ancient times, to the outskirts near to what remained of the surrounding forest.[43] It would be worth while to verify whether this was a common phenomenon and if so to find an explanation for it. Was the movement provoked by the desire of the smaller gentry to emphasize the legal differences between them and the peasants at a time when their economic superiority began to be in doubt? Did they wish to give themselves room to practice a new aristocratic fashion, that of digging a moat round the house and fortifying it like a smaller copy of the great castle? Or were the motives perhaps purely economic ones? Did the smaller gentry, dispossessed of their main possessions by the charitable gifts of their forebears, wish to move their barns and stables closer to the new arable furlongs which their servants had brought into use by reclamation and to the pastures which they kept for their own use? Traces of undertakings of agricultural reclamation which aimed at reforming demesnes of the gentry away

[41] Epperlein, 526   [42] Document No. 36, p. 391   [43] Duby, 261, p. 590

from their older lands are not lacking. Many small French backwoodsmen tried to extend their inheritances as did the knights who in 1219 received from the chapter of Notre-Dame de Paris one hundred *arpents* to reclaim and who were forbidden to lease them to settlers. And in the middle of the thirteenth century in the Ile de France we meet many houses and 'purprestures' with enclosed and moated gardens built by members of the lesser nobility and completely surrounded by woods.[44]

The removal of the houses of the gentry ought in any case to be compared with the creation of *gagnages* and *bastides* by patrician town families. These important and compact farms were composed by joining together parcels of land acquired on the outskirts of arable areas and they were kept voluntarily separate from the agrarian community of the village. This phenomenon has been well studied around Metz where within a radius of ten kilometres many bourgeois farms of this kind made their appearance between 1275 and 1325.[45] But the parts of the waste which were not absorbed into extensions of the village clearing were not wholly dotted with the new, large houses of the wealthy. Most of the isolated farms created at that time were those belonging to peasants, like those which were erected in the middle of the common lands between two villages in the Ile de France, Corbreuse and Brétencourt. We know about these thanks to a law suit settled by an inquisition in 1224. The settlers came from Corbreuse; the Brétencourt men broke down the hedges around the new cabins and their grazing cattle devastated the new meadows and gardens. Witnesses called by the commissioners recollected that the first house was built in 1175 and a second one twenty years later. In this place some peasants had obviously preferred solitude to being members of a community[46] before the end of the twelfth century.

In the course of the thirteenth century an isolated homestead became the common choice of settlers who went into the sparsely populated areas in the heart of the wide tracts which still separated one village enclave from another. This is quite clear in Brie. After 1225 and the foundation of the last *villeneuve*,

[44] *Cartulaire de Notre-Dame de Paris* (ed. Guérard), I, p. 399; II, p. 297. Professor M. Postan, in a seminar at the Ecole Pratique des Hautes Etudes in 1961 and again in a lecture at Aix in the same year, expressed the opinion that one of the most pressing of the motives behind reclamation was the exhaustion of the anciently cultivated soils. In the thirteenth century in England certain manorial lands suffering from an overintensive cereal cultivation had, according to him, lost their fertility and become incapable of producing bread grains. To compensate for this deterioration the lords had then abandoned these fields to peasants and had ventured cultivation on the virgin lands which were of lower quality: reclamation was thus allied to migration. We must await the appearance of his forthcoming book before we can examine this hypothesis further. But we must point out that it would provide an attractive explanation for the removal of the lordly demesnes which is discussed above.

[45] Schneider 351, pp. 394 *et seq.*

[46] *Cartulaire de Notre-Dame de Paris* (ed. Guérard), II, p. 307

a final wave of settlement carried the isolated farms into what remained of the 'wilderness'. The same happening can be seen on the high ground of the Massif Central. In Margeride, a scattering of isolated houses, which is the present-day arrangement of the district, was completed as the fourteenth century approached. Maine was colonized in the same way. We know that a number of isolated farms were created after 1240 in Bresse and the Beaujolais mountains which are areas of *mas* (isolated farms) rather than hamlets, as were the Mâconnais hills not far away. We can see the same thing in England on the verges of the royal forests. On the fringe of the Peak forest the bailiff authorized 126 peasants to construct a 'purpresture', i.e. the enclosure of an isolated house, between 1216 and 1251. Devonshire and north Warwickshire, which were settled after 1086, were also regions of separate dwellings. The same was true of the Bavarian plateau, the Austrian Alps and the *kampen* around Bois le Duc, where peasant settlement took place after the twelfth century.[47]

*   *   *

This new system of land settlement reflects an extremely important change in man's attitude to and his relationship with nature. It encouraged the extension of a special type of landscape in which permanent enclosure predominated.

The origin of the hedgerow is a complex one. Examples from the most distant past can be quoted. It appears also in very recent times. But a good deal of research has shown that most of the enclosed countryside in France and Germany corresponds to regions where settlement was late and usually after the thirteenth century. We have seen that when reclamation went on around villages the assarts remained enclosed for a time. But as soon as they could form a compact entity like the old arable, the permanent fences were destroyed and they coalesced into open fields. On the other hand, when the solitary farmer settled on a farm in the midst of a waste where he was able to organize his holding in one lot surrounded by pasture land, he erected an enclosure of durable materials, either a wall or a living hedge.[48] In fact in medieval documents enclosures without exception went hand in hand with dispersed habitation. An enclosure actually fulfilled three important functions. As a vestige of and substitute for the woodland, the hedgerow provided first of all some of the traditional forest products, posts, stakes, leaves for litter or fodder. It protected crops which were otherwise exposed to the depredations of grazing animals and wild beasts. Lastly, and most significantly, the permanent fence was a symbol of ownership, the sign as well as the defence

[47] Brunet, 43; Fel, 54; Latouche, 227; Duby, 261; Finberg, 187; Hilton, 161; Jansen, 671; Wiesner 544   [48] Document No. 48, p. 403

of an individual farm isolated in the midst of land enjoying collective use. It placed the whole farm in the protected position once monopolized by the homestead toft.[49]

Settlement by dispersed habitation, and thus by enclosure, profoundly modified the economic position of a farm. The old collective economy which by communal usage and the periodic construction and destruction of temporary enclosures enabled individual cultivation and communal stockrearing to alternate on the arable portions, was replaced by an individualistic agrarian system. A close study of the movement towards dispersal from the chronological and geographical points of view would be of very great interest. Had it begun to spread everywhere by about 1220? And at what point of time should we place its most intense phase in different parts of Europe? In my opinion such a study ought to be conducted jointly with another devoted to fiscal powers of lordships. In some regions one can indeed observe in the course of the thirteenth century a kind of explosion of the village lordship. It became usual to levy customary dues on households, while forcing men subject to tallage to live generation after generation in the *manses* they occupied.[50] Ought we not to consider such changes as an adaptation of methods of levying dues to the new fragmentation of habitations?

If we enquire into the reasons which induced small cultivators to set up separate dispersed farms we can begin by looking at the direct effects of assarting. A moment came when in order not to have to return home each evening after a day's work in the fields, the squatters constructed overnight shelters which they later occupied permanently. But was it really only a question of adapting themselves to the distance from their work? One can also imagine that the acquisition of better tools in the thirteenth century often allowed a rural family to manage by themselves and to forgo the old need for mutual assistance.[51] It could also have been a question of the possibilities of the soil. We ought to ascertain whether this last phase of agrarian conquest did not take place on land which required a different and more individualistic handling of cereals and stockraising, and favoured the predominance of the latter. Lastly did the wealthy men, lords or burgesses, who put up the money needed by the settlers, discover that they could expect a better return on their invested capital by creating separate farming units than from agricultural clearings farmed collectively by villages? This final method of settlement reflected a profound change in the rural economy, a swing of investment towards pastoral activities.

[49] Juillard and Meynier, 66; Brunet, 43; Bader, 38, pp. 100 *et seq.*; Chaumeil, 46
[50] See p. 250
[51] Thus in northern Italy the spread of the dispersed dwelling appears to have been favoured by the investment of urban capital which reinforced the equipment of peasant farms and permitted their individualization.

It is possible therefore to believe that the modification of the system of cultivation, which found an expression in certain methods of colonization was stimulated by the opening up of the movements of exchange, and particularly a more active trade in meat, wool and leather.[52] In support of this assumption it appears that the initiators of these changes were not peasants but masters who were engaged in commercial speculation. The Cistercians showed the way from the twelfth century onwards; the wealthy gentry and patricians imitated them later to be followed by their humbler fellows. A house standing alone, and a compact parcel of land contained within fences (which not only offered protection against wandering cattle, but also enclosed the master's animals and preserved the grazing for them alone) appears to have provided a unit of production where stockraising on the natural grassland made up the chief resource and where grain-growing made an important but nevertheless secondary contribution. Thus the movement of dispersed settlement in the twelfth century could well appear, after the period of the foundation of the *villeneuves*, as a slowing down of the impulse towards agricultural development. During the last stage of the reclamation of cultivable soils therefore we can see the extension of the arable taking second place to the growth of pastoral activities and a more intensive exploitation of grassland.

*   *   *

Whatever may be the value of these hypotheses and the fate which future research may have in store for them, according to all present indications the force of agricultural expansion was spent by the beginning of the thirteenth century. In some countries, such as the eastern end of the Germano-Slav plain, Lombardy where the harnessing of the alpine torrents was going on, the Juras, and the northern half of Warwickshire, it did not seem to flag until after 1300. But it can be seen to halt before 1230 in the Paris region, and in the middle of the thirteenth century in upper Provence and in Picardy, where by that time all usable land had been brought into cultivation. The end came also in England at about the same time where cereal growing predominated, on the estates of Ely cathedral for example. And the end of the colonization of the Brie can be seen as the fourteenth century drew near.[53]

[52] It is also necessary to put it in context with changes of diet which can be guessed at, such as the increased demand for meat and dairy products, which was especially strong in urban and aristocratic circles. In northern Italy the extension at the same period of an enclosed landscape, in which the hedgerow was one of the chief features, ties up with the increase of vines and orchards. The penetration of the urban economy appears here again as the principal factor in the change.

[53] Hilton, 161; Gaussin, 293; Bishop, 278; Miller, 198; Brunet, 44, pp. 446 *et seq.*; Sclafert, 83, p. 37

It is true that these chronological divisions which provide the rural history of Europe with its most important milestones are far from being everywhere erected in the right places. Detailed verification is still required. Thus the general consensus of opinion is that no more assarts were created in Artois after 1270; but in spite of this in 1316 a lord in this area divided up one of his woods and settled seven families there in a hamlet specially created for them.[54] Nevertheless it remains firmly established that here and there the retreat began in the last years of the thirteenth century. Some soils which deteriorated very quickly after they were put into cultivation began to be abandoned. I take an example from the mountains of Beaujolais. About 1240 a small landlord wished to create a dozen dependent peasant farms; by 1286 three of these *manses* were deserted and the lord sold the whole reclaimed area on very unfavourable terms.[55] We can confidently believe that about this time (except perhaps in the new isolated farms devoted primarily to stockraising) human settlement had filled up the available soils on which the yield of arable cultivation could repay the effort of the cultivator.

These reflections present a framework for research. They invite us to distinguish between types of agricultural settlement, and to place them more accurately in time and space. Already what we know today about the regions best provided with survey-like records, northern and central France, the Low Countries and the German Rhineland, enables us to envisage provisionally the lines which agrarian reclamation followed and its general aspect. It seems to fall into three successive phases. The enlargement of the primitive clearings was almost entirely the work of peasants and was carried out in the setting of the village community. It appears to have begun here and there by the tenth century, and it is perfectly possible that this growth merely continued in certain cases an earlier and equally slow expansion. The foundation of new villages encouraged by the leading landlords began in most parts later, and we must place the most intense phase of this second wave of settlement between 1150 and 1200. Lastly, a third period is characterized by a slowing down which was in some areas quite abrupt. Apart from northwestern Germany, where new villages were still being created,[56] the only notable progress which occurred in forested regions appears allied to dispersed settlement and the growth of pastoral activities. But even to go as far as erecting this tentative hypothesis is to invite its amendment or even its demolition.

---

[54] Martel, 316; *La chronique et les chartes de l'abbaye de Marœil* (ed. Bertin), No. 195
[55] Perroy, 269, pp. 129 *et seq.*
[56] Timm, 570, pp. 98 *et seq.*

CHAPTER II

Work in the Fields

Of all the various aspects of agricultural expansion the retreat of the wastelands is the one most easily observed. This is the reason why, in order to outline the features of the movement which are the least vague, I began with the reclamations. But the forward march of reclamation was itself also closely connected with two other parallel movements, of which one, demographic growth, urged it onwards, while the other, improvement in farm technique, followed in its wake. The variations in these movements are not always easy to see; let us nevertheless start by examining the technical progress which had to follow and keep pace with the spread of the cultivated area.

*　　*　　*

Abundant information about agricultural equipment and practice is available in the books on agriculture which were written and circulated in many European countries during the second half of the thirteenth century. Amongst those which achieved the greatest success were the treatise of Pietro de Crescenzi of Bologna, the various manuals of *Housebondrie*, that is to say domestic economy, the most famous of which was written by Walter of Henley, and above all the collection of *Fleta*, also from England, which contains both a strictly practical description of model agricultural practice and advice to landlords about the management of their property. All these books were penned in the vulgar tongue. They were addressed to an educated public, but one which was not composed solely of the clergy.

The spread of literature of this kind was notable enough in itself. It continued and spread still wider the popularity enjoyed ever since Carolingian times by the writings of Roman agriculturists, which had urged an increase in the output of the soil and had recommended more efficient farming methods. It also reflected the continuing diffusion of the spirit of enterprise amongst manorial administrators. Already alive in the great monasteries of Seine and Meuse in the time of the Franks, when the treatises of Varro and Columella attracted the founders of the intellectual 'renaissance', this spirit permeated the Cistercian abbeys of the twelfth century. Agriculture was considered by them to be a 'mechanical art', worthy of scientific interest and susceptible of systematic improvement.[1] But that this curiosity should then have moved beyond ecclesiastical and intellectual circles where Latin was spoken and should have infected certain representatives of the nobility and the higher administration, was an event of the very greatest importance. It is more significant still to see this interest spread and intensify in certain countries like Italy and England around 1250, i.e. at the moment when demographic pressure, the increased exchange of goods and the resulting social changes made landlords aware how important it was to pay attention to their manorial activities and to direct them rationally. The appearance of agricultural treatises in the language of the lords is a landmark in the all too vague chronology of agricultural expansion, and provides solid arguments for those who think that agriculture from the eleventh to the thirteenth centuries had in all western countries become steadily more intensive while its area was extending.

We ought, therefore – and the task should be relatively easy as well as useful – to examine all these writings in detail to find out what success they had and what field they covered. Were they in fact practical manuals and were they used as such? It is important, too, to extract the didactic part of these treatises and to separate it from the sections that are mere anthologies, slavishly copied from other authors or the Latin classics, so that we can find out how much was the result of direct experience and contact with the land.[2] This should then enable us to compare the theoretical ideas proposed by these books with the state of technique as it was actually practised. This is the only way in which we can be sure whether the period really benefited from an improvement in farming methods.

At this point the enquiry becomes tiresomely complicated and may prove something of a disappointment. It runs head on into two interconnected difficulties. The first difficulty is that the evidence is practically non-existent for the period before the thirteenth century, is rare after that date, and is always unrevealing and discontinuous. The second obstacle is the complexity of agricultural practices. Many such practices were interdependent and formed coherent systems of which all the interlocking elements ought to be simultaneously observed in operation. This of course would be impossible. For this reason, as well as for the sake of clarity of exposition and simplification of research, we must resign ourselves to considering the two important aspects of agrarian practice consecutively, even though by so doing we separate arbitrarily practices which were by their very nature associated. These two aspects are the sequence of the crops and the manner in which the land was cultivated.

[1] Südhof, 134
[2] Documents Nos. 25 to 30, pp. 387-390

I. CYCLES OF CULTIVATION

The agricultural treatises contain much advice on crops and on how to organize their rotation amongst the fields in order to reap the most profitable harvests. How far was this advice followed? To help us select more easily from unpromising documentary evidence, and to avoid transposing into medieval times the model biennial or triennial rotations which are so familiar to traditional agriculture in modern Europe, we shall have for the moment to leave on one side the somewhat obscure question of what is properly called the rotation (*assolement*), i.e. the management of homogeneous 'courses' or portions of the village lands in which all the strips were treated each year in exactly the same way, and were either all sown with one kind of corn or all left fallow.[3] English surveys of the twelfth century reveal the existence of fields which were apparently subject to compulsory rotation of crops, but on the continent clear evidence of collective usage of this sort is nowhere to be found before the fourteenth century; besides, it was strictly a part of the relationship between field and forest, arable and stockraising; we shall have to discuss it later, but here we need only consider two distinct points.

The arrangement of the cycle was in the first place controlled by the distinction between the fields under winter crops, such as wheat and rye, and those under spring crops, such as barley and oats. But this distinction itself depended largely on dietary habits. Since at that time bread constituted man's basic foodstuff, he was naturally forced to produce bread crops before all others, and this meant winter grain. Even if the yield of rye on sandy soils had not been much higher than that of wheat he would often have preferred to sow it because it was less demanding and easier to thresh. However, the wealthy ate white bread made only from wheat flour. Whether the lord was priest, nobleman or townsman, the needs of his table required wheat to be sown on lands which would often have been otherwise devoted to rye. And it is also possible that the cultivation of wheat increased during the twelfth and thirteenth century because of the spread of aristocratic fashions amongst lesser folk which is always a characteristic of social habits in times of economic growth. It is not necessary to point out that wheat found purchasers at a higher price, for it was a commodity of high quality subject to a fairly regular trade. These then were the considerations which gave wheat a large place in cultivation.

However, medieval bread, the horrible black substance which was the staple food of common people, were they peasants or servants, contained all kinds of grain, sometimes millet,[4] often barley which gave such a high yield,

[3] D. Faucher 'L'assolement triennal en France', *Etudes rurales*, 1961
[4] Millet appears to have been the most frequently cultivated grain in Comminges

and also oats, although these were sometimes eaten in the form of gruel (*bouillie*). The bare necessities for human subsistence, therefore, encouraged the growing of spring corn, '*mars*' or *tramesium*, as part of the sequence of crops. Neither must the part played by oats in the care of war-horses be forgotten. After all, the aristocratic civilization of the Middle Ages in western Europe was primarily a horseborne one. Village overlords demanded dues in the form of oats for use in their stables. In the eleventh and twelfth centuries, before the payment of the tallage in money became widespread, the occupiers of castles, whose cavalry protected the countryside, exacted oats from their subjects before anything else. These demands – to which in the thirteenth century must be added the substitution of the horse for the ox in the ploughteams of many regions[5] – all helped to extend the share of the arable lands devoted to spring grain.

A system which was not limited to the production of winter grain but associated the *tramesium* with it, also presented certain technical advantages. Alternate crops encouraged the growth and vigour of the plants. To sow wheat or rye on some fields and barley or oats on others enabled the risks of a bad harvest in the uncertain climate experienced by a large part of western Europe to be spread. As recent research into the thirteenth-century accounts of the bishop of Winchester has shown, excessive moisture, and especially heavy autumn rainfall, could often be disastrous for winter cereals.[6] In such years spring grain came to the rescue. A mixed cultivation which introduced a new season of ploughing in Lent helped to spread agricultural work more evenly throughout the course of the year, and to utilize domestic labour and draught animals more economically. Gangs and teams of the same size could thus work a larger area. The agricultural treatises published in England in the thirteenth century all draw attention to the fact that one plough could cultivate 160 acres sown with wheat or rye, but as much as 180 acres if the seed was divided between winter and spring crops. Consequently we can assume from the increase in spring grain that progress had been made and that farm management was in this respect more efficient. The distribution of the different crops can be seen in detail, since medieval sources contain a great deal of information on the kind of grain which reached the lord's barns. It is true that the composition of dues exacted by any lord is misleading since it depends less on peasant production than on the personal wishes of the master. To meet the latter the tenant would deliver perhaps all the wheat and oats

---

during the twelfth century, and in the forest of Orleans during the thirteenth century; Higounet, 454; *Cartulaire de l'abbaye de la Cour-Dieu*, No. 13. In medieval Lombardy millet played a considerable part in human diet, just as *po enta* does today; Toubert, 651.

[5] See p. 110.   [6] Titow, 86

that he had harvested, and consequently we know nothing of what he kept for himself. Tithes are a more faithful reflection of the composition of the harvest. The best sources are obviously demesne inventories or manorial accounts. The quantity of different seed which was sown or harvested each year on each demesne was recorded in them, and such records are plentiful in the thirteenth century. At the same time there is valuable information to be found in leases and share-cropping agreements which incorporate instructions about farming activities. Except in England this material has hardly been touched, and it awaits the prospector's pick.

This gentleman will have to look much farther, however, before he unearths the second factor in the farming sequence, and perhaps he will never strike the golden lode. This factor is of course the duration of the fallow. What we want to know is whether the land was allowed to rest every other year, every third year, or more often. Was the sequence biennial or triennial or was it an even looser one, i.e. was the cultivation of winter and spring grain interspersed with long unproductive phases? Was the area of the village lands devoted to food crops widely utilized or was it, for lack of manure and because of the need to prevent yields falling to an absurd level, restricted to a few strips surrounded on all sides by the intermittent return of natural vegetation?

This is a fundamental question. If we could but answer it, we should be able to measure the real intensity of medieval agriculture, place human labour in its true context, and define the limits of what was economically possible for the men reclaiming the land. Unfortunately, this problem is almost insoluble. The fault lies with the documents, because neither commissioners, administrators nor scribes bothered to give any estimate of the extent of the uncultivated fields. But our enquiry runs up against another insurmountable difficulty: the duration of the fallow depended directly on the quality of the soil which naturally varied considerably from place to place. Because of this factor, modern peasants in different localities make use of different sequences, and their ancestors would certainly not have behaved otherwise. But this very diversity seriously limits the significance of the information provided by our sources, since they refer to pieces of ground whose fertility is unknown to us.

Having explained these considerations and made these reservations we can now resume the discussion and analysis of what, in the present state of research, can be discerned of this fundamental aspect of rural economy.

*   *   *

If we are to believe some passages in the *polyptyques*, a triennial cycle, sharing the area cultivated each year between winter grain and the *tramesium,* was applied on certain lands of the big abbeys between the Loire and Rhine in the Carolingian period.[7] After this darkness falls until the twelfth century. So far as the composition of the crops is concerned, the few explicit documents then show how widely practices differed at that time. About 1150 a very conscientious inventory described ten dependent demesnes of the abbey of Cluny all of which lay close to the monastery. Here is what this inventory has to say about the point in question. In only two of these farms did the area occupied on the lord's land by spring grain equal that occupied by winter grain; in others the proportion was two-thirds, a third, or a quarter; one of the demesnes produced only rye and a little wheat.[8] The division of the crops, then, corresponded mainly to domestic needs. The monastery, a huge manorial household with vast stables, consumed wheat above all else and a great deal of oats. But it appeared that locally the cycle was entirely governed by the natural qualities of the soil, and the system selected was both flexible and complex.

Some sources of the same period have something to tell us about the fallow. They tell us that a shifting cultivation interspersed with long resting times was very generally employed, especially on sectors recently won from the wastes. In 1116 the inhabitants of one village in the Ile de France were granted the right to plough anciently reclaimed land in the royal forest and permission to open up new assarts; but only on condition 'that they cultivated them by taking a crop for two harvests only, and that they then moved on to other parts of the forest'.[9] This prohibition was probably intended to avoid the risk of a total exhaustion of new lands by continuous and prolonged cultivation from which the king, who, as the lord, exacted a part of the harvest, would have suffered. But the injunction implies also that fallow would normally cover much more than a third of the fields. The very fact that it was subject to an edict proves that primitive methods of periodic 'slash and burn' were far from being abandoned here. The region was not amongst the most backward, and a century later it appeared in the vanguard of agricultural progress. I shall quote one other example which dates from the beginning of the thirteenth century. In the *villeneuve* of Bonlieu in Beauce the nuns of Yères used to oblige the settlers to cultivate 'according to the season', that is to say to follow a regular sequence; they left no more than one year in three fallow. Their preference for a triennial cycle thus appears incontestable, but the rule nevertheless authorized peasants to leave their arable uncultivated in certain cases: 'because of poverty' (that is, if they found themselves temporarily without draught animals), but also 'to improve

---

[7] See p. 22   [8] Duby, 442
[9] *Cartulaire de Notre-Dame de Paris* (ed. Guérard), I, p. 258

the ground'.[10] This text is illuminating. It proves that there was a great deal of liberty in the choice of rotations and that small farmers found themselves less tied down by routine or collective constraint than we might sometimes imagine. They were free to organize their own sequence of crops after taking as much account of the quality of the soil and climatic conditions as of agrarian traditions. We can see that on these fully occupied village lands the triennial sequence was assumed to be the most desirable practice, but was also, so to speak, a luxury device. It could only be followed on a fertile soil and exploited by husbandmen well enough equipped to turn over the soil to the depth required to restore fertility. It was therefore an exacting method and probably for this reason was not so widespread as is sometimes believed.

*   *   *

We come next to the thirteenth century which is less scantily served by its documents. Towards the middle of the century the first formal evidence of the use of a rotation wholly based on a three-year cycle appears. In 1248 the 1,000 odd acres cultivated on the grange at Vaulerent in the Ile de France were divided into three 'years'; 'corn', *marsage* and fallow in three courses whose area was all but equal.[11] Observe that the farm in question belonged to the Cistercians, and consequently was run on the most advanced principles. On this great peripheral demesne, situated far from village lands, the alternation of crops could, of course, be very easily organized. But it is also certain that a similar sequence was generally followed in Normandy during the second half of the thirteenth century,[12] and on many farms on the Ile de France in the early fourteenth century. In 1334-1335 for instance, on the demesne which the abbey of St Denis possessed at Tremblay 136 *arpents* were sown with winter grain and 164 with spring grain, while 163 were left fallow.[13] These observations may be compared with what we know about the English countryside, where in some villages peasants occupied a third 'field' taken from the grazing grounds of the 'outfield'. By doing this they intended to replace the two-field system, in which every year half the village lands carried no crop, with a less extensive system which distributed the land equally between autumn sowing, spring sowing, and fallow. This clearly represents a progressive extension of the triennial cycle.[14]

However, closer scrutiny reveals that we must not assume that the area where the triennial cycle was employed as the fourteenth century approached was too widespread. In this connection there are four points to be noted.

---

[10] Archives Nationales, LL.1599 B p. 143   [11] Higounet, 304
[12] Strayer, 276   [13] Fourquin, 551
[14] Stenton, 275, p. 122; Hilton, 667; Darby, 47, p. 239

1. Three-course rotations are not unknown in the Midi countryside. One reference taken from a notary's register tells of land granted in a village in Haute Provence 'for the next six years or for four seasons'. This formula signifies that the communal practice was to cultivate the field in two years out of three. And the inquest of 1338, which describes in great detail the demesnes farmed by the Hospitallers in the southern Alps, shows that in several of them the manorial fields were submitted to a regular triennial cycle.[15]

2. The documents I have quoted show clearly, it is true, the limits of such a practice. The stipulations of the first example are ambiguous: it leaves it to be understood that the four productive years (and since it is a *métayage* contract, it is these alone which matter) could, if necessary, be spread over a longer or shorter period. As for the inventory of the Hospital's demesnes, it mainly shows the flexible way in which the crops could be distributed, and, moreover, the limited place allotted to spring grain. The composition of the tithes raised on the neighbouring parishes reveals that peasant households, more conscious of the need to extract as much from the land as it could give, more often risked a March sowing, which was hazardous in this climate. But only 22 of the 120 manorial demesnes devoted half or more of their crops to barley or oats; on 46 demesnes only winter wheat was harvested; on 52 demesnes wheat or rye occupied most space. Furthermore the administrators most frequently decided that it was necessary to leave fallow much more than one-third of the fields. The fields lay fallow one year in 79 of the demesnes, and longer still on 21 more; the servants of one commandery even abandoned the soil to the waste for four years out of five.

3. It appears too that the production of winter grain carried the triennial cycle into many northern village lands. In 1249 in one village in the Ardennes tithes amounted to 14 measures of wheat and 14 of rye against 20 measures of oats.[16] If more evidence could be found which would allow harvest and sowing to be calculated it would be of the greatest interest.

4. Evidence confirming the existence of prolonged fallow is more significant still. It must have been considerable, since lack of manure, insufficient ploughing, and the inability of man to maintain the fertility of the soil artificially, prevented the 'free' period in the fields from being too much reduced. The intelligent author of the agricultural treatise which we call *Fleta* adjured his readers to prefer one good harvest every other year to two mediocre ones every three years. His advice was to cling to the old 'two-field' system, one field lying fallow and the other growing partly winter and partly spring grain. In fact the English countryside, where the landlords were

---

[15] Arch. des Bouches-du-Rhône, 369 E 17, fol. 71; Sclafert, 131
[16] *Cartulaire du l'abbaye cistercienne de Val Dieu*, No. 101

at that time probably more anxious than anywhere else to raise the productivity of their lands, adopted the strict triennial cycle much more gradually than is sometimes admitted. No certain details of its use can be found in Lincolnshire before the fourteenth century.[17] Certain written documents still badly in need of cataloguing reveal how common was the practice of long fallow periods in France. At the end of the thirteenth century in the Beaujolais hills, some manorial fields remained uncultivated for a year after having grown oats; they were then sown with rye and again allowed to rest the whole of the following year.[18] At the same period lands in Forez are known which were cropped only three times in thirty years. The custom of temporary cultivation, snatched at intervals from the waste and pasture, remained popular, especially on the fringes of land reclaimed by dispersed settlement where arid conditions had up till then restrained the pioneers. The *garrigue* of Provence and Languedoc was exploited in this way by means of sporadic slash-and-burn cultivation.[19] The necessity for prolonged fallow probably reflects the grazing and pastoral activities of the peripheral farms, established after 1250 in lands newly enclosed and hedged.

When all is said and done most of the documents known today which expressly prove the strict limitation of the fallow to a third of the arable area for France in the second half of the thirteenth century come from the alluvial soils of the Paris basin, i.e. from the same regions where the lands of the great abbeys of the Carolingian epoch had been intensively cultivated. What happened in other places? Everything leads us to believe that on less homogeneous soils the sequence of crops was everywhere irregular, and that every year a vast part of the cultivated area remained unsown. There is enough evidence to permit us to speak of the progress of the three-year cycle since the ninth century, but only if we do not conjure up a picture of its total victory. The three-year rhythm was certainly more widespread than is usually accepted in the southern parts of France. But on the other hand it was much more narrowly restricted in the north. We should be wise, therefore, to conclude that during this stage of agricultural growth the extension of the area sown with crops resulted more from reclamation than from a shortening of the fallow period.

*   *   *

In any event, towards the end of the thirteenth century some remarkable changes in the regions where economic expansion was taking place come to light from documents which become somewhat more informative. They all

[17] Stenton, 275, p. 123; Stenton, *Documents of the Danelaw*, pp. xxx-xxxi
[18] Perroy, 269, p. 143   [19] Sclafert, 83, pp. 25 *et seq.*

bear testimony to the desire to work the cultivated lands in a more rational manner and for greater profit. It should also be noted that in some places this urge could result in a retreat from the triennial rotation, as for instance in the Alsatian countryside where a biennial cycle was adopted based on a single but much more abundant wheat crop every other year.[20] This particular attempt at adaptation was a response to the food requirements of the rapidly developing Rhineland towns, and to the consequent rise in the price of wheat. Here, giving up spring grain and extending the fallow yielded a better return. Higher yields and production concentrated on the crop with the highest commercial value henceforth made up for the reduction of the area under the plough in the peasant economy.

Elsewhere in England, north-western France and Westphalia spring sowing was retained, but arranged differently. Barley was often mixed with oats and sometimes replaced it completely. The introduction of barley was sometimes dictated by the need to keep up yields, since the yield of oats was absurdly low; elsewhere again changes in dietary habits which are as yet ill understood were the cause; lastly, in some cases the lure of commercial profit was probably the determining factor; in countries bordering the North Sea the growth of brewing brought about a rise in the price of barley.[21]

Frequently, too, leguminous plants replaced oats. In 1314 on the demesne which Thierry d'Hireçon farmed at Roquetoire in Artois the spring crop was made up of 25 to 30 per cent oats, 50 to 60 per cent vetches, 15 per cent peas and 5 per cent beans.[22] This changeover affected the economic structure of the farm very profoundly; not only because these crops yielded more, nor even because they possessed a higher nutritional value,[23] but because so far from exhausting the soil, their cultivation improved it; left where it was the green stuff became a natural fertilizer; so much so that an extension of leguminous crops could sometimes take place at the expense of the fallow. This practice opened the way to a rotation which put the land in a state to produce food crops three years out of four. It may well be that on closer examination the sequences of cultivation at the end of the thirteenth century

[20] Juillard, 67, p. 35
[21] Raftis, 201, p. 161; Verhulst, 137; Schröder-Lembke, 130
[22] Richard, 473. Right at the end of the fourteenth century the crops on the fields of one of the demesnes of the *seigneurie* of Neufbourg in Normandy were divided in the following way: winter grain, 20 *setiers* of wheat; *trémois*, 2 *setiers* of barley and a little oats, 12 *setiers* of vetches. Plaisse, 681.
[23] At the beginning of the twelfth century to alleviate the shortage of food, the count of Flanders 'decreed that whoever would sow two measures of land in seed time, should sow another measure of land with beans and peas, because these kinds of vegetables germinating more freely and growing more quickly at a more convenient time of year, would feed the poor more quickly if famine and scarcity persisted in that year'. Galbert de Bruges, *Vie de Charles Le Bon*, (ed. Guizot), p. 245.

will already reveal the arrival in some places of a four-course rotation.[24]

*   *   *

As soon as they become sufficiently explicit, our sources reveal before all else the multiplicity of rotational systems. This is the first point to consider. It forestalls any hasty generalizations, and emphasizes the infinite variety of methods of cultivation in the west where quality of soil, climatic conditions and distribution of land were nowhere alike. A flexible system corresponded to an economy unequally and imperfectly affected by commercial exchanges and it sometimes also reflected the divergent development of dietary habits. We can guess how easily local usage could in this way be changed, and we can observe at least some large-scale farmers trying to improve their methods and adapt them to market conditions, and thereby demonstrating a genuine spirit of enterprise.

The material remains, however, much too scarce and irregularly distributed to allow us to observe any general progress at all clearly. For this reason we cannot say with certainty whether there was a new movement in the thirteenth century, or whether it was part of a wider impulse whose origin dated back to Carolingian times. We may, however, risk the following more cautious hypothesis.

During the two first periods of the movement of reclamation, while clearings were being enlarged and the *villeneuves* established, i.e. right up to the second third of the thirteenth century, the continued creation of new fields at the expense of apparently inexhaustible virgin land made it unnecessary to apply more intensive cycles of cultivation on the older village lands. If there were improvements in the practices employed in the Carolingian period we can assume that they must have spread at a very leisurely pace.

On the other hand, half-way through the thirteenth century the extension of the cultivated area could not be carried further except by dispersed farms and semi-pastoral activities. Indeed, in certain places fields were abandoned while yields gradually shrank on many which had been carved out of the waste and put under the plough. What happened, therefore, was that the 'external' advance by the conquest of the dunes and woods was, under the pressure of a sustained need for subsistence, succeeded by a phase of 'internal' conquest, when an effort was made to extract more food from the same area by reducing the fallow as much as possible. It is in fact at this moment, in the very same regions where reclamation halted soonest, and where demand for food was most pressing, that we can pick out the first signs of four-course

[24] See the texts quoted by N.S.B. and E. C. Gras, *The Economic and Social History of an English Village, Crawley, Hampshire*, Cambridge (Mass.), 1930, and by L. Delisle, *Normandie*, p. 297.

rotations. This is the only important change in the direction of more intensive cultivation which can be borne out by written sources.

2. YIELDS

When we consider the effort medieval agriculturists devoted to organizing the cycle of cultivation, we are at once struck by the fact that their first concern was to raise yields, and at all costs to prevent them from dropping. This vital preoccupation was an obstacle everywhere to a reduction of the fallow; sometimes it even helped to extend it. Anyone who seeks to gain an accurate picture of the improvement of agricultural technique or to follow the movement of expansion ought to take note of the changes in crop yields, and to compare their levels to those of the ninth century which seem, even by the most conservative estimates, to be derisory. To this end we must collect patiently, but not too hopefully, any information bearing on this subject, even though there is not much to be learnt before the last years of the thirteenth century.

At this point in consequence of more advanced methods of manorial management and of the attitude of certain lords who had become more sensitive to fluctuations in output and who tried to increase the return from their land.[25] manorial documents begin to record a great deal of detailed numerical information. English manorial documents in particular contain abundant material much of which can be arranged in continuous series over many decades. It must be realized of course that this documentary evidence is not easy to handle nor can its teaching be utterly relied on. Measures of capacity vary from place to place and make comparisons difficult. Besides, we can never be quite sure what the figures of harvest totals in the text represent. Was the harvest measured at the time of reaping? Or later, in the barns, after the wages of harvesters and threshers, the tithes and the servants' food had been deducted?[26] But in spite of the lack of precision these facts are supremely valuable when set against the obscurity which veils the story of agricultural production. The most vivid impression we gain is one of extreme diversity, although this is hardly surprising.

1. The yields of different crops from the same fields could vary widely. I have already spoken of the different returns from barley and oats which led some farmers to modify their distribution of crops. On one of the abbey of Ramsey's manors the yield of barley oscillated between 6 and 11 to one, but the oat harvest barely exceeded what had been sown – an almost negative return.[27]

2. Striking regional contrasts also affected average yields. On some allu-

[25] On this change of psychological attitude see document No. 29, p. 389.
[26] Farmer, 338   [27] Raftis, 201, pp. 176-178

vial plains these remained high and came close to present-day yields on poorer soils. In Artois for example, on leased-out church lands admittedly indirectly farmed and which do̅ not seem to have enjoyed exceptional fertility, the return of wheat at the beginning of the fourteenth century sometimes exceeded 15 to one; on average it was about 8 and that of oats about 6. In the same province, the demesnes of Thierry d'Hireçon rendered equally generous harvests: at Roquetoire wheat yielded 7·5 to one in 1319 and 11·6 to one in 1321; at Gosnay 11 to one in 1333, 15 to one in 1335. The yield of wheat was equally high (8 to one on average) on the lands farmed by the abbey of St Denis at Merville in the Ile de France,[28] On the other hand, at the same period on the manorial demesnes throughout the Provençal Alps it was between 3 and 4 to one. In some alpine villages it sometimes even fell to a Carolingian level; it was only on some of the small *ferrages* (homestead gardens) near the towns, on exceptionally well manured soils, that it reached 6 or 7 to one, as it did also in some very fertile parts around Arles and Fréjus.[29]

3. Yields of course varied greatly from one year to another. From equal sowings of 216 measures of wheat, the administrators of Merton College harvested 869 in 1334 and 1,040 in 1335, and on the Burgundian demesne of Ouges the yield of wheat, which rose to 10 to one in 1380, fell in the following year to 3·3. We should note too that the yields of different grains did not move together. On the lands of Gosnay in Artois the level of wheat yields was twice as high as that of oats in 1333 and three times as high in the following year.[30] This variation in space and instability over time, much more pronounced than nowadays, originated in the limited efficiency of agricultural practices and man's inability to control natural conditions. It imposed one basic feature on rural economy which must always be emphasized, that of the extreme irregularity of cereal production.

But beyond these variations is it possible to determine average productivity? English agriculturists of the thirteenth century set down in their treatises levels which seemed to them normal. Here they are: 8 for barley, 7 for rye, 6 for leguminous plants, 5 for wheat, and 4 for oats.[31] In reality, studies of long series of accounts on certain English manors lead us to think that these figures, even under favourable conditions, were very optimistic. Between 1200 and 1450 on the well-worked lands of the bishop of Winchester, wheat yielded an average of 3·8 to one, barley the same and oats only 2·4.[32] These

[28] Fossier, 607; Richard, 473; Fourquin, 551   [29] Duby, 286

[30] J. Saltmarsh, 'A College Home Farm in the Fifteenth Century', in *Economic History Review*, 1937; Martin-Lorber, 536; Richard, 473   [31] Document No. 29, p. 389

[32] Beveridge, 'The Yield and Price of Corn in the Middle Ages', in *Economic History Review*, 1927

are modest levels. They seem definitely lower than those revealed by documents relating to Artois and the Parisian region. On the other hand, they are not far off the levels of yields registered by surveyors on the strength of returns of the administrators of the Provençal demesnes of the Hospitallers, and they hardly differ from those which then served as a base for the establishment of the *métayage* leases in the region of Toulouse.[33] The average yield of wheat which nowadays reaches 20 to one in the country around Neufbourg in Normandy never exceeded 3·2 in the manorial fields there on the eve of the fifteenth century.[34] All these supporting indications lead us to realize that the alluvial fields of north-western France were exceptionally fertile and to think that most western farmers of about the year 1300 expected to harvest about three or four times as much as they sowed, and that they could hardly hope for more.

* * *

The accounts of the Winchester series do not reveal any marked long-term changes. In the first half of the thirteenth century average yields of wheat, barley and oats respectively range between 4·3-4·4 and 2·7; in the second half of the century they can be put at 3·6-3·5 and 2·2, and in the fifty years following at 3·9-3·7 and 2·6. A slight fall can be noticed after 1250, followed fifty years later by a recovery. These fluctuations are, it is true, very slight. But yields themselves were so low and the useful portion of the harvest so limited that an apparently unimportant variation could have very marked repercussions on the volume of foodstuffs available. In addition, the figures relate only to the well-cultivated manorial lands, and the period of fluctuation coincides with the abandonment of marginal fields, and the concentration of the demesne on soils of higher quality upon which all the lord's means of production could be deployed. According to appearances then, the fall in productivity should have been more marked on the smaller farms. Sagging yields after 1250 probably encouraged peasants, at least in certain regions, not to reduce the fallow too much and raised their doubts about the three-year cycle. It led them to abandon the assarts as soon as fertility began to be exhausted. It is tempting to ascribe this phenomenon to the first recoil from the farthest extensions of cultivation which began in the second half of the thirteenth century.[35] It is also probable that the fall, even though limited, stimulated the effort to improve the sequence of crops as the fourteenth century approached, and set in motion the improvements which, as the

[33] Sicard, 617   [34] Plaisse, 681, pp. 165 *et seq.*
[35] But also, according to M. Postan, to certain reclamations which had as their object the transference of cultivation to yet unexhausted lands.

movement of the curve shows, sufficed to raise yields almost to their previous level.[36]

However, the recovery itself was rather feeble. On the eve of the fourteenth century the return on seed sown remained much below that which has normally been obtained in European countries since the agricultural revolution of modern times. It has been calculated that for England it was five times less.[37] Selection of seed was imperfect, the harvest incomplete, the preparation of the soil insufficient: as a result of all these factors medieval fields yielded very little. It should nevertheless be noted that they were hardly less productive than those of the sixteenth century, nor even in certain countries than those at the beginning of the nineteenth century. In his *Théâtre d'Agriculture*, Olivier de Serre remarks that seed 'even on good soils, multiplies itself no more than five- or six-fold',[38] and in 1812 the *sous préfet* of Marseilles, in reply to an enquiry, stated that 'the average harvest over a ten-year period is from $4\frac{1}{2}$ to 5'.[39] The coincidence is striking: the yield at that time thought to be normal was not sensibly more than on the lands farmed by the Hospitallers in the same region five hundred years earlier. A most enlightening comparison, for it proves that medieval agriculture had at the end of the thirteenth century reached a technical level equivalent to that of the years which immediately preceded the agricultural revolution.

On the other hand when we compare average yields with those which we can estimate for Carolingian times, the superiority of the thirteenth century is clear, except perhaps for some very ill-favoured village lands. Crop yields do not in fact seem to have exceeded two to one in Frankish times.[40] But Walter of Henley in his treatise estimates that land which does not yield more than three times its seed, brings no return, 'unless', he adds, 'the price of corn is very high'.[41] This condition and the allusion to prices are very significant. They suggest that in the view of the agriculturist, a return of less than three times would no more than allow the farmers' family to keep alive (do not let us forget that peasants at that time were very near starvation level). On the other hand, in years when the return was above three to one, the harvest left an excess which could be sold to merchants. Walter's view is evidence that

[36] It is as well to note that if, in the accounts of the bishop of Winchester, the levels of yields per amount sown rose after 1300, those of yields per acre continued to sag. The improvement was the result of a thinner sowing and the adoption of less intensive cultivation. Less was asked of soils which were thought to be exhausted. It should be pointed out that seed had always been thinly sown. On all French and English manors teams of women weeded the crop every spring and pulled out unwanted plants from among the sprouting shoots. Duby, 445.

[37] The difference for wheat was as 1:6 between 1400 and modern times in the Norman district of Neufbourg; Plaisse, 681, p. 170.

[38] II.4, §8   [39] Archives des Bouches-du-Rhône, M.13
[40] See p. 25   [41] Ch. XIX; Bennett, 149, p. 86

for his times and in the countries he knew such conditions were usually fulfilled. This mention by an expert, as well as all the figures which English
manorial documents produce, lead us to suppose that a great change in productivity, the only one in history until the great advances in the eighteenth and
nineteenth centuries, occurred in the countryside of western Europe between
the Carolingian period and the dawn of the thirteenth century.

The chronology of this movement will always remain uncertain, since it
took place at the very moment when written records were so scarce. One
source, the Cluniac inventory from which I have already drawn material on
the question of the development of cultural cycles, provides some facts for
the middle of the twelfth century. But its isolation in the midst of a documentary desert takes away most of its value. However, let us place these few
figures side by side with those, equally scanty, which refer to the ninth century. In the year when the commissioners visited the demesnes of the abbey
of Cluny the harvest had not been good; they mention this accidental short-
fall in their account of revenue, and they note that the administrators estimated the deficit on the wheat harvest as one-fifth of a normal harvest. If the
quantity of grain stored in the barns is compared with that devoted to the
new sowing, the yield is shown to be mediocre and very uneven as between
one farm and another. In one of the demesnes – the best tended and equipped
– the harvest was valued at six times the seed; rye on the lands of another
'hall' yielded five to one and wheat four to one. Such returns approach those
of the thirteenth century. Conversely, on the four other farms at which the
inventory valued the harvest and seed, the yield remained that year between
two and two and a half to one. This level nearly corresponded to the one
revealed by the Carolingian documents.[42] It would be rash to draw general
conclusions from this unique source. It might, however, provide support for
those who consider that the rise in agricultural yields was in full swing in the
middle of the twelfth century, although still imperfect and confined to the
most carefully managed demesnes.

3. WORKING THE LAND

It cannot at any rate be denied that between the ninth and the thirteenth
century crop yields rose. If I were to be pressed very hard to give an estimate
of this growth, I should risk the following hypothesis: average yields, which
could be put at about 2·5 to one, increased under the least favourable conditions to around 4 to one. To put it in another way, the portion of the
harvest at the disposal of the producer doubled.

It does not appear, however, as if the practice of manuring had in the
meantime noticeably improved. We find long passages in agricultural treatises

[42] Duby, 442 and Document No. 114, p. 465

devoted to manuring and these show that the larger farmers recognized its advantages.[43] English landlords obliged their tenants to fold their sheep overnight on demesne land to fertilize it; they also sometimes claimed the privilege of holding cattle fairs on their fields. In addition corn was cut high on the stalk and the straw which was left uneaten by the cattle during the period of common grazing on the stubble was then ploughed back into the soil to enrich it. If Walter of Henley is to be believed, this was worth a good deal. However, methods of stockraising remained the same. In many regions the number of animals was small. Cattle lived in the open and were rarely stabled. The little manure that was collected was very thinly spread over the arable. In the neighbourhood of Paris, one of the regions where economic progress was most advanced, one lease of the thirteenth century required the farmer to manure the land 'once in nine years, in the fifth year'.[44] Normally the manure was reserved for the few enclosed fields, small in size and under constant cultivation, such as the Provençal *ferrages*, which were almost like gardens. It is possible that the progress of enclosure which was evident in the thirteenth century was a response to the wish of the larger farmers, who possessed more animals, to use the manure from their vaccaries and sheep runs on their own lands well away from others. In any case the special crops, and, in winegrowing countries like the Ile de France, the vineyards absorbed almost entirely the farmyard refuse. Cereal-growing did not appear to have gained anything from the growth of stockraising,[45] since the surplus manure was diverted to commercial vegetable production, which developed at the same time. Perhaps it was only the more extensive cultivation of leguminous crops in the thirteenth century that helped to restore the soil of the fields to greater abundance. This change in the cycle of cultivation could have been partly responsible for the slight rise which the curve of English yields showed after 1300. However, in the light of such scanty information as exists it is permissible to think that the rise in productivity after the Carolingian epoch was chiefly set in motion by greater effort on the land, simultaneously made more effective by improvements in ploughing implements.

In the first place the practice of harrowing became more widespread, and its effects were very beneficial. The Bayeux tapestry, which dates from about 1100, already shows a harrow in action; a century and a half later many documents testify to the general imposition of labour services 'to cover the winter sowings'.[46] Above all the number of ploughings increased. Owners of the great Carolingian demesnes demanded three ploughings each year from their men subject to labour services, two on the fallow before sowing wheat and rye, and another one on the winter corn stubble to prepare for the March

[43] Document No. 30, p. 390
[45] See p. 146 *et seq.*
[44] Fontette, 340; Bennett, 149, pp. 77 *et seq.*
[46] Document No. 125, p. 482

sowing. It seems as if this ancient sequence changed but only slowly. On ten demesnes of the Abbey of Cluny of which we have a description in the middle of the twelfth century, the ploughing services were organized as in the ninth century; on a single manor only was a third ploughing of the fallow required. Progress consequently remained very limited. But even so it appears to have been very profitable: on the demesne where the winter sowing was prepared by three ploughings, the result was a yield of six to one, that is two or three times greater than on the other farms.[47]

One hundred years later at Villeneuve St Georges and at Thiais, i.e. on the same lands as those described by Irminon's *polyptyque*, the peasants, like their forebears, were required for 'the first and second ploughing' and for 'the March ploughing' on the lord's land. However, at Villeneuve, double work was expected for the second fallow ploughing[48]: a further slight improvement. As far as can be seen, it was only in the second half of the thirteenth century that the practice of a fourth ploughing became widespread in the French countryside.[49]

Progress followed thereafter, perhaps at an increasing pace. On the model farms run by Thierry d'Hireçon in the first decades of the fourteenth century winter sowing was prepared by four successive ploughings of the fallow.[50] It must be noted that evidence of improvements of this kind appears at the same period when and perhaps in the same regions where a rearrangement of the sequence of cultivation was attempted in order to extract a greater output from the soil. More frequent ploughing in fact accelerated the restoration of the powers of the soil, and contributed actively to the renewal of its fertility. It is therefore not impossible for us to conclude that the improvement of agrarian methods which it constituted could by itself appreciably raise yields.[51] This is why all the evidence in written documents which allow it to be discerned, dated and followed up ought to be the object of a systematic review. It happens, of course, that the rhythm of work on the land is directly connected with the organization of labour services, and it is reasonable to hope that manorial documents, inventories, rentals and custumals

---

[47] Duby, 442   [48] Document No. 157, p. 514

[49] The same is true for Germany. G. Von Below, *Die Hauptsache der älteren Deutschen Agrargeschichte*, p. 71.

[50] Richard, 473. In the country around Toulouse the *métayage* leases of the fourteenth and fifteenth centuries required the tenant to plough six or seven times to prepare the seed bed, Sicard, 617; it was of course a question here of shallow ploughing with the primitive plough (*araire*), which needed repeated cross furrowing to break up the land efficiently.

[51] It will be noticed that on the manorial farms of Neufbourg in Normandy, where yields were very low at the beginning of the fifteenth century (3·2 for wheat, 3·4 for barley, 3·1 for oats, and 2·9 for rye), three plough 'seasons' was the custom. Plaisse, 681, p. 147.

will disgorge much more material relating to this point, even in periods when documents are rather scarce.

* * *

It was thus, above all else, human toil which finally drew from the land the extra output and, allowing for the defective state of our knowledge, this redoubled effort on the part of men appears definitely to have been the chief motive force in agricultural growth. But we still have to ask ourselves whether this was merely the result of a proliferation of workers, or whether such workers as there were had more efficient methods at their disposal. We know hardly anything about the actual numbers of labourers; but Carolingian documents lead us to believe that by the ninth century manpower was over-abundant. On the other hand it seems to have been badly provided with tools. This leads us to imagine that real progress came first of all through improvements in agricultural implements. It is the most attractive hypothesis, and we must combine the study of the increased number of ploughings with a similar study of tools.

Such a study is in fact very disappointing. The enquiry has not yet been taken very far and is subject to great difficulties. The thirteenth century has bequeathed us a great many pictures of peasant tools. Traditionally, they provided artists with symbolical representations of the calendar months either to be carved on porches of churches or painted in pious books.[52] But we can never be sure that these images were copied exactly from life and did not take the form of iconographic types fixed by the style of the particular workshop. As for the descriptions of tools to be found in the works of academic philologists like Jean de Garlande or Alexander Neckham, or in literary fantasies like the *Dit de l'outillement du vilain*, they tell us almost nothing. One major source remains, i.e. the mass of inventories, accounts and terms of farming leases, which is quite exceptionally abundant for the thirteenth century, and remains up to now largely unexplored.

The diffusion and progress of hydraulic machines are nearly alone in having been subjected to detailed enquiry. It has been established that grain mills operated by water power continued to spread throughout the period. They can be seen penetrating parts of the country until then poorly provided with them, such as Devon where the abbots of Tavistock made great efforts in the twelfth century to equip their demesnes with mills.[53] More than anywhere else they multiplied in towns where large milling businesses were concentrated on banks of rivers, often around bridges. Two mills existed by

---

[52] J. le Sénécal, 'Les occupations de mois dans l'iconographie du Moyen Age', in *Bulletin de la Société des Antiquaires de Normandie*, 1924
[53] Finberg, 187

a stream in one district of Rouen in the tenth century; five new ones were built in the same place during the twelfth century, ten more during the thirteenth, and fourteen in the fourteenth century. Eleven mills were established at Troyes between 1157 and 1191. At Toulouse, burgesses wishing at that time to make a good investment bought shares in the business of the great mills at Bazacle. And we must not forget wind mills, recorded at Arles for the first time in 1162-1180, the use of which also began to spread at the end of the twelfth century in Normandy, England and Flanders.[54] The old hand mills, hunted out and destroyed by manorial agents everywhere where the obligation to bring grain to the lord's mill was imposed, became tools of the poor or substitutes, like the ten handmills and the horse mill which operated in times of siege at the end of the thirteenth century in the city of Carcassonne.[55] It must also be mentioned that the action of paddles and cog wheels could equally be utilized to work other machines, to brew beer or press oil in the twelfth century, to move hammers and flails. The latter appeared for the first time, in texts listed up to the present, in the middle of the eleventh century in Dauphiné, where they were used to full cloth. A hundred years later they are to be met everywhere. Tilt-hammers and water forges spread with the same speed. The first ones we know about were working at Issoudun in 1116 and in Catalonia in 1138.[56] Their spread is evidence of metallurgical progress.

Progress is clear and it was decisive for the rural economy. From the end of the eleventh century documents contain a host of clues which would be well worth listing. They testify that iron then occupied a much more important position in the daily life of country people than it did in Carolingian times, and that its use was spreading fast. In market regulations and toll tariffs for instance, references to iron in bars and ingots, or objects in wrought metal, particularly agricultural implements, proliferated. Iron production was very dispersed, because the ore usable in the then state of metallurgical technique was to be found almost everywhere. But, since charcoal constituted the most essential basic material, forges were localized in the forest. Iron workers therefore lived in wooded areas, like the itinerant workers of the royal forests of England, or the 'smithy' which Louis VI owned in the forest of Othe and which he gave as a gift in 1131 to the Hospitallers.[57] The count of Champagne ran several 'forges to make iron' around Wassy and offered one as a gift to the abbey of Crète in 1156, to Clairveaux in 1157, to

[54] Gille, 111; Sicard, 685

[55] G. J. Mot, 'L'arsenal et le parc du matériel de la cité de Carcassonne', in *Annales du Midi*, 1956

[56] Gille, 110; Joris, 344; E. Carus-Wilson, 'An Industrial Revolution of the Thirteenth Century', in *Economic History Review*, XI, 1941

[57] Lennard, 268, pp. 13, 242; A. Luchaire, *Etudes sur les actes de Louis VII*, No. 479

Igny in 1158 and to Trois Fontaines in 1171.[58] These repeated offerings perhaps prove that production increased, and they at any rate show that the Cistercian monasteries, as great centres of rural activity, felt at that time the need of assuring the replenishment of their toolsheds with iron.

The manufacture of tools in fact was not itself established in the forest. It seems as if it was concentrated in the towns. The poor man whom Geoffrey Martel, count of Anjou, met one day in the wood where he made charcoal for the blacksmith, went to sell it at Loches, the nearest market town.[59] In the town of Metz the manufacture of ploughshares (*socherie*) was the most important craft in the twelfth century; several *sochiers* held their office from the bishop for an annual payment of twenty-eight ploughshares. The bishop kept twelve for use on his demesnes outside the town and sold the others.[60] But craftsmen working in iron were probably to be found at this period scattered in villages. According to Guibert de Nogent's account, about 1100 another charcoal burner (an important man, since he was the former knight of Puiset, who had given up the world as a penance) sold charcoal for the forge *per rura et oppida*.[61] Amongst these rural blacksmiths many former manorial servants were to be met with. Originally charged with shoeing the lord's horses and repairing harness, they put their anvils at the service of the peasantry; continuing to pay dues to the lord of the manor, they manufactured for payment field tools for a rural clientele. Against these village artisans the *sochiers* of Metz could no longer defend their monopoly in the thirteenth century. In the fourteenth century we find them at work everywhere: they often received the basic material from their customers, and often too they undertook to maintain the machinery of the large agricultural enterprises in return for an annual pension of cereals.[62] The growing activity of country forges is one of the most reliable indexes of the improvement of peasant tools. A searching enquiry into manorial accounts, toll charges, lawyers' registers and even the study of surnames (by tracing the occurrence and diffusion of significant family names like Schmidt, Smith or Lefèvre) which would establish more clearly the story of the medieval blacksmith would be of obvious interest.

It is harder to find any information about the tools themselves. Manorial inventories – most frequently dating from after 1300 – contain many iron

[58] Maas, 73   [59] *Historia Gaufredi Ducis* (ed. Halphen), p. 134
[60] Schneider, 351, p. 227
[61] Guibert de Nogent, *De vita Sua*, I, IX. Metallic articles occupied a considerable place in a list of toll dues drawn up at Poitiers in the second half of the twelfth century; it mentioned the sale of billhooks, saws, knives, scythes, nails and horseshoes, as well as ingots, hammers and anvils, which labourers from round about perhaps came to buy in the town. D. Claude, *Topographie und Verfassung der Städte Bourges und Poitiers bis in das 11. Jahrhundert*, Lübeck-Hamburg, 1960, p. 141.
[62] Duby, 445; Richard, 473

tools, incomparably more than on the great royal and monastic demesnes of the ninth century. The grange owned by Thierry d'Hireçon at Bonnières in Artois was in 1315 equipped with eight long and eight short pitchforks, five iron two-pronged forks, five iron-tipped shovels, four spades, a pickaxe, a billhook, a hatchet and two harrows.[63] But how useful were these tools? Were they better than those of the Carolingian peasantry? And what in particular do we know of the agricultural labourers' principal implement, the plough?

It was still almost entirely built of wood: a priory of Marmoutier received in 1180 the rights of usage in a wood for its tenants who went there to collect materials 'for their ploughs, their handles and their fences'.[64] But frequent references inform us that in the twelfth century its cutting edge was always reinforced with iron, even in backward countries like the Corsican Balagne.[65] On the other hand, we are utterly ignorant about the shape of the shares, either the ones forged at Metz for the bishop or others. There is no information on this essential point. Did peasants normally use ploughs which, like some illustrated in manuscripts, were fitted with a mouldboard?[66] Joinville's astonishment when the waters of the Nile fell and he saw Egyptian peasants 'each one ploughing his land with a plough without wheels', proves that the plough in Champagne in the thirteenth century normally had wheels. But this is a rare clue. It would hardly avail to examine the texts and especially the iconography of the period more closely in an attempt to discover others which would help to dissipate the mists which shroud the history of the wheelless and the wheeled plough, and to support the hypothesis of a progressive spread of the latter throughout the northern countries, for it is doubtful whether these sources can ever throw sufficient light on this point.

However, another improvement which was of great importance is easier to follow up. It was perhaps by this means alone that the use of the plough was extended beyond the easily worked soils to which Carolingian cultivation had been limited. This advance affected not only the shape of the instrument, but its power. It consisted of a threefold improvement in traction. It seems that in the course of the eleventh century better methods of harnessing were adopted, the shoulder collar for horses, the frontal yoke for oxen, as

[63] Richard, 473

[64] *Cartulaire des possessions de l'abbaye de Marmoutier dans le Dunois*, CXC; Archives des Bouches-du-Rhône, B.161, fol. 53 2⁰ (1341): some burgesses of Digne received the use of a wood, *causa edificandi, aratoria et alia quacumque*.

[65] Archives de la Corse, H.9. In some *métayage* agreements drawn up in the Toulouse region in the second half of the fourteenth century, the tenant is enjoined to 'keep the plough (*araire*) in good condition, well provided with wood and iron'; Sicard, 685. In 1338 the Hospitallers of Provence provided the blacksmiths they employed with iron and *fustes* (timber); Archives des Bouches-du-Rhône. H.(OM), 156.

[66] See plate I, facing p. 390

well as shoes for both animals. In the second place a little later in western Europe (which since the Carolingian era had held the lead in agricultural advance) we see the horse taking the place of the ox at the plough. When exactly did this happen? Probably not before the twelfth century. Knights who took an oath of peace at Verdun-sur-le-Doubs in 1016 promised not to commit an aggression against the *caballarium ad carrucam*,[67] although the word *carruca* in this text probably meant a vehicle. A royal gift at the end of the eleventh century in the Ile de France refers to land 'which six oxen can plough'. A hundred years later we can sense the transformation which was taking place although it was still incomplete. A document of the Orleans region speaks of plough animals 'either ox or horse or ass', and Jean Garlande, in his description of the wheeled plough, represents it as provided either with a yoke or a collar. On the other hand, in 1218, the arable furlongs of Palaiseau near to Paris were all ploughed by horses; the latter appear alone in 1277 in an enquiry conducted near there at Gonesse as well as in the drawings which at the same period decorated the *Veil Rentier* of the lords of Audenarde.[68] It is not too hazardous to guess that the change took place on the plains of France, in Picardy, Flanders and Lorraine, around 1200.

The change was advantageous, although probably less so on the fringes of the assarts, where extirpation of roots required bovine strength, than on the well-worked lands. The adoption of the draught horse was less suited to the extension of the agricultural area than to the intensification of cultivation. The change, contemporaneous with a slowing up of reclamation, thus appeared as one more sign of a general transformation of the rural economy in the course of the thirteenth century. In fact the horse was speedier, much speedier, than the ox, and its use accelerated considerably the work of the farm and made it possible to increase the number of ploughings and to drag the harrow, shown in the Bayeux tapestry being pulled by a horse in the eleventh century. Giving up the ox team in favour of the horse also meant the spread of oat growing, which in its turn was connected with a more regular practice of the three-year rotation. Countries where this took place witnessed an improvement in the preparation of the land and thus in its fertility, a reduction in the duration of the fallow, and a rise in return on seed sown. The whole process marked the advent of a much more productive agrarian system.[69]

However, in many regions peasants continued to harness oxen to the

[67] Ed. Bonnaud-Delamare, in *Bulletin philologique et historique*, 1955-1956, p. 151

[68] *Recueil des actes de Philippe Ier*, No. 121; Archives Nationales, 48 J, fol. 80ro; Archives Nationales, L.885, 114 et 115; S.196 B; *Veil Rentier* (ed. Verriest), Brussels, 1950

[69] 'In every case the ox disappeared because it was too slow to respond to the invasive cultivation of corn, most frequently required by demographic pressure,' G. Braudel, *La Méditerranée au temps de Philippe II*, p. 298.

plough. We could learn a lot if we could define the regions where this backward state prevailed, but a geographical study of this nature has never been made. We do know, however, that, perhaps because oats did not grow well there, the horse as a plough animal did not penetrate the Mediterranean lands. But large areas unwilling to accept it also existed in northern countries. In Burgundy ploughs with eight oxen were still working in the thirteenth century. In 1274 peasants compelled to do labour service in the Brie were required to harness horses and asses as well as oxen. All the valuations in Norman inquests at that period were made in terms of 'bovine animals'. As for English agricultural treatises, they all counselled against using horses, which cost too much because it was necessary to pay for shoes and oats.[70] The substitution of the horse for the ox in the thirteenth century was thus perhaps more restricted than has been thought. For this reason it would be interesting to plot more accurately the limits of this change and to establish its relationship with little-known aspects of the economy and technique of which it affords us a glimpse.

Lastly, there was yet another – the third – improvement in the manner of drawing the plough which made it more effective whether the team was composed of horses or oxen. It is true that we know little about the strength of the beasts themselves, although it is more than likely that this increased in many parts by selective breeding and as a result of more abundant fodder. But thanks to certain accounts and inventories we can at least count the animals, and measure the increase of the teams of draught animals on certain of the larger estates. In the two generations following the Domesday Book the number of plough animals increased by 20 to 30 per cent on nine manors of Ramsey Abbey.[71] In this context the attention which the manorial commissioners devoted to the farmyard animals is very significant. In the middle of the twelfth century when the abbot of Cluny caused an inventory to be made with the intention of raising output his agents took good care to make a note of the number of supplementary 'plough teams' with which it seemed to them desirable that this or that farm should be equipped by the acquisition of oxen.[72] In the eyes of these administrators an adequate number of well-equipped teams was the basic condition for economic progress. Why should we too not assume, as they did, that agricultural growth at the height of the Middle Ages was largely the result of the greater efficiency of the ploughing team, and that this was due perhaps less to improvement in the actual implements than to the increased strength of the animals which worked them?

Nevertheless, these improvements in equipment did not extend to all

---

[70] *Cartulaire de Saint-Etienne de Dijon*, 117; Archives Nationales S.11 583; *Delisle, Normandie*, p. 302; Document No. 27, p. 388
[71] Raftis, 201, p. 66; Darby, 47, p. 197　　　　[72] Duby, 442

agricultural enterprises. It is probable that their very uneven diffusion reflected economic differences, especially between regions. Detailed research
would most likely bring into relief an ever widening contrast between the
Ile de France, say, and the French Midi where emaciated oxen pulled coulter-
less ploughs as in earlier days, and where iron was still a great rarity. In the
villages of Haute Provence a scythe was worth a fortune in the fourteenth
century and the iron tools in the toolshed at the commandery of the Templars
of St Eulalie-du-Larzac looked very much the same as those of Carolingian
times. There were only cauldrons, pot-hooks, carpenter's axes, augers and
files to be seen, as in the workshop at Annapes in the ninth century.[73] It is also
probable that technical progress could not be introduced into the mass of
peasant households because they were too poor to improve their equipment.
In fact it was not enough to know about the plough with a mouldboard in
order to give up the wheelless plough. It was still necessary to be in a position
to acquire the share and above all the beasts capable of pulling it. The infiltration of technical improvements into humble farmsteads certainly proceeded
very slowly and for this reason as time passed differences between the farms
of the wealthy and their poorer neighbours appeared to become more profound than ever.[74]

[73] Archives des Bouches-du-Rhône, 396 E.18, fol. 109; Higounet-Nadal, 457
[74] The medievalist will be interested to know how slowly the plough was adopted
for general use in the course of the seventeenth century in Canada. We learn this from
very detailed references. The first pioneers dug with their spades for more than 20 years,
'until an inhabitant of the country sought a way to lighten the toil of men who usually
worked by hand to till the soil, which was turned over by plough share and oxen on
27th April, 1628' (*Œuvres de Champlain*, 6 vols, Quebec, 1870, I, ch. V). The use of the
plough was not general before the middle of the century. R. L. Seguin (*L'Equipment de
la ferme canadienne aux XVIIe et XVIIIe siècles*, Montreal, 1959, p. 21) gives three reasons
for this delay. The plough was made on the farm, but certain pieces, particularly the
mouldboard (*versoir*) (made of wood tipped with iron until the nineteenth century) had
to be constructed by specialized craftsmen. Secondly, the supply of draught animals was
insufficient. Lastly, it was hard to manoeuvre the plough between the calcined stumps of
the felled trees. In fact land was still being partially dug over *à la pioche* in 1672.

CHAPTER III

Agricultural Expansion
and the Structure of Society

The story of medieval economic expansion is punctuated with many gaps. Any study of Italian conditions is at present quite out of the question, in spite of a mass of what appears to be promising documentary evidence. Of the history of technique in western Europe as a whole there are no more than occasional glimpses. An immense task here awaits the research worker and in particular the archeologist, who must turn his attention to the relics of everyday life, homes, village lands, food supply, farm equipment and livestock. On the other hand, related changes which affected the means of production also modified the very structure of society and in turn reacted on economic conditions. It is much easier to find traces of these changes in manorial records, and this is the right place in which to summarize what is known of them.

I. THE CONDITION OF THE PEASANT

Agricultural progress stimulated certain changes in legal status. Expansion into the new lands hastened a lightening of manorial obligations and the areas of reclamation appeared usually as zones of liberty. To take an English example, in the thirteenth century free tenants made up half the peasantry of north Warwickshire, a country of assarts, but they only represented one-third in the southern part of the country; two out of five villages in the north escaped labour services, but only one in five enjoyed this advantage in the south. *Liberi tenantes* swarmed also on the lands of Ely Cathedral which adjoined the Fens in process of colonization. We know, too, that the fringes of the great forests of the twelfth century were invaded by small allods settled without the lord's leave and that the settlement charters created in the *villeneuves* a system of manorial rights and monopolies (*régime banale*) more flexible than elsewhere. In 1159, the settlers established on the polders of the Flemish abbey of Bourbourg enjoyed personal liberty and were directly dependent for public justice on the count; they possessed hereditary and alienable tenures, and they owed to the overlord no more than light payments of 'recognition'. The condition of the *Freibauern* whom the Salic kings had established in the Saxon and Thuringian forests was similar, as was that of all the rent-paying tenants freed from servitude who reclaimed the lands of the abbeys of St Dié and Remiremont in the Vosges, and the pioneers who settled the Bavarian plains and the Austrian and Styrian mountains.[1] Finally, to prevent their men from being tempted by colonizing landowners to move out to the new lands where they were promised better conditions, lords of the old villages were forced to relax their exactions.

But has not too much been made, perhaps, of the freedom which reclamation conferred? The immigrant often arrived on new lands empty handed, without worldly goods, even without anything to eat until his assart could yield its produce. He had first to be admitted, to be helped and to submit to the collective discipline without which the new land could not be brought into production. It is a striking fact that many settlers arriving from a distance and calling themselves free, were soon 'commending' themselves to the local lord, placing themselves under his protection and falling under his sway. In Auvergne the heaviest labour services were to be found in the districts of recent occupation, and there they lingered longest. Nowhere did the manorial system show itself more tenacious than in Combraille or the Jura where reclamation was very late.[2]

Indeed, if the weight of the lord's power did not make itself felt equally in the different regions where colonization took place, it was probably because this did not take place everywhere at the same time and in the same way. In the first phases of reclamation, in the eleventh and early twelfth centuries, free migration into the immense areas opened to cultivation by the somewhat more powerful plough teams of this time, probably caused a noticeable lightening of the lord's control by relieving demographic pressure. But what happened in the twelfth century? It is just possible that the kind of settlement characterized by the isolated farmstead favoured the personal independence of the peasant. Far from the lord's prying eye and hidden behind the leafy branches of his hedges, a tenant could more easily conceal the sheaves of which he knew he must render a share. On the other hand land became scarcer and scarcer. To receive the right to settle the peasant had now to pay a heavy entry fine, and sometimes even to surrender his own liberty and that of his descendants.[3] It seems indeed as if, at any rate in certain parts, the settlers

---

[1] Hilton, 161; Miller, 198; Boutruche, 184, p. 65; Mollat, 319; Documents Nos. 36, 40, 41, pp. 391, 396-397; Bosl, 489; Van den Linden, 328; Perrin, 200, pp. 662 *et seq.*; Dollinger, 159; Harley, 300. It must be admitted that the legal status granted to the pioneers in Flanders and Germania in the twelfth century proceeded from the primitive statute of the *Königsfreien* collected in the Frankish era in the *Centena*, Bosl, 516.

[2] Duby, 261, p. 13; Gaussin, 293; Fournier, in *Cahiers d'Histoire*, 1959

[3] Documents Nos. 147 and 148, pp. 506-507

of that period were unfortunates cruelly exploited by the owner of the waste land.

★   ★   ★

The condition of the peasant was also altered in other ways. The improvements in ploughing equipment and harness, as well as the different ways of tilling the soil which formed the basis of technical progress, raised the importance of ploughing compared to other agricultural labour. From the accounts of the Hospitallers of Provence we can see that in 1338 ploughing cost four times as much as all the rest of the work on the demesne.[4] This progress also raised the relative value of tools and equipment. In thirteenth-century Italy a pair of oxen was worth as much as all the land of a family holding. The rise of yields, the improvements in equipment and agrarian practice brought about a gradual shift in the values of farm capital in rural society. The value of land fell in relation to livestock. The effects of this shift can be observed in the terms of leases and merits further consideration.

The gap which had separated 'ploughmen' from men who worked with their hands widened after the year 1000 as is shown by the distribution of manorial dues. In the eleventh century the exactions of the territorial lord did not bear as heavily on the poor peasant without a team, who worked with a hoe and got his living from the homestead toft and temporary employment in the great households, as they did on those 'who perform their work with oxen or other beasts'.[5] The contrast between ploughman and manual worker became more pronounced in northern countries than in the Midi where the plough (*araire*) remained easy to handle, to pull, as well as to construct, and used very little iron.[6] The devaluation of manual services in relation to those performed with the help of animals, and hence the social decline of the 'cottars', 'bordars' and all manual workers, can be much more clearly seen in northern manors. In every country from England to Provence the *bouvier*, i.e. the driver of the team, had since the twelfth century become the true farm servant.[7] The 'plough', by which is meant the entire team composed of the implement itself, the oxen or horses capable of drawing it and the man who drove them, ended by representing the basic economic unit, the yardstick by which the landlord could estimate the value of his dependants and the services he could expect from them. It was by 'ploughs' that

---

[4] Duby, 445

[5] *Cartulaire de Saint-Vincent de Mâcon* (ed. Ragut), No. 476

[6] At Manosque, however, the lord required two ploughing services each year from those 'who worked with a plough, oxen, asses or other animals' and merely carrying services and days (*journées de main*) from their other dependants. *Livre des privilèges de Manosque* (ed. Isnard), p. 20.

[7] Postan, 414; Duby, 445

labour services were reckoned in the Cluniac inventory of the mid-twelfth century, as in others drawn up a little later for the English landlords.[8]

On the other hand, manual labourers without draught animals underwent no technical progress and sustained no rise in yields: on the contrary there was a relative fall in their living conditions. At the end of the thirteenth century they formed a large proportion of village society and thanks to some documentary evidence we can say exactly how large. Lords who levied dues wished to know the movable property of their subjects and from time to time ordered surveys of their livestock. Registers in which taxes levied on the inheritance of dependants were recorded have also been preserved. Recent researches which throw a vivid light on medieval peasant life, and which are based on the records of the bishop of Winchester, show that in certain villages on these estates 40 per cent of the villeins paid their 'heriot' in money, whereas normally they would have been obliged to deliver to the lord the best animal from their stable: in other words, they did not own any animals.[9]

That the increased value of farming equipment strengthened the hold of the wealthy over the peasantry cannot be denied. By loans and advances for the purchase of cattle, or by hiring out oxen, the power of urban capital penetrated the *contado* of Italian villages. Everywhere the lord maintained his authority over his men by helping them to acquire livestock or by threatening them with its confiscation. When in some provinces in the thirteenth century servitude was born anew and flourished,[10] it was the need to acquire agricultural equipment, efficient though costly, which led poorer peasants to bind themselves into dependence. The same needs held them in servitude, for although they had the right to decamp, to take another master, or to proclaim themselves free, they could do so only by abandoning their movable goods, in other words, by giving up their plough animals. In fact because of this, agricultural growth appears to have been a very powerful agent of social differentiation.

2. THE FAMILY FARM

Agricultural growth, by hastening the disintegration of the *manse*, broke up the ancient framework within which the daily life of the peasant family was contained. It is difficult to believe that what dissolved this fundamental unit was a change in the structure of the family or a dislocation of the kinship group. Households based on single married couples already occupied *manses* described by Carolingian inventories.[11] The fragmentation of the *manse*

---

[8] Duby, 442; Documents Nos. 113 and 114, pp. 464-467
[9] Postan-Titow, 539   [10] See pp. 248 *et seq.*
[11] See p. 32. Nevertheless if it is remembered that some tenants in Frankish times employed domestic slaves it is possible to imagine that the increasing shortage of servile

resulted in part from the combined effects of demographic pressure and changes in the methods of manorial taxation. But its principal cause was undoubtedly the higher productivity of human labour. To survive, a household had no longer any need of such extensive lands. The reduction in the size of the plot of land considered sufficient to support a family, and the average dimensions of a peasant farm generally, thus appeared as one of the criteria of agricultural progress. The chronology of this process is worth establishing.

In Lorraine where the study of this process has been most detailed, the *quartier* (this fraction of the ancient *manse* did not of course always correspond to an exact quarter of its size) already appears sporadically in the *polyptyques* at the end of the ninth century. However, the lords definitely adopted this type of holding as the new basis for rents in the twelfth century. The average area of land attached to each *quartier* then reached fifteen or sixteen dayworks (*journaux*), i.e. about 7 to 10 acres. In fact, the farm was nearly four times smaller than the *manse* of the early Middle Ages.[12] Since there is no proof of any decline whatever in the peasant group which lived on each of these family holdings we must accept that reduction in fallow periods together with a rise in agricultural yields had nearly quadrupled the productivity of the arable between the ninth and the twelfth centuries. Or else we must assume that the tenants, by assarting the fringes of the village clearings, had acquired control over free or rent-paying holdings, supplementary parcels of land which completed the *appendicia* of a *quartier*. Or again, and this is the most likely assumption, that the resources of a peasant family had been increased by reclamation and more intense cultivation simultaneously.

The breaking up of agricultural units in the early Middle Ages can be seen generally in all the regions which benefited from agrarian expansion. The course of this movement tended in its turn to disintegrate the Lotharingian *quartier*: in the country around Namur in the thirteenth century some of these new holdings supported several families each, who held them and farmed them jointly.[13] Here and there the *manse* put up a more or less tenacious resistance. It had entirely disappeared after the eleventh century in the Norman countryside. About 1150, in one village of southern Burgundy only three *manses* out of nineteen mentioned by documents still possessed 'appurtenances' which could be ploughed and formed really coherent farming units; all the others were completely fragmented and their memory was only preserved in place-names. In the thirteenth century all the ancient *manses* in the Parisian region and Flanders, as well as in Alsace and Swabia, had dis-

---

labour on peasant holdings may have hastened the disintegration of the *manse* after the year 1000; Perrin, 256.

[12] Perrin, 200, pp. 644 *et seq.*   [13] Genicot, 189, pp. 231 *et seq.*

integrated and been cut up and redistributed in small plots.[14] In other countries, however, the family farming units still firmly retained their cohesion. They had sometimes been protected by the managerial methods of the manor or by customs of inheritance, as in Bavaria where division of holdings originating in reclamation was forbidden, or in north-western Germany, where the institution of primogeniture in the peasant class made a precocious appearance.[15] But what is remarkable is that the most resilient *manses* which survived in the Middle Ages and whose outlines are revealed intact by modern aerial photography were usually situated either in the southern countries where the new organization was never adopted or else in the zones most recently won by reclamation, such as upper Beaujolais, Bresse, western France and the mountains of the Massif Central.[16] In these latter areas, of course, the farming units took shape at a period when the consequences of technical progress had already made themselves felt and on the poorest of soils where productivity was unlikely to rise any further. Considerations of this nature strengthen the impression that the disintegration of the *manse* between the year 1000 and the thirteenth century was largely determined by improvements in agricultural technique.

Progress of this kind and the demographic changes which were so closely connected with it worked themselves out inside the village community itself. The most productive village lands could support more people and accommodate both immigrants and the new hearths set up by local children living in their birthplace. In this way the group of newcomers and settlers grew up outside the close and traditional circle of heads of the older households who thought of themselves as the only rightful custodians of communal rights on the common lands.[17] Their cabins, *bordes*, and cottages, which had already appeared here and there in Carolingian inventories, multiplied in the eleventh and twelfth centuries as they were erected one after another outside the old enclosures. Then towards the middle of the thirteenth century isolated farms appeared on the edge of the cultivated land, and thereby broke up the solidarity of the village. The people who lived in them were only seen at mass; they closed their land to collective grazing and thus limited the areas where

[14] Duby, 261, p. 373; Bloch, 3, p. 166; Duby, 443; Dubled, 236; Fourquin, 551

[15] Dollinger, 159; Wittich, 210. In Westphalia the most ancient reference to primogeniture appears in the *Hofrecht* of the abbey of Abdinghof which dates from 1152. Rothert, *Westfälische Geschichte, I, Das Mittelalter*, 1949, p. 266. It is to be noted that in England the hide had given place in the twelfth century to smaller agricultural units: the virgate, which was a quarter, and the bovate, which was an eighth; but one or the other always served as a basis for peasant dues on the manor, which kept them stable and prevented the fragmentation of holdings beyond this level. Nevertheless the family possessions of tenants did not exactly fit into the structure of manorial rents and services. See document No. 124, p. 479.

[16] Higounet, 60; Fournier, in *Cahiers d'histoire*, 1959   [17] Bader, 512, p. 51

the communal flocks could roam freely. This latter form of existence profoundly modified customary ways of life. By provoking a defensive reaction on the part of the village community, they called into separate existence zones where the interests of the individual were paramount over those subject to collective control.[18]

3. DEMOGRAPHIC GROWTH

The improvement in agrarian technique increased to a very considerable extent the output of foodstuffs. It removed the obstacles which held population in check in the same way as the extension of arable. It opened the gates wide to a process which in its turn gave a further impetus to reclamation and farming methods. Nobody denies that the population of western Europe grew, but historians lack the means to measure this growth with any precision.

There is plentiful evidence pointing to a sharp growth of population during the eleventh and twelfth centuries – although factual details are vague and figures are altogether lacking.[19] These appear in the thirteenth century, and they multiplied after 1250 when tax collection emerged from its rudimentary state. Princes and lords were anxious to know exactly who owed them taxes, and specifically how many *feux*, hearths or households there were, which from then onwards became everywhere the basis of taxation. The information found in these fiscal documents is supplemented by manorial records of various kinds, rent rolls, surveys and registers of the courts of justice, which reveal from time to time movements of land and those occupying it, and sometimes enable us to analyze the structure of the family. It is true that these sources are too imperfect for us ever to hope to follow satisfactorily the demographic trends of this period. Nevertheless they deserve close scrutiny, and in some cases scholars have begun to use them. The history of population has recently made great progress.

Most of the definite facts which have been suitably analyzed are both local and late. But they clearly indicate the vigour of the movement. I shall take Provence as an example, where the number of hearths doubled between the middle of the thirteenth and the beginning of the fourteenth century.[20] If we accept that the census of hearths was not merely a fiscal device and that the composition of the household did not undergo significant change, this suggests that within 50 years human beings in this province became twice as numerous although many were very poor. In nine villages in the *viguerie* of Nice, 440 hearths were counted in 1263 and 722 in 1315. The rise affected different villages very unevenly; while one with 25 hearths remained stationary, another increased in two generations from 66 to 157 and a third from 30 to 103.[21]

It is not possible to measure so precisely demographic growth over wider areas, and historians' estimates vary considerably. Recently W. C. Robinson has stated that the average annual rate of growth at that time could have been no more than 0·2 per cent for the whole of Europe, while W. Abel estimates it as 0·39 per cent for France and 0·48 per cent for Germany.[22] The truth is that the kingdom of England appears to be the only country where demographic estimates can be supported upon a solid documentary foundation, thanks to the exceptionally abundant material such as the Domesday Book and the Poll Tax registers of 1377. The most authoritative estimates would have us believe that the population of the kingdom rose from 1,100,000 inhabitants in 1086 to 3,700,000 in 1346. According to J. C. Russell the average rate of annual increase should be placed around 0·46 per cent.[23] However, if we examine the facts more closely it appears again that growth was very different in the various regions. Expansion followed dissimilar trends from one village to another. Some, such as the hamlets situated on the edge of the Holland fens of Lincolnshire, were caught up in an active forward movement. It has been estimated that the number of men there increased six times in some places and twenty-four times in others during the 200 years which followed the drawing up of the Domesday Book.[24]

Such local variations therefore invite prudence. They particularly forbid the application of rates of growth calculated for England to the whole of Europe, because this county was still backward at the time of the Norman Conquest and relatively empty compared to certain French provinces. It is far from impossible, for instance, that certain villages in the region of Paris supported almost as many men in the ninth century as they did in the fourteenth. On the other hand in one Burgundian village territory, one out of every five of the 400 inhabitants enumerated in 1248 was a settler who had come to win from the wastes the fields which supported him.[25] Consequently, to assume that the population had trebled uniformly in all parts of the country in the twelfth and thirteenth centuries would be as fallacious as to attribute the heavy density of population of Villeneuve St Georges and Palaiseau revealed in the *polyptyque* of Irminon to the whole of Carolingian Gaul. We should do better to explore in detail the limited areas where accurate observation is possible.

★   ★   ★

[21] Baratier, 92, p. 180
[22] Robinson, 97; Abel, 'Wachstumsschwankungen mitteleuropäischer Völker seit dem Mittelalter', in *Jahrbücher für Nationalökonomie und Statistik*, 1935
[23] Russell, 98, p. 246   [24] Hallam, 299
[25] Martin-Lorber, 534; Fourquin, 549

Latent demographic pressure, which had only been held in check by the deficiencies of agricultural technique in the early Middle Ages, appears to have populated the empty or sparsely inhabited places as soon as it was released by improvements in equipment and the rise in productivity. In this way, it is estimated that from 20,000 to 30,000 new inhabitants spread into the forests of Brie between 1100 and 1250. From all our evidence the rate of population growth in the areas of great reclamation was much higher. In the villages of south Warwickshire, already heavily colonized in Saxon times, population increased only slightly between 1086 and 1279, and in seven parishes it had even declined. On the other hand in the northern part of the county it doubled or trebled.[26] To begin with, therefore, the agrarian conquest encouraged large movements of rural population.

The study of these migrations in those far off times is less difficult than some. Amongst the men of the twelfth century whose names appear in manorial documents, many bore surnames which connected them with their birthplace. In this way we can recognize many peasants who emigrated and populated the outlying parts (*faubourgs*) of the growing townships of the neighbourhood. But many others also left the lands of their forefathers for pioneering ventures and assarts. Such was the case of the man who, in the eleventh century, settled in a village on the banks of the Saône and married a girl who was also not a native of the place, but had moved there without her family, from a village about 9 miles away. Rural population at this period is shown to be far more mobile than it is usually supposed to be. In 1181 in one canton of Lombardy 12 per cent of those who farmed, some of them very humble people, did not live in the village of their forebears. At this period we can also trace substantial migrations of Flemings and Dutch towards northern and eastern Germany, and of people from La Vendée and Brittany into the country of Entre-Deux-Mers between the Garonne and the Dordogne.[27]

Nevertheless, these movements from the overpopulated areas into the empty lands, and the outflow from the ancient villages towards the *villeneuves* did nothing to equate regional densities. There were still sharp contrasts between the various counties of fourteenth-century England: the well populated parts of East Anglia and Leicestershire against the wilderness of Devon. In 1328 Hurepoix was almost unpopulated whilst the neighbouring plain of France with 19 'hearths' per square kilometre can be described as the most densely occupied countryside of Europe. Thus it can be seen that the rich, anciently settled lands, nurseries for courageous pioneers, not only supplied

---

[26] Brunet' 43; Hilton, 161
[27] *Recueil des chartes de l'abbaye de Cluny*, V, No. 3649; Cipolla, 518; Boutruche, 93; Epperlein, 526; Documents Nos. 36 and 38, pp. 391, 394

the colonizers of the wasteland, but also underwent an internal growth so powerful that it widened the old clearings, and stimulated technical progress and the rise in yields which fostered it. The region of Paris, already teeming with men in the ninth century, supported twice as many five hundred years later.[28]

*　　*　　*

Finally, we must consider whether demographic trends were alike for all social groups. The study of these differences, in the rare instances when sources are available, is fascinating. English historians have proved that variations in mortality were more marked amongst the depressed classes of cottars, those all-but landless people who lived by hiring themselves out on the manorial demesnes.[29] Were not these families whose chief livelihood came from wages tempted to increase their real capital by rearing more children? Were marriage rates throughout the hierarchy of wealth the same? The study of the economy of the medieval countryside calls for detailed research into the structure of rural families of a kind which is by no means impossible.

Lastly, it must be pointed out that population movements could be either slowed down or accelerated by legal conditions, and, especially, by different systems of inheritance. Very dissimilar population trends have recently been discovered at the end of the thirteenth century in two dependent villages of the Benedictine priory of Spalding, both situated on the edge of the Fens and on soils of the same quality. In one village, there were many young married couples; in the other, delayed marriages, few children and a tendency to settle elsewhere. The former village was inhabited by sokemen, free peasants who could divide their property and inheritance without restraint, and furthermore each share of the free inheritance, no matter how small, carried with it pasture rights on the neighbouring fenland. Because of this a family could exist without arable merely by owning a few score sheep, and all the children were able to have families and set themselves up in the same village. This was the source of a dynamic change within the village itself. On the other hand the people living in the other village were *operarii*, of servile status, whose lord forbade them to divide their patrimony. This ban enforced prolonged celibacy, restriction of births or else emigration.[30]

4. OVERPOPULATION

Though stimulated by the continued growth of population, agricultural progress appears to have been powerless in the last resort to free the peasants from food shortages, as the record of famines shows.

[28] Fourquin, 574　　　　[29] Postan-Titow, 539　　　　[30] Hallam, 298

In the eleventh and twelfth centuries irregular harvests resulted here and there in scarcities, and hordes of famished people in search of food periodically besieged the gates of monasteries. In these religious establishments the giving of alms was an institution that fulfilled a regular economic function. The monks of Cluny every year at the beginning of Lent distributed 250 salt pork carcases amongst 16,000 people; the monks of St Benoît sur Loire fed in good years and bad anything from 500 to 700 beggars.[31] There were some amongst the lower ranks of society who owned nothing at all, and such people suffered severely from harvest failures, falls in yields during wet seasons, or excessively hot summers, when food which had become unfit for human consumption brought on fatal epidemics of dysentery. It seems, nevertheless, as if the widespread famines, which were still terrible in the first thirty years of the eleventh century, became thereafter more widely spaced out, less intense and, at last, disappeared altogether. The last threat in old Germania was averted in 1217-1218 by importing grain from the new lands of the east. No further general shortage was felt in Germany and the Low Countries between 1215 and 1315, and only a few periods of scarcity hit relatively backward provinces such as Austria.[32]

Nevertheless, catastrophic shortages of wheat again appear to have struck the English and French countrysides in the middle of the thirteenth century. It is true that our knowledge of famines remains somewhat doubtful, for what value can we put on the accounts of the chroniclers, who were by nature given to romance and to magnifying dramatic events, the echoes of which had already reached them in a distorted form? It seems, however, as if demographic pressure, relieved after the first 1,000 years A.D. by the opening up of new arable, once again became acute after 1250 as soon as reclamation ceased. The sustained rise in the price of cereals from the time when sources allow us to observe it (that is, in England after about 1160) furnishes proof of the growing pressure of demand[33]; further evidence of it can be seen in the stagnation and even gentle decline of wages. In any case the overpopulation of the countryside is obvious in the second half of the thirteenth century (although this may perhaps be due to the sudden abundance of documentary material).

The clearest signs of it can be found in manorial documents describing peasant land. Repeated division amongst heirs had by then multiplied small farming units. 'In the assart of Jeannenque there are shares, a sixth of which was given to the men of Lactote; five parts were made of the other five shares, and one of these parts was divided into three, and in one of these three

[31] Duby, 441; *Recueil des Chartes de Saint-Benoît-sur-Loire* (ed. Prou), I, Nos. 149-150
[32] Curschmann, 606
[33] Documents Nos. 62 and 63, p. 417

parts they had one half and Bertrand Carbonel the other. . . .'[34] The fate of this parcel of land in the neighbourhood of Arles is by no means unique. At the time of Domesday there were 68 tenants living in one Norfolk village; in 1291 there were 107 sharing 935 holdings which were in turn broken up into 2,021 plots of land. One such piece measuring about 6 acres was shared by 10 tenants. In another East Anglian village a strip of land was divided between 1222 and 1277 into 20 fragments. At Rozoy in the Ile de France an inheritance comprising 160 *arpents* was carved up into 78 plots.[35] Fragmentation on such a scale gives an indication of the proliferation of families which utterly broke through the administrative organization of the manor. Documents of the second half of the thirteenth century also show the rapid accumulation of population on farmholdings. 89 rent-paying tenants were counted in one Lombard village in 1248; 100 only twenty years later. At Weedon Beck in eastern England the number of tenant families increased from 81 to 110 between 1248 and 1300 without any extension of the village lands through reclamation.[36]

Changes in mortality rates are the final and the most telling witnesses in the indictment of the excessive population which oppressed certain western countries at the end of the thirteenth century. In effect, the only important study of this kind concerns England between the years 1240 and 1350, and rests on the extraordinary series of accounts preserved in the records of the bishopric of Winchester.[37]

It emphasizes how precarious was the existence of the peasant population, which in some districts appears by 1300 to have exceeded that of the eighteenth century by 20 per cent. In 1245 the expectation of life for a man over 20 years of age was 24. For the entire period the death rate can be estimated at 40 per 1,000. Since the evidence only takes into account adults and since we know nothing of infant mortality, the rate for the whole population might have been somewhere around 70 per 1,000, that is to say far higher than for any population, even the most backward, which is covered by modern statistics. Furthermore this rate rose after 1290. It became 52 per 1000 for adults between 1297 and 1347 and the expectation of life therefore fell to 20 years. Fluctuations in the curve of mortalities were very frequent and expressed the sensitivity to epidemics of such a physically debilitated population; the fluctuations appeared also to be closely correlated with the curve of harvests, and an approximate analysis by social class shows that the richer peasants were less likely to die than their poorer neighbours. These statistics,

---

[34] Archives communales d'Arles, authentique du chapitre, fol. 116 (1182)
[35] Bennett, 149, p. 47; D. C. Douglas, *The Social Structure of Medieval East Anglia*, Oxford, 1927; Fourquin, 551; Morgan, 408
[36] Romeo, 481; Morgan, 408   [37] Postan-Titow, 539

imprecise as they are, provide the most striking proof of how utterly insufficient agricultural improvements were. In spite of the various changes in agriculture in the last years of the century, technical progress never succeeded in meeting the needs of a teeming population which lay at the mercy of a shortage of food as cruel perhaps as it had ever been in Carolingian times.

CHAPTER IV

The Growth of Exchange and its Effects

Agricultural expansion was accompanied throughout its whole course by another long-term movement, the gradual awakening of economic life and the slow growth of commercial activity which penetrated little by little into the world of the countryside, and in doing so contributed to its prosperity and helped the rural classes to support an excessive population. In fact cultivators of the land were required to produce, apart from their own food supply, enough to provide the ever more pressing demands of purchasers. For, since the dark age which followed the Carolingian era, the level of material existence in the west had continued to rise. The small group of wealthy men who depended in the ninth century on peasant labour for their food and the raw materials from which the ornaments of their life of display were fashioned, became ever more demanding and numerous. The pressure of demand breathed life into the processes of exchange, although not all the latter resulted in what could properly be described as commercial transactions.

Throughout the Middle Ages the growth of economic activity followed two parallel but overlapping paths. In the manorial setting the currents bearing the products of woodland and field direct to the country halls and town residences of the aristocracy grew larger and swifter: at the same time a network of exchange founded on buying and selling and the use of money spread and ramified.

I. DEMAND

This more active traffic was chiefly in response to increasing luxury consumption. Two major embellishments made up the amenities of high life at that time: high quality wine and cloth of fine wool, dyed in brilliant colours. In knightly circles the fashion for wine drinking had spread to the frozen and misty frontiers of Christianity. As for the taste for precious stuffs, it dominated the economic outlook of the noblity to such an extent that thirteenth-century princes, in order to prevent their vassals from ruining themselves, were forced to limit by statute the number and quality of garments which the different ranks of society were each year permitted to purchase. Such sumptuary laws are remarkable but much more so was the way the wearing of such adornments penetrated into the lower ranks of society and little by little took its place among the habits of village squires, town patricians, and even peasants. About 1333 in one village lost in the mountains of upper Provence, when a country bumpkin married off his daughter custom required him to clothe her in a robe of cloth from Ypres or Champagne, and if he were genuinely too poor and unable to find a moneylender willing to make an advance against the security of his sheep, the husband-to-be would have to go to the neighbouring market town to buy the stuff.[1] Anything which the systematic examination of notarial registers, merchants' account books, descriptive literature, or the archeology of everyday life could tell us about the diffusion of luxuries would immeasurably enrich our knowledge of rural economy since the twelfth century. For the raw materials of these beverages and garments came exclusively from the countryside, and they encouraged the development of other products side by side with the cultivation of cereals. The pyramid of medieval society whose apex was an all-powerful and spend-thrift aristocracy mainly animated by the desire to show off, concentrated in the lords' hands the new income generated by agricultural expansion. It channelled the money towards the purchase of items of luxury. The fact that the traffic in consumption goods was the first to increase at all extensively can thus be explained. This is also the reason why when capital formed by the progress of cultivation returned to be invested in the countryside it was not cereal production which benefited to begin with, but consumption goods for the nobility, such as wine, meat and the materials for fine craftsmanship.

However, agricultural activity more narrowly defined was also stimu-lated by an increased demand for foodstuffs, since the numbers of men who were not producing supplies for their own households with their own labour continued to grow. While numerical details which would allow us to esti-mate the growth of this group of consumers is altogether lacking, we can guess at its composition. It was primarily made up of all those specialists and craftsmen whom the general rise in the standard of life and the increase in the division of labour was constantly throwing up. Some lived in the castles and homes of the aristocracy, like the workmen who made the actual luxuries, or the companies of professional soldiers which multiplied through-out the whole of Europe during the twelfth century.[2]

But the greatest demand for food and supplies came from the towns. The growth was earlier in some places, more active in others: the first signs of urban development can be seen in the last years of the tenth century at Marseilles and Toulouse, and only sixty years later in the Mâconnais; early

---

[1] Archives des Bouches-du-Rhône, 396, E.17

[2] Garrisons and armies in the field had to be victualled. In 1203, 2,210 smoked pork carcases were sent from England to Rouen for the king's army. A. L. Poole, *From Domesday Book to Magna Carta*, Oxford, 1945.

and very intense in Italy, the urban movement did not affect England and central Germany until the thirteenth century and even then not very actively. Historians of rural economy are waiting for their colleagues who study urban phenomena to establish the chronology and rhythm of the renewal of activity experienced by towns in the various regions. For without examining the location, size and function of towns, we can neither know nor understand the mechanics of production nor the traffic in commodities in the surrounding countrysides from the eleventh century onwards.

*　　*　　*

One of the most important effects of urban expansion was to absorb part of the rural overpopulation and to relieve demographic pressure in the surrounding villages. We now know that towns and *bourgades* grew mostly through immigration from the local peasantry.[3] We know also that urban places exercised an attraction for country folk. For this reason many new 'burgesses' remained half farmers and continued to cultivate their family lands and to get from it their food supply and that of their neighbours. Peasant activity always remained considerable in the economy of medieval towns, which were, especially when they remained small, in fact no more than growths deeply embedded in the life of the countryside which gave them birth. Because of this symbiosis every town produced itself a large part of its own food supply.

Nevertheless there were at least some men who had to buy what they needed to feed themselves. This was primarily the case with travellers. Every town was the centre of a network of constantly increasing road traffic. Documentary evidence shows the appearance everywhere in France in the eleventh and early twelfth century of hospices and inns to cater for travellers. They show also that some of the permanent inhabitants of the town gradually gave up working on the land to devote themselves to more profitable specialized 'crafts'. Many documents of urban manors relate to the problems of landlords who were obliged by the defection of their tenants to take over the management of plots of land in the outskirts of the town originally cultivated but subsequently abandoned.[4] Finally some built-up areas became too populated to draw all their supplies from the *suburbium*. A town of 3,000 souls – and many surpassed this size in the thirteenth century – consumed each year at least a thousand tons of grain: to produce such a quantity of food it was necessary in the existing state of agricultural technique and yields to sow about 4,500 acres, and consequently, in order to allow for the land to have the necessary resting period, to dispose of an arable area at least twice as big. The purveying zone had thus to extend far beyond the walls. *Trecento*

[3] Plesner, 538; Duby, 261, p. 340　　　　[4] Document No. 85, p. 438

Florence could not live off its neighbouring lands for more than five months in the year. It depended for the rest of its supplies on goods brought sometimes from a long way off.

These reasons explain why we see merchants who dealt in foodstuffs living in eleventh-century towns and prospering too. I have found, for instance, former servants of the bishop at Mâcon who set up a bakehouse by the bridge and sold bread to travellers. They quickly made their fortune.[5] Butchers had the same success everywhere, and they often formed the first and most powerful of the professional town associations. There were a dozen of them in the thirteenth century at Montbrison, a small market town in Forez which had no more than 2,000 inhabitants, and they got rich by selling meat, as well as salt, leather, wool and cattle on the hoof.[6]

Nevertheless, even when supplies came from afar, the provisioning of centres of consumption was to a large extent not true commercial activity, for it was effected by the operation of manorial institutions. In fact every town was the centre of one or more great manors. And to these 'houses' was drawn the surplus from a great number of farms both large and small, which filled the tithe barns of bishops and chapters and the cellars of the nobles. Whether as their servants or as customers, a large proportion of town dwellers were fed by manorial households, and the latter also supported many paupers. Rural demesnes and renders of rents in kind supplied hospices with their provender. Those specializing in trade or handicrafts quickly learnt to use the manorial organization to supply their booths and workshops, and to avoid dealing with country producers or having to haggle with them over the price of goods. They took over the 'farming' of demesne revenues; they took the place of the landlords in exploiting vineyards and in collecting tithes; they sought to bind peasants and lesser nobles by means of credit and wove a web of contracts, engagements and rents around the neighbouring countryside in which the masters owed them sometimes a portion of the harvest and at other times half of a flock. Finally they bought land or became lords themselves of possessions alienated by debt-ridden nobles or of new farms created by the regrouping of land.[7]

However, increasing activity stimulated by the growth of demand inaugurated a widening and loosening of economic conditions. Money was convenient and necessary, its use spread and the share of trade extended. Manorial documents reveal the increasing intervention of commerce even in the heart of the manorial complex. I mentioned earlier the convoys which in the early Middle Ages brought to the abbey of St Bertin the produce of the vineyards it owned near Cologne. A monk used to fetch them, but by the

[5] *Cartulaire de Saint-Vincent de Mâcon* (ed. Ragut), No. 13
[6] Perroy, 348   [7] See p. 83

end of the twelfth century he no longer brought back casks but money obtained on the spot by the sale of the *vendange* instead.[8] In one year about 1100 the monk who directed a Cluniac deanery in the Dombes sold horses and corn for nearly 2,000 livres. As for the abbey of Cluny which itself supported several hundred people, it had ceased at that period to expect all its provisions to come from its manors. It spent an enormous sum, more than 1,000 livres, every year to buy grain, and by this means 240,000 pieces of money were put into the hands of the rural producers of the district.[9] Thus, continued recourse to buying and selling encouraged the development of regular commercial methods and the growth of the machinery necessary for exchange.

2. THE MECHANISM OF TRADE: MONEY AND MARKETS

Will it ever be possible to follow very closely the story of money in rural life? A number of things prove that the use of currency was becoming less and less unusual. We can guess that mints increased from the early Middle Ages onwards in all countries where they were needed. The Saxon and Salic emperors created many beyond the Rhine where none existed before.[10] It seems, also, as if issues of coinage became more frequent and perhaps more abundant without, however, completely fulfilling new requirements. One recent enquiry into southern European charters has shown that, when it was a matter of prices or payment, references to equivalents in cattle or goods became more and more common until 1075, and then became rarer and rarer until they disappeared around 1140.[11] This is a sign that exchange developed more quickly than the circulation of cash and that a more frequent striking of coins appeared later to reduce the shortage of the means of payment.

More obvious is the diffusion in the rural world of the notion of exchange value, of the different and variable worth of the various coins in circulation. We know now that the custom spread in most French provinces between 1050 and 1100 of distinguishing in written instruments between the coinage struck by the different mints, of specifying the kind of coins required for each transaction, and of speaking of a current coinage.[12] At the same period the part played by cash in life pensions, in prebendary payments, and in wages grew. From 1080 the infirmary servants at Cluny, completely kept by their masters, received in addition a small wage of 40 *deniers* every year. On one of the abbey's demesnes 360 *deniers* was distributed in 1155 to the vineyard workers.[13] All this evidence points to the same thing. But it is desirable that by means of a detailed examination of the sources and active numismatic research we should establish for each region of western Europe the timetable

[8] Dion, 105, p. 419   [9] Duby, 441   [10] Suhle, 145   [11] Herlihy, 341
[12] Duby, 261, p. 357; *Les origines des villes polonaises*, Paris, 1961, p. 230
[13] Duby, 441

of a movement which obviously did not follow the same course everywhere. It should be noticed that an awareness of the instability of monetary values was manifest earlier in Aquitaine than in the valley of the Saône even though the latter was traversed by one of the chief axes of road traffic. We can also see that cash was relatively abundant from the early eleventh century in Normandy and in the English countryside,[14] even though these areas lacked towns, which admittedly prevents us from associating the growth of urban habits too closely with the use of money. In 1115 a landlord of Mâconnais could extort 500 *deniers* from one peasant and 1,200 from another[15]; but 200 years later money was still very rare amongst the mountain folk of upper Provence whose cattle continued to provide their sole movable riches. To depict the geographical distribution of monetary practice is a delicate task for which the economic history of the medieval countryside nevertheless still cries out.

The setting up of new tolls and the income they brought in are other symptoms of the way country folk reacted to increased economic activity. The principal phase took place in France in the second half of the eleventh century: the profit of the local tolls of St Lô was forty times higher in 1093 than it was in 1039; towards 1075 the lords of Mâconnais began to levy taxes from traders crossing their districts, while in the west the first toll tariffs were drawn up.[16] A second wave occurred in the middle of the thirteenth century, at least in the French Midi. Protests were then made against the exactions on travel instituted by the lords of upper Provence on the country roads leading towards Aix and Marseilles; at the same period a small landowner on the Garonne thought of throwing a barrier across the river and taxing wine ships.[17] However, these fiscal innovations were mainly the concern of those specializing in long-distance traffic and affected peasants only indirectly. The multiplication of weekly markets and fairs in small towns and villages present a much more immediate reflection of the activities of these people.

This phenomenon can be seen all over western Europe, with the exception of Italy. There the network of country markets was in fact set up much earlier in the tenth century; but in the eleventh century the early growth of urban economy drew the main traffic in agricultural commodities into the towns and quickly allowed the village markets to atrophy.[18] On the other hand, we can follow their proliferation in Germania, at first through the royal records in western provinces in the eleventh century, and then through the foundation deeds of the villages in the new lands of the east in the twelfth

[14] Musset, 347   [15] Duby, 261, p. 359
[16] Musset, 347; Duby, 261, p. 335; Document No. 56, p. 409
[17] Sclafert, 83, p. 69; Higounet, 343
[18] Skaskin, 649; Luzzatto, 22, p. 127

century. In France, the richest set of documents relating to this topic are the charters of enfranchisement granted after 1100 to the small townships, the principal clauses of which always concern the trading activities that the inhabitants wished to exercise without restraint. A weekly market was set up or regularized; the commercial monopolies of the lord, his privilege of selling wine at certain times of the year, and his right to buy on credit in the village were restricted; the inhabitants demanded for themselves custody of the weights and measures for wine or cereals; sometimes a cattle market was set up.[19]

All these stipulations show a growing interest on the part of rural society in trade in the products of the soil, and a detailed list of them would be very illuminating. We can guess that these preoccupations were already making themselves felt towards the end of the eleventh century, but the culminating phase of this reversal in attitude for the whole of western Europe must be placed at the eve of the thirteenth century. At that moment a close constellation of small seasonal fairs grew up in the interior of Provence. In south-west France at the same time were founded all the *bastides* whose principal function was to shelter not only garrisons but country markets. At the same moment also England was criss-crossed with a dense network of markets in towns and villages which played an extremely important role in this country where there were no fully developed towns. Thirty-three active markets could be counted in Leicestershire alone, i.e. one for every 25 square miles; 27 (one for every 45 square miles) in Gloucestershire; and 80 in Devon.[20]

In the localities where periodic trading sessions were located a few specialists would set up house and serve as intermediaries between the long-distance businessmen with a distant clientele and the local producers. They were often described as *mercatores*, like the two bakers and two butchers 'who used to buy and sell everything necessary for food' and for whom, about 1100, a charter of settlement in the region of Blois was the preliminary to their establishment in the future *villeneuve*.[21] At Ferrières-en-Gâtinais around 1180 tavern-keepers fulfilled this function of go-between and, because they acted as brokers for buyers strange to the country, the lord forced them to shut up shop during the period when he alone held the right to sell wine.[22] Around these local markets traders of all kinds flourished, like Armanno of Bonifacio who, when he died in 1238, had stocked in his home 947 lamb- and goat-skins, bought in small lots from the graziers of southern Corsica.[23]

It is certain, however, that in spite of limitations established by charters of enfranchisement, the manor played a much more extensive and powerful

---

[19] Documents Nos. 58-59, pp. 412, 413   [20] Sclafert, 83, p. 83; Hilton, 590
[21] *Cartulaire de l'abbaye de Marmoutier pour le Dunois*, p. 56 (1064-1119)
[22] Perroy, 269, p. 87   [23] Lopez, in 6, p. 326

part in the country than in towns to forward the transactions which put products of the soil into circulation. The lords held control of most of the means of transport, thanks to cartage and carrying services, which were usually the last labour services to disappear.[24] They also maintained many outlets for sales in the towns. For instance at Montlhéry in 1265 the monks of Vaux-de-Cernay ran a tavern where they sold grain as well as wine. The priory of St Pierre de Jusiers possessed a house in the market of Mantes which enabled it to trade in the products of their vineyards until the commune tired of allowing this competition, and bought it back in 1290.[25] Finally the lords, through rents and tithes, kept in their own hands the most important and valuable commercial cargoes, since they usually required their dues from peasants to be paid in the shape of commodities, such as wheat and wine, which could readily be sold.[26] The big buyers from the towns dealt first with them, and it was often through them that the small producers disposed of their farm surpluses. English abbeys can thus be seen selling to Italian and Flemish traders quantities of wool which were much greater than the clip from their own sheep on their own manors; they bought what small farmers produced in order to sell it at a profit,[27] and as early as 1216 the General Council at Cîteaux was worrying about the profits which the English communities were able to draw from such intermediary trade.[28]

Nevertheless the important fact, and one which little by little modified the economic position of the rural world from top to bottom, was the dispersal and extreme decentralization of commercial activity permitted by the growth of the innumerable small markets between the year 1000 and the first years of the thirteenth century. In this way a very flexible and complex system of trade came into operation. It can be held responsible for the great diversity of prices between one district and another recorded by fourteenth-century documents,[29] with which the shrewder traders no doubt made play, buying in one place and selling in another.

In any case, all over the place, within areas comprising ten or twenty villages, small but busy townships became centres of a commercial activity in which even the most modest households participated, and which continually grew. Peasants found there iron for their tools and cloth for weddings; they took there grain which was regularly bought by merchants from the

---

[24] Duby, 444

[25] Olim, I.206, 3; *Cartulaire de Saint-Père de Chartres* (ed. Guérard), II, p. 721. The canons of St Paul and St Denis sold the wine from their cellar. Archives Nationales, LL.1157, p. 234 (1243).

[26] At Origgio in the thirteenth century, the monastery of St Ambrose of Milan levied rents in wine, which was sold in the neighbouring market. Romeo, 481.

[27] Carus-Wilson in 6, p. 375; Hilton, 667

[28] Martène, IV, col. 1249   [29] Document No. 64, p. 417

towns or monastic houses for their own consumption. We know that the provisioning of the monastery of Cluny depended from 1120 onwards on the surrounding towns, just as, in the thirteenth century, did the Leicestershire abbeys.[30]

However, documents mention most frequently transactions relating to two commodities. In the first place in France and the Rhineland, they mention wine. Thus the small town of Ferrières-en-Gâtinais appears in 1185 to have been above all a wine market; vintners from elsewhere had to acquire a part of their consignment in the manorial cellar; for the remainder they could go to other sellers who were without any doubt peasants. For the rest, it appears as if the most obvious activity of local markets throughout the west concerned animal products. The fairs were primarily cattle, wool and leather fairs, whose occurrence was regulated by the pastoral calendar, some taking place in the autumn and some in the spring. The conditions of animal husbandry in fact forced small farmers to sell their animals at the first of these seasons and to buy others at the second. This is what the peasants of Orsonville did, who were in the habit of going to Etampes or Gaillardon at the beginning of the season to acquire draught oxen which they got rid of at the beginning of the following winter.[31] But even if we cannot trust entirely the evidence, still only partially assembled, of written documents, at any rate they suggest that the growth of exchange and the requirements of traders, encouraged, particularly in the country, activities which were outside and parallel to the cultivation of cereals.

3. THE CORN TRADE

We must not, because of all this, underestimate the extent of the corn trade. But signs of it have mostly to be sought in urban records. It is indeed difficult to pick out such signs; in the documents which have up till now been studied hardly any appear before the end of the twelfth century. The trade which went by sea is far easier to track down, since customs dues were levied from very early times and for this purpose cargoes were valued and recorded in registers. The nature of the sources explains why, in the present state of research, trade is most in evidence for two European regions. To begin with England. Here, by way of example, are three of the earliest references in the records of this country: in 1198 a duty was levied on corn exported to Flanders; in the following year merchants undertook to transport grain harvested in East Anglia to Norway; we know, finally, that a network of cartage services linking the estates of Ely Cathedral to the port of embarkation at Lynn served particularly 'to sell the lord's corn'.[32] The second active

[30] Hilton, 667   [31] Archives Nationales, LL.1351, fol. 82ro
[32] Miller, 198; Documents Nos. 66 and 68, p. 417

area was the Mediterranean. Genoese traders frequented the Fréjus fairs from the end of the twelfth century,[33] and Provençal lords organized labour services to bring the crops grown in the mountains in long mule trains down to the ports where purchasers could always be found. Apart from these two maritime outposts we shall have to wait for progress in urban history to reveal the direction and size of the grain trade.

It can, however, be stated categorically that all over Europe grain was the object of a sustained demand at this period. The rise in prices from the thirteenth century onwards which records in some well documented fields reveal to us is proof of this. A study of these trends has not been made except in England, and it is doubtful whether such a study would be possible elsewhere except in the notarial archives of Italy and the south of France. From the English series which extend from 1208 to 1325 it has been possible to discover first of all that the four kinds of grain, wheat, rye, barley and oats, behaved very much in the same way,[34] and that they all suffered very violent short-term fluctuations. Prices were thus very closely linked with seasonal variations in harvests. This, in an overpopulated society which did not know how to store grain or accumulate reserves, and in a world which considered bread as basic foodstuff and had very few substitutes available, is not surprising. Over the long period the rise was continuous. It was steep before 1250 and seemed to prolong a movement whose beginning was probably in the mid-twelfth century. This sharp rise represented 'the most violent movement of prices in English history', and in fact the average price of grain doubled or even trebled between the third quarter of the twelfth century and the first quarter of the thirteenth. The rise continued thereafter but at a slower rate: in 1320 it appears that prices were four times higher than in 1180.[35] The behaviour of the curve leads us to think that farmers were constantly required to produce more in response to the growth of consumption.

Can the lessons of the English sources be applied generally? What was the real degree of elasticity of prices elsewhere? An inquisition of 1338 in the southern Alps shows prices to be very localized; they varied as one to two or to three from one village market and another, and the geography of local

---

[33] Février, 613

[34] The curves of their fluctuations are more or less parallel, but as the prices of the grain consumed by the poor were at a lower level, this parallelism in reality meant that the amplitude of fluctuations was much greater. The average prices for the period 1266-1277, recorded in the town statutes of Brescia show that the prices of the inferior grains were more unstable. Toubert, 651

[35] Beveridge, 139; Farmer, 338; Documents Nos. 62 and 63, p. 417. The correction and interpretation of the evidence supplied mainly by the account rolls in which manorial administrators transcribed the totals of harvest sales presents great difficulties, which are the cause of the differences between the curves drawn by various historians.

trade can do nothing to explain these disparities; so one wonders whether force of custom did not confer on them the rigidity they possessed.[36] Indeed to what extent were country dwellers sensitive to these long term variations? In this connection we have to distinguish clearly between the mass of small producers and the more important ones. If cereal production was directly stimulated by price movements, it was primarily through the large estates. Furthermore, is it not probable that the advantages of the market were understood not by the lords themselves but rather by their agents, those managers in whose favour new forms of association with the sharing of profits were devised? The stimulus of prices originating in the consuming towns was transmitted to the countryside by this group of entrepreneurs who were now invested with great economic power, but were not as yet quite won over by the aristocratic fashions and prejudices that condemned the spirit of gain, and who represented almost certainly (and we shall return to this point) the chief dynamic and progressive element in rural economic life. However this may be, manorial documents, in England at any rate (for elsewhere the material is so scattered and inaccessible that its study has hardly begun), show that from the early thirteenth century the amount of grain harvested on the large estates and destined for sale was considerable. On the thirty-two dependent manors of the bishop of Winchester in average years 13,000 bushels entered into commercial activity, that is, nearly half the gross product of the demesne fields; consequently, it reached nearly 80 per cent of the net product after deduction of the seed corn.[37]

However, it does not seem to have been until about 1300 that the large-scale trade in cereals reached its culminating point throughout Europe. It was, it must be noted, at that precise moment that the administrators of the great estates were preoccupied with the problem of increasing the output from cultivation. As we know, all the economic phenomena which are neither manorial nor urban escape our notice. But at least we can see that even manors of modest size were at that time geared to produce for the market. In Provence the Commanderies of the Hospitallers drew most of their income from the sale of cereals and on six of the Duchy of Lancaster's manors in Wiltshire, 1,200 measures of grain out of the 1,300 available after sowing were sold.[38] Maritime trade, profiting from technical progress in navigation which greatly increased the capacity of ships, had grown: traders from the Mediterranean conveyed 20,000 hectolitres of wheat in 1317 to Bruges which was then suffering a famine[39]; barges from the Elbe and cogs from the Baltic

---

[36] Duby, 445; Document No. 64, p. 417
[37] Postan in 6, p. 195
[38] Duby, 445; Postan, in 6, 195
[39] Van Werveke, 610

then began to ship surplus grain westwards from the new lands of the Christian east; the first signs of an export trade can be traced in the 1260's in Brandenburg and twenty years later in Prussia.[40] We can see everywhere regular lines of supply leading in the direction of the urbanized regions. Thierry d'Hireçon, who farmed extensively in Artois, and some of whose administrative accounts have been preserved, negotiated the disposal of his surplus harvest directly with traders from Ghent and Bruges; sometimes he himself organized convoys by water to Flanders. The one he sent to Ghent in 1329 brought him a return of 225 *livres* of which 39 had to be deducted to cover transport charges.[41] A catchment area of supply, whose limits advanced or retreated according to whether the year was one of shortage or abundance, grew up round each town, large or small. For instance, at Nice the purchase of grain was the first concern of the municipality and its chief expense. It was purchased everywhere, in the mountains around, in Marseilles, Montpellier, Genoa, Pisa and sometimes even in Flanders. Paris was usually supplied from the French plain; but in the event of scarcity its food supply came from much further away; in 1304 the lifeline extended to Vexin, the region of Orleans, and as far as Sens and Tours.[42]

4. WINE

The seasonal instability of the trading forays which kept the towns supplied with corn, like the violent oscillations which upset the price curve from one year to another, are evidence that the grain trade was utterly irregular. It seems, on the other hand, as if the products of enclosures and homestead tofts, watched over and tended by hand and protected by fences, together with the products of the wild domain of woodland and grassland, supplied in the thirteenth century a much more stable trade. Even though not always the most remunerative, these sales channelled a regular flow of cash into manorial coffers and peasant households.

The homestead tofts sheltered a number of valuable, tender and demanding plants which went into the preparation of luxury goods. There were to begin with the plants providing textile fibres and dyestuffs: 'Hemp, flax, woad and pastel, madder, dyer's weed, teasels, rushes and other materials which go into the making and dyeing of linen, the preparation of woollen cloth and leather, and other processes, are contained', according to Trévoux's eighteenth-century dictionary, 'within the surrounding walls of the homestead toft (*jardinage*).'[43] Once upon a time they were raised for the manufacture at home of garments for the family or the lord's household. When textile crafts

---

[40] Małowist, 703 and 704; Carsten, 8. For instance the burgesses of Prenzlau used the river Ucker to take loads of grain down to the Baltic; Zientara, 604

[41] Richard, 473   [42] Fourquin, 551   [43] Meuvret, 124

began to concentrate in certain towns the opportunity to sell them arose. Originally produced in the homestead tofts of the Somme valley, afterwards introduced into the rotation of cereal cultivation on the sandy fields of the Picardy plateau, crushed in mills operated by river power and then exported as far as London, woad was largely responsible for the great prosperity of the neighbourhood of Nesle, Corbie and especially Amiens.[44] Nevertheless the typical product of the enclosure, at least in France and Lotharingia, was wine.

R. Dion has written a magnificent history of the vineyards of France.[45] We can do no more here than draw attention to the very early establishment of vineyards around the cities which were abodes of the nobility and the higher clergy and the growth of the cultivation of vines for the purpose of export. Around Laon, Paris and on the slopes above the Moselle, in other words as near as possible to the provinces whose climate was unfavourable but where the taste for wine had taken hold, the light white wine which was the one most appreciated at aristocratic tables was produced in quantity for distant consumers. After the year 1000 the vinegrowers of these districts were continually being approached by merchants, and their customers increased particularly in the cities where wine became one of the status symbols of bourgeois wealth. Vineyards therefore spread along the waterways which alone offered a means of transporting the casks cheaply and without excessive jolting.[46]

The first beginnings of commercial viticulture can be seen in the Moselle in the direction of the Rhine (the traders of Cologne exported Rhine wines to the Low Countries, England and Scandinavia) and from Paris and Laon in the direction of Noyon, Soissons and Beauvais. However, in these regions exposed to the north the vintage produced little when the season was not a favourable one and the irregular harvests led merchants to seek their supplies further south. The fame of wines from Auxerre, Anjou, St Pourçain and from the coastal regions of Aunis and Saintonge spread in the thirteenth century.[47] One hundred years later the play of politics which left the English kings only one continental possession, Guyenne, saw the birth and speedy growth of the great vineyards of the Bordeaux country, which penetrated far up the course of the rivers.[48] At the same time the dukes of Burgundy were working to promote the popularity of Beaune wines whose expansion had for long been held back by their unfavourable position in relation to the network of waterways. Their heaviness and strength was also considered excessive and it took customers by surprise. But a traveller in France in the

[44] Carus-Wilson, in 6, pp. 376 *et seq.*; Joris, 344
[45] Dion, 105   [46] Renouard, 144
[47] The first mention of La Rochelle wines is at Liège in 1198
[48] Higounet, 342

middle of the thirteenth century would have recognized three great wine-producing regions, around Auxerre, la Rochelle and Beaune. In one French province only, the Midi of the Rhône and Mediterranean, perhaps more favoured by nature than any other, production of wine for sale did not increase at all. It was too far removed from the large centres of consumption. Furthermore at the Burgundian and Languedoc frontiers vinegrowing communities, powerfully supported by their princes, jealously barred the passage of southern wines.

A vast number of vinestocks were therefore planted. Such undertakings were, it is true, more localized than the great reclamations with which they were contemporary. They were, nevertheless, comparable because of the considerable effort they called forth as well as because of their effect on rural life. The 'plant' itself required the close co-operation of landlord and peasant in conditions which were noticeably different from the reclamations. Here it was a question of a garden-type cultivation, requiring patience and rewarded by slow returns. Although needing hours of hand labour and a great deal of manpower, viticulture did not require much material equipment or the help of animals. In the regions which benefited from it the development of the vineyard caused a revaluation of manual tasks. It offered work to the cooper and to all peasants not provided with equipment whom the improvements in ploughing had thrown back on miscellaneous jobs. As far as providing employment was concerned the growth of viticulture compensated to a certain extent for the progress of agricultural technique.

It sometimes grew at the expense of the wastes. In the Bordeaux region, the *palus* (marshes) were covered by vinestocks, and Edward I opened up his forest to planters of new vines. But the vineyard gained from the arable in a more general way in the eleventh and twelfth centuries. Contracts between equals were concluded not between lords, like the *pariages* which prepared for the foundation of the new towns, but between the master of the field and the worker who agreed to transform it into a vineyard. According to the terms of these contracts, known as *méplant* or *complant*, and whose use was general from Mâconnais to Aunis and the Trier district, the plots had, at the end of five years when the vinestocks began to bear, to be divided into two halves, of which one became the free holding of the peasant who created the enclosure. The parcelling out of the vineyard, like that of the newly ploughed lands, thus multiplied the peasants' free holdings, although in a more legitimate way. It follows that the small folk, men who were too poor to keep plough oxen and who possessed no more than their own strong arms and spades, participated largely in wine production and its direct profits. As soon as it spread to the peasantry the vocation of vinedresser assumed the democratic character which distinguished it from that of ploughman. Some of the special features of rural society in France, the home of the greatest vineyards, stem from this.

Some of the best vintages, nevertheless, the ones most sought after by merchants and for which they paid the most, came from the *clos* of rich men, high dignitaries of the Church, nobles, or in the thirteenth century, town patricians. It was a point of honour with these grand people to maintain and improve the standing of their wines. They took the trouble to supervise in person the preparation of the land and the *vendage*. Good vineyards were thus abandoned to peasant farmers only with reluctance, either as holdings or in *métayage*. They were by preference entrusted to servants or, increasingly, to hired workmen. At the expiration of the contract of *complant* the landlord took over himself the management of his share of the new vineyard.

Viticulture was thus much more closely linked with direct cultivation than was cereal-growing. From the twelfth century onwards it was also much more closely linked with hired labour and the use of money. In 1148 the abbot of Cluny devoted the large money rents which his English manors brought in to the upkeep of the vineyards.[49] In the thirteenth century the best practice was to establish in the vineyard a *closier*, a manager of domestic status, fed and housed by his master, who directed the work of the vineyard labourers paid by the day in cash. The vineyard was also the support of the small allod and of the humble wage-earner. The lord's *clos* provided the chief livelihood of a vast number of small households without capital, possessing no more than tiny personal vineyards where, in time stolen from their working day, householders went morning and evening to dig their own ground.

The masters were bent on keeping their vines under their own supervision. For this reason the best vineyards remained confined within the limits of the towns where the leading ecclesiastical lords had been established from ancient times, and which became again in thirteenth-century France the chosen residences of high society, as well as the seats of the great commercial enterprises. The vineyards formed a wide belt round the towns. Similarly the small vineyards and the vinegrowing wage-earners, the *affaneurs* as they were called at Lyons, were not distributed over the countryside; they constituted semi-urban groups, narrowly localized on a few lands on the outskirts. From these zones the cultivation of food crops could be completely eliminated. Passing through Auxerre in 1245, Fra Salimbene was amazed to find that 'these people sow nothing, reap nothing and gather nothing into their barns. They only need to send their wine to Paris on the nearby river which goes straight there. The sale of wine in this city brings them in a good profit which pays entirely for their food and clothing.' This reference ex-

[49] Duby, 441

plains the extent to which the establishment of vineyards injected life into the rural economy by stimulating a new and important demand for cereal supplies and by animating currents of exchange between wine and grain countries: between Picardy, for example, and the country around Laon, between the Parisian hillsides and the French plain. Activity was generated in small townships and links were forged between districts whose occupations were complementary.

5. PRODUCTS OF FOREST AND PASTURE

The uncultivated lands were being put to good use at the same time as the enclosed tofts. The woodlands and the scrub regenerated after periodic slash and burn, the heathlands, the *terre gaste* and the *gâtine*, which encircled the village land or were at the disposal of adjacent village communities had always provided their share of the food supply, and systems of sharing in its utilization had from ancient times been in operation. The village community laid down how many beasts each householder could send out to pasture. Or else the lord, in exchange for a small payment, a pig, a sheep or some handmade objects, made over to his own tenants or neighbouring peasants precisely regulated rights of usage over the uncultivated portions of his estate. In France custom distinguished the 'pannage', that is the right to pasture swine in the forest, the *glandée*, the right to gather acorns, and lastly 'estover', or the right to collect dead wood or the permission to cut a certain quantity of standing wood in one part of the forest. After the year 1000, as in the very early Middle Ages, small-scale animal husbandry provided an indispensable contribution, and often an important addition, to the profits of cultivation.

Records show that above all else peasant households kept pigs in the forest. In one Essex village described in the Domesday Book the manorial demesne supported only 40 pigs, whereas the tenancies could have supported 2,200. On the other hand the large flocks of sheep which browsed on the fallow and manured it with their dung belonged for the most part to the masters, at least in England. At the end of the eleventh century in Southminster close to the previously mentioned village, 700 sheep were tended by the shepherds of the manorial 'hall'.[50] Lastly, at that period there were still districts of woodland and grassland where stockbreeding was not merely a by-product, but the principal activity. In the eleventh century certain demesnes of the abbey of Fécamp in Normandy presented an altogether pastoral appearance; these manors had received as alms from the Duke as an initial establishment, cows with their calves, oxen and pigs.[51] The whole of Domesday England, apart from East Anglia, appears to have been basically devoted to animal husbandry. Farms isolated in the forests of the Weald and

[50] Lennard, 268, pp. 257-281   [51] Musset, 465

specializing in the fattening of pigs are to be found delivering to the lord's manor dues in the form of dried meat, and the great inquest listed the swineherds of Devonshire and Wiltshire in a separate category. At Doddington on the edge of the Fens, the bishop of Ely possessed a *vaccaria*, i.e. a dairy farm, on which there were one hundred cows and 24 mares. But on the agricultural manors of eastern England, livestock rearing seemed undeveloped and quite insufficient for a healthy exploitation of the soil.[52]

Records allow us to perceive, however, that from the end of the eleventh century the development of the waste lands was intensified especially through pastoral activities. The stimulus came in part directly from the progress of assarting. We know that the reclaimers tended to begin with enclosed pastures and meadows producing hay. The movement of conquest in its first phase is revealed as an attempt to extract more from the woodland and marshland grass. For long the North Sea polders and the English fenlands supported first sheep and then cattle on the wet ground while the salt was leached from the meadows. For a long time the settler lived on milk products and vegetables from his garden plot, and this was also the diet of all those hermits who went at the end of the eleventh century, either singly or in religious communities, to live in the 'desert'. Cistercians lived the pastoral life and developed primarily by stockbreeding the open spaces which they had been granted. The monks of the Great Charterhouse quite soon after the foundation possessed about 50 cows. By 1226 they maintained 750 ewes, 300 lambs and 180 goats. The records of all these new monasteries are full of titles which give them grazing rights on other people's land, either manorial demesnes or village, and rights of free seasonal passage for their flocks (transhumance); they are full also of the echoes of disputes over grazing with surrounding peasant communities and even their brothers from other abbeys. Bitter rivalry developed between the Great Charterhouse from its foundation and Chalais, and between the Templars of Lus and the Carthusians of Durbon over the use of the alpine pastures.[53] Monks and lay brothers of the desert places in the twelfth century appear obsessed by an acquisitive aggressiveness; their attitude, pettifogging and quarrelsome, was typical of stockbreeders. Very soon we see them preoccupied with obtaining exemption from tolls. In 1195 the abbey of Boscaudon on the region of Embrun obtained the privilege of trading at Marseilles.[54] In fact the monks could not themselves use all the produce which the wastes upon which they lived yielded in such abundance. They quickly became sellers of large quantities of cattle, wool, wood, leather and footwear, which they found very profit-

[52] Lennard, 266, pp. 258 *et seq.*; Miller, 196; Darby, 42, p. 204
[53] *Recueil des plus anciennes chartes de la Grand-Chartreuse* (ed. Bligny), Grenoble, 1960, Nos. 26, 27, 28, 42, 43   [54] Sclafert, 81, p. 13

able. Completely isolated from the world and lost in inaccessible solitudes as they were, the first Carthusians had at their disposal in 1173 500 *sous viennois* with which they purchased the withdrawal of a competitor;[55] at this period the wealth and business acumen of the Cistercians were proverbial among the French nobility who could ill conceal their distrust and envy of them.

It seems too as if the last years of the twelfth century marked the beginning of a period particularly favourable to the sale of such goods. The astonishing detail of English manorial documents allows us to trace about 1180 a marked rise in the prices of livestock, which had for some time remained stable. An ox worth three shillings a generation before could be sold for twice as much; and six pence instead of four were now needed to buy a sheep.[56] The trade in wood and the different animal products underwent a growth similar to the wine trade in the thirteenth century.

* * *

In the open forests of the early Middle Ages, badly maintained and damaged by unplanned utilization as they were, fine timber trees had always been rare. We know the story of Suger who in 1130 sought twelve large beams for the abbey buildings of St Denis. He felt sure of finding them on the monastery estate in the great forest of Iveline, but the Parisian carpenters were amazed to discover that the lord of Chevreuse who held half the wood in fief from the abbey had used all the best trees during his wars against the king and Amaury de Montfort 'to build his fortifications'. They advised the Abbot to send to the Morvan for the beams. Suger did so and found the trees it is true, but spoke of it as a miracle.[57] Later in the thirteenth century castles had almost ceased to be constructed of wood. On the other hand large numbers of houses were built in the fast growing towns, and many ships were under construction on the rivers and sea coasts. They were lightly built craft which deteriorated quickly and had to be rebuilt at least every ten years. These and other needs created by the progress of material civilization constantly raised the price of timber.

The forest was also the source of quantities of materials which became more essential as the conditions of daily life grew less primitive; firewood for hearth, oven and workshop, resin for torches, bark for ropemakers, wax for candles, lime and ashes for various uses; and charcoal for the forge. The extension of vineyards created a heavy demand for wood to make into casks and vats, the winemaking receptacles which had to be partially renewed

[55] *Recueil des plus anciennes chartes de la Grand-Chartreuse*, Nos. 30, 43
[56] A. L. Poole, 'Livestock Prices in the Twelfth Century,' in *English Historical Review*, 1940; Raftis, 201, p. 62
[57] Suger, *De consecratione* (ed. Lecoy de la Marche), p. 221

every wine harvest, and for vine props whose use alone enabled the plants to stand up to hard frost and which were cut every season in enormous quantities from the heart of oak and chestnut. In this way viticulture and forest management were closely linked together. If land was enclosed for vineyards, it was immediately feared in the neighbourhood that 'because of the vines, damage to the woods would result',[58] and the forest lords increased the level of fines for the wrongful use of trees.

In fact, it is clear from written records that men, by the end of the twelfth century, began to regard the woodland spaces as a precious possession well worth special protection.[59] But at that very moment, they were being attacked and reduced by the activities of the reclaimers, who were probably never so numerous nor so invasive as then. In addition the peasants with rights were no longer content to get wood 'for their kitchen, their house and their fences'. Tempted by the profits of trade they went into the woods to load their donkeys and carts with faggots and logs to sell in the local market town. After 1160 we meet more and more often amongst the archives of France and Old Germany deeds which regulated the forest usages, which defined the rights of foresters and strengthened their authority over peasants and herdsmen, which sometimes granted a great local lord, as guardian, not only the revenue from the woodlands, but also (the better to protect them) strong judicial powers.[60] Here, selected from many others, is a deed in which in 1205 the monks of Chelles entrusted the protection of their coppices to William of Garlande, and in which at the same time the sequence of exploitation was regulated. A cutting was to be made at the end of five years; then during the following seven years the wood was to be left intact and protected; thereafter it was to be put up to auction; during the four years after each cutting access by sheep was to be prohibited.[61]

What profound changes! The forest in the early Middle Ages had been a bottomless reservoir open to all, in which every man could plunge according to his needs. Above all else, it had been a vast pasture where domestic animals like pigs, sheep and oxen, as well as the herds of wild horses from which the cavalry of the great lords was drawn, had roamed in complete freedom. In the thirteenth century trees became a specialized and protected form of plant life intended to supply the needs of building, manufacture and heating. Indeed the contribution of wood sales to manorial income was considerably enlarged. A systematic study of these profits would be worth undertaking

[58] *Cartulaire de l'abbaye de Val-Dieu*, No. 262
[59] Lamprecht, 20, I.1, p. 137
[60] Timm, 570. Philip Augustus caused the Bois de Vincennes to be closed in 1183; Rigord, *Gesta Philippi regis*, 21
[61] Bibl. de Meaux, Ms. 59, p. 105

and sources for it are not so scarce as they might seem. In the receipts of the count of Beaumont-le-Roger after 1250 the total for the forests exceeds that for fixed rents from land.[62] Through these sales the great landowners entered into intimate dealings with professional traders who sometimes, relying on the shortage of cash from which most rural landlords chronically suffered, bought trees more cheaply before felling. The monks of St Denis who had in 1201 disposed in this way of the right to exploit parts of the woodland received 133 livres every St John's Day for the next seven years.[63] However the right to cut wood was usually sold by auction to the highest bidder. It was decided for instance in 1307 that the wooded part of the abbey of St Benoît-sur-Loire's demesne at Varty should be sold – 'cried up' – at the market of Clermont and 'he who would give more for it, should step forward and another should outbid him (*recherra*)'. Thierry d'Hireçon did likewise, or else instructed his foresters to recruit weekly workers and to sell the timber and firewood in small lots.[64] Just as in viticulture, forest exploitation in the thirteenth century attracted merchants and their money into the most remote districts. It increased the profits of direct cultivation; it also provided employment and additional wages for manual workers who had neither land enough nor the necessary tools to produce all their own food by themselves.

*   *   *

At the very moment when cattle were being excluded from the forest, the increasingly varied diet which can be guessed at from some documents and the consumption of meat and cheese which it entailed, the ever present need for leather and, even more, for wool, encouraged country folk to widen their pastoral activities. Butchers, who were so active in all small townships, incited them to follow this occupation. Sheep-rearing made great strides in the course of the thirteenth century, and has been studied closely in England. It constituted a large part of the prosperity of this country, where farmers of all ranks had become aware of the profits to be obtained from the sale of skins to parchment-makers and of milk (according to Walter of Henley, 20 ewes could provide as much as 2 cows and could give each week 250 pounds of cheese and half a gallon of butter). But it was of course wool more than anything else that attracted buyers from Flanders and Italy. To satisfy them the breeds were improved. The ever greater size of parchments preserved today in muniment rooms is tangible proof of the biological im-

---

[62] Strayer, 475, p. 77. In 1289 Pierre le Bouvier of Verrières bought from Notre-Dame de Paris in the woods of Chatenay the right to fell two plots covering 2½ and 27 acres respectively for the very high sum of 994 livres. *Cartulaire de Notre-Dame-de-Paris* (ed. Guérard), II, No. 63.
[63] Archives Nationales, LL.1157, I, p. 529
[64] Richard, 473; Bruwier, 482

provement of the animals from whose skins they were made. The improvement continued throughout the thirteenth century and the Cistercian abbeys where the most rational methods of breeding were practised probably played a leading part in it. Long-stapled breeds were gradually developed in certain districts, such as Lincolnshire and Shropshire.[65]

Regional specialization introduced differences in the price of wool. In regions like Devonshire where wool was less good and consequently cheaper, sheep-farming did not grow much. In 1420 in the accounts of the abbey of Tavistock the yield of corn sales exceeded that of the sales of wool.[66] This shows how dependent pastoral activities were on the market. Breeders felt this acutely and did not hesitate to devote large sums of money to improving the quality of their animals. In 1196 the manor of Sulby in Northamptonshire spent 33s. 4d. to replace 100 sheep bearing coarse wool with others bearing fine wool. This was a profitable investment for the annual income of the demesne rose from £9 2s. to £10.[67] Above all the size of the flocks increased considerably.

The larger manors alone have left records in sufficient abundance for this growth to be followed in detail. Here is one example. The demesnes of the bishop of Chichester supported 3,150 animals in 1220 and 5,900 in the fourteenth century.[68] Nevertheless numerous references convince us that the sheep runs of the humblest peasants were also proportionately more heavily stocked, and that the largest number of English sheep (their total numbers are estimated at 8,000,000 in the middle of the fourteenth century) were maintained by villagers. In 1225 on the manor of Damerham and the neighbouring hamlet of Martin near Salisbury, the abbot of Glastonbury owned 560 sheep on the demesne but the flock belonging to 198 villagers amounted to 3,760 head.[69]

Research on the continent has not been taken nearly so far, but it is probable that it will not be slow to reveal details on the same scale. Already during the thirteenth century a rapid and sustained growth of pastoral activity can be discerned in several regions. It was at this period, it seems, that the opening up of the 'alps' and the meadows on the high mountains was organized. A large number of *Schwaighöfe* were established in the Tyrol and the Bavarian Alps. On the alpine slopes which had until then been uninhabited and unproductive, the lords would instal at great altitudes herds of 50 to 100 cattle, both cows and sheep, and entrust them to families of herdsmen. The latter tilled homestead tofts and a few fields out of the pasture, but

[65] Power, 142; Pelham, in 47; Trow-Smith, 32   [66] Finberg, 187
[67] A. L. Poole, *From Domesday Book . . .*, p. 54
[68] *The Chartulary of the High Church of Chichester* (ed. Peckham), Sussex Record Society, 1964   [69] Pelham, in 47; p. 240; Power, 142, p. 30

they lived mostly on milk, wild foods, and a little grain supplied by their masters. They delivered every year in rent several hundred cheeses and forty pounds or so of butter.[70] At the same period the peasant communities of the valleys in Béarn and Auvergne organized the development of the great hill-top grasslands. It was often the opportunity for agreements with stock-breeders from the plains or from more distant parts to whom pastures were opened up during the summer months. One such agreement concerning the pasture land around the Lake of Issarlés in Velay was concluded in 1295 be-tween the Cistercians of Aiguebelle and the prior of a small local monastery acting on behalf of the mountain dwellers. The latter reserved their freedom to erect enclosures on the grazing grounds to protect their fields and mea-dows; they authorized the monks to bring up 120 *trentains* of ewes each summer, but they demanded an annual rent of nine sous and half a quintal of cheese and required that, except in rainy weather, the animals should be folded every night on the cultivated parts of the village lands to manure them.[71]

In southern countries the first written agreements to do with trans-humance appear also in the last years of the twelfth century. This great seasonal see-saw which regularly moved tens of thousands of animals in search of greener grass from the Provençal mountains to the great winter pastures in the region of Arles and back again, was set up and canalized through a series of agreements covering grazing and rights of free passage along the approach routes concluded between the drovers of the flocks and the various agricultural communities. In the records of the counts of Provence a fragment from an account of 1300 reveals that that winter more than 20,000 animals descended from the valleys of the Ubaye, the Bléone and the Asse alone on to the territory of the *bailliages* of St Maximin and Barjols. On 12th June 1345 the flock of the Hospitallers of Manosque, ready to leave for the alpine pastures, was reckoned as 63 rams, 534 ewes, 443 sheep and 381 lambs. At that period the high pastures of the southern Alps appear to have been overrun and overgrazed. Village communities attempted to prohibit entry to outsiders and the mountain folk who, ruined by the invasion from the low-lands, had not already emigrated groaned under the burden of the flocks of the lords and the graziers from the valley towns. Many of the animals who trod the lanes of Provence at each change of season belonged in fact to nobles or professionals. Sixteen stockbreeders owned 6,500 sheep listed in one account of 1300 and the lord of Digne himself owned about 2,000. However, many came also from peasant sheep-runs, since village custom authorized each village household to run eight *trentains* on the common land. Goats and

[70] Haussman, 301
[71] *Chartes et documents de l'abbaye d'Aiguebelle*, No. 115

ewes formed the sole worldly goods of many households in the villages of upper Provence at the beginning of the fourteenth century.[72]

One might expect that manorial records in France, Germany and Italy, hitherto so little explored, would reveal enough for us to gauge the importance of the part played by stockbreeding in the demesne economy of the thirteenth century. In 1229-1230 the administrators of the abbey of St Denis's demesne at Maisoncelles in Brie sold 516 sheep, 40 pigs, 30 cows and 7 oxen, and those of the demesne at Tremblay more than 400 sheepskins,[73] The flocks of the Templars of Cavalerie in Larzac numbered 160 goats and 1,725 sheep in 1308, and the Hospitallers of Manosque in 1300 maintained more than 1,500 sheep, 300 pigs, 77 goats and 90 cows.[74] The estate accounts of the demesnes which Thierry d'Hireçon ran in Artois provide very valuable information for the early fourteenth century about the purchases and sales of cattle of a large-scale cultivator, and also about the profits derived from them. He maintained horses (24 at Bonnières alone) and fed them in winter on straw and spring grain; but these were kept solely for plough and field work. Only the foals and the animals which were no more use were sold; mainly strong beasts were bought. Pig-breeding seemed to be carried on more for profit: of the 300 reared at Bonnières in 1328, 12 were fattened and slaughtered for the lord's table and 37 sold at market. The sale of calves, and especially milk and cheese, so easily disposed of commercially, made the rearing of cows more profitable still.

Nevertheless, as in England, the most lucrative transactions concerned sheep. Between the farm of Roquetoire and the fairs of St Riquier there was an incessant and profitable movement of buying and selling. In 1320 for instance 160 sheep were bought for 8½ sous each; the following year after only two had died the remainder were sold for 10½ sous each. Thierry d'Hireçon invested 68 *livres* into this transaction and it brought him back 83, but by selling wool from the same animals he gained another 52 *livres*, which brought his final profit on the whole operation up to 100 per cent.[75]

* * *

Like the development of forest and vineyard, stockraising was largely a matter of money and trade. It brought cash into country homes and placed the latter in contact with hucksters and wool merchants; it linked them especially with the little local town and its end-of-season fairs. For, as the affairs of Thierry d'Hireçon show, stockraising implied that cattle and sheep should continually change hands. This circulation was particularly lively in the thirteenth century, since, except in the transhumance regions, most

[72] Sclafert, 83, p. 50   [73] Fourquin, 551
[74] Higounet-Nadal, 457; Reynaud, 472   [75] Richard, 473

farmers could not muster sufficient reserves of fodder to keep many animals through the winter. Meadows were few, hay was expensive and the price of acorns could reach astronomical levels.[76] Men themselves were too obsessed by the fear of famine to dip freely into their small stocks of grain to feed cattle. There remained only straw or leaves collected in the forest and hedgerow. During the lean months therefore cattle had to fast; they grew thin to the point of dying and lost all their strength and value. English agricultural treatises estimated that a cow could produce in the 34 weeks between April and October milk worth 42 pence; but during the 28 weeks of winter, even when milk was three times as dear, the value produced fell to no more than 10 pence.[77]

Animals were therefore slaughtered freely every autumn. First there was a mass killing of pigs because their meat could be salted, one reason incidentally why this commodity was so important to the rural economy. Purchases of salt formed perhaps one of the heaviest and most frequent expenses of a peasant household. The larger cattle were disposed of at the September or October fairs: at the Étampes fair the peasants from round about brought for resale the horses and donkeys which they had earlier bought for the 'season'.[78] The need to get rid of animals as winter approached thus offered an opportunity for speculation which some farsighted individuals who knew how to obtain winter feed, or who had accumulated hay or other fodder, could turn to their own advantage. This explains the enormous profits which people like Thierry d'Hireçon and the urban butchers made. It is possible that hope of such profits encouraged considerably the spread of leguminous crops in the rotation of cultivation during the last years of the thirteenth century. Peas and vetches were fed to the ewes in the sheepfolds in winter at Roquetoire and Bonnières.

From all this it can be seen why pastoral activities so closely connected with commerce and money were dominated by the richer people. On modest farms, stockraising was controlled by the capital of the lords and still more by the capital of the townsmen. In the thirteenth century the butchers of small towns like Digne and Seyne-les-Alpes, of great regional markets like Metz and Coventry, as well as burgesses of all professions who desired to put their money to good use, concentrated a very important part of their business on stockbreeding. They advanced cash to peasants and helped them to start a flock or to build one up; they reserved for themselves part of the profits by the terms of one of those contracts of diverse legal form which were known as livestock leases, *'gasaille'*, or in Italy *soccida*. These partner-

[76] Duby, 445
[77] *Walter of Henley's Husbandry* (ed. E. Lamond), 1890, p. 77. Bennett, 149, p. 91
[78] Archives Nationales, LL.1351, fol. 82ro

ships all in fact veiled usurious loans; nevertheless in 1226 the chapter general of Cîteaux authorized houses of the order to contract them. Sometimes such contracts entailed the organization of part-time wage-earners, like an agreement concluded in 1334 in Cipières in upper Provence, covering five *trentains* of ewes; the stockbreeder brought one-third of the livestock into the business, and after five years when the partnership had to end, he would keep half the flock; but before the conclusion of the contract he received from his associate 22 *sétiers* of grain, 20 sous for the *companage* and 4 *livres* in wages. More often, under what was really called *gasaille* in southern France, the peasant received the whole flock, and had to return it all after one, two or three years, keeping only half of the increase; this was what happened to the two peasants of Auribeau to whom, in 1309, a burgess of Grasse entrusted a cow and its calf, estimated at 55 sous, 'for half the profit, common peril and fortune'.[79] It was a disguised loan, and at the end of the lease the peasant, if he possessed enough money, could buy the animals. Contracts like this lent themselves to innumerable combinations, permitting one villager to take over in *gasaille* the cattle that he would have had to sell to a butcher to get hold of a little cash, and another to entrust his flock to a shepherd for the transhumance. But the principal function was to establish links between the money available in the hands of townsmen and the humblest country households.

Our sources show too how some burgesses created for themselves pastoral demesnes in the neighbourhood of the towns managed, as were the vineyards, by agents and domestics, but often given over to share-croppers, since the need for supervision was in this case less pressing. We know that on the new farms of the burgesses around Metz animal farming was commoner than cereal cultivation. The profits to be expected from pastoral activities in the thirteenth century stimulated the wealthy classes, ecclesiastics, nobles, burgesses and the better endowed peasants, to take a growing interest in the grasslands. They were encouraged to cultivate isolated lands, shut in by hedges, so that they were cut off from the collective constraints of village fellowship, and were thus able to evade the obligations of the common flock and the communal grazing. The infiltration of capital into the countryside through pastoral speculation was evidently not a new trend in the spread of the different forms of settlement which written documents, place names and observation of the countryside reveal to us. The profits of stock-farming accelerated the progress of enclosures and dispersed habitation, and contributed to the formation of the *bocage* or hedgerow landscape.

6. COMMERCIAL GROWTH AND SOCIAL DEVELOPMENT

Only a detailed survey co-ordinating all these scattered clues and allow-

[79] Archives des Bouches-du-Rhône, 396 E 17, fol. 80; Aubenas, 331

ing for all differences of time and place would enable us to advance reliable theories about the pace at which an exchange economy penetrated rural life in all the provinces of western Europe. And we are of course far from finding ourselves in this position. We cannot even be certain that the increase in exchange is not an illusion created by the greater amount of information and more communicative sources. By all appearances, however, the movement rapidly intensified in the thirteenth century, which throughout its course appears as an era of expansion and proliferating transactions. In any case the play of commercial operations in the countryside on the eve of the fourteenth century was astonishingly widespread and vigorous. To give an idea of the ramifications of trade I shall only cite three examples. The first will demonstrate how powerful the currents which carried certain agricultural products over long distances could sometimes be. At the beginning of the fourteenth century ships exported from the Gironde in good years and in bad some 80,000 casks of Gascon wine, that is about 700,000 hectolitres.[80] My second example shows the part played by purchases and sales in manorial management in the first half of the thirteenth century. There have been preserved, in an imperfect edition, fragments of accounts kept by master Richard de Toury who between 1236 and 1242 ran the finances of the Cistercian abbey of Maubuisson, situated, like all houses of this order, in an isolated site in the depths of the forest. Among the cash receipts come first of all the sales of the proceeds of the tithe probably negotiated on the spot; then certain woodland products, such as pigs, iron, charcoal and bark; then finally the sale, settled in three instalments, of the right to cut wood and pasture swine. All the money thus acquired was spent at the fair of Lendit on horses with their harness, iron fittings for carts, cauldrons, shoe leather, parchment, linen and woollen cloth, wine and oats; it was also used to pay the wages of carpenters, woodcutters, and transport drivers.[81] Lastly, to give some idea of the weight of traffic in a region where trade was purely local, here are details of a register compiled in 1307-1308 by the count of Provence's tollkeepers at Valensole. This plateau dominating the middle reaches of the Durance was crossed by one of the routes followed by merchants and muleteers between the mountains of Gap, Digne, Barcelonette and Castellane and the lowland districts of Avignon, Aix, Marseilles and Grasse. In the summer between June and August beasts of burden brought huge logs of wood down to the timber-yards of Aix and the workshops of Marseilles. It was the main season of traffic (that year 715 journeys were recorded). But from March until July

[80] Y. Renouard, 'Recherches complémentaires sur la capacité du tonneau bordelais', in *Annales du Midi*, 1956
[81] H. de L'Epinois, 'Comptes relatifs à la fondation de l'abbaye de Maubuisson', in *Bibliothèque de l'Ecole des Chartes*, 1857-1858

convoys with ever-increasing loads of grain passed towards the mountain country of pasture and forest whose barns were the first to be emptied. In September there began and continued for three months the traffic in linen cloth which the traders of the plain took to sell in the market towns of the hill country after the late summer fairs had put money into the pockets of the peasants. In the spring convoys carried salt up country and travelled down again with wool and raw hides. Lastly, throughout the winter the *nourri-guiers*, the big stockbreeders of Digne, Seyne, Marseilles or Aix, passed through, driving oxen to and from places which offered opportunities for trade.[82]

★ ★ ★

This commercial traffic and the possibilities it offered of small additions to the returns from agricultural activities made more bearable the over-population of the villages which all the documents of the late thirteenth century bring to our notice. Bordars and labourers were able to support themselves almost without land by rearing during the summer months such small animals as pigs and sheep, whose purchase price the lord or a butcher had advanced, and which could be easily fed on the wastes. Wage-earning provided another and important means of making both ends meet.[83] As the great estates came into contact with the outside world and their owners and agents could renew their stocks of cash at fair time by the sale of surpluses, they were more ready to hire labourers and offer them money instead of an allowance of food. In 1338 the Hospitallers of Bras in Provence paid out more than 50 *livres* in day wages (that is more than double the money they received from manorial rents and taxes, and 20 per cent of what the sale of harvested grain brought in) to hundreds of harvesters and reapers and to women employed in April to weed the crops.[84] The main function which the great cereal-growing estates performed at the end of the thirteenth century was to set in motion movements of capital, to introduce large quantities of agricultural commodities into commerce and to redistribute part of their value in the shape of wages amongst landless and ploughless peasants. We must remember also that the development of skilled crafts offered supplementary rewards to a rural population for whom agriculture could not secure a living. Prominent among these skills was viticulture, an occupation which provided manual employment in the winter months. Many thousands of people got their livelihood as vinedressers.

[82] Sclafert, 83, pp. 74 *et seq.*; Documents Nos. 60 and 61, p. 414

[83] The pious life of St Thibaut, hermit, shows that from the mid-eleventh century men could 'support themselves on small earnings', by hiring themselves out to perform 'vile farm work', such as carrying stones, cleaning out stables and cutting hay. *Vita S. Theobaldi*, AA.SS. VII.544.   [84] Duby, 445

But we must also try and find out, in spite of the difficulties and the enormous gaps in our knowledge, how it was that certain peasants gradually came to specialize in making articles for sale. In the early Middle Ages every countryman was perforce an artisan who had to make with his own hands all household objects from his house and clothing down to his pots and pans and agricultural tools; he worked also for the lord's household, since he had periodically to deliver certain handmade articles, shingles, vineprops, battens (men's work) and pieces of woollen or linen cloth (the work of his wife and daughters). Dues of this kind continued for long to burden peasant tenancies. They proved very long-lasting in Germany. In 1301 the dependent *manses* of the abbey of St Emeram at Ratisbon were still for the most part obliged to provide cloth woven by women from manorial wool to be worn by the monks themselves or to be distributed by them as charitable gifts. A *polypty-que* drawn up at Fulda about 1150 reveals the existence of dues in the form of forged tools, woollen coverlets and linen thread. And on some Alsatian manors in the thirteenth century domestics were still clothed in very rough material made in their homes by some of the tenants. Lingering remains of this custom are to be seen in certain places in the English countryside. The Black Book of Peterborough, compiled in the first quarter of the twelfth century, enumerates how many ells of cloth dependent villages of the monastery were obliged to provide on the festival of the patron saint. Finally in France, amongst the different instructions which the canons of Notre-Dame of Chartres issued about 1130 to the mayors who were their representatives on their demesnes was one telling them not to demand weaving services from the peasants.[85] The rural household was therefore for many years a workshop upon whose services the lord could call.

The time came, however, when the lord relinquished his claims on handmade articles. They disappeared earlier in Italy where they had altogether vanished from manorial inventories before 1100, and much later in Germany. The lapse in France can be dated to the first half of the twelfth century. The reason why they lapsed is that small workshops where such articles could be obtained more cheaply and of better quality sprang up near the town markets. As standards of life were rising customers were becoming more numerous and harder to please; demands were now met by the new urban districts and smaller boroughs growing up round the fairs and markets. To begin with the customers were lords, but soon they were joined by peasants who did not hesitate to buy more efficient ploughshares or better-made shoes if they had money to spend. One would like to be able to distinguish the tools in a peasant's stock of equipment which came from the workshops of skilled

[85] Heimpel, *Das Gewerbe im Stadt Regensburg*, p. 35; Maitland. 168; *Cartulaire de Notre-Dame de Chartres* (ed. Lepinois and Merlet), I, No. 58

RE F*   153

artisans. But inventories describing the movables of modest households are unfortunately very rare, even in the thirteenth century.[86]

In any case the first artisans we are aware of in the little country towns at the end of the twelfth and the thirteenth centuries were blacksmiths and shoemakers. The monks of Marmoutier and the lord from near Blois who were in 1190 endeavouring to settle population in a *villefranche* intended to instal there two ironworkers, a shoemaker, two bakers and two butchers.[87] If in the course of the twelfth century the Cistercians of La Ferté in Burgundy paid for many of their purchases with shoes made by lay brothers in the domestic workshop, leather workers were also numerous at Ferrières-en-Gâtinais in 1185 when that little commercial town received its franchise. Amongst the different things contributing to the prosperity of the provost of a castle on the banks of the Saône in the first half of the thirteenth century was the sale of shoes from a stall at the castle gateway.[88] At that period, craftsmen were to be met with in the smallest villages. At Ouges in Burgundy at the beginning of the fourteenth century, bakers, shoemakers and wheelwrights[89] were in business, and to judge from the speedy increase in the thirteenth century of names like *Sabatier* and *Schuhmacher* it would be worth following up in the lists of peasants which appear in manorial records references to surnames indicating a professional skill.

The first village artisans were, at least until the twelfth century, slaves absolutely dependent on their lords, who were to begin with employed on the tasks of the demesne, but who gradually received permission to work for others as well. About 1300 the blacksmiths and harness-makers (and also millers who were specialists partly supported by those who had recourse to their services) were to some extent manorial servants and remained closely attached to the great manorial estate which was their chief customer and which often paid them a retaining salary. They nearly always held their workshop, mill or forge, and its equipment, from the lord for rent. Nevertheless it was their special skill which provided their livelihood. The appearance on the rural scene of such small teams of artisans widened employment in the villages and gave many a man frustrated by the insufficient resources of his agricultural holding an occupation and the means of existence.[90]

[86] See p. 282   [87] *Cartulaire de l'abbaye de Marmoutier pour le Dunois*, XLIV, p. 56
[88] *Recueil des Pancartes de l'abbaye de la Ferté sur Grosne* (ed. Duby, Nos. 46, 57, 115, 127); Perroy 269 p. 87; Duby, 261, p. 525. The charter of franchise of the town of Louhans in Bresse enumerates in the middle of the thirteenth century 'cloth merchants, clothiers, skinners, mercers, shoemakers, butchers, ironmongers, grocers, salters, bakers, and money changers'; M. Pacaut and F. Gauthier, 'Louhans au Moyen Age', in *Cahiers d'Histoire*, 1960.
[89] Martin-Lorber, 536
[90] The following reference appears in a notary's register at the beginning of the fourteenth century. The priest of a Provençal mountain village apprenticed his brother in

Nevertheless, it was easier for families of cultivators to supplement their income by working part-time in the slack seasons of the agricultural calendar and by making at home a few articles for sale such as had once been required by the lord. Woollen and linen cloth which had for generations been woven in peasant homes to pay manorial dues was carried to market or offered to the town dealers as soon as the master's 'hall' ceased to call for it. This change-over, though most important, is very obscure. Again English evidence throws a few shafts of light. It has been noticed there that the towns where hitherto the high quality woollen industry had been concentrated declined in the thirteenth century and that the manufacture of woollen cloth was dispersed in the countryside. This fact is connected with the spread of the fulling mill. Many lords built these on the banks of country streams after the end of the twelfth century. Fullers set up in the villages where they developed weaving. As winter employment, weaving could, like spinning, bring a little money into labourers' households.[91] An enquiry of this kind is still to be undertaken for other western countries, but a few details gleaned here and there lead us to suppose that textile crafts in the thirteenth century offered everywhere an addition to the livelihood of many country dwellers. In France, at least in certain provinces, fulling mills were perhaps no less numerous than in the English countryside. Many of these fulling mills can be traced in the southern Alps, an overpopulated pastoral country with poor soil. Fustian-making spread in the vicinity of the towns of northern Italy; in the second half of the thirteenth century a workshop of the Umiliati was in operation in the little village of Origgio near Milan.[92] We know that in the southern fringes of Christian Europe the ranks of craftsmen were such a fruitful field for heresies that the name 'weaver' eventually came to be used for the supporters of any religious movement of the poor whether heterodox or not. We know also that, hunted out of the towns, the heretics spread in the thirteenth century into the villages. A study of the inquisition records could be, in Languedoc and in Lombardy, one of the points of departure for research on the rural craftsman, for the lack of which some of the fundamental processes of the economy still continue to evade the historian of the country-side.

However, even at the present state of our knowledge, there is no doubt that many villagers had subsidiary occupations. This occupation could be connected, like the forge or the mill, with the improvements of agricultural technique, or else, like cartage and mule transport, with commercial growth,

---

the neighbouring village to learn the cobbler's craft. Archives des Bouches-du-Rhône, 396 E 18, fol. 292.

[91] Carus-Wilson, 695

[92] Sclafert, 83, pp. 61 *et seq.*; Document No. 145, p. 504; Romeo, 481; Borlandi, 692

or again, like weaving, with sheep-farming, or else again, like the making of vineprops or casks, with forest management and viticulture. The diffusion of craftsmanship, like the growth of vineyards and the spread of sheep flocks, loosened up the social relations in rural society. Based on the prosperity and the widening purchasing power of the well-to-do, the continued specialization of some peasants in the production of commercial goods made possible the extraordinary build-up of population on the fragmented holdings which is revealed in some manorial inventories. This build-up would remain quite inexplicable unless there had been the possibility of earning money outside agriculture.[93]

7. THE VILLAGE COMMUNITY AND THE ENTREPRENEURS

The growth of trade based on cattle and forest products had considerably raised the value of uncultivated land. In the thirteenth century it sometimes far exceeded the price of arable. On the outskirts of Paris an *arpent* of meadow was on the average twice as expensive as an *arpent* of ploughland[94]: In 1297 a *bonnier* of fullgrown trees in the region of Liège was let for 5 sous per annum, i.e. for twice as much as a *bonnier* of farmland. This enhancement in value encouraged owners of grassland and copse to put obstacles in the way of their haphazard use and, especially, to oppose the activities of settlers. The slowing down of the reclamation movement in the second quarter of the thirteenth century was in many cases mainly caused by the change in the value of the wastes. A little later this change in value even precipitated the desertion of some marginal clearings on very infertile soils. It was evident that exploitation of natural vegetation was more profitable than raising crops. And yet population was always getting denser and the fear of hunger more insistent.

The thirteenth century does not seem to have witnessed any rivalry between ploughmen and vinedressers. The production of wine for sale (it was of course exclusively high quality wine from the hillsides and suburbs and not yet wine from the plain) was confined to enclosures and vineyards and hardly encroached on the cereal-growing area. On the other hand foresters and shepherds began with increasing bitterness to cross swords with the men who wished to sow grain. In the early Middle Ages ploughland and pasture had been peacefully associated, since running the sheep flocks over the

[93] In 1267 in the district of Elloe in the English fenland, population was so closely packed on the village lands, even though these had been considerably enlarged by reclamation, that each inhabitant had hardly more than an acre of cultivated land at his disposal. How could these men have existed without getting from the neighbouring marshland not only a supplement to their food supply by fishing, stockrearing or salt extraction, but also considerable quantities of saleable products? Hallam, 299.

[94] Fontette, 340

fallow enriched the soil, and space was so abundant that the two could exist and develop side by side without hindrance. The progress of reclamation on the one hand and the new anxiety to protect hay and trees on the other, however, required the two to be more closely integrated. The area providing the food supply was much more restricted than before and consequently it had to be organized in an elaborate and rational manner. Competing interests met in head-on collision over attempts to decide the forms which this re-organization should assume. For this reason the thirteenth century was a period of interminable law suits, the accounts of which fill the muniment rooms and archives.

★   ★   ★

On one side was ranged the village community. It combined, in mutual interdependence, all the inhabitants of ancient *manses* who were primarily cultivators, but who also wished to enjoy the supplementary profits of stock-rearing, and this ambition was held most strongly by those who were not very well provided with land. For these men had at stake their collective rights in pasture and grazing over the whole of the village lands (with the exception of the homestead tofts close to the village) and especially over what remained after reclamation of the woodlands and pastureland. They resisted all attempts to reduce further the space still open to the communal flocks by those who wished to construct new cabins on the commons or plough up new fields there. They fought against permanent enclosure which was re-garded both as a symbol of individual appropriation and an obstacle in the way of the free run of cattle. As examples of the struggle, chosen from many other disputes whose traces are preserved in the rolls of the royal courts, here are two lawsuits brought in the same year 1221 by English village communi-ties against one of their members. In the first case the culprit had erected an enclosure in the middle of the grazing grounds; in the second he had ploughed up eight acres on the common land. At exactly the same period the whole village of Brétencourt in the south of the Forest of Rambouillet banded them-selves together behind their provost for a punitive expedition of reprisal in-tending to destroy the hedges and dwellings erected by the men of another community on their collective pasture.[95]

Villages also defended themselves against their own more enterprising inhabitants who tried to develop their sheep-farming activities to excess, or who, under a livestock (*gasaille*) contract or otherwise, introduced animals belonging to other people on to the grazing grounds. As a protection against such activities the rest of the inhabitants fixed the number of sheep and cows

[95] Document No. 49, p. 404; Darby, in 47; Archives Nationales, S.206, No. 29 (1224)

which each household had the right to send to the common, and levied taxes on beasts from outside. At the end of the thirteenth century in the southern Alps, Lombardy and the Apennines, village assemblies began to elaborate the first statutes of the forest which restricted within precise limits the use of the woodland by the inhabitants and kept closer watch on the flocks of the butchers. Finally the villagers rebelled against the lords who prohibited peasant access to the 'forest' reserved for hunting, from which deer, boar and other game emerged to damage the crops.[96]

The need to fight to defend themselves strengthened the peasants' feeling of solidarity. Throughout the west, the village community, as an association of all the heads of families created by neighbourly interests and welded together by the need to regulate the relationship between the private owner-ship of field and the collective ownership of uncultivated land, drew closer together. The built-up site became the hard kernel in the heart of the village lands. The prohibition on setting up house away from it became stricter, as a disciplinary measure against freelancing reclaimers and those who erected fences. It can be assumed that the large villages still to be seen today, sited in the middle of a largely open space, acquired their cohesion in the course of the thirteenth century. This concentration usually took place with the appro-val of the lord whose interest it also served, since he could thereby more conveniently control his assembled subjects. The religious authorities also encouraged a grouping of population which helped them to enforce dis-cipline and made it easier to ferret out heretics and those who attempted to evade their parish obligations.

★   ★   ★

However, at the same time the village was confronted by the growing appetite of the lords, who wanted to keep a larger portion of the as-yet-uncultivated land within the demesne. As dispensers of public justice and as the source of police authority over the fields the lords protected the com-mon lands; but under the pretext of defending them they also tried to arro-gate to themselves the right to regulate their use in their own way and to their own benefit. An increase of lordly power over the village lands and the customary fields, and its ever-heavier pressure on the common land, can be seen throughout the thirteenth century in every country in Europe. The transformation coincided with a closing of the ranks of the village com-munity. The two tendencies were certainly precipitated by the new econo-

---

[96] Documents Nos. 52, 53, 54, 55, pp. 407-409. In 1211 Philip Augustus promised not to introduce stags into the Bois de Boulogne; *Recueil des Actes*, No. 1279. In one Picardy village, according to an inquest conducted in 1317, 'the crops are devoured and destroyed by the beasts from the woods of Piquigny'; Archives Nationales, U.737, No. 23.

mic conditions; by the bait of the anticipated profits of forest management and sheep-farming as well as by the shrinking of the common grazing grounds. One significant fact is that the peasant communities in the Germanic countries which were able to maintain their rights over extensive pastures in the face of encroachment by the lords were situated in the only region where reclamation still left vast wildernesses untouched.[97]

In fact the nobles and monks who wielded power in the village tried to use it to appropriate for themselves the pasture rights and to exclude the community from them. Thus, in 1322 in the Provençal village of Sénas, the lords tried to reserve for themselves the exclusive privilege of sending their flocks to graze on the stubble.[98] At other times, the masters simply added a portion of the commons to their estate. Finally, they closed the commons entirely and excluded others from it. Very ancient custom recognized the right of neighbours to enter and to share in the free use of the uncultivated portions. But by the end of the twelfth century lords and their officials were endeavouring to restrict such use. The dues which the users had to pay, formerly light and merely a formal recognition of the lords' rights, were increased and little by little took on the appearance of a manorial levy on the profit of the sale of wood or the produce of sheep-rearing. The lord's forester began to be the peasants' most dreaded enemy. Then certain parts of the waste were declared 'forest' or 'warren', or 'hay' (enclosed wood). A ban was put on assarting or on pasturing, and infringements incurred heavy fines. By 1160 the settlers on the *villeneuves* of Bonneville in Beauce could not take their flock into the woods for three years after felling; and according to the *Établissements de Saint Louis*, 'if the customary tenant takes oxen or cows into the lord's wood if it is less than three years old, or a goat, he must pay a fine of 60 sous'. In the thirteenth century this protection of the young trees generally lasted until the 'fifth' or the 'seventh leaf', that is to say the period of exclusion protecting the saplings from flocks was prolonged to five or seven years.[99]

To these boundaries and limitations imposed with the lord's authority which continually forced the peasants' flocks back towards the village and into cultivated lands, were added others, which owners of the newly created peripheral demesnes on the fringes of the common land attempted to impose. These owners were often the lords who chose to set up house outside the

---

[97] Timm, 570   [98] Archives des Bouches-du-Rhône, B.3343, fol. 429ro

[99] *Établissements de saint Louis*, I, CLVIII; Olim, III, p. 59. Some villagers of Champagne obtained the right to send into the woods belonging to a knight *vaccas ad quintum folium equos post duos annos completos a tempore scissionis dicti nemoris, et communiter omnes bestias, absque etiam garda, tempore quo terra in tota patria et territoria cooperta est niva, et omni anno in die veniris in Passione Domini ac in die Resurrectionis ejusdem*; Olim, III, p. 56, No. XXII.

village proper in the middle of a demesne which to an ever greater extent they hedged round by protective regulations. These competing estates injured the rights of the village community and were sometimes formed at the expense of the collective grazing grounds and with the consent of the lord. At the beginning of the fourteenth century in many villages in Provence the lords let out as individual tenancies large sections of the outfield (*terre gaste*) to richer peasants who sometimes banded together to exploit the large grazing grounds outside and against the interest of the community.[100] All these lands lying in large blocs on the frontiers of the cultivated land tended to be surrounded by permanent hedges so that the grass could be wholly reserved for the owner's own flock. New conflicts and lawsuits were inevitably born as a result of these enclosures and attempts at farming in severalty.

* * *

The consequences differed from one place to another, since the relationship between the opposing forces also varied very greatly. But the new organization of the village lands they helped to establish was to last for many centuries. The first result was the partition of the huge grazing grounds common to several village groups; there was an end to the tacit intercommoning agreements so frequent between neighbouring communities in the early Middle Ages when the land was still largely waste. Within the cultivated area itself, the agreements which settled these quarrels imposed partition, that is, a strict delimitation of the sectors known as 'forbidden' (*défens*) or 'warren'. These were henceforth legitimately removed from collective use. In 1224 the monastery of Montmartre agreed to the division of its woods at Rouvray into two parts; one remained completely open to use by the peasants but the other was 'put out of bounds to animals', and the abbot kept the sole right of pasture there. In the same way the dean of the chapter of Meaux renounced in 1228, in favour of the count of Champagne, the right of usage held by five village communities bordering on the woods who were dependants of his manor in the forest of Brie. The dean received in exchange the entire disposal over another portion of the forest zone.[101] In the centre of

---

[100] Sclafert, 83, p. 29

[101] *Recueil des Chartes de l'abbaye royale de Montmartre* (ed. de Barthélemy), No. 122; Bibliothèque nationale, Ms. lat. 5993, A, fol. 483ro. Here is another more complicated example of partition. In 1276 the enclosed nuns of the Trinity at Nouaille in Poitou came to the following agreement with the villagers. The wood was to be divided into two equal parts. In the first the nuns reserved the right to fell trees for sale, and during the three following years to exclude the village flock. Thereafter the latter could graze freely, but the other part of the wood was then to be felled and the animals excluded for three years. The nuns kept their right to transform the whole wood into ploughland; but in such a case they agreed to leave the peasants to enjoy the right to graze freely on the harvested fields. (M.S.La Pu, 'Chartes et documents poitevins du XIIIe siècle en langue vulgaire', in *Archives historiques du Poitou*, LVII, 1960, pp. 66–68.)

the Paris basin the movement to divide up the woods appeared to get under way at the same time as the lords ceased to create new townships. The watershed between these two successive stages in the organization of the countryside was the twenties of the thirteenth century when the attitude of the local aristocracy towards the profits of the forest changed and they discovered that selling wood was more advantageous than exploiting new peasant communities by exacting dues from them. At more or less the same period – though north-western Germany was in this respect a good century behind – a very similar reorganization was taking place all over western Europe. By blocking agrarian expansion as irrevocably as backward technical conditions had done in the ninth century, these rearrangements helped to increase demographic tension in the villages. At the same time the conflict between woodland and 'plain' was accentuated.

*   *   *

All the measures in fact aimed at a definite segregation of peasant and manorial flocks and herds. In 1255, as a result of arbitration, the lords of a Provençal village were authorized to prohibit access to some woods, but were in return deprived of the right to cut hay and graze their oxen on the village lands; the right of common grazing there belonged solely to the peasants.[102] These agreements often legalized the formation of some permanent enclosures which reserved for individual use enclaves taken out of open spaces. The lords were usually the instigators of these enclosures and benefited from them. We know how in England the Statute of Merton in 1236 allowed them to plant hedges on the manorial waste on condition that they left enough pasture for their tenants, and then how in 1285 the Statute of Westminster extended their rights to enclose the commons.[103] Permanent barriers like these reinforced the protection of the prohibited areas which up till then had been assured by custom and by the threat of fines alone. They were erected mostly around portions of the demesne, whether these were cultivated by domestics or let out on lease. But permission to create permanent enclosures was also often given to other large cultivators, such as townsmen who had bought land and pasture within the cultivated spaces, or the better-off peasants. Both types wished to evade the communal constraints which did not benefit them as they did the poor.

All these enclosures were erected either on the ancient common land or else on its fringes. One rental drawn up in the fourteenth century in north Warwickshire allows the position of the enclosures to be traced; they were

---

[102] F. Allemand, 'Histoire de Jarjayes', in *Bulletin de la Societé d'études des Hautes-Alpes*, 1895
[103] Darby, 47, p. 189

almost all located on the site of former woodlands on the edge of the open field; but some had bitten into the anciently cultivated village lands around plots held in severalty. We can also see that most of these hedges had been planted by the more enterprising villagers who were closely linked with wool merchants and who had abandoned agriculture for sheep-farming. To such an extent that here and there in the second half of the thirteenth century hedgerows began gradually to reappear in the midst of open country on the parts of the village lands where the rights of the peasant community had been less well defended, and allowed to fall into abeyance. But, as we have seen, hedges spread more thickly in the less densely settled regions in which the village communities were faint-hearted and unresisting and where later, individualistic forms of reclamation, clearly based on sheep-farming, helped its progress.

★　　★　　★

On the old village lands the new arrangement prevented the peasant flocks from entering a large part of the woods and pastures, and permanent fences also closed off some of the arable. How in these circumstances could the smaller folk obtain sufficient keep for their animals? Probably many of them were forced to reduce their livestock. The growth of a pastoral economy dominated by capital, like the improvement of agricultural equipment, helped to create the powerful antagonisms between rich and poor which wracked village society at the end of the thirteenth century. But the small cultivators struggled hard to avoid losing completely the essential support which they obtained from keeping animals. While the rich reserved the best meadows and most extensive pasture for their speculations, the poor endeavoured to find a substitute for grassland on the arable land which was left to them. The archeology of farming equipment suggests that in Germany of the fourteenth century the sickle, which had once left the stalks of corn standing in the fields, was replaced at reaping time by the scythe. This change indicates the new interest which small cultivators began to take in straw. The straw provided litter for cattle when the shrinking grazing grounds made it harder to collect bracken or leaves; above all it was a substitute fodder. Fields were now treated in the same way as meadows; they were cut close to the ground. This was a preliminary expedient.[104] Apart from this, and most important, the collective right of communal grazing was strengthened on the portion of the cultivated lands which still escaped enclosure. The lords lent themselves to these arrangements because they saw in the proliferation of detailed regulations more frequent opportunities to penalize infringements and thus to collect fines. A strict calendar was laid down which protected the

[104] Timm, 135

grass and young corn on individual plots between certain dates, raised the penalties for damage by animals and permitted cultivators to mark with 'signs' strips which carried a crop and were temporarily out of bounds. But any illegal enclosure was rooted out. In documents of the thirteenth century from Lorraine, mention of hedges becomes less frequent at the same time as the first references to the communal shepherd appear. At the heart of the ancient village lands given over to peasant cultivation these measures made the open-field landscape more homogeneous. Henceforth it was in striking contrast to the landscape of enclosures.[105]

The increasing price of wood in fact made it impossible to go on erecting temporary wooden enclosures, while repeated divisions among heirs, which from now on were to be permitted by the lords, divided the land into an infinite number of parcels and broke it up into tiny lots. In these conditions the surest way of safeguarding the crops from the dangerous proximity of sheep flocks was to reassemble piece by piece the lands which had to be ploughed and harvested at the same time. It was also necessary to impose on all the inhabitants of the village (on all, at least, who had not acquired the right to enclose their property), a common discipline of crop rotation, and thus to form compact courses, some for winter and spring corn, on which the flocks came to graze the stubble after harvest time, others for the fallow, open for one or more entire years to free grazing. It appears that compulsory rotation became established on certain village territories at the very moment when the intensification of cereal cultivation and the shrinking of the wastelands required a stricter dovetailing of arable with pasture. The institution of compulsory crop rotation was favoured by the strengthening of the manorial authority and the concomitant consolidation of the village communities. In the German Rhineland, the only region where up till now research in depth has been carried out, obvious traces of this practice cannot be seen before the end of the thirteenth century.[106] It was the period when reclamation succeeded in reducing the extent of the surrounding belt of grassland and pasture, and when consequently it became very urgent to regulate the grazing on the fallow of animals whose numbers had now become excessively large. But the control of crop rotation did not penetrate into the southern regions of France. There on soils which were much less homogeneous there still existed in the proximity of each arable settlement sufficient areas of 'wooded land' *saltus* or *garrigue*; furthermore transhumance often made it possible to send livestock to find its keep further afield. One can think of highly regulated field systems with complete management of crop rotation as one of the remedies against the shortage of food sought by a population whose agricultural progress and the development of exchanges had for three long cen-

---

[105] Planhol, 79   [106] Juillard, 66; Schröder-Lembke, 130

turies permitted a free expansion but who at the approach of the year 1300 found themselves again too numerous.

Our survey has with some difficulty traced the stages of economic development and the many changes it made on the face of the medieval countryside. Can it now provide us with a chronology? We cannot but be aware that our knowledge is too full of holes and is too patchy to permit an ambitious scheme, and we have to recognize the immense disparity between the rhythm of development in Italy, which was already full of active towns before the year 1000, and Saxony, which on the eve of the thirteenth century was still in a prehistoric state, all forests and pastoral life. Yet, since the sole aim of this account is to encourage the pursuit of research, the attempt has to be made, and an outline must be sketched whose provisional character will be sufficient excuse for its temerity and lack of precision. Allowing a wide margin for the obvious discrepancies between advanced and backward regions, the following may be said, in the present state of historical knowledge, to be the main phases of economic development.

1. The beginnings of expansion are lost in the mists of the tenth century.

2. The growth of population and all-but invisible improvements in technique raised crop yields and carried agricultural progress forward. In the second half of the eleventh century, first developments of exchange began to make economic relations more flexible, to quicken the circulation of money in the countryside, and to stimulate the activities of craftsmen. Little by little the cultivated areas grew larger, helped perhaps by the diffusion of iron tools. It is tempting to place the most intense phase of the agrarian progress at about the middle of the twelfth century.

3. The four or five decades which precede and succeed the year 1200 mark a turning point in the expansion. Agricultural growth continued very briskly, encouraged by the rapid rise in the price of cereals evident in certain regions. But the financial difficulties from which many great lords then suffered, and which were widespread among the middle ranks of the aristocracy, are proof of a sudden commercial growth and the opening up of markets in various products, many of which came directly from the land. All these were signs of economic change, which showed itself through the institution of a succession of fairs and the organization of regional markets and a powerful urban growth. The rapid success of viticulture in France is another sign of economic progress.

4. After the first quarter of the thirteenth century the rise in the level of material culture, evident mainly through the enrichment of the diet and the spread of aristocratic fashions amongst people of lower rank, continued and

inflated the arteries of commercial life. We can sense that there was a growing demand for non-agricultural commodities, the value of which constantly rose. At the same time amongst those in charge of agricultural production appeared many men well versed in rational methods of management who were as attentive to the fluctuations of the markets as they were to the theories of the agriculturists.

5. The halt in grain expansion came in the period which can be dated between 1275 and 1330. In most regions, including those that had most benefited from it, arable ceased to gain from the wastes, and even began at certain points to lose ground; production of cereals faltered. This did not prevent the rural economy as a whole from wearing at this moment an air of solid prosperity. But nevertheless we notice that the antagonism between the small country people and the increasing band of entrepreneurs became sharper. The condition of the former deteriorated; they became too numerous and found it hard to feed themselves; when they were not scattered and isolated from each other, as in the areas where colonization was carried on by dispersed and isolated individuals, they formed themselves into vigorous defensive communities in the villages, closely linked together by the joint interest of the compulsory crop rotation. The entrepreneurs succeeded in building up individual farming units directly linked with trade; they went on improving their tools and perfecting techniques. In order to intensify grain production, in particular, they applied more complex rotational systems and engaged more labourers to till the soil more thoroughly. Nevertheless their special interests were the vineyard, the woodland, the grassland, and the management of their flocks, which yielded the larger part of their profits.

BOOK III

XI-XIII Centuries

BOOK III

XI-XIII Centuries

The Manor and the Rural Economy

The existence of small allods of land which were farmed in freedom by peasant families can only be surmised from the documents of the early Middle Ages. But after the year 1000 references to them appear much more frequently. Peasant free ownership can be assumed to have existed everywhere except in England, where the legal basis of landownership was entirely built upon the notion of tenure. In France recent research has brought to light the widespread existence of free holdings throughout the feudal period, of which I shall quote two examples. By a piece of good luck we know all the landowners in one small village territory in the Mâconnais about the year 1100 because one after another they ceded their possessions to the abbey of Cluny. Amongst these landowners were 15 peasants. Six of them held portions of their farms from a lord, but the lands of all the rest were absolutely free and untrammelled by any obligation. Fifty years later, of 65 landowning peasants on a part of another Burgundian village only two were tenants in the real sense of the word. True enough, the others possessed a few fields held of one or more lords, but the *manses* where their families lived and the plots they had recently won from the forest they owned fully and freely.[1] Furthermore, the documents often mention quite humble people, serfs and men who could not freely dispose of their bodies, as being in possession of free land.

The documents also indicate that the existence of these small free properties was threatened. To begin with they were menaced by the custom of charitable donations. Nearly every time one of these peasant properties appears in a written deed it is because it had just been added by gift to the possessions of a great religious foundation. They were also apt to be broken up through division amongst heirs: such division caused the general and continuous decline of all lay estates, but land held in tenure was much better

[1] Duby, 261, pp. 296, 374

protected than land in the absolute ownership of a single family. Lastly these allods had to resist the heavy pressure of the manorial system. In the Mâconnais village territory which I have just referred to, the six peasants who owned freely only portions of their land had very recently lost the completely independent status of some of their property by surrendering the eminent domain to one of the great landowners of the district. Did they do this freely in return for protection? Or did they submit against their will to the superior force of an invasive power? Whatever may have been the reason in this particular case, large estates always benefited at the expense of the smaller; they surrounded them, overshadowed them and finally swallowed them up.

At the same time everywhere on the continent free peasant properties were being re-assembled in a hundred different ways. They grew through contracts of *complant* by which in the eleventh and twelfth centuries humble men as well as lords created their vineyards.[2] They grew also, and perhaps most often, by fraudulent means, by the surreptitious appropriation of badly supervised lands, by lords neglecting to demand rents and thereby losing the legal right to do so conferred by collective memory and custom. When for years no rent had been paid, this or that field or meadow was assumed to owe nothing and everyone considered it to be free. In this way reclamation created a fringe of independent land on the borders of the manorial wastes. The uncultivated lands on the banks of the Garonne had remained unsupervised for many years and when, in 1309, the rights of the duke of Guyenne were being overhauled, the commissioners discovered small allodial holdings all over them. They found themselves at loggerheads with the owners, many of them very humble, who energetically refused to admit that their land was subject to anyone else.[3]

Lands without a lord, constantly in the process of recreation, were to be found everywhere: and not only in countries like Frisia where the manor had never taken root. Nowhere did manorial possessions in fact encompass all village lands; the latter often comprised vast areas consisting of small peasant proprietorships.[4] Moreover small proprietors often banded together to defend the legality of their independent property and to resist the encroachments of their masters. They formed the most active element in the village community which was everywhere in the thirteenth century the constituent cell of rural society juxtaposed to the lord's household. Even in England historians have for some time admitted that peasant society was not organized solely around the 'manor', and that even though the custom of the country did not admit the principle of allodial holdings, there were many so free that in practice they evaded nearly all real tenurial obligations.

[2] See p. 139   [3] Boutruche, 184, pp. 66 *et seq.*
[4] For example in the Lombard village described in Romeo, 481

Nevertheless, the manor of the feudal period appears as an extraordinarily complex institution. It was not restricted to rights over land; the term itself is an ambiguous one with a variable meaning. The individual whom the peasant of that time called his lord, and the man described by contemporary documents as *dominus*, *sire* or *Herr*, did not always own the superior title to the land. A small cultivator might well consider he was an allodial holder, but he could none the less be subject to an overlord to whose economic domination he submitted. The master could be his personal lord, to whom he was bound by strict ties of loyalty, and who could impose upon him strict obligations which would continue to be binding on his children. The master could be his leader in time of war, a holder of private justice and exclusive rights (*ban*), charged with policing the district, responsible for defence and in return able to levy dues from local inhabitants. If there was none other, the master could be the king, and the peasant could suffer directly from his demands and requisitions. Although called free, the small allod was thus always answerable to an economic overlordship which in one way or another appropriated a part of its output. Furthermore, the condition of a small farm was always influenced by the mere presence in its neighbourhood of a large manorial household. The latter dominated the local market through its purchases and sales. It controlled the agricultural calendar by the manner and the order in which it cultivated its fields scattered all over the village territory. Because at certain seasons of the year it engaged day labourers; because it sometimes acted as a go-between to negotiate with outside buyers of farm products; because at times it offered help and credit – for all these reasons the manor, without appearing to do so, held the small free proprietors of the district in thrall. In Carolingian times this domination can only be surmised, but after the year 1000 it emerges into the open. None of the independent peasant properties was ever very far from a manorial centre. Because of the activity it generated in the heart of the surrounding farmlands, as well as because of the traffic of wealth and employment it called into circulation between the peasant households legally subject to it and its administrative headquarters, the manor, large or small, was undeniably the chief motive force of the rural economy. Thus when in the earlier pages of this book we outlined the general conditions favouring expansion we found that the manor always occupied the commanding position.

The economy of the manor therefore merits special consideration, especially since the light thrown by our documents during this period falls directly upon it. Yet even so, its story remains full of uncertainties. The destiny of every manor was individual and its structure unique. Finally its economic organization was largely dependent upon the personality of the man who at any particular moment administered it.[5] It is difficult to make proper allowances for all these variables. Far too few monographs yet exist for us to have the hardihood to depict regional types or to describe a simple outline of development through the ages. We must, nevertheless, try to see how the history of the manor entered into the general development of the economic life which we have so hesitantly analyzed and hedged around with so many preliminary hypotheses. In doing so, we may be advised to use, despite its imperfections, the chronological outline with which the last chapter terminated, and I therefore propose to keep the year 1200 as the dividing line, and shall begin by formulating the principal problems of manorial history in the eleventh and twelfth centuries.

[5] See, for example, the abbey of Fécamp, Musset, 465, and the monastery of Saint-Martin of Tournai, Haenens, 663

CHAPTER I

Wealth and Power
in the XI and XII Centuries

The early period is obscured by the poverty of the sources. The use of writing was almost exclusively restricted to the narrow world of high ecclesiastics, and, as even in those circles hardly anyone troubled to keep accounts, there are few or no figures. All documents, therefore, come from religious establishments. The most communicative are the inventories compiled in the tradition of the Carolingian *polyptyques*, the rentals (*censiers*), or lists of obligations; these were called custumals (*coutumiers*) since they included the *coutumes* or impositions, taxes which were no longer levied on holdings, but on 'men', who were dependants and subjects.[1] Nevertheless, even these invaluable documents are scarce. Most of our information comes from cartularies, collections of different kinds of deeds which vouchsafed the integrity of the manorial patrimony, registered the acquisitions which constantly enriched it and recorded successful lawsuits, the victories over rival manors. Domesday Book, the royal inquest of 1086, which sheds such extraordinary light on the English countryside, is quite unique.

All this documentary material thus yields relatively little evidence about economic phenomena. It deals mostly with juridical matters, such as titles to land and the relationship of one man to another through ties of protection and obedience. This, however, reflects very faithfully the main trend of the period. In the eleventh and twelfth centuries commerce was beginning to come to life, yet it remained in a subordinate position: it was (except in Italy which always led western advance in these matters by at least a hundred years) too superficial and peripheral to modify at all profoundly the traditional structure inherited from the early Middle Ages. The dominant force influencing the direction in which the manorial economy developed came from the changed distribution of the powers of authority.

I. THE LANDED PATRIMONY OF THE GREAT RELIGIOUS FOUNDATIONS

The documents of this period have most to teach us about the history of the great estates, and particularly of the great ecclesiastical estates. The latter

[1] Perrin, 200, pp. 589 *et seq.*

173

continued to be enriched by an inexhaustible flow of alms. Religious opinion, still somewhat simple, considered that offering the material things of this world to God's servants was an act of piety deserving salvation. All Christian men gave, and gave often. They gave what they had in plenty and what they judged to be most valuable, which was naturally land. The religious attitudes of this period were thus responsible for immense transfers of wealth which, at the expense of lay estates, created and nourished innumerable Church-owned manors. The largely ecclesiastical origin of our sources should not blind us to the fact that this stream of pious donations was indeed the most powerful current animating the economic life of the time.

The flow of donations can in fact be divided into several phases of unequal intensity and direction, and it is both useful and relatively simple to outline the chronology for the different regions.[2] The culminating phase for Europe as a whole should probably be placed at the end of the tenth and the beginning of the eleventh century. At that period any act of mortal sin was an occasion for a devout man to make a gift of atonement proportionate in size to his resources; a king for instance might present a whole district. Benedictine abbeys and cathedral churches were the chief beneficiaries. The entire landed possessions of Ely Cathedral in England, for example, were built up between 970 and 1020,[3] and it was during the same period that the deeds of acquisition by gift were most closely concentrated in the cartularies of Cluny.

The zeal of the donors gradually waned in the second half of the eleventh century. We can see here the effects of a greater spirituality, of the discovery of a more heroic and truly charitable principle of Christian behaviour. Probably men came to attach greater value to other 'good works', such as undertaking long pilgrimages and succouring travellers; these works were harder to perform than simple acts of giving and therefore more certain of earning salvation. But the reduction in pious donations must also be related to a movement of retrenchment on the part of the lay aristocracy. Impoverished by the generosity of their ancestors, noblemen began to show a greater inclination to protect their landed inheritance, the chief bulwark of their social standing, from being imprudently dissipated. Gifts, then, became much smaller and less frequent; we can see from the cartularies that they were gradually reduced to funeral offerings and the niggardly endowment of services in memory of deceased persons. Almsgiving of other kinds, however,

[2] The statistical method suggested by D. Herlihy in 249 merits attention. It begins by establishing the proportion of ecclesiastical lands among the parcels of landed property dealt with in the documents and proceeds to analyze the extent to which these proportions varied. They reached 40 per cent of the total at the beginning of the tenth century and declined to 15 per cent towards the year 1200.

[3] Miller, 198, p. 23

remained active. Around the year 1100, shaken by the sermons of reforming priests, lay lords surrendered the ownership of nearly all rural churches and ceded them to chapters and monasteries; these churches formed the nucleus of new ecclesiastical demesnes to which were added, little by little, the small donations of humble parishioners. At the same time, all lords of any standing founded collegiate churches in their castles, since they wished to have near them educated men able to conduct their affairs and to educate the younger members of their households.

The twelfth century was for the ancient religious foundations preeminently the age of disputes and lawsuits. In these quarrels they did not always succeed in making their neighbours refrain from infringements of their temporalities. The rights of the older church foundations, therefore, were at this period to a certain extent encroached upon, and, as we have seen, they were receiving hardly any additional land from charitable gifts. They were able, however, to an increasing degree to buy land. Money, particularly through important gifts of cash from the newly-rich town burgesses, came more readily into their hands than into the hands of the lay lords. It should be noticed besides that the flow of gifts of land had not entirely dried up; it had merely been diverted to other religious houses which, by following a way of life more in keeping with new concepts of piety, now caught the favour of the faithful. Such gifts speedily enriched the ascetic and solitary Cistercian communities, the regular or Carthusian canons, the commanderies of the Knights Templars, and Hospitallers. In this way new religious estates grew, especially in the regions into which the possessions of the old churches had not previously extended. Nevertheless, whatever success the latest wave of foundations achieved, their domains were usually confined to the most unproductive sites; they were concentrated in the immediate vicinity of the established monastic headquarters within reach of direct exploitation, and they never achieved the tremendous rate of growth which had, at about the year 1000, spread the possession of the great abbeys throughout whole provinces.

*   *   *

In actual fact the possessions often proved to be too large. Many religious foundations received more land in the eleventh century than they knew what to do with, certainly more than they required for their own sustenance and for their charitable needs, and much more than their administrators could manage. Economic life was of course still too limited for anyone to dream of organizing a manor for the purpose of regular sale of its surpluses. Even had this possibility occurred at that time to the heads of these communities the notion of gain and enterprise would have seemed repugnant to the ecclesiastical conscience. As in Carolingian times only one thing mattered to the administrators of a monastery or chapter: how to support the 'family' in plenty without pinching or fear of shortage.

A large part of the property of these establishments was therefore granted to 'friends', members of great families with whom the Church had connections and whose protection and favours it wished to enjoy. In law these were purely temporary concessions, although they were in most cases regularly renewed at each generation; the land was thus incorporated into the family possessions of the beneficiaries. The concessions were furthermore almost all gratuitous. Some took the form of fiefs which required no more from their holders than homage or 'services', which were often vague. More frequently these possessions were the subject of a contract of *precaria* or, as it was called in Italy, of *livello*[4]; the church retained the nominal ownership and levied an annual charge of a few coins serving as a symbol of allegiance, but not economically significant. As the influence of Gregorian ideas established itself and as almsgiving declined, some ecclesiastical administrators began towards the end of the eleventh century to condemn these gifts, to forbid them and to endeavour to recover the 'benefits' bestowed by their predecessors. The greater number, however, continued in the hands of the lay lords, and in this way somewhat compensated for the losses of private patrimony caused by the pious offerings of their forefathers.

Despite this, however, the estates of many of the older foundations remained enormous. Their extent and their dispersal presented the administrators with intractable problems of management. How were properties so immeasurably vast and often so remote to be profitably used? How could they be supervised and how could their output be gathered in?

*   *   *

In the eleventh century the landed property of the monasteries and cathedral churches which had not been granted on leases of *precaria* or as fiefs was usually divided into several units of manorial administration. Each was of a sufficiently restricted size to be capable of direct and efficient supervision. Thus the estate of St Emmeram of Ratisbon was in 1030 divided into thirty-three demesne groups. The monastic lands of Cluny were divided at the end of the eleventh century into a score of 'deaneries' and in most chapters of canons the joint property was arranged in portions called 'prebends' or 'obediences'.[5] Each of these administrative units was as far as possible entrusted to one of the members of the religious community, who had the sole charge and performed his function autonomously. In many

---

[4] Déléage, 218, p. 599; Fiumi, 141; Didier, 433, p. 257
[5] Dollinger, 159; Duby, 441

abbeys a broad interpretation of the Benedictine rule authorized a monk to be installed in each rural manor. Those canons who were not under the strict compulsion of communal life resided from time to time on the lands belonging to the prebendary offices they occupied. Very often these men exercised by delegation the lord's functions over the very same lands which their families had once upon a time given to the monastery. Bequeathed from uncle to nephew and enriched from one generation to the next by the generosity of the family many such canonical prebends became satellites, indeed almost annexes, of the estates of the great families of the region.[6] By introducing one of their sons as a novice or lay brother into a local monastery and ensuring that he would later be allowed to administer the lands given by their ancestors, many lords could keep an eye on the former family property of their relations. Situations of this sort added to the confusion between the lands of the church and the nobility and minimized the effects of the excessive charity of the latter.

Religious duties nevertheless prevented ecclesiastical managers from residing permanently in the 'hall' in their care, and even when they were on the spot they could not devote all their attention to manorial business. In general, and especially during their absence, they delegated their powers to lay officials. Documents call these lay servants *villici*, as in Carolingian times, or else 'reeves' or 'mayors'. These men, who were perfectly competent, although often very humble, performed the true managerial function.

The activities of the lay managers brings us to the concrete realities of the manorial economy. Its boundary was limited: lands and various rights were normally dispersed over several villages and the surrounding uncultivated spaces, but they were always within reach of supervision and so situated that a man on foot could easily visit the most distant dependency within a day. The 'manor' was all grouped around the 'hall', the residence, the house of the master, but this focal point also harboured the agent, wholly in command of his job, who knew each tenant and dependant personally and whom they respected; who remembered what each man owed, what each field could be expected to yield, and what the sales of the last market brought in. In this way the economic unit of the ecclesiastical manor differed very little in extent and form from the *villa* as described in the *polyptyques* of the Frankish era.

*   *   *

The chief difficulty, as it had been in former times, was to maintain the link between these subsidiary centres and the household of the masters which they supported. The problem presented itself in exactly the same way as in

[6] Raftis, 201, p. 11; Duby, 261, p. 216

the ninth century. For some ecclesiastical landlords the solution was simple. Bishops, like kings and counts, could move about freely and could travel in person from one demesne to another. They possessed in each a well-built mansion. In the twelfth century French bishops fortified these rural dwellings; they settled down with their retinue and cavalry on each one in turn, consumed the contents of granary and cellar on the spot and gave their orders directly to their agents. The procedure was precisely the same as in Carolingian days. Similarly, the prebendary canons consumed a part of the fruits of their endowment on the spot and arranged for the transport of the rest to the headquarters.

But monks lived together in communities and were obliged to stay there. Furthermore their diet and the necessities of their daily life were subject to strict rules. Their manors had thus to be directed from afar, as well as to provide the exact requirements for their needs which had to be conveyed to the refectory. To achieve all this the manorial economy had to be most meticulously regulated. There could be no question of extracting as much as possible from the land. On the contrary the first care was to even out fluctuations, to ensure a stable revenue falling due on regular dates and closely adjusted to rates of consumption which were themselves not subject to change. Good monastic officials were thus those who knew how to estimate exactly the domestic consumption of brethren and servants, and the requirements for alms and the sustenance of travellers, in terms of rations and weight of grain. The persistence of the formulae applied in the ninth century is very striking, for in fact the Statutes of Adalard of Corbie served as a guide for many officials of eleventh- and twelfth-century monasteries.[7]

In order to provide for such precisely defined requirements, the main task was to allocate the responsibility for provisioning amongst the different manorial units according to their respective capacities. We know from several documents how Peter the Venerable, abbot of Cluny in the early twelfth century, resolved this problem. He directed some of the twenty-three deaneries to specialize in particular commodities: for instance, one, on which the oat crop was highest, had to supply the stables, the rest had to take their turn in providing the general requirements of the household. Each manor had to be the sole supplier during a given period of time, and all together had to provide enough for the whole year. The theoretical period of supply was one month and so the word *mesagium* or *mesaticum* was used to describe the system, and we can see that it was employed throughout the Christian world. It was in use in the abbeys of north-west Germania from the tenth century onwards: their *villici* had to supply the refectory in turn. In the English manors of Ely the provision of supplies was distributed weekly between

[7] See the case of Cluny in Duby, 441

thirty-three manors, while on the Rochester manors the order of succession
– *ordo maneriorum quomodo firmas facere debent* – divided the year from Michaelmas to Michaelmas into periods of 24 days each.[8]

The difficulty was obviously to adjust the period of supply to the real
output of each satellite manor; their crops varied considerably from year to
year; their area and output was constantly being modified by the flow o
alms, the outcome of lawsuits and grants. In 1148 Peter the Venerable, after
much trial and error and many alterations, thought he had achieved an
equitable distribution, but by 1155 he had to undertake another enquiry into
the deaneries in order to balance more equally the revenue and the charges on
each of them.[9] Normally in order not to restrict unduly the rations distributed to the members of the community in bad years, a large margin had to
be allowed for and in practice a limited portion only of the normal profits
of each manorial unit was demanded, and the remainder was left at the disposal of the local manager. It is true he was expected to transmit what was
left over to the household and especially to hand over all the money which
the sales of the surplus had brought in. But in reality he was allowed great
freedom of action and the system turned him into a completely independent
entrepreneur.

In this way the particular system of management came very close to
'farming'. Besides, the 'farm' itself was employed in conjunction with the
organization of the *mesaticum*, especially in England. There such a system was
an ancient custom. Before the Norman Conquest Saxon villages had to
render to the kings and earls fixed quantities of food. The unit of service here
was the 'night'. This was in fact the obligation of shelter and maintenance at
a fixed rate (*droit de gîte*). In this connection the word *feorm* was used, which
meant provision. After 1066 the word was quite naturally confused in the
minds of the Norman clerks with the word and concept of *firma* or 'farm'.[10]
In any case in English documents at the end of the eleventh century and the
twelfth century it is common on church properties to find at the head of a
manorial unit a man called *firmarius* who was neither the delegate of the religious community nor a servant. He was the holder of a concession who for a
certain period, most often for his lifetime, wielded the powers of the lord.
The land and the peasants living on it, the labour services which they owed,
the whole process of cultivation, the *instauramentum*, the cattle, sometimes
even the stock of cereals, were given to him. The contract by which he was
bound was comparable to the contract of *precaria*, with the difference that it
entailed a heavy service of provisioning. The 'farmer' undertook to maintain
the estate in good condition. In principle, if liveries of food were not kept

---

[8] Duby, 441; Miller, 198, p. 38; Lennard, 268, pp. 130-133
[9] Duby, 442   [10] Lennard, 268, p. 128

up and the property was neglected the concession was terminated. The contract was thus essentially one of 'lease' and when the beneficiary was not an important person the lord preserved control of his manor. The lord was also permitted to increase the total of annual supplies which he expected from the manor if its capacity was increased. For this purpose periodic assessments were made which permitted an appreciation of the *valor* of the property and made it easier to revise the dues. In fact the output of the 'farms' on the properties of Ramsey Abbey doubled between 1086 and 1140.[11]

It does not appear as if this process, so convenient for monks wishing to spare themselves the troubles of direct management, was employed in the English countryside alone. In Saxony and the Rhineland at the end of the twelfth century, manors owned by the Church were often granted for life or for a fixed period to a *villicus* in exchange for a *pensio* or a fixed participation in provisioning the household.[12] In the Ile de France lands were also granted in *mainferme*. How widespread was this practice? We can see that the proportion of leases for life decreased in the twelfth century. But Abbot Suger notes that he confided the manor of Beaune-la-Rolande in the Gâtinais to agents under contracts renewable annually. The spread of such lease-like arrangements in feudal times is still badly recorded, and the charters would have to be examined in detail to reveal the exact information we need.[13]

The managers of the Church manors, whether they were 'farmers' or stewards, were obliged, as in the early Middle Ages when their masters were unable to consume the produce on the spot, to transport it. In the mid-twelfth century a flotilla of boats was still hauled up the Rhine each year by the men and horses of the abbey of Deutz in the direction of the demesnes which it possessed near the river. They made regular halts in the vicinity of each manor and the managers fed the men and their animals and loaded the boats with grain, poultry and smaller animals while the pigs were driven in herds along the bank.[14] This activity continued Carolingian practice and, like it, wasted a great deal of labour. Some administrators, however, considered it advantageous to commute liveries in kind by transferring money. Local managers had for some time been accustomed to sell part of the demesne surplus; and the growth of exchange and increasing flexibility of the monetary media permitted an extension of commercial operations. The more frequent intervention of cash in the contacts between dependent manors and the headquarters of their masters was the most conspicuous change affecting the properties of the Church in the eleventh and twelfth centuries.

The example of England shows clearly, however, that this change was

[11] Raftis, 201, pp. 76 *et seq.*; Lennard, 268, pp. 190 *et seq.*
[12] Latouche, 227, p. 336; Document No. 122, p. 476
[13] Schnapper, 474   [14] Sloet, 205, No. 302 (1155-1165)

not always one of continuous progress. Very early, from the time of our first documents, a mixed system of money dues and supplies of provisions was in force on certain demesnes, like those of Ramsey Abbey; both *censa* and *firma* were combined in 'farming'.[15] If there was commutation of liveries, this was always because of the particular needs of the headquarters, and the relative ease of buying or selling commodities on the spot. And we do not always see the conversion taking place in the same direction: the proportion of cash sometimes shrank. Thus during the first half of the twelfth century the practice of 'farming in kind' was maintained and even extended in a general manner on the English abbeys; a rebirth of monasticism augmented the numbers of the different communities and increased the volume of domestic consumption and the difficulties of victualling; so that more had to be brought to the refectories. By the same token after 1150 the movement was reversed although for different reasons. On the manors of Canterbury it was the reduction in the number of monks which caused a diminution in the proportion of agricultural commodities from the demesnes. But the administrators of the abbey of Ramsey were forced in the same direction by a greater weight of indebtedness and the need to find money at all costs. On the other hand financial difficulties at Cluny provoked by the drying up of the flow of precious metal from Spain led to the reorganization of the system of *mesaticum*; in order to cut down expenditure, more abundant liveries of the produce were required from each subsidiary manor.[16]

The situation peculiar to each community and the personal actions of those in charge thus produced very different solutions – a warning to historians to be very chary of hasty generalizations. The documents, however, lead us to think that the part played by money in the internal economy of the great ecclesiastical properties was less restricted at the end of the twelfth century than it was around the year 1000. I take as an example St Paul's in London, whose estate consisted of twenty manors. In 1181 only six out of the twenty delivered a 'farm' entirely in agricultural commodities: the dues from eight others were mixed, while the remaining six remitted only money to the community.[17] Here the bond between masters and their land was very loose. The responsible administrators enjoyed very great autonomy. Their attention was directed to the movement of prices and market conditions and they were encouraged to indulge in buying and selling; the spirit of profit-making began to motivate them. This changed attitude and the transfer of initiative to intermediary agents, were they deans, stewards or farmers, no doubt helped to set in motion the general advance which the economy of the countryside was experiencing at that time.

[15] Raftis, 201, p. 10; for Ely Cathedral see Miller, 198, p. 40.
[16] Lennard, 268, p. 139; Duby, 441 and 442   [17] Lennard, 268, p. 179

2. LAY FORTUNES

Although the destinies of the lay fortunes were intermingled with those of the great Church patrimonies, their history was subject to very different influences. They were in fact dominated by forces whose effects were mostly those of disintegration. Lay fortunes were not only reduced by charitable gifts, but also frittered away by divisions amongst heirs. In the few regions where eleventh-century documents are able to dissipate some of the obscurity we can see aristocratic families gradually being deprived of the best lands by pious gifts and replaced as lords by the Church: while some collateral branches of prolific families found themselves in a few generations reduced by the splitting up of the inheritance to the level of modest free allodial peasants.[18] In this way lay estates went through a gradual process of erosion.

There were nevertheless defensive measures. Most great families managed to maintain themselves in an economic position which was well above that of the peasantry. They profited from the sometimes spontaneous and sometimes forced liberality of the Church; from grants of *precaria*, of fiefs, and of *livelli*; and there were even some lay lords who did not disdain to take on the 'farming' of demesnes. Furthermore, they were drawn together by family solidarity. By controlling more strictly individual alienations of the ancestral lands, families succeeded in reducing the effects of charitable gifts. The effects of the customs of inheritance which had everywhere conferred equal rights in allodial land on heirs of equal rank were noticeably relieved by maintaining the property undivided in the joint possession of groups of relations, by limitation of marriages, and finally by the institution in the twelfth century of dowry money which in certain regions excluded married daughters from a share in the land.

Finally agricultural expansion at that period increased returns from all aristocratic properties. Higher yields from demesne fields, larger revenues from tithes, mills and the taxes levied on users of woods and pastures, gave noble families a higher standard of living than their ancestors had enjoyed, although their landed properties were less extensive. More important still, these families took a much closer interest in reclamation than did the ecclesiastical lords. In Germany the unflagging vitality of the nobility from Carolingian times onwards was upheld by the uninterrupted conquest of the new arable lands. In France the demesnes of the aristocracy, which were being inexorably eaten away by the advance of the Church estates into the anciently cultivated portions of the village lands, were gradually reconstructed at the expense of the forest. The demesnes thus slowly detached themselves from the village, and in documents at the end of the twelfth century they appear

---

[18] Duby, 261, pp. 58 *et seq.*

to have been removed to the fringes of the remaining forest and to the hills. In most of the *pariage* contracts which founded new villages and in which religious foundations were associated with lay lords, the latter reserved for themselves on the assart the nucleus of a little demesne, the house and court-yard where the new revenues expected from the enterprise could be gathered.[19]

All these forces of restoration explain how the aristocracy in the eleventh and twelfth centuries emerged as dominant and secure economically as they were in the Frankish era. Owning most of the land which did not belong to God or his earthly representatives, the aristocracy dominated the peasant world from the same height. Possessing hereditary privileges of wealth and leisure the nobility were separated from those who were forced to work for their living by an unbridgeable gulf. Religious thought in the tenth century had constructed a rigid interpretation of the social framework; it divided Christian men into three 'orders', each dedicated to perform a particular social function. On one side were placed the non-producers, monks, clerks and men of war; on the other, the *laboratores*, the workers, the *rustici*, the peasants.[20] Indeed the economic reality which had once inspired these ideas appeared unchanged to everyone in the last years of the twelfth century. Étienne de Fougères in his book of *Manières* described the '*laboureurs*' as created by God to toil for the support of other men and reduced to eating what the lords rejected:

> *ne mangera ja de bon pain,*
> *nous en avons le meilleur grain*
> *et le plus bel et le plus sain. . . .*[21]

*   *   *

Nevertheless, landed wealth was not at all equally divided amongst the members of this vigorous aristocracy, and the little we know of the distribution of lay lands suggests that there were two clear economic levels and two distinct rungs of the ladder. A small group of 'magnates' – *principes, optimates, proceres,* whose special eminence is recorded in eleventh-century documents and who are called 'barons' or *sires* in later sources– lived on a much higher plane than the rest of the nobility. Their families usually held positions of leadership connected with public power, the title of count or the guardianship of a fortress. This high office was immune from the division amongst heirs which broke up the landed estates. It reverted to a single in-dividual, a son or a brother, and consequently maintained the elder branch of the family in a position of superiority from one generation to the next.

[19] Document No. 37, p. 393   [20] David, 217
[21] He will not eat good bread / We have the best grain / The finest and the most nourishing. . . .

It was well placed by this superiority to receive further gifts from the king, bishop or abbot, all of whom were anxious to attract and hold the friendship of a magnate, the head of the clan. Apart from this, these 'princes', by the simple fact of their monopoly of public authority, dominated the great uncultivated spaces and thus disposed of an enormous untapped wealth, which the efforts of pioneer peasants were little by little bringing into production.

Their wealth in terms of land can thus be compared to that of the cathedrals and monasteries most favoured by donors of charitable gifts. It was structurally the same: huge, geographically dispersed, and divided into innumerable manorial units. The *sires*, like the bishops and the Carolingian magnates, moved about from one manor to another. From references in the charters which they granted we can follow the kings round on their perpetual nomadic progress. But the habits of counts and castellans were no more sedentary even though they stayed longer in their favourite residences. Of the six great barons who possessed manors in Oxfordshire at the end of the eleventh century only one lived almost permanently on his manor; the others appeared only at long intervals.[22] On such manors the bailiffs, the *villici*, the *maires*, living in their masters' houses for which they were entirely responsible in his absence, played a role of the very greatest importance, which was very like that of the agents on monastic lands. For lack of documentation their activities elude us. It seems, however, that the practice of 'farming' was very widespread because it relieved the lord from the cares of management, which were both irksome and unworthy of his rank. At the time of Domesday all the manors which formed Odo of Bayeux's demesne in Kent were, with one exception, 'at farm'.[23] As on ecclesiastical demesnes, the 'farmer' rendered either money or goods according to the needs of the household. In the time of Henry I commutation into money made rapid progress on the demesnes of the English crown let out 'at farm', because the king and his court spent a great deal of time in Normandy. Although it was no longer necessary to purvey victuals across the Channel, money was needed instead.[24] It seems as if most of the reeveships on the Capetian demesnes in the twelfth century were also let out at farm in return for money payments. On the lands of the magnates, as on church lands, local managers gradually won economic independence.

Nevertheless, much of this land – and the analogy with the great ecclesiastical estates is again very striking – was granted as 'benefices' or as fiefs. It was in this way incorporated in small parcels into the patrimony of the

[22] Lennard, 268, p. 43
[23] Lennard, 268, p. 113-117 (even though Odo was in fact holder of a Norman bishopric his English possessions must be considered as a lay *seigneurie*)
[24] Lennard, 268, p. 140

'friends' of the lord, his vassals, and those whose loyalty he sought. These men usually occupied a more modest economic position; they formed the lower ranks of the aristocracy and for some these grants represented their entire wealth. This was so in England after the Norman Conquest for many of the smaller landowners, adventurers who had a share, and often an important share, in the landed wealth of the barons. In Oxfordshire, which has been so well studied by R. Lennard, at least a third, and sometimes two-thirds, of the possessions of the great lords were in the hands of vassals.[25] On the other hand in Mâconnais, the knights' fiefs were usually minute. The fief never represented more than a very modest addition to their own possessions, which were chiefly composed of the allods handed down from their ancestors.[26] But whatever their size, these noble tenancies, inalienable and indivisible, were never broken up by almsgiving or by division amongst heirs. They were almost always held free of payments and economic obligations and were consequently independent of all ties of economic subordination towards the superior landlord who had granted them. They consequently brought the family who enjoyed their use an important and useful income.

Whether made up of allods or fiefs, the land of these vassals who were described in documents in all parts of the Christian world by the word 'knight' or its equivalent, was sufficiently extensive and productive to allow the owners to live without themselves setting their hands to the plough. They drew enough from the land to be able to take part, with the leisure and equipment appropriate to their rank, in the political and military life deemed worthy of a man of breeding in the retinue of the magnate who was their benefactor. Differences of wealth certainly existed amongst these warriors; but all lived like gentlemen, and their landed property was much more extensive than the holding of a simple peasant. The English *thegn* at the beginning of the eleventh century was supposed to own a 'hall', a kitchen, a church and five hides of land, i.e. five times as much as the largest peasant family. The 'manor' held by Hardwin de Scalers at Whaddon in Cambridgeshire from his lord the bishop of Ely after the Norman Conquest was of this size and value. The property assigned by the bishop of Magdeburg in 1159 to the *locator* of a newly founded village near the Havel was also of similar proportions. In Mâconnais from fifteen to thirty peasant *manses* were usually dependent on each knightly house and rendered dues to it.[27] But the fiefs of some Norman knights, spread over several hundreds of acres and equal in size to several canonical prebends, appear to have been much larger.

It is extremely unusual for documents of this period to describe in detail the landed property of lords of the second rank. But when we catch glimpses

[25] Lennard, 268, p. 27   [26] Duby, 261, pp. 291 *et seq.*
[27] Stenton, 232, p. 482; Miller, 198, p. 72; Duby, 261, p. 422

of its structure, it appears everywhere similar. It was organized around the 'house', the headquarters of the family. From the eleventh century on the name of this residence served as a surname common to all members of the family. It was not a fortified place, but the centre of agricultural pursuits, full of servants and cattle. The parish church usually stood alongside the house; built by an ancestor, it remained in the possession of the family until the time when the denunciations of reforming priests obliged the family to sever its connection. The family then gave it to one of the ecclesiastical foundations but usually retained the best tithes. A demesne was usually attached to the house. Finally, peasant farms dispersed in various directions, but never very far away, were dependent on it. This organization was basically the same as the portions of the very great estates which were in charge of domestic officials or 'farmers'. It also resembled the estates which grew up in the twelfth century around the recently-founded religious establishments such as the houses of the Templars or Cistercian granges. These men of the lower aristocracy lived in close contact with the land; they managed their own property and when they were absent their wives or brothers deputized for them; their landed possessions produced enough to satisfy all their wants but left little surplus for trade; they gave their orders directly to the farm labourers; they had peasants as neighbours and shared the same anxieties when harvests were bad.[28]

To sum up, in discussing the landlords it is essential to distinguish between the two quite distinct economic categories. We can place in one group the magnates, such as the abbots, bishops, counts and princes. These men did not maintain direct control of their estates; they were separated from them by their entourage and especially by their agents who came between them and the countryfolk who worked their fields; moreover they were not able to lay their hands on more than a small part of the return from their landed wealth. The position of the smaller landowners and the canons or monks responsible for a rural priory was quite different. Their economic situation differed little from that of the domestic officials and the 'farmers' of the great lords. Both of these latter groups managed property small and compact enough to be run by a single individual and both were able to collect the entire profits from them directly. They interposed between the peasants and the great lords an entrepreneurial class which was at that time the principal dynamic element in the economic life of the countryside.

3. POWER OVER THE PEASANTS

If, in the eyes of economic historians, the lords of the small manors and

---

[28] Duby, 261, p. 425; for two examples of such knightly demesnes see documents Nos. 79 and 80, pp. 433, 434.

the manorial managers of the great lords are comparable, their eleventh-century contemporaries recognized profound legal distinction between clerks, monks or knights who were able to escape the constraints and obligations placed upon the common people, and those who had to support them. In fact during the years which preceded and followed the year 1000, the evidence of a reapportionment of authority appears in documents throughout western Europe. Although it had come to be embedded in the collective consciousness, it differed in many respects from ideas accepted in the early Middle Ages. By it the mass of labouring peasants, whether proprietors or tenants, were subject to the private domination of a few leaders. It reserved real liberty, the right to carry arms and the immunity of their habitations, for no more than a small élite of well-born men, and more precisely for those owning enough land to permit them to live in idleness. It protected them from all obligations save those of honour and pledged word. Such a political transformation, and the economic submission of the peasant masses which it entailed, exerted great influence on the development of the rural economy. In fact it determined the system of taxation and through it the most important transfers of wealth which took place at that period. To a large extent it also governed the productivity of labour. It must therefore be closely examined.[29]

* * *

In the kingdom of France the change was perhaps at its greatest. The relaxation of the royal authority in the first half of the tenth century followed fifty years later in the southern provinces by a similar weakening in the power of the count, and balanced by the rise of the movement known as 'the peace of God', placed the castle at the centre of a new political organization. The fortified place, almost always very ancient, had originally been erected by royal decree, but its guardian was henceforth to hold it as a personal possession; around it he appropriated to himself the *ban*, i.e. the very same power that had been wielded by the kings of the early Middle Ages and delegated by them to their representatives. Throughout the surrounding territory the lord of the castle undertook to maintain law and order, and arrogated to himself the power to pursue and punish criminals, to call up soldiers in case of need, and to enact ordinances. In the larger villages the courts of lower justice, which had once upon a time brought free peasants together in public assembly, passed into his hands. He himself adjudicated or charged one of his servants with the task, and therefore collected the fines. Furthermore, as a payment for the protective duties which he performed he demanded an 'aid' and he levied the taxes called in contemporary documents

[29] Italy, Germany and France are very well treated in this respect in Tabacco, 206.

'customs'. All this is important for the history of the rural economy; the castellan claimed thereafter the right to exploit the whole population of the district as he pleased.

His authority and his power to extort money did not, it is true, extend to lords of rank, to his relations, his friends or his vassals, from whom he merely expected faithful service and the bearing of arms. But the entire peasantry was subject to him. In the past serfs had not been subject to royal authority, and were responsible only to their masters. But now greedy to add to his receipts, the castellan would have liked to ignore this old limitation – it was in any case disappearing fast – which separated the mass of country folk into serfs and free men. The legal distinctions which formerly excluded men of servile birth from attending the assemblies of public justice or from partici-pation in the community became blurred in face of the demands of the castellan. In 1050 it would still have been common knowledge which family in any village was servile and which was free. But in the second half of the eleventh century the words *servus* and *francus* and their equivalents fell little by little into disuse in most French provinces.[30] They disappear from manorial inventories and deeds of gift because the appropriation by private lords of royal powers deprived these words of any perceptible economic significance. All that mattered for the lord of the *ban* and for his officials was the fact that they were workers, which brought all peasants residing in the territory of the castle within the power of the *sire* and his authority to raise taxes.

Some country folk, however, continued to escape. In fact in face of the pretensions of the castellans the private authority exercised by the heads of noble families and religious establishments over their own dependants and men of their household was strengthened, developed and extended. Theirs was a domestic power which from time immemorial had removed from royal control the site of the habitation and placed under the protection, justice and rule of the head of the household or the *manse* (*caput mansi* say some docu-ments of the end of the eleventh century), his kith and kin, his servants, and his 'family' in the widest sense. The latter included serfs, of course, but also some men of free birth who, having commended themselves to a master with their offspring came to be incorporated in his household. These de-pendants, servile or protected, did not escape from the family authority when they quitted the house of their patron to live on a holding in their own *manse*. The lesser nobility and church lords therefore claimed the exclusive right to direct, judge and exploit all 'their' men. They stubbornly defended them against the demands of the castellans and, as far as they were able,

[30] Except north of the Seine and on the plateau of Langres, where these terms were kept in usage, although their legal significance changed considerably.

prevented 'their' men from submitting. In fact they looked upon the individual possessions of their dependants as an extension of their own patrimony, and they considered any tax which these men paid to somebody else as an unwarranted levy on the income due to their own households.

The resistance put up by the religious lordships was perhaps the most active, since their dependants were more numerous and more dispersed. (Many men and women, some of whom were nobles and belonged to wealthy families, had formerly entered and still at this period continued to enter, the *familia* of the patron saint of a sanctuary for pious reasons and to obtain salvation.) Moreover most of the great ecclesiastical foundations could show charters of immunity, formerly granted by the sovereign, which prohibited local magnates from exploiting the dependants of the church. Finally, in the course of the eleventh century Gregorian ideas helped to revive the belief that ecclesiastical property must not be subject to temporal authority. In any case the evidence illuminates with great clarity the conflicts over the control and taxation of their men which brought the ecclesiastical lords and the castellans into fierce opposition. These rivalries between the lordship which we can describe as appertaining to the *ban*, since it was founded on the territorial power derived from the king, and the lordship which can be described as 'domestic', since it emanated from the power wielded by the heads of families over their households, produced some widely differing results.

Most frequently the authority derived from the *ban* prevailed. Many masters lost control over those of their former slaves who lived too far from the homestead, and the right of protection over some free men. The wardens of fortresses could usually dispose of larger forces. The support they could promise to those who placed themselves under their guardianship appeared more likely to be efficacious and thus their patronage was sought after. We can well see why in the twelfth century the men of the *sauvetés*, founded by the Templars in the region of Toulouse, which by virtue of the cross symbolizing God's peace provided sanctuaries from illtreatment and exactions, sought of their own free will the patronage of the castellans in the vicinity.[31] The 'domestic' lords surrendered their least defensible and most marginal rights to the profit of the 'territorial' lords. Frequently, also, there occurred a division of power between the domestic and the territorial lord, the castellan taking over the superior instruments of authority, such as military power and punishment of the most serious crimes.[32] The peasant then had to submit to two masters whose demands were superimposed on him. However, no territory of a castellan ever became a unified whole; scattered enclaves remained in all of them. All domestic lordships, even the most modest con-

[31] Ourliac, 320   [32] Document No. 105, p. 455

trolled by the least well endowed of the country gentry, in fact kept their authority within and around the actual habitation of the master over a group of subjects who were in this way completely removed from the power of the territorial lord. Within these residual enclaves a uniformity quickly established itself. There ceased to be any distinction between slaves and free men amongst the 'men of the house'. At the beginning of the twelfth century when a lord spoke of someone in his 'family' he said: 'He is my man.' A vague term, but one which emphasized the feeling of ownership.

★　　★　　★

Outside France developments are not so easy to observe and they sometimes fell out of step chronologically, even though the general direction was the same. In Italy about the year 1000, the city, with its precocious power, was at least as important as the rural castle; urban communities therefore frequently appropriated the power of the *ban* over the surrounding country. But in the first half of the eleventh century the same rivalry for the exploitation of the peasants can be seen south of the Alps between territorial *ban* and personal protection. There also the humble folk were torn between the authority of the man calling himself *dominus loci*, the lord of the place, who because of this title claimed control over everyone, and the patron to whom some peasants had commended themselves, in order to be, according to the eleventh-century formula, 'fed, clothed and shod' by him as a member of his household.[33] This domain of Italian social history remains very imperfectly explored. We find, however, in the Lombard, Piedmontese or Tuscan countryside manorial documents of the feudal age making a clear distinction between domestic servants still held in the grip of slavery, entirely subject to the lord's right of correction over their bodies and subject to his orders (these were the individuals known as 'other people's men' whom the urban communities of the twelfth century refused to welcome into their midst unless the bond which tied them had first been severed), and on the other hand the villeins whose residence in a certain place made them liable to certain services.[34]

The royal power did not seem to have crumbled away so completely in the north of the Christian world, in Germania, England and the principalities of north-western France, Normandy and Flanders. The castles there were retained in the hands of the princes, the kings and the counts. The power of the *ban* was not broken up and was not divided between separate autonomous and competitive territories. The vigour of the rural assemblies of free men where justice was still dispensed by virtue of 'the law of the country'

[33] Muratori, I., *Rerum Italicarum Scriptores*, 837
[34] Jones, 191; Fiumi, 141; Luzzatto, 166; Gabotto, 108, p. cxli

(*Landrecht*) and the 'common law', kept alive the idea of a public authority. Responsible throughout their principality for the punishment of crime and the maintenance of peace, the leaders of the people kept to themselves the privilege of levying certain of the heaviest exactions. The peasants did not avoid taxes, but at least they benefited by having fewer masters, of higher degree, and more remote. The concentration of the power to levy taxes was not, however, complete. Private powers of protection and domination over certain men which permitted many lords greatly to increase their incomes also existed and developed in these countries. Nevertheless these developments assumed different forms in the Germanic countries on the one hand and the countries bordering the English Channel and the North Sea on the other.

★   ★   ★

In Germany and its western borders, the Low Countries and Lotharingia the dividing line between freedom and servitude was still as clearly marked as in Carolingian times. Regional customs recorded in the mid-thirteenth century group the free peasants separately. They were not to be confused with 'nobles' who were exempt from exactions, nor with 'knights' who, since the mid-twelfth century, alone had the right to carry arms. Nevertheless they continued to be answerable exclusively to the counts' tribunals. They could not therefore pass as *servi*, or slaves. Like the *francs* of Carolingian times, they had to take part in judicial assemblies and the richest were obliged to sit on them as aldermen. In times of war they were called up for military duties; and in north Germania and on the frontiers of the Slav world continued to be so obliged for a long time. In less exposed areas where warlike activity became, as in France, a professional occupation, the free peasants helped in the communal defence by supplying oats. There was one significant difference, however: it was the count and not the private lord who levied 'protection money', the *Grafenschatz*, in the king's name. And it was also to the count, margrave or bishop, invested with the count's authority, that the colonizers in Thuringia, the Flemish polders and the banks of the Elbe, paid their rent as a token of their freedom.[35]

The continued vigour of public institutions did not, however, prevent every religious house and, judging from our evidence, also every noble from imposing upon men of their 'family' the various obligations which the slow but prolonged decay of royal authority in the twelfth century made it easier to enforce. Who were these dependent men, so often strictly subject to a lord, living on clearings in the vast forests and only visited by the king's agents at infrequent intervals? They were mostly slaves, since the primitive notion of

[35] Bosl, 489 and 516; Van der Linden, 328; Document No. 36, p. 391

slavery still survived. In the documents many are called 'household slaves', *servi salici*, and 'slaves in perpetual service'. The 'prebendaries' – the ones who were 'fed' and housed in the master's residence, or installed in a cabin close by, but continued to take their meals in the refectory or barn of the 'hall' – these men and women possessed nothing of their own. Their master could punish them and give them orders as he pleased. Some others, however, were described as 'slaves eating their own bread'. They lived on a *manse* which they cultivated and which provided for their families. They also gave service 'with their bodies' and had to obey all the lord's commands; but as they lived somewhat further away from their master they possessed a slightly greater degree of independence. Those who lived furthest away could almost be confused with the quite free men of the *familia*.

The latter were especially numerous on the church manors. In southern and western Germany, in Lorraine, Flanders and Picardy, persons of all classes, the aged, the widows, the pious seeking to ensure their after-life, and others who were simply looking for earthly protection or material help, all commended themselves in large numbers to various sanctuaries during the tenth and eleventh centuries. These 'men of the altar' – the great Bavarian abbeys each counted a following of several thousand – dedicated themselves and their descendants to a patron saint.[36] Like emancipated slaves, dependent but free, they were not compelled to do 'body service'. They belonged none the less to the 'family' of their master, and their possessions were to some extent integrated into his patrimony.

In the German countries bitter competition developed between public authorities and private patrons over the exploitation of the dependants of differing status. The much-studied evolution of the advowson – that delegation of royal power within ecclesiastical immunities – reveals the existence of attitudes and conflicts comparable to those of which traces were to be found in French monastic cartularies. By the end of the tenth century the Germanic 'advocates' considered their function as part of their heritage. They claimed the right to dispose of it at will and to distribute its fragments as fiefs to their friends. Above all, they used it as a pretext to profit from the peasants settled on the church's demesne, to exort presents from them and to inflict fines on them in the exercise of justice. The monastic administrators fought against these pretensions; in the course of the eleventh century written laws limited the activities of 'advocates'. The latter were allowed to preside three times a year over courts of general pleas, solemn judicial assemblies; they were given police and military powers; they were also allowed to levy certain customs on the tenants, to punish them for serious crimes and to collect part of the profits of justice. However, the abbots

[36] Document No. 91, p. 442

energetically defended their domestic lordships and succeeded in enforcing the total exemption of their 'household slaves' and often of their whole *familia* as well.[37]

* * *

Anglo-Norman developments were more complex. There is no doubt that the political and economic influence of private protectors did not spread until after the year 1000. The king might grant to certain magnates the *feorm* of this or that village, and some free men of modest rank, harassed by the obligations of war and driven by hunger in years of bad harvest, might also seek a 'lord' to whom they could commend themselves. We can see how in this way appeared and spread the institution of patronage, as well as the custom of 'sake and soke' (the expression appears in 965), which obliged dependants to present themselves at the 'hall' of their patron, to plead their suits before him and to offer him their services. Some of the ties of dependence, which bound not only men but also their land, were tight and some were slack, and we can distinguish at that period many gradations between the free devotion of the thegn, the man-at-arms who was himself a lord, and the harsh compulsion which forced the peasant, fed in the household, to place his bodily strength at his master's disposal.[38]

After the Conquest, in 1086, the 'hall', the house of the chief, where people came together to render service and to receive justice, had already acquired sufficient importance in social relations for the Norman clerks who compiled the Domesday Book to base their description of the kingdom on what they called 'the manor', rather than on the framework of the village. In their country 'the manor' signified the dwelling of the man of power. When the invaders settled down, having liquidated the Saxon leaders and occupied their habitations, they placed their yoke firmly on the necks of the natives and immensely strengthened the authority of the heads of 'households'. Many domestic slaves were still to be found, especially in the west of England: 25,000 were counted in 1086, as many as sokemen, i.e. free men subject to 'sake and soke'. At a guess they formed almost one-tenth of the male population. 300 of them worked on the demesne of Ely Cathedral, distributed on almost all its manors.[39] None the less ancient notions of servitude within the circle of men attached to the manor began to fade. Synods and preachers denounced slave traders. The compilers of the Domesday Book used the word *servus* when describing domestic servants with reluctance. In most counties, when classifying men according to their degree

[37] Perrin, 200, p. 675; Dollinger, 159; Documents Nos. 101, 115, 117, pp. 450, 468, 470.
[38] Stenton, 232, pp. 463 *et seq.*
[39] Miller, 198, p. 44

of dependence, the king's clerks adopted other criteria: the nature of the service men owed to the lord and especially the nature of their land.

They described the 'sokemen', the men who were not compelled to work on the fields of the manor, or who at least toiled there only occasionally, as 'free tenants'. The peasants who participated in the cultivation of the demesne by regular labour service, and who had to present themselves once or twice a week at the manor to receive the lord's commands, were classified in two groups according to the size of their own holding. Those who possessed enough land to support their families were described as 'villeins'. The rest, whose holdings, simple cabins with gardens attached, did not suffice to provide a living, but who depended on employment at the master's house or elsewhere for supplementary income were called 'bordars' or 'cottars'.[40] The number of free tenants was reduced by the Conquest, and by the revolt which followed it, as well as by the demands of the new lords. On one small manor of a vassal of Ely Cathedral, the demesne formed one-quarter of the arable land in 1066, and fifteen sokemen shared the rest; twenty years later the demesne had doubled in area, there were no sokemen, only nine villeins and twenty bordars. Of the 900 sokemen in Cambridgeshire before the Conquest, no more than 213 preserved their state of relative independence when the Domesday Book was compiled.[41]

In any case land tenure and personal ties tended to be confused in England at the end of the eleventh century. Inside the 'manor', authority over men and over land, domestic lordship and land lordship, coincided. On the other hand the autonomous *seigneurie banale*, the independent territorial lordship, did not, properly speaking, exist at all. William the Conqueror held all the castles. He had, it is true, distributed huge domains amongst his companions in arms, but they were scattered all over the country. For instance, eleven barons, all great lords, owned land scattered and intermingled amongst twelve villages in Oxfordshire.[42] The possessions of the lords were so fragmented that it was very unusual for a single manor to cover the whole territory of a village. For this reason, most peasants lived cheek by jowl with men who, being tenants of other lords, were answerable to other manors and were therefore under different 'protection'. If a dispute arose between them they were more inclined to take their case not before their own lords, but before the village assembly, or before the public court of justice which held regular assizes in the shire or its subdivisions, the hundreds. In fact, as in Germania, the tradition of local assemblies remained very much alive; assem-

---

[40] This took over the distinction already established between the different classes of free dependants before the Conquest and described in particular in the text entitled *Rectitudines singularum personarum*. Document No. 92, p. 443.

[41] Miller, 198, p. 73; Maitland, 168, p. 62; Document No. 74, p. 428

[42] Lennard, 268, p. 59

blies where free men periodically met together to receive judgment in the king's name. The Norman kings did nothing to weaken this custom; and, as in Germania, the sheriff, the king's representative in each shire, levied fines in his name, mobilized men in time of war, and imposed the taxes needed for defence. The greater lords, however, in the first half of the twelfth century, attempted to appropriate the royal prerogatives. They were most successful in doing so on the wild borderlands of Scotland and Wales where a perpetual state of emergency persisted and where the military leaders held power and prestige over a scattered population always in fear of invasion. But, these frontiers apart, the sovereign succeeded after 1155 in taking the superior powers of justice and peace firmly in hand throughout his small kingdom. Almost all the gallows erected by the lords on their demesnes were pulled down and the right to punish crime and to judge free men reverted again to the shire and hundred courts, and to the itinerant royal judges.

Nevertheless the king recognized the personal authority of lords of manors, and this helped to consolidate the 'domestic lordship'. Amongst the manorial tenants a distinction arose. The 'free men', i.e. those not burdened with regular labour services, were held to be subject to public tribunals (thus, in the inventories of the lordship of Ely, the free tenants are called *hundredarii*, the hundred men).[43] On the other hand, the villeins and bordars were no longer answerable to 'common law'. They were abandoned to the justice and punishment of the master according to the custom of the manor. They became in the common estimation 'customary men'. In other words, they fell wholly under private power.

Regular courts continued to be held in the hall of the manor to settle the quarrels of dependants. The free men of the village sometimes carried their suits before this court of conciliation, because it was nearer at hand than the hundred court, because they felt more at ease there and because its judgments often proved more effective. Furthermore, the manorial court shared in the keeping of public peace. It dealt with offences committed against the king's peace by members of the 'family' and by neighbours. On some of the more powerful lordships, the manorial courts took the 'view of the frank pledge', i.e. the presentation of 'tithings', the small groups of ten men into which all the adult males of the kingdom were grouped for purposes of criminal police and jurisdiction.[44] Thus every lord of a manor administered justice of some kind, and was thereby able to collect the money proceeds of fines. Furthermore, the ideas of jurists who had even at this period rediscovered Roman law identified the status of a villein, excluded as he was from public assemblies, with that of the slave of antiquity. He was declared to be *servus* and as such

[43] Miller, 198, p. 117   [44] Documents Nos. 150 and 151, p. 507 *et seq.*

hereditarily tied to the glebe, he was considered as the object of unlimited exploitation and delivered over to the arbitrary will of the master so completely that 'he did not know in the evening what he would be required to do the following day'. Thus, by the end of the twelfth century a large part of the English peasantry had slipped back into a state of complete servitude. As a consequence it was subjected to heavy economic oppression, much heavier indeed than that borne by free men at the hands of the royal agents.[45]

* * *

Throughout the west in the eleventh and twelfth centuries, through the exercise of a territorial *ban* and through personal dependence, protective authorities both private and public bore hardly upon humble people, the peasantry and all those condemned by their inferior status to labour for the support of their betters. This authority grew steadily heavier, and the profits of justice, requisitions and 'aids' demanded from subjects were added to the revenue which came from the ownership of land. These sources of wealth were merged with the patrimony of princes, the great religious establishments and the wealthiest families and helped to swell the lords' incomes.

However, if what we mean by the word *seigneurie* (and this indeed is the sense in which economic historians have to use it) is the power of economic exploitation, there were several kinds of *seigneuries* (lordships) in the eleventh and twelfth centuries. The language of the times did not distinguish between them, and neither did contemporaries who were solely interested in the amounts which they could expect to receive or to give, and were totally unconcerned with the definitions of the legal source of their incomes or dues. Seigneurial inventories of the twelfth century had become 'customaries', *coutumiers*, because alongside of rents attached to fields, and confused with them, they now recorded the 'customs', the taxes demanded of men because of their dependence. Nevertheless, if we aim at a deeper understanding of the economic mechanism, separate consideration of these different profits will not come amiss. For this purpose we must treat the landlordship (*seigneurie foncière*) apart from the *seigneurie banale* and the *seigneurie domestique*. The basis of the former was the demesne and the holdings attached to it, while the latter applied to men, and bound groups of peasant families to the household of the individual who exercised his power through a network of services and dues.

[45] A. L. Poole, *From Domesday Book . . .*, p. 39 *et seq.*

CHAPTER II

Lords and Peasants in the
XI and XII Centuries

I. MANORIAL LANDOWNERSHIP

The scarcity of written sources in the tenth and eleventh centuries raises a particularly serious obstacle to research into the history of manorial land-ownership. The few manorial territories in western Europe which were the subject of inventories in Carolingian times hardly ever appear again explicitly in documents of later centuries. Thus, all continuity of development, such as there could have been, escapes observation. However, some of the parchments on which the text of the *polyptyques* are written carry subsequent alterations, erasures and interpolations. These corrections were intended to adapt the administrative documents piecemeal to the perpetual changes taking place in economic and social relations. In this way it is sometimes possible to date successive changes; and they deserve the closest attention. It was patient research on material such as this that enabled C. E. Perrin to uncover the gradual transformation of the Lorraine *seigneurie*. In addition the habit of making inquests and inventories and compiling at intervals lists of tenants and statements of their services remained alive in religious establishments on the continent and even spread to England. We thus possess for some demesnes a series of twelfth-century rentals, thanks to which we can follow various developments in the manorial economy.[1] These developments pose many important questions, to some of which we can suggest answers.

(a) The size of the demesne

Medievalists generally consider that the size of the demesne diminished a great deal between the ninth and the twelfth centuries and they are fond of contrasting the immense demesne fields which the serfs of the great Carolingian abbeys had to cultivate with the compact estates in the vicinity of the house from which the lords drew supplies for their tables three centuries later. In fact it is not hard to find in documents of that period evidence of the dissolution and partition of demesnes. Many lords behaved like the monks of Tournus in Burgundy who, in 974, divided up the huge furlongs given to

[1] Perrin, 200; Didier, 433; Document No. 109, p. 460

them in charitable gift by the count into parcels of land attached to new *manses* on which seven tenant families were established.[2] But it is most likely that the arable parts of the demesne slowly dwindled away as a result of small and repeated amputations. Small plots were detached and granted and handed over to cultivators, to begin with as temporary concessions, soon to be made permanent. Thus in 1147 a priest received from the abbot of Waulsort a *possessiuncula* taken from one of the furlongs of the monastery; he had to hold it 'according to the right of the tenants of the *manse*' and to pay a rent proportionate to the area of the granted land.[3] If we are right in assuming that agricultural technique gradually progressed during the period, it would explain the continuous reduction of the lord's demesne. As yields rose on the master's fields, provisioning the 'hall' no longer required such extensive cultivated areas.[4] Why indeed should superfluous lands be directly cultivated when it was easy to find men willing to take the fields and to pay rent for them?

Nevertheless neither in France nor in England nor in Germany do the documents permit us to assume that any considerable portion of the masters' arable had been deliberately distributed to tenants. On the contrary, until the end of the twelfth century such a process appears to have been exceptional. In the texts it is usually seen as an expedient; when the lords had recourse to it, we can guess that it was forced upon them either by a temporary shortage of labour or by the difficulty of cultivating newly acquired or remote territory. Indeed they were most unwilling to separate themselves permanently from the demesne lands. For most of the time, therefore, it must be assumed that the division of the demesne was accidental and often resulted from an enlargement of the patrimony itself.

Here pious gifts played a part. Almsgiving often added new land to church property, but without including the labour necessary to cultivate it. Without servants or men subject to labour service this land had either to be added to the ancient *manses*, granted to settlers or else, as was done by the monks of Tournus, converted into new farms. Another cause of the decay of demesne arable and furlong and their break up into parcels was division amongst heirs. To be sure of possessing an equal share heirs divided up between them the fields of each *villa*, and in the course of generations these 'shares' were reduced to collections of fragmented plots scattered amongst several villages, the most distant of which were let out as tenancies. Finally the creation of fiefs and *precaria* intervened. The endowment of vassal knights

[2] Duby, 261, p. 73

[3] *Les chartes de l'abbaye de Waulsort* (ed. Despy), No. 25; '... *ex indominica cultura in villa Pondrem nobis jure mansionarii cessit, et secundum quantitatem terre censum solvere precepit ...*'.

[4] Document No. 109, p. 460

and domestic officials and the favours granted to 'friends', broke up the demesnes of the magnates and especially the enormous estates possessed by the religious establishments in the early Middle Ages.[5] These estates were divided into parcels of a much more restricted size. But it must be noted that for the most part they were still directly cultivated.

In short, it may be doubted whether many landlords' fields at that period became peasants' fields. It would probably be more correct to say that the demesne arable, without losing much in extent, was divided by inheritance and 'benefices' into ever smaller units of cultivation. This fragmentation largely resulted from demographic growth, the proliferation of aristocratic clans, and the multiplication of lords.

If we examine the documents carefully we can also note that signs of enlargements of demesnes are hardly less numerous than those of their contraction. It is clear that some lords were actively extending their direct cultivation. This was usually the case with the religious communities formed after the end of the eleventh century in reaction to the monastic system of the seigneurial type in favour at Cluny. These new-style communities undertook the task of tilling the soil themselves. Thus the Cistercians were forbidden to acquire tithes, mills, *cens*, (i.e. rents), and *colons* (i.e. tenants). In so far as these rules were respected – at any rate until the mid-twelfth century – the estates of these institutions, which were enormous and much enriched by almsgiving, were entirely cultivated as demesnes; they were divided into a large number of 'granges', each entrusted to a team of domestic workers. This much is well known. What is less well-known is that the older religious orders were also preoccupied in the twelfth century with extending the direct cultivation of their lands. The case of the monastery of Cluny appears to me very significant. Around 1090 the chamberlain of the abbey, i.e. the official in charge of the money revenue, took steps to acquire the whole territory of a certain village which was sold to him at a very high price by the noble and peasant landowners. After having expelled the inhabitants, as the Cistercians often did elsewhere,[6] the monks created a 'grange' on these lands. About thirty years later, Peter the Venerable sought to remedy the serious difficulties which had befallen the monastery's economy. In an attempt to reduce the purchase of foodstuffs, and to assure the direct provisioning of barn and cellar, he did not hesitate to devote substantial sums to increasing the number of ploughs, and planting new vines.[7] We can attribute the same intention to

---

[5] It was, it seems, the usurpations of the magnates and the troubles arising from invasions which broke up the demesnes of the great monasteries of the Frankish kingdom in the tenth century. For the abbey of Saint-Wandrille, see F. Lot, *Etudes critiques sur l'abbaye de Saint-Wandrille*, pp. lxv and 59; for St Germain-des-Prés, see M. de la Motte Colas, in *Mémorial du XIVe centenaire de l'abbaye de Saint-Germain-des-Prés*, Paris, 1959.

[6] Document No. 83, p. 436   [7] Duby, 441

Abbot Suger of St Denis at the same period. He set aside twenty livres for the creation of a vineyard at St Lucien, which would enable him to avoid pledging the precious altar ornaments at the Lagny fairs each year in order to pay for the purchases of wine. At Rouvray he had the 'hall' rebuilt and 'established three ploughs there', and immediately the profits of the demesne increased fivefold.[8] We have already seen that reclamation was often carried out by the lords with a similar intention of raising the yield of domestic cultivation. It is true that many new tenures were created on the lands won by assart. But a considerable portion of the new fields were often kept in demesne. On the fringes of the Burgundian forests the 'demesne assarts', the *condemines* (arable land belonging to the demesne) 'with the assarts which adjoined them', flourished in the eleventh and twelfth century and in many 'new villages' the lords kept for themselves a house, its purpresture, and a parcel of arable land which could employ one or two ploughs.[9]

What else do such investments signify if not the very real attachment of the landlords of those days to the direct cultivation of their land, and the persistence of the same types of management as those exemplified by the Carolingian documents? In fact it is impossible to find in the eleventh and twelfth centuries either a manor without a demesne, or a lord drawing nothing from his land but rents. For instance there is no manor in the Domesday Book without its demesne, and the remarkable figures which the inquest produces show that this demesne always occupied a considerable proportion of the arable land: 22 per cent on the possessions of the bishop of Winchester, and 58 at least of the 85 'ploughlands' which belonged to Odo the Seneschal; on 6 of the 20 manors owned by Burton Abbey the demesne occupied an area equal to all the tenancies; and on two others it was larger still.[10] Evidence provided by the ecclesiastical cartularies of southern Burgundy agrees with this. In this region every knight about whose affairs something is known had five or six times as many fields under cultivation as the average peasant farm; we even come across manors with no apparent dependent holdings and entirely composed of demesne fields.[11] Arable formed the greater part of the latter. It was either concentrated in large parcels or else dispersed in small plots over different parts of the village lands. In the mid-twelfth century one small noble in the county of Chalon owned apart from woods, five carrucates of meadow, twelve 'worklands' (*ouvrées*) of vines and fourteen dispersed fields intermingled with those of the village peasants.[12]

Such estates indeed appear considerably more modest than the immense areas cultivated in the ninth century by the menservants of some of the great

---

[8] *Liber de rebus in administratione sua gestis* (ed. Lecoy de la Marche), I, pp. 158, 169, 170
[9] Duby, 261, p. 304; Document No. 37, p. 393   [10] Lennard, 268, pp. 74 *et seq.*
[11] Duby, 261, p. 78; Document No. 80, p. 434   [12] Duby, 261, p. 424

Frankish monasteries. But it must, of course, be remembered that the *polypty-ques* always described exceptionally large demesnes. The demesne estates after the year 1000, although much smaller, were no less full of vigour, and we must picture the manorial housholds of the period as centres of great agricultural activity.

(b) Domestic labour

Methods of cultivating the demesne do not appear very different from those which were practised in the ninth century. The principal tasks, and especially ploughing, were in the first place performed by domestic servants. The 'plough', i.e. the team comprising the machine itself, the draught animals and the menservants who drove them, formed the basic equipment of all the 'halls'. The economic power of the latter was reckoned in 'ploughs'. In fact throughout western Europe every household, religious or noble, maintained a small band of domestics employed full time, and amongst them a few *bovarii*, i.e. those men who operated the plough in pairs, one leading the harnessed animals and the other guiding the plough itself. At the end of the eleventh century twelve families lived on the demesne of one Burgundian knight, attached to his farm. There were twenty of these *famuli* on one of the abbey of Cluny's deaneries fifty years later. In the thirteenth century there were thirty on one of the English manors of the abbey of Bec.[13] All references to this social class of labourers, and especially any which allow us to understand the real conditions of their lives, deserve to be carefully studied.

The lords took upon themselves the entire responsibility for maintaining a certain number of such men. Many in fact appear in documents under the name of 'prebendaries'. In a document compiled in 1122 for the chapter of Notre-Dame of Paris, we read 'of the drivers (*bouviers*), and of the *familia* of ploughmen, and of others who lived on the bread of the brothers'. In 1195 a charter of the same region speaks of a knight's *famulus* 'living on the bread of his master'.[14] On the demesne of Cluny they were fed on the grain received by the lord as profits of his mills and ovens. In Italy the texts present these men as 'living regularly on the distribution of food of the master'.[15] Legally they were described as *servi* in all regions where the notion of slavery had not yet disappeared. They formed the hard core of the *familia*, the most rigidly subject to domestic authority. All of them were exempt from any other authority and obeyed no one but the head of the household. In the new religious communities in which manual labour was deemed honourable,

[13] Document No. 80, p. 434; Duby, 442; Morgan, 408
[14] *Cartulaire de Notre-Dame de Paris*, I, p. 408; *Recueil des Actes de Philip Auguste*, II, No. 512
[15] Document No. 113, p. 464; Muratori, I, *Rerum Italicarum Scriptores* 589 (1034)

similar services were performed by monks of peasant origin, the *conversi*, or lay brethren. They were treated as brothers by the congregation of monks and formed a single community with them. But as they were uneducated, lived apart and were obliged to perform only the simplest liturgical exercises which left them a great deal of free time, they undertook the heavy labour of the 'granges'. For the monks this was a happy solution, and in the twelfth century the Benedictines of the older observance also adopted it.

However, about this time another category of servants, whose numbers were on the increase, begins to appear in documents. These servants were still full-time domestics, mixing in the daytime with the team of 'prebendaries'. But unlike the latter, they had their own homes. They dwelt on tiny holdings (a cabin with a garden and sometimes one small field) quite close to the hall where they worked. They led family lives and lived on the distribution of foodstuffs which they consumed at home, i.e. on a wage. This slightly less dependent condition was probably that of the *servi quotidiani*, the 'day labourers', whose services are described in the German *censiers*, and also of the *sergents*, the *servientes*, of one demesne in Bresse who, each provided with a family cabin, together cultivated the demesne lands, looked after the fabric of the 'hall' and undertook the convoys of foodstuffs to the house of their lord, the bishop of Mâcon.[16]

The English ox drivers or *bovarii* (in the English inventories at the end of the eleventh and the twelfth centuries references to these labourers increase and take the place of slaves who were already disappearing) seem to have occupied a very similar economic situation. Even though their daily labours were entirely confined to the demesne, they did not live in the 'hall'. We see them in possession of a holding exempt from dues in money or in kind, which compelled them to follow their 'calling', i.e. to fulfil the task to which professional capacity dedicated them. Consequently we should consider these *bovarii* as *ministeriales*, specialized domestics, boarded out of the lord's house. Certainly the plot of ground which they had at their disposal was obviously too small to provide them with subsistence, or for it to be considered as a true wage. What it could produce, a few sheaves of corn, some garden vegetables and roots, could provide no more than a supplementary food supply. The major function of these minute holdings, similar to those of the German *quotidiani*, was rather to attach these labourers more firmly to the service of the 'hall' at a time when population was sparse and hands were short, and when peasants willingly moved about. Such a holding also enabled them to lead family lives and to bring up their children. But the real remuneration of the English *bovarii* was made up of other advantages, such as the right to use the lord's plough on certain days, and to sow their fields with

[16] Dollinger, 159; Document No. 112, p. 463

the lord's seed; but above all it was wages, in the form of food and money.[17] The *bouviers* of the Mâcon region also received at this period cereal rations which they were wont to eat at home.[18] Certain remarks in documents concerned with manorial administration also suggest that what the servant could lay his hands on and carry away clandestinely was far from insubstantial. Altogether, the existence of a group of satellite hovels, clustered round the 'hall' has the appearance of an extension of the master's household. Refectories and dormitories were more than half empty and the wage-earner began to occupy the dominant position in the domestic economy.

Besides, these full-time servants, bound to the demesne by their holdings, were joined at intervals by temporary auxiliaries, 'hired men', taken on to complete certain tasks like harvest, vinedressing and the care of animals. Thus on the English manor of the abbey of Bec, which I referred to above, eight wage-earners came to the assistance of the thirty domestic labourers at harvest time. In 1134 the chapter-general of the Order of Cîteaux regulated the employment of paid workers recruited in the *granges* to help the lay brothers. The Carthusians and their neighbours the monks of Chalais also paid the shepherds who took their flocks to the mountain pastures.[19] Finally we can consider as part-time paid workers, occupying an economic position hardly different from that of the *bovarii*, the bordars of the English manors, and the cottars whom the Anglo-Saxon texts call *kotsetla*. They were provided with holdings which were in fact no more than a few acres in size; an area equal to at most one-sixth of the farming unit which could be considered capable of maintaining a peasant family. These labourers owed the master on account of the holding one or two days free labour each week. But the rest of the time they hired themselves out either to other cultivators, or what was probably more often to their own lord. On certain 'halls' the *lundinarii*, the Monday men, came each Monday to work for nothing. If they came back on other days, they received wages. Liable to so little labour service, we can assume them to be more than half-time day labourers.

(c) Labour services

Labour service throughout Europe in the eleventh and twelfth centuries remained, however, the principal means of obtaining during the period of heavy seasonal labour reinforcements of manpower for the team of servants installed in or near the household. Documents of that period all mention the labour services imposed on tenants and dependants. We often see new labour services established immediately a new manorial field was created, as in one parish in lower Auvergne where about 1050, in order to plough a *condemine*

---

[17] Postan, 414   [18] Document No. 113, p. 464
[19] *Recueil des plus anciennes chartes de la Grande-Chartreuse*, pp. 80, 124

(demesne arable) recently brought into cultivation, ploughing services had recently been imposed on each of twelve families of tenants. It was partly in order to attract additional bodies subject to labour service who could help to cultivate the demesne arable enlarged by reclamation that the lords of Normandy and Maine founded so many *bourgs* in the countryside in the eleventh century.[20] However, these ploughing or labour services appear everywhere to have been less heavy, and sometimes much less heavy, than those listed in the Carolingian inventories. And when more closely examined, forced labour appears to be very differently organized in the various parts of western Europe. We need to know much more about the geography of labour services, but until a closer examination of the sources allows the frontiers to be exactly drawn and the differences to be carefully tabulated we have to be content with the broadest of outlines.

★   ★   ★

On the southern flank of the area in which we are interested, in Italy and in France south of Burgundy and the Loire, labour services were light and of very limited economic value. Most of the holdings mentioned in cartularies were wholly exempt from labour dues. We do not find here the *lot-corvée* or *ansange*, i.e. the plot of land to be cultivated by the compulsory services of the tenant for the benefit of the master: the most southerly *ansange* of which I have found a trace in France, is no further south than Chalon-sur-Saône. Finally, in cases where the documents record labour services, these by no means overwhelmed the family who had to perform them. At the end of the twelfth century, for instance, the monks of Vallombrosa in Tuscany demanded only three services with oxen and three services with a donkey each year from one tenant, and two services and some manual services from another. In the whole *censier* of the Auvergne manor of Sauxillanges no more than a few days ploughing are recorded. In one manor of the bishopric of Mâcon which was listed after 1100, thirteen of the dependent *manses* co-operated to some extent in the cultivation of the demesne: each had to supply every year the team for eight days ploughing, two men for vineyard work, a mower and a haymaker; in addition they had to bring in two loads of hay, perform two woodland services, and help with the harvest and threshing. But fourteen other *manses* were obliged to do no more than ploughing service and the remaining eight participated in demesne work only to the extent of two or three man-days. Altogether throughout the year the 35 subject peasant farms put 220 days work at the master's disposal. In the ninth century a single dependent *manse* of one of the great abbeys between Loire and Rhine had often provided more than that. The inquest drawn up about 1150 in the

[20] Fournier, 452; Boussard, 279

home deaneries of the abbey of Cluny accounted for even fewer contributions. No labour services at all on three manorial units; on the others, 'workers' were called up at mowing time, and 'ploughs' from the village were required for ploughing, but only on odd days, and never on more than four in the whole year.[21]

Thus, it seems clear that in these regions the lords often neglected to claim from peasant cultivators placed in their power much assistance in the form of work. Even if they did, what they mostly expected was help with ploughing, that basic agricultural task, the value of which was emphasized by technical progress and which needed equipment rather than manpower. Ploughing equipment obviously concerned the lords more than manual labour service alone. Thus, on the Cluniac demesnes the contribution of men subject to labour service was reckoned as 'ploughs'; the commissioners looked upon the requisitioned peasants as forming gangs, in which there is no doubt their draught animals were included. It must be added that in documents of the twelfth century these labour services with equipment appear often to be based not on holdings, as they were in Carolingian days, but on 'inhabitants', or 'neighbours' as the commissioners of Cluny called them, i.e. on the menfolk of the village. Did such services in this case in fact come from the landlordship? Ought they not rather to be considered as one of the *aides* which the territorial lord by virtue of his power of the *ban* now required from all those whom he protected? Everything seems to point to many of these ploughing services being dues appertaining to the *ban*, assumed in the course of the eleventh century for the cultivation of the lord's demesne and consequently recent additions to the demesne estate.

By the same token simple labour services seemed in the mid-twelfth century to be dwindling away. This appears quite clearly on the lands of the abbey of Cluny. On one deanery 150 mowers came to work on the manorial fields; but the services of one hundred more were dispensed with in exchange for dues of two deniers per head. The carting and vineyard services were similarly commuted: to be exempt from them the dependants paid all together 60 sous every year. On this one manor alone, the conversion of the services brought the steward more than 5,000 deniers every year. Money levied in this way served to pay the wage-earners who performed the same jobs. But hiring these day labourers cost only a part of the money paid by those subject to labour services. The lord thus profited from commutation. For example half the tax paid by peasants in order not to have to work in the vineyards was enough to pay the hired labourers who replaced them. Put in another way, the productivity of a paid labourer, if converted into money

[21] Luzzatto, 165; Fournier, 451; Duby, 261, pp. 314 *et seq.*, and 442; Documents Nos. 87 to 90, pp. 439-442

terms, had doubled. On manors such as these, which cannot be considered as particularly progressive, recourse to money and recruitment had caused forced labour to shrink very significantly by the middle of the twelfth century.[22]

Ought we to assume further that similar, but much earlier, commutations had in the obscurity of the tenth and the early eleventh centuries gradually put an end to the 'demesne system' in all these regions? Should we consider the rarity of labour services in 1150, as well as their lightness, as the effect of recent developments which reduced to next to nothing a combination of services once comparable in size to that which absorbed in the Carolingian *seigneuries* of northern Gaul such a considerable part of the tenant force? A hasty reply would be unwise: the early medieval sources in this region are too uninformative for us to base any firm hypothesis on them. But some trial soundings in Italian documents encourage us to think that the southern provinces, where, in the twelfth century, the most heavily burdened peasants toiled no more than a few days in the year on the lord's fields, had never known a system of compulsory labour as strict as the countries north of the Alps and the Loire. A very clear distinction can be drawn on the great estates of the early Middle Ages between the great 'families' of domestic serfs wholly burdened with the demesne tasks on the one hand, and the other peasant households who gave the lord a part of their harvest. Probably at that period there existed few exchanges of manpower between the lord's land and that of the tenancies.[23] One is thus led to ask instead whether at least some of the light labour services recorded in certain documents drawn up after 1100 were not innovations. The improvement of agricultural technique and the desire to till the soil better may perhaps have encouraged lords to impose such labour services in very recent times. Some lords had succeeded in doing so by using new powers which the extension of the rights of the *ban* had put into their hands. It is thus far from impossible that in these regions the system of reduced labour services known in the twelfth century was not so much the residue of a decayed structure, as, at least in part, a recent creation.

* * *

In the northern half of the continent, i.e. in the zone in which the agrarian structure of the early Middle Ages is much better illuminated by the great Carolingian *polyptyques*, labour services in the twelfth century remained quite clearly much heavier. The tenants of the demesne of Manise in the Meuse country had then to work two or three days a month with their animals, if they had any, for nothing. To this regular co-operation supplementary labour services were added at the time of spring and autumn plough-

[22] Duby, 442; see also Document No. 84, p. 437. [23] See p. 53

ing and at haymaking and harvest. Each *manse* provided in this way fifty-seven days of labour every year; furthermore each holding fulfilled certain 'tasks', such as the ploughing in May of a plot taken from the demesne fields.

The abbeys of Lorraine required from the peasant farms which flanked the demesnes services of the same kind as in the ninth century: supplies of cut wood; the cultivation of an *ansange* made up of two parcels taken from the demesne, one sown with winter corn and the other with spring; and finally seasonal services. Every *manse* had to construct in March an enclosure of a given length; in July it had to mow the hay, toss it and carry it; in August it had to take part in the harvest, in carrying the crops, in cleaning the barn; finally and above all else it had to lend its plough at the three ploughing seasons.[24]

However, these obligations all appear considerably less onerousthan those supported by even the least burdened Carolingian *manses*. Labour services were reduced between the ninth and the twelfth centuries; it is impossible to doubt it. We can glimpse some details of this reduction in manorial documents. On the demesnes of the monastery of Marmoutier in Alsace, the *manses* still owed in the eleventh century the *servitium triduanum*, the free service on three days weekly which once characterized the servile tenancies in Carolingian Germania. A written deed tells us that it was suppressed by the abbot in 1117. He converted it into a rather heavy money payment, since it was worth as much as all the other money dues to which the tenant was liable. The manorial administrators had taken this decision in consideration of 'the negligence, the uselessness, the slackness and the idleness of those who serve'.[25] Useless because the manpower was underemployed; idle because the forced labourers hung around the yard at a loose end. Since forced labour no longer served a purpose, it would surely be much more profitable to lay hands on the spare cash which peasant households now had at their disposal. The peasants would pay a good price to buy back the time they wasted away from home, and it would be preferable to hire the few workers necessary to perform their tasks.

This example is revealing. It is possible that here and there in the northern part of the former Carolingian Empire, some labour services had disappeared as a result of a reduction in the area directly cultivated by the lords. In particular we can see that some *lots corvées*, i.e. plots of land to be cultivated by the compulsory services of the tenants, were detached from the demesne and came to be included in the appurtenances of the *manse* which once cared for them and which received the entire disposal of these arable plots in exchange

[24] F. L. Ganshof, 'Note sur une charte de saint Gérard pour l'église de Brogne', in *Mélanges F. Courtoy*, Gembloux, 1952; Document No. 115, p. 468
[25] Perrin, 467, p. 102

for supplementary dues. We can guess also that the dissolution of the links of manpower between estate and tenancy was hurried on by the dismemberment of the *seigneurie* through the partition and almsgiving which separated certain tenancies from the manorial fields they had for generations helped to cultivate. The fragmentation of the *manses* also played its part: it was not always easy in fact to divide the labour services between the autonomous tenants of each fragment of a dismantled tenancy. It was often preferable to convert these services into a cash sum which was more easily divided. Many labour services were probably lost in this way.

Nevertheless it appears that there were two principal economic reasons why forced labour dwindled away between the ninth century and the twelfth. Firstly the manpower provided by those subject to forced labour became superfluous – 'useless' in the phrase of the Alsatian text. The improvement of the ploughing equipment and the increase in productivity which it caused made purely manual labour less sought after. The use of better ploughs, stronger animals, more efficient methods of harnessing, made it no longer necessary to collect together huge teams of workers to till the soil with their hoes, or to transport goods on their backs. But just at this moment demographic growth, the creation of new holdings, the break up of old ones, and the formation of territorial lordships increased the numbers of those subject to forced labour. Many lords no longer knew what to do with these excessive numbers of men. On top of this a second factor intervened. It was the period when the growth of exchange introduced more money into the small dependent cultivations while at the same time it facilitated the recruitment of wage labour. The masters were encouraged, as in the southern regions, to commute the services. In short we can assume that the decay of the Carolingian system of labour services was gradual and had probably spread widely in all directions by the year 1100. But according to the evidence, technical progress and the quickening of monetary circulation in the course of the twelfth century hastened this decay at the very moment when, as we have said above, the masters for the same reasons renounced their demands for liveries of manufactured products.[26]

*   *   *

England has to be considered separately. On certain ecclesiastical manors at least, the only ones where we can even guess at economic conditions, the connection of labour on tenancies and demesnes remained much closer in the

---

[26] See p. 153. It is worth investigating whether this phenomenon cannot in some way be related to a change in economic and social relationships within the peasantry itself. In Carolingian times some tenants owned domestic slaves who helped them to discharge the labour services owed by their *manse*. Now this auxiliary manpower appears itself to have been absorbed after the year 1000. Perrin, 256.

twelfth century than anywhere else, and certainly as close as the *polyptyques* suggest it to have been on the continent in the ninth century. Such a relationship already existed in the Saxon era, as is proved by a text drawn up shortly after the year 1000, which describes the services of the *gebura* or 'peasant'.[27] Such services had not very much changed by the second half of the twelfth century when inventories of the great monastic estates proliferated.

The manors then owned all their own ploughs and the *bovarii* who handled them. Even so, these teams could not till all the demesne land, and the tenants had to carry out one-third and sometimes one-half of the ploughing. The tenants were not all subject to the same dues, and documents of the period place them in two distinct categories according to the incidence and nature of their obligations. One group merely performed some seasonal and supplementary services such as 'boonworks', or *precariae*, which generally made use of draught animals and consisted of definite tasks like carting or ploughing. The manorial tenants whose assistance was limited in this way were considered 'free' in terms of the legal criteria recognized by custom. From the point of view of demesne cultivation their economic position differed little from that of the German or northern French peasants. These casual workers ate in the refectory on their working days and shared the servants' allowance. On the other hand the second group of tenancies was much more closely associated with the cultivation of the lords' land. Let us take the bordars' and cottars' tenancies: these men's work in their master's 'hall', unpaid for one or two days a week and remunerated for the others, was, as we have seen, very similar to that of the *bovarii* and the domestic menservants. The principal share of the compulsory manpower was supplied by these men whom English texts after Domesday Book called 'villeins', true peasants.

The tenancies 'in villeinage' of the monastic manors of the twelfth century, like the Carolingian *manses*, comprised arable of very unequal extent. On average, however, an area of land which a plough could till in thirty days was about able to feed a peasant family; but it required no more than half the time and physical power of the villein and his tools. The other half was available to the master to dispose of in several ways. The villein tenants were obliged like others to perform boonworks. It should be noted that these tasks were often performed in the lord's household. For instance the villein washed and sheared the sheep or prepared malt for the manorial brewhouse at Christmas and Easter. Villein labour always made a significant contribution to manpower: on the demesnes of Peterborough Abbey in the first quarter of the twelfth century, the villein had to lend his plough for three days in the autumn, three days in the spring and one in summer; on top of this he had to

---

[27] Document No. 92, p. 443

prepare and sow four acres with spring grain. However, the specific obligations of villeinage consisted of weekly services, 'weekworks'. Each tenancy in this category sent a man three mornings a week to the manor to perform whatever he might be ordered to do.[28]

This regular assistance was in fact adjusted in such a way as to fit in with the needs of the agricultural calendar. In 1185 on one of the demesnes cultivated by the Templars in Gloucestershire, villein tenancies provided only two man-days per week during the slack season from Martinmas to haymaking. On the other hand they had to give four days a week as long as haymaking lasted, and then again two until 1st August. When harvest began and the need for manpower became more pressing than at any other time of the year, six man-days were required from them each week, two on Monday and Wednesday and one on Tuesday and Thursday. As soon as the corn was carried the service fell to four days a week until 11th November.[29] This arrangement of labour services demonstrates clearly that they were not, like the 'boonworks', or the services demanded on the continental demesnes, supplementary to the demesnes' normal needs. The interdependence was so close that on certain manors villein households were integrated into the team of permanent manorial servants in August every day except Sunday. Like the serf settled in a household of his own on German estates in the ninth century, the English villein in fact bore the appearance of a half-time domestic, fed by his master on the days of whole-time service and remunerated by a parcel of fields comprising his tenancy from which he was expected to be able to provide his family's basic subsistence. He therefore occupied an intermediate position between the two categories of workers employed on all the European *seigneuries*, the permanent servants of the *familia* and the persons subject to periodic labour services who at intervals came together on the lord's fields to help in their cultivation.

It should be noted further that on English manors (at any rate, to repeat, on those whose economic structure we can trace, that is those belonging to certain religious establishments, mostly Benedictine of the ancient observance) a slow movement of commutation developed during the twelfth century. As on the continent money dues tended to be substituted for labour services. The lords did not actually abandon their right to require peasants for such and such a 'task', but they agreed to 'sell' it to them for a year. I take as an example the manor of Fontmell in Dorset, belonging to Shaftesbury Abbey, which is known from two successive inquisitions. In 1130-1135, in addition to the three days of weekwork, it was incumbent on the villein tenant to plough an acre and a half, to harrow one acre, and to pay one

---

[28] Stenton, 275, p. 136
[29] A. L. Poole, *From Domesday Book . . .*, p. 42 (Temple Guiting)

measure of corn and sevenpence halfpenny. Finally he had to pay a tax of tenpence levied in lieu of delivery of wood for enclosures, which can be considered as the first commutation of a labour service. Forty years later, the 'weekworks' were no longer claimed. The lord kept only the disposal of the seasonal labour of haymaking, harvest and cartage. On the other hand he levied much heavier dues, varying between 35 and 50 pence on each tenancy, which represented the price of services from which the villeins were now exempt.[30] The conversion is exactly like the one which the abbot of Marmoutier instigated in 1117, and it was most likely inspired by the same considerations. In the same way the monks of Burton renounced the services of some villein tenancies in exchange for a payment of two or three shillings.[31] We must not imagine that analagous changes took place on every manor, but they can be traced on a great many of those observable through their documents. It appears that the lords were more willing to adopt such changes when their residence was not too close and when, as a result, they found the supervision of the demesne troublesome. On the eve of the twelfth century at Minchinhampton, a remote manor of the abbey of the Trinity of Caen, labour services were actually exacted from twenty-six tenancies while on nine others dues only were levied; fifty years later no more than twenty tenancies remained to perform the labour services, and finally about 1170 even these had disappeared completely.[32]

* * *

The system of forced labour and the existence everywhere of large teams of domestic workers confirm what can be learnt from the study of the demesne lands: landlords in the eleventh and twelfth centuries had not divorced themselves at all from direct cultivation. Whether it was retained in the hands of the master or whether it was entrusted to an agent or to a 'farmer', the demesne undoubtedly formed the most productive portion of manorial landownership. To demonstrate this I shall use figures from the inquisition covering the deaneries of the abbey of Cluny about 1150. On six of these manorial units, and during a poor season at that, the lord's land produced four times as much grain and wine as was delivered by all the tenancies. Domestic needs were thus very largely covered and the harvest itself provided a large surplus for sale. The administrator of one of these manors negotiated the sale of one-eighth of the wheat harvested on the demesne furlongs; and another sold the whole wheat harvest and one-third of the rye harvest.[33]

[30] Stenton, 275, p. 140   [31] Document No. 107, p. 457
[32] A. L. Poole, *From Domesday Book . . .*, p. 45
[33] Documents Nos. 113 and 114, pp. 464, 465 *et seq.*: Duby, 442

It can be seen, however, that methods of management did not remain identical with those we are familiar with in the early Middle Ages. They appear to have been especially modified in the course of the twelfth century in England as well as in France and Germany (Italian developments are still veiled in darkness). The growing importance of ploughing in the preparation of the arable and the greater efficiency of draught animals in cereal production, encouraged the strengthening of plough teams in the manorial household where the oxherds, servants skilled in handling the plough, became more and more the centre of the domestic economy. These two considerations made it equally advisable to avoid losing any labour services with animals due from the tenants at different ploughing seasons. They caused labour services to be more keenly claimed, and to be extended; they caused harrowing services to be instituted, and the rights of the *ban* also to be utilized to make the draught animals of villagers who were not tenants available for work on the demesne fields. The value of labour services with animals was undoubtedly enhanced in the twelfth century.

On the other hand it became increasingly unprofitable to bring into the 'hall' famished and thieving labourers who wasted their time. The lords often preferred to send these compulsory workers back to their holdings and to allow them to produce there additional goods which they could easily sell on the expanding local market. The master was then tempted to turn a part of his dues into money, and with it to pay hired workers who could be engaged at the appropriate times. Commutation affected particularly vineyard work, since the vines needed skilful attention and were better not entrusted to compulsory labour liable to scamp the work.

This development was bound to loosen the ties between the holdings of dependent peasants and their lord's estate. The peasants were much freer to dispose of their own productive power. They could cultivate their own land better and obtain more from it. They became accustomed to attending markets more frequently in order to raise the money with which to pay the lord's exactions. They appeared at the manor much less often, and then mostly to bring their dues or money payments. Personal relations became easier. As for the lords and their agents, their economic position changed but little. They acted perhaps more often than before as employers who provided sustenance and wages for their servants; on the other hand, their role of recipients of rent became more predominant.

(d) The structure of manorial rent

Carolingian inventories show that landlords had already succeeded in appropriating a significant part of the produce grown on the confines of the manor by letting peasants make use of certain constituents and equipment of the manor in return for payment. Rents could be derived from woods and pastures, the mill, the bakehouse, the brewery, and even the parish church through oblations and tithes. These demesne profits, directly siphoning off part of the output of the neighbouring peasant farms, were considerably inflated in the course of the eleventh and twelfth centuries as the number of village inhabitants increased and the soil became more fruitful. We might even think that it was through exploiting the mills and levying tithes that the lords drew most of their advantages from the reclamation and settlement of the wastes.[34] As soon as outsiders were settled in a corner of the woodland the amounts of oblations and death duties began to rise and tithe barns to fill up. Certainly all the inquests in the mid-twelfth century show how important was the contribution of these sources to the profits of landownership. The description of the demesnes of Cluny, to which I have several times referred, reveal this clearly. In two deaneries the mills yielded enough to feed the whole of the domestic staff; one single church brought in 600 deniers and 50 measures of grain each year, i.e. more corn than all the rents in kind levied on one of these two manors, and more money than the lord received from all the tenants on the other. The barns of a third demesne received seven times more grain from the church and tithes and five times more from mills, bakehouses and rights of usage in the woodlands than was delivered by peasant tenancies.[35] At that period the highest rents did not come from tenancies; it was far more profitable to own mills, a church in a large parish, or better still, tithes. This was the reason why the aristocratic families who held tithes did not give them up when the spread of Gregorian ideas about 1100 compelled them to renounce the ownership of the actual churches. This is also why so many lawsuits in areas of reclamation related to the destination of the tithes of *novales*. And finally this is why so many of the tithes supposed in modern times to be of a religious nature and claimed as such by the Church had probably originated in tithes arbitrarily imposed by lay lords in feudal days.[36]

★   ★   ★

Charters of gift and inventories drawn up in the twelfth century describe peasant holdings as being mostly organized as they were in the early Middle Ages. All over France and Germany there were *manses, demi-manses* or *quartiers*, i.e. the units of manorial taxation, formed, as in the Carolingian

---

[34] See pp. 71-72   [35] Document No. 114, p. 465; Duby, 442

[36] *Les dîmes en Forez, Chartes du Forez XV*, Mâcon, 1959; Kuujo, 359; Van der Linden, 328. In Rouergue in the eleventh century all tithes were in lay hands and some only were subsequently given to the Church; J. Bousquet, 'Vie sociale et vie religieuse en Rouergue. Les plus anciennes chartes de Saint-Austremoine (XIe-XIIIe siècle)', in *Annales du Midi*, 1961.

period, of buildings where the family lived and a related group of 'appurtenances' rounding off the farm. The inhabited plot was the basis for reckoning the services even when several tenant households lived on it. Each plot
was recorded in the rentals under the name of all those who held it and who
were together responsible for the charges. The same structure existed in the
English countryside: the 'virgate' and the 'bovate', even though their areas
were far from equal, appeared in the eyes of the lords and their officials as the
nucleus of the manorial organization, created to support a peasant family.
'This land was counted as two virgates, but because two men could not live
on it the two virgates have been made into one'[37]: alterations of this sort are
proof of the real connection between the institution of the family and the
agricultural unit. In France units called *tenures* which seem to be of more
recent formation are sometimes encountered in manorial documents of the
period; but they show a similar structure. The house and land, firmly linked
together, was entrusted *en bloc* to a family of cultivators who were collectively liable for its entire service.

The liabilities of tenancies formed in this way usually comprised, apart
from the labour services which already existed or were subsequently added,
a complicated bundle of dues. The composition and amount of these charges
could vary markedly within the same manor even though the area of the
taxable unit was not so very different. In one Mâconnais village twelve
manses were dependent on the same lord; their various dues were organized
in seven distinct ways, and revealed inequalities which doubled their burden.[38]
As a general rule the burden of obligations which neighbouring tenants owed
their landlord differed a great deal. In the twelfth century the lists of rents
preserved in archives are infinitely more complicated than the Carolingian
inventories; they are lengthy and elaborate since they record innumerable
differences from one tenancy to another.

The dues themselves were frequently mixed and were paid at one and the
same time both in agricultural and animal produce and money. In the texts
of the Mâcon region which analyze the composition of rents, about half the
tenancies had to pay at least a few pence; in English documents the proportion
was much higher, for it was exceptional for tenancies not to be obliged to
make regular payments in cash. Nevertheless, generally speaking, dues in kind
prevailed, and – this is worth underlining – the preponderance is much more
obvious than in Carolingian inventories. The dues were mostly contributions of wheat and oats, the two kinds of grain so essential to the lord's table
and stable. Frequently also the *manses* kept the master's house provided with
meat and delivered 'haunches of cows', lamb, pork or fowls raised in the

[37] A. L. Poole, *From Domesday Book . . .*, p. 48, n. 3 (1189)
[38] *Cartulaire de Sainte-Vincent de Mâcon*. No. 516

farmyard. In the regions where small cultivators produced it themselves, they also supplied some wine. There were also obligations to bring hemp and other minor crops grown in the homestead toft. These liveries were spread over the year. Here, for instance, is how the rents due from the dependent *manses* of a priory in Dauphiné were distributed: a loaf and some meat on the first of January; a capon in Lent; a lamb and bread at Easter; several sacks of grain after the harvest; and pork or mutton on St Julian's day.[39] Not much, after all.

It is quite impossible to observe anywhere at this period a definite tendency to replace supplies of food with money payments. In an occasional document a money rent appears to have been substituted for a former obligation in the shape of livestock, as for instance the tenancy in Comminges which paid twelve deniers 'instead of a pig'.[40] But examples of this kind are too scattered to prove the existence of a pronounced tendency amounting to a commutation of dues parallel to that of labour services. Actual conversions, when we find them, did not all work in the same direction. Some of them tended to increase the volume of money rents: others, on the contrary, reduced them, as happened in northern Italy, where many money dues were transformed into liveries of agricultural produce at the option of the lords, who were townsmen wishing themselves to profit from the widening market for cereals and wine. It would thus be rash to assume that the conversion of rents had increased the flow of cash into the coffers of the landlords to the same extent as the partial commutation of manual services.

⋆   ⋆   ⋆

In later inventories we can observe at the end of groups of compact family tenancies, further lists of tenancies of a different kind, simple parcels each liable for a particular kind of rent. Some of the fields or meadows separately rented in this way seem to be fragments of the demesne, like former *ansanges* (plots cultivated by forced labour) now leased out for rent. Others seem to be erstwhile free lands of poor peasants who had become clients, and in doing so had placed their lands as well as their bodies under the protection of a master, and thereby burdened them with a money charge as a sign of allegiance.

---

[39] Didier, 433

[40] Higounet, 456. One part of the manor of the Chapter of Beaujeu yielded 20 *setiers* of grain and 36 sous in 1090. Sixty years later, on a neighbouring demesne group belonging to the abbey of Cluny, the corn dues were about the same but the cash yield was valued at 850 sous (Duby, 261, p. 313). In fact, then, as the structure of obligations from one demesne to another varied infinitely, comparison between the two types of payments cannot prove that the value of money payments (*cens*) was generally inflated in this region in the first half of the twelfth century.

However, when we look at them closely, we become aware that most of the little plots of land granted separately were situated in the recently occupied parts of the village lands. They resulted directly from this recent occupation, the lord having given out the land in small parcels to the villagers who undertook the necessary work of reclamation. Of these new-style tenancies many were undoubtedly conceded for limited terms, for one, two or three 'lives'. But these have left little trace in the archives which never preserved titles to leases after they had expired. Almost all the tenancies we find were hereditary, though much less rigid than the ancient ones and, above all, transferable as a whole or in part. In southern countries they assumed the legal form inherited from Roman antiquity, such as the Italian *livelli*, or the emphyteutic lease, thus named in the twelfth century by the lawyers of southern Gaul brought up in the traditions of legal scholarship.[41] Wherever they were, their obligation was neither labour service, nor submission to the justice of the lord, but rent alone. They were rent-paying lands, *terres censales* or *censives*, and they multiplied as vineyards and reclamations extended.

Except in the regions where the vine had for long been indigenous and wine the everyday drink, *manses* did not include in their appurtenances any enclosures planted with vinestocks. The master's residence was the only one to be so provided. But in the twelfth, and even in the eleventh, century we know that many lords wished to extend the areas under vines. They entrusted these new plantations as far as they could to their household servants. But the undertaking required a great deal of manpower, and so the vineyards were often enlarged with the help of neighbouring peasants to whom certain demesne fields were granted to be turned into vineyards. The first of these contracts, traces of which are to be found from the tenth century in the Mâconnais and in the twelfth century in Saintonge,[42] resulted, as we have seen, in the division of the new close as soon as it began to produce into two halves of which the peasant kept the sole ownership of one. But generally in the twelfth century the owner of the land preferred to leave the vineyards entirely in the hands of the vinedresser in exchange for participation in the crop; he kept for himself a quarter, a third or a half of the *vendange*. It was not strictly speaking what is usually called a *métayage*, since the costs were borne by the cultivator, but more a means of adjusting the rent of the land to the extremely variable returns from viticulture. During the first five or six years the young plants yielded nothing, and it was then not possible to impose a fixed rent on a man who toiled in the close without profit; the latter did not wish to bear single-handed the risks of production, even when the vines had begun to bear. A method of levying a share of the fruits, familiar to country-men since it resembled the tithe, was therefore applied to the vines. It had only

---

[41] Document Nos. 87-90, pp. 439-442   [42] Dion, 105, p. 360

one disadvantage for the lord; he had to watch carefully to avoid being cheated.

A similar system of dividing the profits between the landlord and the peasant entrepreneur was applied to the fields and the meadows won from the wastes of the lordship which the lord had not reclaimed with the labour of his domestics. The conditions of cultivation differed little from those of the vineyard: a prolonged period of unproductive work, and uncertain future yields. An annual levy of the fourth, ninth or twelfth sheaf of the harvest – called *champart* or *terrage* in northern France, and *tasque* or *agrier* in the south – became the characteristic charge on the plots in the new parts of village lands.

Nevertheless rent of this kind also had its inconveniences. For the peasant to begin with, it seemed often unjustly burdensome. In an age when average yields seldom surpassed four to one, and often fell below that mark, to give up a quarter of the harvest to the lord meant to let him have at least a third of the disposable crop. Manorial rent was thus raised to a substantially higher level than on the ancient lands of the *manses*. *Champart* had advantages for the cultivator when the occupation of the soil was still recent and the cultivation shifted, with the result that certain plots were left resting for several years in succession and no liveries had to be made from them. But as soon as cultivation became regular and intensive the peasant became conscious of the excessive weight of the charge. Besides, the master required his share 'on the spot'; i.e. on the stalk, and the peasant had to wait for the rent gatherer to make his rounds before he could remove his sheaves to shelter:

> '*son blé remaint de l'autre part*
> *qui est au vent et a la pluie*
> *au vilain malement ennuie*
> *de son blé qui gît par le champ.*'[43]

On his side the lord could be the victim of fraud. On new lands still dotted with trees and shrubs nothing was easier than to conceal a few sheaves of corn. The master who wished for a stable income also found it harder to adjust himself to fluctuating levies. Indeed, the habit had already grown up of exacting from new, but immediately productive, meadows, the return from which varied much less from year to year, a rent different from that exacted from arable. These lands were leased for an annual money rent fixed in proportion to their area. Thus, according to an agreement drawn up in 1208, the peasant user of the woods at Favières in Parisis, on occupation of a

---

[43] 'His corn remains outside / exposed to wind and rain / The villein is greatly concerned / about his corn which lies in the field.' *Conte des vilains de Verson*, verses 66–69, in L. Delisle, *Normandie*, p. 669.

meadow, had 'to give the lord one penny for the *novale*, and for each *arpent* of meadow one halfpenny in annual rent. If he were to transform the meadow into arable he would have to pay tithe and *champart.*'[44] A fixed levy appearing more convenient to all parties, lords and peasant agreed together to extend it to arable when the assarts came into full production. In fact to-wards mid-twelfth century both *champarts* and *tasques* become rarer in the records and rents more numerous. It was at this moment that the *terre de sarte* (as it was called in Lotharingia), forming a girdle around the *terre de mes*, the ancient portions where the plots remained attached to the *manse* and were granted with them, became in peasant vocabulary the 'rented lands'. They were similar to the *nova terra* which little by little grew at the expense of the great marshes in the English village lands on the edges of the Fens. The strips of arable bore a cash rent, levied according to the units of area. This was usually a minimal charge well below the site value of the land, the reclaimers in effect receiving a bonus.[45]

The settlers who came to settle in the heart of the forest in the new villages were granted entire tenancies of the same form as the *manses*: a measured parcel of land tied to the house – known as the *hôtise* in the Ile de France, the *casal* in Aquitaine and the *Hufe* by the German colonists – and its homestead toft. If the lord of the assart kept for himself a demesne in the new cultivated area, he might impose two or three days of forced labour at ploughing time,[46] but usually the pioneers were not subject to any labour service and the charge imposed on their holding was of the same type as the charges on the assarted plots on the fringes of the old village lands. For the house a fixed rent in cash and poultry[47]; for the land, tithe, *none*, *champart* or *tasque*. But in these new villages, also, levies on harvests were relinquished without too long a delay and fields were charged rents. The canons of Notre-Dame of Paris set a fixed rent, reckoned on the measured area, on the *hôtises* which they estab-lished in one such village in 1199; it was six *deniers* per *arpent*.[48]

*   *   *

To sum up: 1. The continued growth of agriculture and, in certain countries, of viticulture caused the progressive expansion of manorial rents through a multiplication of rent-producing units. This explains why so many religious houses flourished, why the aristocracy was so prosperous, and their standard of living, civilization and material culture made such vigorous pro-

---

[44] At Bois-Rufin a rent is levied on the meadows and a *terrage* on the fields (Document No. 37, p. 393).

[45] Document No. 129, p. 487; Miller, 198, p. 98; Verhulst, 208; Génicot, 189, p. 239

[46] *Cartulaire de Saint-Père de Chartres*, II, p. 438 (1111–1129)

[47] In the oldest of the *villeneuves* the rents of the plot containing the buildings is in kind; Higounet, 305   [48] *Cartulaire de Notre-Dame de Paris*, I, No. 79

gress. It must, however, be emphasized again that most of the profits came from exploiting mills and levying tithes and *champart*, i.e. from direct charges on harvests.

Most masters had to entrust this function to intermediaries. Servants were stationed at the mouth of the winepress to measure the wine, and scoured the woods to discover the sheaves of corn, while the mill and the parish church were usually leased to 'farmers'. These agents, of course, kept back a part of the taxes for themselves. In this way there grew up and prospered a new class who were strategically placed in village society between master and peasant, who were parasitic on the manor and who enriched themselves at the expense of both parties.

2. It must also be noted that in the course of the twelfth century, but especially after 1150, the quickening circulation of money encouraged lords to extend the part that money played in rent. As a result of the changes which new affluence and more worldly preoccupations made to their way of life, many masters gradually detached themselves from the farmyard and assumed a more sophisticated way of life. The small fines imposed in the private court where the master settled the quarrels between himself and his tenants over services, 'new rents' to replace *champarts*, and cash payments to buy off labour services, drew into the manorial household a larger share of the cash which passed through peasant hands.[49]

3. Nevertheless the proportion of money income remained small. We can see this clearly from the inventory of the Cluny manors where the commutation of services actually appears to have been well advanced. And all manorial enquiries before 1180 reveal a similar preponderance of dues in kind. They also show the generally light incidence of ground rent. From the 72 tenancies responsible to one of these manorial units at the beginning of the twelfth century, the cathedral church of Mâcon received each year, apart from the 57 measures of wine, 8 measures of oats and 107 loaves (and these quantities of foodstuffs correspond very nearly to the annual food allowance of a servant family), only 40 sous, that is hardly more than the price of a second-rate horse. Such an income would allow no more than one or two households to be maintained in a modest style of life.[50] In fact, then, rent did not usually represent more than a small contribution to the lord's income, the greater part of which came from cultivating the demesne. It is only necessary to add that the system of land ownership, as revealed through contemporary documents, was favourable to a peasant economy. It did not overwhelm the small cultivator, nor did it exact more than a small portion of his revenue. The men who, in the eleventh and twelfth centuries, raised the yield of agriculture and won so many fields from the wastelands, were not apparently

[49] Raftis, 201, p. 93   [50] Duby, 261, p. 313-314

prepared to toil for their masters' gain alone. A tenancy in the hands of a peasant was hardly less profitable than an allod. But we must not forget that all these humble people, free holders as well as tenants, had still to yield part of their profit to another lord, who claimed to control not their land alone, but also their bodies.

2. THE EXPLOITATION OF MEN

(a) The familia

The numbers of landlords were great and they belonged to all ranks of society. Twelfth-century documents record peasants who owned more land than they could cultivate themselves, who leased out plots to other villagers less well provided for, and who acquired in this way economic power over their tenants. It is true that to have power over men as well as land was a less common privilege, but we may assume that every noble family, monastery or chapter controlling and exploiting a *familia*, a group of dependent peasants, in its vicinity formed the centre of a domestic lordship. The importance of this kind of economic domination was indisputable, since it was certainly most highly valued by twelfth-century lords. Men were still relatively few in number and worth much more than land, which was after all valueless without men to work it. A lord's wealth and the very foundations of his power were based on his 'house', the number of his servitors, the devotion and service which he could expect from the retinue of men loyal to him. The most highly prized of a lord's possessions were neither his fields nor the small amount of gold and jewellery locked away in his inner chamber, nor were these objects of envy to others. The real wealth of that period was to be found only in the 'family'.

The complex social group known as the 'family' included first of all the domestics. It contained also peasants set up in their own homes; some, but not all, of the lord's tenants; freeholders who had become clients; and occasionally tenants of other lords. The domestic lordship did not in any way correspond to the boundaries of landlordship. Former serfs, or descendants of free men who were once placed in commendation, all, with their progeny and their personal possessions, in fact belonged to the lord, who had the power to give them away, sell them, or enfranchise them. He considered them 'his men'. What then did he expect from them?

* * *

Above all he expected them to work. The eleventh- and twelfth-century 'family' constituted before all else a reservoir of manpower into which the master could dip freely for help in the cultivation of his demesne. The first duty of a dependant consisted in 'service', by which was meant that he was bound to fulfil all his lord's orders. To make the most of the labour force which was entirely at his disposal the lord kept it as far as possible under his own roof. The huge quantities of grain produced by landed estates went primarily to feed the domestic workers who were mostly young men and girls, either unmarried or childless. The labour force was of no use unless it was full of vigour and to that end it had constantly to be renewed. For a long time, while the slave trade remained active, i.e. at least until the early twelfth century in Germany and England, this was accomplished by purchase. The masters also claimed bastards born in the house. Lastly, and this eventually became the normal method of recruitment, they chose their servants from among the children of those of 'their men' who lived with their families in huts of their own. A diploma given in 1035 by the king of Germany, Conrad II, laid down the powers of the abbot of Limbourg over 'the unmarried sons (of men of his *familia*); he may place whoever he wishes in the kitchen, whoever he wishes in the bakery, whoever he wishes to do the laundry, whoever he wishes to look after the stable, and he may assign whoever he wishes to do each task. As for those who are married, the abbot may appoint them at will to be cellarers, seedsmen, collectors of tolls, or foresters. . . .' On the manors of Gloucester Abbey in the thirteenth century the villeins were inspected every year; the youngest and most active were selected for domestic service in the master's house. At the same period at Chalgrove manor in Oxfordshire villeins with adult sons had to present them to the master at Michaelmas for him to choose those whom he wished to retain for his home.[51]

We may well think that in the eleventh century the essential economic value of the *familia* centred on this group of domestic servants. The men whom the master had housed in their own cabins (*casés*), were still obliged, it is true, to perform personal service, as distinct from the charges and labour services incumbent on their tenancy. They came to work in the household on certain days; their wives wove the lord's flax and wool at home or in the workshops of the 'hall', they fashioned at home various wooden objects for use on the demesne.[52] But this labour supply remained insufficient. Their master mainly expected from them what was later called in Germany *Gesindedienst*: he wanted them to rear children and put them at his disposal when they were old enough to serve. Like the servile *manses* of Carolingian times, the cabins inhabited by the men of the familia were nurseries of young domestic workers.

*   *   *

However, as the eleventh century advanced, and as techniques improved,

[51] Diplomas of Conrad II, No. 216; Document No. 134, p. 495; Bennett, 149, p. 184
[52] Document No. 117, p. 470

less manpower was needed in the 'hall'. The roughly woven cloth and planks produced by the dependent households lost their value. Little by little the lords reduced their domestic staff, housed more of their men under separate roofs and allowed these households greater economic independence. In the domestic lordship, as in the landlordship, and probably at about the same pace, the physical relationships were being relaxed. Henceforth it was by periodical claims on their men's property that the masters sought to profit from the rights they had over them.

In the Germanic regions and northern France, religious foundations had always had in their 'families' dependants whose status was too exalted for performance of manual labour. These *sainteurs* manifested their submission by paying an annual rent, sometimes in the form of wax for lighting the church, but mostly in the form of cash, and usually very little of that. The single coin that the *censuales* placed each year on the altar on the feast day of the saint was often sufficient token of their dependence.[53] The charges could sometimes however, amount to several *sous*, and assume real economic significance. In Bavarian abbeys in the thirteenth century the 'men of the altar' were listed in three categories according to whether they owed one, five or thirty *deniers* each year. The annual payment of a small personal charge (*cens*) in money, a 'poll tax', *chevage*, considered as a symbol of the tie binding dependants and due from all individuals not living in the house, was certainly the earliest of the levies created by the domestic lordship.

Probably a good deal more profitable was the exercise of justice. Servants and slaves had from earliest times found themselves wholly subject to correction by their master. As public justice became enfeebled, masters claimed from private lords wielding territorial jurisdiction the right to punish their men and even to judge strangers who had inflicted injury on a member of their family. According to a custumal of a manor in Berri, when a member of the *familia* suffered an injury, the lord levied a fine on the culprit, and besides, in virtue of his position as a protector, he appropriated a third of the damages awarded to the victim.[54] The bitterest disputes which raged between the abbeys and their 'advocates' in Germany and in eastern France, and their 'guardians' in central France, concerned the administration of justice and the right to impose fines on personal dependants. For a culprit had to pay five or seven *sous* for the least misdemeanour. This was frequently more than the ready money he had in his possession. The lord who tried him was thereupon empowered to impound anything of value in his house.

Lastly, in certain circumstances the lord acquired the habit of claiming

---

[53] See p. 192
[54] Van der Kieft, 458, Document in proof No. 13 (1073), No. 30, p. 244. (My own interpretation differs slightly from the author's, pp. 123-125.)

gifts from his 'men'. These gifts began with marriage. A dependant was not in fact his own master and could dispose neither of himself nor of his children. If his son or daughter got married they could no longer take up domestic service, and if they left their father's cabin the labour force which the lord could expect from it was depleted. Therefore, before the wedding could take place, permission had to be obtained which, little by little, no doubt, as peasant households gradually became more prosperous, ceased to be granted free of charge. The English villein paid 'merchet' at the marriage of his daughter, a sum equal to that demanded of him when he sold an ox. Besides, the lord generally required the marriage to be arranged within the ranks of his own *familia*. In fact if one of the intended spouses was of free status, or belonged to another master, a part of the service due from the household might be lost permanently to the lord, and he might also lose possession of any children of the union. 'The men of the land of St Peter shall not take strange wives, so long as they can find wives whom they could marry in the "hall". It must be the same for the women. . . .'[55] It was perfectly true that endogamy was frequently impossible, for ideas about incest held at that time prohibited a union between quite distant relations. Members of the *familia*, especially if it was a small one, soon all became cousins, making *formariage*, as it was called, necessary. But before they were given permission they had to offer the lord compensation. In the eleventh century a slave of Cluny had to give up the ownership of his own serfs in order to be allowed to marry a woman of free status who was a dependant of another master. Levies of this kind are mentioned about 1120 in the oath taken by mayors of Notre-Dame de Chartres.[56]

The death of a dependant offered another opportunity for a demand. In fact the movable goods acquired in his lifetime by a bondsman were considered to belong in the first instance to his lord, who claimed to be his chief heir. The master in fact took upon himself the right of 'mortmain', i.e. he did not take everything, but reserved for himself a portion of the personal estate. He exacted a third or a half of the movable estate (this was the German *Buteil* claimed from some dependants), or else he took first choice of one head of cattle at the death of a man, or one garment at the death of a woman; he took the *meilleur catel*, according to the expression in use in northern France. This prerogative gave the *seigneur de corps* an excellent opportunity for appropriating periodically the goods accumulated in the houses of dependants. In addition, the protector probably demanded other 'aids' from his men whenever he was pressed by special need.

[55] *Cartulaire de Beaulieu*, No. 101
[56] *Receuil des chartes de Cluny*, IV, No. 3649; *Cartulaire de Notre-Dame de Chartres*, I, No. 58

It is unfortunately true that we still do not fully understand these taxes. We cannot say precisely at what moment they became part of established custom. *Chevage* certainly existed in the tenth century, and appeared to be an even more ancient practice. The first references to lords' tapping the inheritances of their dependants, and the first mention of *formariage*, date from the last years of the eleventh century in southern Burgundy. All the indications lead us to believe, however, that the claims of the masters became more insistent during the twelfth century at the period when labour services began to decline in importance, and peasant prosperity was growing. Thus in Bavaria 'men of the altar', dependants of free status attached to the great monasteries, had mortmain and marriage taxes imposed on them, descended into an inferior servitude and lost what honourable condition their subjection had hitherto preserved.[57] It is permissible to think that since the eleventh century the levies of the domestic lordship had followed in the wake of the fiscal powers of its great counterpart, the lordship deriving its revenue from monopolies and privileges (*seigneurie banale*).

(b) *The* ban

Lords able to exploit the rights of the *ban* i.e. of exclusive privileges and monopolies, were very few. In more than half of western Europe, in England, Normandy, northern France and Germania, kings, dukes and counts themselves exercised the *ban* over extensive territories. Even in the regions, like Aquitaine and the ancient kingdom of Burgundy, where the decay of royal power had gone farthest, entire groups of villages of a score or more acknowledged the same protector, 'Lords' in the real sense of the word, these princes, castellans, and 'advocates' of the great abbeys, imposed the heaviest, and of course the most lucrative, judicial sanctions. They levied 'exactions' and 'customs' on countless rural homesteads as the price of the peace they were able to maintain. The archives are too scanty to let us see at all clearly the forms which the *ban*, in its economic aspects, assumed in the eleventh and twelfth centuries. We know only a little about the rights which churches in possession of 'immunities' preserved (and their prerogatives were not usually of the highest order), and sometimes also about some of the rights which their lay rivals had wrested from them.

In France, where the study of 'customs' has been carried farthest, the chief phases of the fiscal powers of the *ban* appear to have been as follows:

1. The system became established in the first half of the eleventh century and the earliest profits came from the exploitation of justice. The lords appropriated the right of *vicaria*: they controlled rural tribunals and collected

[57] Dollinger, 159

fines. Probably simultaneously (these taxes appear about 1020 in the documents of the Mâconnais) the castellans responsible for police functions in the area carried out requisitions intended to maintain the cavalry of their men-at-arms. They levied dues for protecting the harvest (*maréchaussée*), or for stabling horses (*gîte des chevaux*), requisitioned hay and oats, which *laboureurs*, wealthier peasants, bore at a double rate. The lord's servants also collected a levy on crops (*moissonage*) and took a share of the sheaves which they had protected until harvest time. All these 'customs' often went under the name of 'gifts', and they were in fact supposed to reflect the gratitude of those protected.

2. Towards the mid-eleventh century we see references to the *droit de gîte* multiplying. This right enabled the castellan to charge peasant households with the upkeep of his agents and their horses and his hunting dogs for the period of one day. The annual protection taxes of *sauvement* or 'ward' (*garde*) imposed on village communities are also first mentioned at this time.

3. It seems as if new exactions became established in the last quarter of the eleventh century. Carting and ploughing services, previously assigned to the upkeep and provisioning of fortresses, were transferred to the lord's demesne to help in its cultivation. In order to take advantage of increasing road traffic, the lords set up new tolls and seized new commercial privileges, such as the *banvin* which reserved the monopoly of wine sales at the end of the season when the wine had begun to turn sour and when hogsheads had to be emptied in preparation for the new harvest. At the same period documents begin to record other monopolies which, under the rights of the *ban*, obliged villagers to use the lord's installations, such as presses or ovens, or else to buy a certain amount of wine at his tavern. From this period also date the first references to the *taille*, the *tolta*, or the right of tallage (*tollir*) which allowed a lord who claimed such power to demand material assistance whenever he needed it from the inhabitants of a territory and to apportion it amongst them. An act of 1090, by which king Philip I granted to the canons of Orleans 'all our justice, our rights and the *tolte* which we have here' over a vineyard in the Ile de France, at the same time as he granted the right of *vicaria*,[58] probably contains one of the oldest written references to this exaction. It seems that it added an arbitrary sum from time to time to the other prerogative receipts. It alone remained variable. *Gîte*, like labour services and *maréchaussée*, seems to have become before the end of the eleventh century a regular annual charge, strictly regulated by custom and based on the heartn and the home of the villager.

4. The finishing touches to this fiscal system were put during the twelfth century. Regulations fixed the rights exercised respectively by the lords in

[58] *Recueil des actes de Philippe Ier*, No. 123

possession of territorial prerogatives and by the lords exercising their powers as heads of families and households. Some time before 1150 castellans took cognizance of the expanding village markets, and established their right to levy a tax on transactions. Two particular changes occurred at this time. To begin with the lords manifested a greater desire to amass money. Dues which were formerly levied in kind were henceforth collected in cash. About 1050 the Mâconnais villagers delivered to their 'warden' a certain quantity of wine, but by 1115 this right of 'ward' (*garde*) was paid for in money. It was the same with the *taille*. To my knowledge the texts refer to it for the first time as the 'collection of cash' about 1180. The second change also affected the *taille*. In the latter half of the century it was losing its irregular and arbitrary character. It was becoming, to use a contemporary expression, *abonnée*; it took the shape of a fixed annual charge or rent. In 1157 the men of Rozoy had to agree henceforth to pay a rent of 18 livres of Provins every year to the canons of Notre-Dame of Paris who levied the *taille* at will; these charges were to be divided amongst all the villagers of the territory. According to the charter of franchise granted in 1185 to the town of Ferrières-en-Gâtinais, every house owed a rent of five sous a year as *taille*. A few years later the *tolte* levied by Etienne de Coucy was 'moderated' in such a way that 'every man owing *taille* pays four deniers on fixed terms'.[59]

This is the chronological outline which I believe it possible to establish on the basis of the documents relating to central France. I put it forward as the skeleton framework upon which an enquiry covering the whole of western Europe could be hung. Such an enquiry is likely to be exceedingly useful, for the emergence of the *ban* as a fiscal authority is consistent with other tendencies in the economy of the countryside, such as the spread of monetary media and the increasing prosperity of peasant households. It is possible through the chronology of taxation, which is relatively easily dated from documents, to divine the deeper and less obvious rhythm of expansion.

* * *

This system of taxation, gradually imposed as village wealth grew, laid a burden on the peasant economy, the weight of which at the end of the twelfth century is difficult to estimate. Contemporary documents are unfortunately much too uncommunicative and contain too few numerical details for the charges to be accurately measured, and there is nothing to enable us to relate the changes to the ability of the country folk to pay, even if we

---

[59] *Recueil de chartes de Cluny*, IV, No. 3115 and V, No. 3920; *Cartulaire de Notre-Dame de Paris*, I, p. 389; Perroy, 269, p. 76; *Recueil des Actes de Philippe Auguste*, I, No. 279; for tallage in England see, amongst others, Bennett, 149, pp. 139 *et seq.*

were in a position to know what this was. We have to be content with vague and scattered clues in the charters. These lead us to believe that the incidence of the different exactions was most inequitable.

The annual *gîte* or *moissonage* may have removed from the resources of each household only a few measures of grain or hay and one or two loaves every year, i.e. even less than the dues owed by the *manse*, which were also very light. But by means of the *taille*, so long as it remained an arbitrary charge, the lord could strip peasant households of all their savings: we know of one Mâconnais peasant in the early twelfth century who had to deliver 40 *sous* to the lord of the *ban*, and another who had to give him 100.[60] Even when regularized, these 'collections' transferred to the lord's coffers a large part of the cash earned by villagers. However, it appears that the most efficient instrument of taxation was still justice. In England at the end of the twelfth century when a wage-earner did not receive more than one penny for a day's work and when the livestock of a peasant of middling rank was not worth more than about ten shillings, the royal judges imposed fines amounting to hundreds of pounds at each sitting of the courts. The 430 fines inflicted in 1202 at the Lincoln assizes amounted all together to £633 – about 30 shillings on average for each offender.[61] It is true that because these fines as a rule greatly exceeded the villagers' available funds, the judge had often to be content with no more than a fraction of the sum imposed even when the convict was put under arrest and pressed to raise the money for his release amongst his relatives. But a village brawl was sufficient, provided that the delinquents were reasonably solvent, to produce at one time more cash for the lord than the most prosperous landownership could earn in a year. This explains why the rights of jurisdiction were so jealously defended and were the object of such bitter dispute. It also explains why the lord's justice proved so invasive. One of the earliest 'franchises' the peasants asked for was to affirm their right to be free of the lord's jurisdiction unless they themselves chose to invoke it.

It is quite impossible to compare the profits of the *ban* with those of land-lordship or domestic lordship derived from the same landed property. Neither inventories nor fragments of accounts make any distinction between the different revenues of a lord, between 'customs' and other kinds of taxation. To add to our difficulties those lordships of the *ban*, and the more powerful ones at that, were secular ones and therefore almost entirely lacking in archives. All the same we should be justified in concluding that the profits emanating from the rights of the *ban* were incomparably higher than those emanating from any other right. In particular, the power of the *ban* allowed its holders to drain off at an earlier stage, and much more efficaciously, the in-

[60] Duby, 261, p. 329 [61] A. L. Poole, 270, pp. 84 *et seq.*

creasing flow of money into peasant households. From a single *aide*, claimed only from the inhabitants of the castellany who were 'men' of the abbey of Cluny, the lord of Beaujeu, could, in 1200, extort the enormous sum of 300 silver marks.[62] For this reason the lordship of the *ban* played an essential part in the development of the rural economy. E. Perroy in particular draws our attention to the differences in the systems of taxation in France and England as an explanation of the divergencies between the management of the great demesnes in the two countries at the end of the twelfth century.[63] If the administrators of the English monastic manors worked unceasingly to raise the output of the manorial fields, it was because the power of the royal authority strictly limited their rights of taxation. Tallage and even justice could not possibly procure for them the huge profits which led the holders of the *ban* in France to take less and less interest in their demesnes.

We could probably find the key to much of the working of the economy in the various ways of applying the powers of the *ban*. Thus, in the hierarchy of wealth, the *ban* raised those lords who were able to exercise it well above the heads of noble houses who possessed only tenancies and small bands of body servants. Conversely, the weight of the exactions tended to level down the economic condition of the peasantry. Clearly heavier than rents on land, it reduced freeholders to the level of dependent tenants. The demands of the lords actively stimulated peasant production. But in so far as the *taille* remained irregular and arbitrary, and periodically drained the small cultivators of their accumulated reserves of movables, it slowed down the economic ascent of the more adventurous and enterprising rustics.

* * *

Although the lord of the *ban* was much richer than other lords, he was also further removed from the source of his receipts. To carry out his functions connected with the maintenance of peace and justice, and to collect his taxes, he needed the assistance of numerous agents who shared in his power and in the economic advantages it brought. The development of landownership produced, as we have seen, a crowd of intermediaries. But these individuals multiplied even more abundantly in the service of the territorial lordships. The advance of the fiscal powers of the *ban* contributed very greatly to the enrichment of the auxiliaries of authority who were usually domestic officials (*ministeriales*). No other group in the society of that time enjoyed an equally rapid economic advancement, at any rate on the continent, since domestic officialdom did not develop to the same extent in England. This may have been because great lordships in England were very much dispersed, because private powers did not develop as fully, and also because the ties binding

[62] Duby, 261   [63] E. Perroy, 'Seigneurie et manoir', in *Annales*, E. S. C. 1961

servants to their masters did not become as loose as on the continent. But on the French side of the Channel, domestic officials rose to join, and sometimes even to dominate, the old noble families in the villages, and appear to have been the chief beneficiaries of the growing prosperity of the countryside in the twelfth century.

These men were all domestic servants. We have seen that when the abbot of Limburg wanted foresters or tollkeepers he appointed the married sons of his slaves.[64] No other members of the *familia* were so closely bound to the master as they. In fact the master entrusted the *métiers*, i.e. the official positions of control in his lordship, to the most trustworthy of his men so that he could keep a tight hold on them and punish them when necessary. As late as the end of the eleventh century an official had to resign his post as soon as he was released from strict subjection by enfranchisement. Nevertheless these posts often brought with them considerable independence. This was especially so when an official managed one of the 'halls' or supervised the forest far away from his master. In the intervals between their lords' visits these officials wielded all the powers of the head of the household over bands of servants of lesser rank. They collected rents, directed the demesne and had control of profits. They commanded others; they dispensed justice; they negotiated with traders. Sometimes they held the entire domestic economy in their hands with no other obligation but to deliver a fixed pension on a certain day.

In all the lordships, even the smallest, the position of these officials slowly improved during the eleventh century. The prosperity of the humblest miller kept pace with his master's. But as the year 1100 approached the charters of the great religious establishments begin to mention with far greater frequency some of these specialized servants who had so enriched themselves as to make their masters apprehensive. Foresters were amongst the earliest of these new-rich. The establishment of rights of forest use, together with the reclamation movement, had increased the importance of their office; as population settled in the woodlands, so the dues these overseers collected became more abundant and their authority and jurisdiction extended over more peasants. Everyone who managed a seigneurial office, 'mayors', 'reeves', 'bailiffs', *villici*, alike, all enriched themselves. The *villici* benefited especially from the extension of the domestic lordship and the establishment of 'customs'. Their power was highest over the peasants whose subjection to their masters' exactions was greatest. And higher powers meant more revenues.

As a reward the lords' agents usually received a fief (a plot of ground granted without payment); its produce was the remuneration for their *métier*. Moreover, in order to encourage their efficiency and their application in the

[64] See p. 221

discharge of their office, they received a share of the rights it was their business to enforce and of the fines which they inflicted. In this way they benefited directly from the rise in the seigneurial receipts. They ran a parasitic lordship inside the one it was their job to manage. In fact, they became the real masters of the peasants, building up their own clientele within and without the *familia*. Many put the profits from their office into land, acquired allods and thus removed themselves one stage further from their dependent position. Many even resided away from the land for which they were responsible and discharged their office through their own agents. Their success was permanently ensured, for most of the officials wasted no time in making their office hereditary. In two or three generations families of bailiffs or foresters built up in this way fortunes comparable to those of the lesser nobility and adopted a similar way of life. When this stage had been reached, their lords found it hard to control them: worse than unmanageable, these servants became rivals threatening to dispossess their masters altogether.

The latter attempted to take counter-measures. From one end of the continent to the other administrators of ecclesiastical lordships (we know, of course, nothing of the inside story of the others) with few exceptions attempted in the twelfth century to regain control over the domestic officials. Whenever it was still possible they brought them to judgment and conviction before the domestic tribunal of the *familia*, confiscated part of their wealth and specified the exact amount of the taxes to which they had a right. They subordinated them to superior officials charged with their supervision who reserved the highest functions, particularly justice, for themselves. In northern and western France and in Germania, the mayors were thus often made answerable to a representative member of the religious community, and domestic officials had to swear not to exceed the limits of their office. Thus the mayors of Notre-Dame of Chartres had to undertake not to hold courts, not to exercise the power of constraint without the approval of the provost, to refuse 'gifts' from the peasants and not to demand labour services for their own use.[65] In the event these counter-measures could never be pushed very far. The offices remained hereditary fiefs and continued to be so profitable that nobles were sometimes tempted to acquire them. At the end of the twelfth century a small Burgundian castellan had purchased a provostship, from which the lord (the canons of Chalon) had the utmost difficulty in dislodging him.[66] The master's best remedy was often to repurchase the office when the official who had by the thirteenth century completely adopted the habits of the nobility, found himself in debt.

We can thus see that the existence of powerful lordships in a world of economic expansion not only permitted great churchmen and the nobility

[65] *Cartulaire de Notre-Dame de Chartres*, I, No. 58   [66] Duby, 261, p. 395

to emerge from rusticity and to live in hitherto unknown luxury, but also supported a large number of servants many of whom were able to amass fortunes which in the end made them wholly independent. The manorial economy was in fact an economy of waste. Not caring to count the cost, the master allowed himself to be plundered by those who followed or represented him and whose prosperity contributed to his glory. This was how a small rural aristocracy was able to raise itself on the shoulders of the peasantry. Legally it remained much inferior to the world of nobles and men of breeding, but it shared nevertheless the authority, prosperity and tastes of its betters. In the Mâconnais at the end of the twelfth century, the fifty or so families of the great officials installed on the manors of bishops, counts, castellans, chapters and great monasteries, and the 150 families of village gentry seemed all to be, economically speaking, equal. There was, of course, one great difference between them, which was that the families of the officials preserved more of the spirit of enterprise and desire for profit and kept their rude peasant commonsense unblunted.

CHAPTER III

The XIII Century (1180-1330): Evolution of Feudal Rent: Peasant Dues

While nothing is known about the history of the smaller non-ecclesiastical lordships in the twelfth century, it is clear that the economy of the larger ones responded, even if at the cost of many crises, to changes in their environment. Our evidence reveals abrupt rearrangements, struggles with rival castellans or officials and, even more clearly, efforts of reformers. Men, like Suger at St Denis, Meinhardt at Marmoutier and Peter the Venerable at Cluny, were faced with the problems of maintaining supplies and managing the finances, and had to find ways of solving them. Generally speaking, it was not their object to invent new solutions; they looked to the past, as did the whole of monastic society, and endeavoured to restore the old order, taking as their model the administrative rules inherited from the Carolingian epoch. Nevertheless, from time to time they introduced changes which rejuvenated the organization of the manor.

After 1180 this movement of change pressed on at an increased pace, and the penetration of money and exchange into rural life was one of its important causes. We can follow these transformations more easily than in earlier periods because the documentation is so much richer. The great increase in the number of inventories and accounts after 1180, and the new passion for numerical accuracy which they reveal, were partly the effects of a general cultural progress. But it also shows a greater familiarity with the use of money; masters and their agents gradually became conscious of values and more accustomed to appraising and accounting.[1] But more than anything else, the wealth of sources came from changes in the organization of the manor itself. The great lords began to surround themselves with educated officials, paid by wages or pensions, trained specialists, whose trade was to write, to keep accounts, to reckon and to administer. While Suger, Peter the Venerable and the other reformers of the demesne economy were, so to speak, amateurs, the great seigneurial complexes, since the two last decades of the twelfth century, were to be professionally managed. The mere presence of these experts could be sufficient to alter the character of management. For

[1] Document No. 26, p. 388; Duby, 444

instance, the officials appointed by the king of France as 'wardens' over the abbey of St Martin of Tournai helped the monks to understand their finances more clearly and to draw up a sort of annual budget.[2] This was a change of considerable importance the effects of which were more than a mere inflation of the archives. In certain regions some of the Church lordships went so far as to abandon the system of 'farming'; the demesne was henceforth managed by responsible agents who had to render periodical accounts directly to the lord. Thus, on the manors of the great English ecclesiastical establishments the 'reeve', the villein in charge of the demesne, had to keep careful note in his head of all receipts and payments of money; scribes came at Michaelmas to draw up at his dictation a summary which had then to be submitted to the 'auditors' for verification. The wealth of manorial documents in England and in particular the continuity of the account rolls, is a direct result of these methods of management,[3] and at last enables economic historians of the countryside to compile statistics and to invest their work with greater precision. On the other hand, bringing order into the material, in some ways so profuse, and in other ways so scanty, and collating research, which has not been carried to the same lengths in all the countries of Europe, creates new difficulties for the historian.

I. THE MOBILIZATION OF SEIGNEURIAL WEALTH

Before this period pious gifts, grants of a feudal nature and partible inheritance had determined the fate of the great landed fortunes.[4] But money now entered the patrimony like a ferment and affected its very stability. Luxurious habits, like the taste for travel, finery and general ostentation, hallmarks of the aristocratic way of life, created in the houses of lay and ecclesiastical lords alike an overwhelming need for money. But most lords' wealth consisted of land, together with the network of 'friendship' and personal dependence; and some of the wealth now had to be liquidated. In the thirteenth century, indebtedness becomes the constant feature of the lords' economic condition.

For a long time the lords had made use of small short-term loans. Since the first half of the eleventh century all lords exercising the *ban* had forced village markets to recognize their right to withhold for a fortnight payment for their purchases of bread, meat and wine.[5] They had abused the privilege,

---

[2] Haenens, 665

[3] Bennett, 149, pp. 166 *et seq.*; Miller, 198, p. 99; Raftis, 201, p. 128

[4] Certain customs set a limit to the disintegrating forces; giving daughters a dowry in order to exclude them from the succession, and also the habit of giving the eldest son the major part of the inheritance, spread. Less prolific after 1250, noble families were also less generous: they no longer gave land to the church and their vassals, but money instead. Genicot, 189, p. 50; Duby, 261, p. 498-502.   [5] Document No. 58, p. 412

thereby provoking the protests of the peasants who tried to obtain its suppression in charters of franchise. But the lords also began to incur loans of precious metals either minted or unminted. The first demands of any size seem to have come from the knights taking part in the Crusades. They applied to the great churches, who were known to be custodians of treasure well stocked with gold and silver. Pending repayment, the monks demanded as a pledge land capable of yielding an income approximately as great as the interest on the sum lent. Debts of this kind, arising from the needs of a distant military campaign, for long remained an unusual occurrence. Indebtedness did not become chronic until after the middle of the twelfth century. The first to find themselves in financial embarrassment were the richest and most powerful lords, who were, naturally, the greatest spenders: first the princes, then the great religious establishments and the castellans. About 1140 the monastery of Cluny found itself enmeshed in debts from which it was never able to free itself. Fifteen years later the Cistercian abbeys began in their turn to fall into debt. For the religious establishments in the region of Metz the critical period was about 1170.[6]

A lower and more numerous social class experienced these anxieties a little later. There is evidence that the debts contracted by the small lay aristocracy in the region of Mâcon became increasingly heavy in the early years of the thirteenth century. It appears indeed that from then on all over Europe nobles and their peers, the great officials, were racked by pressing financial problems. Although these men possessed substantial fortunes their revenues were not large and still consisted mostly of agricultural products. But in order to take part in ceremonial life, to follow sartorial fashions, to go to war and to maintain a good stable they had to incur the expenditure of more and more money. They were obliged to turn to moneylenders. When in 1230 one knight from the district of Metz died, he left an annual income of 19 livres and movable wealth valued at 30 livres, but his debts amounted to 33 livres and a little later his wife was forced to sell part of her inheritance.[7]

In fact an increase in the number of purchases and sales of land and land rights followed on the heels of the loans. This was one of the most characteristic features of the new phase in the development of the manorial economy after 1180. The allod had up till then been protected against sale by family solidarity, and the fief by the lords' vigilance. But judicial proceedings to loosen these constraints developed in the first years of the thirteenth century. After 1220 we can see the use of the contract of sale, which had for generations fallen into disuse, spreading anew in the Paris region and also in

---

[6] Duby, 441; Schneider, 351, p. 300
[7] Duby, 261, pp. 404 *et seq.*; Schneider, 351, p. 327; Tits-Dieuaide, 505; Document No. 70, p. 424

Mâconnais.[8] The approval of the other members of the family or the feudal lord which had to be obtained before any sale soon became a formality. If a man felt really pressed for money he could sell a few parcels of the demesne, and one or other of the dependent, rent-paying families, for the best price he could get. From now on these sales and compensating aquisitions transformed seigneurial fortunes much more speedily than almsgiving and partible inheritance had done two centuries earlier. As a result the lords as a social class became more fluid and after 1200 the nobility appeared, particularly in France, to be a much less strictly enclosed society.[9]

The documents reveal a ceaseless and growing flow of transfers of fragments of manors from noblemen's to churchmen's hands. Religious establishments were themselves immersed in debt, but they constantly received money and precious metal as alms; the wills of donors often prevented them from using these assets to satisfy their creditors, so they had to find other outlets for them. In 1191 the chapter-general of Cîteaux had forbidden the purchase of landed property; but the rule was soon abolished, and had in any case been very quickly circumvented. In one Burgundian village where in 1202 they had received rights over the tithes, the Cistercians bought the lord's authority in 1225; during the forty years after 1260, profiting from the fluctuations in the land market, they continued to acquire parcels of land of all sizes for money. In a single year, 1322, between harvest and seedtime they acquired fifteen fields. Through similar purchases St Ambrose of Milan, which held only one-sixth of the village lands of Origgio in 1240, owned half of them by 1320.[10] It was by deliberate investment of their liquid funds that the ecclesiastical lords rounded off their patrimonies at this period. It followed that the establishments which collected the largest cash revenues were able to make the greatest progress; such establishments were the Cistercian abbeys, in so far as they carried on active trading, and the urban chapters, who lived in the heart of merchant societies and were closely linked with commercial circles.

Nevertheless, some part of the lords' prerogatives passed by purchase into the hands of men of low birth. There were plenty of *nouveaux riches* in the thirteenth century. Literature written for a wellborn public, full of sarcastic references to these jumped-up 'villeins' with absurd manners who set themselves up on manors and attempted to take their place in polite society, is proof of how frequent was social climbing, and what offence it caused. Many of these *parvenus* came from the towns. Traders who had made money would lend cash to knights and receive pieces of land as a pledge; later on they

---

[8] Fontette, 339; Vigneron, 148

[9] G. Duby, 'Une enquête à poursuivre: la noblesse dans la France médiévale', in *Revue Historique*, 1961   [10] Martin-Lorber, 536; Romeo, 481

would acquire the land and its rights. Thus, about the year 1200 a usurer of Toulouse was able to buy all the lands owned by the abbey of St Sernin in a certain village, together with 32 dependent peasant families; and in 1265 a merchant of Cluny received in return for a loan of 800 livres the disposition of a castle held in fief from the duke of Burgundy, with all the 'high' justice and the prerogative powers (*ban*) which appertained to it. The financiers of Metz created in this way their landed demesnes in the surrounding countryside between 1275 and 1325. We can even see some peasants who succeeded in rising sufficiently high to acquire noble property for ready money, and especially the right to levy the *taille* and to dispense justice.[11]

After the mid-thirteenth century references to seigneurial property sold to non-nobles abound in all the repositories of archives, particularly in the most highly urbanized countries, such as Italy, the Low Countries and France. They have attracted the notice of historians, focussed naturally enough on new and unusual phenomena. But it must be pointed out that most of these transactions concern small fragments of manors. To believe that at this period the economic difficulties of the ancient nobility were acute and their impoverishment great is a temptation to be resisted. The material superiority in rural society of even the humblest knightly families was only rarely imperilled by the rise of a few exceptionally successful business men. On the eve of the fourteenth century the share of burgesses or country folk in possession of manorial property remained limited. Take, for instance, the case of the Alberti dei Giudici, leading Florentine merchants; in 1315 they owned no more than one demesne of 200 acres, flanked by about a hundred parcels of land let out to peasants. Like other merchants of their city or of Pisa, they held their wealth chiefly in precious metals and urban property. Bourgeois infiltration into manors in the Parisian region at that time remained likewise almost imperceptible.[12] Most ancient noble families had still not relinquished more than a few scraps of their ancestral property. Moreover, generous princes would often step in to repair noblemen's losses. In short, with a few exceptions, all the *seigneuries* in 1300 remained in the hands of churchmen or warriors.

Nevertheless, even if the social position of the lords had not markedly altered, certain changes in their economic behaviour can be observed. All were becoming accustomed to buying and selling and handling money. As a result, they probably felt much more responsible for the fortunes of their manors than did their predecessors. They were aware that their wealth was not static and that they could arrest its decline and contribute to its growth. We may also assume that the lords of the church who commanded the

---

[11] Duby, 261, p. 524; Mundy, 346; Schneider, 351, pp. 394 *et seq.*
[12] Fourquin, 551

largest financial resources were prepared patiently to aggregate and re-assemble their rights over men and land into compact units. For the ecclesi-astical demesnes in Lombardy, Burgundy and the neighbourhood of Paris, it was a period of concentration. They assumed the appearance of great co-herent estates, both better run and easier to manage than heretofore. The success of agricultural writings in vulgar tongues proves, at least in certain regions like England and northern Italy, that an interest in the demesne economy and a desire for more rational management was not entirely the monopoly of clerks. Like the latter, knights were more farsighted than their ancestors had been, more conscious of the profit motive, and more business-like, even when they were financially embarrassed. Many of the new aspects of the manorial economy in the thirteenth century came from this changed attitude.

2. THE DECLINE OF RENTS

Our sources are too discontinuous, widely dispersed and unevenly utilized, to be able to show clearly the development of manorial dues. More-over the developments followed different trends in different regions and even on different manors, and cannot be represented by one simple outline. We must be content to trace only the more obvious tendencies. At first glance it appears that in the thirteenth century the income of the peasant household was subject to deductions which, though no lower than in the past, were yet different in nature.

For many lords the most pressing problem was to obtain money, and this led them to demand cash rather than labour or agricultural produce from their tenants and men. The conversion of services and dues offered a simple and immediate solution to the problem of finance. It was acceptable, if not to all, then at least to the most enterprising peasants, who were prepared to pay money provided they could dispose of their crops and profit from the grow-ing opportunities for taking their surpluses to market.

This is why commutations, already frequent at the end of the twelfth century, continued to multiply thereafter. It does not appear, though, as if all masters abandoned what remained of labour services; we can even see that on some English monastic manors direct cultivation was for a short time intensified and thus reversed the trend and constrained villeins in the first half of the thirteenth century once again to perform the work which they had for years been free to redeem for money payments. On the other hand, apart from tallage, merchet and heriot were henceforward levied in cash. In the payment of rents specially, until then usually demanded in kind, money was substituted for cereals, wine, livestock and meat. But there is no proof that commutation was universal. In certain localities the larger portion of rents continued to be levied in kind. Elsewhere, however, they were speedily and almost entirely commuted. One example is the Bavarian abbey of Baumburg: where on the eve of the thirteenth century *manses* and isolated parcels of fields or vineyards had provided the lords with nothing but agricultural products; but by 1245 58 per cent of the *manses* and 98 per cent of the parcels provided nothing but cash.[13] Briefly, then, there is enough evidence for us to assume that at the beginning of the fourteenth century a money rent had replaced many of the fixed dues in kind on most of the manors all over Europe.

In effect, in a period of continuously rising prices, the benefit which lords could derive from this transformation quickly proved to be illusory. The real value of money rents fell constantly in the thirteenth century, and the fall was heavier in rural localities than elsewhere. For rents there were laid down in locally minted money which continued to weaken relatively to the great regional currencies. When, at the end of the thirteenth century, increase of population caused land to become even scarcer and its price to go up, rents of hereditary tenancies on which services had for long been converted into money remained at absurdly low levels. The tenant of a Mâconnais *manse*, the annual yield of which was valued at a score of livres, paid the lord rent amounting to no more than ten *sous* per annum; to put it in another way, he retained nearly 98 per cent of the revenues. In the region of Namur landlords commonly received two *deniers* per *bonnier* for pieces of land which they could easily have let for thirty times that sum; this meant that their property was as good as valueless to them.[14]

Undoubtedly tenancies changed hands more frequently than formerly and thus returned more often to the lords. The latter could then, before installing new incumbents, re-negotiate rents with them and in this way readjust them to the real value of land. This explains why at the end of the thirteenth century on the same manor, contiguous lands sometimes produced striking differences in rents. In one Flemish village, the lords of Pamele-Audenarde levied on two *bonniers* of land of apparently identical fertility one *denier* and two and a half *sous* respectively. On one great hayfield belonging to the same manor the rent from one parcel yielded the lord one hundred times as much as another neighbouring plot of the same size.[15] However, other indications lead us to suppose that, perhaps restrained by the strength of local custom and faced with a tacit coalition of peasant interests, the landlord did not have the power to raise the level of money rents much each time land was relet. In addition, through lack of supervision, or through inability to overcome the passive resistance of unwilling rentpayers, many other dues

[13] Dollinger, 355
[14] Duby, 261, p. 513; Génicot, 189, p. 247   [15] Duby, 443

slowly dwindled away or even disappeared completely. The proportion of land rents in seigneurial income thus became so infinitesimal as hardly to count at all. Around the year 1300 they amounted to no more than one per cent of the annual receipts of the monastery of St Denis. At the same period a Burgundian knight could not extract more than about thirty *sous* every year from sixty-two tenancies, i.e. hardly a third of the wages which he then had to pay a single ploughman in addition to his keep.[16]

3. RISING PROFITS: FINES ON TRANSFERS OF PROPERTY

The depreciation of rents from land confused the economic condition of tenancies and allods. While it considerably relieved the burden on the peasantry, the actual money which such farming households were thereby able to save was taken away from them in other ways. A compensating rise in other manorial revenues helped to reduce the losses suffered by the masters through the fall in rents.[17]

The desire of all peasants to have a greater control over their land gave the lords an easy opportunity for increasing their demands. The need for money was also spreading amongst villagers many of whom were willing, like the nobles, to pledge a part of their lands, or even to sell them in order to obtain cash. They could sell their entire tenement only in the last extremity, but they might perhaps be allowed to alienate fragments and thereby to break the integrity of their holdings. They might also wish to endow their daughters with a little land. Furthermore, hoping to benefit from legacies, the Church itself applied pressure wherever it could to persuade people to make wills as they wished. Finally, as economic relationships grew to be more flexible, the laws of inheritance prohibiting the division of tenancies became very irksome. A variety of forces thus combined to release peasant and from the shackles hindering its mobility.

[16] Fourquin, 551; Duby, 261, p. 509. The situation in northern Italy was the same; Luzzatto, 22.

[17] It is hardly necessary to point out the profits which the lords continued to draw from agricultural growth as long as it continued. Great lords in France and Germany, like the Sire de Pamele-Audenarde, as well as others of modest rank – like those squires who, though owning no more than a part of the tithes of a Mâconnais village, drew five times more from them than from all their land at rent – always drew the larger part of their income from directly tapping the surplus of peasant harvests through tithes, profits of the mill and the church (Duby, 443, 247). Similarly, in their final stages, reclamations continued to add to the numbers of holdings. Note also that in later periods the lords of the woodlands could grant assarts on much more advantageous terms since more men were searching for places to settle. When in the second half of the thirteenth century the monks of St Bavo of Ghent decided to let out their remaining wastes they had no trouble in finding burgesses to take up the plots, even though these were burdened with a heavy rent of ten to twelve *sous* per *bonnier*. It was mainly the creation of new rentpaying plots in the drained fens which caused the money revenues of Ely Cathedral to rise by 20 per cent between 1222 and 1251. Verhulst, 208; Miller, 198, pp. 96 *et seq.*

This tendency threatened the lord's interests. To allow the break up of the ancient *manses* or other complete tenancies which still preserved their integrity (and in 1180 most of them did), would have made the collection of dues much more difficult. The dues would have to be apportioned to different lots and there was always a risk that the most remote ones would, after a few years of neglect, be transformed into allods. However, throughout western Europe in the thirteenth century landowners allowed the release of parcels which had up till then formed family tenancies. The general disappearance of the *manse* and its equivalents as units of cultivation and taxation dates from this period. The backward districts proved, of course, to be the exception. In such places peasants were shackled by traditions preventing division, and there was little trade with the outside world; moreover settlement on newly colonized land took the form of isolated farms whose compactly arranged and enclosed lands for long preserved their integrity.[18] The *manse* remained the family unit in Graisivaudan until about 1250. In 1280 it still provided the framework for an inventory of the rights of St Lambert of Liège.[19] Elsewhere, however, tenancies were usually much divided. In one village in Mâconnais twenty-five groups of tenants in 1260 shared one former *manse*, and the officials were hard put to it to identify in the village territory the parcels which had once formed the holding. In the *Veil Rentier* drawn up about 1275 for the lords of Pamele-Audenarde, the rents were spread over a multitude of parcels. Even in Alsace and Swabia where the lords were vigorously opposed to fragmentation, the average area of tenancies described in the inventories did not at this time exceed two dayworks: an absurdly small size. Two hundred and fifty acres of arable in one village in the Ile de France were shared between 160 concessionaries.[20]

When dealing with those who owed him rent, the administrator of a manor no longer had before him the simple picture of a score or perhaps thirty households in which at any given moment he could find a certain quantity of supplies; he had to keep count of the position and dues of hundreds of pieces of land. Such a break-up of individual tenancies strongly favoured the institution of money rents and entailed a simplification of the timetable of rent collection, which was usually reduced to single annual payments. On the other hand it made the organization of the rent-bearing land extraordinarily complicated, since these multitudes of parcels of land changed hands very often. Indeed, many parcels eventually vanished altogether: in 1222 the agents of the chapter of St Paul in London failed to find three acres

---

[18] See pp. 117-118. A proper study of inheritance customs in the peasant world would permit the demarcation of the regions where, as in north-western Germany, the institution of primogeniture helped to safeguard the unity of family farms.

[19] Didier, 433; Document No. 129, p. 487

[20] Duby, 261, p. 505; Document No. 130, p. 489; Duby, 443; Fourquin, 551

of land listed in a recent inquest.[21] Before the end of the twelfth century the use in France and Germany of the *censier-coutumier*, records listing dues, began to disappear. Other ways of registering the lord's prerogatives, better adapted to the complexity and mobility of the tenancy, came to replace it. The *Weistum*, the 'record of custom', was adopted in the Germanic countries and their western borders: all the inhabitants of the manor assembled together in the lord's house each year to acknowledge their obligations to him orally.[22] In central and south-western France the *terrier* registered the boundaries of each parcel within the village territory and identified it.

On the other hand, when the lord, acceding to the pleas of his peasants, authorized them to divide their tenancies, he himself could often profit by raising the rents considerably. Comparison of successive lists of dues shows that frequently the combined total of the charges imposed on portions of an ancient *manse* exceeded, and sometimes greatly exceeded, the total of the original service. Nevertheless the principal advantage the lord derived from division was that he was able to levy on such scattered and mobile land the fines on the transfer of property imposed by usage since the twelfth century on new tenants.[23]

These fines were levied first of all on heirs. To enter into possession of an inheritance they had to pay the lord an entry fine, a 'ransom'. Sometimes confused (when the owner was a personal dependant) with heriot (mortmain) this right was often equal to a year's rent. For the whole tenancies owned by the villeins of the English Ramsey Abbey it sometimes reached 40 shillings, a large sum, and if the heirs could not pay such a heavy tax, the land escheated. When that happened the heirs remained in possession, but they had to deliver all the produce to the lord until they had paid off the debt.[24]

Taxes were likewise imposed on purchasers of tenancies. Sales in fact soon became as frequent perhaps as transmission by succession: from the first years of the thirteenth century, the peasant land market can be seen opening up everywhere. The lords always kept the privilege of authorizing these alienations. They wanted to be able to prevent nobles, clerks or townsmen from becoming their tenants through purchase, for men of such social standing would have been more difficult to exploit. Thus in the neighbourhood of Metz the landlords took care that the *terres de meix*, possession of which still entailed submission to the manorial justice, were not acquired by burgesses.[25]

---

[21] Bennett, 149, p. 47

[22] Document No. 117, p. 470; Perrin, 200, pp. 686 *et seq.*

[23] These fines appeared in 'custom' in the course of the twelfth century; Didier, 433. In the rentals of a priory in Dauphiné they were called 'pleas' (*plaids*), which meant that their amount was the result of an amiable agreement, but gradually they became fixed. They also became yearly payments (*abonnés*).   [24] Raftis, 201, p. 222

[25] Document No. 157; p. 514; Schneider, 351, p. 362

Between peasants, on the other hand, transactions were entirely free. But in exchange for his *lods*, i.e. his approval, which was no more than a formality, the lord deducted a part of the sale price. It was usually a *treizain*, a thirteenth part, or else one *denier* per *sou*, which was nearly the same thing. Sometimes the lord took more; in eastern France he demanded for himself up to fifteen per cent of the sum paid.[26] Finally it must be added that the growing scarcity of land resulted in very high entry fines being paid by peasants prepared to do anything to be allowed on to a tenancy which would give them a livelihood. The fine of *entrage*, and the right of *abergement* (settlement) became widespread and extremely lucrative. All these fines on the transfer of property were paid in cash. They gave the lords' finances much-needed support. It has been estimated from documents relating to the Forez that, taking good years with bad, they raised the value of rents by a quarter.[27]

4. THE EXPLOITATION OF THE POWER OVER MEN: TALLAGE

The earlier tendency of associating and combining the taxes derived from privileges and monopolies of lordship, or from domestic lordship, with rents from land continued in this period, and eventually prevailed. Nevertheless in the thirteenth century the manner of exploiting men changed significantly as a result of two separate factors. On the one hand, as 'franchises' were spreading the powers of exaction were becoming more regular; on the other hand, with regional principalities getting stronger all over Europe, fiscal powers gradually established themselves on two different levels.

*   *   *

In many countries agreements concluded at different places between the lord and the rural community fixed limits to the lord's rights. It would be useful if a co-operative enquiry, based on an exact chronology and a detailed map, could trace the spread of the village 'liberties' in different parts of western Europe. In the present state of research all we are aware of is that there were whole areas where villages never obtained charters laying down 'good customs' in writing. In Lorraine only large towns benefited from such concessions. Further east beyond the Rhine, grants of charters of liberty were always exceptional. In England some rural towns were founded in the thirteenth century with the promise of 'liberties' for those who settled in them, but such privileged villages continued to be very unusual in a country where the sovereign kept for himself the supreme ruling powers.[28] In Italy, and

[26] For the district of Namur, Genicot, 189, p. 155

[27] Perroy, 269, p. 127; Hilton, 391; Documents Nos. 145, 147, 148, pp. 504, 506. The growing value of these taxes explains why the lords had tried to control changes of ownership very strictly in the thirteenth century. It was one of the principal functions of the rural courts of justice.   [28] Perrin, 537; Bennett, 149, p. 296

perhaps in Provence, where large numbers of peasant communities of a semi-urban nature existed at quite an early date, possibly even before the beginning of the twelfth century,[29] there emerged communal institutions comparable to those of the towns which deserve to be considered separately. In France the movement of enfranchisement penetrated everywhere even though, whether early or late, it varied widely from province to province. In certain districts in the Paris basin many communities had received their 'liberties' by the first half of the twelfth century: the little vinegrowing villages in the neighbourhood of Laon, for instance, acquired in 1129 the same franchises as the town itself. On the other hand in the Paris region the great time for the drawing up of 'good customs' of the peasants was much later, between 1245 and 1275. The franchises were drawn up later still in Burgundy where only one village in five benefited from them. They were even rarer in Dauphiné. In the little county of Comminges about sixty localities were enfranchised between 1202 and 1300.[30]

Considered from the economic point of view the 'enfranchisement' movement chiefly resulted in transferring to the lords who owned territorial monopolies and privileges the large sums of cash which the most prosperous peasants had succeeded in saving up. For charters of liberty were almost always sold to communities and very dearly. The high commercial value placed upon franchises in the French countryside is a valuable pointer to the damage inflicted on the peasant economy by the random exercise of the *ban*, but it is evidence above all else of the prestige which personal liberty enjoyed in popular estimation. In order to obtain a franchise the inhabitants of Thiais in the Ile de France in the mid-thirteenth century offered their lords 2,200 *livres*, and the inhabitants of the neighbouring village of Orly offered 4,000. These enormous sums far exceeded the funds available to the villagers,[31] and the latter had to be allowed easy terms of payment and long-term credit. The second consequence of franchise concessions was thus to aggravate peasant indebtedness and to extend the hold of the moneylenders and business men over the countryside. Many lords speculated on the intense desire of the countryfolk to have their 'liberty' proclaimed and to be rid of the obligations which they regarded as symbols of servitude – *chevage, formariage* and mortmain, and all the other 'blemishes' which were degrading and intolerable in the common view. By advancing credit for this purpose they succeeded in obtaining a permanent stranglehold on the village economy; and laid hands on money long concealed from the tithe collectors. The sale of charters enabled them to overcome their financial difficulties for a while

[29] Leicht, 164; Aubenas, 509
[30] Brelot, 517; Chomel, in *Annales E.S.C.*, 1956, pp. 353-355; Bloch, *Rois et serfs*, Paris, 1920, p. 112   [31] Fourquin, 551; Document No. 156, p. 513

without noticeably lessening their future profits. It was nearly always a very good business proposition for the lords.

The liberties did not in fact abolish the lords' power to levy exactions. They suppressed intermediaries, officials and agents, whose demands and chicaneries were often less bearable than the masters' if only because as persons they were less respected. The villagers also often received the right to police the countryside by agents appointed by themselves. In addition they could themselves allocate the 'customs' between the households and arrange the assessment of the tallage according to the capabilities of each; or at least according to the apparent signs of prosperity, such as the numbers of livestock or the length of the frontage of the house. But the weight of authority and the lords' demands continued to bear down over the whole territory of the franchise, very carefully defined by the charter, and over all its inhabitants. The poor wretches had wished above all things to know in advance what they would have to pay; they were willing to pay so much, and maybe more, merely in order to ensure that the impositions should no longer be arbitrary. In this way the charters of enfranchisement did not so much reduce the fiscal powers of the *ban* as regularize them, introduce them into custom, and thereby legitimize them, and even entrench them more firmly. So much so that enfranchised villages did not finally find themselves in a particularly privileged economic position compared to the many localities which had not received charters, but which benefited from the growing fixity of custom.

It often happened in fact that the rivalry of several lords over the profits of the *ban*, or simply the progress of methods of administration and the spread of writing, led to the, at least partial, recording of the customs. These written records established customs and at the same time simplified them. The rules of 'advocacy' and agreements about the *garde*; the lords' attempts to fix the rate of exactions so as to ensure a more regular flow of money (this was the case in many Lorraine villages assessed by the lord who held the power of the *ban*); the practice adopted in Germany of writing on a *Weistum* roll the 'yield of obligations' hitherto recited by the village community[32] – all these transcriptions of the collective memory helped to deliver the country folk from arbitrary imposition and to stabilize the privileges and monopolies of the lower order (*ban inférieur*). But, like the charters of liberty, they established this power ever more firmly within the limits of the village territory.

★   ★   ★

In all the regions where the princely authority had disintegrated in the tenth century, a new power, remote but insistent, began to make itself felt

[32] Duby, 261, p. 612; Schneider, 351, p. 330; Perrin, 537

after the year 1200. This was the power of the king, the duke or the count, and it was henceforth to be permanently represented on the spot by ubiquitous agents. These officials, foreign to the district and frequently changing their posts, were eager to extend the prerogatives of sovereigns upon whose prestige their own power rested. They were even more zealous to raise money in their masters' names, for some of it stuck to their own fingers. Thus, without being relieved of the demands of the lords close at hand, the peasants had also to support other, more distant, but none the less burdensome fiscal powers. And, after the end of the century the demands of the Pope had also to be met. From the thirteenth century onwards, then, the weight of growing states added to the burdens already carried by the rural world, sometimes to the point of nearly crushing it; in any case from then on we have to consider the princely levies as an important part of the economic machinery of the countryside.

In some countries, the pressure of the higher authority was exercised directly. Recruiting sergeants of the English kings dragged young men away from their villages to fight against the Welsh, the Scottish or the French. Similarly, the Brandenburg peasantry, mobilized in the event of invasion, had to pay a tallage called *Bede* and to provide war transportation for the Margrave. In 1185 when the inhabitants of Ferrières in the Gâtinais received their charter of franchise, the rights which the king of France reserved to himself were enumerated: they were a special levy of fifteen *livres* raised in the community by his provost, and military service.[33] Nevertheless, the princes' demands were most frequently made to the lords, although the latter passed them on to their own peasants as soon as they were able. Forced to incur debts in order to fulfil royal or pontifical demands, the abbots of Ramsey increased the weight of the dues on their manors; they inflicted entry fines and relief more ruthlessly. At the same period the Count levied directly on each peasant household in the villages of Upper Provence the '*albergue*', his ancient right of shelter (*gîte*); but he left the lords to raise the 'cavalcade' and to provide him with men-at-arms. In effect the burdens, whatever they were, fell entirely on the peasantry.[34]

In the thirteenth century and at the beginning of the fourteenth, the princely demands were still mostly intermittent, and therefore unforeseeable. For this reason they disturbed economic activity all the more profoundly. The arrival of the collectors heralded a catastrophe, a scourge whose surprise

[33] Bennett 149, p. 119; Carsten, 8, p. 39; Perroy, 269, p. 75

[34] Raftis, 201; Document No. 156, p. 513. In the thirteenth century the dependent peasants of the church at Hildesheim suffered three superimposed taxes: a general tallage (*Landessteuer*); subsidies claimed from time to time by the bishop; and lastly the tallage of the 'advocate'; A. Peters, 'Die Entwicklung der Amtverfassung im Hochstift Hildesheim', in *Zeitschrift des hist. Vereins für Niedersachsen*, 1905.

and whose incidence could be likened to a climatic calamity or an epidemic. This is why they so often provoked a chorus of complaints and sometimes a defensive reaction. For the same reason, the taxes of the rulers did not result in the disappearance of the customary charges which the holder of the *ban* and the owners of bondmen considered as an integral part of their fortune. The growth of the state merely suppressed the intermediary powers of the castellans. These men forfeited to the princes the highest of their prerogatives, the power of military conscription, the punishment of serious crimes, and the 'high' justice. In the lesser manifestations of territorial *bans*, however – the 'low' justice, the *gîte*, the *taille*, the direction of country life – the private character of the privileges was merely accentuated. These rights were wholly merged with the patrimony of those who had owned them. Consequently they tended to be subdivided with sales and partible inheritance. They declined to the level of domestic lordship. The remains of the former territorial power came to be confused with the prerogatives which once upon a time the heads of houses exercised over the men of their 'family'. They sometimes even became mixed up with charges on land. In any case the power to levy exactions, and especially the *taille*, ceased to be a privilege reserved for a few powerful men; it became debased. From the thirteenth century the *ban* had come to be exploited economically on a lower level than that of princely taxation system, and in a purely local manner, for the benefit of humbler masters, lords of single parishes or of a few peasant households.

⋆   ⋆   ⋆

All over Europe, from the marches of Brandenburg and Franconia to Milan and Provence, we find in the thirteenth century men who possessed the lordship of no more than a single village. An authority on such a small scale originated in the break-up of ancient castellanies into smaller portions, usually conforming to parish boundaries. The lord's power established itself at the village level as a counterpart to the growing cohesion of the community of inhabitants, as well as to the new severity with which the ecclesiastical authorities treated parishes in a society riddled with heresy. A further source of these lordships was reclamation created by the *villeneuves*[35] and grants of 'franchises'.

The actual lord of the village was sometimes one of the prince's officials. In 1229 the duke of Brabant enfeoffed Arnoud de Wesemael his official with the 'high' justice in a territory, and made him the 'lord' of the place. Sometimes the lord was a younger son, or a son-in-law, of a castellan who had received part of the *ban* within the limits of the parish as his heritage. In eastern Germany the position of lord was usually occupied by the descen-

[35] See p. 76

dants of the colonizing *locator*, who had built the mill and the forge with the prince's permission and who, after the creation of the village, had filled the office of *Schultheiss*, a minor judge rewarded by a third of the fines. However, the *dominus loci* was for the most part the largest landowner in the cultivated area, ecclesiastical or lay, who had by purchase or gift also acquired the right to punish petty offences committed within the village confines or on nearby roads, to control communal usages, to protect the harvests and to collect the fines and 'customs' as payments for his supervisory and judicial functions. Sometimes this parish lordship was itself divided. In the south of France it was often held jointly by many co-lords: associations like this in villages in Languedoc on the eve of the fourteenth century frequently comprised a dozen or more individuals.[36]

At this period the village lord generally lived on the spot. He was therefore much closer to the peasants than the former castellan had been, and much closer than the prince and his agents, against whom the villagers often sought the local lord's protection. Only moderately wealthy, he was himself a cultivator, but because his social position obliged him to spend freely, such a country gentleman, well aware of the prosperity of his rustic neighbours, would be inclined to advance his economic claims as far as he was able. To begin with, he would use his power to raise the output of his own land; he would monopolize the few general labour services and use all the draught animals in the village two or three days a year to plough his fields or to cart the crops he wished to sell in the neighbouring town. Above all, he would attempt to turn to his own profit the collective agrarian constraints and use of the common lands.[37] For all these reasons, relations between the fortified house, where he lived somewhat apart from the village, and the village community sometimes led by the curé, were often strained. But if the main use which village lords made of their hold over the lesser *ban* was to help them exploit their demesne more actively, they could also wring from it a regular money income, fixed by the charter of franchise or the *Weistum*. They drew a revenue from the weekly market. They collected various small fines from the infractions of agricultural practice which had by then become much more strict. They claimed financial aid from the inhabitants on certain 'occasions' recognized by custom, as for instance when they had to expend large sums for a daughter's marriage, to fit out their eldest sons with arms as knights, to pay ransom or to make journeys overseas. Finally, and most important of all, they levied the *taille*. This exaction, sometimes allocated by the parishioners' own representatives, but always based on the 'rooftree', the family house, often yielded more than any other profit of lordship.

[36] Tits-Dieuaide, 505; Duby, 261, pp. 586 *et seq.*; Document No. 122, p. 476; Dubled, 435   [37] See p. 158

Personal servitude was abolished on all territories which enjoyed charters of franchise. Bondsmen were no more: after a residence of one year to prove their wish to remain permanently, immigrants were protected against the lords' claims and demands on their persons. In the enfranchised villages what is sometimes called the *baronnie*, by which is meant the supplementary profits arising from the exploitation of men, belonged exclusively to the *dominus loci*, or the village lord. But elsewhere, i.e. in the great majority of localities, other lords as well as the lord of the territorial *ban* levied payments, and particularly the *taille*, on certain households. These lords had preserved the right to exploit their own dependants.

There was, it appears, a revival of servitude in the thirteenth century, at any rate in some regions. To demarcate exactly these areas, and to make an accurate count of the free and non-free men in them would need much more detailed and extensive research than has so far been done. If in some villages the legal status of a section of the inhabitants was lowered and the ties binding them to their masters became stronger, this may have been connected with the extension of the franchises. To proclaim the freedom of some country folk was to bring out, by way of contrast, the web of servitude in which the rest were still caught up. This can be seen clearly in documents where terms denoting a state of dependence are brought into relief by the use of honorific expressions intended to show how superior were the 'free'. The rebirth of juridical studies had also a powerful influence. Lawyers (and many manorial administrators in the thirteenth century were trained in schools of law), had revived the notion of slavery and were thus encouraged to look for similar conditions in the social structure of their own time. Finally, with increasing differences in peasant wealth and with the gradual formation in the villages of a class of poor people who expected to be supported by the generosity of powerful men, the ties of subordination in the lower ranks of economic society were bound to become closer. We have already seen how, by the mid-twelfth century, public opinion in England began to equate the status of the villein with that of the slave, and thereby strengthened the power of the lords over their bondsmen. On the continent developments were slower, but after 1250 the existence of a special social status considered as that of 'dependent men' was generally recognized.

This was the condition of the 'serfs' in Champagne and in Lorraine, of the *Leibeigene* of Swabia, of the Burgundian 'men subject to *taille* and exploitation', of the *questaux* or *hommes de queste* in Aquitaine and of the Provençal *malservi*. The bodies of all these men belonged to their masters. The hereditary attachment was often made closer by an oath of fealty or by a ceremony of allegiance, the varied rites of which recall the homage of vassals. Some dues were required from them alone; *chevage*, mortmain, *formariage* and the *taille 'à merci'*, all seem to be characteristic of their status. Even the names by which they were known showed that they were subject to a more arbitrary exploitation than men whose status was free. Finally they were usually compelled to reside in certain places. They were called *couchants et levants* in Burgundy, or, according to the Provençal expression, *hommes de casement*. The jurists had in fact exhumed from Roman law the idea that the serf had to be bound to the soil.[38]

It may seem surprising to see these hindrances to the mobility of peasant families reappearing at the precise moment when land was becoming increasingly scarce, when many landless peasants fought for the privilege of taking up vacant farms, and, in order to be admitted, were willing to pay a heavy entry fine. In fact the attachment of the bondsmen reflected the masters' desire to keep a closer hold over their dependants, to prevent them from escaping their authority by settling on a *villefranche* or by yielding to the attractions which urban life with its supposedly easier conditions, exercised on the poorer country folk. One Provençal villager who, outwitting the vigilance of the master to whom he was bound, had settled in Grasse, the nearest town, had eventually to agree to set up his son on his majority on the tenancy which he had himself abandoned and the cultivation of which was temporarily in charge of another inhabitant of the village. His successors had to live there for ever, and were threatened, if they failed to do so, with an enormous fine of fifty livres. Forced residence was a guarantee that the typical charges of dependent status would always be paid. Even though they fell mostly on the poor, they could still be worth a great deal to the lord; the fines of *formariage* which the royal tax collector levied in 1282-1284 in the bailiwicks of Senlis and Vermandois varied according to the household from 12 to 74 *sous parisis*.[39] But on the whole it would be true to say that, for thirteenth-century lords, to own 'men' meant above all else to be able to impose on them the *taille*. The significance of the juridical status of *taillables* or *questaux* was that these men had to perform the demands of their master and that they had to pay taxes. Dependants no longer formed, as they did in the eleventh century, a reserve of man-power. They offered instead opportunities for taxation: they were the 'tax fodder'. This change shows more

[38] Jacques De Vitry, B.N. Ms. Latin 17, 509, fol. 133, distinguishes four categories of *servi*, 'man', of the 'soil', by 'birth', and by 'hiring'; Dollinger, 159; Hubrecht, 637; Aubenas, 622; Samaran, 647; Archives des Bouches-du-Rhône, B.169; Documents Nos. 147, 148, p. 506

[39] Archives des Bouches-du-Rhône, 396 E 17; reference in M. Bloch, *Rois et serfs*, Paris, 1920, p. 185. In 1234 the monks of St Denis imposed a fine of 500 *livres* on one of their bondsmen, most likely a *ministérial*, who had married the daughter of a knight; Archives Nationales, L.848, No. 32.

clearly than anything else what after 1200 became the new relationship between lord and peasant.

If thirteenth century dependants were obliged to 'make a fire', i.e. to maintain a hearth, in a certain house, and if they were forbidden to leave under pain of having the lord confiscate all their movables, it was because the latter had above all else to be sure that he controlled his main source of movable wealth, the value of which had greatly increased through improvements in technique. But as a result of these requirements servile conditions became closely bound to residence in certain specified places and the fiscal obligations of a dependent tenancy were transferred from the man to his habitation. In fact certain lands upon which houses were built were recognized as 'servile'. In some villages there were *meix taillables* or *feux serfs*. To settle on them was to fall into servitude. Freedom could be regained by leaving them, but only on condition of leaving empty-handed. Thus the connection of personal dependence with 'domestic' lordship was blurred. The new servitude more often assumed a 'real' character which was increasingly accentuated.[40] It was transferred to certain specific lands and by this means became an intimate part of landownership.

At the end of the thirteenth century the lords of some tenements would no longer let them to peasants who did not acknowledge themselves to be their bondsmen; the lords now wanted to collect from the households not only rent and fines on the transfer of property but also the *taille* and other personal rights. For this reason the *taille* became to an ever greater extent a burden on the poor and unfortunate. As soon as a dependant got together a few savings, he would, drawn by the mirage of personal liberty, offer the lord the price of his freedom, i.e. a capital sum on which the interest was approximately equal to the *taille*. This was the way many individual franchises were sold. In 1268 the monks of St Maur des Fosses freed twenty-nine families living in Vitry for 250 livres payable in five years. And in the second half of the thirteenth century many English villeins became 'free tenants' by the redemption of the services which were the cause of their servitude.[41] Furthermore, the most enterprising bondsmen decamped and sought their fortune elsewhere. To replace them only poor men burdened with children and threatened with starvation were willing to occupy the servile lands and to bind themselves by the oath of fidelity. As the fourteenth century, a time of grave overpopulation, approached, the reappearance of serfdom in certain countries was one of the most obvious manifestations of the recent economic submission of the new peasant proletariat to the lords of the soil.

[40] Duby, 261, pp. 591, *et seq.* Documents Nos. 147 and 148, p. 506
[41] Archives Nationales LL.46, fol. 118; Bennett, 149, pp. 283 *et seq.*; Documents Nos. 159 and 160, p. 517

In any case almost everywhere in the second half of the thirteenth century the most effective method of profiting from the power over men was the *taille*, whether it was levied on villages wholly subject to a territorial lord, or inhabited by free peasants and hereditary dependants living side by side, whether it was collected from an entire community, or from separate hearths recognized to be subject to *taille*. Sometimes still demanded in kind, but much more often in money, the *taille* almost always took the form of an annual and fixed payment.[42] Before that time many lords had imposed it only at long intervals when they experienced a specially pressing need for money. In one village of the Paris basin a *taille* of fifty *livres* was levied in 1190 and another one of eighty *livres* in 1248 and no one living could remember any other. So widely spaced as not to be fully absorbed into custom, these irregular demands were much resented by the rural population. They were even the cause of rebellions. In the Ile de France the dependants of the abbey of St Denis refused to accede to their lord's demand in 1250, and 2,000 peasants of the neighbourhood joined with them. By general agreement the *tailles* which still remained arbitrary were then converted to regular payments (*abonnés*). The regularizing movement, begun a hundred years earlier, was concluded after 1250: almost all the *tailles* recorded in written documents after that date show fixed rates and dates of payment, even for the humblest and most subject of the dependants. Like rents, they were henceforth levied at certain dates on the houses of subject individuals.

The landlord owning the peasant home frequently also succeeded, either by purchase or by exchange, in appropriating the *taille* on the family who dwelt in it, with the result that this imposition became very closely bound to the land. This was logically followed by the practice at the end of the thirteenth century when *manses* were sold with the *taille* incumbent on them. By purchase, sale, gift, or bequest, the privilege of levying this exaction, once a symbol of the highest power, was now broken up and fell into diverse hands. At the end of the thirteenth century many new-rich French peasants exploited the *taille*. In any case the *taille* appeared, in countrymen's eyes as well as lords', to be complementary to rents on land and a partial compensation for the latter's extraordinarily low level. On many tenancies it formed the chief return and doubled, even sometimes trebled, the value of the rent.

Thus, added to rents and dues, and sometimes based on each parcel of land, the *tailles* went far to reinforce the profits of landownership in a manner much more efficient than fines on the transfer of property. As personal taxes

---

[42] Fourquin, 551. In the middle of the thirteenth century the *taille* was also fixed in many villages of the Rhineland. Epperlein, 526, p. 46.

they had come to form the principal value of bondsmen.[43] In the aggregate they represented the largest part of the revenue received by lords, large and small, who happened to hold any kind of authority over men. In one of the villages of the lordship of Pamele-Audenarde, they produced in 1275 twice as much money as all the combined rents.[44]

★   ★   ★

The process of adaptation whose opening phases occurred in some countries around the beginning of the twelfth century, ended after 1180 by profoundly transforming the composition of the lord's rent: a gradual fusion of landownership with personal lordships and lordships of the *ban*; a decline in rents; but much higher profits from tithes, mills, fines on the transfer of property and *tailles*. In all these ways the economic pressure on the generally more prosperous peasantry was never relaxed. In certain sectors of the rural world, it even became heavier. Two opposite forces actually encouraged this development. The masters made use of their prerogatives in order to satisfy their needs, especially their need for money: the peasants resisted, the strongest amongst them most successfully. In fact the entire reorganization of manorial taxation, the new forms of servitude, the conversion of dues into money, and above all the regularizing of the *tailles*, benefited the richer peasants. The lords' impositions had never corresponded to the wealth of the subjects except very roughly, and the correspondence became less and less exact. In the thirteenth century the poorest people were crushed by the lords' fiscal power and were thereby thrust ever lower. The development of fixed rents combined with and favoured other changes in economic conditions. The latter were more recent – no trace of them is found in documents before the year 1200 – and they helped to swell the already powerful currents which were transferring the larger part of the profits of small cultivators into other hands.

5. PEASANT INDEBTEDNESS AND ITS EFFECTS

The thirteenth century witnessed a steadily growing demand for credit in the peasant world, together with vast opportunities for investment by those who had ready money available. Superimposed on the old rents and customary taxes, arrears on newly created perpetual rents encumbered the lands of the country folk ever more heavily.

The quickening circulation of currency not only sharpened the need for money amongst nobles, clerks and monks. Villagers also were induced to

---

[43] In 1340 a lord from the neighbourhood of Blois sold sixteen bondsmen for 80 *livres*; this sum obviously represented twenty times the yearly *tailles*, which shows that in the eyes of the seller the other dues hardly counted. Tessier, 650.   [44] Duby, 443

buy more than their forebears. They needed money to acquire animals and to improve their methods of cultivation, to enlarge their stake in stockraising, to settle on lands the price of which was constantly rising, to achieve juridical freedom and acquire the lord's franchise, or finally, to buy the artifacts, tools and clothing manufactured by artisans in market town or hamlet. Nor must we forget the considerable growth of taxation. Every man now had to find ready money with which to satisfy the lord's tax collectors, in order to avoid having his animals seized or his house ransacked. Thus, all those who possessed little more than their land and cattle were forced to borrow, and the immense increase of rural credits is incontrovertible proof of economic expansion in this period.

Many of the loans granted to peasants were really investments. Such, for instance, were the sums of money which the abbey of Bourbourg advanced in 1218 to settlers who wished to dig a new canal in order to extend the polder. Or the numerous contracts *ad medium lucrum*, with shared profits, which fill the notary's registers in the southern countries. In 1309, for example, the wife of a knight from the neighbourhood of Grasse entrusted the trifling sum of 40 *sous* to a household of peasants dependent on her husband on condition that it was put to good use; the following year the capital was to be repaid and the profit shared.[45] Nevertheless, peasants contracted more debts for consumption than for any other purpose. They turned either directly to merchants – most goods, and particularly cloth, were sold on credit – or to professional moneylenders.

At the end of the thirteenth century the 'Lombards' had penetrated the whole of eastern France, from Dauphiné and Lorraine to Namurois and Hainault, setting up their loan shops in the towns and offering money to those who were financially embarrassed. The recognizances for debt which Lombard moneylenders made their debtors sign in one little town near Namur between the years 1295 and 1311 have been preserved. By stipulating repayment in grain these transactions provided short-term subsistence loans, and, most probably, represented advance payment on crops.[46] Jewish financiers also exploited a considerable peasant clientèle. In order to keep in touch with their interests, the Jews of Perpignan travelled regularly about the neighbouring countryside, but it is impossible to discover traces of all their debtors. Those in the humblest positions, who borrowed at very high rates of interest, do not appear in any of the surviving documents; but 65 per cent of the debts registered before notaries by the moneylenders of Perpignan

[45] Mollat, 319; Aubenas, 331

[46] Document No. 73, p. 427; Chomel, 627; Genicot, 189, p. 187, n. 3; Tihon, 352; F. Vercauteren, 'Documents pour servir à l'histoire des financiers lombards en Belgique (1309)', in *Bulletin de l'Institut historique belge de Rome*, 1950-1951

about the year 1300 were contracted by countrymen. Repayment on these loans was less frequently stipulated in money and more often in agricultural produce than on loans to townsmen. Most peasants borrowed in the autumn, their need for money coinciding with the seasonal migration of the flocks and sowing time; loans were usually to be repaid at harvest time, and they too probably concealed advance sales of the crops.[47]

Peasants in financial need, however, often received help from better-off neighbours. This appears frequently to have been the case in Provençal villages, whose notarial registers, still far too little utilized, reveal at the turn of the fourteenth century the details of endless loans repayable in grain or money, entered into to buy a donkey, an ox, a house, or grain. Grain had to be repaid at its price in May and sometimes the debtor was himself obliged to carry the sacks to the local town, sell them to the highest bidder and bring back the proceeds. Most of the loans made in the mountains, where the standard of life of the peasants was markedly lower than in the neighbourhood of Perpignan, were secured by mortgages. One of the count's statutes of 1266 prohibited foreclosing on ploughing implements or animals; thus the house or the future harvest usually provided security for the debt. Land was also mortgaged. In 1334 a peasant in this region ceded the produce of his land for the next twelve years to one of his better-off neighbours (who had just given his daughter a dowry of 53 gold florins) in return for twelve *livres*: he was to work the land and the debt was to be reduced by two *livres* after every sowing. This small husbandman had in fact sold, in exchange for an immediate provision of money, a rent in kind on his property.[48] Innumerable transactions of this type are to be found in the records after 1250. They transferred to moneyed men the harvests of this or that plot of land for four, ten or even twenty years; and thereby assured the domination of the richer inhabitants of the village over their poorer neighbours.

In the Provençal mountains rents acquired in this way encumbered the land temporarily. They were gradually extinguished as the liveries of crops freed the peasant from his debt. Such operations were the equivalent of purchases of standing crops, practised on a large scale and under the cloak of a loan on grain by moneylenders of all kinds from boroughs and towns. The practice of rent charges, i.e. charging properties with new fixed annual payments, which spread in the second half of the century, must, however, be considered as an economic phenomenon of equal importance, but quite different in scope.

*   *   *

---

[47] Document No. 72, p. 425; Emery, 335
[48] Archives des Bouches-du-Rhône, 396 E 18, fol. 75 *et seq.*

Their earliest traces can be found in France in the twelfth century.[49] The process spread slowly after 1200, and became universal after 1250. The procedure was very simple and began with a man in possession of land, either an allod or a tenancy (for after the mid-thirteenth century at least in France, tenants for rent received the right to create a new rent on their holdings on condition that they recompensed the lord by an 'entry fine' or tax on the transfer of property similar to one they would have paid on a sale). In exchange for the exact sum he needed this man would cede an annual and perpetual rent with which he would charge his land. The purchaser would levy on the property each year five to eight per cent of the sum he advanced. The payments could be made in money, but also, very frequently, in kind, and especially in grain. Around Namur most perpetual rents, even those collected by the highest lords, were paid in grain.[50]

By no other method could a land-holder obtain so easily the funds he needed. And this facility outweighed for the seller the disadvantage of the practice; the impossibility of repurchase, which meant that the land was permanently subject to rent; and the overwhelming burden imposed in years of bad harvest by the obligation to pay in cereals. The need to pay a fine on the transfer of property inconvenienced the purchaser. On the other hand the title of possession thus acquired was completely mobile, easily transferable, negotiable, and transmissible to heirs. Above all, the process offered a perfectly safe investment, since in the event of default, the purchaser was authorized to seize the property on which the rent was charged; he ran hardly any risk of losing his payments and a complete code of laws developed favourable to him.[51] These considerations, together with the growing financial embarrassment of certain groups of countrymen, explain the continued success of the 'creation' of rents. They were used for the transfer of funds for all kinds of purposes, from providing a dowry to the raising of alms on a patrimony while maintaining its integrity. The faithful whose piety induced them to make donations to their church to found masses, anniversaries or chaplaincies, frequently gave sums of money to buy fixed rents of which the annual yield would be sufficient to pay for one of these services in perpetuity. The universal spread of the practice in the second half of the thirteenth century shows that the market for rents was both an open and an active one, especially in the countryside. Peasants who happened to fall victim to passing financial crises attempted, it is true, to find other ways of obtaining short-term credit against security which did not bind them so completely for the future. But the main flow of capital into peasant cultivation took place through the purchase of 'created' rents. It allowed the possessors of ready

[49] Document No. 69, p. 417   [50] Génicot, 189, pp. 264 *et seq.*
[51] Document No. 143, p. 503

money to acquire a direct and permanent share in agrarian production. By stipulating that their payments should be made in grain they kept their households supplied without recourse to commercial channels; they evaded the continuous rise in the price of cereals; above all they escaped the great seasonal variations in prices. People who had ample funds available even succeeded in laying hands on quantities of agricultural commodities which they could themselves put on the market, and many recipients of rents replaced peasant producers as sellers of surplus grain. At the end of the thirteenth century rents had come to play an important part in the mechanics of the grain trade.[52]

By this means a new kind of economic domination was established over allodial and rent-paying land alike. It was less stable than the manorial lordship since it was so deeply entangled in trade and business transactions of all kinds, but it was none the less firmly entrenched and burdensome. Like landownership and personal and territorial lordships, it syphoned off a large part of the profits of field and vineyard. By purchasing these rents, which were freely available, many members of quite humble social classes could share in the exploitation of the tillers of the soil. It should be noted, however, that the largest holders of 'rents' belonged to the old upper classes, and especially to the clergy who used a substantial part of their liquid funds in this way; and it was in this manner that rural indebtedness helped to strengthen seigneurial rent.[53] Many lords exploited their own dependants' need of money. They bought perpetual rents on lands worked by their bondsmen, and also on many properties of which they held the lordship and which were cultivated by their tenants. The perpetual rents they purchased from the peasants then supplemented, and were additional to, the rent on land, and had the effect of permanently increasing the charges on the tenancy. This effect can be seen very distinctly in the mid-thirteenth century in the Paris region. In order to pay for franchises and the yearly payments of *tailles* and tithes the villagers needed ready money, and their lords offered to provide it by buying permanent rents. At Orly and l'Hay Chevilly, as well as in many other localities, the granting of franchises, paid for by instalments, resulted in the creation of numerous rents in the lord's favour during the early years following the grant of charters.

This is how a new system of regular charges was created which largely compensated the master for what little he had lost in making the *ban* more flexible. These charges were of course borne by the least prosperous peasant

---

[52] Génicot, 189, p. 275

[53] Fourquin, 551; Godding-Ganshof, 484. In 1240 the chapter general of Cîteaux authorized the abbeys of the Order to buy *rentes* when they received a gift of money for this purpose. Martène, IV, 1253.

households. Only the better-off individuals, who did not need to apply elsewhere for the money to pay for enfranchisement, were ever liberated in the real sense of the word.[54]

★　　★　　★

In the second half of the thirteenth century one more method was available to lords to compensate them for the fall in fixed land rents and to protect them against the general movement of prices which was gradually eroding the value of their money incomes. The growing overpopulation of the villages, the immense number of peasants prepared to take land on almost any condition, the instability of rural society, the frequent transfers of property and migrations, gave the landlords an opportunity to change, in spite of the weight of custom, the status of the rent-paying land which had fallen vacant. They could impose a new system of leases which were no longer hereditary, but could be either revoked by the lord at will, or granted for a short term only. On these lands the lord could alter the rent periodically to take account of the increased productivity of the soil, of the change in the value of money and its gradual depreciation, of the state of the demand for tenancies, or even of the apparent prosperity of the tenants.

We do not know much about these new tenancies, but in certain regions the main outline of the story is clear. In the most anciently occupied portions of Bavaria where demographic pressure was most powerful, we can see during the thirteenth century a kind of revokable tenancy appearing, known as the *Freistift*. In the *Bauding*, the assembly at which all tenants were gathered together, the landlord proclaimed new land leases each year; generally he gave them back to the men who had held them previously, but only after prolonged bargaining; he then received a gift or else required an adjustment of the rent.[55] On English manors, written contracts for short-term leases, *per cartam*, increased in numbers in the second half of the century. In 1299 50 per cent and in 1342 57 per cent of the rents collected by Ely Cathedral came from contractual tenancies, and, by a gradual process of adaptation, their yield trebled between 1251 and 1336.[56] In the Cotswolds many villeins lost the hereditary condition of their tenancy after 1260. It was granted to them by a lessor for one or two lives on payment of high entry fine and of an annual rent in cash.[57] At this period most peasant cultivations in north-western Germany were let on leases for nine, twelve or twenty-four years. A similar system of temporary leases can also be seen operating widely in the Flemish polders. According to an inventory of the income of the abbey of St Bavo of Ghent drawn up in 1281, perpetual tenancies brought the monks

[54] Fourquin, 551　　　　　　　　[55] Dollinger, 159
[56] Miller, 198, pp. 94 and 109　　[57] Hilton, 391

in a return of no more than 32 *livres*, while they got as much as 196 *livres* from lands let out on lease.[58]

The practice of short-term leases renewed by mutual agreement spread on Italian manors at this period, and enabled the monastery of Saint Ambrose of Milan nearly to double the yield of rents from the manor of Origgio between 1250 and 1320. Tenancies at the Cistercian abbey of Settimo in Tuscany were in 1338 almost all let for five years at most by the contract of *affictum*. Nevertheless the economy of the Italian countryside was dominated by the towns inhabited by provision merchants, whose main preoccupation was food supplies; and these landlords preferred rents in kind. Around Settimo, as at Origgio, tenancies on short-term leases paid a rent in grain. The practice of *métayage*, or *mezzadria*, linked with a short-term lease, became common in these regions at an early date. For a few years the peasant received the farm fully equipped on condition that he gave the owner half of the produce.[59]

Whether they helped to raise money rents or increased dues paid in agricultural produce, these changes in the condition of leases affected the structure of landownership more than any other single factor. They originated in methods used since early times in the management of demesnes and in the contracts of 'farm' concluded between masters and their managers. Now the landlords found in it the most efficient method of countering the threat of dwindling rents, but in actual fact what made possible changes so exceptionally unfavourable to the small cultivator was the depressed condition of a large part of the peasantry consequent on the growth of population and the circulation of money.

*   *   *

By exploiting these tendencies and by breaking the strict rules of custom, the lords were able to make use of the economic condition of the peasant to compensate themselves for the decline of the older type of dues. Pressed by necessity, and much more aware of economic realities and relative values than their predecessors, they took advantage of the increase in productivity and the more thorough circulation of money in the countryside. At one and the same time they exploited the enterprise and thrift of the better-off villagers, and the difficulties of the less fortunate ones. They took advantage of their monopolies and such powers of command which the renascent states left in their hands. Finally their superior position gave them control of increasingly scarce and valuable arable land and sometimes of the cash balances

[58] Wittich, 210; Verhulst, 208
[59] Romeo, 481; Jones, 673; Imberciadori, 478; Luzzatto, 'Contributo alla storia della mezzadria nel medio evo', in *Nuova rivista storica*, 1948

which the peasantry were slowly able to create. All these various compensations kept up and even in some cases considerably raised the level of manorial rents. In the last analysis the lords were the principal beneficiaries of rural prosperity.

It should, however, be noted that with the general relaxation of the economy and the new mobility of property the *seigneurie* had not only become more complex but also much more flexible. The sharp demarcations which had formerly kept apart men on different rungs of the social ladder and which had restricted manorial profits of lordships to a small élite, were now becoming blurred. At the end of the thirteenth century, merchants and some new-rich peasants drew rents, tithes and the various forms of perpetual rents on land and even enjoyed the immense profits of the *taille*. All these rights, even the ones which originated as part of the royal prerogatives, were bought and sold, or were handed down from one patrimony to another. The manorial prerogatives were thus dispersed and the currents bearing the products of peasant toil into the lords' households flowed into innumerable channels and constantly changed course. This new-found flexibility – we might even call it instability – was obviously due to the dominance of money in the relationship between the masters and the tillers of the soil. To what extent had the changes and the facilities offered by the use of money detached the lords from the direct cultivation of their rural properties? Had they become nothing more than ground landlords? What did the manor now mean to them?

CHAPTER IV

The XIII Century (1180-1330):
The Exploitation of the Demesne

I. ENGLAND

Conditions in England must be considered first, since much more is known about them. The wealth of surviving documents makes it possible to study the attitudes of the ecclesiastical lords in great detail. After the end of the twelfth century the demesne seems to have become more important to the men administering the affairs of the great English monasteries. At that time, as a result of rapidly rising prices of foodstuffs, the yield of 'farms' paid in money was insufficient to keep the refectories provisioned. The English monks thus found themselves in a situation very similar to that of Peter the Venerable fifty years earlier at Cluny.[1] Manorial administrators tried to cut down their expenses and to balance their budgets by not renewing the contracts of 'farm' and by resuming the direct management of the demesne. At Ely and Ramsey the 'farm' was abandoned after 1175. From then onwards we can observe in the collections of surviving documents a greatly increased number of surveys intended to estimate the resources of the manors more precisely, to discover which items could have their yields enhanced, and to plan a consistent policy of investment. Much money was now devoted to improving livestock. More still was relinquished because cash was no longer taken in lieu of labour services. The system of 'selling' labour services to the peasants had been encouraged in previous decades by the spread of the money economy, but now the services were again claimed in kind.[2]

The revival of ties which bound men together, and the strictly dependent condition in which the political developments placed so many of the inhabitants of the manor, made it possible for a form of servitude to raise its head again. Labour services, and especially ploughing services, as onerous as they had ever been in the eleventh century, oppressed villein society. Neither widows, nor the sick, nor even peasants administering the demesne itself,

[1] This similarity ought to stimulate a detailed enquiry into the chronological relationship between what we know about continental experience and the economic growth of the great monastic demesnes in England.

[2] Miller, 198, pp. 85 *et seq.*; Raftis, 201

were exempted: all dependent men had to work in the lord's fields. On the manors of Ely Cathedral the strict enforcement of peasant obligations resulted in a ten per cent extension of the 'weekworks', or weekly labour services, between 1221 and 1251.

At the same time the management of the demesne was reorganized. On each manor, one of the villeins was appointed 'reeve'. Under the supervision of a 'provost' or a 'bailiff', he had to carry for one year the heavy responsibility of directing the cultivation and mustering the men subject to service. His principal task was to sell the surplus output; indeed commercial transactions came to occupy an ever larger part in the manorial economy. Amongst the money receipts of the canons of Leicester in 1254 the total of rents was still greater than that of sales, i.e. 44 per cent against 41 per cent; but by 1297 rents formed no more than 32 per cent while sales of grain formed 27 per cent and sales of wool 35 per cent. On fifteen English manors of the abbey of Bec at that time, the returns from rents and fixed payments were 287 *li* and from direct cultivation 360 *li*.[3]

After that time, however, direct cultivation on the largest monastic manors began to decline. In 1255 the demesne provided Ely with half its income: in 1298 with no more than 40 per cent. The manorial accounts of Ramsey Abbey have been analyzed in great detail and they show that during the third quarter of the thirteenth century the lords were rapidly giving up the cultivation of their demesnes. Even though agricultural yields were buoyant and a prolonged rise in prices offered ever great opportunities for the sale of surpluses, the monks' agents no longer sold grain, and villeins could once more redeem their labour for which there was no call. The decline of the demesne exploitation seems to have been caused by the burden of royal and pontifical taxation. Immersed in debt, the ecclesiastical lords were once again forced to convert their rights into cash in order to escape their difficulties, even if this meant sacrificing future prospects. They reverted to the practise of the eleventh century: leaving the dependent peasantry with economic initiative, enabling it to increase its own production and to sell its surplus, and appropriating a large part of these profits by steeply increasing monetary imposts. The reduction in the demesne on the Ely manors, at the expense of which new tenancies were created, began in the second half of the thirteenth century.[4]

★   ★   ★

The economic development of the great monastic lordships of eastern and midland England is particularly vividly illuminated, but it does not

[3] Hilton, 667, pp. 25-26; Morgan, 408
[4] Raftis, 201, pp. 217 *et seq.*; Miller, 198, pp. 110 *et seq.*

necessarily follow that an identical system of exploitation was in force on demesnes all over England. Monastic methods were in fact relics of the past and were not at all typical. To associate the tenants with the labour of the demesne in the thirteenth century was an anachronism embalmed in the few tradition-bound communities of monks and canons. Besides, even on these manors belonging to the ancient religious foundations the return to direct management entailed a greater reliance on paid labour: the permanent employment of domestic servants and the seasonal recruitment of day labourers. In 1316 one Ely manor employed a *familia* of eleven men who did the ploughing and carting and looked after the livestock; grain was threshed by workers paid by the piece; in addition a man was engaged to do the sowing, two boys were taken on to spread manure, and five more ploughmen were paid for 147 days at the rate of a penny a day. From the very earliest years of the thirteenth century the administrators of the estates of the bishops at Winchester spent hundreds of pounds every year on wages. On one of the Crowland Abbey manors where labour services were extremely heavy, they were valued in the annual accounts in 1322 at 4 *li*, while more than 9 *li* were distributed to the paid labour force. It must also be pointed out that when, in the counties further to the west, those in charge of ecclesiastical estates expanded their direct cultivation, they did so without restoring the forced service of the villeins. Thus, on the lands of Worcester Abbey the growth of the demesne economy was entirely achieved by equipping the manors with extra draught animals and by taking on wage labour. Finally, the great royal inquests at the end of the century show that the vast majority of landed estates in England, belonging both to the aristocracy and to many of the religious houses, bore an appearance totally different from that of the huge but old-fashioned estates of the bishops and monasteries.[5]

Such immensely rich series of documents as the Hundred Rolls – the survey drawn up in 1279 listing all the lordships in the kingdom, their estates, their revenues and the men who were subject to them – an echo of the Domesday Book of two centuries before – and the Inquisitions Post Mortem– drawn up to value the estates of the royal tenants-in-chief at succession – demonstrate more clearly than anything else how small most manors were at that time. In the south Midlands only 36 per cent of the manors mentioned in the Hundred Rolls possessed more than 500 acres of arable land. For that

[5] Miller, 198, p. 90; F. M. Page, *The Estates of Crowland Abbey; a Study in Manorial Organization*, Cambridge, 1934; *The Red Book of Worcester*, 393. The example of England in the thirteenth century deserves to be studied by historians of the Carolingian estates. Might not the types of farming described by the *polyptyques* in the ninth century perhaps also be exceptional by comparison with the majority of landed estates of lesser importance, for which no single source survives to give us any inkling of what conditions on them were like?

matter many villages (in Leicestershire, one in two) contained several landed estates; in one there were five manors, two lay and three ecclesiastical. The general surveys also show that on the smaller manors the demesnes were proportionately much larger and they consequently comprised fewer villein tenancies. It has been calculated from the Hundred Rolls that demesne lands occupied more than 26 per cent of the area of the great estates and villein tenancies 51 per cent, while on small estates no more than 33 per cent of the land was let out to villeins, and 41 per cent was retained for the demesne. Furthermore on small manors labour services were mostly levied in money.[6] The accounts of Henry de Bray, a knight of no great wealth, show that men subject to labour service played hardly any part in the cultivation of the demesne, which was wholly worked by hired labour.[7] The revival of forced labour in England in the thirteenth century seems, therefore, to have been very limited: it was only temporary, since it declined definitely on the great monastic estates after 1275, and was restricted in scope, since labour services were only used to reinforce those of manorial employees.

The practice of direct management was none the less very much alive. It showed no sign of weakening on small estates, i.e. the vast majority of manors, during the third quarter of the thirteenth century. It was supported by the extensive use of wage labour. Indeed we ought to consider the villeins themselves as part-time wage-earners because they were fed in the lord's house on some of the days on which they worked there and were sometimes allowed to take home in the evenings sheaves of the grain they had just harvested. Changed economic conditions were unpropitious for a recurrence of forced labour. They in fact favoured the greater use of paid labour by more widespread use of the twelfth-century practice of 'selling' the services to those liable to them and buying with the proceeds the freely offered services of paid workers. Even though the forced labour of villeinage was carefully allotted throughout the agricultural calendar, paid work still had the advantage of greater flexibility and made it possible for employment and seasonally fluctuating manpower needs to be much more finely adjusted. Finally the determining factor – and this should be underlined – was that money wages remained all but stable throughout the thirteenth century and the first half of the fourteenth; in a period of gently and continually rising agricultural prices, wage stability obviously favoured the employers.

In fact, the vigour of demesne farming, for which there is so much reliable evidence in all English villages, appears closely linked with an abundant labour supply favourable to the lords, and was consequently also linked with the overpopulation of the countryside. Cottars, bordars, all the freeholders

---

[6] See, especially, the table in Kosminsky, 403, p. 100
[7] *Henry de Bray's Estate Book* (ed. D. Willis), London, 1916

whose holdings were so reduced by partible inheritance as no longer to provide them with a living, and all the villeins' sons for whom there was no employment on the parental holding, composed a ubiquitous proletariat, living in increasing misery, in a country where the towns were still small, where the reclaimable wastelands were all but gone, and where perhaps the more anciently reclaimed lands had lost their fertility. Often excluded from the village community and the collective pasture rights and thus unable to obtain a supplementary income from sheep and pigs, large numbers of ill-nourished men and women offered their labour to the smaller landlords and manorial managers. This was what kept wages so low and made the direct farming of the demesne profitable not only as a way of provisioning the lords' households, but also as a method of production for the market. The very existence of these day workers who had to buy their daily bread helped to sustain the price of grain. If we add to these highly favourable market conditions, the existence of a powerful monarchy which put a brake on the spread of private taxation and which limited the profits of manorial and seig-neurial dues, we can easily understand why the lords of the English manors did not develop into mere recipients of fixed payments, but remained agri-cultural producers right up to the eve of the fourteenth century. Not only did they rear livestock which enabled them to profit from the high price of wool for export, but they also sold grain on the home market. An easy labour market, and an overpopulated country crowded with landless peasants, underpinned their prosperity.

2. THE CONTINENT

The history of demesne farming on the continent is much more obscure, since the study of manorial documents has not yet gone very far. The present state of researches does not enable us to discover what was the most usual size of the demesne or whether it tended to increase or to shrink.

It is better to take separately the case of the great estates run by the reli-gious orders whose rules specifically enjoined manual labour and the direct cultivation of their land. Like the English monastic estates, they were a dis-tinct group whose exploitation is clearly shown by the evidence as being different from the general practice. It is obvious that after the year 1200 these large estates, in France as well as in Germany, suffered a crisis of manpower. Religious houses were finding it very difficult to recruit lay brethren. It is hard to put a finger on the reasons which now turned the sons of peasants away from a vocation to which so many of them had been drawn in previous generations. Was there a gradual change in religious attitudes in rural society. Was town life more attractive? Or was, perhaps, the appeal of other religious activities greater? Whatever the reason, the Cistercians and other working orders were forced to engage more and more paid help. From the thirteenth century onwards such employment upset the balance of abbey budgets. The obligation placed on the monks to cultivate by their own labour the whole of their land had for a long time been surreptitiously evaded in most Cistercian monasteries, and the evasion was officially sanctioned by the chapters-general in 1200. They authorized the leasing of the 'least useful' lands in 1208, and in 1224 the whole of the 'granges'.[8] Many were parcelled out, for there was no difficulty in finding peasants ready to take up tenancies of land. Often the monks joined with other lords in *pariage*, and jointly founded new villages on the sites of their 'wilderness'. In this way direct cultivation suffered a marked setback of which a clear-cut change in labour supply was the cause.

In the archives of other estates some traces of a parcelling out of the demesne can also be discovered. There are clear indications that it was more frequent than in the twelfth century, and though this may be partly because documentary sources were now more numerous, it was also because land was more mobile. Innumerable manors were broken up by partial sales and portions of demesnes were transferred into other hands. The new owners, not always themselves in a position to cultivate them, therefore transformed them into rent-paying holdings. We find in inventories and rentals at the end of the century a number of plots of land whose names, or that of the locality in which they lay, prove that they had previously formed part of demesnes. Many *condemines*, *crouées*, *coûtures* or *dimanche-près* had been detached in this way in small portions and leased to peasant farmers in exchange for rent or a share in the harvest. One charter of 1230, for instance, describes the lands belonging to a knight of the district of Mâcon which had formerly been a demesne. The fields were now held by burgesses of the neighbouring town for high money rents; the vineyard was held by the tenants, who handed over a quarter of the *vendange* to the master in addition to a small rent. The lords preferred to levy on these fragments of the demesne lands share-cropping dues which enabled them to claim a part of the harvest. It gave them the feeling that they were still in some way associated with the cultivation. Dues of this nature were at the beginning of the thirteenth century received from the parcelled-out portions of the demesne on the estate of the monastery of Baumburg, as well as at St Bavo of Ghent.[9]

All this evidence, however, does not dispel the impression that in he thirteenth century, as in the twelfth, the parcelling out of land affected only a very small portion of the demesne. There were too many psychological

[8] Jones, 673

[9] *Recueil de chartes de Cluny*, VI, No. 4655; one furlong brought in 14 *sous*, another 15, a mill 20 *sous*, the vines 14 *sous* and one-quarter of the *vendange*; the lord kept in hand only the tithe and a newly planted vineyard which he would probably let when it was in full bearing.

obstacles; such as the reluctance of masters to be separated from land which had been farmed by their fathers, and the strength of custom which would not allow on the same village territory ancient manorial fields and plots traditionally leased to peasant farmers to be treated in the same way. Furthermore written documents show that amputations of the demesne land were largely compensated for. What one demesne lost here, another would gain there, very frequently by the cultivation of wastelands. We have already said that the arable demesnes of countless knightly houses of the Ile de France, established in the mid-thirteenth century on the fringe of the woods, were probably created, at least in part, from the waste. We see, for instance, in 1219, some members of the lesser nobility leasing for reclamation from the chapter of Notre-Dame of Paris one hundred *arpents* of woodland at a rent of four *deniers* per *arpent*, in addition to a tithe of the eleventh sheaf; they were strictly forbidden to put settlers there; the labour of breaking up and cultivating the soil, therefore, fell upon their own servants.[10] Other demesnes were extended by purchase. Between 1200 and 1270 the administrators of the Lorraine monasteries acquired for money many small plots of land which they assembled piece by piece into small enclosed demesnes devoted partly to sheep-rearing, but mostly to cultivation. A little later burgesses undertook similar enterprises. Chance has preserved the documents which show us a village lord in the same region who succeeded between 1302 and 1320 in adding to his estate 23 peasant tenancies of which he had purchased the entire possession.[11] Growing activity in the land market encouraged such consolidations.

Indeed so great was the encouragement that the demesne appeared everywhere at the end of the thirteenth century to be secure, except perhaps in Italy. It is true that the greatest lay lords had by then entirely given up direct cultivation. We know about the 25 manors of the count of Namur from an inventory drawn up in 1289. Nine of them no longer had demesnes, and demesne land covered only nine per cent of the area of the whole patrimony. The proportion was even smaller in the *Veil Rentier* which describes the possessions of those extremely wealthy Flemish lords of Pamele-Audenarde.[12] Nevertheless the movement restricting the demesne is hardly visible except on the princely estates. The larger religious foundations at this period still kept fields, meadows and good-sized vineyards in hand. It is true that the demesne in the village of Thiais, attached to the abbey of St Germain-des-Prés, was three times smaller in the fourteenth century than it had been in the time of Irminon's *polyptyque*. Nevertheless it still covered 225 acres. And the

10 *Cartulaire de Notre-Dame de Paris*, II, p. 287
11 Schneider, 351, p. 355
12 Génicot, 189, pp. 99 *et seq.*; Duby, 443

abbey of St Martin of Tournai had 12,500 acres of demesne spread over 37 'halls'. The damage which in 1250, or thereabouts, the burgesses of Arles caused to the arable and meadows of the Archbishop was estimated at 20,000 *sous*. At Tremblay in the Ile de France, where its rent-paying holdings covered 1,400 hectares, the abbey of St Denis farmed 200 hectares of fields and 937 acres of meadow as demesne. The description of the lands belonging to the Walloon priory of Grand Bigard drawn up in 1296 tells that the demesne occupied a quarter of the whole patrimony.[13]

These, of course, were all huge estates. But the study of modest landed possessions reveals that on them demesne lands played an even more vital part. About 1300 very many estates of the petty nobility, of the smaller religious communities, and of the new-rich burgesses who had settled in the country maintained before all else 'granges', well stocked with cattle, served by teams of permanent servants, and containing large hay-fields and extensive arable strengthened by recent consolidation. All the 'houses' of the Templars in France at the time when their order was proscribed were of this kind; the demesne, upon which huge flocks were raised, formed the principal wealth of the commandery of St Eulalie-du-Larzac, as was also the case at Caen, where a score of domestic servants cultivated 155 acres of fields and tended 33 cattle, 26 horses, 280 sheep and 108 pigs. At the same period the Templars of Berlin cultivated a demesne of 25 *Hufen*, i.e. an area five or six times larger than the average size of a peasant farm. Some of the 'granges' were also in the process of being assembled. The Premonstratensians of Gergovie formed theirs in the course of the thirteenth century by a number of small purchases. While at Ouges in Burgundy the Cistercians assembled piecemeal 550 'dayworks' of plough, two-thirds of which were grouped in large fields, meadows and more than 400 'dayworks' of woodlands. In Tuscany in 1338, despite recent amputations, the abbey of Settimo preserved as a demesne a grange, a garden, an orchard, a vineyard, mills, fisheries, a bakehouse and a fine flock. And what little information we can glean about lay manorial property allows us to assume that most households of the rural nobility controlled farms of similar content. 600 sheep, two ploughs and several plough horses were counted in the mid-fourteenth century on Pierre d'Orgemont's demesne at Gonesse near Paris. High up on the moors of the Beaujolais mountains there was in 1286 an arable furlong of about six acres which forty years earlier a small nobleman had tried to reclaim. He was forced to sell it, together with the 125 acres of woodland which he had kept in hand with the intention of assarting. On one estate belonging to some knights of Mâcon in 1267, the demesne lands brought ten *livres* in every year

[13] Fourquin, 551; Haenens, 666, p. 56; Archives des Bouches-du-Rhône, III, G 3 No. 208; Engelmann, 336, p. 191; Godding-Ganshof, 484

while the tenant lands brought in only one hundred *sous*. Everything leads us to believe that, like the small English lords of the Midlands, all the knights, squires, *Ritter* and officials of France and the Empire derived the greater part of their revenue from the demesne throughout the thirteenth century, and even beyond.[14]

*　　*　　*

At the turn of the thirteenth and fourteenth century, the master often ran most of these demesnes himself, at least if he lived on his land and could supervise it in person and watch over his domestic servants, or if he had trustworthy agents upon whom he could rely. Thierry d'Hireçon was a typical example of a landowner sharing in this widespread partiality for direct management. He was a churchman (and perhaps for this reason a meticulous administrator), and one of the countess of Artois's councillors; in his later years his sojourns in his house in Paris became shorter and shorter and his residences in the houses he had acquired in Artois longer and longer. He looked after his household at Roquetoire personally; in 1310 he took the demesne of Bonnières, a huge farm of 1,450 'dayworks' of ploughland, into his own hands, and in 1325, when the termination of the lease allowed him to evict the 'farmer', he also decided to manage the lands at Sailly and to set up there a *mesnie* of twelve menservants and two maidservants. He also employed agents whom he required to keep detailed accounts during his absence, which is why we know so much about this country estate of medium size.[15]

On most demesnes the area given over to the plough was large. It is true that lords often wanted to eat bread made from the grain they grew themselves, and consequently had to have arable lands extensive enough to fill their barns as a safeguard against poor harvests, but they were also concerned with the sale of grain. Thierry d'Hireçon, for instance, despatched cereals to Flanders every year and the Hospitallers of Provence sold a large proportion of the demesne-produced grain.[16]

The cultivation of cereals required much equipment, many draught animals and, above all, abundant manpower. At harvest time, and during the summer and autumn ploughing, in the thirteenth century a small amount of labour services still brought a few tenants and bondsmen with their horses and oxen to the demesne fields.[17] In some regions, as in Normandy and

---

[14] Higounet-Nadal, 457; Delisle, *Normandie*, p. 721; Carsten, 8, p. 34; Fournier, 450; Martin-Lorber, 676; Fourquin, 551; Perroy, 269, p. 141; Duby, 261, p. 507

[15] Richard, 473　　　　　[16] Richard, 473; Duby, 445

[17] In 1234, for example, the Templars of Manosque agreed with the community to limit the work due by dependants and their animals to two days in the year. *Livre des privilèges de Manosque* (ed. Isnard), Digne, 1894, p. 20.

Flanders, even the *lot-corvée* (cultivation of a plot of demesne arable) remained in use. On their demesne of Vliezde in 1227 the monks of St Bavo of Ghent distributed three and a half acres of arable to each dependent *manse* to be ploughed five times; the holding had also to supply two labourers in the month of March, two days weeding in June, sixteen days reaping and finally two men and a cart had to be put at the lord's disposal twice a year to spread manure on the fields.[18] This example demonstrates that, in the north of Europe at least, forced labour still occupied a far from negligible place in the demesne economy at the beginning of the thirteenth century.

Such obligations, however, were quite insufficient to ensure the entire cultivation of the arable land. Furthermore, lords and peasants sometimes agreed to substitute payments in money for forced ploughing services. Labour service rapidly dwindled on some estates in the course of the thirteenth century: in 1290 the tenants of the same Flemish manor of Vliezde were no longer compelled to do more than a manuring service. The detailed statistical data which we have now begun to uncover in certain manorial documents of this period reveals what a low value was set on forced labour. On the great Thuringian demesnes the work done by a man subject to labour service was set at a half, or even one-third, of that done by a paid worker. Nor was the labour service performed entirely gratuitously; as a rule the forced labourer had to be fed. A man who came to harrow the lands of the church at Bayeux could claim a white loaf, a brown loaf, a measure of beer and three herrings or five eggs. The cost of the food often exceeded the value of the work done. In 1315 the eleven four-horse ploughs subject to forced labour which ploughed Thierry d'Hireçon's land for a single forenoon in fact cost thirty sous, i.e. a third of the annual wage of a domestic servant. In an inventory of 1338 the services owed to the Hospitallers of Provence by the men subject to labour service were worth only half as much as could have been done by a day labourer in their place, but the meal which was served to them was worth two or three times more than a domestic's ration.[19] Many labour services were therefore abolished in the lord's interest. On the Provençal demesnes of the Hospitallers hardly any remained except in the most backward mountain districts, and even there they were not always claimed. In the administrators' opinion carting services alone were still worth their value for the transport of surplus crops to the borough markets. In the *Veil Rentier* of Audenarde the rare ploughing services still imposed on tenancies (the most heavily charged owed three days per annum) were without exception redeemed by the peasants very cheaply.[20] The cultivation of the

[18] Verhulst, 208, p. 370
[19] Lütge, 360; Delisle, *Normandie*, p. 80; Richard, 473; Duby, 445
[20] Duby, 443 and 444

demesne arable on the continent, as in England, fell, therefore, on the paid workers, temporary or permanent.

The three demesnes which Thierry d'Hireçon ran employed a great many such men. For sowing a man was hired whose wage was proportionate to the area to be sown. Women who weeded the corn in springtime were paid from four to six deniers per day. Reaping provided countless temporary jobs, paid either by the day, by contract, by area, or by piece, the workers receiving every eleventh, fifteenth or twentieth sheaf to be gathered. Lastly in winter the threshers received wages paid in grain and in money. Nevertheless, the most important tasks of agricultural labour, i.e. ploughing and harrowing, were performed by domestic servants who worked full time in the household. Out of 23 persons living in the hall of Bonnières, 12 were ploughmen each of whom received between 45 and 100 *sous* a year besides their food (bread, oat gruel, peas, herrings during Lent and the heavy August labour, and meat on Sundays). They were an unstable group: at Sailly nine out of fifteen jobs changed hands between 1325 and 1328. The labour situation on the Provençal estates of the Hospitallers in 1338 was exactly the same. One estate employed twenty servants throughout the year, whose food bill was 80 *livres*, and whose upkeep and wages accounted for a further expenditure of 36 *livres* in cash. They received help from temporary labourers of both sexes for weeding the crop, reaping and for the transport of the grain; for these 1,280 days work, the house had to pay out 50 *livres* every year.[21]

★   ★   ★

Offering regular employment to peasants of the neighbourhood, distributing considerable sums of money in the form of wages (more than one hundred *livres* was thus dispersed denier by denier amongst the innumerable seasonal workers on the commandery of Comps in Provence), and thereby transferring a useful portion of the profits realized by the sale of surplus crops into the hands of the most depressed rural classes, were not the least of the manor's economic functions. Large numbers of labourers of humble status obtained from the demesne considerable additions to their incomes. Their situation was often an advantageous one. It has been calculated that the income earned by a high-grade servant, like the 'first oxdriver' employed in the Provençal houses of the Hospitallers, was at least the equivalent of that of the cultivator of a good-sized farm, and furthermore the servant had far greater economic security. Such men were always certain of being able to eat their fill at their master's table, even in times of scarcity.[22] As for casual wages, they were indispensable to the almost landless peasants, the *brassiers*, the *Söldner*,

[21] Richard, 473; Duby, 445   [22] Duby, 445

the *Gärtner*, and to all the tenants of tiny holdings in France and Germany who occupied the same position as the English cottars. The wages earned by wives and daughters at weeding, by the father and other men of the household at harvesting or threshing, could save their families from total destitution. We can also imagine seasonal migrations at harvest time on the frontiers of mountain and plain: hordes of wage-earners moving from the plains where the grain ripened earlier to the less favourably situated upland fields and thus earning for several weeks wages of from sixteen to twenty-four *deniers* per day. This was enough to see them through the winter. The relatively high cost of labour hired for seasonal work, especially the heavier summer tasks, need not surprise us. The work required a huge labour force, it was all performed by hand and against time. Large-scale farmers, therefore, competed for casual labour and the economic structure of peasant society was organized to meet their demands. The existence of a labouring proletariat, prepared to earn its living in a short working period, corresponded to the notion of agricultural employment telescoped into a few short seasons. A new link was forged by the wage system between the demesne and the peasantry who had drifted apart after the decay of forced labour: an infinitely more flexible link and one, moreover, which was essential to both parties.

However, the burden of wages, added to the cost of maintaining equipment and animals, considerably reduced the returns from cereal cultivation, except on those demesnes which, being either near large towns or exporting harbours found themselves in specially favoured trading locations, or on those demesnes where normal yields were above four to one. About the year 1300 a vast number of inventories and accounts provide data sufficiently detailed for us to draw up balance-sheets for some agricultural enterprises. The results lead us to conclude that the profit margin was often extremely small. On one commandery of the Provençal Hospitallers the crops were worth 266 *livres* in a normal year; but expenditure properly attributable to field work and the handling of the crops amounted to 222 *livres*, thus swallowing up to 84 per cent of the gross receipts.[23] Probably some costs could be cut down in a bad year – e.g. fewer reapers would be hired – and we can guess that the fluctuations in cereal production affected the economic condition of the small peasantry at least as much because the opportunities for seasonal employment varied as because prices of foodstuffs were very unstable. But not all the menservants could be discharged after a bad harvest, nor could all the oxen and horses be sold. The largest items of expenditure were irreducible, and pushed the enterprise into the red in inclement seasons. In fact the surviving fragments of manorial accounts give the impression that meadows

[23] Duby, 445; document No. 137, p. 498

and vineyards produced the most reliable sources of demesne income, and, thus, in the eyes of their owners, were the most highly valued.

Indeed in the thirteenth and early fourteenth centuries the sale of cattle on the hoof, and of leather and wool, produced large profits and, on the continent as well as on the English monastic estates, yielded much more money for the lords' chests than did the sale of cereals. I have written above of the great profits which Thierry d'Hireçon made from sheep bought in the autumn and resold in the new season, and the determined efforts made by burgesses of Metz to build up large pastoral estates.[24] Even when the lord did not deliberately maintain close business relations with butchers and wool merchants, he willingly kept direct control of wasteland on which to feed his plough animals and to raise his horses. Livestock-rearing was in fact the least costly branch of farming. The menservants looked after the stables and only the cutting of the meadow hay demanded much additional manpower. It is most significant that haymaking services proved most tenacious in France and in the Low Countries. They were the last services to be claimed by the officers of the lords of Pamele-Audenarde; men subject to forced labour mowed the larger part of the hayfields of St Bavo of Ghent; on St John's Day the villeins of Verson in Normandy worked for long hours on the lord's meadows.[25] But even when the master had to hire men and women to perform these tasks, the cost remained low compared to the value of the hay.

On the other hand, work in the cultivated part of the tofts and the care of the vines demanded the expenditure of a great deal of manpower. We know that vineyard work was the first to be entrusted to workers paid by the day, to those *ouvriers de vigne*, especially numerous on the outskirts of towns where most of the vineyards were situated. Added to the large outlays for wages there was the heavy expense incurred each autumn in maintaining and renewing vats and casks, and *vaisselles vinaires*. The costs of viticulture were exceptionally high. Nevertheless the lords bore them cheerfully, for the wine produced on their land and by their own care was essential for entertainment and gifts. Besides, no other agricultural product sold better than wine. So well indeed, that, in spite of their high level of wages, vineyard workers usually cost less than half the value of the wine harvest. But in regions where the vine was widely cultivated and where the wine was neither particularly distinguished nor atttractive to merchants, the lords sometimes relinquished the direct cultivation of their closes. The vineyard of Rivoli in Piedmont, for instance, was parcelled out in 1337.[26] More often, however, the vineyard,

[24] See pp. 148 and 150
[25] Duby, 443; Verhulst, 208; Delisle, *Normandie*, p. 678
[26] Daviso di Charvensod, 656

together with the enclosed meadow, was the last part of the demesne from which the lord allowed himself to be separated. Agricultural treatises edited in the fourteenth century, like the one composed in the region of Bamberg by Gottfried von Franken,[27] dealt extensively with the art of gardening and the care of vineyards which, of all forms of peasant labour, were of the greatest interest to men of quality.

*   *   *

The demesne, therefore, was cereal-growing by tradition, viticultural by the lord's inclination, and pastoral by financial interest, and it remained, on the eve of the fourteenth century, on small and middle-sized estates, on the continent as well as in England, under direct management. On the larger estates, however, where the lord did not live in such close contact with his property, the demesne lands were no longer directly cultivated. It is not that they were parcelled out: they preserved their boundaries, and their constituent parts were kept quite distinct from the rent-paying lands. But the lord, who often retained the meadows, enclosures and vineyards in hand, would entrust the cultivation of the arable fields to 'farmers'. He would no longer concern himself with growing grain, a crop which needed so much toil for so little return.

We have already seen how ancient was the practice of 'farming out'. In the early eleventh century it is rare to find a monastery which had not entrusted the complete direction of some manor to an agent in exchange for an annual 'pension'. In the thirteenth century this practice was considerably modified. It has been pointed out that the great English ecclesiastical estates had for a time given it up. On the continent, on the other hand, the 'farm lease' spread, although it was modified in two ways. On the one hand the demesne alone, the economy of which was now much more independent of the tenancies, was usually farmed out. On the other hand, the duration of the lease was gradually shortened as landowners as a group gradually became aware of changes in prices and production. As our sources have been only partially explored it is not yet possible to uncover the beginnings of the changes in the practice of 'farming'. But it seems as if the practice of leasing the 'farm' of the demesne alone began to spread slowly everywhere in the last years of the twelfth and the early years of the thirteenth century – in Normandy, and Maine, as well as Flanders, Burgundy and Roussillon, in northern Italy, Hainault and Saxony. In Namur it was at first only applied to the demesnes of the greatest lords. About the year 1200 the lands of the count and the chapters were the only ones to be farmed out; the abbeys did not follow suit until the middle of the century, and then but reluctantly.[28]

----

[27] Südhof, 133   [28] Génicot, 189, p. 107

The practice probably spread by copying the methods first used by princes, bishops and other great lords not intimately involved in the care of their lands. In 1300, out of the whole vast demesne of St Lambert of Liège a few meadows only were not farmed out, while the much smaller demesne of the neighbouring priory of Grand Bigard remained almost entirely under direct management. Nevertheless the new methods caught on speedily or slowly according to the region. In Lombardy in 1250 *conductores* managed a great many demesnes, while in the Ile de France, even fifty years later, administrators of monasteries and collegiate chapters made use of such managerial methods very seldom, and then only with regard to their arable. In about 1280 (at the same moment as the practice of demesne leasing was reintroduced in England on the lands of the abbey of Ramsey), these methods were adopted by the monks of St Bavo of Ghent on their lands in Zeeland; but they tarried much longer before giving up the direct control of the ancient *villae* of inland Flanders.[29] Research is still too sketchy for us to see what induced the lords to relinquish direct cultivation. Were the administrators mainly sensitive to price changes, or to the local deterioration in the labour market and to the growing difficulty here and there of recruiting agricultural workers? We need also to know more about the lords' way of life. Was it not then that many of them ceased to pay frequent visits to their country residences? If the story of the 'farm lease' after 1180 were better understood, and we knew more about its geographical spread and its time-table, we could probably discover the underlying reasons for its success.

It seems as though the latter was hastened by the gradual shortening of the length of leases. In France, during the whole of the first half of the thirteenth century it was the custom to entrust the cultivation to a 'farmer' for his whole life, and often to prolong the grant for the life of one of his heirs. But leases 'for two lives' decreased rapidly after 1250 in face of the expansion of short-term contracts.[30] It seems that these became customary first in northern Germany and in the Low Countries. Adjusted to fit the rhythm of crop rotations, the lease lasted six, nine, twelve, or twenty-four years; it rarely extended for longer periods, for at the end of a term as long as this the land had to be marled; an expensive operation for which the 'farmer' could not be made responsible. However, in the Italian countryside, and perhaps also in southern France, leases were usually much shorter, for three years and often even for one year only, probably because the peasants there were economically worse off.

It sometimes even happened that the demesne land was 'farmed out' in parcels. In 1280 twelve peasants divided between them in unequal shares the

---

[29] Derveeghde, 483; Godding-Ganshof, 484; Fourquin, 551; Cipolla, 611; Raftis, 201, p. 124; Verhulst, 208   [30] Schnapper, 474

24 *bonniers* of arable in a village which were formerly cultivated by the canons of St Lambert of Liège themselves; and in the rental of the lords of Pamele-Audenarde one demesne furlong was farmed out each year, *bonnier* by *bonnier*, and another one was cut up into several parcels.[31] But this leasing by parcelling out appears to have been quite exceptional in the thirteenth century. The usual practice was to lease out the whole unit of cultivation (with the frequent exception of meadows, vineyards and the master's house) provided with all the necessary equipment, tools and domestic servants including the few labour services which were still needed, and even supplied with cattle. Often a special agreement concerning the livestock completed the contract and fixed the detailed allocation of the profits of stockrearing. Lastly it was by no means exceptional for the lord to advance money or seed to the 'farmer'. By this arrangement the 'grange' kept its integrity; there was no change in its economic structure, only the person running it was different. And even this replacement sometimes did not occur since it was not unusual for the 'farmer' to be the former mayor, agent, or *villicus*, or sometimes indeed the whole group of domestic servants.[32]

The lord often expected from the individual taking over the business of cultivation a share of the crops which had to be put aside for him in the barns after threshing; the contract was then one of *métayage*. This custom had been applied on certain demesnes for many years. Already in the mid-twelfth century the monks of Cluny had on one of their manors concluded an agreement of this kind with a villager, granting him temporarily a few *arpents* of arable, providing him with the seed and the two oxen he needed in order to equip a suitable plough, and in exchange reserving half of the crop. And before 1149 the mayors of Notre-Dame of Chartres had to promise their lords not to use the contract of *medietates* in dealing with peasants.[33] At all events in the thirteenth century the contract of *métayage* or *facherie* as it was called in Provence, was everywhere in great favour. Its stipulations were very diverse. It gave the master a widely differing share in the produce according to the quality of the soil and the condition of the 'farmer': sometimes it gave him two-thirds of the crop, more often a half or a third, but occasionally much less, especially when the soil was not very fertile. In 1338 the Provençal Hospitallers were unable to find a peasant willing to take at farm certain land on their demesne, even when he was offered nineteen-twentieths of the produce to keep for himself.

Métayage offered the masters one great advantge. It allowed them to profit from the hoped-for growth of demesne productivity, as well as from

[31] Duby, 443; Derveeghde, 483, pp. 30-31
[32] Documents Nos. 138, 139, 140, 141, 142, pp. 498-503
[33] Duby, 442; *Cartulaire de Notre-Dame de Chartres*, I, No. 58

the rise in agricultural prices. An advantage perhaps specially precious to them was that it allowed them to keep the produce of their own land which gave them the feeling of closer contact with it. Even when the lord's participation was minimal, the contract assured him an important share in the net profits. For we must not forget that the *métayer* had to deduct seed and sometimes tithes from the portion which was left to him, and this was a heavy charge burdening the normally low yields of agriculture. Nevertheless the system also presented inconveniences of which the lords were well aware. The wide fluctuations in crops necessitated close supervision. Also, in order to spare themselves trouble, many masters, as soon as the duration of leases was reduced and it became possible to readjust at frequent intervals the rates of payment, preferred a fixed 'farm' discharged either in grain or money, or both, usually supplemented with a few produce liveries, and 'entry fines'. Frequently the amount of the 'farm' was calculated in relation to the area sown. Thus, on the demesne of Sailly before Thierry d'Hireçon took it in hand, the 'farmer' had to provide six measures of wheat and five measures of oats for each measure of land sown with cereals.[34]

When leased, the demesne was not in any way alienated. It remained 'the master's land' which he could one day repossess. Thus the lord did not feel himself deprived of it. Relieved of all the burdens of management, he continued to benefit from the gradual rise in income, whether the property was held in *métayage*, or whether the 'farm' was periodically adjusted to the growing value of profits. The accounts of the Capetian demesne in Normandy, totally 'farmed out' in 1260, show that the rates of fixed payments faithfully followed the curve of prices and land rents in the second half of the century.[35] It was only necessary to watch that the 'farmer' did not exhaust the soil by taking too much out of it, or let the buildings fall into disrepair. Contracts, therefore, carefully laid down the duties of the cultivator, obliging him not to break the rhythm of cultivation, to use on the demesne all the manure and straw, to work all the animals and to maintain the tools. A system of obligations and safeguards guaranteed the masters against 'farmers' who broke their agreement.

*   *   *

For all these reasons the first contracts of 'farm' probably appeared more profitable to the landlords than to those responsible for the cultivation, and in any case it cannot be said that they loosened the grip of the manor on the rural economy. So conscious now were the lords of the advantages of these arrangements that they tried to adjust tenancies to the legal forms originally contrived for the exploitation of the demesne. In this they succeeded when-

[34] Richard, 473   [35] Strayer, 475

ever the position of the peasants favoured changes in custom. Thus, in the second half of the thirteenth century the East German *Höfe* and the Italian *podere* became subject to short-term leases, either at 'farm' or in *métayage*.[36] These new formulae, flexible and secure, were apparently favoured by manorial administrators.

Economic historians have not until now given much attention to the condition of 'farmers'. Who were these men who were willing to manage the labour force on the demesne and to dispose of its surpluses? What were their personal circumstances which made it possible for them to profit from so doing? For how long did they keep their farms? Did they become rich? All aspects of these social problems remain to be explored, but we can expect results of the utmost importance to emerge. It appears that many of these *amodiateurs, grangiers, Meyern,* belonged to the clergy, the bourgeoisie or even to the petty nobility, just as did the *locatores* who had undertaken the reclamation of the first half of the thirteenth century. Many others came from the ranks of the domestic officials. Lastly we are not short of examples, particularly in Germany, of farms which were leased to the village community.[37] But how many peasants were able individually to take charge of the cultivation of a demesne? Unless it had been parcelled up (and this, to repeat, appears to have been very unusual, except perhaps in Italy), most villagers lacked both the experience and the means to take on the management of enterprises on this scale; they lacked the authority for issuing orders to teams of servants or for requisitioning forced labour. The peasants who became 'farmers' of demesnes, could only have come from among the better-off who had already risen well above the common run. The mass of the peasantry could derive no profit from the abandonment by the lords of direct management of their demesnes – an abandonment which, in any case, did not take place in the early fourteenth century except on the very largest estates.

In fact, it does not seem as if the vast majority drew any benefit at all from the 'farming' of the demesne. In any event the poorer peasants were not given an opportunity to lease the few pieces of land they needed in order to be able to feed their families by the produce of their own cultivated land. With few exceptions, the system of 'farming' did nothing to modify the economic relations between the household of the lord and the men of the village, any more than it changed the labour situation or the conditions of employment of the permanent servants and day labourers, unless maybe it were to hasten the disappearance of forced labour. The most which the 'farm' lease did was to transfer responsibility in the rare cases when the lord himself or one of his agents was replaced by the richest peasant in the village, who in small ways,

---

[36] Wittich, 210; Luzzatto, 197; see p. 258
[37] Documents Nos. 141 and 142, p. 502

by lending on security or by buying fixed payments, had begun to extend an economic domination over his neighbours. Such a man might in these cases occupy a position similar to that of a lord. Henceforth it was he who dealt with traders, tried to profit from the disparity between wages and prices and exploited to his advantage the difficulties of small husbandmen who were forced to sell their livestock in the autumn. He assumed the attitude of the master in relation to the village community: and he kept it at a distance. In order to increase his own profit he attempted to remove more of the demesne fields and meadows from collective constraint, to interfere with the common right of pasture and the obligations to the communal flock. Closer to the earth, less extravagant, and craftier than the nobleman, he was able to add to his wealth by all these means. As a result, the early progress of the 'farm' mainly loosened agricultural solidarity and sharpened the tensions between rich and poor in the heart of peasant society.

CONCLUSION

Peasants and the Manor
on the Eve of the XIV Century

A cursory survey of manorial economy in western Europe at the dawn of the fourteenth century will reveal to the surveyor a number of disparate features. The patchwork advance of historical research in the various countries is perhaps partly responsible for this, but regional contrasts were nevertheless very profound and were largely due to the uneven pace of development. To take the most obvious instance, the story of Italian landownership throughout the Middle Ages seems always to have been a whole century ahead of French. Whatever we happen to consider, be it the decline of direct management or the spread of *métayage*, we can observe in Milan and Tuscany in the second half of the thirteenth century tendencies that did not reach the neighbourhood of Toulouse or the Ile de France until three or four generations later. It is tempting to connect this precocity with the earlier emergent power of an urban economy. Conversely, in Thuringia, a land without towns, the structure of the manor seems archaic and still close to its Carolingian prototype. Similarly, in England, where urban centres were few and limited in size, the evolution of the manorial economy was in certain respects obviously slow in comparison to continental trends, and particularly slow on monastic properties more closely tied to traditional ways. Indeed, the old forms of slavery seem to have remained alive longer on the lands of the English abbeys than anywhere else. They left an indelible mark on the relations between peasant and master, especially in the persistence of forced labour, which was probably the means whereby the large-scale agricultural undertaking managed to prolong its existence.

Local diversities in the institution of landownership, however, were even more profound. Even in the same province differences in economic structure could often be considerable. Here, as an illustration of this point, brought simultaneously to light by an inventory drawn up in 1338, are three separate manorial units all situated in the same region and all forming part of the same landed property, that of the Order of the Hospitallers. They are Salliers near Arles, le Poët-Laval in the hills above Montélimar, and Puimoisson on the plateau between Durance and Verdon. Salliers made a handsome profit;

expenses, including the lord's maintenance, amounted to only 150 *livres*, and receipts to 720 *livres*. This prosperity was due to arable situated on fertile soils and close to a large grain-exporting market, but also mainly to the deliberate leasing of the demesne fields in *métayage*. Cultivation costs were low, returns in marketable goods were very high. Le Poët, where the manorial household was large and demesne arable almost non-existent, was in the red. Most of the receipts came from tithes and seigneurial rights which needed a large staff of tax collectors. Its revenue was 613 *livres*, but disbursements came to 656 *livres*. As for Puimoisson, it was a huge cereal-producing undertaking, which was profitable because of the low level of wages; but as the lords disbursed more cash than they collected, the key to the demesne economy lay in the sale of surplus crops.[38]

We should note first of all in these examples how complex were the economics of landownership. Indeed it may well be dangerous to talk in this book of 'the' manor, or 'the' *seigneurie*, because by overemphasizing its general characteristics we may conceal the uniqueness of its particular features. Each manor had its own destiny. Its internal organization was peculiar to itself and its problems of management needed individual solutions. The men who had to solve these problems did so well or badly, but they always solved them in the light of their own abilities and experience, and, on any given land, with regard to existing customs and peasant habits. This said, it is obvious that every manor throughout the long drawn out period of rural expansion, that began before the year 1000, adapted itself gradually to changes in its economic and social environment. Broadly speaking, on the threshold of the fourteenth century we can see no weakness in the manorial economy. On the contrary, we can see everywhere revealed the vigour of medium-sized estates, controlled either by the petty nobility living on their ancestral lands, by the agents of prince or prelate, or increasingly by 'farmers', some of whom had risen from the village community. This affluence was supported by the universal prosperity of the countryside. However, was this prosperity shared by all country folk alike?

*   *   *

There is no doubt that the return from most small farming enterprises rose in the course of the thirteenth century as a result of the general widening of economic horizons, the expansion of stockraising and viticulture, and new facilities which allowed all and sundry, rich and poor, to sell freely their muscle power and the surplus of their domestic production. Despite the total inability of historians to estimate the exact incidence of the seigneurial de-

[38] Document No. 137, p.498

mands or the share deducted by the owner of the eminent rights of the soil and the lord of the justice or the *ban*,[39] we can see that the surplus value of peasant cultivation was not entirely absorbed by the increasing pressure of payments and taxes. In fact, it is clear that no landlord ever succeeded in raising rents on land as fast as the value of land and its profits increased. It is equally easy to see that peasants were never in a hurry to pay either their landlords, or the holders of the fixed rents they had created on their property, or the collectors of the *taille*. It is also true that creditors had few weapons to use against such passive resistance. Manorial accounts and legal registers all confirm that most payments were collected only after long delays and at the cost of threats and repeated dunning. The same documents also show that lords had often to come to terms with peasants and to remit large parts of the debt. It is obvious that the village community was united against extortioners, and that agents responsible for seizure or confiscation of land often found the whole population combining to prevent them from carrying out their mission. Ill-will, inertia and at times active resistance on the part of country folk were important factors in the whole business of debt collection, and were obstacles impeding the flow of peasant profits into the money chests of the lords and their minions.

Nevertheless the very few sources which allow us a glimpse of the economic position of individual villagers at that time do not create the impression that many peasants lived a life of affluence. Peasant dwellings described in inventories at the beginning of the fourteenth century were little more than unfurnished huts. A few sticks of furniture, such as a chest, a rough box, or a cooking spit, one or two bed coverings, an occasional pewter or copper vessel, a small stock of grain (but no money): such were the usual 'chattels', the movables recorded by the bailiffs responsible for collecting heriot from the hovels of the English villeins.[40] The lists were, it is true, drawn up by the lords' men, with the purpose of seizing a small portion of the movables; in such circumstances concealment was natural and allowances for these frauds must invalidate all evidence from sources of a fiscal origin. But inventories after death, wills and marriage contracts contained in notarial registers of the southern French and Italian countryside, are less suspect, although they are not very different. They confirm that the standards of life

[39] Any attempt to reconstruct a peasant family's budget (see, for instance, Abel, 585, pp. 157 *et seq.*) founders on the lack of sources. We could use the few inventories of movables, drawn up by manorial tax collectors (see Document No. 161, p. 517) and the more plentiful evidence about the area of land which such and such family held from a master. But how can we estimate the means and the needs of any small cultivator when we know nothing at all about the cycles of cultivation, yields, prices of grain and even the composition of his household, his diet, or the contribution provided by wages? Any hypotheses which can be formulated on this subject are surrounded by an enormous margin of doubt.   [40] Stenton, 275, p. 249; Bennett, 149, p. 233

hardly rose between the eleventh and the fourteenth centuries and at all events significantly less than that of the nobility. Very rarely do we find peasant families who had succeeded in saving large sums of money. Their wealth appeared almost wholly to take the form of land, agricultural equipment and livestock. More direct information has been preserved about the economic condition of village priests, which doubtless never sank below the average condition of their parishioners. One such priest of Beaujolais, who died in 1269, left his heirs no money at all: he bequeathed his sister the rye which he had lent her, his niece a mare, and his nephew a cow.[41] In all European countries at the beginning of the fourteenth century the number of animals in the flock was the outward sign of peasant wealth.

As for the average size of the holdings it often seems to be much reduced. In Namur, in Flanders and in England most peasant households cultivated between five and 7½ acres of arable. For example, in 1305 70 per cent of the tenants of the abbey of St Bertin at Beuvrequem had less than ten acres and 43 per cent less than five.[42] Owning a plough team and a few sheep, these 'labourers' were the mainstay of village communities. Since the twelfth century the latter had become stronger everywhere through self-help and the use of collective property, and they provided their inhabitants with a safe refuge in adversity. There is no doubt that by closing their ranks small husbandmen were better able to defend themselves against poverty and the excessive demands of the lords. None the less, it is a fact that two classes grew up above and below this middling rank, one richer and the other poorer, both of which tended to remain outside the village community. The poorer class was often rejected by it, while the richer class detached themselves in order to make better use of their economic independence.

*   *   *

The growing disparity of wealth can be regarded as the most obvious change affecting the structure of peasant society during the final phases of thirteenth-century agricultural expansion. Formerly class distinctions had been drawn according to the hereditary and juridical lines separating free men from unfree. But by 1300 it was a man's economic condition which counted most. In those regions where the borderline between liberty and servitude had not been erased from the collective memory, or where it had been reintroduced, hereditary differences did not impose the clear-cut dis-

[41] Archives du Rhône, G.3, No. 2
[42] Coopland, 431, p. 77. This lack of landed property implies that most peasant households derived supplementary income from activities of a pastoral or artisanal nature, or from wages.

tinctions experienced in daily life due to differences in wealth. For instance, in the English countryside the prosperity of many villeins contrasted strongly with the poverty of a growing number of free tenants.[43] On the continent, new conditions of personal dependence fettered the poor with ties of servitude, while allowing the rich to escape easily. Economic position now entirely governed the legal status of individuals.

Lively exchanges of goods and mobility of holdings gave new openings for peasant wealth, and activity was stimulated by the number of payments which had to be made in cash. The whole process by which the relations of lords and country folk were to an ever greater degree based on money, compelled the least wealthy husbandmen to sell. While the process animated village trade, it also caused a large part of the peasant world to fall into the hands of moneylenders and merchants from the local towns. At the same time it offered rewards to the more astute villagers who knew how to take advantage of the market. Favouring the rich at the expense of the poor, it helped to reopen those economic disparities in the heart of peasant society which arbitrary exactions in the previous feudal era had done so much to narrow down.

This explains why few premonitory signs of social differentiation can be seen in documents of the second half of the twelfth century. In one of the Shaftesbury manors described in the first inventory of 1130-1135, only two men, one of whom was the village priest, owned holdings very much larger than their neighbours; fifty years later a new inquest revealed a third large tenant. Amongst the peasants who had all their property confiscated at Northampton Assizes in 1176, there was already considerable difference in wealth. One man possessed no more than sixpence: another more than seventy shillings. But it was in the course of the thirteenth century that the gap between rich and poor widened everywhere. In one village in the plain of the Saône, where in 1180 all the inhabitants appeared to be on the same economic level, a hundred years later we find five distinctly wealthier families prospering. They had begun to acquire fixed rents on the properties of less fortunate neighbours.[44] At the end of the thirteenth century all manorial inquests, in France, Italy and England alike, show evidence of marked differences in the size of dependent holdings, and this is confirmed in notarial registers. Here, for instance, are two peasants in the same village in Upper Provence who married off their daughters in 1330. One gave his daughter a dowry of 75 *livres* in money, a tunic of Chalons cloth, a robe of Ypres cloth trimmed with fur, a chest and two sets of bedding; the other could not offer more than two pieces of cloth and a coverlet, and had to let his future son-in-

[43] Miller, 198, pp. 113 and 149
[44] Poole, 270, p. 73; Duby, 261, p. 518

law pay for the tunic and robe of cloth which custom decreed that the bride must wear. It appears that the handful of larger peasants in that village at that period who could give their daughters a dowry of fifty golden florins had almost risen to the level of the petty nobility.[45]

It is true we still meet a very few rich peasants in documents drawn up about 1300, but they had already begun to assemble small manors and to impose themselves as masters over their less fortunate neighbours. As a group they were mostly the lord's officials (amongst whom were the priests who sometimes took up their church and its tithes on 'farm' and turned out to be large purchasers of land rents), and the few peasant 'farmers' of ecclesiastical and noble demesnes. In addition, there were to be found enterprising tenants who, profiting by the disappearance of obstacles to the alienation of tenancies added piecemeal parcels of land to their own holdings. They managed to lease plots of land taken from the lord's demesne, and thus to cultivate fifty or so acres of good land. Conditions favoured medium-sized arable and pastoral farmers. It was they who sold to the merchants of local towns the largest part of the surplus production of the village: the produce of tithes and *terrages*, their own and the manorial crops, as well as the standing harvest or the wine harvest which the poorer peasants had been forced to sell in order to find at short notice the cash they needed to pay rents and *tailles*. In peasant society it was they alone who really profited from favourable market conditions. They placed their money skilfully; they joined, in contracts of *gasaille*, with more modest village husbandmen in stockrearing operations from which they kept most of the profit; they practised usury amongst those around them, they advanced money to their neighbours in various advantageous ways. Here is the case of two brothers, substantial peasants in a hamlet in the Provençal Alps. In 1334 they bought for twelve *livres* from a small cultivator in the same village the whole of his crop due to be gathered from one piece of land for the next fifteen years. The following year they lent their neighbours four *livres* and ten *sous*; this sum had to be used to sow and plough two fields whose harvest the creditors most likely kept for themselves.[46]

New-rich men of this type often sent one of their sons to school and thus prepared him for a career in church or administration. It was at these points that the peasant world began to intrude into the higher ranks of ecclesiastical circles. In Italy and the south of France men of this type often tried to move into the local towns and to insinuate themselves into the company of merchants and notaries. In France they sometimes achieved matrimonial alliances with noble houses by marrying the daughter of a knight, or took a burgess son-in-law. Many, like the well-to-do Austrian peasant who aspired

---

[45] Archives des Bouches-du-Rhône, 396, E. 18, fol. 75 and 17, fol. 27
[46] Archives des Bouches-du-Rhône, 396 E.17, fol. 71 and 18, fol. 73

to drink wine, [47] acquired some of the habits of the upper classes. But it seems as if, at least in France, they were seldom wholly absorbed into the nobility. Indeed their very exclusion protected them from some of the wasteful habits of the great world and safeguarded their future. In any event they were carried along by the rising tide of economic improvement which lifted them ever higher and enabled them to bid ever higher for the sale of woods or the leasing of the demesnes. In short, we can regard this group of men as the most active agents in the movement of expansion characteristic of this period.

But on the other hand, on the eve of the fourteenth century the depression of the much more numerous group of vulnerable peasants was also speeded up. We have seen how the whole evolution of the rural economy took place at the expense of the poorest. The regularizing of the *tailles* and the sale of franchises, the spread of fixed rents on land, even the facilities for borrowing the necessities of consumption, all these many ways by which the money economy spread, enmeshed the less well-off peasants in a web of debts and bound them in effective slavery to the towns or to their better-off neighbours. The condition of personal dependence, the rise in the price of plough animals, indeed the very replacement of labour services by money payments, served to aggravate the precarious situation of the English cottars, the French *manouvriers* and *malservis*, the German *Höldner*, and all men whose holdings were too small to feed their families, much less provide them with anything to sell or enough cash to satisfy their lords and their creditors. Rearing smaller animals could have helped, but this group of tenants often found themselves excluded from the commons and the rights of common pasture by the lord, by the larger cultivators, or even by the village community. As the century drew to its close the last hopes of reclamation and settlement on marginal lands disappeared.

Having sold the remnants of their inheritance many of these men left for the towns in search of easier livelihood. The exodus sometimes took the form of seasonal migration. One man who made leather bottles at Toulouse in the winter returned every summer to work his land in the village where he was a serf. In one village in the southern Alps a tax inquest in the winter of 1340 listed 110 inhabited and 42 uninhabited houses: the families who lived in the latter had gone down to the plain to earn a little money in the slack season. [48] For such people the best remedy against complete destitution was to go into service. All such labourers expected to receive their keep during temporary or permanent employment in the fields, meadows or vineyards of the larger estates. We have already seen how this mass of available labour encouraged both the abandonment of labour services and the continuation of direct cul-

[47] E. Patseltt, *Österreich bis zum Ausgang der Babanbergerzeit*, Vienna, 1946; pp. 154-155   [48] Wolff, 709, p. 67; Baratier, 92, p. 73

tivation. Nevertheless the static level of wages combined with the rise of grain prices, both of which were caused by the presence of a growing multitude looking for work, kept day labourers in a state of chronic undernourishment. A detailed study of death rates, which has recently been made possible by certain extraordinarily revealing English manorial records, shows the disastrous effects of a bad harvest on these landless, or all-but landless, peasants. They suffered in three ways: by being forced to buy more grain, to pay more for it, and lastly by the reduction of employment at harvest and threshing time. The years of meagre harvest were, for the poor, years also of sickness and death. And the rise in the average rate of mortality at the end of the thirteenth century revealed by these documents was incontestably caused by the rapid increase in the numbers of destitute villagers.[49]

Social differentiation in peasant society, a secondary effect of rural economic growth since the mid-twelfth century, was, to begin with, favourable to the lords, who made what they could out of it and in doing so accentuated it further. But it became in its turn one of the most active factors in the changes in the manorial economy about the year 1300. In any case the gradual disturbance of the social structure involved future developments. Prosperous, nearly all its wasteland cleared, teeming with labourers and covered with growing crops, the countryside of Europe on the brink of the fourteenth century was really overpopulated and was burdened with a growing number of peasants in a condition of semi-starvation. We can believe, too, that the economic activities of a small band of entrepreneurs – lords and their agents, and townsfolk attracted by speculation in grain and cattle – slowly, but inevitably, exhausted certain soils, lowered the level of wages and reduced the purchasing power of nearly all the peasant families. Thus this basically vulnerable world, with its few reserves of wealth, unconsciously built up for itself difficulties for the future years. The scarcity which hit England in 1258 and rapidly assumed famine proportions was the first sign of these difficulties. In 1309-1311 the German countryside suffered a far crueller shortage of foodstuffs.[50] The hard times were at hand.

[49] Postan-Titow, 539   [50] Curschmann, 606

BOOK IV

Change and Upheaval
in the XIV Century

BOOK IV

Change and Upheaval in the XIV Century

Introduction

The documents in most western European archives through which the economic life of the countryside after the mid-fourteenth century may be studied are considerably more numerous than those available to historians of earlier periods. These vast accumulations of manuscripts, often so hard to decipher, so badly docketed and awkward to handle, seem at first sight somewhat discouraging. Their very abundance chokes the path of research; their perusal demands special techniques, such as random sampling and selection of representative examples. They call for teamwork and for new methods of analysis and for the use of card indexes. Finally the actual sources are not entirely suitable for publication. Their exploration in fact remains very imperfect. Furthermore, except in England and north-western Germany, economic historians interested in the last two centuries of the Middle Ages have concentrated their attention almost exclusively on towns, merchants, and the 'business' of trade. For all these reasons, rural conditions of the time remain, in spite of such a wealth of material, shrouded in greater obscurity than those of the twelfth and thirteenth centuries.

It is also very noticeable that the nature and the provenance of the sources have changed. The deeds drawn up at the lords' behest, the inventories and accounts, all become relatively scarcer after the first quarter of the fourteenth century than in the immediately preceding period. Many of course, such as those drawn up and studied in England, still exist, and the muniment rooms of German, French and Italian manors contain bundle upon bundle. Nevertheless, at least in certain regions, considering the extent of seigneurial property, their paucity at the end of the thirteenth and during the first decades of the fourteenth century is very marked. Instead we find many more documents drawn up by officials of state and principality, particularly registers drawn up for taxation and legal purposes, censuses, and assessments of wealth. Thus the observation point is gradually altered. Henceforth the rural world is viewed from a different angle and the researcher must take this into account if he does not wish to make it appear as if the facts themselves have changed when there has merely been a shift in the perspective. Finally, it was more than just the texts that changed. In all the deeds regulating the economic relations of lords and peasants, as well as in the petitions addressed to the public powers asking for tax relief, assistance, or letters of pardon, complaints and references to the miseries and catastrophes of the time abound. The decay of manorial institutions, to which the contents of our documentary material bear witness, the general note of pessimism, the obvious political tension between states and the almost permanent state of war, all communicate a clear impression of a rapidly deteriorating rural economy. Should we not consider this whole century connecting the great period of growth, which lasted right up to the eve of the fourteenth century, with the rise about 1450 of a new wave of prosperity, as a time of recession, or at the very least, stagnation?

English economic historians were the first to attempt to adapt for medieval conditions the models constructed by economists to explain changes in economic movements in modern times, and a few years ago they suggested that there were two consecutive long-term trends affecting the rural economy, the first positive and the second negative, the transition from one to the other taking place during the first half of the fourteenth century. About twelve years ago, E. Perroy, in an article analyzing in great detail the reversal of the upward trend in England and northern France, put forward an elaborate hypothesis, namely that several 'crises' affecting wheat harvests, monetary circulation and population occurred between 1315 and 1370 and finally ushered in a long period of recession. The author urged other historians to verify these hypotheses from documents and in fact more recent studies have suggested even greater refinements. They have distinguished in the interpretation of economic data profound geographical differences and have marked out zones where economic conditions evolved at different rates. These studies effectively destroy the picture of western Europe as a homogeneous society and prevent us from applying without further thought conclusions based solely on facts relevant to the countries bordering the English Channel and the North Sea. But, more than anything, they bring to light the lesser fluctuations which lie behind the major trends. Can we perhaps discern the first symptoms of depression well before the end of the thirteenth century? And, by the same token, temporary bursts of prosperity in the midst of the late fourteenth-century slump? We also have to account for the theories of Marxist historians. Rejecting models of 'cycles', condemning explanations based on demographic catastrophes or price movements, they are determined to see in the difficulties of which the sources provide not so much evidence of a malaise affecting the whole economy of the countryside as of signs of the collapse of 'feudalism' – meaning by that the breakdown of the system of manorial exploitation. The changes which were caused by the transference of the forces of production did not in the end appear to be favourable to the peasantry. But they directly prepared the way for the movement of recovery which we can see commencing about the middle of the fifteenth century.[1]

[1] See particularly the discussion on the report on the economic history of the later Middle Ages presented to the Congress at Rome in 1955, *X⁰ Congresso internazionale di science storiche, Roma*, 1955, *Atti*, Florence, 1955; Perroy, 564; Hilton, 554; Graus, 552.

CHAPTER I

New Features in the Rural Economy

At the very outset of this sketch it must be repeated that any study of conditions at this period must be undertaken within certain geographical limitations. Fourteenth-century documents, being very plentiful, enable us to derive from systematic research a much sharper and more detailed analysis of the conditions determining the evolution of the rural economy, and also demonstrate effectively how the different rural communities still preserved their distinct character. To begin with, it appears quite clearly that wide areas of Europe continued in this period to enjoy sustained prosperity prolonging the rising trends of the thirteenth century. This was so in Holland, where the growth of the commercial centres, the ceaseless efforts to regain land periodically engulfed by marine inundations and to conquer new land, the rise of animal husbandry and beer-brewing, provided the rural economy with continuous stimuli. Lower Lombardy experienced similar conditions. In the second half of the fourteenth century, i.e. when the difficulties experienced by France and England were worsening, this region benefited simultaneously from a forward leap in population and an agricultural and pastoral expansion quickened by massive investment and the activities of a new generation of entrepreneurs. Finally, conditions in the east German countries were peculiar. They experienced difficulties, it is true, especially heavy depopulation. But certain favourable factors, notably the maintenance of agricultural prices, made possible the establishment of large-scale cereal-growing estates whose prosperity lasted well into the modern period.

We must also take account of regional diversities on a smaller scale. Neighbouring districts could provide violent contrasts. Censuses contained in fiscal documents such as the *Etat des Paroisses et des Feux* of 1328 for royal France, or the registers of the Poll Tax drawn up in England in the last quarter of the fourteenth century, reveal what these differences were. They continued and even widened in times of crisis. Sharp contrasts can be seen throughout the fourteenth century between the wooded and almost uninhabited slopes of Hurepoix and the lush plain of France, and between the counties south of the Thames and the rich lands bordering the Wash.[1] Our

---

[1] Fourquin, 574; see the map of population density in rural England drawn up from data in the Poll Tax of 1377 by Pelham, in Darby, 47, p. 232.

evidence leads us to picture the economy of the countryside organized into small regional units, each firmly attached to a market town and formed during the expansion and commercial growth of the thirteenth century. There was a close network of relationships which were never broken throughout the later Middle Ages. Some, indeed, were knit together even more closely. In each of these regions, population movements, opportunities for employment, occupation of the soil and production, the state of the markets, agrarian conditions and even family circumstances, present individual characteristics. Studies which set out to analyze the peculiarities of these economic entities, because they could draw upon copious material in princely archives, such as inquests covering huge properties much more extensive than the area depicted by manorial documents, could take account of geographical considerations and would without doubt open up entirely new perspectives. They would allow a reappraisal of general impressions over the whole field, and perhaps even provide an answer to, or at any rate a more exact definition of, the problems of a rural economy so dependent on purely local factors. For the time being, however, we are forced to be content with a hastier and a less clear cut view based on the evidence of the most generalized sources. These indeed, point definitely in the whole of the west and even for Italy itself (we look in vain in Tuscany and Liguria for traces of comparable growth to that animating the economic life of the Milanese countryside)[2] to a recession of activity in the face of mounting difficulties.

I. THE CATASTROPHES

References to these troubles are innumerable, even if we discount, as we must, the exaggerations which are natural in our sources, and even more the selectivity which has sometimes moved scholars to give too much prominence to evidence of desolation. We have first of all to consider all the signs of catastrophe, everything that points to sudden shocks, unexpected external accidents which destroyed reserves of wealth, dispersed factors of production and disturbed the flow of exchanges. Contemporary documents are excellent reporters of such calamities, which were of three kinds.

The earliest to make an appearance were the troubles connected with food supply. Production of the basic foodstuff, grain, was always highly irregular, practised as it was in climatic conditions which can hardly ever have been favourable and on soils which were often unsuitable and exhausted by primitive farming methods. In the twelfth and thirteenth centuries, lean years followed fat years and even in the best seasons many people had to be content to live from hand to mouth in springtime and in the weeks before the

[2] Intervention by R. Lopez, in *Xº Congresso internazionale di Scienze storiche, Roma, 1955, Atti,* p. 401, 402

harvest. But even so, after the decades which followed the year 1000 Europe seems to have escaped famines and crises in the food supply serious enough to cause a considerable proportion of the population to starve to death. It is true that this aspect of the history of food supply remains very imperfectly explored. It must also be admitted that its study is very complex. Monastic chronicles of the feudal epoch groan with references to the lack of food; but they never provide information from which the real gravity of these crises can be measured, nor do they describe the boundaries of the areas where they raged. Nevertheless we can subscribe to the opinion of those historians who consider that difficulties of victualling got worse in the last years of the thirteenth century, at least in the westernmost areas of Europe, and that after 1300 an age of catastrophic shortages commenced.

In particular it seems that a succession of wet seasons made chronic difficulties much more acute, and provoked in 1309 in the south and west of Germany a crisis in the supply of wheat which then spread to the rest of western Europe. The worst period was reached in the years 1315-1317. Between May and August 1316 one inhabitant of Ypres in every ten died of hunger; the poorest people who possessed no reserves and who could not meet price rises of such extraordinary amplitude were obviously worst hit. Town records bear witness to the periodic return of similar famines. Seven can be traced from the archives of Toulouse between 1334 and the middle of the fifteenth century.[3] The problems of food supply became everywhere a permanent and acutely felt burden on all municipal bodies, in Italy as well as in Languedoc and Germany.

It should nevertheless be noted that these anxieties about food supplies always appear in contemporary records to be specifically urban phenomena. Rural documents, much less communicative, have never been examined on this point. What should we expect to find in them? It might be supposed that the countryside was less vulnerable and that most peasants could always have found enough to prevent them from starving even in the worst years. To what extent was the destitute section of the village population affected? We have seen that, from the end of the thirteenth century, mortality rose markedly in years of bad harvest among the landless cottars on the English manors who were dependent on wages and had to buy their bread.[4] It is therefore not at all impossible that the rural proletariat was also decimated by these waves of shortage. The shortages in any case troubled village economy deeply in other ways. The disordered fluctuations of cereal prices which they caused on the urban market disturbed the conditions of trade and had repercussions on production and employment.

*　　*　　*

[3] Van Werveke, 610; Capra, 605　　　　　　[4] Postan-Titow, 539

War was another external cause of disturbance. Actual hostilities, pillage and burning of crops, had always been common accidents of feudal times. However, after the end of the thirteenth century the growth of opposing principalities, the formation of groups of professional soldiers trained for armed conflict and with an interest in its prolongation, and perhaps other profound changes still imperfectly understood, stimulated military tension throughout Europe. Henceforth war became a semi-permanent state of affairs, and flames were rekindled in some places as soon as they were quenched in others. Furthermore, methods of warfare altered and gained in destructive power. Conflicts were still localized it is true, and never engaged more than insignificant numbers of combatants. But companies of professional soldiers, badly paid by their princes, lived off the country and exploited it to the full. The main victim of the devastation was the countryside, since cities were well protected by ramparts and troops of burgesses. Moreover, *dégat*, the systematic destruction of wealth, again mainly rural, was often employed as a tactical weapon, or as an object lesson. Are historians perhaps wrong not to attach greater importance to acts of war in their analysis of economic conditions from the eleventh to the thirteenth centuries? An attentive reading of the Domesday Book leads us to think that wars in that period could have widespread results.[5] At all events it is certain that after 1300 war could intervene effectively at the local level to alter the evolution of rural economy.

There was no single province in the west in which villages did not suffer periodically from the passage of troops, fortunately, of course, often rapid and at long intervals. In certain regions, such as Flanders at the beginning of the fourteenth century and the environs of Paris or Bordeaux later, devastation through military operations was prolonged. In the patrimony of St Martin of Tournai 22 'halls' and 7 mills were burnt down in 1302. In the Paris region, the grain tithe which normally produced 35 *muids* at Antony fell in 1384 to 20, and that of wine from 120 *queues* to only 20. These figures show the extent by which the presence of soldiers could reduce the output of a village. In the same year, because of the same military campaign, 22 *arpents* of vineyard out of 32 and 90 *arpents* of arable out of 190, had to be left waste on the lands of the abbey of Lys near Melun. As a result of similar

[5] Darby, in 47, pp. 166 *et seq.* The collapse of royal power and the fierce struggle between lords fighting over the royal prerogatives in thirteenth-century Germany fed the flames of conflicts which laid waste the countryside. Records are full of allusions to destruction of crops and peasants reduced to poverty and flight; Epperlein, 526, p. 136. See also document No. 144, p. 504. Destruction on this scale could certainly not have been without effect on economic development; perhaps it favoured the progress of the farm lease in north-west Germany. In fact hardly anywhere was the contrast between thirteenth-century peace and fourteenth-century military disorder more vivid than in France.

restrictions on cultivation provoked by events of the same kind the monks of St Denis, who had in 1342-1343 sold 133 *muids* of grain, could offer traders in 1374-1375 no more than four.[6]

Nevertheless, if the economy of the countryside suffered from war, the damage was usually less serious than appears mirrored in over-pathetic accounts. Modest holdings were less badly affected. The peasant population, who fled at the first alarm and waited in the shelter of woodland or marsh till the alert was over, did not suffer physically from hostilities, except by accident. It must also be remembered that agricultural equipment was so rudimentary that it did not take long to put it back into working order. When peace returned, cultivation could be resumed; after an enforced rest the earth again bore a harvest. The incursions of the soldiery never affected the production of cereals for long. On the other hand cultivation of the homestead tofts, and especially vineyards, suffered more lasting damage. If the vinestocks had been destroyed or were too long neglected, they had to be replanted and the vineyard had to be tended for several years before grapes could once more be gathered. Above all, cattle offered a tempting prey to the soldiery. If the villagers had not had time to disperse their flocks and herds in forest hide-outs, passing troops usually destroyed some of the livestock. These were the ways in which war dealt the most damaging blows to the peasant economy. When oxen and plough horses were killed there were enduring repercussions on agricultural labour and its output.

But of course it was the lords' dwellings, more exposed because relatively richer, which suffered most, together with their appurtenances, mills, bakehouses, enclosures, orchards, in short all the luxury capital of the countryside. The fact that war struck the manorial economy harder is worth remembering. Damaging the rich more than the poor, it helped to level down the differences in rural wealth. At all events the capital losses it caused were very unequally distributed amongst rural society.

There was the same inequality between regions. Everywhere, as soon as the danger retreated, repairs were energetically undertaken. All productive equipment, even the most fragile, was quickly restored. Phases of reconstruction alternating with phases of devastation can be seen, for example, in the Bordeaux country.[7] This explains how even in the worst pillaged regions, war damage was never complete enough to disturb for long the distribution of habitations and the agrarian structure. But it is also obvious that the poorer and less populated areas suffered more from the destruction, and that on them reconstruction was slower. Indeed, being less resilient, they succumbed more easily to the blows. If the restoration was slower it was because the effort of reconstruction and investment was turned first of all towards the

---

[6] Haenens, 663; Fourquin, 551   [7] Boutruche, 547, pp. 193 *et seq.*

more fertile areas. The good arable lands of Valois had for some time before the end of the fifteenth century been fully restored and were as populous and productive as before the military troubles, while in the neighbouring, but poorer, district of Brie, the wounds of war were still waiting to be dressed.[8]

*   *   *

There were other calamities besides famine and war which shook the foundations of the rural economy even more deeply. These were the epidemics and pestilences, especially the most grisly one of all – the Black Death – which in 1348 and 1349 ravaged the whole of Europe with the exception of a few German cantons. It is probable that cities, where overcrowding, bad hygiene and food shortages favoured contagion, suffered most from this final calamity. But it did not spare country-dwellers. In one Surrey locality fifteen times as many deaths were registered in 1348-1349 as the normal, and ten times as many in 1349-1350. Observation of rural society shows particularly that the intensity of the plague varied considerably from place to place. In one English village 747 persons died in 1349, whereas only five died in the neighbouring place with a population of the same size. We do not lack examples of villages being totally spared by the Black Death. In the census of Garges near Paris, drawn up in 1351, two-thirds of the men bear family names already registered twenty years earlier, which is evidence, in a society where names were transmitted from father to son and inventories were drawn up, of considerable demographic stability.[9] But it is still clear that the rural world suffered heavily from the Black Death, the effects of which lasted for long. For more than half a century the sickness reappeared in periodic waves which proved here and there to be more deadly than the great epidemic of 1348-1349. It must also be realized that if famines and military campaigns remained superficial accidents, deaths from plague, which affected demographic progress permanently, attacked the very structure of rural life. Here we touch on those deep-seated reversals of trends which are revealed to us by a new series of facts.

2. THE DEPOPULATION OF THE COUNTRYSIDE

The most obvious of these reversals is the decline in population which proved to be not temporary but of long duration. It seems that the collapse began very abruptly and succeeded a long period of uninterrupted growth. This is borne out by a good deal of indirect evidence, such as the rise in wages, the restriction of sown areas and the abandonment of inhabited places, all of

---

[8] Fourquin, 551

[9] Fourquin, 551. The province of Béarn was almost completely spared. Tucoo-Chala, 688.

which suggest the same thing. But it is more immediately obvious from the censuses which multiplied all over Europe precisely at this period. These documents, however, suffer from serious shortcomings. To begin with they are all essentially fiscal documents. They were drawn up as a basis for the distribution of the subsidies payable to the princes which it was customary to divide between the villages according to their population. The result was that the declarations upon which they were based were from the very beginning falsified, in spite of being taken on oath, because of the desire of the communities to reduce the burden of taxes. Furthermore, individuals were not counted, only taxable units, i.e. households, or 'hearths'. How many people on average lived in each rural household? Estimates made by the various experts differ wildly. In addition the lists which have been preserved are frequently only concerned with the households which were financially solvent, since the surveyors did not wish to add to their task by registering households to poor too participate in the levy. To make the necessary adjustments, we should need to know the proportion of destitute people; but as the number of the latter varied greatly, any estimate can only be a conjectural one.[10] Some other documents which account for only a part of the rural population, like recruiting lists for the militia and lists of tenants or persons liable to the *taille* used by seigneurial collectors, complete the evidence of the censuses. Although far from perfect, the material does permit some useful observations to be made, and in particular it allows the historian of the rural economy revealing glimpses of demographic movements. It should be noted that while these sources still remain mostly unexplored, the study of population movements is one branch of research which has shown the most remarkable recent advances.[11]

So far as the actual investigations go, very pronounced differences can be discerned between the few regions which have been the object of detailed examination. Some of them, in fact, betray no tendency to decline, but on the contrary, clear signs of growth, as for instance, according to some estimates, in northern Italy. In northern Brabant the censuses show a rise in the number of hearths between the last quarter of the fourteenth century and the second half of the fifteenth century which varied, according to the village, from 6 to 32 per cent.[12]

---

[10] See, on this point, some remarkable critical analyses in Arnould, 571, and Baratier, 92. Extraordinary cases of the overcrowding of households are known. In 1484 70 persons lived in one house in a Norman town 'because they feared the *tailles*, since if each married person kept, as it is commonly called, a separate home, they would certainly be forced to pay a much higher *taille* . . .'. An interesting proof of the direct effect of fiscal methods on the structure of population is in Guenée, 578, p. 321.

[11] According to the report presented to the Congress at Paris, 86.

[12] Cipolla, 548; J. Cuvelier, *Les dénombrements de foyers en Brabant* (XIVᵉ-XVIᵉ siècles), Brussels, 1912-1913; Hilton, 668.

Nevertheless, in most provinces investigations have revealed a very pronounced decline. In Provence, where the plentiful sources have but recently been explored, the fall is shown by the first years of the fourteenth century, and consequently it preceded by a long time the outbreak of the great epidemics: in the village of Maillane, for example, one hundred 'hearths' were counted in the mid-thirteenth century and only 80 in 1319.[13] However, the fall in the Provençal population was greatly accelerated after 1320, and for most of western Europe the most critical period in population history must be placed in the twenty years which followed the Black Death. It is then that the curves revealed the most violent falls. This shows that the shock administered to society by the Great Plague, coming on top of existing deficiencies, was the determining factor.[14] After 1370 demographic depression prevailed throughout the European countryside for several decades.

We can guess how profound it was from the details of one small Burgundian village which I take as an example.[15] There were 41 households in 1375, that is, half as many as in 1268. The number was then stabilized at a slightly higher level: 54 households in 1378 and 53 in 1400. Then came the terrible collapse: in 1423 no more than 13 households. This then is the general outline of the trend which does not seem to have any connection with military catastrophes. A similar decline can be found everywhere. The Florentine *contado* was proportionately reduced; nor can one single solvent household be found at Maillane at that period. In the same general manner the curve of population starts to recover in the second quarter of the fifteenth century. The Burgundian village selected as an example counted 28 households in 1436, 42 in 1450. After 1460-1470 the impetus increased in the richer regions of France and England, while population stagnated in the poorer areas, and sometimes even continued the downward trend.

Apart from some exceptionally favoured rural enclaves, the disaster had been astonishingly far-reaching. Thus, we find that, taken as a whole, the county of Nice lost two-thirds of its population between 1320 and the beginning of the fifteenth century, and the poorest districts in the mountains suffered an even worse depopulation. In one small town on the upper reaches of the Var 268 households were counted in 1313 and only 89 in 1471. Around Senlis the density of hearths per square kilometre fell from about 15 in 1328 to 3 or 4 in the middle of the following century.[16] Towards 1470, when recovery was in full swing, in most European villages households were still only half as numerous as at the beginning of the fourteenth century.

[13] Baratier, 92 (see in particular the table dealing with the Sisteron region, pp. 172-173) and 420; Document No. 162, p. 520

[14] According to the English evidence used by Russell, 98, infant mortality appeared to rise greatly after 1348; at the end of the century it was fertility which declined.

[15] Martin-Lorber, 536   [16] Baratier, 92, p. 186; Guenée, 578

3. THE SHRINKING OF THE CULTIVATED AREA

To match the reduction in the numbers of men there was a corresponding retreat in the extent of the arable, a phase of *Entsiedlung*, a contraction in the occupation of the soil, which followed soon after the end of colonization. These alterations in cultivated space have been made the object of detailed study in Germany and England. In these countries we see in very many village territories that some fields, usually those situated on the fringes of the cultivation in the zones most recently taken by man from the wastes, were abandoned. Records also show the desertion of some *manses* and inhabited plots situated either inside the villages or in the belt of dispersed habitations. Finally, we see whole villages completely disappearing with their territories. Nothing remains of them today except their place-names. Sometimes the outline of ancient streets and enclosures, or the grid of long strips of cultivated land, almost flush with the ground, appear thrown into relief. Aerial photography in England has revealed with the help of oblique lighting some of these remains covered over and preserved by the meadow turf.[17] Research has disclosed the existence of a large number of these 'lost villages', or *Wüstungen* as the Germans call them, whose desertion can be dated to the second half of the fourteenth century or early in the fifteenth. In England traces of about 2000 rural settlements which were thus abandoned have been found. Most of them lay to the east in the country anciently devoted to cereal production. It is true that most of these sites were not totally abandoned until the sixteenth century; but this was but the final step in a partial desertion which took place after 1348 and which affected profoundly these smaller and more marginal rural centres whose lands were for one reason or another unfavourably situated. In the east and south-west of Germany between 20 and 30 per cent of settlements disappeared. The retreat was on an even larger scale in central Germany.[18] In northern Thuringia, of the inhabited places known in the early Middle Ages, 146 out of 179 were completely deserted before 1600. It would be very useful to extend the same enquiries to France and to plot, region by region, the areas of human occupation which were subsequently abandoned. We already know that some hamlets in Brie and Provence disappeared in the second half of the fourteenth century.[19]

To provide the means of interpreting such a metamorphosis of the agrarian scene, research would also have to establish as precisely as possible the chronology of desertion. By matching up archeological observations with written evidence it has been possible to discover that many English villages

[17] Document No. 168, p. 526   [18] Document No. 170, p. 527
[19] Beresford, 586; Abel, 545, p. 8; Brunet, 43, p. 431

lost their inhabitants at the time of the Black Death and were never re-occupied. Topographical studies are more complicated since the 'lost villages' themselves must not only be traced, but also the belt of contraction marked out from those village territories which continued to be partially cultivated. The fertility of the deserted fields and their relationship to the great forest areas and to urban settlements must be noted, and particular attention paid to what vegetation replaced arable. Sometimes fields would be replaced by meadow. In England examples of this abound. The hamlet of Tusmore, a 'lost village' in Oxfordshire whose foundations can still be seen at sunset under the smooth turf, contained 53 peasant households in 1279. By 1357 it was empty and its lord was authorized to enclose the whole territory for the purpose of feeding his flock: the site was never again inhabited.[20] However, most parcels which ceased to be cultivated were overwhelmed by woodland or waste, either temporarily, as in France during the worst moments of the Hundred Years War, or permanently. The natural regeneration of the forest in central Germany at the expense of the clearings which were made between the eleventh and the thirteenth century, was truly amazing. Pollen analysis carried out in the peat bogs at Roten Moor shows clearly that cereals re-treated between 1350 and 1420, but also that the retreat was matched by the advance of tree species. Birch and hazel, both fast-growing scrub trees, were the first to re-establish themselves in the deserted fields; they were the fore-runners of beech and the high forest which once more covered the soil cleared by man's labour for a short space of time.[21] The return of natural vegetation in the fourteenth and fifteenth centuries is an episode in the history of European civilization of equal importance to the adventure of clearing the wastes.

4. EVOLUTION OF PRICES AND WAGES

The final changes in economic conditions concern the relative values of agricultural products and peasant labour. It must be admitted that these changes are not at all easy to understand and indeed the whole history of prices in medieval times is infinitely more complicated and conjectural than that of the occupation of the soil or even of population. It is possible to con-struct a few continuous series in some places, mostly remote from each other, by using the accounts of the few great lords, nearly all of them English, who continued after the beginning of the fourteenth century regularly to sell the output of their demesnes. Most of the data, however, come from urban documents. The mechanism of agricultural prices, and especially grain prices, is much too complex for observations made at widely scattered points to

[20] Beresford-St Joseph, 40, pp. 111-112 and figure 43
[21] Document No. 35, p. 391

provide general conclusions. Everything leads us to believe that the grain market remained as narrowly localized as it had been at the beginning of the fourteenth century.[22] so that price levels could vary by as much as two to one from one village to another, and that in any case the transactions carried out in the markets of the larger towns and in the barns of cultivators took place in utterly disparate conditions. These factors invalidate much of the significance of the various price series reconstructed from the archives of Montauban or Frankfurt. Nevertheless it is possible to establish from the scanty documentary material a few very important conclusions.

In the first place it appears that the grain market was agitated by violent short-term fluctuations. These seem to have been very much magnified during the fourteenth century. The extent of the regular seasonal variation each year is especially obvious. The tendency to scarcity, and, even more, the new psychological reaction, fear of the famine which was once more known to be possible, made demand very sensitive to the vagaries of the harvest. The great spring price rise which normally followed the September fall, was accentuated when the preceding crop had been mediocre; it could soar to fantastic heights when the new harvest also threatened to be bad. And if several lean years followed each other, the oscillations linked up and got out of control. During the wheat crisis of the year 1316 people in Flanders paid twelve or even twenty-four times as much as was customary. Under the combined effects of scarcity and monetary disturbances, the price of a *setier* of rye in Paris rose between 1415 and 1421 from six *sous* to 448; in 1422 it fell to 28 *sous*.[23]

However, when we examine the prices of different cereals over a long period (they were all affected by largely parallel fluctuations) we notice that they were stagnant, or that at certain points they fell regularly. It is easy to grasp the main change from the previous period of agricultural expansion in the twelfth and thirteenth centuries which brought in its train, as we know, a slow and sustained rise in prices. It appears indeed that the reversal in direction was not the result of a sudden upheaval or external shock. After 1300 the trend altered but gradually. The famines of the second decade of the fourteenth century which followed several years of great plenty probably did not produce, even in the countries bordering the North Sea, such prolonged repercussions on the movement of agricultural prices as has been thought. At the time of the great shortages prices show a clear rise on the Parisian market, but they quickly returned to the average level which prevailed before the crisis and remained there. Prices kept low and steady between 1320 and 1432 in the accounts of the abbey of St Denis. In England, the price of grain fell

[22] Document No. 64, p. 417
[23] Van Werveke, 610; Fourquin, 551

rapidly after 1325; it was, on average, 20 per cent lower in the second quarter of the fourteenth century compared to the first quarter. The Black Death produced a sudden fall in production which immediately raised the price level. But it fell again after 1370.[24]

In the accounts of the monastery of St Denis the level of selling prices changed little between 1374 and 1410; between 1410 and 1440 prices were disorganized by military operations and monetary disturbances; after that they can be seen stagnating and then gently declining until the approach of the sixteenth century. We can reconstruct curves for other regions with trends which were hardly different. Some series based on English documents reflect a rapid collapse during the years 1375-1380. At Frankfurt prices returned in 1371-1380, after a marked rise, to the level of 1351-1360, fell by a quarter in the following decade and rose afterwards by 15 per cent, to sag gently throughout the fifteenth century. Nevertheless, on the whole, a fall in the price level is borne out by all, or nearly all, the records, and showed itself to be often profound. If, in the accounts of the Norman manor of Neufbourg, the value of a measure of wheat remained practically at the same level between 1325 and 1400, it has been calculated that at Caen grain was worth half as much in 1428 as in 1270. The loss in value between the middle of the fourteenth century and the middle of the fifteenth century has been estimated at 35 per cent in lower Austria, 63 per cent in England, and 73 per cent in Frankfurt. The decline in the price of the basic foodstuff probably appeared the more obvious because the price levels of wine and other peasant products kept up firmly throughout the whole period. It has been calculated that the average prices of cattle fell by only 11 per cent in England between 1350 and 1450. The price of butter rose throughout the fourteenth century.[25]

In large- and medium-sized agricultural undertakings the consequences of declining cereal prices were aggravated by the marked rise in rural wages. Here, also, it was a question of a complete reversal of the trend. The effects were rather violent, since wage rates were directly affected by demographic movements. In the English countryside the existence of a plentiful labour supply prolonged the stability of money wages until 1320. Thereafter we see them rising a little here and there. It was, however, the Black Death which precipitated the rise. On the demesnes of Tavistock Abbey, a labourer who received 3½d. weekly in 1298, demanded 4d. by 1334; but he had to be given 6d. in 1373, 7d. in 1381 and 8d. in 1385.[26] Calculated from data taken from the bishop of Winchester's records, the index of money wages moved from 100 in 1300-1319 to 124 in 1320-1339, then to 133 in 1340-1359; to 169 in

[24] Fourquin, 551; Postan in 6, p. 198
[25] Plaisse, 681, p. 229; Abel, 545
[26] Finberg, 187

1360–1379 and 188 in 1380–1399; it then settled down at that level. In the accounts of the abbey of St Denis wages doubled between 1349 and 1370 and then stopped moving.[27]

We can also see everywhere that wage differentials closed up. It was, in fact, the wages of unskilled labourers which reacted most to the rise. At the end of the thirteenth century, a thatcher at Winchester was paid three times as much as a reaper; in the first half of the fifteenth century the former received only one-third more than the latter. The significance of these wage rates for the fate of the great agricultural enterprise was that the increasing cost of the day's labour occurred at the very moment when the price of grain was collapsing. On the manors of the bishop of Winchester, where the index of wages doubled between the beginning and the end of the fourteenth century, that of corn prices moved in the opposite direction and declined from 100 to 65. The discrepancy increased further towards the middle of the fifteenth century: if the index of wages did not markedly change, that of prices began again to sink after 1440; it stood at 53 in the period 1440–1459 and 47 in 1460–1479.[28]

5. AN INTERPRETATION

These then are the facts. How should they be interpreted? It cannot be denied that in the fourteenth century and the first half of the fifteenth the rural economy was disturbed by accidental calamities of a purely external nature. Neither can the hypothesis of climatic changes be rejected without examination. In the belief that, for similar reasons, the cultivation of cereals in Iceland was abandoned, that Scandinavian colonies in Greenland were no longer able to support themselves, that the altitude of the forest limit descended in the Sudentenland, that viticulture ceased in England and became more uncertain in Germany, some scholars have in fact concluded that the climate of central and northern Europe became colder between the early fourteenth century and 1460.[29] The argument can certainly be countered by pointing out that some of these phenomena can be explained simply by changes in commercial habits. But it is worth taking the study of climatic variations further and data can still be obtained from research into the few and imprecise sources for ancient periods. Good indications of long-term

---

[27] Postan, 582; Fourquin 551. Here are some detailed facts about the changes in day wages of vinedressers at Marseilles: (Baratier, 100).

	1306	1331–1336	1349–1363	1409 and 1439	1480
Male wages	10–15d	15–18d.	4–5s.	5–6s.	7s. 6d.
Female wages	5–6d.	7–8d.	2s.–2s. 8d.	2s. 8d.	3s. 4d.

[28] Postan, 582; see also, the table drawn up by Slicher von Bath on a different base, Document No. 167, p. 526   [29] Steensberg, 569

climatic variations are obtained from the chronology of glacial flows. But observations of this kind for the Middle Ages lack precision. As proof of a continued deterioration in climatic conditions it seems as if European glaciers did in fact extend downwards, but not till later, i.e. between 1450 and 1600. Nevertheless North American studies of the growth of ancient trees over the centuries reveal that in the fourteenth century rainfall increased in the western states. Can we assume that such rainfall changes affected the whole of the northern hemisphere, and consequently that there was at that time excessive moisture, so inimical to cereal culture, in European countries also? At all events, it is not unlikely that about 1300 western Europe entered a long period of adverse climatic conditions which could in part explain the return of food shortages and the desertion of certain lands.[30]

Another external change in rural conditions had a direct influence. This was the growth of states and its consequences: the reappearance of war and the immense development of princely taxation. In a world which did not command a stock of money commensurate with its needs, the cumulative and disproportionate financial demands of princes and their officials, pillage, ransoms and the greed of warriors during a century and a half, served to upset the distribution of wealth, disturb the circulation of money, and create disorder in price levels. The general feeling of instability and insecurity which resulted caused economic activity to contract. It encouraged hoarding, restricted production, and limited exchange. All these anxieties were obviously felt much more strongly in the towns, but the countryside was not immune from them. The final blow from outside, which was certainly an accidental one, was the Black Death and its aftermath of morbidity, which afflicted Europe for half a century.

*   *   *

Nevertheless these catastrophes cannot by themselves explain the changes which affected the economy of the countryside. These changes were to a much greater degree the result of internal movements affecting the relationship of production and consumption. There is no doubt that we have to look back into the past to find the origins of the economic ills. The gradual impoverishment during the thirteenth century of an ever-widening circle of the peasantry and the overpopulation which was forcing reclamation on to infertile soils, prepared the way for them. The poor lands, completely exhausted after bearing a few crops, had soon to be abandoned for ever. The first contractions in the arable area occurred, as the year 1300 approached, on the fringes of the village lands on the always speculative extremities of the

[30] Le Roy Ladurie 70 and 71

assarts.[31] Meanwhile the death rate was, it seems, mounting from 1290 onwards amongst the mass of undernourished labourers who were at the mercy of variable harvests and climatic hazards.[32] Thus agrarian recession, like the demographic collapse, started before the beginning of the fourteenth century.

The two movements achieved their greatest momentum between 1320 and 1370, and we can place the decisive phase of the reversals during those years. In the heavily overpopulated country regions (the unproductive mountains of Oisan, for instance, supporting 2,828 households, had to feed at least as many men in 1339 as they did in 1911),[33] demographic pressure was from then on quickly relaxed and the economically least-favoured group of peasants was eliminated in a few decades. This calamitous reversal, obvious traces of which can be found in the censuses, was the apparent outcome of many forces. The death rate in the lower ranks of rural society around 1300 was already so high that a quite small increase, such as that reflected by the profits of succession taxes in English records in the last years of the thirteenth century, was sufficient to upset the balance between births and deaths in one generation. The latter preponderated to such an extent that for many years the growth of the population was slowed down and then eventually turned into a decline. In some regions troubles arising from wars aggravated the consequences of the biological failure. The movement of armies and the recruiting of troops carried away many peasants who were without family ties and sucked them into their wayward progress. They were thus removed from village life and scattered abroad. The rural exodus towards urban settlements has likewise to be superimposed on the picture of shrinking village populations. Indeed, almost everywhere at the beginning of the fourteenth century in Europe we find the towns growing. They must have been peopled by immigrants, since what we know about the birth rate shows us that it was far too low to ensure by itself even the natural renewal of the population. Many villagers moved to town to enjoy better protection. Walled cities provided refuge in times of danger, and we know, for instance, that during the political troubles of 1358 to 1360 and 1410 to 1420, many country folk crowded into Paris.[34] Other country workers also moved to the towns in the hope of more lucrative employment. At that time urban wage rates were definitely higher than average. In Artois at the beginning of the fourteenth century, a woodcutter earned from 9 to 12 *deniers* a day, while a mason, if he worked in a town, received 15 to 18.[35] Thus the number of day

[31] Examination of manorial accounts of the late thirteenth century, the collapse of yields and the removal of the arable fields of the manorial demesnes which are thereby revealed, has led M. M. Postan to think that the exhaustion of the soil had affected in England the central portions of the village territories as well.　　[32] Postan-Titow, 539
[33] Allix, 36　　　　　　　　[34] Fourquin, 551　　　　　　　[35] Richard, 473

labourers slowly diminished in the decades after 1300. The decline in the numbers of the rural proletariate contributed without doubt to the fall in grain prices, as it did to the rise in wages, and these movements were visible on the eve of the fourteenth century and gradually became more marked. The changes in conditions of employment in the countryside perhaps caused a preliminary decline in cereal production in some regions (especially in Artois and southern Flanders which suffered more from military operations and the repercussions of the wheat crises).[36]

Then the Black Death supervened. The epidemic of 1348-1349 dealt a crushing blow to the already fragile demographic structure. It must be recognized, however, that the immediate effects of the shock were to some extent mitigated. People of middle age resisted the disease better than others and the high mortality was soon followed by a great wave of births which rapidly filled the gaps. The periodic returns of the plague probably produced much more prolonged consequences, and had a decisive influence on the population curve. Everything leads us to believe that the real fall in the rural population occurred between 1350 and 1380.

It was during this period that the numbers of working men were so decisively reduced in the countryside. The poor were eliminated partly for physical reasons: the epidemic struck them harder than others. But the survivors made the most of the opportunity to establish themselves on the holdings rendered vacant by death. Families which for generations had lived in misery and under the economic heel of their employers, were able to rent land, and good land at that. It was offered to them on every side. To all appearance, the evacuation of the infertile soils and the desertion of the badly situated villages also occurred during these three decades. It was not so much that deaths had been more numerous in the zones of *Wüstungen*, but that the men whom the plague had spared had no further need of the barren soils. Intense demographic pressure alone had peopled land so ill suited to grain growing. As soon as the pressure was relieved these areas were abandoned. Thus the rural exodus and the catastrophic wave of mortalities caused a realignment of the factors of production in the countryside, a huge reorganization which affected both the conditions of employment and the utilization of the land. The ranks of the least-favoured labourers were considerably thinned out, and the bad lands, moorland, mountainside and woodland, reverted to wilderness.

Such conditions encourage a less pessimistic interpretation of the evidence of a reduction in arable. In most cases it was a direct result of demographic decline, but it also reflected a concentration of agriculture on the more productive soils. Furthermore, the most recent research on *Wüstungen* in Ger-

[36] Fossier, 607

many shows that at least in certain backward provinces, the retreat was certainly less widespread than would appear from a simple enumeration of abandoned lands permanently reoccupied by the forest. Most of these areas were never in effect more than very precarious settlements, temporarily exploited by shifting and extensive husbandry, whose function in the rural economy was in reality ancillary to that of the wooded areas. We must consequently be on our guard against considering the abandonment and regrouping in the fourteenth and fifteenth centuries of all the fields into a few coherent village territories subject to strict agrarian constraints as signs of economic malaise, agricultural failure or a too sudden decli ne of the population. On the contrary, these topographical transfers reflect a critical phase in the growth of the cereal economy, postponed for a century or two, but quite comparable in their development and nature to those of which the Ile de France was the scene during the thirteenth century. Thus, in north-western Germania the lords enclosed their woods whose value was increasing. They surrounded them with hedges, shut out the peasants' swine and henceforth forbade periodic beat burning. The power of the lords, enforcing this enclosure, caused the families who in these woodland zones drew most of their subsistence from forest, animal husbandry and related cultivation to change their objectives. They were obliged to alter their way of life and the *Waldbauer* became an *Ackermann*, a genuine cultivator settled on permanent fields. By concentrating together all the dispersed settlements and dwellings, habitation in large villages was strengthened, and encircled by the oaks whose acorns from henceforth fed the swine. Around these communities, reclamation created homogeneous village lands of a kind those countries had never known before.[37]

★   ★   ★

In France, England and the Low Countries, the various movements which changed the structure of peasant society reduced permanently the number of men seeking hired employment. All the ordinances of princes, therefore, failed to lower wages to their pre-Black Death level. In fact exactly the opposite occurred and wages continued to rise throughout the fourteenth century. This permitted the peasants who remained in service (the registers of the Poll Tax show that servants, *servientes*, and households of labourers, *laboratores*, still formed a good third of the population of the English countryside in 1377) to improve significantly their standard of living.

Generally speaking, it certainly appeared in the new equilibrium which gradually established itself about 1380, after the great demographic disturbances in some regions and the migrations and transfers of population in other

[37] Timm, 570, pp. 98 *et seq.*

regions, as if most country folk led a rather less precarious existence than their ancestors had done. They were, perhaps, more exposed to transient injury, and to unpredictable calamity but they probably lived a more restricted and self-contained life, and in general their economic position was stabilized. Population trends and price indices suggest that the following sixty years was a period of stagnation interrupted only intermittently by catastrophes. If we attempt a rough analysis of this new state of the economy, it will be noticed in the first place that it was characterized by a marked weakening in demographic vitality. It is possible that the reduction in the relative number of landless labourers helped to restrict opportunities for growth. Peasants settled on their own land were probably more careful to limit their families in an effort to prevent the break-up of their inheritances. They managed this by not allowing all their children to marry and by encouraging the unmarried ones to leave the holding and try their luck in the towns. The lack of adequate studies into peasant family life is acutely felt here, particularly as in certain regions fourteenth- and fifteenth-century records would provide material for these to be made in great detail. Thus it can be observed that around Fribourg in Switzerland the average number of children per household amongst cultivators remaining in the country was significantly lower (2·5) than amongst those who, having settled in town, had cut their ties with landownership (2·9).[38] In any case, at the end of the fourteenth century, density of human settlement was in many countries light, land relatively abundant, rents low, and labour dear.

The permanent fall in rural population appears also to have prolonged the stagnation of the grain trade in the country. Fewer in number than formerly, wage-earners on agricultural estates henceforth lived mostly as domestic servants; they were fed by their employers and did not have to buy their own bread. Moreover, for various reasons the volume of grain purchases in the towns remained lower. In the first place, the population of most urban settlements in Europe fell markedly at the end of the fourteenth and the beginning of the fifteenth centuries, in spite of the constant influx of country folk. This was partly due to epidemics aggravated by overcrowding and partly to the general slackening in exchange activities. Furthermore, the provisioning of households in these declining towns had become less dependent on the specialized grain traders: fear of famine had actually induced many citizens to arrange direct supplies either by buying land or fixed payments (*rentes*), or by concluding contracts with rural producers for the supply of cereals.[39] We should also take account of the changes which appear to have

[38] F. Bromberger, 'Bevölkerungs- und Vermögensstatistik in der Stadt und Landschaft Freiburg um die Mitte des 15. Jahrhunderts', in *Zeitschrift für Schweizerische Statistik*, 1900   [39] See p. 355

affected diets. A movement which tended to reduce the consumption of bread in certain regions and inversely to increase purchases of other foods, already visible in thirteenth-century documents, can be remarked and it increased in a regular manner thereafter. It can be seen in the *Weistümer* of southern Germany in which the amounts of meat and cheese which managers of manors had to serve to demesne workers were fixed. The same thing appears also from domestic accounts. One small Saxon noble is revealed as spending relatively large sums on providing his house with sausages, fish and honey; there is the same distribution of purchases of foodstuffs in the registers of the Parisian college of Ave Maria, or the *hôtel* of the king of France, where in 1417 the supply of meat cost eight times as much as the supply of grain.[40]

All these related phenomena help to explain the prolonged slump in grain prices, at first sight so surprising in a period in which one sees the area devoted to cereal cultivation everywhere considerably restricted. At this point it must be recalled that only the less fertile soils had been deserted and that the concentration of agriculture on the more favourable lands probably caused a rise in average yields. In this way, in between the seasonal or periodical scarcities, supply kept ahead of demand on the cereal market. To this may be added the facts that the variations between crops encouraged all cultivators to extend the sown area in anticipation of bad harvests, and that the ever-increasing weight of tax collection forced all peasant households to produce a surplus for sale. For all these reasons, agricultural holdings, on which the demographic purge had increased productivity, produced in normal times abundant supplies of cereals for sale.

Nevertheless the ever more pronounced decline in the price of grain compared to rural wages, which were maintained at such a very high level by the competition of town crafts and the spread of textile workers into many country districts of Europe, sealed the fate of all excessively large agricultural enterprises. Indeed it certainly seems as if the eclipse of the demesne and the great decline in direct manorial cultivation occurred in the years after 1380, at any rate in France and England. We must, however, seriously consider whether the eclipse of the manorial economy necessarily meant that medium-sized enterprises employing purely family labour, or run with the aid of no more than two or three domestics assisted from time to time by a few day labourers, had in any way lost their vitality.

[40] Abel, 545, pp. 147 *et seq.*; Rey, 707

CHAPTER II

The Decay of the Manorial Economy

If the rural economy of the last two centuries of the Middle Ages is, in fact, painted in sombre colours, it is because the sources throw light on hardly any but manorial enterprises and because economic trends were unfavourable to them. It is quite reasonable to conclude that the fourteenth-century recession was chiefly manifest in the countryside in the decline of the manor. In addition, manorial undertakings suffered most from political disturbances since they were directly affected by the deterioration of the cereal market and the supply of labour. We have already seen that what military operations damaged was mainly manors and manorial capital. Furthermore, after war was over, the manorial master had to help his peasants to rebuild their holdings if he did not wish them to emigrate and to abandon his land for ever, or even if he simply wished to conform to the popular notion of the lord's tutelary role in rural society which public opinion expected of him. Aristocratic and ecclesiastical fortunes, therefore, suffered heavily. They also suffered more than is commonly realized from the increasing weight of taxation. A recent study leads us to think that it was papal demands which were largely responsible for the economic deterioration of one great Flemish abbey during the first decades of the fourteenth century; the financial loss it sustained from taxation was at least three times as heavy as that resulting from war damage.[1] Finally, perhaps most injurious of all, because they interfered with the mechanism of manorial economy, were the tumultuous movements then agitating the secular world. The lay lords, deeply involved in political events, were dragged into warlike adventures in which many lost their possessions, sometimes for ever. Almost all were compelled to absent themselves from their estates for long periods. R. Boutruche has shown only too clearly the damage caused by the campaigns which so cruelly ravaged the Bordeaux region. Not only were the management of the estates, the relations between master and peasants, and the loyalty of tenants and managers, affected by the long absence of the landlords, but the old landlords were often replaced by new landlords, unknown and often grasping, who felt no hereditary attachment to men or soil.[2] It is certain that the shocks to which the political structure was subjected in many provinces

[1] Haenens, 663, pp. 124, et seq.   [2] Boutruche, 546, pp. 233 et seq.

hastened the slow removal of country gentry into the towns which had been going on since the thirteenth century. Many nobles, monks and high dignitaries of the Church spent less and less time at their country residences. They cut themselves off from contact with their land and from its cares and became strangers to the men who dwelt on their manors. This preference of lords for city life caused profound changes in farming methods and in the distribution of agricultural produce. It also transformed the psychology of management, and economic historians would do well to take this into account.

Highly complex, vulnerable, tied to the unstable destiny of an aristocratic élite and deeply interwoven with the feudal system which was being torn apart by the convulsions of the dying Middle Ages, the manor was thus subjected to violent stresses and strains, and was able to resist them much less successfully than did the peasant holding. We must, it is true, be on our guard against unduly exaggerating the depression of the manorial economy. It must be admitted that the same calamities and changes in society affected ecclesiastical properties much less seriously and that in many villages after the troubles the latter appeared more firmly entrenched than ever before. Moreover, when lords were forced to sell large parts of their patrimony, they generally retained the most favourably situated and productive lands. At moments of crisis they usually preserved after each wave of destruction sufficient resources to survive, to rebuild and to reinvest. We must not forget that in the second half of the fifteenth century both nobles and churchmen took a prominent part in the new movement of expansion, and in most cases led it. At that time the aristocracy dominated the rural world from the same eminence as before, and the focal point of the rural economy still was, as it had always been, the manor. We may speak of its decline, but only so long as we remember that the decline was limited, temporary and relative; and that it did not take place everywhere to the same extent.

*   *   *

Not all western provinces were agitated by political troubles to the same degree, and, as we have seen, some actually benefited from having found themselves in more favourable conditions. But we still lack enough comparative studies for it to be possible to distinguish clearly the particular features displayed by the manorial economy in different parts of Europe. We can, however, see certain regions where manors remained both vigorous and prosperous. Northern Italy was one such region. It is true, of course, that all we know about country life in this part of Europe comes from the relatively few soundings made in the enormous quantity of surviving records. These records are unluckily widely scattered and sometimes difficult of access, but we can at least catch glimpses from them of the persistence of demesne exploitation and labour services around Genoa in the fifteenth century. We also know that on the lands of one Cistercian abbey in Tuscany the levying of fixed payments did not decline at all during the fourteenth and early fifteenth century, and that the structure of the manorial economy was very little disturbed by the Black Death. We get the same impression of stability and affluence on the landed estates of the bishop of Pavia near Bobbio where the number of tenants actually rose during the period.[3] Further detailed investigations will probably one day permit us to assess how much the general prosperity of Italian manors owes to the persistently expansive tendencies throughout this area where demographic vitality and the opening of markets continued to stimulate the rural economy. But they should also help us to analyze more closely social conditions, which were so markedly different in all regions. The resilience of manors of the ancient type in the Ligurian mountains and the highlands behind Nice was, it seems, due to a deeply entrenched feudalism in those remote and backward areas. In the plains and along the main routes, on the other hand, it was the strength of the urban economy which supported and quickened manorial prosperity by providing capital and opening up outlets, and which harmonized and renewed relations between lords and peasants by means of the various flexible forms of contracts of association. The stimulus of the town entrepreneur and the virtual urbanization of the countryside particularly during the fourteenth century by a continuous expansion into the *contado*, especially into the hills, transplanted into the countryside a system of cultivation which had originally been evolved in the suburbs of the great cities: by this system, the *coltura promiscua*, plantations of vines and fruit-bearing trees on irrigated plots, were intimately linked to arable cultivation in a combination of fruit and cereal production requiring a great deal of skilled labour. The new landscape, visible for the first time in Tuscan paintings of the *trecento*, shows clear signs of a prosperity diffused throughout the countryside by activities emanating from the towns.[4] Here the lords were almost all denizens of the cities; they were either nobles who had gone to live in the neighbouring town, or else men of the city who had bought, or leased, land from the Church on very advantageous terms.[5] Did these townsfolk apply the same spirit of enterprise which animated their trading and banking affairs to the management of their rural properties? Was this their contribution to the process of expansion? Or were they so fascinated by the aristocratic way of life that they also adopted the traditionally idle and negligent behaviour of a lord? Were they content

[3] J. Heers, *Gênes au XVᵉ siècle*, Paris, 1961, pp. 511 *et seq.*; Jones, 673; Luzzatto, 22

[4] Sereni, 84, p. 93. Another sign of the overwhelming influence of the town economy was the spread at this period into neighbouring districts of the system of weights and measures used in the great Lombard communes. Toubert, 651.

[5] Cipolla, 549

to profit passively from a prosperity which owed nothing to their own initiative? Controversy between historians on these points is still open[6] and detailed study focussed upon particular cases alone will eventually decide the issue.

*   *   *

The development of the manorial economy on the eastern flank of the Germanic countries proved also to be very different. In these new countries it was the profound upheaval associated with depopulation and desertion of the cultivated land which revived the vitality of manorial institutions. In the immense void caused by the *Wüstungen*, huge demesne exploitations became firmly established. The *Landbuch*, which describes the agrarian structure of Brandenburg in 1375, reveals clearly that the land cultivated by the nobles was then much less extensive than peasant land. On demesnes cultivated by labourers of free condition,[7] the small nobles, holders of only the inferior justice, were in the position of 'neighbours' to peasants who did not owe them any labour services. But during the last quarter of the fourteenth century the lords, without any effort on their part, saw their estates acquiring all the lands left deserted by the sudden demographic collapse. At the same time the labour supply which would have permitted an extension of the kind of farming based on wage-earning disappeared. A belated political disintegration, comparable to that experienced in Gaul at the end of the tenth century, allowed the manor to revive. The decisive factor in these countries was the feebleness of the State. In return for money subsidies from the lords, the princes handed over their royal privileges and thereby put the peasants completely into the power of the local lordlings. It was this that enabled the masters to bind countrymen to the soil, to prevent migration to the towns, and to impose the heavy labour services which their disproportionately swollen demesnes demanded. The manor benefited from depopulation in this case, through the decay of the public authority. Throughout the fifteenth century, little by little, a peasantry which had hitherto enjoyed greater liberty than any other in Europe, was burdened with a rigid servitude; and this servitude prepared the way for the great prosperity enjoyed by the vast agricultural estates of the clergy and nobility in modern times.[8]

*   *   *

We must therefore distinguish some sectors in which the manorial economy in general seems to have grown. Equally we have to recognize that

---

[6] Sapori, 29; Fiumi, 141

[7] In the 148 villages of Uckermark there were counted in 1375 2,695 households of *Kossäten*, poor peasants who hired themselves out on the great agricultural undertakings; Zientara, 604.   [8] Carsten, 8, p. 23; Tyminiecki, 33

in other parts of Europe all the manors did not decay to the same extent. We retain, indeed, an impression of great diversity amongst manorial institutions. The internal structure of the manor protected it, more or less, against the forces which tended to break it down. Its fate also depended on the personality of the man who was at its head, on his needs and wishes, on the attention he devoted to his task, and on his attachment to his land. This can be seen very clearly on Church demesnes where the phases of prosperity and depression are almost always found to be closely connected with a change in the dignitary responsible for the domestic economy.[9] In the Low Countries, in England, France and indeed every country where calamities and political troubles aggravated the effects of a reverse in the economic climate, chance helped certain demesnes to escape devastation and even strengthened them through the failure of their neighbours. Very many castles were held by the same family without a break throughout the period. There the continuity of manorial administration did not suffer the damaging interruptions which elsewhere loosened the bonds between master and labourer.

Generally speaking, it seems that manors belonging to princes and the great families, as well as those belonging to the church, suffered less. Less disorganized management, better kept records, greater determination to preserve the integrity of the patrimony and to return at whatever cost to former levels, fortified the ecclesiastical manors against disintegration. As for the princely manors, they benefited first from the concentration of compulsory powers. This process protected them and also facilitated their restoration; the all-embracing taxation strengthened them by providing a constant stream of liquid funds and a part of this capital at least helped to stimulate the manorial economy. Lastly, the top ranks of the lay aristocracy were everywhere reduced in numbers and power lay in fewer hands. This tendency helped the landed fortunes of every great family to accumulate. In England, where the phenomenon has been studied in detail, the patrimonies of the wealthiest magnates increased throughout the fourteenth and fifteenth centuries by matrimonial alliance and inheritance as well as by investment of the huge money profits which came from their proximity to the king and from their political influence.[10] It is also possible to imagine that noblemen in the lowest ranks, intimately connected with peasant life as they were, were also able to manage their properties more successfully. This hypothesis could probably be verified from notarial registers of the Mediterranean countries. In any case the present state of research certainly shows that the most obvious signs of malaise revealed themselves in the middle ranks of manorial wealth.

[9] Haenens, 663, pp. 98 *et seq.* is very convincing on this point with reference to the abbey of St Martin of Tournai.
[10] Holmes, 670

I. THE DECLINE OF DIRECT CULTIVATION

It is clear from all available records that fourteenth-century lords of every rank were, no less than their ancestors, deeply attached to their demesne lands. They all liked eating and drinking the produce of their own fields, orchards, vineyards, and those well-stocked fishponds that were usually to be found near the mansions of the rich.[11] Every wealthy man expected to live off the produce of his own land and by the labour of his own servants. This attitude of mind explains why there was no waning in the interest shown in agrarian literature during the last two centuries of the Middle Ages and why it was eagerly perused in the town houses where so many notabilities now lived. The interest extended even into the rarefied atmosphere of the royal court: for it was King Charles V of France who commissioned for his own library the translation of Pietro de'Crescenzi's *Ruralium commodorum opus*, and also the treatise, *De l'état, science et pratique de l'art de bergerie*, from Jean de Brie. Every reigning prince privately nursed the image of himself as a shrewd manager of his own estates.

In fact, of course, the noble and religious houses described by contemporary documents were always shown surrounded by lands which had to supply them with bread and wine, inhabited by plentiful domestic labour, and equipped with all the tools necessary for agricultural work. It is obvious from the accounts of English manors at the end of the fourteenth century that direct farming still provided for almost all the master's wants. One religious house in Leicestershire obtained all its food from three demesnes which it kept in hand and the sale of wool from its flock was sufficient to pay for domestic purchases.[12] In the same period south German lords were bitterly disputing common lands with peasants and were forcing new demands for labour services upon them. In fact they could not bring themselves to admit that their demesnes, so reduced by partible inheritance, could no longer provision their households, for they simply could not imagine any other system of subsistence. In France a similar interpretation of household economy gave new courage to the lords in the regions most devastated by the war; once the danger was past they set out to recruit labour for ploughing up their own demesne furlongs and patiently to put their enclosures and meadows back into cultivation. The same motive caused many masters to undertake reclamation: as, for instance, the superior of a country priory near Boulogne who, about 1440, had 'newly assarted, broken up (*derrechier*) and ploughed about 150 dayworks, all in one piece and in three courses . . . which had not

[11] On the importance in the fifteenth century of the revenues of ponds in the profits of the manors of Sologne, see Guérin, 553, pp. 131 *et seq.*
[12] Hilton, 667, pp. 131-133 (Owston Abbey)

been cultivated during the life, age or memory of man'.[13] On the Norman manor of Neufbourg, the accounts of which have been carefully analyzed, the function of the demesne can be clearly seen. In 1397-1398 its output did not form more than 6 per cent of the total revenue, but the lord's table was almost entirely supplied from the vast kitchen garden and farmyard. The necessary complement of oats and wheat came from peasant dues, which were levied in money or kind, according to whether the harvest on the few demesne fields had been good or bad.[14] The lords of those days tried above all things to avoid disbursing money on provisioning their households. Thus we are not surprised to see from successive surveys that the area of demesne arable, meadow and vineyard on the manors of St Germain-des-Prés[15] increased during the fifteenth century: tradition, convention and most deeply held conviction all inclined the richer landlords to manage their lands themselves, and to watch their own harvests ripen, their own flocks increase, and to drink wine from their own vineyards.

* * *

Historians of the medieval countryside must treat these psychological attitudes as fundamental and stabilizing features of the economic structure, as well as a major obstacle to prevailing economic tendencies. Nevertheless, their braking power was not sufficient to halt the slow march of events already under way in the thirteenth century on the largest manors in France and the Low Countries by which the large-scale agricultural enterprise was doomed to eventual eclipse. Studies of individual manors in fact plot the course in the fourteenth century of this movement, which was separating lords from their fields without their being aware of it. In the present state of research it appears that the movement passed through two successive phases.

The retreat of direct cultivation continued its slow pace until 1350. But in the second quarter of the fourteenth century we can see that the retreat followed two different routes. The first of these ways was, of course, as in the past, by the 'farming out' of the whole demesne. Already widely used about 1320 on the great estates of north-west France belonging to the princes and the most powerful monasteries, this system of management continued to spread slowly, and the early changes in economic conditions hardly seem to have hindered its progress. Between 1290 and the middle of the following century we do not see many differences in the terms of the leases by which the abbeys in the region of Paris granted the entire exploitation of their

---

[13] *Chartes de Lucheux*, No. 53
[14] Plaisse, 681, pp. 222 *et seq.* This evidence of the flexibility of dues restrains us from coming to any too definite conclusions about the movement of conversion into money of dues in kind.   [15] Fourquin, 551

manors to lessees for periods of years. Neither does it seem that the violent disturbances agitating the grain market in certain towns in this part of Europe had any influence on the total number of 'farms'. Recent investigation into the demesne of St Martin of Tournai reveals continuity of arrangements during the first half of the fourteenth century. The monks did no more than take precautions to avoid monetary changes lowering their manorial income. They required that the 'farm' should be partially paid in cereals. They laid down in the lease that the remaining sums should be calculated with regard to the market value of the currency and not merely to its legal value: a simple precaution against monetary instability.[16] Formulated and introduced into the manorial economy during the great prosperity of the thirteenth century, the versatility of the 'farm lease' was amply demonstrated. Its gradual extension on the largest landed properties was neither slowed down nor unduly precipitated by the preliminary difficulties of the new era.

Nevertheless, we can also observe that, after about 1320, demesne cultivation began in a parallel movement to contract in new ways which were more disturbing to the very structure of the manorial economy. Certain lords were active in promoting a policy of letting out the peripheral fringes of their demesnes by carving off new holdings. It seems as if by doing so they were responding to the needs of the poorer peasants who had not yet been markedly reduced in numbers by demographic decline. These people wished to add a few scraps of land to their exiguous family holdings and were prepared to pay high rents in order to have access to arable land. It thus became more profitable to let out land than to cultivate it. The lords were aware of this, for they got rid of the most remote fields, where the labour of their servants was least effective. They also gave up those recently conquered reclamations on marginal land whose productivity was rapidly falling. They decided to concentrate their own farming activities and the productive effort at their disposal on the better lands. Existing research shows such a contraction of demesne fields, particularly in England. It appears to have been a long-term movement which also began in the middle of the period of agricultural prosperity. Thus on eight of the bishop of Winchester's manors the area of manorial arable steadily diminished from 37 per cent during the second half of the thirteenth century to 24 per cent during the first half of the fourteenth century and to 20 per cent in the second.

Nevertheless, when we look more closely, the curve of lettings seems to show a violent rise between 1320 and 1340. This was the moment when the English demesnes belonging to the Norman abbey of Bec suffered their heaviest losses of land, while the marginal portions of the demesne lands of Leicester Abbey were also being let out to peasants in small parcels. The in-

[16] Haenens, 663

come from the demesne on one Ely manor fell by two-thirds; on another it fell from 80 *li* in 1319 to 10 *li* in 1333-1334.[17] This then, was a moment of crisis, of a first and violent shock. The contraction of demesne cultivation which the statistics derived from the records of the great English ecclesiastical estates indicate was probably the combined result of the chaotic behaviour of grain prices after the famine of 1316 and the rise in wages caused by the slowly thinning ranks of the rural proletariat. These problems turned demesne administrators away from direct management. They were encouraged to pass on managerial cares to peasant tenants who were less affected by wage levels and agricultural prices. The area of the demesne seems to have been stabilized on some English ecclesiastical estates after 1340; on most of the others, however, it continued to contract after that date.

★   ★   ★

Apart from northern Italy and eastern Germany, in every European country in which the study of manorial enterprises has been sufficiently developed, it is clear that the decline of direct management began to take on a new aspect after the mid-fourteenth century. On the one hand the process was accelerated; on the other hand it so operated that it had a marked effect on the general economy of the countryside.

The first task incumbent on historians of the countryside is to establish the time-table of this movement of contraction more precisely. The results of work done so far are very scanty, but they give the impression that the movement attained its greatest intensity in the 'seventies and 'eighties of the fourteenth century. The period when, around Liège as well as Brandenburg, the Cistercian abbeys gave up the direct management of their last granges can be placed between 1350 and 1370. The leasing out of land taken from the demesnes of ecclesiastical estates in the Parisian region multiplied after 1356. Thus the canons of Notre-Dame of Paris detached from the large demesne which they managed in the village of Mitry-Mory 75 acres between 1346 and 1348, and a further two hundred acres between 1352 and 1356; the disintegration then paused for a while, but was resumed between 1380 and 1390. We see the Premonstratensians 'farming out' their grange at Gergovie in Auvergne in 1381 and the Cistercians their grange at Ouges in Burgundy in 1382. It was at this period that the Hospitallers of Provence let out most of their estates to 'farmers'. And if we turn to the English countryside we discover that the monks of Ramsey began about the year 1370 to let off the demesne fields on their manors to peasants; twenty years later their demesne was wholly 'farmed out'; the demesnes of Leicester Abbey and many other religious establishments were abandoned to 'farmers' at the beginning of the

[17] Hilton, 667, p. 88; Morgan, 408; Miller, 198, p. 105

fifteenth century.[18] Trying to fix this process more precisely in time and space encourages a more searching approach to the problem: why did aristocratic resistance to the relinquishment of direct management, which had previously been so stubborn, finally crumble?

Why this should in fact have happened on many manors about 1380 is at first sight understandable. Indeed at this period, even without taking into account local accidents of war, the manorial economy experienced violent shocks and was overwhelmed by demographic collapse, the slump in agricultural prices and the rise in wages. Occasional inventories and fragments of accounts exist which allow us to understand better the lords' decisions and to discern their motives.

We are right to doubt whether the masters, especially the humbler ones, were at all clearly conscious of price movements. The deterioration of the grain market took place very slowly. Could it have been evident to them when conditions of sale varied so strikingly from month to month and from one town to another? On the other hand, they were immediately aware of the difficulty in recruiting workers. The flight of domestic servants and the disappearance of labourers, carried away by the military or struck down by the plague, left the land untended and swiftly reduced its output. The fall in manpower made it obviously advisable to let other people bear the anxieties of management. The sudden rise in wages, above all else, unbalanced manorial budgets and this was enough to condemn direct management. The accounts of the Cistercian manor of Ouges show this clearly. In the year 1380 its arable produced hardly any profit. Out of 131 *setiers* of harvested grain, 27 had to be kept for seed, while the domestic workers consumed 80. Money receipts amounted to 173 *livres*, but expenses were 168, of which upkeep of buildings accounted for 29 *livres*, equipment and tools for 35, and wages for 100. Thus the entire revenue was swallowed up. Two years later the whole grange was farmed out and from then on the monks, without troubling themselves at all, received good quantities of grain. We can also see how heavily wages weighed on the budget of small Saxon manors. One small country landowner, who was faithful to tradition and had not given up cultivating his ancestral demesne, spent almost as much money in paying his twenty-one domestic servants as in keeping up his table, clothing himself and maintaining his family in a fashion worthy of their station.[19] It is significant that the parts of Europe where direct exploitation remained vigorous, such as eastern Germany, certain south-western Germanic countries and northern Italy, were precisely those where the princely or urban authorities

---

[18] Carsten, 8, p. 75; Van Derveeghde, 483; Fourquin, 551; Fournier, 450; Martin-Lorber, 676; Raftis, 201, p. 259; Hilton, 667, pp. 90 *et seq.*
[19] Martin-Lorber, 676; Abel, 545, p. 147

had taken measures energetic enough to keep conditions of employment favourable to the lord, notably by hindering the flight from the land and by binding the peasants to the soil. Already in the thirteenth century the structure of the economy of the great agricultural enterprises was showing its fragility, overburdened as it was with administrative expense, wasteful habits, managerial peculation, and endless lawsuits; in short with all the practices which in happier years had kept an army of parasitic intermediaries in affluence.[20] It appears that the shifts in the economic climate after 1348, whether they were directly felt or not (like for instance the price trend), were sufficiently powerful to impede the free working of the mechanism and to persuade lords reluctantly to restrict their own farming activities and to hand over their managerial function to 'farmers'.

In order to explore the sudden decline in direct management in the decades before and after 1380, we must also take account of the changes which affected the structure of manorial society. The lords loved their land, but their affection ran counter to other considerations. R. Boutruche has rightly pointed out that the adoption of the farm lease 'was the response to a mentality which flinched from the cares and risks of direct management or of temporary *métayage*, and which preferred a fixed to a fluctuating income, even a high one'. Shall we ever be able to measure the unfolding of economic awareness in the minds of the lords? It is simpler merely to state that the abandonment of direct management, and recourse to rent-paying holdings or contracts which made over the demesne to another manager for a time, particularly suited the masters who had often to absent themselves and to let the demesne out of their sight. Does it not seem as if manorial society in many western provinces was greatly disturbed, and that during the period many lords changed their way of life, mainly by leaving their country homes? In the manorial records of one village in the highlands behind Nice there is a gap between 1353 and 1453; the mountains were then completely desolate. Later, when the owners reappear, we find them established at Nice, and managing their property from a distance.[21]

What effect did such migrations have on the demesne economy? In one Provençal commandery of the Hospitallers, the demesne, extensive in 1338, was almost entirely farmed out by 1411. But in the interval the household, formerly composed of twenty-four persons waited upon by eight servants, was reduced to six, and the home farm, although reduced in size, was sufficient for their maintenance.[22] Which came first, then, the contraction of

[20] Duby, 445

[21] Durbec, 'Chartes du val de l'Esteron', in *Provence Historique*, 1953

[22] Duby, 660. Whether the master did or did not live on his land made a great difference to the manorial economy. In Normandy, on the royal manor, there was no more income in kind after 1260; while at the end of the fourteenth century, the lords of

the demesne or that of the household? It would be useful, in any case, to trace in detail the composition of manorial households and to see whether the great company of persons which in feudal times formed the '*mesnies*' of the country gentry or the rural religious communities, did not vanish everywhere in the west during the fourteenth century. Finally, we must not forget the concentration of wealth, that accumulation of landed property in the hands of the great magnates who had at all times regularly leased out their demesnes at farm. All these changes of residence and ownership, about which so little is still known, could well have been amongst the most powerful incentives towards leasing out the demesne lands.

*   *   *

It appears, furthermore, that during the second half of the fourteenth century, the lords found new ways of putting the management of their lands into other hands. These changes deserve the close attention of historians, although here also our knowledge is at the moment quite inadequate. Future research should attempt to fill in the gaps in the following very provisional sketch which is based on exiguous data.

1. Many demesnes were broken up by letting out small parcels as rent-paying holdings on terms which followed the various legal forms traditionally given to peasant tenures. This method of erosion of the demesne integrity, which had already greatly affected English ecclesiastical manors fifty years earlier, seems to have spread across France after the middle of the fourteenth century and in the early fifteenth. This leasing of peripheral plots from the large fields on the edges of great arable areas reduced the extent of the manorial demesne by one-third in the village of Ouges in Burgundy, and by one-half at Lorgues in Provence. A large part of the vineyard which the monks of St Denis owned was also distributed in small lots to the tenants after 1345. Sometimes, indeed, whole demesnes disintegrated completely in this way and disappeared: in Brandenburg in the second half of the fourteenth century many monastic manors were entirely parcelled out.[23]

2. Nevertheless, most demesne lands which the lords ceased to exploit themselves were granted not as rent-paying holdings on a hereditary basis, but for a limited period only. It is true, we notice a general tendency for the terms of years of temporary concessions to get somewhat longer. The life-lease, which had gone out of use in the thirteenth century, largely regained ground: after 1370 it was frequently used on the lands of Ramsey Abbey in England, as well as in villages around Paris.[24] In fact, the troubled times and

---

Neufbourg received a great deal of grain from their tenants; Strayer, 475, pp. 16-20; Plaisse, 681, p. 226.   [23] Martin-Lorber, 676; Fourquin, 551; Carsten, 8, p. 75
[24] Raftis, 201, p. 260; Fourquin, 551

the scarcity of men encouraged the permanent attachment of 'farmers' in areas devastated by the soldiery. It also appears that the lords sometimes, in prolonging the length of the lease, laid down that the cultivators had to undertake all repairs and particularly to restore the devastated land. However, according to all appearances, the short-term lease which lapsed after a few years, gained the masters' favour everywhere.[25] Contracts of this sort abound in every repository of records. Researchers will do well to follow up selected topics with a few exhaustive and essential statistical studies. As for the legal status of these leases there was no significant change. Two important modifications, however, altered considerably the position of the short-term lease in the working of the rural economy at this period.

3. The first was concerned with the obligations of the lessor. *Métayage*, or share-cropping, seems to have rapidly spread in southern Europe. We have already seen that contracts which associated the owner of the soil with the cultivator and which required him to provide half the seed, to pay in part for the labour, to contribute to the upkeep of the tools, and sometimes to advance grain and even food for the *métayer* and his family in the first year, were widespread in Italy from the thirteenth century onwards. More than three-quarters of the leases drawn up in the country surrounding Siena in 1316 specified associations of *mezzadria*. This system of management also prevailed on the lands of the Tuscan abbey of Settimo in the second quarter of the fourteenth century and it was then that the references to *métayers*, *massarii*, and *partiarii* increased in the communal statutes of Lombardy. The practice of *facherie* and *mégerie* then invaded Provence, as well as Toulousain, Quercy and the whole of Aquitaine as far north as Poitou, Limousin and Sologne.[26]

4. Even more important may have been the second change, which concerned the size of the parcels granted 'at farm' or in *métayage*. Obviously the ideal purpose of the transaction from the lord's point of view was to preserve the integrity of the demesne he had inherited from his ancestors, to maintain

[25] In fact the lords wished to preserve the possibility of taking back the land into their own hands. This happened more often than one would think. Against 2,500 acres of holdings, the three demesnes of the Norman lords of Neufbourg occupied only 250. At the end of the fourteenth century they were all farmed out to a large peasant. In 1405, at the expiration of the lease, the demesne of Canteloup was again taken in hand. The lord engaged three servant families who, employed by the year, received a money wage paid quarterly and a monthly allowance of grain and peas. In fact these wage-earners had formerly been in the service of the 'farmer'. Which shows, as we should do well to remember, that in the fifteenth century the effects on the basic structure of cultivation of leasing or taking in hand were often minimal. Plaisse, 681, p. 138.

[26] According to the census of Siena, 6,500 out of the 15,000 properties were the subject of a contract of lease, and 5,000 of these contracts established a *métayage*. Imberciadori, 478, p. 49; Jones, 673; Toubert, 651; Ourliac, 199; Sicard, 685; Guérin, 553, p. 262.

his authority over the whole territory, and to grant it in its entirety to one farmer in a single coherent unit of arable, meadow and vineyard, with its stables full and its flock intact. We know that demesnes were usually leased out in this manner in the prosperous years of the thirteenth century. In the last quarter of the fourteenth century, and even up to the middle of the fifteenth century, many masters still succeeded in finding individuals who, alone or in company with others, were sufficiently audacious and provided with enough resources to take over the demesne as a whole and as a going concern. But during the periods of great distress, in the most ravaged areas, on the least fertile soils and when labour and market conditions made management onerous and uncertain, potential lessees became harder to find.[27]

Indeed, the difficulties forced many lords, for all their disinclination to do so, to scale down the demesne by reducing its size. Since they could not resign themselves to lease the whole of the demesne to different tenants, they could at least trim its outlying parts and offer these to farmers and *métayers* in portions of modest size which could be cultivated by the labour of single families. The *bordes* of the Toulousain, about 100 acres in size, equipped with one or two pairs of oxen and leased by *métayers*, had, it seems, their origin in some such reductions of demesnes. In the fifteenth century they formed family agricultural units whose management did not demand much capital and, above all, did not need much wage labour. The small share-cropping farms (*métairies*) which appeared then in Poitou were of the same dimensions and this was also the average size of the *mezzadria* of Tuscany. It is true that after 1450 we meet here and there much larger farms in the fertile localities of the Parisian basin or in eastern England.[28] One dreams of a vast research project which, by using the abundant material, would establish for each region the average size of farms formed in the mid-fifteenth century out of the old manorial demesnes. Everything leads us to suppose, however, that in general the average size was rather small and that we should date the period when units of this size were created to the fifty years after the Black Death. The large-scale cereal-producing enterprises which were still able to exist in western Europe disappeared at this period. The size of the agricultural undertaking adapted itself to the behaviour of the grain market, as well as to the more pressing requirements of labour supply. And here we catch sight of one of the fundamental transformations of country life which merits closer scrutiny.

★　　★　　★

[27] Already by 1338, the Hospitallers of the Provençal mountains had, in spite of themselves, to keep in their demesnes certain poor lands which no peasant would take up under a contract of *facherie*; Duby, 445

[28] Sicard, 685, p. 25; Merle, 677; Imberciadori, 478; Fourquin, 551

Here again, in order to explain the advance of *métayage* by the reduction in the size of farms, it seems necessary to extend our social investigation and our inspection of changes in economic attitudes from the world of the lords into that of the actual cultivators. Who were the men who assumed the management of the manorial land and who thus helped to modify so profoundly the structure of the manor? What means did they command? What were their motives and what their hopes?

The answers to these questions still lie in the thick bundles of documents stacked in historical archives. We get the impression that among lessees, clerks, former officials and administrators, were relatively fewer than in the thirteenth century. The evolution of the feudal system in England after the year 1400 probably caused the number of gentlemen 'farmers' to increase; nevertheless many of the better-off peasants also began to 'farm' lands belonging to the ecclesiastical landlords. In the region of Paris burgesses willingly took on the 'farm' of collecting the tithes and manorial rights. But it was most frequently the husbandmen who took over the cultivation of the demesne fields. This last point could help to clarify certain hypotheses of research. Was not the practice of 'farming out' facilitated by the general trend which had, since the thirteenth century, raised some village families above the level of others – a trend which was accelerated by the demographic troubles of the fourteenth century? In any case if recent investigations confirm these first impressions of demesne lands being taken over by modest cultivators of small means, this by itself would explain the necessity for destroying the unity of the demesne by carving it up before letting it out.

The contrast between the land farmed out in the north and that in the south, where *métayage* was all-pervasive, remains to be elucidated. We must make sure, first of all, whether the contrast is not exaggerated by the nature of the evidence. For the northern lands, the records continue to tell us almost exclusively about the typical manors of the Church, whilst the notarial archives of the Midi largely illuminate the practices commonly in use amongst different classes and specially amongst urban communities. Ought we to give equal value to the effects of such different legal traditions? Or should we really consider the uneven penetration of urban economic influences to be responsible for the differences? Was it not, perhaps, the *métayage* contract, associating capital with the exploitation of the soil, that attracted business men, eager to invest their money, accustomed to risk and profit, and able to drain off the surpluses of agricultural production? Some evidence from Italian sources leads us to think this was the case. In the middle of the fourteenth century, when most citizens of Siena had for long been accustomed to apply to their property in the *contado* the system of *mezzadria* cultivation, the monks of a nearby abbey still leased out most of the land *a fitto*, i.e. for a fixed payment. Tuscan records also show that, one hundred years later, three-quarters of the lessors in *mezzadria* were members of the bourgeoisie. But here again it is to be feared that the perspective may be distorted by the origin of the documents, and even more by the more advanced state of urban economic studies in the Midi; for, after all, two-thirds of the sixteenth-century lords who patiently built up and consolidated the *métairies* in the Gâtine of Poitou were landowning nobles, deeply rooted in rural traditions and amongst the wealthiest and mostly highly born persons in the land.[29] The victory of *métayage* in the south, if it proves to be as complete as the imperfect exploration of sources at present suggests, could then best be explained by the depressed economic condition of the peasants. While the 'farmer' of the northern lands lived in affluence, most of the *métayers* of the Midi seemed to be wretched individuals settling on the lords' lands empty-handed and expecting immediate help in the shape of an advance of seed, provision of tools and even sometimes of food for their families during the first year. The contracts of *mezzadria* and *facherie* seem to have held the defenceless peasantry, working on land whose productivity had probably not been increased by improvements in technique as in the north, tightly in a net of economic dependence the strings of which were held by wealthy bourgeois and nobles. It is obvious that only a vast extension of the present limited researches into social history will reveal to us the real reasons why direct management declined and allow us to understand clearly the many forms of the system which took its place.

2. FIXED PAYMENTS

We must not rush to the conclusion that the lords of those days were no more than receivers of fixed payments from the land. A landlord who entrusted his property to a *métayer*, who used often to visit him, to supervise his work, to keep an eye on store room and stable, to help negotiate sales and to associate himself alike with profits and losses, was very close to the soil and remained at least partially a cultivator.[30] He was almost as much involved in the problems of management as the landlord who directed a team of servants through an agent. The extension of all the forms of share-cropping, such as *facherie*, *mégerie* or *gasaille*, ensured that the manor was intimately connected with the business of production, the disposal of surpluses and the day-to-day vicissitudes of the agricultural economy. Nevertheless, it cannot be denied that changes affecting the management of the demesne increased the proportion of fixed payments in most manorial revenues. But it seems that at the same time dues themselves unmistakably sagged. The decline of the manorial economy was largely the result of this fall in fixed payments.

[29] Imberciadori, 478; Jones, 673; Merle, 677   [30] Document No. 184, p. 540

There is a definite relationship between this phenomenon and external and accidental troubles, such as the prolonged absences of the lords, the havoc caused by the military, and other calamities. Each time the political climate worsened the dues registered in manorial accounts correspondingly fell. Receipts from tithe barns also fell, since tithes and proportional payments levied on harvests (*terrages*) were the first to be affected by any disaster.[31] Revenue from destroyed mills and bakehouses fell immediately and they would produce nothing for several years afterwards. Catastrophes thus not only lowered dues abruptly, but kept them low for a long time, because peasants pleaded poverty for many years and made the ruinous condition of their land a pretext for their inability to pay: the accounts of the Norman manor of Neufbourg show that in 1436-1437 60 per cent of the heritable rents were wholly or partially remitted. After the Ile de France had been ravaged in 1360, dame Marguerite of Clermont was only able to levy six *livres* on her land at Montreuil-sous-Bois instead of fifteen, and six *setiers* of oats instead of 46. Exactions which had to be remitted in hard times were then quickly forgotten by the common memory, and thus ceased to be guaranteed by custom: it was hard to re-establish them in the restored villages. When in 1390 the canons of Notre-Dame of Paris demanded the annual *taille* of 33 *livres parisis* from the peasants of Suçy which they had not required since the hostilities of the 'fifties, they had to invoke the king's aid to overcome their men's resistance and to fight them for years in interminable lawsuits.[32] The drying-up of manorial revenue was thus largely the result of war, and this is why French historians, whose attention is focussed on a country that suffered more than others from military action, often tend to exaggerate this decline.

However, it is clear that there was a more general decline caused by depopulation. In deserted villages, and on parts of the village territory which reverted to waste, hereditary dues were lost. Fewer hearths meant fewer individuals subject to *taille*: at Ouges, where all peasant homes owed *taille*, the fall in population reduced by half the receipts from that tax between 1380 and 1445, while on one manor in Sologne, receipts fell in the mid-fifteenth century from twenty livres to two: there were no more than six servile families left.[33] The growing scarcity of men exercised a less direct, but perhaps deeper, influence on manorial profits. Dependent families, sure of finding elsewhere vacant land on which to settle on more favourable condi-

---

[31] We have seen how much the yield of the tithe fell at Antony in 1384, and especially the wine tithe, because the vineyards suffered most from the passage of the troops.

[32] Plaisse, 681, p. 328; Fourquin, 551

[33] Martin-Lorber, 676, Guérin, 553, p. 207; 'of the others there is no knowledge', said the lord of La Ferté-Hubert, 'and I am left with tenancies partly in cultivation and partly in ruin'.

tions, threatened to abscond. To retain them, landlords had to consent to 'moderate' the rate of taxation. They lowered it even more if they wished to reconstruct the village territories devastated by mortality, to attract new cultivators, and to encourage those who had not run away to greater efforts to put everything in order. All attempts at repopulation entailed endless bargaining. Only with great difficulty were adjustments made between landlords' concessions and peasants' claims. The landlords always lost: to appreciate this we have only to read Boutruche's lively and penetrating descriptions of what happened in the Bordelais.

Another factor in the decline is the contraction of peasant activity at the end of the fourteenth and the beginning of the fifteenth century, i.e. at the very time when conditions were most disturbed. The closing of the market for land significantly lowered the product of the *lods et ventes*[34]; the dwindling numbers of livestock directly affected receipts from the right of mortmain; the lords owning markets and rural tolls suffered from the stagnation of trade. It is only necessary to add that the collapse of agricultural prices reduced the value of fixed dues in kind. Between 1430 and 1456 the income of the Teutonic knights at their commandery at Coblenz from this source fell by 40 per cent.[35] In many regions landlords renounced what remained of *champarts* and *tâches*, and attempted to commute grain dues into cash; and also in areas of damage, by forcing the tenants to pay in money, they encouraged them to speed up repairs. But from that period onwards revenues also suffered from the consequences of changes in the value of money; particularly from the continued depreciation of the weak local currencies in which in many regions taxes were reckoned. Many lords probably endeavoured at the time of new rent agreements to stipulate dues in a strong currency. In upper Dauphiné, money rents, which in any case did not form more than a third of total dues, were constantly adjusted at this time by reference to the rate for 'good money', which effectively prevented them from being devalued.[36] This, however, could entail even greater losses since, in order to bind peasants to the land, many manors had abandoned the practice of revokable leases. Long-term or perpetual concessions made adjustments impossible.

Thus, manorial profits were everywhere dwindling away. The fall appears to have begun early. Some English sources show that the decline was under way by 1320. The movement accelerated with the coming of the Black Death and became a rout after 1370. Here are some figures. An *arpent* of vineyard at Argenteuil which was leased in 1300-1320 for an annual rent

---

[34] The yield of the taxes on the transfer of property in the Norman manor of Neufbourg fell from about 13 livres in 1397, to less than 9 livres in 1405 and to 18 sous in 1444; Plaisse, 681, p. 324   [35] Abel, 545, pp. 136 *et seq.*   [36] Chomel, 655

of 12 to 24 *sous parisis*, was let between 1400 and 1410 for a rent of 5 to 15 *sous* and 8 *pintes* of wine; 50 years later the annual rent was between 6 and 12 *sous* besides the 8 *pintes* convertible into 8 *deniers parisis*. Eliminating the variations due to the changes in the currency standard, we can estimate the average value of the rent of an *arpent* of arable on the lands of St Germain-des-Prés at 84 *deniers* in 1360-1400, at 56 *deniers* in 1422-1461, at 32 *deniers* in 1461-1483. At Beaufour in Normandy the revenue from the rent-paying lands rose in 1397 to 142 *livres*; it fell to 112 *livres* in 1428, then to 52 *livres* in 1437; in 1444 it was reduced to 10 *livres*. On the English manor of Forncett, an acre of land was let for an average rent of 10¾d. in 1376-1378, of 9d. in 1401-1410, of 7¾d. in 1421-1430, of 8d. in 1431-1440, of 7¼d. in 1441-1450, of 6¼d. in 1451-1460; but these figures actually understate the real proportions of the fall since the currency in which they were reckoned lost much of its value in silver between 1368 and 1459. An equally sudden fall can be seen in German manorial accounts in the fifteenth century. The lords of Holloben in Saxony had levied 30 measures of rye, 54 of oats and 33 pieces of money in 1394; in 1421 their income fell to 5 measures of rye, 9 of oats and 5 pieces of money. Reckoned in terms of the price of wheat, the index of 'farms' in the county of Göttingen tumbled from 100 to 14 between about 1430 and the middle of the sixteenth century.[37]

*   *   *

In fact the fall in fixed payments, together with the decline in direct management and the necessity to spend money on repairs, significantly affected the financial standing of all lords during this period. Everywhere they appeared to be short of money and on the look-out for outside profit, and for this reason often launched out into careers or adventures which took them away from their estates. However, the various ways of supplementing their incomes, such as taking employment with the more powerful princes who were in search of allies, or the hazardous path of political intrigue and matrimonial alliance, assured the maintenance of nearly all the great aristocratic fortunes. Many manors changed hands. Some passed to the new-rich who belonged neither to the nobility nor to the Church. But we must not be misled by the excessive importance which some historical researchers have tended to confer on the movement of urban capital. Wealthy burgesses who had ousted families of gentle birth from their estates were comparatively few in 1450; and among those who had done so, most had adopted the habits and behaviour of the ancient aristocracy. European society therefore remained solidly a noble one. It is true, notarial records in Provence and in Forez show us some lesser nobles, living like peasants, whose landed property, combining

[37] Fourquin, 551; Plaisse, 681, p. 326; Davenport, 186; Abel, 545, p. 143

free and rent-paying holdings, fragments of tithes and 'tasks', appeared similar to that of some villagers, and who, like them, gave a few measures of grain and one or two head of cattle to their daughters as a dowry. The lower ranks of the gentry were not easily distinguishable from other rustics.[38] Nevertheless, in the fourteenth and fifteenth century, from the point of view of influence and particularly of prestige, an enormous distance always separated the lowest members of the village squirearchy from their peasant neighbours.[39]

Generally speaking, of course, the world of the landlord had considerably relaxed its hold on the rural economy. A large part of the revenues extracted from the soil by the peasants still found its way into the lords' hands, but the endless progress of taxation had greatly enlarged the share taken by the agents of the State. And above all, those receiving fixed payments now no longer lived in a rural society. Although vestiges of the lordship based on the *ban* (*seigneurie banale*) still existed amongst the various dues, it had been bereft of all its significance by the advance of the monarchies. The lords no longer took part in the trade in agricultural produce, profits from which now went to the 'farmers' of their revenues and demesnes. They had even given up the cultivation of the land. In the fifteenth century, agriculture was in most cases, no longer conducted by the masters, but rather by the peasantry.

[38] Gonon, 632   [39] Fourquin, 551

CHAPTER III

The Peasants

As the decline of the manorial economy and especially the cessation of direct management meant that farm accounts were no longer kept, the number of documentary sources available to us has thereby been greatly reduced. Peasant farming, indeed, has no records and hence no history. Evidence, however, is not lacking to convince us that very many branches of the rural economy lost nothing of their vitality during this period, and that the centre of activity moved from the manor to peasant units. This transfer had been in preparation for many years. During the prosperity of the last years of the thirteenth century, many medium-sized agricultural undertakings in the hands of managers and more substantial peasants had been gradually growing in strength though this was concealed by the nature and arrangement of manorial records and obscured by the spotlight thus projected on to the lord's habitations, his rights and his needs. On the great English monastic estates the gradual reorganization of management at that time, by lightening labour services and increasing the weight of money dues, as well as by instituting regular tallage, had shifted the business of the manorial economy on to the shoulders of an energetic peasantry who produced and sold farm surpluses and paid their rents from the proceeds.[1] Already the England of the manor was in the course of becoming the England of the peasant cultivator, and if we take the trouble to look we shall see that the same thing was happening on the continent. The Black Death and its aftermath precipitated the changeover. But in any case, the study of manorial farming in the fourteenth century can never illuminate more than one facet of the rural economy and, moreover, one which was continually shrinking. A parallel investigation into peasant farming, which is both harder and less complete, appears to be more than ever necessary.

I. POPULAR REVOLTS

The more accessible sources all communicate an impression of difficulties and decline. The same fortuitous crises which in the fourteenth century struck the manorial estates with such force that they were shaken to their very

[1] See particularly the suggestive study of the development of the domestic economy of Ramsey Abbey, in Raftis, 201, pp. 217 et seq.

foundations did not spare the households of the poor. These households had in the first place to suffer the repeated attempts of the masters to deal with financial difficulties by squeezing the last drop from manorial rights, and by constantly scaling up their demands on dependants. The latter could not always resist, and indeed ransoms were often paid, and burnt manors and devastated fields repaired, out of peasant savings. Calamities also affected country folk more directly. It seems that the least bearable of these disasters and the ones which engendered the most spirited reaction were those of a political nature. It was not so much sudden accidents like hostilities, pillage or the arrival of troops; much could be hidden from them and they passed by. The rulers' agents, however, remained, and so did resident garrisons defending the country, for whose upkeep the villagers had to provide. They lived off the countryside and imposed not only collective ransoms on hamlets, but also personal exactions on the richer individuals. Threatened with having their houses burned about their ears the villagers of Antony had in 1358-1360 to give the men-at-arms holding the castle of Amblainvilliers wine, flour, salt, wax, and on top of this 20 *moutons d'or*.[2] There was little to choose between foragers from friendly or enemy armies: one took as much as the other. Then the tax collectors appeared and swept up all they could find. And lastly the lords recovered from their men the amount of the 'aid' that they themselves were obliged to pay their sovereign. There is no doubt, that of all the ills which afflicted them, the peasants suffered more painfully and less patiently from the burdens of war and remote taxation. These obligations were the direct cause of much social and religious agitation. The risings reflected the troubles and tensions at the heart of country life.

Throughout the Middle Ages, even at times of great prosperity, spasmodic movements of resistance to taxation plagued the peasant world. They sometimes came to the surface in an abrupt upsurge of feeling, like the coalitions which every so often in the thirteenth century united the inhabitants of neighbouring villages in the Paris region against the *taille*. In north-west France, waves of emotion also dragged bands of rural labourers into hopeless adventures; in 1251 the 'crusades' brought together 'shepherd boys' and 'children', and in 1320 a 'mob of peasants and common people' who started off to march to the Holy Land.[3] In such cases religious motives were at the back of an agitation which could not be controlled and which was perhaps over-stimulated, as when these gangs of supposed pilgrims looted and massacred. The currents of popular discontent became even more widespread in the course of the fourteenth century, and increasingly caught the

[2] Fourquin, 551
[3] P. Alphandéry and A. Dupont, *La Chrétienté et l'idée de Croisade*, vol. II, Paris, 1959, pp. 125 *et seq.*, pp. 259 *et seq.*

imagination of a world which was only too conscious of its own grievances. These developed into purely social movements and as such provoked the combined opposition of the lords, all the more ready to defend themselves since their own economic position was becoming less secure.

A chain of peasant uprisings clearly directed against taxation exploded all over Europe. The earliest occurred in northern Italy which appeared actually at that time to be rather prosperous. After the year 1300 the latent rural unrest became closely interwoven with the powerful movements imbued with the ideal of religious poverty which flourished on the borderlines of Christian orthodoxy. It finally came to a head around Vercelli and, being confused with heresy, was quickly crushed by fire and sword. Then ten years later, in coastal Flanders, peasants, most of whom lived in easy circumstances, took up arms against taxation and attacked the prince's agents; they soon turned their rage against the entire nobility and for years resisted all efforts of the aristocracy to crush them. In 1358 the Jacquerie, a crazy outburst of violence, was at first also turned against the men who bore the king's arms. A few peasants without real leadership had in unreasoning anger begun to kill and in their futile madness they swept with them blind mobs whose doings earned for them their ill-repute. They burned the houses of the rich and were soon exterminated in their turn by the knights. It should not escape our notice that this revolt took place in the north of the Paris region, i.e. in one of the richest countrysides in Europe. Little is known of the riots of the *Tuchins* which swept southern France, but they also seem, on existing evidence, to have been protesting against taxation. England's famous Peasants' Revolt broke out in 1381 in East Anglia – again in the most populated, advanced and prosperous region.

A long period of social ferment had prepared the way for this rebellion which has been studied in greater detail than any of the others. Its origins can be traced back to about 1325, when the lords, reacting against the first marked deterioration in agricultural markets, had increased their demands. The hardening of the manorial system evoked lasting bitterness amongst the peasants, which was manifest in interminable wrangling in the public courts and in a general attitude of insubordination. The royal measures after the Black Death, regulating labour and forbidding rises in wages, affected many rural wage-earners, and aggravated the social discontent. On top of everything came the Poll Tax, a new and yet heavier imposition by the king. Its burden was the immediate cause of the explosion. Conditions were not, however, so bad and country-dwellers were certainly better off economically than they had been fifty years earlier. Indeed, it is clear that the revolt, like others before it, was chiefly caused by the pressure of the authorities and by an increase in taxation felt to be intolerable. It is true the revolts were triggered off by a double current which had its origins in the complexities of peasant society. Bound together against the political authority, the 'workers' in fact belonged to two economic groups whose interests were quite distinct. The most numerous were obviously the prosperous peasants. What they desired was no more than a relaxation of the manorial system in favour of free enterprise, the abolition of serfdom and forced labour, and a reduction in rents. They demanded a greater share in the trade in agricultural products. But by their side stood the real poor, the landless men, the day labourers, the Kentish cottars led by John Ball. These men hoped for much more profound social and agrarian reforms. They wished to see all restrictions on the liberty of labour suppressed. They wanted Church lands to be confiscated and re-distributed in small parcels and the common lands restored. The underlying incompatibility of these two attitudes doubtless caused the revolt to come to grief sooner than it might otherwise have done.

The whole movement of rural unrest that afflicted western Europe during the fourteenth century merits a study in depth. For instance, were the ring-leaders of the rebels always drawn from the most depressed classes? The important thing to note is that in spite of the influence of the half-heretical wandering preachers on the rioters, and especially on the humblest people, and their discourses on Adam and Eve and the fundamental equality of all God's children, and the inspiration of the mystic communities of artisans vowed to holy poverty, all these revolts attacked the lords' wealth only accidentally. If they pillaged and looted the luxurious homes of the rich, it was because they were in the grip of mob violence fired by primitive greed and personal rancour. In reality, the rebels were not aiming so much at the manorial system itself, as at the exploitation practised by the princes and by the military leaders. They expressed the disarray of certain districts oppressed by taxation and the presence of garrisons, and impatience in face of excessive demands and physical damage, rather than actual impoverishment or a general depression of the peasantry. It need only be added that these outbursts were extremely brief, were not repeated and had no permanent consequences. But their very frequency and ubiquity makes it highly desirable that we should examine what there is to be known of the true economic condition of the peasantry in the fourteenth and the beginning of the fifteenth century. For this purpose we must make use of all our sources of information, and for certain regions the information is abundant. Research into notarial records, surveys and what remains of manorial inventories in some selected areas would allow us to verify our hypotheses and to answer the questions which must now be asked.

2. THE RICH AND THE POOR

At first sight, at least two features in the new economic situation helped to ameliorate the peasant's lot. These were depopulation and the consequent relaxation of pressure throughout society. In the apparently desolate landscape, where the wastelands were encroaching and the villages were falling into ruin, the labourer in field and vineyard was obviously – at least in the intervals between waves of destruction and the passage of soldiers and tax collectors – much less poor than his ancestors had been, because the land which supported him was not so inequitably distributed. In addition, the entire peasantry gained from the fall in manorial rents, which was itself a sign of economic liberation. The relaxation occurred gradually, almost imperceptibly. In France in the later Middle Ages charters of franchise were fewer and more limited and granted no more than small exemptions. Peasants were able to free themselves by bargaining and digging in their toes, although, it is true, some manors held firm. But the signs of a gradual enfranchisement were evident everywhere. In one place tenants, evading their master's supervision, would succeed in transforming a rent-paying holding into an allod, as in one Provençal village where in 1308 almost all the land had been held in dependent tenancies, but became in the next hundred years independent property subject only to the authority of the prince and his taxes. Elsewhere again, long-term leases more favourable to the lessee spread at the expense of the precarious and uncertain tenancies so widespread when land was scarce and men starving. Thus in west Midland villages, tenancies 'at will' appeared by the end of the fourteenth century to be definitely declining in relation to long-term leases. Finally, personal dependence was coming to an end as well. Registers of mortmain show that the numbers of *hommes de maisnie* belonging to the counts of Hainault fell by 70 per cent between 1317 and 1350, and then again by half before the end of the fourteenth century. When the lords of Nivernais about 1440 tried once again to exploit their serfs, they encountered stiff resistance; their dependants, fewer in number than their ancestors, commanded a much more favourable economic position; several maintained four or five servants in their own homes. If we are to believe their lords, many who grumbled at paying a *taille* of 50 *livres* in fact possessed more than 2,000 *écus*; and if they protested against *formariage*, it was only because they wished to marry their daughters 'into the nobility and bourgeoisie'.[4]

Nevertheless it is very difficult to be certain that the extra weight of royal taxation did not largely compensate for the lightening of manorial rent, and whether, in the final analysis, peasant households were really able to keep for their own use the larger part of the fruits of their toil. This uncertainty

[4] Juglas, 639; Bossuat, 624

explains why historians have been able to come to such very different conclusions about the economic condition of peasants at that time.[5] Many have held that they were in a very depressed state, and it must be admitted that there is much evidence of widespread destitution. Thus it appears obvious that loans for purposes of consumption obtained by poor people from moneylenders in the rural market towns were very frequent at that period: the financiers of Asti made their fortunes from exploiting peasants' money difficulties and in the fourteenth century their counting houses multiplied and prospered in the territory of the counts of Savoy.[6] English villagers, as described by John Langland in his writings, were badly fed and lived on milk and gruel; to eat bread and drink beer was for them a luxury. As for the French peasants, to a visitor from England, Sir John Fortescue, they seemed to be half starved and clad in rags at a time when economic recovery was already well under way. Inventories of goods seized for mortmain in the fourteenth century and sold for the benefit of the duke of Burgundy in his bailiwick of Montagne describe the chattels of the poorest kind of folk. A few tattered clouts or thin quilts, a chest, some old garments, an animal or two, and a few measures of grain were all the tax collectors could find in a peasant hovel. And when Gaston Fébus found himself hard up in 1378 and proposed to sell his bondsmen of Béarn their liberty, 40 per cent of them replied that they had not the necessary money with which to pay.[7] We must take care when considering the condition of peasants at that time not to take too favourable a view, because the decline in manorial rent was largely due, as we have seen, to peasant impoverishment. Two obvious signs of the general worsening of their economic condition are revealed by wills of the Forez after the year 1380; these signs are smaller dowries and the introduction of associates from two households (*pariers*) to farm the same tenancy jointly and to form a single hearth.[8]

To go beyond these general impressions, indeed, and to come closer to economic reality, we shall have to find out exactly how wealth was distributed amongst the peasants. Did those who lived in the precarious state described by some tax surveys and contemporary literary writings (which ought not, of course, to be accepted as evidence without a double check) form the whole of rural society? Was there not another class of cultivators alongside them who were more prosperous? In other words, what became of the movement already gaining ground in 1300, by which the differences in wealth between villagers were getting wider, and by which some of them had raised themselves well above the mass of their poorer fellows? Our

---

[5] Abel, 545, pp. 157 et seq.   [6] Document No. 73, p. 427
[7] Vignier, 652; *Bulletin de la Société des sciences, lettres et arts de Pau*, 1879
[8] Gonon, 632

enquiry is not a straightforward one. Certain manorial documents, such as successive lists registering the rents due from tenants, show clearly how, little by little, the plots granted by the master were dispersed in some cases and were concentrated in a few hands in others. But this evidence is only valid if the whole village formed part of the manor. Neither can we be sure whether a peasant's holding really constituted the whole of his property. One man, who held what seemed an absurdly small strip, could easily have other possessions elsewhere, which would lift him into another, much higher, rank in the hierarchy of wealth. Taxation records are more reliable, and significant results can be expected from an examination of the numerous surviving series of censuses, especially in southern Europe.[9] Finally, there is hope that rural archeology, so little exploited in the west, will produce evidence. Excavation of villages deserted in the fourteenth and early fifteenth centuries would not only furnish decisive information about the structure of the peasant farms themselves, of which the dwellings in the built-up areas of habitation were but the centre. It might perhaps also help us to assess the real gap separating rich and poor and the size of the latter group. However, even in the present state of our researches, we can already state four preliminary points.

1. We can see that differences in peasant wealth continued to grow during the first half of the fourteenth century. Here for example are some figures extracted from the records of an English manor, Weedon Beck. They allow us to group the dependent inhabitants at three moments of time according to the rent that they paid.[10]

Amount of rent	Number of tenants		
	1248	1300	1365
More than 1 *li*			2
From 15 to 20 s.			1
From 10 to 15 s.	3	4	7
From 5 to 10 s.	46	33	26
From 2·5 to 5 s.	15	26	8
From 1 to 2·5 s.	7	18	8
Less than 1 s.	1	19	18
Labour service only	9	7	3

Sources of this type always leave a wide margin of error. In this case it is

[9] Wills must not be neglected either; 3,228 have been preserved for the single county of Forez, dating from the fourteenth century, and more than two-thirds of these relate to peasants; Gonon, 632   [10] Morgan, 408

certain that commutations and consolidation of dues had changed the classi-
fication of landed rents between 1248 and 1365; besides, it is very likely that
many tenants whose dues were less than one shilling were not peasants but
occupiers of houses in Weedon Beck, which was a little urban centre. If we
leave this last group out of our computations, and also those tenants who
were only burdened with labour servives, it appears nevertheless – (*a*) that in
the second half of the thirteenth century the number of tenant families rose
from 71 to 81 and that this growth caused some holdings to be broken up;
(*b*) that the number of small tenants paying less than 5s. and probably being
in possession of less than a quarter of a virgate grew; and their proportion
rose from 30 to 60 per cent; (*c*) that the number of tenants in 1365 was
definitely smaller than in 1248; (*d*) that the proportion of small tenants paying
between 1s. and 5s. was, as in 1248, once again 30 per cent, and (*e*) that the
decline in the population merely allowed the regrouping of some tenancies,
and the formation of a dozen farms considerably larger than the average.
The movement appears similar, and even more pronounced, when reflected
in the documents of Stoneleigh Abbey in the Midlands: the percentage of
peasants whose holdings exceeded 45 acres was 5 in 1280 and 57 in 1392.[11]

2. We can in fact guess that, after the 'seventies of the fourteenth century,
depopulation and the adoption of less rigid forms of leases encouraged the
change. In one Leicestershire manor in 1341, 625 acres were held by 26
villeins, most of whom cultivated tenancies of customary size, the 'virgates'
of 25 acres; in addition 50 acres were leased in minute plots to 25 cottars. In
1477 there were no more than three cottars, and only 17 other non-free individuals remained, but the area of land which they shared was the same, even
though seven of their number each possessed holdings made up of between
2 and 3 virgates. Amongst the free tenants of the manor, the redistribution
had been more rapid still. 19 of them cultivated 160 acres in 1341; in 1477
four only held more than 225 acres between them. A similar tendency can be
seen in Sologne at the same period. Mortality and migration here produced
many gaps (in one locality in the mid-fifteenth century only 18 out of the 32
hôtels (houses) on which tithe was levied were occupied) and this gave some
peasants the opportunity to assemble a great deal of land. In 1448, one rent-
paying tenant was installed in a large *cheseau* (holding) which had all the
appearance of a real manor ('a tall house placed on the said mount . . . with
a double chimney . . . surrounded by great square ditches'); he held as well
a grange, two stables, a huge assemblage of arable land in a single block, and
three other *cheseaux* on which no houses were built. Serfs had also occasion
to round off their possessions substantially. The possessions of one of these
dependants, put up to auction in 1411-1412, was sold for 117 *livres*: it com-

[11] Hilton, in 669

prised, apart from fine domestic equipment and cattle let out on livestock leases, a great deal of land and four houses.[12]

It must be noted, moreover, that in the more fertile village territories the places left vacant by depopulation were often very speedily reoccupied by migrants moving in from poorer soils. Density of settlement was not therefore necessarily reduced and it does not seem as if, in spite of plague, destruction and the migration to Paris, peasant farms in the rich grainlands of the Ile de France were either reduced in number, or redistributed, in the period between the mid-fourteenth century and the end of the fifteenth century.[13] We know that the concentration of men on soils most favourable to cultivation corresponded with the progress of *Wüstungen*.

3. It is obvious, indeed, even on the few village territories on which the population did not become more thinly distributed, that the leasing of the manorial demesne, let on long or share-cropping leases in very small parcels, considerably extended the area of land which peasant families had at their disposal. Some of the poorest could in this way have managed to add to their farms enough land to provide for their needs and to have been able to stop working for others. We must assume, however, that the break-up of the demesne profited mainly the larger cultivators, who were in a better position to conclude advantageous leases. In this way, they consolidated their possessions and demonstrated their superiority. Already in England at the end of the thirteenth century – documents of St Peter of Gloucester prove it – there were well-to-do peasants who employed labourers. One hundred years later day labourers and servants who no longer found work in the houses of the lords could still be employed on the large peasant farms which were probably less unusual than formerly. The English Poll Tax returns of 1380 show that wage-earners, still very numerous in some villages, mostly worked in the service of the well-to-do peasants: in one Midlands locality where 16 servants and 18 heads of families lived, one of the latter gave work to seven of the former.[14]

The village community, drawn closer together by the misfortunes of the times[15] and the necessity to oppose the lords' demands, the tax collectors' impositions and the exactions of the military, often tried to put obstacles in the way of the progress of these large peasant farms. But it rarely succeeded in halting their growth. It is true that in face of fortuitous calamities these

[12] At Stoughton, Hilton, 667, pp. 100-102; Guérin, 553; *ibid.*, pp. 240-241, the movables were sold for 12 livres, they comprised a bed with bedding, vats and casks, a bin, a table, chairs, and a mortar; document No. 163, p. 521. [13] Fourquin, 551

[14] R. H. Hilton, 'Some Social and Economic Evidence in late Medieval Tax Returns', in an unpublished paper.

[15] We can see it opened in Lombardy, after the middle of the fourteenth century, to the poorest peasants, who had until then been rigorously excluded; Toubert, 651

large-scale enterprises proved, as had formerly the lords' demesnes, more vulnerable than others; the collectors of tithes had their eyes on their wealth and extorted more from them. But, closer to the soil and connected with men in the market towns, well-to-do peasants were in fact more favoured by economic conditions than any other group in rural society. There was nothing, therefore, to hold back the slow movement towards the accumulation of land and movable capital in the hands of larger tenants, 'farmers', petty manorial officials and priests (one *curé* of the Burgundian mountains owned in 1377 much ready money, a gold chain, a whole set of copper and pewter vessels and a quantity of linen and he had 714 animals on livestock leases distributed amongst about 50 cultivators in his own and neighbouring parishes).[16] Together with a few enterprising petty nobles, and some intelligent administrators of ecclesiastical property, these men, often associated with business men from the towns, continued to stimulate economic activity in a period of apparent recession and to keep up the level of agricultural production.

3. AGRICULTURAL PRODUCTION

In order to take a balanced view of the general atmosphere of depression communicated by contemporary records, we should be wise to check by a detailed investigation whether the material conditions of rural labour were not in reality somewhat ameliorated by circumstances, such as the decline in population or even by the stimulus of the troubles themselves. The massive transfers of population which sometimes modified the geography of agrarian settlement so profoundly in certain regions, like north-west Germany, actually facilitated the transition from a very primitive economy based on the destruction of the forest to an intensive and organized cereal-growing agriculture, closely linked with stockraising. Elsewhere the changes corrected the effects of an excessive extension of arable cultivation which the over-population of the later thirteenth century had pushed forward on to so many infertile soils. Migrations relieved poorer countrysides of their starving and excessive multitudes, returned unproductive lands to woodland and pasture, and concentrated dwellings in more appropriate localities. Less is known about this period of beneficial readjustment than about the times of the great reclamations. It would seem, however, that most features of the European landscape visible today took shape during this period. Many villages were regrouped, lost their outlying holdings and dwellings and were more closely knit into a built-up agglomeration. Around them the reorganization of the field systems which, here and there, had been in preparation since the year 1300 was put in hand. Outside these better organized arable lands controlled

[16] Vignier, 652

by communities of individuals acting in close co-operation, on the fringes set free by retreating settlement, sometimes even on the very site of former villages vacated by death or flight, better opportunities now presented themselves for the deployment of larger farms worked by single incumbents enclosed by hedges and protected against division by stricter family laws unfavourable to partition.

Many grew up in the thirteenth century and their increase seemed to be encouraged by depopulation. Here and there, in the few regions where excavations have been conducted, archeological study of village lands reveals that the substantial farms, the *bordes*, or large *métairies*, were relatively numerous. In any case they achieved complete autonomy and their compact lands were wholly relieved of collective constraint. Indeed, the easing of demographic tension temporarily softened the bitter conflicts in which the users of the commons and the owners of the new farms, scattered as freelancers on the borders of the village arable, had been engaged in the thirteenth century. In this way pastoral or woodland economy was encouraged on the soils which were less suited to cereal-growing. We might assume that on grassland and arable fields alike this would have resulted in a rise in the productivity of each unit of labour.

It is probable that productivity was also raised by the increase in the average size of the farms which (except perhaps in the exceptionally prosperous districts where repeated immigration obstructed the reorganization and simplification of the much subdivided fields) everywhere brought the dimensions of most cultivated units into line with the capabilities of single families assisted by few servants.

Indeed, on some English lands where figures for grain yields are available, these rose significantly, although in the early decades of the fourteenth century they had been declining, probably because the arable was over-extended and perhaps also because the soils were exhausted by an over-intensive cultivation. Historians still lack perfectly reliable figures for the demesne lands of the bishop of Winchester, but in their present form, subject of course to revision, the data so far shows that the average yield of wheat sown rose gradually from 4·22 to 1 in 1300-1349 to 4·35 in 1350-1399, and to 4·45 in 1400-1449; that of barley rose from 3·8 to 3·96 and then to 4·31; that of oats from 2·42 to 2·85 and to 3·62. Giving up the less fertile fringes and concentrating the agricultural effort of the manor on productive soils favoured the tendency.[17] But it may also have been stimulated by more efficient equip-

[17] Beveridge, W., 'The Yield and Price of Corn in the Middle Ages', in *Economic History Review*, 1927. These figures are only those of the master's lands, which, merely by giving up the marginal areas, had gained in average fertility; furthermore, the whole effort of the available domestic labour was then concentrated on a much more restricted area. What was the state of the tenants' lands?

ment and methods. Indeed, we ought not to accept without closer enquiry that the fourteenth century was a period when technique stagnated, although actually the history of the rural economy at this point raises a whole series of questions to which we cannot yet give precise answers.

Can we assume, for instance, that the tools used by medium-sized farms deteriorated and that peasants reduced their purchases of iron and returned to the home manufacture of makeshift ploughing equipment? Should we not rather assume that they made greater use of the services of specialized craftsmen? In a period in which there is abundant evidence of the forward movement of material civilization and a gradual diffusion amongst the lower ranks of society of utensils and tools of which previously only the more well-to-do had had the monopoly, the latter hypothesis should not be considered too outrageous. Research in this direction could it seems rely on evidence likely to prove much more rewarding than that of the thirteenth century. For instance, the iconography of the period is far richer and the greater realism with which objects were portrayed makes their use as source material possible. There is also a good deal of information in written sources, in the stipulations of lease contracts and domestic registers. Valuable evidence also comes from inventories of post mortem inquests and merchants' accounts. The early fifteenth-century ironmonger's shop in the little episcopal town of Riez in Provence, where iron shoes for animals could be bought, as well as ploughshares and nails, had an extensive peasant clientèle.[18]

The story of livestock and of plough teams during the fourteenth century would also be worth special attention. *A priori*, we may suppose that cattle belonging to the peasantry would have suffered badly from pillage and looting.[19] But can we not also assume that the retreat of the sown area and the corresponding advance of grassland permitted them to be better fed and therefore more efficient at their job? The speed with which flocks were replaced during the reconstruction phases is most striking, as also is the abrupt growth of stock after the economic recovery of the mid-fifteenth century: in the village of Maillane in Provence where in 1430 there were about 40 draught animals, in 1471 this number had gone up to 200.[20] And the progress of cattle-raising, stimulated by urban speculation, probably helped to fertilize the fields. It meant that they were better cultivated (*métayage* contracts of the Toulouse region imposed a greater number of ploughings on the farmer[21] and better provided with manure.

Finally we have to take account of the improvements which took place

[18] Baratier, 691
[19] Accounts of the receipts coming from the passage and rights of pasture in the Norman manor of Neufbourg show that the number of cows raised by peasants fell from 190 in 1397 to 30 in 1437 and the number of pigs from 2234 to 430 in 1444; Plaisse, 681, p. 323.   [20] Baratier, 420   [21] Sicard, 617

in the rotation of crops. Clearly to be observed in certain English demesne records, changes in the traditional cycles prompted before 1300 by the growing demand for food and the exhaustion of the soil, became more widespread during the fourteenth and early fifteenth century. As is shown in the following table, constructed from material referring to certain great ecclesiastical demesnes, there was an extensive decline in winter wheat in favour of higher-yielding barley and of leguminous crops.[22]

Manor	Year	Wheat	Oats	Barley	Leguminous plants
Wistow (Ramsey Abbey)	1307	50%	4%	30%	16%
	1340	38%	7%	19%	36%
	1379	19%	3%	34%	44%
Leicester	1363	21%			17%
	1401	17%			32%
Sherborne	1425	40%	13%	42%	5%
	1435	34%	10%	50·5%	5·5%
	1452	20%	10%	61%	7%

Similar developments went on at the same pace on peasant farms. This can be verified in the accounts of Leicester Abbey by comparing the proportion of different cereals taken for tithe from the parish crops with the demesne harvest. It corresponded with certain new trends in the market: brewing, for instance, increased purchases of barley in the towns. It kept pace also perhaps with gradual changes in dietary habits (the consumption of pea soup appears to have been widespread). It was stimulated more directly by the need to provide more nourishing fodder for the cattle sold for meat, as well as by the wish to shorten the fallow period by sowing legumes as fertilizers after cereals. In Flanders, where the existence of large towns provided such a marked stimulus to economic initiative, already by 1328 the cultivation of peas on the fallow was widely practised (the harvest which one peasant of Bourbourg complained he had lost during the risings of western Flanders was composed of one-third each of wheat, oats and beans).[23] Written records in that region refer in 1323, 1368 and 1372 to the first known efforts to combine ploughing and pasture in a new rhythm: these were agreements with urban butchers, by which enclosed meadows on harvested fields were set up for three, four or even six years. They reveal a little later the extension of turnip cultivation on stubble.[24] Were these innovations really as sporadic as they appear to be from the documents which today make them known to us? Were they confined to a few of the more advanced country districts? In

[22] Raftis, 201; Hilton, 392 and 667   [23] Pirenne, 644, p. 208
[24] Lindemans, 123, 1, pp. 83-84, 412; Verhulst, 137

Sologne, a poor and backward country where beat burning was widely practised on the heathland (*brandes arces*), and where, even at the end of the eighteenth century, a third of the ploughland of a parish had to be left fallow for ten years in succession, there were fields in the fifteenth century which produced turnips, rape and *potage*, i.e. peas and beans, in the intervals between rye crops.[25]

4. PEASANTS AND TRADERS

One last problem, as hard as any posed by the history of peasant agriculture: to what extent were agricultural undertakings engaged in commercial activity?

Much of our evidence gives an impression of a general recession in rural trade during the fourteenth and early fifteenth centuries. If we look at the grain trade, we see in fact from the accounts of many English manors that price levels sag and profits from sales disappear. We also see that, in order to protect themselves against violent fluctuations in prices, townsfolk attempted to take the provisioning of their households out of the hands of professional traders: one Genoese merchant went to great trouble to buy grain at the source himself, even though he had to do it from a distance through his agents, in order not to have to use local retailers. We see grain universally hoarded: one enquiry conducted at Carpentras in 1473 shows half the householders possessing large stocks of foodstuffs.[26] The climate seemed to be one of a general contraction in exchange. Armed conflict upset commercial connections, the instability of money seriously disturbed trade and fear of scarcity distorted the traffic in cereals. All our hypotheses must therefore start by assuming a slackening of activity and a deterioration in the markets.

Nevertheless a study of the economy of the countryside suggests that we should to a certain extent mistrust the conclusions put forward by historians of long-term commercial trends. Their field of observation is, of course, trained on much wider horizons and is fixed on the few great trading centres. But often the threads connecting these large markets with the small country ones followed devious routes in the course of which economic tendencies changed both in intensity and direction. Of course we could never ignore the fact that customs dues levied at the English ports on the export of wool and the import of wine suffered a constant decline in the fourteenth century. But,

[25] Guérin, 553, p. 74

[26] Heers, 700, p. 42; R. H. Bautier, 'Feux, population et structure sociale au milieu du XVe siècle: l'exemple de Carpentras', in *Annales, E.S.C.*, 1959. If, indeed, many rural lords in France, Italy and the Low Countries transferred their place of residence at this period to a big town, they deflected into that town the stream of fixed payments and dues which nourished their household; such lordly migrations could well explain in part the slowing down of trade.

even so, we must consider that such a trend, closely connected as it was with political decisions and a control made all the easier to supervise and manipulate since it was exclusively a maritime one, could reflect not only restriction of exchange in general, but geographical transfers of production and consumption. It would be dangerous to interpret them, without closer examination, as signs of a general slowing up of trade at the local level of the producer or even of the country towns where buying and selling took place. The problems of commercial activity in the countryside have to be studied on a smaller scale. Greater knowledge of the main streams of trade, such as the huge and regular traffic in cereals from the Baltic ports to Flanders, or from Languedoc to Genoa in the fourteenth century, certainly permits some aspects of these problems to be better understood. But a different approach is, nevertheless, required. The rapid progress of historical research in the urban economy of the later Middle Ages is a useful step. But to unravel the whole story it is still necessary for historians of cities and business men, whose participation in this task is absolutely indispensable, to direct their enquiries into particular channels.

★   ★   ★

We must not really expect to find the most copious and valuable evidence in the archives of the countryside itself. It is obviously essential to extract carefully statistics of sales from the documents of manors, notaries and princely agents concerned directly with rural affairs, and to interpret them in relation to local conditions. But, with few exceptions, all these transactions of which we find traces in local records refer only to the surpluses from the great demesnes. Some of this material is evidence of a still considerable connection with outside trade: in 1448 on the Wiltshire demesne of one great lord, it was possible to sell 86 per cent of the net revenue in grain.[27] As for the decrease in the volume of sales which most manorial documents reveal, we must be careful when we relate it to the development of demesne farming. Was the fall always evidence of a general decline in exchange? Did it not, rather, in most cases reflect the giving up of direct cultivation? While dealings between lords and merchants shrank, we might suppose that tenants, who have not left us any records, replaced their lords in the trading nexus.

It is not impossible to trace in records of the rural scene some of the stimuli which continued to induce villagers to buy and sell whatever the state of production or market. Searching through marriage contracts and dowries, we can gauge how far social convention and the need to appear prosperous combined to force peasant households to conduct commercial transactions. Many country folk obviously endeavoured from motives of

[27] At Winterbourne Stoke on the land of Lord Hungerford; Postan, in 6, p. 195.

pride to keep more animals in their stables than they really needed to maintain their farms in good heart. Thirteenth-century prosperity had introduced habits of consumption into the countryside which the harder times had not everywhere eradicated. To the profit of travelling pedlars and town shopkeepers, girls continued to be arrayed in foreign cloth and 'merceries' on their wedding day. All peasant women in Forez, even the poorest, owned after their marriage the 'garland' which had held their veil in place. In Lombardy during the fourteenth century we can see that the sale of spices grew and that village communities took steps to curtail waste at betrothal feasts and funeral bakemeats.[28]

According to all the evidence, rural trade continued also to be vigorously stimulated during the fourteenth and fifteenth centuries by the development of taxation, which forced peasants to obtain cash at certain seasons by all means available to them. In England taxes had never been a very great burden relative to rents on land, and they remained light. But on the continent the need to pay taxes was the force which drove countrymen into the arms of the merchant. The dealers who collected saffron in the Abruzzi mountains on behalf of the great Nuremberg merchants knew this well: they timed their visits for February, the very moment when the villagers had not only to scrape together enough to pay for the transhumance of their flocks to Apulia, but also when they had to discharge the royal *taille*. And how many tax gatherers were not in some way interested parties in trade? In addition country folk who were pressed by tax obligations sold not only their goods but also their labour. The increasing weight of *tailles*, while sharpening the need of peasant households for cash, probably also hastened the growth of a class of rural artisans which up to now historians have found mostly in connection with urban commercial undertakings. These tendencies call for a better sifting of tax records and manorial rent books for details of the pressure exerted by the cash demands of prince and lord on country farms, and the collection of all the evidence, however scattered, which gives some idea both of peasant wealth and the sums of money that it was made to disgorge. No other method of investigation would produce a more reliable estimate of the volume of transactions at village level; we might sometimes even hope to plumb by this method some of the underlying and obscure factors which motivated the entire rural economy. For instance, by keeping prices and wages very low did not the demands of the princes in the fourteenth century favour the exploitation of the countryside by the city-dwelling holders of liquid funds? Did they not in some way create the very favourable conditions for the diffusion of the textile industry in the hamlets around Augsburg and Bourg en Bresse or in the Languedoc countryside? Was not the vitality of the

[28] Gonon, 632, p. 157; Toubert, 651

establishments providing village credit, which multiplied all over the place at that time, primarily supported by the need for cash to pay taxes?

All the frequent, but scattered, references in manorial documents which illuminate other aspects of the local market must be re-examined. There is no need to point out the importance of all records concerned with taxes levied in the village, even on merchants themselves, and on the effects of the measures on commercial transactions[29]; or of all the infrequent entries in accounts which, listing wage-earners and describing the nature of their wages, allow us to glimpse a little of the purchasing power thus liberated in the neighbourhood of the demesne. The archeological evidence relating to material culture, such as peasant clothing, furnishings, and even dwellings, would also be of incomparable value. More abundant and accurate than for previous epochs, we could expect it to enable us to make a less arbitrary estimate of how self-sufficient was the domestic economy. The knowledge that an Inquisition Post Mortem of a widow's house drawn up in 1377 in a village of Sologne includes a wool comb, a spool and two pounds of spinning wool is enough to prompt much-needed research on the domestic manufacture of textiles and on the manner in which skilled crafts were combined with agricultural occupations.[30] Nevertheless scarcity of direct evidence in the countryside itself about the relations between peasants, middlemen and retailers cannot be denied.

*   *   *

The best vantage point from which to observe the process of exchange, and from which the most fruitful researches can be made, is without doubt the small town. It was almost always the seat of justice and finance, that lower machinery of princely administration which, provided with a clerical staff, frequently left a legacy of well-stocked archives behind it. In addition, scriveners and notaries permanently pursued their vocations there, and finally the town offered the most favourable meeting ground for country and trading interests. In every region the town was the centre of a flexible network of lively local fairs, which was still growing in the fourteenth century and was matched with the principal dates of the agricultural calendar. At the end of the agricultural season, when the fruits of harvest and vineyard were sold and when farmers bought their plough animals, the entire population of the surrounding villages would assemble there: the fairs determined the customary dates of peasant marriages, for which even the poorest families pre-

---

[29] The product of the farm of 'customs' levied on sales in the Norman borough of Neufbourg in 1444-1445 reveal, for instance, that 60 per cent of the transactions usually concerned cattle, 10 per cent grain and that much wine was bought from retailers; Plaisse, 681, p. 111   [30] Guérin, 553, p. 230

pared by purchases of wedding ornaments; attendance did not drop even at moments of great danger from war or epidemic. In each of these smaller centres lived a few of the entrepreneurs who acted as intermediaries between peasants and large-scale commerce.

The registers or account books kept by these men have sometimes been preserved. They permit us to observe in detail how during the space of a few months their businesses were organized. I take as an example a man who was active on the eve of the fifteenth century at Riez, a little town in the southern Alps. A notary by profession, he owned land in the village territory and in the neighbouring countryside, and he was still in the process of enlarging his landed property. But he also owned two shops. In one he sold ironmongery, ingots, nails and spare parts for tools, and his clientèle for this kind of commodity appears to have been largely a peasant one: in his other shop, the smaller gentry and churchmen of the district bought imported cloth. However, the merchant himself was more interested in the grain trade, which offered much higher profits through the many openings provided by the enormous variations in price levels. He sold a little grain in the town itself, but the larger part he lent to the small folk of the neighbourhood, either in the spring when the corn-bins were nearly empty, or at seed time. He was repaid at harvest time, at high interest rates; sometimes, though, he accepted payment in the form of labour for his own land. His largest profit, however, came from the huge mule trains which he sent to distant places where demand was strong and permanent, and especially to Fréjus, a regular port of call for Genoese cargo ships. In 1417-1418 he sent more than 2,000 *setiers* there. The grain came partly from his own demesnes, but he also bought large quantities. He would, for instance, trade wine imported from lower Provence for grain harvested by the mountain folk: in this way in the year 1417-1418 1,500 *setiers* of wheat and 500 *setiers* of oats, barley and spelt passed through his hands. Finally he kept himself supplied with cereals by taking over the 'farm' of the manorial revenues in the neighbourhood of the borough: in 1420 in return for 200 florins he was entrusted with collecting tithes which commonly produced more than 1,200 *setiers* of different cereals. This notary – and we know the important role he played in the everyday life of the rural society from the very fact of his profession – was at one and the same time landlord, rent collector, direct cultivator, 'farmer', moneylender and merchant, and combined in his person all the common services which the town performed for the score or so of villages around about. Through his business dealings we can see quite clearly the working of exchange at the local level. At that time, of course, the trade in the south of France was going through a sombre and restricted phase.[31]

[31] Baratier, 691

The records put particular emphasis on the magnitude of the speculation in the little country centres on the products of animal husbandry, on the animals themselves, their meat and leather. Upon them rested the prosperity of the richest and most enviable men, those butchers who swaggered on the sidewalks, exhausted the communal grassland by overgrazing it with their flocks and flouted the nobles. At the little town of Digne in 1407, one grazier was denounced to the authorities for keeping 80 cattle to the detriment of others, but to his own great profit. The people of Montferrand in Auvergne, who were surprised that in 1440 no more than three or four mercers' shops remained active in their little administrative borough, and who looked askance at the prosperous butchers, supposed that the cleverest business men 'found more profit in cattle than in other merchandise', and consequently proceeded to keep their flocks in the suburbs; 'so much had the cattle multiplied' they said 'that all else, such as arable and vineyard, was ruined'.[32] On this point opinion from all parts was agreed. The changes in economic conditions had not weakened the interest in pastoral economy which small-scale business men had shown in the thirteenth century. On the contrary the activity at cattle fairs and the prosperity of traders in meat and fleeces at Lincoln and Coventry, as well as in the most remote towns of Auvergne or the Alps, give the impression that trade in animal products was more actively sustained than any during the troubles of the fourteenth century because it was so lucrative and was little affected by any of the factors which contributed to the general recession.

These considerations lead us from the town to the neighbouring villages to examine the method of production. We find confirmation in all the evidence – ample in certain countries and likely to be multiplied even further by a systematic study of the structure of the farmhouse and its contiguous buildings for cattle and fodder – of an extension of stockraising to the detriment of all other branches of farming. Its growth was not restricted to the proximity of towns, for it reached up into the highest mountain pastures where at the end of the fifteenth century whole communities would arrange to spend the summer months in grazing cattle on the alpine meadows.[33] Here and there in the countryside we can see a new enclosure movement unfolding, and an increase in the number of individual farms where cereal-growing and the use of grassland were dovetailed together, free from collective constraints. Depopulation, the return of unoccupied land, and shortage of manpower, certainly encouraged many small farms to change over to a pastoral economy based either on common grazing or on the letting of pasture by the owners of wasteland, or again on the use of privately-owned

---

[32] Sclafert, 83, p. 140; Bossuat, 693, pp. 131-132
[33] See, for example, Ilg, 310, on the Austrian mountains

meadows protected by hedges. It is also possible that the retreat of the area put down to cereals was hastened by the desire to obtain greater profits. There are good reasons for thinking that many a furrow buried today beneath the English turf, and many a field reverted to grassland and pasture in north-west Germany, ceased to be sown with crops because cattle prices, unlike grain prices, kept high at this time and because the fattening of cows or sheep was more profitable than producing cereals.[34] This is yet another reason why we should not accept too pessimistic an interpretation of *Wüstungen* and other signs of apparent agrarian contraction.

When in the 'forties of the fifteenth century it was clear that a recovery was taking place, the first signs were the rapid growth of flocks. Like those of the princes, for instance: René of Anjou, Count of Provence, in order to equip a recently acquired demesne bought 1,300 sheep in 1458 through two cattle-dealers of Manosque, and in the following year 29 oxen at an alpine fair; he rented pasture and sold the fleeces of 3,000 animals.[35] It must not be thought, however, that the cattleyards of the lesser gentry, farmers and peasants of every condition were restocked more slowly. In 1471 in 8 parishes near Vence 28,000 sheep and more than 1,100 cattle were recorded; every country family there owned between 100 and 200 head of stock.[36] This taxation document reveals most strikingly the importance of pastoral capital and the speed with which it was replaced reflects the reality of the general progress. Another sign is evident too: at that period there was a revival everywhere of the antagonism between cultivators and flockmasters, which the fall in population had damped down for two or three generations. The conflicts about common lands, prohibitions (*défens*), hedges, rights of common pasture, which had since 1350 been assuaged became universally more acrimonious; obvious evidence of an agricultural recovery and a rise in population. But while we can see the tension gradually building up to its former level in village territories which were actually less populated than before, we must suppose that the space occupied by graziers was considerably enlarged, and consequently we must conclude that during the period of recession, pastoral expansion had in fact benefited by the retreat of arable. On many peasant farms had it not, at least in part, compensated for it?

Nevertheless, even after having allowed for this switch towards animal husbandry, the actual proportions of which incidentally need to be separately measured in each region, the final impression remains that the level of economic activity in the smaller towns, and therefore all rural trade, contracted markedly during the fourteenth century. The reduction in the number of shops at Montferrand was really the result of a decline in the rural clientèle

[34] Hilton, 668; Timm, 570   [35] Sclafert, 83, pp. 237-238
[36] Document No. 195, p. 551

which, by depriving the traders of customers, caused them to turn to stock-raising. We can compare two fragments of toll accounts. One set covers the winter of 1299 at Pertuis, a country market town, and the other set, from Aix, the small regional capital quite close, covers the last months of 1348 and most of the following year, i.e. the period which came immediately after the impact of the Great Plague. The second set of accounts, it is true, shows that the countryside was still travelled by mule drivers and pedlars, and penetrated by traders, many of whom lived in the villages and were more than half peasants, buying grain, fruit and wine and selling salt, leather, dried fish and draught animals. The economy of the countryside, therefore, was still largely an active one. But we see, nevertheless, that the volume of traffic as measured by those paying tolls, was actually three times smaller in Aix, the great crossroads of trade, than it had been at Pertuis, the modest staging post, during the three corresponding months of 1299, half a century earlier.[37]

*   *   *

The example of Aix shows quite clearly that the working of the rural economy was inevitably involved in commercial machinery, the key to which must be sought in urban records. Research monographs devoted to the commerce of a town can contribute fundamentally to our knowledge of exchange at the village level if, like the researches of Philippe Wolff at Toulouse and J. Schneider at Metz, while they are based on an exhaustive examination of the city archives, they do not lose sight of the rural area surrounding the town.

I have purposely used the word 'monograph' since this problem, more than any other, demands to be set in a regional context. In the first place, it is important to plot the exact limits of the zone in which the influence of the individual urban area was exercised, and also to gauge the intensity of its effect, all the more because the degree of urbanization was in fact so different in the various provinces of western Europe in the fourteenth century. In England it seems that the power of the towns was considerably weakened and much of their activity was transferred to the countryside. This was particularly the case with certain crafts. We know that textile manufacturing spread into the country and went on developing there. In some Norfolk and Suffolk and, later, Cotswold villages, a few capitalist clothiers, who continued to farm their lands and some of whom were still bound by ties of servitude, controlled weavers, fullers and dyers scattered in peasant households and closely connected with their work. By providing them with wool and selling the cloth they produced, the clothiers captured both the trade and

[37] Archives des Bouches-du-Rhône, B.1595 and 1477

the management of capital. In these regions we can talk of a real escape from the control of the towns.[38]

The opposite happened in the Germanic regions where at that time many new towns were being founded and old ones were growing. There had never been so many peasants begging to be admitted as burgesses of Colmar as between 1362 and 1371, while many of the vinegrowing villages of Alsace grew into towns. The same growth was taking place in the forest regions of north-west Germany where many deserted villages emptied at that time because the inhabitants left to set up in neighbouring markets, which had turned themselves into little towns. There are studies which show us how the enormous demand for timber created by the construction of new town quarters made exploitation of forests worthwhile, encouraged lords to protect their woods, and helped the formation of *Wüstungen*. Anyone who seeks to understand the development of the German countryside, to discover its original features and to explain the signs of growth which were displayed, especially in the eastern and northern provinces, must take account of this movement of urbanization.[39]

The situation in France was more complex. It cannot be denied that some towns declined. Nevertheless depopulation further served to concentrate urban wealth, to increase the resources of some great houses and therefore to inflate their consumption and expenditure as well as the amount of capital they could invest in the country. The connection between rural and urban world was thus only partly relaxed. On the other hand, the two were drawn more closely together in northern Italy, where the power of the urban economy continued to expand. As we have seen, the entire growth experienced by lower Lombardy about the year 1400 was set in motion by townsmen. In the hope of profits even higher than those expected from usury or trade, the townsfolk rented church lands in the *contado* and improved them. They took their place in the countryside at the head of the group of entrepreneurs and carried with them on their path to prosperity the wealthier peasants.[40]

★   ★   ★

In spite of the marked falling-off in trade throughout the greater part of Europe, the presence of large inhabited centres thus continued to act as a ferment in the rural economy even in regions where urban influence suffered a decline. Above all, it continued to stimulate the life of the satellite towns. Without making use of urban documents, which at this period become very

---

[38] Carus-Wilson, 695
[39] Timm, 570, pp. 83 *et seq.*; document No. 170, p. 527
[40] Cipolla, 611

abundant and explicit, it would be impossible to isolate some facts which are indispensable to our understanding of the formation of wealth in the country-side. For instance, we could not compare the relative position of workers in urban workshops and in agriculture and thereby appreciate what exactly were the conditions of employment in villages. Urban records also contain invaluable data about the consumption of agricultural commodities and thus about what was required from producers. The last point is especially useful for our study of an economic phenomenon of the first importance, still imperfectly understood, but which nevertheless contributed most effectively in keeping the peasant economy active in spite of all the new factors which tended to slow it down. This was the question, more obvious in the large towns, of the growing popularity of commodities which had previously been the perquisites of aristocratic society. Thus, the demand for wine in towns appears in the fourteenth century to have been greater than ever before. To point out that the daily wine ration of the abbot of St Peter of Ghent was $3\frac{1}{2}$ litres, and the monks' ration was not much less, that the merchants of Paris sold to the royal court in 1417 10,000 hectolitres of 'French' and Beaune wine, merely confirms that the long-established lines of supply were still operating. It is of greater interest for the student of viticulture to learn that the people of Bruges drank an average of 100 litres of wine per head per year, that taverns proliferated in Paris and that townsfolk acquired the taste for drinking '*petit vin*',[41] because the large-scale supply of everyday beverages directly affected the economic position of a host of small vinegrowers. As for the history of animal husbandry, it would be immensely illuminating if urban archives could confirm what we already guess, i.e. that the consumption of leather increased significantly in the fourteenth century, and that meat appeared more frequently than formerly on the table of citizens of small estate.[42]

Likewise only documents of urban origin allow us to observe the economic links which in various ways attached a whole country region to a large town. These links may well appear very close. Many townsmen in fact continued to put what money they had into the acquisition of rural property.[43] Fear of famine was a universal motive, and, for the richer men, the upper class way of life traditionally connected with landed estates had lost none of its glamour. We must be wary, it is true, as in the thirteenth century, of exaggerating the magnitude of these purchases and their consequences and we should accept that the intrusion of the merchant or the richer artisan into the

---

[41] Craeybeckx, 697; Rey, 707; Dion, 105, pp. 472 *et seq.*
[42] Reflecting on two German articles, R. Mandrou clearly puts the question 'Théorie ou hypothèse de travail?' in *Annales, E.S.C.*, 1961, pp. 965 *et seq.*
[43] Document No. 190, p. 546

direct cultivation of land was generally rather limited. Business men and burgesses of middle rank mostly interested themselves in property producing the most easily disposable commodities, such as vineyards or meadows for grazing; when arable came into their possession they leased it on 'farm' or *métayage* to peasants. A few ennobled officials alone succeeded in assembling large landed estates of the manorial type in the vicinity of the greater or smaller administrative capitals. This was the case around Paris, where genuine burgesses had by the fifteenth century hardly acquired any but small rent-paying holdings. In the suburbs of Lyons the most rapidly assembled landed estates were formed by officials, like one Jossard, master of laws, and servant of the king of France, who within twenty years had become the owner of two great castles and manors extending throughout the countryside.[44] Men of this rank indeed lost their spirit of enterprise more quickly than newly enriched merchants. They were in a hurry to display the free and easy attitude towards money of the born gentleman. When they were established on a country manor the process of management and the destination of profits were not markedly altered.

We must, however, recognize that fourteenth- and fifteenth-century towns, and especially the smaller regional capitals which were the seat of the superior lords and the organs of political power, succeeded in appropriating a larger proportion than formerly of rural produce. They had in fact become a more effective point of concentration for all manorial profits. The movement of the noble families into urban residences and the practice which had become usual amongst the great lords of letting out the collection of some of their revenues to townsmen 'at farm' had in combination helped to consolidate the latter's dominating economic position. By townsmen, of course, we do not only mean merchants, or even burgesses, but members of urban ecclesiastical communities, and noblemen plying a profession, or officials who seemed already to have proved themselves one of the most dynamic elements in society. These individuals rarely leased land; what they leased was much more frequently tithes or other seigneurial rights. For them the transaction was usually a form of forward purchase which put into their hands huge quantities of agricultural commodities capable of being resold at a profit. In villages these men, better placed to conduct business and probably using more efficient methods of collection, took the place of traditional lords. The share of the peasant-produced surpluses levied by the manorial institution which they took passed into the town economy by a more direct route.

In the vicinity of those great towns which historians have studied in detail we can also see that many townsmen continued to exploit as far as they were able the chronic shortage of money in the rural world still intensified by

[44] Fourquin, 551; Fedou, 698

355

the demands of the tax collectors. They thus employed in credit operations a large part of the cash resources accruing to the towns. Such observations in the Paris region as have been made give the impression that economic and political troubles then made the purchase of rent charges a less secure and profitable venture. The widespread movement which had in this way forged many links in the thirteenth century between town and country slowed down and practically stopped in the fifteenth century.[45] On the other hand no decline can be discerned in moneylending, short-term credit or loans for immediate consumption. All these operations closely connected with trade, like contracts for forward delivery which concealed scandalously high profits, provide through the notarial registers in Mediterranean lands our most fertile source of information. Innumerable money loans were camouflaged by advances of grain repayable after harvest and threshing. In fact at this period the economic condition of most villagers remained too depressed, and the circulation of money too restricted and disturbed by the expansion of taxation, for the business relations of peasants and burgesses not to be clearly marked by usury. Townsfolk abused the superior power they owed to their reserves of money. One great burgess of Montferrand had in 1451 to seek the royal pardon for having exceeded acceptable limits when lending money on excessively hard terms, buying grain and wine from poor people before the harvest and selling them later at much more than the normal market price.[46]

Nevertheless, various flexible practices of great complexity enabled many business concerns engaged in both trade and credit to link townsmen and country men in genuine partnerships, many of which contributed most effectively in keeping very modest rural farms in contact with the outside world. Take, as an example, a merchant of Toulouse who in December 1382 bought from a peasant a stock of wool to be delivered in May: he paid the wages of the shearers, for whose keep however, the seller was responsible; he paid half the price immediately and the money thus advanced sufficed to keep the animals through the winter; between them these two men co-operated in a genuine partnership to make the most of their capital.[47]

We can see that there was not much difference between purchase, credit and those innumerable contracts which brought farmers and burgess moneylenders into association with each other. Here too it would be invaluable if we could ascertain for certain selected towns if such practices were really limited in this period or if these associations did in fact help the rural world to overcome its difficulties. These partnerships provided a firm support for middle- and small-sized agricultural units. The contract of *métayage*, so widespread in the locality of Italian and French Mediterranean towns on lands

[45] Fourquin, 551   [46] Bossuat, 693, p. 133   [47] Wolff, 709, pp. 205-211

made vacant by migration where the townsmen had been able to assume control, was in fact one form of co-operation between burgesses and peasants adopted for the purpose of cultivating the arable and producing cereals. Many other forms limited to the supply of equipment, a pair of oxen, a plough with or without a ploughshare, or seed, can also be distinguished, but they all pre-empted a portion of the harvest for the city granaries. Large numbers of associations of this type, it seems, were also formed in the branches of agricultural activity which were of particular interest to business men, namely viticulture and stockrearing.

The obvious vitality of vineyard and pastoral economy and the close association of peasant labour and the bourgeois capital which supported it were by no means new to the fifteenth century. Historians can see them more clearly at this period, because the sources cast a brighter light on them; but everything leads us to suppose that economic phenomena of the same kind brought towns and boroughs equally close to their rural environment from the thirteenth century onwards. To my mind, the important thing is that these activities had not weakened during this period in the history of the countryside. While the manor struggled in the throes of the inescapable problems arising from natural calamities, accidents of war and depopulation, the conduct of village economy passed decisively into the hands of peasants backed by townsmen's money. To illustrate this marriage of town and country interests, I shall quote a contract signed in Toulouse in 1489, which stipulated that in times of pestilence the master could go to stay outside the town in the house of his *métayer*, while in time of war the latter could take refuge in his master's house inside the shelter of the ramparts.[48] The participation of townsmen's capital resulted, indeed, in transferring to urban society the fruits of rural toil and in subjugating the country to the town. But the process was none the less a stimulating one. We must see in it a manifestation of the spirit of enterprise which had not been weakened by adversity in spite of all the damage and destruction. Thanks to this spirit of enterprise there was a slow accumulation of the forces which after the middle of the fifteenth century were to launch the rural economy and the whole country life of western Europe into a new leap forward.

[48] Sicard, 685, p. 33

Documents

I IX-X Centuries

About the year 800, documentary material suddenly becomes available; it illuminates the countryside which until then was veiled in obscurity. Most of the texts were drawn up by order of Carolingian rulers who wished to modernize the cultivation and administration of their lands. That is why these documents are to be found in those provinces of the Empire which were most completely under the royal influence: Lombardy, the Rhine valley, the old Frankish territories of Neustria and Austrasia. Outside these regions written sources are very rare.

A. THE CAPITULARY *DE VILLIS* AND ITS ANNEXED DOCUMENTS

I

This is a unique manuscript, dated to the first third of the ninth century, which presents the text of a long series of decrees divided by the editors into 70 paragraphs. It concerns the management of the royal demesnes, but the sovereign who caused it to be drawn up is not named. Was it Charlemagne himself before his imperial coronation – in which case the Act would be valid for the entire Frankish kingdom – or was it his son Louis while he was king of Aquitaine between 794 and 813 – which would restrict the range of the capitulary to that province alone? The debate is still open (an exposition of the controversy and a bibliography can be found in F.-L. Ganshof's La Belgique Carolingienne, Brussels, 1958, p. 162). At all events it is clear that the Act does not aim at innovation, but is rather a re-statement of good practices. It is a very exact document and immensely useful.

*   *   *

1. *The royal intentions are clear: to supervise the administrators who, far from their lord, managed a vast section of his patrimony. They had to be prevented from enriching themselves, from distributing the property in their charge amongst their friends and from oppressing the peasants and craftsmen on the estates. One of the major difficulties of manorial economy in the early Middle Ages is touched on here. Landed property was immense, and given the methods of transport available, impossibly dispersed. How then were the managers to be controlled?*

2. *Each estate supported a huge number of domestic servants who had to be fed and supervised, but who also formed its principal wealth: there were specialized workers, women who wove cloth, ploughmen, and slaves housed under their own roofs on individual plots who were equipped with draught animals by their lords. The amount of arable appeared to be limited. Livestock rearing was very important on the royal estates: it supplied plough beasts, leather and wool, which together with wood were basic raw materials, and above all else, war horses, and meat the main foodstuff of the armed men. Finally there was great wealth in the*

*forest which had to be protected against beat burning, depredation and the progress of clearing,
since swine were fattened there and it harboured game. Hunting and fishing were an essential
source of food supply.*

3. *What did these estates mean to the king? They were, first of all, well-equipped residences where he could always find meat, wine, grain and raiment for himself and his retinue.
They were centres for victualling his army on its annual expeditions. Finally they were storehouses of provisions in which to dip when supplies failed elsewhere. The king also hoped to
extract some money income from them.*

4. *Moreover, the estate economy had trade connections through the purchase of seed and
wine and the sale of harvest surpluses. The market, where the dependent peasants could exchange a part of what they produced for the money required to pay their dues, was never very
far away.*

1. We desire that our great estates which we have established to serve our needs
should be wholly at our service and not at those of other men.

2. That our domestic servants should be well treated and should not be impoverished by anyone.

8. That our stewards should look after our vineyards which belong to their office,
and see that they are well cared for; that they should put the wine in good vessels and
that they should watch carefully that it should not be in any way spoilt. If they should
have to procure other wine, that they should arrange to buy it in a place from whence
they may bring it to our estates. And if it should happen that more of this wine should
be bought than is needed, that they should inform us so that we may express our will
on this subject. That they shall appropriate for our use the produce of the vinestocks
of our vineyards. That they should place in our cellars the dues of our estates which
must be delivered in wine.

23. On each estate, our stewards shall raise cows, pigs, sheep, goats, he-goats, as
many as they are able. And they must not in any way fail to do this. And let cows be
given over to our slaves as well so that they may accomplish their service, without
allowing the numbers in the stables or the ploughs earmarked for the service of the
lord to be reduced. When they make their liveries of meat, let them take oxen which
are lame but not sick, cows and horses which are not scabby and other animals which
are not sick. And as we have said, let not the numbers in the stables and ploughs be
reduced because of it. . . .

28. We desire that, every year in Lent, on Palm Sunday, they take care according
to our orders to bring the money arising from our profits, after we shall have learned
the total of our profits that year. . . .

30. We desire that, out of the total crop, they shall arrange to put on one side that
which must be earmarked for our service; that they shall similarly put on one side that
which must be loaded on the army waggons, from the houses as well as from the
herdsmen, and that they shall take account of how much they have used for this
purpose.

31. Similarly, let them arrange to set on one side that which they ought to give to
the prebendary slaves and to the work shops of the women, let it be distributed at the
right time and let them tell us what they have given and where it came from. . . .

32. Let each steward take care always to have the best seed; by purchase or in some other manner.

33. When all has been thus distributed, sown and done, what remains of the harvest must be kept to be sold or stored according to our orders . . . .

36. Let our woods and forests be well supervised; let them clear the places which ought to be cleared, but let them not allow the fields to encroach at the expense of the woodland; where woods ought to be, let them not allow any cutting or damage; let them watch well over the game in our forests, let them maintain fowlers and hawks for our use, and let them diligently raise the dues for these things. And if administrators, our managers and their men, allow their swine to fatten in our woods, let them be the first to render the tithe in order to set a good example, and after that let other men pay the whole tithe . . . .

45. Let every administrator have around him good workmen, such as blacksmiths, goldsmiths and silversmiths, shoemakers, tanners, carpenters, shield makers, fishermen, bird trainers, soapmakers, men who can brew beer, cider and perry and other beverages, bakers who can make small loaves for our use, men who know how to make nets for hunting, fishing and how to take swarms of bees . . . .

54. Let every administrator take care to see that our domestics apply themselves well to their work and do not waste their time at market . . . .

60. In no case should powerful men be made managers, only men of middling condition who would be faithful.

Capitulare de villi et curtis (ed. A. Boretius),
in *M.G.H. Leges, Capitularia regum Francorum,*
I, 1881, pp. 83-89.

*   *   *

Three fragments of inventories were transcribed immediately before the capitulary De Villis on the sole manuscript by which it has been preserved. The editor entitled them Brevium exempla ad describendas res ecclesiasticas et fiscales. *They were indeed models intended to guide the ecclesiastical administrators anxious to take account of the material condition of their houses. The models were not imaginary ones, but were copied from descriptions of estates which were subsequently been lost.*

2

This fragment described the 'hall' of the royal estate at Annapes on the borders of Flanders and Artois. Within a great enclosure was the house of the lord and numerous less solid buildings to shelter the domestics, the cattle and the provisions. The equipment was miserably poor; a few pieces of household linen for the reception of the lord; a few precious and carefully-listed metal tools. But the five mills for the use of the house and the peasants of the surrounding country yielded a good return. The importance of animal husbandry was quite evident. There was little money in the store-rooms, but everything needed for the larder. Amongst the stores, the balance of the previous year's crop should be noted. The proportion of spring cereals (oats in this case) is very limited. The ratio of crop to seed appears to vary from one year to another and to be in the year of the inventory almost unbelievably low.

We have found in the *fisc* of Annapes a royal palace built of very good stone, with three chambers, the house surrounded by a gallery with eleven small rooms; below a cellar and two porches; inside the courtyard seventeen other houses built of wood with as many rooms and the other dependencies in good condition: a stable, a kitchen, a bakehouse, two granges, three storehouses. A courtyard provided with a strong palisade, and a gate of stone surmounted with a gallery. A little courtyard also surrounded with a hedge, well ordered and planted with trees of different kinds.

Equipment: a set of bedding, linen to cover the table and a cloth.

Tools. Two copper basins, two drinking vessels, two copper cauldrons and one of iron, a pan, a pot-hook, a firedog, a lamp, two axes, an adze, two augers, a hatchet, a scraper, a plane, a chisel, two scythes, two sickles, two iron-tipped shovels. Plenty of wooden tools.

Farm produce: old spelt from the previous year: 90 baskets[1] from which 450 measures of flour can be taken. Barley, 100 *muids*. From this year: 110 baskets of spelt; 60 have been sown and we found the rest. 100 *muids* of wheat, 60 have been sown and we found the rest. 98 *muids* of oats. One *muid* of beans, 12 *muids* of peas.

From the five mills: 900 small *muids*; 240 *muids* of which have been given to the prebendaries, and we found the rest.

From the four brewhouses, 650 small *muids*.

From the two bridges, 60 *muids* of salt and two sous. From the four gardens, 11 sous, three *muids* of honey. From dues one *muid* of butter.

Bacon from the previous year, 10 smoked porkers. 200 this year's smoked porkers, with sausages and lard. This year's cheese, 43 loads.

Livestock: mares: aged, 51; three-year-olds, 5; two-year-olds, 7; yearlings, 7. Horses: two-year-olds, 10; yearlings, 8; stallions, 3. Oxen, 16; donkeys, two; cows with calves, 50; heifers, 20; this year's calves, 38; bulls, three. Old pigs, 250, young ones, 100; boars, 5. Ewes with lambs, 150, yearling lambs 200, sheep, 120. She-goats with kids, 30; yearling goats, 30; he-goats, three; geese, 30; chickens, 24; peacocks, 22.

Brevium exempla ad describendas res ecclesiasticas et fiscales
(ed. A. Boretius, in *M.G.H. Leges, Capitularia regum francorum,*
I, 1881, pp. 254-255).

3

1. *This inventory of a property of the Bavarian abbey of Staffelsee, a dependancy of the bishopric of Augsburg, illustrates once more the paucity of equipment and tools, the abundance of domestic servants, the marked reliance on pastoral activities and the insufficiency of the reserves of grain (no more than could feed the servants until the Feast of St John; what did they eat during July?)*

[1] Measure of volume equivalent to 12 *muids*.

2. *The estate consisted of about 625 acres of arable and hayfield. The 42 manses – all 'furnished' that is, inhabited, and therefore useful – were divided into two juridical categories.*

3. *The system for the servile tenures was uniform. They had to deliver a few products of the smaller animals, but chiefly they had to provide labour: their occupants were in fact domestic servants, enabled to feed themselves on the land which had been granted them. Nevertheless a limit had been set to some of their tasks: changes which would bring their status closer to that of the free manses had begun.*

4. *The latter were quite differently burdened. We can ignore the five almost noble tenures which owed no more than riding service; they did not assist in the estate labour. Others delivered quantities, sometimes considerable quantities, of food. They further participated in the cultivation of the estate in three ways: by cultivating a set piece of land of about 3 hectares for their masters; by putting a labourer at the disposal of the master during a certain number of weeks; and by fulfilling certain definite tasks.*

We found there, attached to that religious establishment, a 'hall' and a lord's house with other buildings. Dependent on this 'hall', 740 day-works of arable land and meadows where 610 cartloads of hay could be gathered. We found no grain except that which we distributed to the prebendaries: 30 cartloads. They have thus received their provender until the Feast of St John and they are 72 in number. Of malt: 12 *muids*. One horse, 26 oxen, 20 cows, a bull, 61 heifers, 5 calves, 97 ewes, 14 lambs, 17 he-goats, 58 she-goats, 12 kids, 40 pigs, 50 hogs, 63 geese, 50 chickens, 17 beehives. Of bacon; 20 smoked porkers with sausages, 27 pieces of lard (*saindoux*); a smoked sheep, 40 cheeses. Of honey: half a measure; two measures of butter, five *muids* of salt, three measures of soap. Five sets of bedding, three copper cauldrons, six iron ones, five pot-hooks, a lamp. 17 casks bound in iron, 10 scythes, 17 sickles, 7 adzes, 17 axes, 10 goatskins, 26 sheepskins, a fishing net.

There is a women's workshop, where there are 24 women. We found there: five pieces of woollen cloth (*drap*), six bands of linen and five pieces of cloth (*toile*). There is a mill which renders 12 *muids* every year.

Attached to this 'hall', 23 free *manses*, furnished. There are six which each render every year: 14 *muids* of grain, four piglets, a piece of linen woven in the workshop, two chickens, 10 eggs, a *setier* of flax seed, a *setier* of lentils. Every year five weeks of work, three day-works of ploughing, cutting a cartload of hay in the lord's meadow and bringing it in, and doing message service.

There are six others which each plough two day-works every year, sow them and harvest them, scythe three cartloads in the lord's meadow and bring them in, work two weeks, join with another to deliver an ox for military service, and when he does not go there, rides wherever he is ordered.

There are five *manses* which deliver every year two oxen and ride wherever it is commanded of them.

There are four *manses* each of which ploughs every year nine day-works, sows them and harvests them, scythes three cartloads in the lord's meadow and brings them in, works six weeks a year, transports the wine, spreads manure on a day-work of the master's land, delivers ten cartloads of wood.

And there is one *manse* which ploughs nine day-works every year, sows and harvests them, scythes three cartloads in the lord's meadow and brings them in, does message service, delivers one draught horse and works five weeks a year.

Nineteen servile *manses*, 'furnished', each of which renders every year one pigling, five chickens, ten eggs, feeds four of the lord's swine, ploughs half a carucate, works three days a week, does message service, delivers a draught horse. The wife weaves one piece of cloth and one piece of woollen cloth, prepares malt and bakes bread.

M.G.H. Capitularia regum Francorum (ed. A. Boretius),
Vol. I, pp. 251-252.

B. THE *POLYPTYQUES*

This is the name given to the most complete of the inventories which analyse the constituent parts of each villa *and which register the burdens of the* manses *after surveying the tenants. They are real deeds used in lawsuits to defend the rights of the lord. Such texts multiplied during the ninth century by order of the rulers who were protectors of religious establishments, as part of the monastic reform of 817 and because of the need to reconstruct manors after the incursions of the Normans. Many of them have been preserved, either as fragments included in more recent descriptions, or, more or less mutilated, in their original state. Examples are those of the abbeys of St Amand, St Bertin (844-848), St Remi of Rheims (861), Lobbes in Hainault (868), Lorsch in the Rhineland, and Prüm, which was drawn up after the Norse invasion in 892. But the most ancient, the most famous as well as one of the richest, was the one drawn up by order of Irminon, abbot of St Germain-des-Prés, between 806 and 829, and edited in a masterly fashion by Benjamin Guérard in 1844.*

4

The extent of the immense landed possessions of St Germain-des-Prés and the network of roads which converged on the monastery can be seen from the map opposite.[2] The contrast between the great villae, *grouped around the abbey, and the much more dispersed possessions in the forested lands in the west and south is very marked.*

5

1. All farming units on the villa *of Villeneuve St Georges, those of the slaves living under their own roof as well as that of the lord, contained fields, meadows and vineyards (the village was situated in the Parisian vinegrowing district). The land grew winter and spring cereals. Double labour was required from tenants on the winter course, since it was ploughed twice over; but the area sown with wheat and rye equalled that sown with grain on the spring course.*

[2] Drawn by M. de la Motte-Colas, in *Mémorial du XIVe centenaire de l'abbaye de Saint-Germain-des-Prés*, Paris, 1959, p. 50.

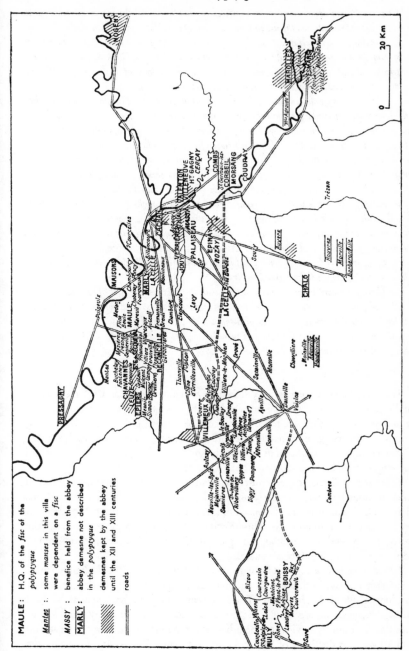

MAULE : H.Q. of the *fisc* of the *polyptyque*

Mantes : some *manses* in this villa were dependent on a *fisc*

MASSY : benefice held from the abbey

MARLY : abbey demesne not described in the *polyptyque*

demesnes kept by the abbey until the XII and XIII centuries

roads

The territorial possessions of the abbey of St Germain-des-Prés in the early nineteenth century

Light fences, thrown down every year, protected the hayfields. All the woodland belonged to the estate, but the tenants had the use of it on payment of dues 'for rights of pannage'.

2. The church was itself a little satellite estate. It comprised three farms (about 75 acres of arable land) held by the priest and the peasants who worked for him. However, the lord drew a profit from the parish church, as he did from the mills, in the form of a customary 'gift' from the serving priest and labour services from the dependent peasants.

3. We can distinguish free and servile manses, as at Staffelsee. The plots of land attached to the former were much larger, but the size of tenures in the same category were very unequal. One servile manse was occupied by eleven people, another by only four. Obligations were not so heavy as at Staffelsee and the difference between free and servile manses was less. Low dues from both groups (note the dues in wine which were the principal object of commercial operations). More extensive, the free manses owed: (a) heavy taxes, replacing military service, levied in cash (one year the tenants paid 48 pieces of silver, which implied considerable access to the market); (b) work which necessitated the use of a plough-team. On the other hand manual services (in the lord's vineyard) and domestic service (note that only female peasants who were not of free birth were compelled to do this) burdened the servile manses. The contrast nevertheless becomes blurred: one cartage service required of a free manse is commuted into a livery of prepared wood, and the tenant had mainly to fulfil, apart from certain fixed tasks, the indefinite services which characterized servitude.

4. There is no correlation between the status of the manses and that of the men who occupied them; marriage between settlers and slaves encouraged such discordance. This shows that legal distinctions were in process of disappearing amongst the peasant population. The commissioners noted that all the villagers were 'men', i.e. the dependants, of the 'lord', The abbey: that was the important thing.

There is a master's *manse* at Villeneuve with a dwelling and sufficient other buildings. 172 *bonniers* of arable land which can be sown to produce 800 *muids*. There are 91 *arpents* of vineyard where 1,000 *muids* can be harvested, 166 *arpents* of meadow, from which 166 waggons of hay can be gathered. There are three flour mills the rent of which brings in 450 *muids* of grain. Another one is not rented out. There is a wood four leagues round where 500 swine can be fattened.

There is a well-constructed church with all its furniture, a dwelling house and sufficient other buildings. Three *manses* are dependent on it. Divided between the priest and his men, there are 27 *bonniers* of arable land and one *ansange*.[1] 17 *arpents* of vineyards, 25 *arpents* of meadow. This provides a horse, as a 'gift'. In the service of the master, nine perches and an *ansange* are ploughed, two perches for the spring grain, and four perches of meadow are enclosed.

Actard, villein (*colonus*), and his wife, also a villein (*colona*), named Eligilde, 'men' of St Germain, have with them six children called Aget, Teudo, Siméon, Adalside, Dieudonnée, Électard. They hold a free *manse* containing five *bonniers* of arable land and two *ansanges*, four *arpents* of vineyard, 4½ *arpents* of meadow. They provide four silver sous for military service and the other year two sous for the livery of meat, and the third year, for the livery of fodder, a ewe with a lamb. Two *muids* of wine for the

[1] Measure of area

right of pannage, four deniers for the right of wood; for cartage a measure of wood, and 50 shingles. They plough four perches for the winter grain, and two perches for the spring. Manual and animal services, as much as is required of them. Three hens, 15 eggs. They enclose four perches of meadow . . . .

. . . Adalgarius, slave of St Germain, and his wife, villein (*colona*), named Hairbolde, 'men' of St Germain. This man holds a servile *manse*. Hadvoud, slave, and his wife, slave, named Guinigilde, 'men' of St Germain, have with them five children: Frothard, Girouard, Airole, Advis, Eligilde. These last two hold a free *manse* containing one and a half *bonniers* of arable land, three-quarters of an *arpent* of vineyard, 5½ *arpents* of meadow. They look after four *arpents* in the vineyard. They deliver for pannage three *muids* of wine, a *setier* of mustard, 50 withies, three hens, 15 eggs. Manual service where they are ordered. And the female slave weaves serge with the master's wool, and feeds the poultry whenever she is ordered to do so.

Ermenold, villein (*colonus*) of St Germain, and his wife, slave: Foucard, slave, and his wife, slave, named Ragentisme, 'men' of St Germain. These last two hold a servile *manse* containing two *bonniers*, one and a half *ansanges* of arable land, an *arpent* of vineyard, two and a half *arpents* of meadow. They owe the same as the preceding one. The female slave and her mother weave serge and feed the poultry whenever they are commanded to do so.

Polyptyque de l'abbaye de Saint-Germain-des-Prés (ed. A. Longnon),
Paris, 1886, pp. 218 and 230.

6

1. *In this forested region, there were no vineyards on the estate; only a few meadows, and small dispersed fields, which had to be enclosed as soon as the grain sprouted, since they were surrounded by a woodland area devoted to pasture. There was much woodland and many pigs: spring crops predominated. There were seven holdings only, but all very much larger than at Villeneuve St Georges, since the yield was much less. Half a manse, with limited service, was granted to one of the peasants who managed the estate.*

2. *There were six and a half manses, but 16 households, although this overpopulation did not mean any visible extension of cultivation at the expense of the neighbouring forest. There were no legal distinctions between the manses, even though they existed between people, such as free women, and slaves, and those men of intermediate status, the 'lides'. Particular services burdened the non-free, such as making things and cartage for the slaves and a money chevage (money, even here, was in circulation) for the lides.*

3. *Labour services were less heavy than in the Paris region, and presuppose the possession of a plough-team.*

(XI. List of Dues at Nully)

There is at Nully a *manse* belonging to the lord, with other buildings in plenty. There are ten little fields there containing 60 *bonniers* which can be sown with 200 *muids* of oats, nine *arpents* of meadow where ten loads of hay can be cut. There is a wood estimated to be three leagues long and one league across where 800 pigs can be fattened.

Éloi, slave, and his wife, *colona*, named Landine, 'men' of St Germain, live at Nully. They hold a half-*manse*, containing six *bonniers* of arable and half an *arpent* of meadow. They plough four perches of winter corn, and 13 of spring corn. They spread manure on the lord's furlong and do nothing and render nothing else because of the service which they give.

Ahahil, slave, and his wife, *lida*, called Berthilde, 'men' of St Germain. Their children are Abram, Avremar, Bertrada. And Ceslin, *lidus*, and his wife, *lida*, called Leutberga. Their children are Leutgarde, Fryshilde. And Godelbert, *lidus*. His children are Gedalcans, Celsovide, Bladovilde. These three live at Nully. They hold a *manse* having 15 *bonniers* of arable and three *arpents* of meadow. They take one cart in Anjou and one to Paris in May. They pay two sheep for military duties. Nine hens, 30 eggs, 100 little planks and as many shingles, 12 staves, six hoops, 12 straw mats. They drive two waggons of wood to Suré. They make four perches of enclosure with little stakes around the 'hall' of the lord, four perches of hedge around the meadow and as many as are necessary at the harvest. They plough eight perches of winter corn, 26 of spring corn. Between ploughings they spread manure on the lord's furlong. Each one pays four deniers for his head.

There are at Nully six and a half inhabited *manses* and one half empty. There are 16 hearths. They pay 12 sheep for military duties, 5 sous 4 deniers for *chevage*; 48 chickens, 160 eggs, 600 planks and as many shingles, 54 stakes and as many hoops, 72 mats (*faculas*). They take two waggons to the wine harvest and 2½ waggons in May, and half an ox.

The slaves are:

Éloi, Galbert, Sinope, Rainard, Gansbold, Fermond, Gilbert, Faroir, Abrahil, Faroin, Aiguin, Gautmar, Hildevoud; these deliver the mats (*faculas*) and do the carrying.

The *lidi* are:

Maurice, Gandulf, Bertlin, Ceslin, Gilbert.

The female slaves (*ancillae*) are:

Frotline, Ansegunde, Aude, Framberte; these fatten the poultry and weave the cloth, if they are given the wool.

The female *lide* are:

Berthilde; Leutberge, Gotberge, Celse, Faregilde, Sigause, Bertenilde; these pay four deniers of *litmonium*.

Rainard holds one *bonnier* of the demesne from the master; Gilbert holds, apart from his *manse*, two *olcas*.

Polyptyque de l'abbaye de Saint-Germain-des-Prés (ed. A. Longnon),
Paris, 1886, pp. 158-161.

7

The polyptyque of St Rémi of Rheims is much shorter. Note the preponderance of winter corn in the cultivation, as well as the introduction of leguminous plants into the cycle of crops. But the country is a vinegrowing one and the estate economy is mainly directed towards stockraising. Each unit of taxation and husbandry corresponds to a single household. All are equally, but lightly, burdened. We can see particularly that the tenants are hardly at all associated with estate tasks: they work separately the individual plots to be cultivated as labour service which have been allotted to them.

At Longeville there is a *manse* belonging to the lord with buildings, two presses, 'hall', stables and an orchard. Eleven fields are attached to it where 60 *muids* of wheat can be sown, also three meadows where five waggons of hay can be cut, seven vineyards and as many vinedressers, where 120 *muids* of wine can be harvested.

Girard holds one *accola*. He works a plot 40 perches long, three wide during the year. He delivers every year one *muid* of wine, a hen, five eggs, a waggon load of wood and does manual service.

Adelus holds one *accola*; the same.

Vulfingus holds one *accola*; the same.

Telgildis, free, with two children, holds one *accola*; the same.

Hrodsindna, slave, with three children, holds one *accola*; the same.

Total: 60 *muids* of wheat can be sown, 120 *muids* of wine and 5 waggons of hay can be harvested. As rent: five *muids* of wine, five hens, 25 eggs, five waggon loads of wood.

*   *   *

Total seed for this year: 63 *muids* of wheat, 1,898 *muids* of spelt, 243½ *muids* of rye, 513 of barley, 883 of oats, 28½ *muids* of leguminous plants.

Total cattle: 31 oxen, 42 cows, 34 calves, 4 yearling calves, 25 barren cows, 8 bulls: in all 113 head apart from oxen.

Total sheep: 607 very young, 561 lambs, 411 geldings, 343 sheep, in all 1,822 head.

Total pigs: ten boars, 100 pigs, 165 sows, 140 young ones, in all 415 head.

Total poultry: 87 geese, 44 *ganders*, 157 hens, 182 chicks, 21 beehives.

Polyptyque de Saint-Rémi de Reims (ed. W. Maas), *Les moines défricheurs,*
Étude sur les transformations du paysage au Moyen Age
aux confins de la Champagne et de la Lorraine,
Moulins, 1944, pp. 17-18.

C. SIGNS OF CHANGE

8

Law of the Bavarians, [Article XIII (before 750)]

This early edition of Germanic law shows that, at the beginning of the eighth century, there was a very marked contrast between the relative economic position of servile and free tenants with regard to their lord. The former were no more than half-time domestics, even more heavily burdened if their master made equipment and draught animals available to them. The

371

latter were responsible only for cultivation of plots of land allocated to them for that purpose, and for carefully defined tasks. As can be seen by comparing this text with the Staffelsee inventory, drawn up in the same region two generations later, changes were already confusing the two classes of tenants by imposing additional limited services on the servile manses and by extending undefined services to the free manses.

Of coloni and slaves of the Church
How they serve, or their dues

The rent of the fields is to be laid down by the judge. . . . Each must give according to what he has: out of 30 *muids* he must give three, and he must fulfil the law of pasture according to the custom of the country.

Plough, sow, enclose, harvest, carry and store the lawful plot, which is four perches (of ten feet each) wide, and forty long.

Enclose, scythe, toss and carry one *arpent* of meadow.

Each peasant must work two *muids* of spring-sown seed, sow it, harvest it and bring it in.

Plant, enclose, dig, layer, dress and harvest the vines.

They deliver one bundle of flax, ten hives, four hens, 15 eggs.

They provide a horse or else go themselves wherever they are enjoined.

They perform service with waggons up to 50 leagues; they shall not be constrained to go further.

They shall take their turn in the maintenance of the lord's houses, in repairing the hayloft, the barn, the stable and if it is needed they shall set about doing all of these things.

If it is near at hand, 50 men shall be charged with providing stone and wood for the limekiln; if it is far away, 100 men shall do this work; and the lime shall be carried to the city or to the estate wherever it is needed.

The Church slaves shall render their dues according to their possessions. A slave serves three days a week on the demesne, and the other three days are for himself. If his master gives him oxen or other things that he has, he serves according to what shall be required of him with the means at his disposal. But nobody shall be unjustly burdened.

G. Franz, *Deutsches Bauerntum*, I, *Mittelalter*, in *Germanen Rechte, Neue Folge*,
Weimar, 1940, pp. 22-23.

9

Edict of Pitres (864)

In these two chapters from the great collections of miscellaneous decrees which Charles the Bald caused to be drawn up, some factors modifying the system of demesne cultivation in the ninth century can be discerned: (a) a few improvements in technique (the process of marling is being extended); (b) a conflict between the lord, who demands always a little more, and the tenants who dissemble (it can be seen that the polyptyques *did not succeed in fixing usages); and (c) the eventual beginning of a land market.* Purchases of parcels of land by men (the text specially singles out ecclesiastics) in a higher economic position; impoverishment of some peasants who then refuse to give service for a holding of which they are in possession of no more than the inhabited nucleus; the fragmentation of lands previously attached to the manses. The entire manorial organization is in a state of disturbance.

29. Certain tenants of the royal and ecclesiastical demesnes owe cartage and manual services according to ancient usage; so much is noted in the *polyptyques* and they do not deny it. But they refuse to carry marl and other things which do not please them because in the old days, perhaps, marl was not carried (in many places indeed its transport began in the time of our grandfather and our father). And for manual service they do not want to thresh in the barn, although they do not deny manual service. Let them carry without any discrimination all that they shall be ordered to carry for the cartage service, since they owe it, and similarly let them perform without discrimination all that is commanded of them for manual service when they owe it.

30. In certain places tenants of royal and ecclesiastical demesnes sell their inheritance, that is the *manses* that they hold, not only to their peers but to clerks of the chapter or to village priests or to other men. They keep only their house, and in this way demesnes are destroyed, because rent can no longer be levied, and it is no longer even possible to know which lands belong to each *manse*. We decree that it shall be enjoined on our officials and those of the Church that they shall prevent this in future, in order that the demesnes shall not be broken up and disturbed. Let all that has been alienated from each *manse* without the authorization of the lord or the master be restored, and let it be given back to each *manse* whose lands have been sold and whose rent has been lost by default of those who can no longer perform the service of the *manse*. And according to the quality and quantity of the land and the vines belonging to each *manse*, when it has been restored, let the rent be levied on each *manse* for the master.

M.G.H. Capitularia regum Francorum (ed. Boretius & Krause),
Vol. II, p. 323.

10

The structure of this manor, a possession of the cathedral chapter of Autun, presents many features similar to those revealed a century and a half earlier at Villeneuve St. Georges or at Staffelsee. But there are some new phenomena—

1. *The fragmentation of the* manses. *The inventory mentions 14 heads of families and 14 manses; but nine of the latter were empty and their lands re-attached to the demesne. The peasant population was concentrated on the other five, which were now sufficient to feed them. A new holding appeared, the* quartier, *occupied by a single household.*

2. *The complete assimila t ion of free and servile* manses *which are now only distinguished by name.*

3. *The increase of dues in cash. Of customary dues, two are paid in money and are not*

373

light (one is paid at the time of the local fair, which shows the connection between the country and trade, as does the mention of the 'port', a place for exchange in the very heart of the manor). But four other services could be 're-purchased' at the wish of the tenant. In this way the ties between demesne and holding, between lords and peasants, were dissolving (even the 'watch', a personal service, is subject to commutation).

The year of the birth of Our Lord Jesus Christ 938, the eleventh of the proclamation, the second year of the reign of Louis and the third of the bishopric of Rodmond, Dean Bernard and the dignitaries of the chapter of St Nazaire found in the *villa* of Tillenay on the Saône, a farm belonging to the master, with barn, garden and 'hall'. There is a church there dedicated to St Denis, which is endowed with three *manses* and pays on All Saints' Day a rent of ten sous. There is a lord's meadow there; 60 carts of hay can be gathered there; three lord's arable furlongs where 30 *muids* can be sown; three woods where two thousand pigs can be fattened, not taking account of the common wood; the port on the river brings some income to the chapter's manor. There is a meadow of five waggon loads which belongs to the 'vidame'. There are five inhabited *manses*. Rictred and Gautier hold a free *manse* which pays two sous in March and 12 deniers in May, or else a pig worth one sou; at the fair of Chalon 12 deniers; labour service[1] and *ansange*[2] is performed. It performs two fortnights of work, or else re-purchases them in mid-March for 12 deniers; a third fortnight of work without the possibility of re-purchase; for the wood, two deniers on St Andrew's day; one *muid* of wheat belonging to the master and one belonging to the *manse* is sown in the *ansange*; if there is any, two waggon loads of manure are spread on the *ansange*; at Easter three chickens or a chicken and five eggs; 100 shingles on St John's day, or else re-purchase for one denier; 12 hoops; for the watch, one *muid* of oats in March. Matusalem and Dominique hold between them a *manse* which owes the same; Aydoen, Constantin, and Constant hold a manse which owes the same, Ildebert, Albert and Thierry hold together a *manse* which owes the same, Lebaud, Agmar, Guinus and Dominique, free men, hold a servile *manse* which owes the same, Bliger holds a *quartier*, inhabited and servile. There are nine empty *manses* which owe what the land yields. There are three other demesne furlongs where 100 *muids* can be sown.

A. Déléage, *La vie rurale en Bourgogne jusqu'au début du XIe siècle*'
Vol. III, Mâcon, 1942, p. 1207.

D. REGIONAL DIFFERENCES

II

This inquest of the end of the ninth century describes a manorial group, a 'hall', dependent on the abbey of Werden in the lower Rhineland. It brings out certain unique features of the great Germanic properties.

[1] Ploughing on the demesne.   [2] In this case a given plot to be cultivated.

1. *Their structure is much looser. The demesne attached to the 'hall' of Friemersheim is dispersed in five localities; as for the 102 manses which belong to it, they are scattered in 19 village territories (the existence of half-manses should be noted).*

2. *Neither mill, nor brewery nor bakehouse is to be found on the demesne. The processing of the grain is handed over to the peasant households who prepare the flour, the bread, the beer and the dogfood. But money is in circulation and forms the most important part of the dues.*

3. *All the manses are burdened with the same dues and services. The latter provides an important addition to domestic labour in three ways: (a) by cultivating the plots worked by labour service, either in the homestead toft zone or in fields cut out of the forest which were protected against the swine by hedges; (b) by fulfilling the 'weeks' of unspecified work in the three principal seasons of the agricultural calendar; and (c) by taking over certain limited tasks, which were all rewarded, of ploughing, haymaking, harvesting, enclosing, gathering the acorn harvest and preparing the grain.*

These demesne *manses* are attached to the manor which is at Friemersheim. To the demesne 'hall' its estate land. At Kumeln the same. At Asterlagen its estate land. At Essenberg a demesne *manse*. At Schwafheim one. Except the church lands which belong to the churches.

To the demesne 'hall' of Friemersheim 30 *manses* are attached. At Kumeln, 20. At Asterlage, 12. At Asberg, 10. At Atrop, 7. At Mörs, 5½. At Ostrum, 9. At Essenberg, 8 and the ninth at Budberg. At Berghem, 9. At Uttelsheim, one only. At Vennickel, 2. At Urdingen, one. At Anheri, 2. At Geldern, one and a half. At Pelden, a *manse* and a half. At Lendingheim, a half-*manse*. At Halen, one half. At Bliersheim, one.

There are the *manses* which are dependent on Friemersheim which the Emperor Charles gave to Bishop Hildegrim and which Hildegrim gave to the monastery of St Liudger.

Rent of each of the *manses*: one once[3] at the Feast of Our Lady, one sou between Martinmas and St Andrew's day, one sou at Candlemas; in the middle of the month of May, one sou, three chickens and ten eggs.

Services: two weeks in autumn; two weeks before the spring; two weeks in June. In each week, five days. In autumn one yoke of land must be broken up, which counts as two day-works; that is the *gibrakon*. Then it must be ploughed and the seed taken to the 'hall', and then harrowed: that is the *giekkian*. If that *manse* does not do the breaking up.... It must plough a yoke and harrow it ... and plough half a yoke, but not harrow it. The same service of first and second ploughing and harrowing must be performed in the spring. The *manse* will also have to care for the yokes, that is to free them of weeds, and to take charge of everything even to taking the harvest intact to the barn. Furthermore in spring, a day-work of labour service must be ploughed, and to each plough shall be given a *setier* of barley beer, a loaf and the allowance that can be found. On the daywork of the labour service the wife must bind the sheaves, collect them and pile them up in five stacks. She takes four sheaves for herself. Her husband brings in two of the stacks to the demesne grange. The rest is taken care of by

[3] Unit of weight used here as a monetary unit.

the 'hall' itself. Similarly for the hay, each person from the *manse* must scythe until midday; and then every two men must be given a loaf, an allowance and a *setier* of barley beer. The hay must be collected in sheaves and taken in a waggon to the barn. Furthermore the *manse* must bring 30 stakes each time it is necessary to renew the enclosure. It takes for its own use the old stakes and branches. The enclosure of the yoke in the field which is called *jucfac* must be cared for, so that neither large nor small beasts may invade the sown fields. If this should happen the *manse* must pay. This enclosure of the yoke must be 5 rods of the yoke long. When this enclosure becomes old, the *manse* will take it for its own and will make a new one. Every year each *manse* must receive 12 *muids* of grain; it must mix it and brew it with its own wood and cauldron and must then receive one measure of barley beer and a half of beer from the second run. Every year the *manse* must receive from the 'hall' two *muids* of rye, and must grind and bake it. When it brings the loaves it can take one out of 24. Furthermore it must grind and sieve two *muids* of wheat and receive half the bran. Similarly it must grind two *muids* of barley for the dogfood. It owes five *muids* of acorns for pigfood. All the *manses* must in turn look after the swine with the swineherd. They are responsible if a pig is lost between the rising and the setting of the sun; but not between the setting and the rising of the sun. It must take entire care of a plot in the homestead toft which must be the length of a rod of the yoke, that is the *jukruoda*, and the width of two cubits. The *manse* must collect in the field one sheaf of flax, which it must take entire care of and present well-prepared seed. But it has the right of *aranfimba* as it is called, that is one sheaf must be given to six *manses*.

G. Franz, *Deutsches Bauerntum*,
pp. 55–59.

12

In this manor of St Ambrose of Milan the slaves are given the entire charge of the cultivation of the demesne; they deliver an annual 'pension' to the masters, in fixed quantities of food. Attached lands support a good rent in cash.

(Before 835)

We have visited in the country of Milan the demesne called Lemonta. There is a little demesne house and a chapel inside the 'hall', dedicated to St Genies, which has no other income but the tithe. Dependent on the said demesne five villeins. They live on the demesne and deliver a rent of 36 *muids* of rye, 12 amphorae of wine, 13 pigs each worth 20 deniers, 18 sheep each worth five deniers, nine hens, 300 eggs. There is also an empty land worked by these slaves for which they pay a rent of five sous. There are two *aldions*, who have delivered themselves to this demesne as settlers and give a rent of eight silver sous. There are olive trees which yield nine livres of oil. . . .

Codice diplomatico sant'ambrosiano delle carte dell' ottavo et nono secola
(ed. Fumagallio), Milan, 1805, p. 217

This 'hall', a dependency of the abbey of Bobbio, was the centre of a smallish demesne. Most of its lands formed holdings in livelli, *from which the lord drew the larger part of his income. The tenants helped a little with the demesne work; they mainly delivered large quantities of grain.*

(862)

At the Tower 700 *muids* a year can be sown; 21 jars of wine and 120 waggon loads of hay are produced. There are 15 *libellarii*. There is one who has four co-farmers on his holding; he delivers in a good year 20 *muids* of grain, one measure of wine, a sheep and he gives three weeks of work. The second with another co-farmer, delivers 23 *muids* of grain, a sheep, chickens and three weeks of work. The third, with his co-farmer, delivers 22 *muids* of grain, six deniers, and three weeks of work. The fourth, with two others, delivers 10 *muids*, a sheep, and gives three weeks of work. The seventh, alone, delivers 12 *muids*, a sheep, and gives three weeks of work. The eighth, with his four co-farmers, delivers eight *muids*, a sheep, and three weeks of work. The ninth, with his co-farmers, delivers eight *muids*, a sheep and three weeks of work. The tenth, with four others, delivers ten *muids*, a sheep, and three weeks of work. The eleventh, with two others, delivers nine *muids*, a sheep, four deniers, two hens and three weeks of work. The twelfth, with two who are in his holding, delivers five *muids*, a sheep, and three weeks of work. The thirteenth, with two others, delivers seven *muids*, a sheep, and three weeks of work. The fourteenth, with five others, delivers five *muids*, a sheep, three chickens, and three weeks of work. The fifteenth, with his co-farmer, delivers six *muids*, a sheep and three weeks of work. The other *libellarii*, who live on individual plots, number 32, and together deliver 520 *muids* in a good year, 15 jars of wine, eleven sous, four deniers, 40 chickens and some eggs, 21 sheep, 50 livres of oil, and 97 weeks of work. All together, the *libellarii* number 47 and the co-farmers 38, which makes a total of 85.

Codice diplomatico del monasterio di S. Colombano di Bobbio *(ed. C. Cipolla), F.S.I. LII, No. 76.*

14

On this demesne, which belongs to the monastery of San Giulia of Brescia, stockraising occupies a much smaller place than in the country of the Franks. The lesser cereals, millet, barley and oats, are mainly cultivated and yield very little: the stocks of grain found by the commissioners on their winter tour hardly equal the total of seed for the year.

On these lands work many domestic servants, almost all of them prebendary (three servile families, boarded out, continue to work in the 'hall' and to deliver as well a few products of the garden and the smaller animals). The tie between the demesne and the tenants, coloni attached to the land or free protected persons, is very loose.

(*ca.* 905–906)

At Porzano a demesne 'hall', four houses, four kitchens, arable land to sow 300 *muids*, vines for 50 jars, meadows for 25 cartloads, woods to fatten 20 pigs, two mills which render 30 *muids* of grain each year. 32 prebendaries, male and female. 20 *muids* of wheat, 53 of rye, seven of leguminous plants, 100 of barley and oats, 140 of millet, ten of millet grass (*panic*). In all 350 *muids*. 21 jars of wine and one urn. Six oxen, four cows, two calves, 24 pigs, 40 ewes, 15 geese, 15 hens.

There are three whole plots and on them reside three slaves who deliver three jars, three pigs, and three ewes.

There are 13 other plots and on them live 13 villeins who together deliver 40 *muids* of grain, five jars of wine, two pigs, four ewes, 26 hens, 130 eggs, and 29 deniers, and each work one day a week. There is another plot on which reside eight villeins who deliver one sheep, three hens and 15 eggs.

There are 15 free men who have given their own property to the 'hall' on condition that each works one day a week.

There are ten other plots on which reside ten *aldions* who only carry letters and messages.

Historiae Patriae Monumenta,
Vol. XIII, *Codex diplomaticus Longo bardiae* (ed. Porro-Lambertenghi), Aosta, 1873, col. 710.

E. THE ECONOMIC FUNCTIONS OF THE GREAT DEMESNE

15

In 822, when the Emperor imposed the use of a new system of measurement, Adalard, abbot of Corbie, the great monastery in the Somme valley, laid down certain decrees regulating the domestic economy.

This rather disjointed chapter deals with the mills. The income to be expected from them was enormous: it was funnelled into the chandlery, that is the internal office charged with collecting all the receipts in cereals and with distributing them to the different refectories where the monks, the guests and the domestics fed. But to administer the mills, trustworthy servants were needed on the spot who would maintain the costly installation, levy the taxes on the users and deliver the exact amount to the lord. This problem of management was solved by entrusting to each miller a complete holding, which would allow his family to obtain its entire living. It was a holding without service (apart from a few dues in the shape of farmyard produce) and it constituted the salary of a specialist official. It was really a fief.

Chapter VII For the mills and brewhouses we desire that the principal shall be thus:

First of all let each miller be awarded a *manse* and *six bonniers* of land, because we desire that he shall be in a position to perform what is commanded of him and that he shall fulfil his multure properly. That is, let him have oxen and all the equipment so that he can plough and, in this way, live himself with his household, feed pigs, geese, hens, take care of the mill, carry all that is needed to repair the mill, repair the weir, bring the millstones, and let him have and perform all that is required.

This is why we do not desire him to do any other service, neither cartage, nor horse, nor manual, nor ploughing, nor sowing, nor harvesting, nor haymaking, nor brewing, nor livery of hops or wood, nor anything else for the needs of the master, but that he shall occupy himself solely with his mill. Let him undertake to feed pigs, geese and chickens which he must feed for the mill and let him deliver eggs. And as we have said, let him apply himself above all things to what is required for the mill and to what must be produced by the mill. . . .

Referring to what we have said above that 2,000 *muids* must be delivered to the monastery by the mills, we do not mean that multure must be put on one side of that which is handed over to the chandler, but that the latter shall seek to evaluate every year what he needs to add or to subtract and how the year must go according to the number of prebendaries, and according to the works which are completed every year, such as the wine harvest, the kitchen garden, the hay, and such like. We desire that he makes an estimate before the millers of the new *muid* in relation to the old one, and states the equivalent, so that they pay the amount of their rent, be it in grain or in malt, according to the new *muid*.

We desire that each miller shall be provided with a complete installation with six wheels. If he does not wish to be responsible for more than half, that is three wheels, let him have only half the land which belongs to the *manse*, that is three *bonniers*, the other three being for an associate with whom he must provide all the multure and the service which is attached to the mill, be it for the work, the weir, the bridge, as is assigned to each mill.

Polyptyque de l'Abbé Irminon (ed. B. Guérard),
Vol. II, Appendices, pp. 313-314.

16

1. *We see in another extract from the* Statutes *of Adalard how the income was distributed. The internal economy of this great house was in the hands of a certain number of offices, allotted to monks, for receipt and distribution. Alongside the chandlery, there was the cellar, which received other foodstuffs; the chamber, which managed the money income and preserved and renewed clothing; the gate, the office charged with relations with the outside world, and which, in particular, levied and distributed alms. The hosteller was responsible for part of the expenditure: he sheltered and fed the wandering poor, those rootless folk on the fringes of agricultural society, who lived upon gifts and temporary employment.*

2. *In these regular distributions, money played a not inconsiderable part: each year more than 1,500 pieces of money were given to travellers who were going to spend them on the road.*

3. *In this part of the country wine was rare. The only person to drink it was the prior, the head of all domestic administration. Bread formed the basic food (white bread for a few privileged people, the sick and those passers by who were priests); the daily ration was about three pounds. But the poorest people expected an 'accompaniment', cheese, peas, meat or fish according to the season and date in the liturgical calendar.*

Chapter IV We lay down that the hostelry of the poor shall be given 45 loaves of maslin weighing three and a half livres, and five wheaten or spelt loaves, of those which the servants receive, which will make 50 loaves in all. These loaves shall be distributed in the following way:

Each of the twelve poor people who shall pass the night shall receive his loaf and in the morning half a loaf as food for the journey. The two hostellers who perform their service here shall each have their loaf. The five wheaten loaves must be divided between the travelling clerks who shall be led to the refectory and the sick who are fed here. This distribution of bread we entrust to the hosteller: he shall decide what is to be done if it should happen that the number of poor people increases. . . .

. . . To the other people who arrive and leave the same day, it is customary to give a quarter, or else, as we have said, whatever the hosteller shall decide according to the numbers and circumstances; the wherewithal to accompany the bread shall be given according to usage.

As for drink, a half-*muid* of beer shall be given every day, that is, eight *setiers*. Four *setiers* shall be divided between the 12 poor people mentioned above, in such a way that each shall receive two cups. Of the other four *setiers* a cup shall be given to each clerk whose feet are washed by the brothers, and one cup to the servant Guilleran. We leave the division of the surplus to the hosteller who shall divide it either between the sick or the poor.

As for the laity who, because of the fief, serve the abbot, the prior or the provosts, inside or outside, on horseback or in another manner, we lay down that at Christmas and Easter they shall receive either two *setiers* of barley beer or one *setier* of wine, but in token of charity and for the honour of the house, and not because of hereditary right; let this remain at the discretion of the abbot, prior and provosts.

What is to be done about wine shall be at the discretion of the prior. The porter shall, according to circumstances, provide for the needs of the poor in food and drink for anything that the hosteller lacks.

If pilgrims from afar come in great numbers, it is the porter who shall provide for their needs so that nothing shall be taken from what is assigned to the daily distribution.

Chapter V To accompany the bread of the poor (either up to 30 rations of cheese or bacon and 30 *muids* of beans), we add a fifth part of the tithe that the porter receives from the cellarer in eels or in that fresh cheese, which according to rule, the ten shepherds deliver, or from that given in tithe by the demesnes. And also a fifth part of the tithe in cattle, that is in calves, ewes and all that is delivered from the flocks to the porter.

Furthermore, we decide that a fifth part of all the money, which comes to the office of the gate shall be given to the hosteller by the porter. As for the money, we desire that it shall be distributed in such a way that every day not less than four deniers shall be given away. And if the fifth part shall not be sufficient for this distribution, the abbot, if he wishes, shall make up the other part; and if there shall be more, it shall not be held back.

The porter shall supply the poor, according to usage, with wood and all things which are not mentioned in writing, such as sheets for the beds, receptacles and the rest. All this shall be given from the revenues of the office of the gate, because of the additional money as it is recalled above. Furthermore, the hosteller shall receive from the chamberer the monks' old clothes and shoes in order to distribute them to the poor according to custom. . . .

Polyptyque de l'Abbé Irminon (ed. B. Guérard),
Vol. II, Appendices, pp. 309-311.

17

Through imperial gratitude, Einhard, the biographer of Charlemagne, had acquired very great landed possessions: the abbatial demesnes of St Pierre-du-mont-Blandin and St Bavo in Ghent, of St Servais at Maastricht, the endowments of Fritzlar in Hesse and in the valley of the Rhine. All these demesnes were situated very far from his usual residences at the monastery he had founded at Seligenstadt on the Main and at Aix la Chapelle where he had periodically to go to pay his court. He did visit his other demesnes, but these were usually left in the care of agents. Letters addressed to these managers show the principal function of these great rural farms to have been storehouses of food and labour. Thus, before a stay at Aix, he enjoins the agents of his nearest demesne to send ahead servants who would prepare the house and arrange food supplies. By slow, wheeled transport, the surpluses from the farm at Fritzlar arrive at Seligenstadt. But the distance prevents efficient supervision and liveries are sometimes disappointing. We also see that, to save money, the lord did not hesitate to utilize the free and unlimited labour of his innumerable dependants in endless transportation, such as this convoy of wax from Ghent to Seligenstadt.

Letter to his agent at Maastricht (ca. 830).

In the name of Christ, abbot Einhard, to his agent and faithful one, greeting.

Know that we desire thee to send men to Aix to prepare and put in order our residence and that thou shalt cause to be sent there in good time, in the accustomed manner, what we shall need there, that is flour, grain to make beer, wine, cheese and the rest. As to the oxen for slaughter, we desire that thou shalt bring them and slaughter them at Lanaeken. We desire that thou shalt give one of them to Hruotlouge, and that the small pieces and the tripes which cannot be kept for our use shall be given to the domestic servants who live there. For ourselves, if thanks be to God we shall be alive, we desire to come to the palace towards Martinmas. Also we desire that thou shalt make all this known to the servants, and that thou shalt order them, on our behalf, to fulfil our needs as we shall order thee to do. Farewell.

Letter LVI (840)

In the name of Christ, Einhard, abbot to N., greetings in the Lord.

We inform thee that we have need of wax for our use and that we cannot procure any here because the honey harvest has been small these last two years in this country. Also we desire that thou shalt agree with N. and thou shalt arrange with him if it is possible to cause a consignment to be brought by our servants who shall be returning to us from yonder after St Bavo. Be in good health and pray for us.

Letter IX (*ca.* 828–830)

In the name of Christ, Einhard, to N. his agent.

We are surprised that all the things that we charged thee to do for us can remain as they have. We have been told that of the grain that thou shouldest have sent to Mulinheim[1] to make flour and malt thou has sent nothing; but only 30 pigs (and these are not good ones, nor even of medium quality) and three *muids* of beans. Nothing more. And this is not all: during the whole winter we have not been able to see thee, nor anyone sent by thee, who would give us news of yonder. If we cannot draw more profit from Fritzlar than what thou hast sent us, we do not know to what purpose this endowment is. Therefore now, if thou carest anything for our good will, we beseech thee to apply thyself to the repair of thy negligence and inform us soon what we may expect of thee.

Einharti Epistolae (ed. Hampe), in *M.G.H. Epistolae,*
Vol. V, 1899, pp. 105-145.

F. THE FATE OF LAY WEALTH

18

Law of the Thuringians (802–803)

Documents describe only royal or ecclesiastical property. Amongst the articles of Germanic law we find the rules determining the transmission of inheritances, which occasionally resulted in the manpower (slaves treated as movable property) being separated from the land.

26. It is the son and not the daughter who receives the inheritance of the deceased person.

27. If the dead man has no son, the movables and the slaves go to his daughter, but the land belongs to the next in line of paternal blood. If he has no daughter, his sister has the movables and slaves. The next in the paternal line receives the land. If he has neither daughter, nor sister, but his mother is still living, she receives what would come to the daughter or sister, that is, the movables and slaves. If he leaves neither son, nor daughter, nor sister, nor mother, the next in the paternal line inherits everything, movables and slaves, as well as land. To whoever receives the inheritance of the land shall belong the trappings of war, that is the breast plate, the vengeance of the kin, and the blood payment.

28. The mother in dying leaves to the son the land, the slaves, the movables, to the daughters the ornaments of her neck, that is necklaces, bracelets, jewels, earrings, raiment, rings and everything that she owns for personal adornment.

29. If she has no son or daughter, but a sister, she leaves the slaves and the movables to her sister, and the land to the paternal next of kin.

---

[1] The modern Seligenstadt.

30. The paternal line inherits up to the fifth generation. After the fifth, the daughter inherits everything, either from the father's side or the mother's, and it is only thus that the inheritance passes from the spear to the distaff.

G. Frantz, *Deutsches Bauerntum*, pp. 34-35.

19

This extract of the Book of Gifts *of the abbey of Freising in Bavaria, is an example of a freely given donation to a religious establishment. The man enters into the service of the patron saints of the church; he becomes a prebendary and gives up all his allod, in this case a modest one. He possesses no more than half the 'halls', divided by inheritance, about 25 acres of arable, which would then have been hardly enough to feed a family.*

(25th December 818)

Of the donation which Perahart made at Marzling

Coming himself to Freising, Perahart fulfilled this donation in the following manner; in the presence of lord Hitton, bishop, and Luitpold, count, and many others who heard and saw him, Perahart gave himself to the service of the Blessed Mary, ever Virgin, or to St Corbinien, confessor of Christ, with all who are dependent on him this day. All that he had this day from his personal inheritance he gave wholly to the house of the Blessed Mary, that is half a 'hall' and half a house, with half of the other buildings, with draught animals, sheep and pigs, one slave, twelve day-works and 30 waggon loads of meadow. I, Perahart, have done all this in order to have food and clothing in this house, and if I receive less than I need, I am permitted to acquire from my property that which I have need of to live. . . .

G. Frantz, *Deutsches Bauerntum*, pp. 40-41.

20

In the region of Corbon, near Mortagne, the abbey of St Germain-des-Prés owned a manor, described in the polyptyque *of Irminon, made up of very widespread lands, mostly small, formerly allods offered as alms. The farm which is described in this passage is clearly larger than the free manses of the* villae *of classical structure and contained amongst its appurtenances woods and pastures. The four children (with their families comprising 20 individuals) continued to farm the ancestral land, given by their father, who had by his gift, made them* coloni *of the monastery. In fact they delivered half of their profits to St Germain. But these men also held an allod which they had recently acquired, and parcels of land dependent on another lord: the heterogeneous nature of this peasant farm, which was probably quite common, is revealed quite by chance.*

This is the gift which Ainhard made in the country of Hiemois, in the hundred of Corbon, in the village which is called Rônel. He gave there 17 *bonniers* of plough land, five *arpents* of meadow, two *bonniers* of woodland, two *bonniers* of pasture. This gift is held by his sons, that is Guinegaud, *colonus* of St Germain and his wife, free, named Ermenrade (their children are Guinegaud, Bernard, Adalgarde) and Guinegard, *colonus* of St Germain and his wife, free, named Rotsinde (their children are Guineran, Unod, Ainard, Guillerad, Roberge), and Elene, *colona* of St Germain (whose children are Grimod, Guinegarde, Guinebert, Guinevoud, Ermentrude, Grime), and Ingeltuide *colona* of St Germain. These four hold the manse. They till it for half the fruit. Apart from this land, they have bought four *bonniers* of arable land, free of the lord. And Géraud has received from a strange manor five *bonniers* of arable land which they have sold.

Polyptyque de l'abbaye de Saint-Germain-des-Prés (ed. A. Longnon),
Paris, 1886, pp. 167-168.

G. THE PARISH CHURCH

21

The slow movement which, in the anciently colonized lands, gradually placed a parish church at the disposal of each peasant settlement was completed in Carolingian times. An area, the parish lands, whose boundaries were drawn by the bishop, was attached to each of these consecrated sanctuaries. The bishop was greatly preoccupied in dividing the profits of the tithe equitably between the patrons of the new churches. Here, parts of four hamlets are attached to a place of worship from which they were separated by a rocky outcrop and an uninhabited forest.

(864-872)

In the name of Almighty God, Bermond, by divine favour humble pastor of the holy church at Mâcon. Know, all ye brethren of the church, that our brother and priest Bedeem, touched by divine grace, has besought our affiliation to grant him the right to build a basilica in the village of Milly. Acceding to his prayers, we have authorized that the work he has conceived by divine inspiration shall be realized. The church built, he has summoned us to its dedication and consecration. On the day of the dedication and consecration in honour of St Christopher, in conformity with the canons, we have given these villages to the parish: Milly, Laly, Viré, half the cultivated land (*finage*) of Cury; and, on the other side of the mountain, of the villages which are called Urny, Montangeran, Corcelles and Mont-Evart, we give two-thirds to this chapel. And in order that this remains well established, we have confirmed it by our hand.

Cartulaire de Saint-Vincent de Mâcon (ed. Ragut),
Mâcon, 1864, p. 231.

H. A GLANCE AT THE ENGLISH COUNTRYSIDE

In three documents, rather less informative than the Carolingian inventories we glimpse the great demense in England and we find that it was organized in a very similar manner to its counterpart in the Frankish lands: an estate worked by slaves; satellite farms held by peasant families; a lord acquires part of the royal rights.

Nevertheless, some distinctive features are evident: for instance, a strong village organization, a system of feorms, tribute in food levied by authority, and a very marked preponderance of pastoral activities. It is true that the 'carucate' served to measure the demesne, but great woodlands, marshes, pastures and swineherds' huts dispersed in the forest encircled the arable on every side. Cheese and bacon formed as large a part of the basic diet as did wheat, and the latter appears to have been sometimes difficult to grind.

22

(793-796)

In the name of Our Lord Jesus Christ.

I, Offa, bestow the land at Westbury, with everything duly belonging to it, i.e. 60 hides and 20 hides in another place, Henbury, on Worcester for the relief of my soul and the souls of my parents, after my death and that of my son Ecgfrith, and it is rightly to remain in all things with the same power and freedom with which King Aethelbald granted it by charter to my grandfather Eanwulf.... We enjoin in the name of the supreme God that it is to be released from all compulsion of Kings and ealdormen and their subordinates except these taxes; that is, all the tribute at Westbury, two tuns full of pure ale and a coomb full of mild ale and a coomb full of Welsh ale, and seven oxen and six wethers and 40 cheeses and six long *peru* and 30 'ambers' of unground corn and four 'ambers' of meal, to the royal estate. This, accordingly with the consent and advice of my bishops, and councillors, they decided by the firm agreement that no authority of king or ealdorman or of any secular kind should demand or strive to get by force or petition from our inheritance any more than these things, in much or in little, except this only which this present charter contains.

English Historical Documents, Vol. I, *ca.* 500-1042, D. Whitelock (ed.), 1955, pp. 467-468.

23

I, King Ethelbert, with the consent and permission of my secular nobles and religious dignitaries, with willing heart will give and concede to my faithful thegn Wulflaf some portion of land of my rightful possession, namely five ploughlands in the place which is called Wassingwell in exchange for other land, namely at Mersham. I, Ethelbert, will free eternally this above mentioned land at Wassingwell from all liability to royal service just as the aforementioned land at Mersham was before. These, indeed, are the marshes which duly and rightly belonged to that same land, which marshes Hega had before: i.e. one dairy-farm of the people of Wye which before was subject to Wye and to Lenham and one salthouse at Faversham, and the right for two waggons to come with the king's waggons to Bleanwood, and pasture for four oxen with the king's oxen; in the dairy-farm of the people of Wye, and 20 lambs and 20 fleeces. And the above-written land at Wassingwell (has) from old these well-known boundaries lying round it: in the west, the king's folkland, which Wighelm and Wulflaf hold; in the north 'Cuthric's down', *Heregetheland*; in the east, Wighelm's land; in the south, the bishop's land at Chart; and two mills belonging to the same land, one in *Wassingwell*, the other in *Hwitecelde*. There are the swine pastures which we call in our language *denbera*, namely, *Lamburnan-den, Orricesden, Tilden, Stanehtan-den*, and the wood called *Sandhurst* which belongs to *Wassingwell*. And I have willingly granted this privilege to this same piece of land at *Wassingwell* and likewise to the said Wulflaf, with the consent and permission of my chief men, that it may remain free and immune from all royal tribute and services exacted by force and penal matters, from the domination of the ealdorman and the capturing of a thief and every secular burden, except military service only, and the building of bridges and fortification of fortresses. . . .

This was done in the year of our Lord's incarnation (858. . . .).

English Historical Docmenuts, Vol. I, pp. 488-489.

24

(899-908)

I, Bishop Denewulf, inform my lord King Edward about the land at Beddington which you were desirous I should lease to you. I have then, my dear lord, now procured from the community in Winchester, both young and old, that they grant to me with all goodwill, to give it by charter for your lifetime, whether to use yourself or let on lease to whomsoever you please.

Then there is 70 hides of that land and it is now completely stocked, and when my lord first let it to me it was quite without stock, and stripped bare by heathen men. And I myself then acquired the stock for it which was afterwards available there. And now we very humbly grant it to you. Moreover my dear lord, the community are now desirous that it be given back to the foundation after your death. Now, of the cattle which has survived this severe winter there are 9 fullgrown oxen and 114 full-grown pigs and 50 wethers, besides the sheep and pigs which the herdsmen have a right to have, 20 of which are fullgrown; and there are 110 fullgrown sheep, and seven bondsmen, and 20 flitches, and there was no more corn there than was prepared for the bishop's farm, and there (are) 90 sown acres.

Then the bishop and the community at Winchester beg that in charity for the love of god and for the holy church you desire no more land of that foundation, for it seems to them an unwelcome demand; so that God need blame neither you nor us. . . .

English Historical Documents, Vol. I, pp. 501.

II   XI-XIII Centuries
The Expansion

A.   TECHNIQUE

1. Estate Management Treatises

The manuals on rural economy which were written in England in the thirteenth century differ little, and indeed often copy each other. They contain much practical advice, some of which appears elementary. However, they were responsible for and reflected a rapid change in the psychological attitude of the landowner. They encouraged the latter to keep accounts, and make calculations, to measure accurately, to watch the market, to supervise the domestic servants and to check their agents' accounts. They drew attention to costs, yields of seed and the variations between them. Thus they introduced the masters to the idea of number, value and profit.

We shall notice on the other hand that all these lessons in good management applied to demesnes in direct cultivation, in the hands of responsible officials, and that they assumed the keeping of account rolls, like those which are preserved in the archives of the great English religious establishments. Furthermore, these documents reflect a demesne economy intimately involved in exchange.

They provide much less evidence of the actual technique of production. However, it is interesting to read their remarks about manure and the elementary chemistry of fertilizers. They show that the best informed farmers were not unaware of the advantages of manuring, but that manure was still a rare and precious substance, which had to be used sparingly and at well spaced intervals.

25

The Office of Ploughmen

The ploughmen ought to be men of intelligence, and ought to know how to sow, and how to repair and mend broken ploughs and harrows, and to till the land well, and crop it rightly; and they ought to know also how to yoke and drive the oxen, without beating or hurting them, and they ought to forage them well, and look well after the forage that it be not stolen nor carried off; and they ought to keep them safely in meadows and several pastures, and other beasts which are found therein they ought to impound. And they and the keepers must make ditches and build and remove the earth, and ditch it so that the ground may dry and the water be drained. And they must not flay any beast until someone has inspected it, and enquired by what default it died.

And they must not carry fire into the byres for light, or to warm themselves, and have no candle there, or light unless it be in a lantern, and for great need and peril.

> *Seneschaucie* (ed. E. Lamond), *Walter of Henley's Husbandry,*
> *together with an anonymous husbandry, Seneschaucie and*
> *Robert Grosseteste's Rules,* 1890, p. 111.

26

How one must pay labourers in August and in time of Haymaking

You can well have three acres weeded for a penny, and an acre of meadow for fourpence, and an acre of waste meadow for threepence-halfpenny, and an acre of meadow turned and raised for a penny-halfpenny, and an acre of waste for a penny-farthing. And know that five men can well reap and bind two acres a day of each kind of corn, more or less. And where each takes twopence a day then you must give five-pence an acre, and when four take a penny-halfpenny a day and the fifth twopence, because he is binder, then you must give fourpence for the acre. And, because in many places they do not reap by the acre . . . keep the reapers by the band, that is to say, that five men or women, whichever you will, who are called half men, make a band, and twenty-five men make five bands, and twenty-five men can reap and bind ten acres a day working all day, and in ten days a hundred acres, and in twenty days two hundred acres by five score. And see then how many acres there are to reap throughout, and see if they agree with the days and pay them then, and if they account for more days than is right according to this reckoning, do not let them be paid for it is their fault that they have not reaped the amount and have not worked so well as they ought.

> *Hosebondrie* (ed. E. Lamond), *Walter of Henley's Husbandry. . .* , p. 69.

27

How you must keep your oxen

I will tell you: the horse costs more than the ox. . . . It is usual and right that plough beasts should be in the stall between the feast of St Luke and the feast of the Holy Cross in May, five-and-twenty weeks, and if the horse is to be in a condition to do his daily work, it is necessary that he should have every night at the least the sixth part of a bushel of oats, price one halfpenny, and at the least twelve pennyworth of grass in summer. And each week more or less a penny in shoeing, if he must be shod on all four feet. The sum is twelve shillings and fivepence in the year, without fodder and chaff. And if the ox is to be in a condition to do his work, then it is necessary that he should have at least three sheaves and a half of oats in the week, price one penny, and ten sheaves of oats should yield a bushel of oats in measure; and in summer twelve pennyworth of grass: the sum three shillings, one penny, without fodder and chaff. And when the horse is old and worn out then there is nothing but the skin; and when the ox is old with ten pennyworth of grass he shall be fit for the larder, or will sell for as much as he cost.

Walter of Henley's Husbandry (ed. E. Lamond) . . . , p. 13.

28

How you ought to inspect your cattle

Sort out your cattle once a year between Easter and Whitsuntide – that is to say, oxen, cows, and herds – and let those that are not to be kept be put to fatten; if you lay out money to fatten them with grass you will gain. And know for truth that bad beasts cost more than good. Why? I will tell you. If it be a draught beast he must be more thought of than the other and more spared, and because he is spared the others are burdened for his lack. And if you must buy cattle buy them between Easter and Whitsuntide, for then beasts are spare and cheap. And change your horses before they are too old and worn out or maimed, for with little money you can rear good and young ones, if you sell and buy in season. . . .

Buy and sell in season through the inspection of a true man or two who can witness the business, for often it happens that those who render account increase the purchases and diminish the sales. If you must sell by weight, be careful there, for there is great deceit for those who do not know to be on their guard.

Walter of Henley's Husbandry (ed. E. Lamond), pp. 23 and 33.

29

The yield of grain

Yield of the contents of the barn, one must see how much of each grain has been sown and how much corresponds to the contents. For, by right and common yield, barley must yield to the eighth grain, it is known that from one quarter comes eight quarters; and rye to the seventh grain and beans to the sixth grain; and peas to the sixth grain; and maslin of wheat and rye, if they are equally mixed, must yield to the sixth grain, and if there is more rye than wheat, by right the yield must be more, and if there is more wheat than rye, less; and wheat by right shall yield to the fifth grain, and oats to the fourth. But the earth does not always yield as much one year as another . . . and before of that, at every count, there should be good opinion and consideration of the soil of the land, and what the weather which has been, for often it happens that the winter sowings take well and the spring sowings badly, and at another time the spring sowing takes well and the winter sowing badly. . . . And then a loyal man should be put in whom there is confidence after the thrashing of the grain, who will take the size of the contents of each part of the barn, himself; and if there is a heap outside let it be measured by cord and by foot, height, length and breadth, when it is threshed; and measure each heap by himself, and then the yield and the contents of the parts and the heaps can be known. And if it is desired to sell the grain wholesale, it can be known, by measuring the height, length and breadth, how much each part or heap should be worth by reason according to the grain market. And when he sells it, it is good that he knows the yield of the parts and heap, for the more he shall put it to the test, the more certain of it he will be. And let the old grain be threshed by him, and the new by him, and let the reeve be charged with the sale of the grain each year himself, to see the contents each year, if it yields rightly.

Traité d'Économie rurale composé en Angleterre au XIIIe siècle, XIV
(ed. L. Lacour) in *Bibliothèque de l'École des chartes*, 1856.

30

How to feed the dung heap

Good sons, feed your dung heaps and raise your dung heap with good earth and mix it with dung. And every fortnight, marl the dung of your sheepfold with clay soil, if you wish or with good soil from cleaning out the ditches. . . . Your dung which is mixed with earth, put on sandy soil, for summer weather is warm, the dung is warm and the sand is warm, and when the three warmths come together, as the great heat withers the corn after St John's Day, and namely barleys which grow on sandy soil, and in the evening the earth mixed with dung cools the sandy soil and produces a dew which greatly saves the corn. Your manured land, do not plough it too deep, so that the dung spoils in going down. Now you shall say rather that you shall have dung which is mixed with soil; if the dung is good and pure, it will last two years or three according to whether the soil is cool or warm, and dung mixed with soil will last twice as long. . . . You should know well that marl lasts longer than manure, for dung spoils in going down and marl in rising. And know that mixed dung will last longer than pure dung, for dung and earth which are ploughed together, the earth supports the dung, so that it cannot spoil in going in. Your dung, when it is spread and watered a little, then is the time for it to be turned, and the earth and the dung will each take better together, and if you put your dung on the fallowed field (*guéret*), it shall be rather at the second plough turned under the soil, and at sowing time shall be thrown up with the mixed earth; and if you put it on the second plough, then at sowing time it will be rather turned on the soil, and then it will be mixed with the earth; and it will not be too much.

Traité d'Économie rurale composé en Angleterre au XIIIe siècle, XIX
(ed. L. Lacour), in *Bibliothèque de l'École des chartes*, 1866.

2. Tools

31, 32, 33, 34
(see Plates I-IV between pages 390-1)

Everything that we know about medieval tools comes from painted or carved representations, of which a systematic collection should be assembled. It is regrettable that the dates of

PLATE I

Document 31: Twelfth-century plough

PLATE II

Document 32
Fifteenth-century plough

PLATE III

Document 33
Twelfth-century harvester using a sickle

PLATE IV

... . c. 7. b. i. z. meli̇ er... clarum quos est.
.atozarlare erpzessii. Juramental impingual corpus. non
.... general uentositatem. remario nocet... eu unno gra
.aro:um.

Document 34
Fifteenth-century press

these figurative representations are often very vague and that they are so difficult to interpret: did the artist copy what he saw, or rather what had inspired previous works of art or studio models?

The drawing of a plough team which illustrates a manuscript of the twelfth century in Moralia in Job of Gregory the Great (**31**), has a distinct air of reality. When it is compared to an illumination of the Vie et des miracles de Notre-Dame of Jean Niélot, which dates from the end of the fifteenth century (**32**), it is clear that the construction – a wheeled fore part, a coulter and a mouldboard – has not changed in any way in the interval. Only the draught has changed: horses with their shoulder collar and complicated harness have replaced oxen with the individual yoke fastened not to their foreheads but to their horns.

The labourer whom Benedetto Antelami, at the end of the twelfth century in the baptistery at Parma, chose to symbolize June, the month of harvest, in Emilia (**33**) handles a sickle and 'scythes' the stalk of the corn quite close to the ear, leaving the straw to provide pasture for the oxen and to fertilize the soil. The press represented in a copy of Tacuinum Sanitatis of Albucassis in the fifteenth century (**34**) was, like the mill, a costly machine; it usually belonged to the lord, who placed it at the disposal of the neighbouring peasants in return for payment of dues.[1]

B. THE EXTENSION OF THE CULTIVATED AREA

1. Stratigraphic Study of Peat Pollen

35

(see graphs on p. 392)

2. Clearing of the Waste Organized by the Lords

36

In this case the archbishop, as territorial lord, wishes to colonize the region; he welcomes the settlers, whom he had probably invited and who are going to put the marshes under cultivation, but who are mainly going to raise livestock. These men came from the Low Countries and were drainage experts; they were led by their priests (who had probably recruited the gangs of pioneers on the spot). They were to form parochial communities, but the uniformly large parcels of land in individual tenancies which they receive, necessitate considerably dispersed dwellings. As for the manorial system set up by the 'contract', it was inspired by what was customary in the polders where the settlers came from. The system was a liberal one and imposed only a single light money tax on each household, which was no more than a token of political submission. The lord of the ban handed over the exercise of justice to the peasants; he was only to intervene at their request in major cases, and furthermore he was to take for himself no more than one-third of the fines: These independent communities administered their own affairs. The lord's only profit was a levy, limited to one-tenth, on future production.

[1] The photographs come from the Maget collection, Musée des Arts et Traditions populaires.

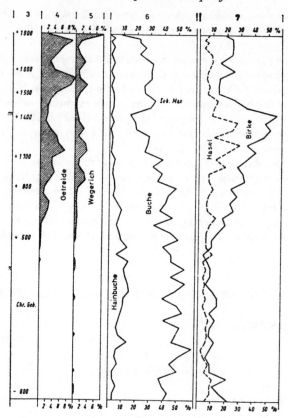

Column labels: Getreide, Wegerich, Buche, Hainbuche, Seh. Max, Hasel, Birke

(See p. 391 document 35)
Variations in the proportion of different species of vegetation throughout the centuries in the peat of Roten Moor
(from W. Abel, *Die Wüstungen des ausgehenden Mittelalters,*
2nd ed., Cologne, 1955, p. 42)
3. Chronology. 4. Cereals (*Getreide*). 5. Plantain (*Wegerich*).
6. Beech and Hornbeam (*Hainbcheü, Büche*). 7. Hazel and
Birch (*Hasel, Birke*).

Frederic, by the grace of God bishop of the church at Hamburg, to all faithful men
in Christ, present and future, perpetual blessings. We desire that this contract which
the men from beyond the Rhine, called Hollanders, have made with us shall be known
to all. Now these men come to find our majesty, requesting instantly the grant of land
situated in our bishopric, until now uncultivated and marshy and useless to the inhabitants of the country, to put it under cultivation. On the advice of our congregation, judging that the thing will be of use to us and our successors, we have not
rejected their request and we have given our consent.

A contract has been established by the terms of which, for each *manse* of the above mentioned land they will give us each year one deniêr. We have judged it necessary to inscribe here the dimensions of the manse, so that there shall in future be no discord amongst the people, that is, 720 royal rods in length and 30 in width, with the streams crossing the land which we grant them in the same way. Finally they have agreed, in conformity with our wishes, to give us a tithe of the fruits of the earth, to wit, the eleventh sheaf, the tenth lamb, pig, goat, goose, the tenth measure of honey and the same for flax; they shall repurchase for a denier the foal raised until Martinmas, and the calf for one halfpenny. They have promised us that they would submit in every thing to the synodal justice according to papal decrees, to canonical justice and to the institutions of the church of Utrecht. For justice and pleas of the secular law, in order not to have to suffer prejudice on behalf of strangers they have agreed to pay every year two marks for a hundred *manses* in order to be able to conduct all the lawsuits. If they cannot agree amongst themselves the pleas or justice of important affairs, let them call on the bishop and bringing him amongst them to judge the case, let them be responsible for his maintenance during his visit; they shall then keep two-thirds of the rights of justice and shall leave the third part to the bishop. We have granted them the creation of churches in this land wherever it shall appear useful to them. We grant to those churches for the use of the serving priest the tithe of our tithes of these same parish churches. As for the parishioners of each of these churches, they agree to give in endowment to their church one *manse* for the needs of the priest.

The names of the men who come to us for the establishment and confirmation of this contract: the priest Henry, to whom we have granted the said churches for his life; the laymen, Helikinus, Arnold, Hiko, Fordolt, Referic, to whom we grant the said land following the laws of the century and established convention, and to their heirs after them. The drawing up of this covenant has been made in the year 1106 of the birth of the Lord, the sixth of the proclamation, in the reign of Henry III, Holy Roman Emperor.

G.Frantz, *Deutsches Bauerntum, I, Mittelalter,*
in *Germanen Rechte, Neue Folge,* Weimar, 1940, pp. 87-90.

37

Associated in this pariage *agreement, the lay lord of the territorial* ban *offers the property, and the monks of St Peter of Chartres are to recruit men to reclaim it, whom they hope to attract by promising them a mild manorial regime (with a very light tariff of fines – on this point the act fixes the custom – and with further remissions of punishment in view). The two co-signatories will each have, in the village lands-to-be, a small demesne and an official whose business it will be to levy dues. They will divide all the profits of the enterprise, that is the re-ceipts of justice (the only privileged 'tax'), the produce of the fixed rent imposed on those new meadows which will immediately yield something to the peasants, a levy on the harvested sheaves, and finally dues levied on the use of the woodland, although this was only a temporary measure as the forest was eventually to disappear completely.*

393

(1113-1129)

The lord Urson, son of Nivelon . . . has given to our church . . . the lordship of all his land which is called Bois-Ruffin, with all the woodland, except two ploughlands of land which, with six *arpents* of these woods to be cleared, the lord Jeremy of the Island had previously given to the monks of Tiron. With this exception, the said Urson has given all the rest to our church in free and peaceful possession; as well as the lordship and the justice of the said land so that all the settlers whom it may please us to place, shall dwell in perpetuity on our property, free and peacefully, with the houses and curtilages as well as the rents borne by these houses and curtilages. . . .

The aforesaid donor has further granted us on this land a house in a place which we shall choose with land for a plough and enough meadows, free of all custom. He has reserved for himself another house of the same status, except that he cannot either sell it, give it away, nor establish settlers there, and cannot have it except for his own personal use.

. . . From the things that follow, the lord Urson has kept for himself the half: that is the tithe (*terrage*), in the rents of the meadows and, as long as there shall be woodland, in the pannage of pigs.

Where these rights are concerned, if the settlers commit an offence and if there is a complaint, the matter shall only be judged in our court and by our judgment, either on our land or at Arrou. The fine shall never be more than five sous however grave the offence. Which our monk shall reduce by however much he wishes, and the rest shall be divided equally with the lord Urson.

The lord Urson, if he so desires, shall have his bailiff for the property which he keeps in common with us; and so shall we have ours. If we desire it, his bailiff shall swear loyalty to us, as ours shall to him, if he desires it.

When he shall be called by the peasant, our bailiff (*terrageur*) shall go to the house of the *terrageur* of the lord Urson. If he finds him, and if the latter wishes to come, he shall go with him to the *terrage*. But if he is not to be found in his house, or if he does not wish to bother, our *terrageur* shall not go back again to find him, and shall not wait to levy the *terrage*. By his oath alone shall he prove that he went to find him, if the other *terrageur* complains that the *terrage* was levied without him. The *terrage* shall be taken, threshed and divided in our barn. . . .

Cartulaire de Saint-Père de Chartres (ed. B. Guérard),
Paris, 1898, II, No. 481.

38

Drawn up in the marches of Misnie, on the eastern borders of old Germany, this charter of settlement differs little from the agreement concluded by the archbishop of Hamburg with his settlers who also came from the Low Countries, with the exception that it mentions the Schultheiss. The latter without doubt organized the colonization, and, provided with a farm twice as large as the other peasant families and holding the lower justice from which he kept one-third of the profits, he became master of the village on the spot.

Gerungus, by the grace of God bishop of the church of Neissen, to all those present as well as future who invoke the name of God, perpetual grace and peace in the Lord. We desire that it shall be known by our congregation now and in the times to come how I have brought together and established in an uncultivated and almost uninhabited place energetic men coming from the province of Flanders, and how I have given in stable, eternal and hereditary possession to them and to all their descendants, the village called Kühren with the following rights. I have given to these Flemings, in memory and as a sign of full possession, four marks, this village and 18 *manses*, with all the customs which exist now and which shall exist in the future, in the fields as well as in the woods, meadows and pastures, in the waters and the mills as well as in the places for hunting and fishing. From these *manses* I have granted one to the church with all the tithes of the *manse*; I have given two of them to the mayor of the peasants whom they call *Schultheiss*, but without tithe. The remaining *manses*, to the number of 15, pay every year 30 sous and 30 deniers for the right called *Zip*.[1] The said men give tithe on all their property except bees and flax, and they shall be responsible for the expenses of the 'advocate' with a small escort three times a year for the pleas which he must hold with them and where they live. From what the 'advocate' or the *Schultheiss* levies in these pleas, two-thirds shall be given to the bishop, and the third to the *Schultheiss*. Let our lands be free of tolls, except for what is sold to merchants. They can sell amongst themselves bread, barley beer and meat, but they must not establish a public market in the village. For all else, we enfranchise them from all exactions coming from the bishop, the advocate, the mayor or any other man. And in order that these statutes shall not be violated in the future, we place them under our *ban*, and we confirm them with our seal in the presence of witnesses. Made the year of Our Lord 1154, third of the proclamation, tenth day of the kalends of December, the first year of the bishopric of lord Gerungus.

R. Kötschke, *Quellen zur Geschichte der ostdeutschen Kolonization*
im 12. bis 14 Jahrhundert
(*Quellensammlung zur deutschen Geschichte*), Leipzig-Berlin, 1912, pp. 27-28.

39

In this case the great lord deals directly with the locator *who is going to construct and settle the village, and who receives immediately, apart from the lower justice, a large hereditary fief. As for the relations between the territorial lord and the peasants, they are to be regulated by a general custom called 'burgess rights' which refers to liberties enjoyed by the inhabitants of urban places.*

(1159)

Let it be known by the whole congregation present and future that I, Wicmann, by the grace of God archbishop of the holy church of Magdeburg, have given to

[1] The lower justice.

Heribert a village called Pechau, with all its dependencies in field, meadow, woodland and pond, for cultivation and to make fruitful, according to the agreement concluded between him and me. For the inhabitants whom he shall himself instal on these properties, I have instituted the jurisdiction which is called burgess rights for all their cases and lawsuits. I have granted to Heribert six *manses* and I have given a *manse* for the use of the priest as an endowment to the church. I have also laid down that neither the count nor the advocate has any right here. It is the same Heribert, and after him his heir, who will give judgment in all the suits in which they shall have to decide between them in the presence naturally of my agent. Of the profits of justice, two-thirds shall be paid to me or to my successor and the other given to the use of Heribert or his heir. Of the *manses* which shall be cultivated here, none shall be given in fief by me or my successor to any man, and the inhabitants shall remain exempt from the service called *burgwere*[2] for the ten years which shall follow their installation. If it should happen that Heribert or his heir should with these same inhabitants buy anything from adjacent villages, they shall have in everything the rights that are given above, and shall acquit to me or my successor in perpetuity the annual tax which must be levied by virtue of burgess rights.

R. Kötschke, *Quellen* ..., pp. 33-34.

40

The settlers who inhabit this marshy 'wilderness' of eastern Hollerland were mainly herdsmen. Manorial rights commonly used in the polders were imposed on them. The tithe and symbolic rent with which their land was burdened did not make a tenancy of it; it was held as an allod which they had complete freedom to sell, to pledge or to divide. The charter of settlement has a 'custumal' as an addition which regulates the exercise of peasant justice, imposes attendance at periodic assemblies, fixes the tariff of fines and establishes the customs of inheritance. Heavy punishments are given to those who evade military service. It should be noted that bondsmen (all the peasants are not of free condition) are compelled to serve like other men, but are liable to corporal punishment.

(18th January 1181)

Let it be known to all present and future that I, Siegfried, by the grace of God archbishop of Bremen, having taken council with my brothers the canons, my men and my officials, have sold a desert named Overnigelant, Rocwinkil, Osterholt and Vuholt, by a contract of free sale. We have laid down that the inhabitants, present and future, of this place shall belong to a single parish. Three times a year they shall attend the synod. The tithe is thus: the tithe of the rushes, the tenth lamb on St Walburga's day, the same for geese and piglings. For a foal they shall give a denier at Martinmas, for the calf, one obole; no tithe for chickens. The *manse* pays annually one denier for the rent at Martinmas. Every six weeks they shall attend the court on condition that

[2] Military service.

it has been announced three days before. After midday matters concerning liberty or the allod shall not be dealt with. He who comes late to the court shall pay eight deniers. For the *ban*, four sous. He who shall have a suit, or who shall have done wrong to another, and shall have been found at fault, shall pay sixty sous. Similarly, if someone is pursued for debt at court and if he admits the debt, he shall pay nothing for this to the judge. But if the judge orders the debtor to pay the debt and if the debtor neglects to do so, at the next court he shall pay four sous. He who claims an allod before the assembly is not permitted to bring witnesses save those who are themselves allodialists, so that they shall be worthy of trust, and of the same parish. It is not permitted to bear witness against a dead man. After the death of the father and the mother, the brother and sister shall share everything equally. If one of them is married and if the other is dead before him without heirs, the property of the deceased shall come to the next of kin. If one of the inhabitants dies and if no one comes during the year who can prove his kinship with the deceased, the goods of the dead man shall pass into royal hands. They are permitted to sell their allod and to pledge it, which shall in no way concern the judge. And none shall be judged elsewhere, but only there where he himself is judge. In my diocese they shall not pay any tolls. In case of *wapenrecht*, he who keeps away, if he is free, shall pay ten sous; the official as much; if he is a bondsman he shall pay horsehair and skin, or else five sous.

R. Kötschke, Quellen . . . , p. 5.

41

Philip Augustus created a 'new town' in his forest and offered the settlers who made their homes there a remarkable lightening of manorial charges; no taille, a much reduced military service, and a big rebate of fines. But on the entire parcel, or half parcel, of land, the assarters paid fixed rents in cereals and money, the latter rather heavy.

(1182)

Philip, by the grace of God king of France. Let it be known to all . . . that we have ordered that the place called Chevrières shall be open to settlers on these conditions: the inhabitants shall be exempt and free of *tolte*, of *taille* and all unjust exactions. They shall not go on military duties and on the riding service (*chevauchée*) unless able to return home the same day, except in case of war. In our forest of Cuise they shall have the right of dead wood. In case of offence the fines shall be: for offences liable to sixty sous, five sous; for the offences of five sous, 12 deniers; he who wishes to clear himself on oath shall be able to do so and shall pay nothing. He who shall commit an offence against the custom shall be banished from the village and shall not return to it without our consent. Every year on St Rémi's day every man shall pay six measures of oats, and at Christmas four capons. And five sous for the entire messuage; for the half messuage half the rent.

Recueil des Actes de Philippe Auguste (ed. Berger and Delaborde),
Vol. I, 1916, No. 51.

Two members of a religious community here take in hand the enterprise of clearing the waste. They reserve for themselves all the profits and take care to stipulate the tariff of dues to be applied to future assarts (a fixed rent in money proportionate to the arable area, matched with a tithe (terrage)). They become farmers of these new lands for the community on conditions which leave no doubt as to their profitability.

(August 1225)

Dean Ernaud and all the chapter of Paris, to all those who shall see the present charter, greetings in the Lord. Let it be known to all that we have given and granted to our dear brothers and co-canons, master Aubri Cornu, provost of Rozoy, and Guillaume Poulet, provost of Vernou, all the woods dependent on the provostry of Vernou, and the new assarts which we once gave and granted to dear Gautier Cornu, formerly our dean and now archbishop of Sens, and Robert, formerly provost of Vernou, by common agreement in order to clear them. The said Aubri and Guillaume shall not without our approval, award any *arpent* of this land for a charge less than four deniers of Provins per *arpent*, and tithe counted in the field, that is the eleventh sheaf. They may construct on these lands one or more villages, according to what shall seem best for the honour and use of our church. All the revenue which shall be drawn from these woods, villages and lands, in grain as well as in money, in justice as well as in every other thing, shall be theirs in all freedom and quietude. The said Guillaume, who holds the provostry of Vernou, shall take a third of it, the said Aubri two-thirds, save in all the right of provostry of the said Guillaume on other lands, so long as he shall be canon of Paris. For this, they shall be held by oath to give us every year thirty livres of Provins on the following terms: the half in the octave of Christmas, the other in the octave of St John. When one of the two shall retire or die, the whole shall come entirely and without division to the survivor, so long as he shall remain canon of Paris. If it shall come to Guillaume alone by the retirement or death of Aubri, the total rent shall be raised: he will render us on the terms above mentioned forty livres of Provins every year.

Cartulaire de l'église Notre-Dame de Paris (ed. B. Guérard),
Vol. II, 1850, pp. 214-215.

3. Peasant Initiative

43

When it was the peasants who took the initiative to clear the waste, the enterprises have left only indirect traces in written records and these are not only scanty but also hard to decipher. This agreement was intended to regulate the sharing of the profits from the tithes, and especially the tithes on newly broken up land (novales) in a village territory surrounded by forests. In it we may at least distinguish the ouches (that is the garden enclosures) and the anciently colonized land on the one hand, and, on the other hand, the new fields dispersed in the wood-

land, which the peasants of the village had created in the years preceding the agreement between the lords.

(1156)

In the name of the Father, the Son and the Holy Ghost. I, Louis, king of France by the grace of God, have desired to make known to all, present and future, that the argument between the bishop of Senlis and the abbess of Chelles on the question of the tithes of the newly broken up land (*novales*) in the forests which are on the territory of the village called Baron, on our advice and by our will, and with the consent of the two chapters, to wit, that of the church of Senlis and that of the church of Chelles, has been settled, and peace made and re-established between them. The bishop of Senlis, in all the lands of the forests above mentioned, which are, were and will be cultivated, and in the other lands of all the village territory above mentioned, shall receive every year one-third of the tithe, and the abbess of Chelles two-thirds, and they shall possess them in perpetuity and in all liberty. Save in the abbess's own demesne furlongs which do not belong to the forests, and of which the abbess of Chelles shall receive every year the whole tithe and shall possess it in all liberty. Save in all the lands dependent on the law of the bishop which do not belong to the forests. Save also in all the garden enclosures (*ouches*) of the said village, of which lands and *ouches* the bishop of Senlis shall receive every year all the tithe and shall possess it in all liberty. The bishop of Senlis shall receive as well every year all the little tithe (*menue dîme*) of that village and shall possess it in all liberty.

A. Luchaire, *Études sur les actes de Louis VII*, No. 365, pp. 402–403.

44

In the early Middle Ages parish boundaries, by means of which tithes were divided between the patrons of neighbouring churches, had not been drawn through the depths of the, at that time, uninhabited and uncultivated woodlands. When these woods were settled the boundaries had to be clearly marked out. In this example we see the birth of a clearing, carved out of a forest in Champagne by a band of peasant families who have migrated spontaneously from the nearest village.

(1190)

I, Matthew, by the grace of God bishop of Troyes, make known to all, present and future, that there has been discord between the abbot of Montier-en-Der and the abbot of Montier-la-Celle because of certain men who, having moved from Fontenay, have built houses at la Brau, a place which the abbot of Montier-en-Der asserts to be in his parish; the abbot of la-Celle also asserts that the place was included within the limits of his parish. After long discussion by my council and the opinion of the two abbots, an agreement has been concluded between them, and it establishes a division of the tithes belonging to the parishes of the said abbots, that is to the parish of

Chavange or Fontenay, dependent on la-Celle, and to the parish of Beaufort or Villeret, belonging to Montier-en-Der. The division of tithes goes in a straight line, from Perthe-Aymon towards the apple tree situated at the side of the public way which leads from Beaufort to Margerie and from that tree by that way up to the stream of la Brau. From that way the division goes towards the source of the stream, and from there by the vale of Bonon up to a tree which the people of the country call Canordel; from there up to the path which passes by the side of the house of Robert de Duma by the side of Chavanges.

Lalore, Collection des principaux cartulaires de l'ancien diocèse de Troyes,
VI, p. 269.

45

Aerial photographs, when taken (as our example is) from vertically above, provide the historian of the countryside with remarkable evidence of the many traces from the past still remaining in the present-day landscape. One only needs to compare the photograph facing page 401 with the ordnance map on page 401 (without which the photograph could not properly be interpreted), to be aware of the wealth of material available. In our example we can see clearly how the great forest of Moulière in Poitou was under assault by the colonizers from Bonneuil. They opened up to cultivation a long marginal stretch of the ancient forest boundary which today follows a winding road almost parallel to the river. They also pushed deeper into the main part of the forest along the stream of Les Touches and, nearer to Bonneuil, following the ancient main road which led from this large town to the south-west. In doing so they founded the hamlet of Traversais.

The difficulty is to put a date to this activity. Place-names (le Mauvais Vent, la Folie, l'Ane Vert), and also comparison with the extension of the woodlands on the ordnance map, lead one to suppose that it was at least in part recent, even very recent. But an inquest, made between 1253 and 1269 to establish limits in the count's forest to the respective rights of the count of Poitiers and the castellan of Bonneuil, brings to light the creation of the little cultivated territory (finage) of Traversais. Twenty-five years before the inquest, huge beeches had covered this spot; then came men determined to cut down the trees, and to sow corn in their place; somehow or other they arranged with the lords and their foresters to be given shelter there and to be recognized as settlers; they paid to one or the other rents in money and a share of the crops or the young animals. This example shows how, in the field of agrarian history, the most fruitful research is nourished by constantly comparing the actual countryside with written sources.[1]

. . . Questioned about the two sous of rent for the assart of Philippe Gaumer, [he] has seen Élie Gaumer holding the said assarts and rendering two sous of rent for them to the knight of Bonneuil. . . . Questioned on the lands and assarts which Pierre Jorget held, said he had never seen corn sown at that place, if not by the man who held it now, and the man from whom he bought it; and they had always been held from the

[1] I owe my knowledge of this combination of documents to the kindness of Monsieur Sanfaçon, professor at Laval University in Quebec.

PLATE V

Document 45
Bonneuil in Poitou: a settlers' village in a forest
(See p. 400)

lord count. When he was asked from what time he had seen corn sown, he replied 25 years, and added that he had seen on these lands and assarts before they had been converted to agriculture, beeches and many other great trees. . . .

Questioned about the assart of the well of Pelac and of whom it was held, he told of having seen the viscount of Châtellerault granting the said assart for rent to Jean Bogot,

Bonneuil in the forest of Moulière

at least ten years ago. But Navier, master of the forest of Moulière, did not allow that the said Jean held the said assart, and granted it to another man, a certain Raimond. Questioned about the assarts of Pierre Jorget, in the valley of the Loubière, he said he had never seen anything rendered from these assarts except to the count of Poitiers. . . .

. . . Questioned on the assarts of Philippe Gaumer, [he] said he had seen Élie Gaumer who cultivated the said assart render to the knight of Bonneuil four deniers per *arpent*. . . . Questioned on the assarts of Pierre Jorget, in the valley of the Loubière, [he] told of having always seen rendered the fifth of the corn of that assart to the men of the count of Poitier and not to others. . . .

. . . Questioned on the assarts of Pierre Jorget, in the valley of the Loubière, [he] said he believed they were held from the lord of Bonneuil, because all around are the lands owing the fourth to this lord. . . .

. . . Testimony of Navier, bailiff of the lord count in la Moulière:

He said that Élie Chalumeau, Jean Godereau and Ayraut Jadin were 'sheltered' by Renaud de Mars, who held that of the count. . . . He said that the lord count has all high and low justice over the 'sheltered people' (*hébergés*), and the lord of Bonneuil the same. . . . Questioned about the two sous of rent on the assarts of Philippe Gaumer, [he] said that he gave the assarts to cultivate to the fifth, because his predecessor, the master of the forest who was called Pujol, had taken away the markers of these assarts and granted these said assarts; he believes that the lord count has a right over them. . . .

. . . Questioned about the two sous of the assart of Philippe Gaumer, and about the other words, says he knows nothing except by hearsay, except that the assart of Pierre Jorget . . . is held of the lord count. Questioned on the manner in which he knows it, says that he has seen at that place the forest of Moulière where there were great beeches; and because that forest belonged to the lord count, [he] says that the assart made in that place was held of the count. . . .

. . . Questioned on the assarts of Philippe Gaumer, says that at least twenty-five years ago, on the order of Pujol and with him, he expelled Philippe Gaumer from the said assarts and took away the boundary stones which he had placed there on the orders of the viscount. . . .

. . . Questioned about the assarts of the well of Pelac, of whom they were held from ancient times, [he] says that he does not know, except that he has heard said to his mother that they were held of a certain Morin. Questioned about of whom the assarts of Pierre Jorget are held, he says that they are held of the count. Questioned whether he knows of whom the assart of Guillaume Bigot is held, he says: of the lord of Bonneuil. Questioned about the manner by which he knows it, he says he has seen the young pigs rendered to the said lord. . . .

Inquest for Alphonse, count of Poitiers (1253-1269) about the rights of the count of Poitiers and the lord of Bonneuil in the hamlet of Traversais and around about. Arch. Nat. J., 1032, No. 12 (ed. Barbonnet), in *Archives historiques du Poitou*, VIII, 1879, pp. 79-113.

46

This document describes once more a plan to clear the woodland on the lord's initiative. The three knights who together owned this forest of Bas-Morvan declare themselves prepared to 'shelter' those ready to break up the soil and agree together on ways of attracting them. They offer a specified parcel of land and grazing in return for a small due, a grant of rights of usage in the woodland (especially permission to put up the necessary enclosures against the wild and domestic animals which roamed the forest), lower fines, and a guarantee not to keep more than one official. By thus strictly limiting the knights' own demands, which were further reduced by a half for the households which had no plough team, these clauses recall the stipulations of twelfth-century charters of settlement. The important thing is that peasant immigration –

already begun when the act of abergement (*settlement*) *was drawn up – took the form of dispersed settlement: an area of thin woodland and hedgerow* (bocage) *was created.*

We, Hugues, sire of Marigny, Hugues de Marizy, knights, and Joceran de Communes, knight, lords of the woodland of Marizy, make it known to all those who will hear and see these present letters, that we lease and live and shelter all those who wish to come and stay in the said woods, to each six *bichonées* of land and a cartload of hay, for seven sous of Vienne, and a customary measure (*bichet*) of oats and a chicken to pay each year at St Martin's Day in winter to our said lords or to our certain command. And if he wishes each of the said 'settlers' (*abergeurs*) can have up to two *mex* (of land) each, for as much as it is divided thereon. And we desire and lay down that each of them has his usage of the said woodland of Marizy, to wit in the dead wood and in the live wood, to house and to enclose his *mex*. And that to the said settlement, there shall be but one official, who swears on the holy Evangelists that he shall well and loyally settle, divide and share between our afore-mentioned lords the revenues of the said settlement (*abergements*). And let the said official have each year from each of the said settlers who shall have oxen one quarter of oats; from each of them who shall not have oxen, half a quarter. Save that we can move and change the official of the said settlement at all times that we may desire. And we desire that when any one of the said settlers shall fall under a great fine of 65 sous, let him be quit for 32 sous and a half, and from all plaint for three or six deniers. And that none other than we three lords can impose on the said settlement our usages. . . . And all these things, we, Hugues, lord of Marigny, and Hugues de Marizy, knights, and we, Joceran, knight afore-mentioned, promise, in good faith and by solemn stipulation, and by our oath on the Holy Evangelists, all these things afore-mentioned, each one for himself, to keep firmly; and if it happens that he should fail, that if any one of the said settlers wishes to leave the said settlement, he may go from it alone, paying his custom, and he may sell and exploit his *mex*, according to the customs of Montchanin. In witness of which thing, we the aforesaid three lords of the woods of Marizy have sealed these letters with our seal. Given and made this year of grace twelve hundred and seventy five, in the month of June.

Copy of December 1311.
Archives de la Côte-d'Or, B.11.476.

4. Other Topographical Traces

47-48

(see between pages 404-5)

From England comes the exciting prospect of systematically exploring the contemporary countryside through aerial photography and thereby revealing traces of medieval colonization. The first of the two oblique views reproduced here[1] shows the structure of a village cleared from the wastes in Derbyshire, fossilized by the later erection of low walls on the edges of the ancient

[1] Plate VI. M. W. Beresford and J. K. St Joseph, *Medieval England. An aerial survey*, Cambridge, 1958, fig. 36, p. 97.

fields. Along the road which serves as the approach axis are aligned houses surrounded by their gardens. Behind each extends a narrow, elongated strip pushed out into the waste, and the garden and the strip together compose the area under permanent cultivation. In the foreground and in the upper righthand corner there are much larger rectangular plots. These probably occupy the position of the medieval 'outfield' in the peripheral area reserved for common pasture, a small part of which was devoted each year to temporary cultivation.

The striking picture of the village lands of Farlow[2] in Shropshire illustrates very well the process by which hedgerow landscape was formed through the piecemeal clearing of woods and heaths. On the right hand side the plots won from the uncultivated land, enclosed because they were isolated, have joined up, but they preserve the network of hedges dividing the landscape. The left hand side of the picture shows a less advanced stage of the conquest: a few islands of cultivation dot the widespread pastures.

5. *Common Lands and Protected Lands*

49

Here is an example of a conflict between a member of the village community holding customary rights of usage through the tenancy he occupies, and the master of a waste who was determined to put it into cultivation, and thus to enclose it, at least temporarily, against collective grazing.

(1236-1237)

The assize comes to recognize if Elias of Leyburn unjustly etc. disseised Wymar of Leyburn of common of his pasture pertaining to his free tenement in the same town of Leyburn after, etc.

The jurors say that the wood was at one time common, in such wise that there were five sharers who had the wood common, and afterwards by their consent partition was made between them that each should have his part in severalty, and it was granted that each might assart his part and grow corn, saving however to each of them common of herbage after the corn was carried, and most of them assarted their part, but the wood whereof complaint was made was not then assarted, and because he to whom the wood pertains has now assarted a part the said Wymar has brought a writ of *novel disseisin*. It is decided that the aforesaid Elias disseised him, and so Elias is dismissed *sine die* and Wymar is in mercy. And it shall be lawful for each sharer to assart his wood, saving to each of them common of pasture after the corn and hay is carried.

English Economic History, Select Documents,
Bland, Brown & Tawney (eds.), 1914, pp. 88-89.

50

This extract from the rolls of the Pleas of the Forest (special courts with jurisdiction over all

[2] Plate VII. *Ibid.*, fig. 34, p. 94.

PLATE VI

Document 47
A Derbyshire village (Chelmorton) showing fields taken from the waste
(See p. 403)

PLATE VII

Document 48
Farlow in Shropshire: an example of hedgerow landscape
(See p. 403)

suits relating to the forests of the English kings) shows that the foresters, in their zeal to protect their master's interests and all that was due to him in the way of game and woodland products, threatened and tried to reduce communal usages.

(1256)

The townships of Ellington, Brampton, Little Stukeley and Alconbury come to say that they are accustomed and ought to have common herbage in Weybridge for all their beasts, on the ground that their arable lands and their meadows which are fit to be mown and abut upon the lord king's demesne wood of Weybridge; and that their lands and meadows are wasted by the deer of the lord king; so that they have not nor can have any profit therefrom; and on that account they had the aforesaid common in the time of the predecessors of the lord king who now is; and also in the fifth year of the reign of the lord king who now is, they were in seisin until a certain Walter the son of Robert who was then steward of the forest in the county of Huntingdon ejected them and kept them out of that common all his time; and every steward one after another until now kept them out in the same way.

The townships of Hartford and King's Ripton say that they are wont and ought to have common of herbage in Sapley, on the ground that the said townships sometime were demesne manors of the king; and at that time it was granted by the kings, ancestors of the king who now is, that they should have common of the said herbage, coming therefor in every year on the feast of St John the Baptist for every four beasts one penny only; and say they had common of the said herbage in the time of the kings, predecessors of the king who now is; and also in the fifth year of the king who now is they were in seisin thereof until a certain Walter the son of Robert, who was then steward of the forest in this county, ejected them and kept them out of the said common in all his time; and every steward one after the other kept them out in the same way.

Select Pleas of the Forest, G. J. Turner (ed.),
Selden Society, 1901, pp. 25-26.

51

This map (p. 406) shows the enormous extentions of the lands placed, after the conquest of England by the Normans, under the 'forest' system, and thus reserved for the royal hunt, in which all damage caused to the woods was severely punished.

*   *   *

The village communities, strongly entrenched in Italy and Provence under the leadership of their magistrates, regulated agrarian life for the collective good. At the end of the thirteenth century one of their most pressing preoccupations was to protect the forest against abuse by its users, and more still against individual assarters who devastated the terre gaste by periodic slash and burn activities. Another anxiety was the proliferation of cattle, which ransacked the cultivated lands and exhausted the grazing. At times helped by the lord, master of the ban and the justice whose interest it was to inflict new fines on possible violators, the communities

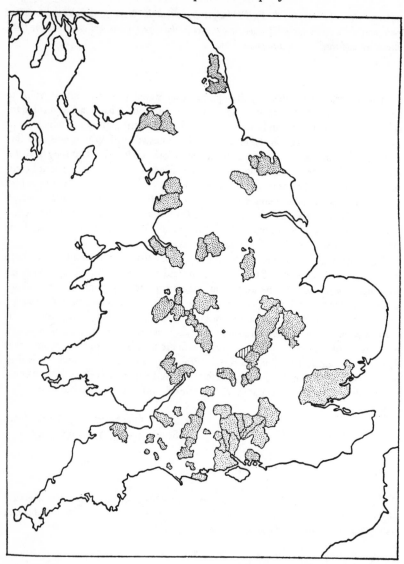

H. C. Darby, *An Historical Geography of England,*
Cambridge, 1936, p. 177.

||||| known extension
▓▓ probable extension

Extension of Royal forests after the Conquest
(see p. 405)

limited the size of the individual flocks and protected the growth of the trees and grass, which in the Mediterranean lands were so easily damaged, by establishing 'prohibited areas'.

52

... Item, we establish that eveiy one of our commune shall be bound to plant each year ten domestic trees, that is each manse, and to this are bound the rector and the chamberlain in the time of their office. And whoever shall go against it shall be punished each time by twelve sous.

... Item, we establish that the rector must call upon three good heads of *manses* in the said commune, who must mark all the common land, and being marked, no one must plough within these limits, and who shall contravene this shall be punished each time by ten sous in cash.

... Item, we establish and order that every head of a family or *manse* of Montaguloto and of the 'hall' shall be bound to plant a garden of leeks to the extent of 200 *brasses*,[1] and a border of chives, and 400 little onions and 50 heads of garlic. He is bound to this by the oath made to the commune; and from the contravener, the chamberlain is bound to take five sous per garden. And the chamberlain must have the order proclaimed that every man must make the said garden, and he is bound to have a search made by two men to make sure the said gardens are planted.

Statuto del commune di Montaguloto dell' Ardinghesca, 1280-1297, Statuti Senesi scritti in volgare ne' secoli XIII a XIV (ed. F. Polidori), Bologna, 1863, Vol. I, pp. 16, 24, 33.

53

(30th March 1315)

In the communal place, in the general assembly of the men of Folgara, these rules have been laid down which must be observed by all.

1. If any person is found by the communal guard in the act of causing damage with his animals, at night, in the meadows and the fields which are not his, he shall pay a fine of sixty sous; if he is found in the daytime, he shall pay twelve sous per beast.

2. If anyone is found in the vineyard with a flock of goats or sheep, he shall pay 20 sous for the whole flock, and five sous if it is in another place.

3. If anyone is found off the public way and crossing the meadow of another with oxen or cows harnessed to a waggon, he shall pay five sous for each pair of beasts.

4. If the guard finds anyone pasturing cattle in the vineyard of another man, he shall inflict on him a fine of five sous per animal.

5. If anyone is found causing damage or cutting wood in the enclosure of a house, he shall pay five sous per stump.

[1] Measurement related to the length of an arm.

6. If a horse is found causing damage in a meadow or sown field belonging to another person, the owner shall pay five sous and the value of the damage.

7. If anyone is caught cutting wood on the hill 'at Galieni' as far as the path of the men of Costa which leads to the mountain, and from the peak down to the plain, he shall pay five sous per stump.

8. Let no one dare to cut larchpoles to make firewood on this mountain, on pain of five sous per trunk.

9. Let no one dare to cut wood from Xomo up to the rock of Slamer and from the peak of the mountain towards Xomo, save to construct a house or for the fire, on pain of five sous per tree.

Fonti di Storia Trentina, Documenti e regesti,
Trento, 1929, pp. 28-29.

54

The year of the birth of Our Lord 1334, 6th November. Let it be known by the terms of this public declaration that the noble and mighty lady Raibaude de Caussol, dame of the said village called Cipières of the one part, and of the other part the men of the community of the said village of Cipières, whose names and surnames are inscribed below, gathered together in public parliament by proclamation in the enclosure of the court of the said lady, on the order of the said lady by the summons of Jean Escoffier, nuncio, public cryer and juror of the said court, have established, ordered and decided in the said village of Cipières and its territory the chapters and statutes below, notwithstanding the chapters and statutes already laid down by the said lady with the men of the said community. These statutes have been written down and ordered by the hand of Jean Mayrgues, of Trets, notary public, as the parties have affirmed.

First of all the said noble lady Raibaude, with the men whose names are written below, has desired, established and directed that all the men of the village of Cipières and persons present and future may hold and pasture freely without punishment a cow inside the protected part of the meadows of Syre and le Plan, at the same times as the oxen and the plough beasts, and that this cow may pasture in all places and in all seasons where the plough oxen are put.

Item . . . that the men of the village of Cipières, present and future, may hold and pasture freely without punishment four goats in the upper protected areas of le Plan, to wit from the road which goes from the village of Cipières towards the hill of Caillol by the gap of le Plan and from there to the said hill of Caillol, and that in the other prohibited areas goats may not enter. The goatherds who shall guard the said goats shall swear each year not to introduce the said goats nor any other like animal into the other prohibited areas, under the punishment and fine contained in the other statutes of the said protected areas. . . .

Archives des Bouches-du-Rhône,
396 E 18, folio 278.

The year of the birth of Our Lord 1337, 25th July. Be it known to all present and future that the noble and mighty lady, dame Raibaude de Caussol, dame of the said place Cipières, on the one part, for herself and for hers, and Michel Guisol and Guillaume André, men of the said village, by virtue of the powers conferred on them by the majority of the men of this community in public parliament, as it appears to me, notary public, by the ordinance made by them in the village of Caussol, assembled yesterday morning by proclamation called by Pierre Brun, nuncio and public cryer of the court of Caussol, on the direction of Guillaume Gaibien, bailiff of the said village....

The said lady with the said men, has established that the protected areas of the *plan* of Caussol and Villevieille shall be prohibited and protected in the following manner: from mid-March of each year, no animal of the said lady or of anyone in the village, shall penetrate into the meadows of Caussol nor pasture in the *plan* until Michaelmas in September; from mid-April until Michaelmas, no small animal must enter the banks of the said *plan* included in the protected area of this *plan*; from mid-April until All Saints Day, no animal must enter the prohibited area of Villevieille, on pain of the customary punishment for this protected area, and thereafter all cattle large and small may enter.

... Item.... If any person or shepherd, of the said lady or of any other person, puts some animal in the said protected areas at a prohibited time, let all the herdsmen of the village enter the protected area with their cattle or the cattle which they guard, once only, without punishment, and let the one who entered first pay the punishment for all the others who shall come in after him. Thus shall the said protected areas be perpetually protected.

Item ... the draught oxen of the said lady or other persons shall not enter these protected places during the periods fixed above, save when they collect the hay in the protected place of the *plan*, or when they sow, or when they gather the sheaves and other corn, or when they plough in the limits of the said protected place; they shall not pasture on pain of the customary punishment for each time that they shall enter or pasture; the ploughmen shall pay the fine from their cash....

Archives des Bouches-du-Rhône,
396 E 18, folio 91.

C. WIDENING OF EXCHANGE ACTIVITIES

1. *Traffic in Goods*

56

This custumal, drawn up by order of the monks of St Aubin of Angers, fixes in a rather haphazard manner the 'good customs' for one of the bourgades on their manor. Details of the rights of pasture are laid down and the nature of certain violations defined. The gradual widening of the rural economy encouraged masters and peasants to set up a tariff of tolls. Its stipulations give us an idea of the ways in which the villagers participated in commercial activity. It sometimes happened that a few of them banded together to undertake a trading expedition, from which they brought back foodstuffs and less common goods to sell locally. But the principal trade was in cattle (it should be noted that a horse which had been shod was more valuable); already stockraising contracts united villagers and strangers. The peasants also 'peddled' such things as honey, wax, pigmeat, wool and skins in the neighbouring markets.

(1080–1082)

The men of Méron will have pasture at Lanthon for their animals, save for their sheep and goats, from Michaelmas until St Aubin's Day, up till the time the bushes bear fruit and foliage. From St Aubin's Day until Michaelmas, the woodland pasture shall be forbidden to all beasts belonging to villeins. Throughout the year, if any animal enters the wood to save itself and if the shepherd can show that he had no hand in knowingly directing it into the woods, he shall not pay a fine for this. . . .

. . . Tolls shall not be paid for what is carried on the neck, save for feathers, wax, lard, beehives and foreign and costly goods. For feathers, a denier; for a table or a honeycomb, a halfpenny; for a hive, a halfpenny; for more than six sous of lard, a halfpenny; for a ham with its lard, a denier; for a bed with bedding one denier; for a wedding outfit, four deniers; for an unshod horse or mare, one denier; if it is shod, two deniers; for an ox, an ass, or a pig, a halfpenny; for three sheep or three goats, one denier; for one load of wool, one denier.

If several men have loaded an ass with different kinds of merchandise, they shall owe toll for the ass, save if it is foreign or costly merchandise. For other things, the toll shall be paid according to its value. . . .

. . . For anything that a man of Méron shall bring in from outside for his own food, whether it be the fruit of his labour or goods that he has purchased, either bread, wine, meat, hay or any other thing, so long as he does not sell it, he shall not pay toll; if he sells anything here, he shall pay toll on the day on which he sells it.

. . . If shepherds or others take secretly in the vineyards fruit or grapes to eat and take home, but not to make wine, or if they steal as much as three sheaves, or take them from one field to another to steal them, and these things shall be found by their owner and taken back as his, this shall not be judged as larceny.

Similarly, little things, like a knife, an arrow, a bow, a shield, or an ass's traces. If such things, or others as small, are stolen, we prescribe that it shall not be judged as larceny.

If a villein of Méron removes his animals to a place outside the manor, and if he brings them back within a year and a day, he shall not pay toll. But if he hands these animals over to another man to be fattened, he shall pay toll the day when they return. Then he shall pay toll according to the increase.

If a villein wishes to sell the skins of his animals, such as catskins, lambskins or other similar animals' skins, he shall pay no toll, unless, in buying and selling he shall act as a merchant.

Cartulaire de Saint-Aubin d'Angers
(ed. Lelong), Vol. I, pp. 262–264.

The castellan of la Ferté Hubert, in the region of Blois, hands over the church of his castle to the monks of St Mesmin de Micy; he completes his gift by the grant of a neighbouring forest to be cleared by a kind of pariage *contract, keeping for himself half the tithe on the crops* (terrage) *raised on the future assarts. But his main intention was that a market town should grow up between the church and his castle; its inhabitants, while remaining very close to the soil and its labours, would devote themselves to trade.*

(1105)

... I give to them also, within the surrounding wall, the land now empty from the nave of the church of St Sulpice up to the moat of my castle, and I give them permission to install as settlers all those who shall come from elsewhere to settle down and to live, and let them build their houses there, with full permission, save only those who belong to my castellany and who may not do so without my consent. These settlers I render free and unencumbered of all demands; nothing shall be required of them by me and my officials, save this: if one of them shall trade on my land, he shall render the just custom, but if they or any others buy or sell or engage in large or small-scale trade on the land of the monks or outside, the justice and the customs shall be the monks'. I make them free of all military duties and riding service, but if some enemy of mine attacks my castle, the prior will mobilize them immediately with my burgesses; if thieves or knights rob me and I wish to recover the goods, the settlers shall follow me on this expedition. ...

I give the monks my woodlands for firewood and building, as my vassals use them and where they use them; but their burgesses shall not take the wood that I have mentioned to sell it, in conformity with the custom of my burgesses. And to those who live in their own homes I give pannage up to one hundred pigs. ... I give them my allod near the wood of Marne, between the roads to Beaugency and St Laurent-des-Eaux, that is, what belongs to my demesne, according to the following agreement. I grant them the rural habitations, that is the barns, which are necessary, to the monks as well as to their peasants who shall come as settlers in the old and new sites; each shall have his *arpent* and they shall be, with their *arpent* and their *hôtise*, in the manor of the monks, not dependent on me, according to the franchise of their men who shall live on their free holding. The said monks shall have in the said land a plough team of their own, without any tithe or share of the crops (terrage) being due to me nor to anyone else. The other men who shall cultivate this land shall render to me a half share of the tithe (terrage) and the other half to the monks, save for their *arpent* above mentioned. The monks shall have their barn where the whole share of the tithe (terrage) shall be taken and stored, to be divided between me and them without any dispute.

J. Martin-Demezil, *Recherches sur les origines et la formation de l'"aireau' blésois,* in *Mélange Cl. Brunel,* Paris, 1953, Vol. II, pp. 262-263.

This collection of customs regulates in great detail the trading activities inside the sanctuary cross which contains the enfranchised zone around the village of Chapelaude in the region of Berri.

1. *The lord arrogates to himself the right to lay up provisions on credit, especially meat, the foremost item on the diet of the nobility, which he was permitted to requisition. His privilege (banvin) was quite arbitrary and allowed him to dispose of the produce of his vineyards before any one else at the moment most favourable to the seller. Custom allowed him to have privileges as a buyer and as a trader.*

2. *He profited in many other ways from the commercial activities of his subjects. In fact the bakers lived in the market town and its other inhabitants usually sold meat and grain by auction, as well as wine which appears to have been the principal object of trade. The lord levied dues in kind on all sales of wine and meat in the village and he taxed all those who took their wine elsewhere to sell it. He also took his share in the profits of the bakers by operating a monopoly on mill and bakehouse (all household ovens were destroyed and their use forbidden).*

3. *On the other hand the villagers expected him to control trading activity. It was for him to guarantee weights and measures; to ensure the circulation of a money that was current in the market towns of the neighbourhood; to maintain prices, but to prevent any unreasonable rise; to see that any travellers who might pass through the village, as possible purchasers of bread, wine, or meat, were not exploited; to protect visitors to the periodic fairs during which the seigneurial monopolies were interrupted.*

4. *Money was scarce, which explains the habitual recourse to short-term credit and the use of deferred payments guaranteed by pledges, which were sold by auction on the spot at the end of the fixed term.*

(Middle of the twelfth century)

... 8. (The prior) will have credit in the village for bread, meat and other merchandises up to fourteen days. For wine which is sold he shall have credit for the fourteen days following the sale of the wine.

9. If a man of importance is lodging with the monks, and if there is no meat to be found in the village, the sergeants shall take pigs and chickens, and on the judgment of two or three men, the prior shall pay the price to those to whom they belong at the end of fourteen days.

10. Whenever he shall so wish, the prior shall sell his wine under privilege (*ban*), save at fairtimes. No inhabitant of the village shall then be allowed to sell his, so long as there shall remain anything to sell of the monks' wine, save if he has put it up to auction before the *ban*. But at fairtime whoever wishes may sell, from one Sunday to the next, even if there is a *ban*; after this Sunday, no one, save those who shall have begun to sell the wine put up for auction before the *ban*. If anyone does otherwise and dares to violate the *ban*, he shall pay sixty sous. The monks shall not sell wine under the *ban* dearer than any other.

11. No one shall dare to increase or decrease the size of the measure of wine or grain which the prior has established. If he does so, he shall pay a fine and the measure

of the wrong size shall be broken. If he wishes to make a second one and hold it as customary, he shall pay sixty sous.

12. If anyone sells bread, wine or meat, to a traveller more dearly than to his neighbour, and is convicted of doing so, he shall first of all indemnify the man he shall have cheated, and then shall pay a fine according to his condition. If it is habitual, as mentioned before.

13. If anyone dares to raise the sale price of wine, such as has been fixed, he must not do so and shall be liable to a fine.

14. If the bakers, save at the fairs, make loaves for sale smaller than they ought to be in relation to the price of wheat, either they shall lose the loaves or else they shall pay a fine.

15. If anyone, living between the four crosses, bakes bread elsewhere than in the oven of St Denis, and this is proved, he shall first pay the charge for baking, and then a fine.

16. If anyone has a damper and habitually bakes his bread below it, the damper shall be broken and he shall pay a fine.

17. Similarly, if it is proved that someone has ground grain elsewhere than in the saint's mill, he shall pay the right of multure and a fine.

18. It is laid down that every inhabitant of la Chapelle who shall expose wine to sell shall give the monks one *setier* per cask.

19. If anyone kills an ox or a pig for sale, he shall give one pennyworth of pork, two of beef.

20. If anyone exports from the village wine on an ass or in a cart to trade, he shall pay a halfpenny per ass, and four deniers per cart.

21. The prior shall impose in the village, with the council of monks and the sergeants, a currency which shall be useful to him and to the burgesses and which shall be accepted around la Chapelle, at Huriel, at St Desire and other neighbouring places. . . .

29. It shall be added that no one, either villager or stranger, may seize a pledge inside the crosses without having carried a complaint before the prior or the provost; if he does so, he shall pay a fine and give back the pledge that he has seized, unless he can prove that he was ignorant of the prohibition. But he may seize a pledge if a promise of payment has been made in the village; nevertheless, he shall not carry the pledge outside the village, he shall not provoke a brawl with the debtor if the latter takes back the pledge and he shall not seize the pledge a second time. He shall first carry a complaint to the prior who shall enquire into his right and that of the other party.

C. van de Kieft, *Étude sur le chartrier et la seigneurie du prieuré de la Chapelle-Aude (XIe-XIIIe siècle,)* Amsterdam, 1960, pp. 241-244.

59

To the inhabitants of this village (who were called 'burgesses' because they enjoyed franchises), an inquest into the customs conducted by the two co-lords, the king and the bishop, assured the right of sale of wine from their houses, and more important still, since in this wine-growing country far from the great consuming centres wine was not the object of much trade, of grain. The villagers had profited by the passing of Louis VIII on his way to the crusade against the Albigensians to obtain a weekly market; the promise of a safe conduct for those who were going to attend it would be likely to attract buyers. But the reduction of the taxes of weights and measures which they enjoyed in this market protected direct sales by the inhabitants from the activities of brokers and outside intermediaries.

(1243)

We Seguin, bishop of Mâcon, and Amaury, bailiff of Mâcon, on behalf of the Lord King ... at the request of our men of Prissé, have been personally in this village to enquire into the customs. Having compared the oldest and the most worthy of belief of the villeins who deposed on oath, we have found the following customs:

... For blood there are three customs: for the blood which is called *volage*, three sous are paid by the one who caused it, but only if the victim brings a complaint; for the blood caused by a weapon, but without danger of death, sixty sous and one denier; for the blood caused by a weapon and followed by death: the culprit falls on the mercy of the lord.

Everyone may sell grain and wine in his house and may possess measures.

The men of the village may take upon themselves, without referring to the lords or their officials, the guard over the grain, the vineyards and the meadows.

... If someone coming from elsewhere lives in the village for a year and a day without being claimed by a lord, he shall be held to be a burgess of the village and be protected as a free man by the lords.

When the king of France, Louis of happy memory, passed through Prissé on the way to Avignon he granted to the men of the village a weekly market on Mondays. For grain, wherever it shall be sold, if it is measured in the village on the day of the market or on another day, one cutting (*coupon*) per *meitier* is due from outsiders, and the half only from burgesses; for measures smaller than the *meitier*, nothing is paid. The measure that we have given shall be used, but services shall be acquitted according to the ancient measure, for we desire to change nothing in this respect.

We promise *guiage* (safe conduct) to those who shall come to the market or who shall come back to it. ...

We confirm all these customs, save the other good usages and customs of the village and save our rights and those of the king. In witness whereof, we have given to these men the present letters with our seal.

Archives de Saône-et-Loire, G. 96, No. 2.

60-61

The count levied toll at Valensole on the principal route connecting the high pastoral valleys of the southern Alps with the sea and the Provençal plains. Thanks to details contained in a fragment of the toll accounts for the years 1307-1308, we can identify the different localities from which those who used this compulsory staging post on the route came. Both specialist and

CALENDAR OF THE TRAFFIC (IN MERCHANDISE) THROUGH VALENSOLE

(Merchandise passing most frequently is indicated by Capitals)

	January	February	March	April	May	June	July	August	September	October	November	December
	Cloth	Cloth	Cloth	Cloth	Cloth	Cloth	Cloth		CLOTH	CLOTH	CLOTH	Cloth
	Fish	FISH	FISH	Fish								Fish
			Grain	Grain	Grain	Grain	GRAIN					
	SALT	SALT	SALT	SALT								
	Wool	Wool	Wool		Wool						Wool	
	Skins	SKINS	Skins	Skins	Skins	Skins		Skins			Skins	
	Sheep		Sheep			Sheep		Sheep	Sheep	Sheep	Sheep	Sheep
						Goats						
	OXEN	OXEN	Oxen	OXEN			Oxen		Oxen		Oxen	OXEN
	Timber	Timber	Timber	Timber	Timber	TIMBER	TIMBER	TIMBER	Timber	Timber	Timber	Timber

Th. Sclafert, *Cultures en Haute-Provence. Déboisements et pâturages au moyen age,* Paris, 1959, p. 80.

general merchants and muledrivers came from some of the smallest mountain and lowland villages.

We know also what their merchandise was and we can appreciate the seasonal balancing of the exchanges between the upland country of herdsmen and woodcutters who sent timber, young plough beasts and skins down to the south-west and coastal Provence. Men from the lowlands provided the peasants in the Alps with salt in winter, fish during Lent, grain between spring and the late upland harvest, and finally, in the autumn, after the great cattle fairs which marked the end of transhumance, textiles.

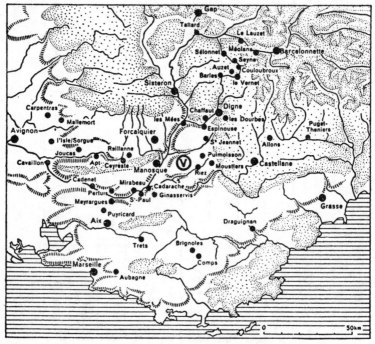

Place of Origin of Merchants and Muledrivers passing through the toll at Valensole in 1307-1308

After Th. Sclafert, *Cultures en Haute-Provence, Déboisements et pâturages au moyen age,* Paris, 1959, p. 73.

*   *   *

Archives of royal and ecclesiastical establishments in England provide a great deal of very detailed numerical evidence about the trade in agricultural commodities. This data can be expressed in statistical curves and represented on maps.

62-63

1. *Compiled from the account rolls of the manors of the bishopric of Winchester, the curve of seven-year moving averages of sale prices of the different cereals (p. 418) shows, by eliminating short-term fluctuations, a slow and continuous rise throughout the thirteenth century. Between 1320 and 1325 a more pronounced oscillation corresponds to the first of the great food shortages from which England suffered in the fourteenth century. It should be noted that the prices of the four principal cereals showed similar tendencies.*

2. *In comparing, for the first quarter of the fourteenth century for which documentary evidence is most abundant, the curve of the price of wheat with the inverse curve of the yield of seed (p. 419), we can see that the movements of prices follow, particularly after 1310, the annual fluctuations of harvests.*

64-65

These two maps, compiled from an inquest drawn up in 1338 on the demesnes which the Hospitallers owned in Provence, show how much prices and wages could vary, and often in different ways, from one district to another in this part of the country. (See pp. 420 & 421).

66

1. *The map on p. 422 shows the principal ports which exported English grain in the fourteenth century. Chief among them was Lynn, close to the great producing regions of East Anglia and accessible to the consuming markets of Scandinavia.*

2. *The dotted lines encircle the zones of low wheat prices (less than 6d. per quarter), where production was most likely to be surplus to requirements. Note the situation of village lands in the East Midlands, marked with a cross, where it is known from written documents that the agrarian system was modified in order to intensify the cultivation of cereals.*

67-68

About 1340 convoys of pack animals, carts and river barges in successive relays conveyed wool and cereals to the exporting ports, from the great ecclesiastical establishments which produced these goods themselves and also collected peasant surpluses in their neighbourhood. (See maps on p. 423).

2. Credit Operations

69

The monks of Cluny bought on the demesne of a small country lord an annual rent in wine and grain which was intended to supply the refectory of the great abbey. It was in fact a period

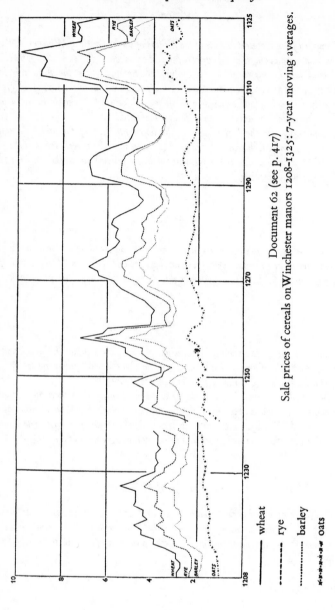

Document 62 (see p. 417)

Sale prices of cereals on Winchester manors 1208–1325: 7-year moving averages.

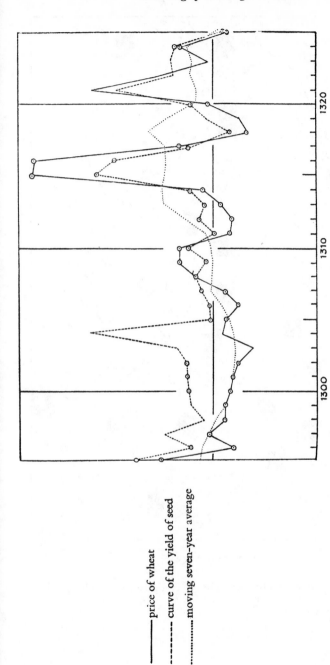

Document 63 (see p. 417)

Winchester Wheat prices & yields compared 1295–1325

The two graphs illustrate D. L. Farmer's study, 'Some Grain Price Movements in thirteenth-century England' in *Economic History Review*, 2nd ser., X (1957).

——— price of wheat

------- curve of the yield of seed

·········· moving seven-year average

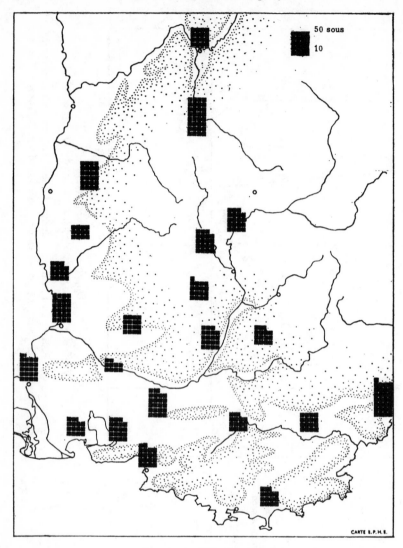

Document 64 (see p. 417)

Ration of wheat allocated to a brother on Provençal demesnes of the Hospitallers

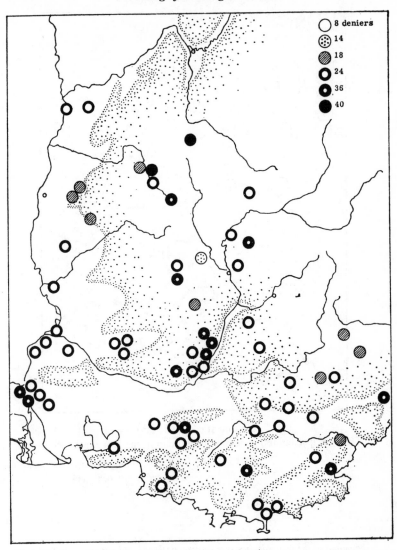

Document 65 (see p. 417)
Day wages of a reaper on Provençal demesnes of the Hospitallers

G. Duby, 'La seigneurie et l'économie paysanne, Alpes du Sud, 1338', in *Études rurales*, 1961, pp. 25, 31.

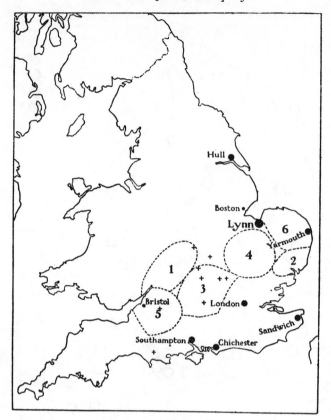

Document 66 (see p. 417)
The principal English ports exporting grain in the fourteenth Century

H. C. Darby (Ed.), *An Historical Geography of England*,
Cambridge, 1936, p. 236.

when the output of the monastic demesnes, so long neglected, did not suffice to feed growing communities. Indeed prices continued to rise and administrators were looking for ways of re-ducing purchases of food. This rent, whose regular payment was guaranteed by a right of seizure on the land, was partly paid for by a spiritual service: the anniversary feast was to re-mind the monks that on that day they must pray specially for the donor and the deceased mem-bers of his family. From one point of view the operation was no more than a pious funerary donation. But the knight Bertrand also needed a large sum in cash. In exchange, his allod was burdened with a service in perpetuity and there was no provision for the vendor or his heirs to repurchase this rent at some future date.

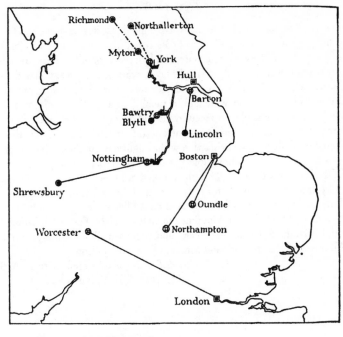

————————— waggon transport
-·-·-·-·-·-·-·-· waggon and pack animal transport

Documents 67 & 68 (see p. 417)
Road and river traffic to English ports

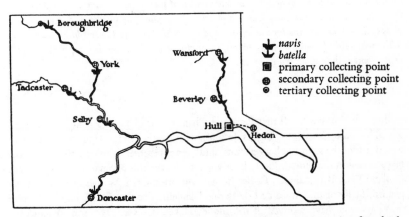

H. C. Darby (Ed.), *An Historical Geography of England*,
Cambridge, 1936, p. 264.

423

(1128-1134)

Know ye all present and future that I, Bertrand de Cortevaix, give, and I confirm this by the present charter, to God, to St Peter and the community of Cluny, two *muids* of pure wine of the Cluny measure, and four *setiers* of pure wheat, and a fifth of beans (or wheat if there are no beans) to be taken every year on my allod in the village of Bresse sur-Grosne. We shall levy nothing, neither I nor my successors, on this allod, in wheat and other grain, in wine and in money, or any other thing, from all the revenues before Cluny shall have received the said quantity of wine, wheat and beans. If I or one of my successors commits some injustice or some fraud against this agreement, and if we shall not give satisfaction within eight days, to the good pleasure of the monks of Cluny, we shall wholly lose the allod and it shall fall in perpetuity to the right of the brothers of Cluny. With the things that I give, a feast has been instituted on the day of my father's birth, for the salvation of the soul of my mother, my father and all my kindred, as well as for the soul of dom Élie, monk, who was hospitaller of Cluny, for that of his father, and mother and all his kindred. For this donation, I have received, I Bertrand de Cortevaix, seven hundred sous in Cluny money, from the said Élie. All this with the approval and consent of my wife Julienne.

Recueil des chartes de l'abbaye de Cluny (ed. Bernard & Bruel), 1876-1903, Vol. V, No. 4002.

70

These two deeds were accidentally preserved in the archives of a chapter because the religious establishment later received as a gift the landed rights which they enshrined. They reveal details of the different business deals which a burgess of Lyons concluded at the end of the twelfth century in three villages in the lower valley of the Saône. Playing upon the need for cash which the rural aristocracy found so pressing, he acquired, by purchase or by taking as a pledge, the income and the produce of the land which he then hoped to sell in his own town. There was a tithe (divided by inheritance), the profits of an office (also shared), and, lastly, the greater part of the output of a vineyard.

(*ca.* 1190)

Let it be known to all that Pierre de Chaintré has given as a pledge a vineyard which he has at Couson to Hugues de Vernay for thirteen livres. Hugues may receive two-thirds of the grapes at harvest time, and Pierre the other third, and this third shall be reckoned in the capital. Pierre has sworn to observe this covenant. Also sworn are Rolland Vers, Baron Bonet, Didier Bonet, who are sureties. Witnesses are the chapplain of St Romain, Girard de l'Ile Barbe, Dieulefit, Thomas, Jean Boudois, Etienne de Vilars, who have received of this money eleven livres and two sous, Rainier de Villon and Pierre de Varay, who have received 20 sous of *lods*, and also Hugues du Puits.

Let it be known also that the same Hugues has bought of Guillaume de Crotet, chaplain, half of the provosty of Sermoyer and the sixth of the tithe of Feillens. Julienne, sister of the said Guillaume, has given as a pledge to the said Hugues the fifth of the tithe of Feillens for four livres of Mâcon. Guillaume, her brother, surety, Guy de Baiviers has given as pledge to the said Hugues half of the provosty of Sermoyer and half of the tithe of Feillens for seven livres and tens sous of Mâcon. The said Guillaume his cousin, surety, with Pons de Chavannes and several others. All this was done by the hand of Acon, chaplain of Sermoyer and of Bernard, his clerk.

Cartulaire Lyonnais (ed. M. Guigue), Vol. I,
Lyon, 1885, p. 86.

71

Here is a Provençal example of a contract of gasaille. *A burgess buys two cows which he hands over to a rural cultivator (in this case a small noble) who is without funds. At the end of two years, after the spring fairs when young animals are sold, the associates will share the profits of the cows' offspring. The lender can then reclaim a sum which corresponds to the value of the two animals, to which is added interest on the loan.*

The year of Our Lord 1256, the fifteenth of the calends of March. . . .

Boniface Arnaud has given for half the increase to Messire Guillaume Pierre, knight of Montaigu, two cows, one of which is white and red and the other yellow and red, by gift and for a price of one hundred sous of Vienne. The two cows above mentioned, the said Guillaume Pierre admits to having received for half the increase . . . and it has been agreed between them that he may keep and feed the said cows, as it is said, from next Pentecost during two complete years to come, and that the said Boniface will receive the said hundred sous at which the said cows are estimated and half the increase at the due term.

Done in the church of St Sauveur, witness R. Santor, priest, R. Laugier, butcher, W. Proprin, Jacques Sellier.

Archives des Bouches-du-Rhône (O.H.), 1088.

72

The information for these two tables comes from the books of the notaries of Perpignan where in the thirteenth century the loans (excluding short-term loans on pledge) made by the Jews of the town were registered. To begin with it can be seen that the surrounding countryside provided the moneylenders with most of their clientèle. 40 per cent of the loans to country dwellers were contracted in the autumn months, the period of marriages and payment of manorial taxes. 53 per cent of the village debtors were bound to repay in August or September after the harvests and wine crops. Probably most of them freed themselves by liveries of grain or wine which the Jews then sold. *The contract for credit often concealed a forward purchase of the crop, concluded at a moment when the need for money pressed most heavily on country folk.*

DATE OF LOANS

Month	Village Debtors		Town Debtors	
	Number	Percentage	Number	Percentage
January	42	4·9	28	6·1
February	74	8·6	45	9·8
March	72	8·4	45	9·8
April	79	9·1	35	7·6
May	82	9·4	44	9·6
June	42	4·9	34	7·4
July	36	4·2	25	5·5
August	55	6·4	35	7·6
September	112	13·0	42	9·2
October	122	14·2	63	13·7
November	104	12·0	45	9·8
December	42	4·9	18	3·9

DATE OF REPAYMENT

Month	Village Debtors		Town Debtors	
	Number	Percentage	Number	Percentage
January	23	2·7	25	5·7
February	29	3·4	24	5·4
March	40	4·8	27	6·1
April	48	5·7	43	9·7
May	37	4·4	36	8·2
June	27	3·2	37	8·4
July	14	1·7	3	0·7
August	229	27·3	66	14·9
September	216	25·7	91	20·6
October	51	6·1	9	2·0
November	77	9·2	34	7·7
December	49	5·8	47	10·6

R. W. Emery, *The Jews of Perpignan in the XIIIth Century*, New York, 1959, pp. 64-65.

In the second half of the thirteenth century, Lombard moneylenders – many of whom came from Asti – began to set up casane, i.e. loan shops, in the countryside west of the Alps. The increasing demand for cash in rural areas promised them rewarding business. This map, drawn up from material taken from the archives of the count of Savoy who controlled these activities, reveals how widespread these shady establishments were during the first quarter of the fourteenth century in the countries subject to him. Almost all these places were villages or small market towns.

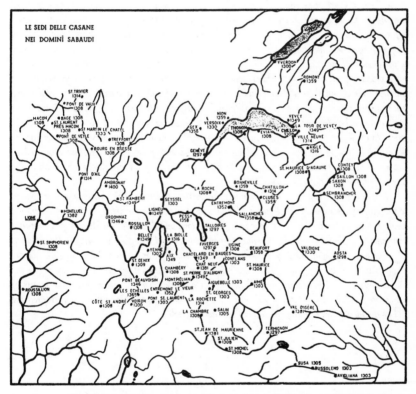

A. M. Patrone, *Le casane astigiane in Savoia* (*Miscellanea di storia italiana*), Turin, 1959.

III   The Manor. XI-XII Centuries

A.   LANDED WEALTH

1. The Domesday Book

When, at Christmas 1085, William the Conqueror held court at Gloucester, he expressed the wish to know what exactly was the wealth of the country he had conquered nineteen years before; he desired to know 'how many hides there were in the counties, what land and cattle the king possessed, and what taxes he could levy in each county'; He also wished to have an estimate of the wealth of the magnates, and the extent and equipment of their possessions. In the following months commissioners gathered evidence from the population, village by village, hundred by hundred. Here and there they met with resistance; a second tour was necessary, and many punishments were meted out because of false declarations. Afterwards all the local inventories were combined and recast into a 'feudal' plan; the possessions of each of the king's 'tenants in chief' in the different shires were grouped together. Thus, two huge volumes were drawn up and deposited in the royal treasury at Winchester. The enterprise and its results appeared so superhuman that already by the twelfth century the inquest had been named 'the book of the day of judgment' – the Domesday Book.

The description is arranged by manors, that is the residences of the lords who were bound to the king by the subordinate status of a feudal vassal. It reckons the area of the demesne and the lands granted in tenure in 'hides' (the unit of taxation) and the actual arable area and working equipment in 'ploughs'. All the dependants were counted and classified according to their status. The inquest also mentions anything that had been added to or taken away from each manor. It gives its total money value. It adds a brief inventory of what the free men attached to the manor possessed. The editors give all these facts as they existed at three successive points of time: 1066 – 'the time of King Edward'; the moment when the Conqueror had granted the fief of the manor; and finally the time of the inquest itself.

74

1. *Here the commissioners have carefully compared the declaration of the men of the manor with the evidence of the hundred court.*

2. *By 1086 the free dependants (sokemen) of the Saxon period have all disappeared.*

3. *The equipment in ploughs is adjusted to the arable area, as well as to the amount of meadowland which could feed the draught animals. The value of the manor had risen by 40 per cent between 1066 and 1086.*

4. *This manor had been threatened in Saxon days with rapid disintegration. A royal manor, it was partly held in farm by the king's representative, the sheriff. The latter had first*

Landed Wealth

of all endeavoured to reduce what he was bound to pay by a half, and then he used his share as security for a huge money loan.

CAMBRIDGESHIRE

In Staplehou (Staploe) Hundred.

The manor of Chipeham (Chippenham) was assessed at 10 hides T.R.E. but a certain sheriff reduced them to 5 hides by grant of the same King because the farm oppressed him, and now it is assessed at 5 hides. There is land for 17 ploughs, and Geoffrey holds it from the King. There are three hides in demesne, and [there are] three ploughs here. Here 19 villeins with 13 bordars have 14 ploughs. [There are] 6 serfs here, meadow for 3 ploughs, pasture for cattle of the vill, [and] 1500 eels from the fisheries. In all it is worth 20 *li*. When received [it was worth] 16 *li*; T.R.E. 12 *li*. This manor, Orgar, King Edward's sheriff, held who was afterwards the man of Asgar the Staller. Five hides of this land were in King E[dward's] farm, and 2 sokemen had 3 hides from the King and could give their land to whom they would, and yet each one provided 8d. or one horse in the King's service, and for their amercements (*forisfactura*) made amends in Forham (Fordham).

Orgar the sheriff himself had 3 hides of this land, and could give [it] to whom he would. Orgar put this land in pledge for 7 marks of gold and 2 ounces, as Geoffrey's men say, but the men of the hundred have seen neither any writ nor any messenger of King E[dward] concerning it, nor do they produce evidence.

Victoria County History (Cambridgeshire), Vol. I,
L. F. Salzmann (ed.), Oxford, 1938, pp. 382-383
(*Domesday Book*, Vol. I, fol. 197a).

75

The value of these manors remained unchanged between 1066 and 1086. They were under-equipped and did not possess enough ploughs to till all the land which could have been culti-vated. It should be noted how much the royal taxation varied from one manor to another in relation to the arable area and how the system of sub-infeudation broke up landed possessions

HUNTINGDONSHIRE

The Land of the Bishop of Lincoln: Toleslund (Toseland) Hundred.

M. In Cotes the bishop of Lincoln had 2 hides [assessed] to the geld. There is land for 3 ploughs. There are 2 ploughs now on the demesne, and [there are] 3 villeins having 2 oxen, and [there are] 20 acres of meadow. T.R.E. it was worth 40s. and [it is worth the same] now. Turstin holds it of the bishop.

M. in Tochestone (Staughton) the bishop of Lincoln had 6 hides [assessed] to the geld. There is land for 15 ploughs. There are now 2½ ploughs on the demesne, and [there are] 16 villeins and 4 bordars having 8 ploughs. There is a priest and a church, and [there are] 24 acres of meadow and 100 acres of underwood. T.R.E. it was worth

10 *li*. and [it is worth the same] now. Eustace holds it of the bishop. The abbot of Ramsey claims this manor against the bishop. . . .

The Land of Rohais wife of Richard son of Gilbert: Toleslund (Toseland) Hundred.

M. in Einulvesberie (Eynesbury) Robert son of Wimarch had 15 hides [assessed] to the geld. There is land for 27 ploughs. Rohais, Richard's wife has 7 ploughs on the demesne there now. In the same place Saint Neot has of her 3 ploughs on the demesne, and in the same vill [there are] 19 villeins and 5 bordars having 7 ploughs. There is one mill rendering 23s. and one fishery which is valued with the manor and [there are] 65½ acres of meadow. T.R.E. it was worth 24 *li*, now [it is worth] 21 *li*, apart from [that which is assigned to] the food of the monks, which is valued at 4 *li*.

William Brito holds 2 hides and 1 virgate of this land of Rohais and [there are] 3 villeins and 4 bordars with one plough. It is worth 30s.

Victoria County History (Huntingdonshire), Vol. I,
W. Page & G. Proby (eds.), London, 1926, pp. 340-341, 353
(*Domesday Book*, Vol. I, fol. 204-207).

76

On these lands, which formerly belonged to a Saxon lord, but which the King confiscated and kept in his own hands, the occupation of the soil was less dense, the free men more numerous, the arable measurements different and the structure of the manor less tightly knit. This was in north-east England where the Danish influence was strong.

LINCOLNSHIRE

The Land of the King: In the Wapentake of Aswardharn.

A manor, At Kirkby Earl Morcar was assessed at 3 carucates. Now the King has 1 plough in demesne, and there are 14 sokemen with 2 ploughs, and 5 villeins and 5 bordars with 1 plough. There is half a church. T.R.E. this was worth 4 *li*; now [it is worth] 8 *li*.

A grange. Evedon depends on the said manor and is assessed at 10 bovates. There is land for 1 plough and 2 sokemen and 2 villeins have a plough. There is a mill worth 5s. 4d., the site of the mill and 6 acres of meadow.

This sokeland depends on the same manor:

Ewerby Thorpe, 1 plough;
Howell, 2½ bovates;
Heckington, 1 bovate;
Quarrington, 1 bovate.

A manor. At South Kyme, Earl Morcar was assessed for 4 carucates and 2 bovates of land. There is land for 2 ploughs. Now the King has half a plough in demesne, and 12 villeins and 3 bordars have 2 ploughs. There are 2 churches and a priest, 2 acres of meadow, and 6 fishponds worth 4s. There are, in all the manor, 210 acres and 700 acres of marsh. T.R.E. it was worth 40s, now [it is worth] 60s.

Domesday Book, Vol. I, fol. 336b.

1. *The second volume of the Domesday Book contains a description of East Anglia (Essex, Norfolk and Suffolk), the most prosperous and heavily populated part of England. The commissioners began their work there and the inventories give extremely detailed figures which include livestock.*

2. *The manor I take as an example is shown in full growth. Its value has more than doubled and the arable portion of the demesne has increased by one-third, perhaps by clearing the waste, perhaps by the absorption of former tenures or free holdings of native peasants, or perhaps, since it was an ecclesiastical estate, by pious offerings. The addition of a fourth plough necessitates an increase in the domestic personnel; there are six serfs (two were needed to handle each plough); three more had entered the household. On the other hand, one of the mills has disappeared.*

3. *A closer inspection shows us how the lord's authority oppressed the rural population. He was all-powerful over his serfs: villeins and bordars were integrated into the demesne exploitation (they were counted along with the other constituent parts of the demesne). A small portion of the manorial land is held by free men, but these possessed other lands over which the lord extended no more than his 'custom', that is, his fiscal rights. There are, finally, the three free men who are much more independent. They are 'commended' to the master and they have only to present themselves at his court. But they own very little land; no more than 30 acres between the three of them.*

4. *Lastly, we can see that this domination was being extended. Near the manor another free man owns a large farm, consisting of a mill, and about 120 acres of land with seven auxiliary workers, two domestic servants (assigned to the demesne plough) and five peasants working by the day. He has given this property to the abbey, perhaps as a funeral oblation, but he keeps the enjoyment of it for his lifetime. In exchange he has received from the church as a* precaria remuniantoria *a life grant of about 60 acres of the demesne.*

SUFFOLK

Theodwardestreo Hundred.

At Pachenham (Pakenham) T.R.E. St Edmund held as a manor 7 carucates [of land]. Then as now 44 villeins and 23 bordars. Then 3 ploughs on the demesne, now 4. Then as now 23 ploughs belonging to the men. Then 6 serfs, now 9. And 26 acres of meadow. Wood[land] for 100 swine. Then 2 mills, now 1. And 3 rounceys, 48 beasts, 65 swine and 190 sheep. And now 8 hives of bees. And 31 freemen and 1 bordar [held] 2 carucates of land. Then as now among them were 11 ploughs. And 3 acres of meadow. These all have always belonged to the Saint with sac and soke and all customs, and to the [Saint's] fold.

In the same [vill were] 3 freemen with 30 acres of land. Then as now 1 plough. Wood[land] for 4 swine. They could give and sell the land, but soke and sac and commendation would remain in the Saint's possession.

In the same [vill] T.R.E. 1 freeman with 1 carucate of land got the Abbot's consent to lease him half a carucate of land on condition that the whole of his land, wheresoever it should be should remain in the Saint's possession after his death. And now out of this [freeman's] land 1 carucate lies in Pakenham in demesne. And 1 plough. And 5 bordars and 2 serfs. And a winter mill. And the Saint had always commendation and sac and soke over him. To the church of this township belong 30 acres of free land as alms. Then Pakenham was worth 10 *li*, now 25 *li*. It is 16 furlongs long and 1 league broad and pays 13½d. to a geld.

Victoria County History, (ed.), Vol. I, pp. 497-498
(*Domesday Book*, Vol. II, fol. 361).

78

Additional inventories complete the Domesday Book. The one quoted here comes from Devonshire. The contrast between West Country manors and those in regions formerly occupied by the Scandinavians is very striking: here no single free peasant can be found amongst the dependants. Note that the provision of fiefs for knights whose names indicate that they were companions of the Conqueror has already been made from abbey land. In these smallish manors the master kept a much larger proportion of the arable land under direct cultivation. The value of all these lands had fallen considerably since the Conquest.

Lands of the Abbot of (Tavistock) Church in Devonshire.

The abbot of Tavistock has a manor called Tavistock which paid geld in the time of King Edward for 3½ hides. These 40 ploughs can till. Thereof the abbot has ½ hide and 5 ploughs in demesne, and the villeins have thereof 1½ hides and 14 ploughs. There the abbot has 17 villeins, 20 bordars, 12 serfs, 1 rouncey, 26 beasts, 12 swine, 200 sheep, 30 goats, 1 mill for the service of the abbey, wood[land] 2 leagues in length by 1 in breadth, 16 acres of meadow, and pasture 10 furlongs in length by a like amount in breadth.

Of these 3½ hides 6 knights hold 1½ hides, which 4 thanes held of the abbot without being able to become independent of the church T.R.E.

Thereof Ermenald has ½ virgate. There Ermenald has 1 plough and his villeins 1 plough, 7 beasts and 40 sheep.

Ralf has thereof ½ virgate, a villein and 3 coscets and they have ½ plough. Hugh has ½ hide, one-third virgate and 1 ferling, and has in demesne 2 ploughs. He has there 1 villein, 6 bordars, and 2 serfs, who have 7 ploughing oxen. Hugh has there 10 beasts, 12 swine, and 60 sheep. Robert has 1 virgate and 2 ferlings and 1½ ploughs in demesne and the villeins 1½ ploughs. There Robert has 3 villeins, 6 bordars, 2 serfs, 12 beasts, 60 sheep and 20 goats. Ralf de Tilio has three-quarters virgate and 1 plough, 1 villein and 4 bordars, who have 2 oxen, 7 beasts, 30 sheep and 10 goats. Gosfrid has 1 ferling and he has there 1 plough, 1 bordar, 6 beasts and 30 sheep.

This manor is worth to the abbot 12 pounds a year, to the knights 100 shillings. When the abbot and the knights received it, it was worth 14 pounds and 8 pounds respectively.

Exon. Domesday. *Victoria County History* (Devon), W. Page (ed.),
Vol. I, London, 1906, pp. 429-430.

2. Lay Property seen through Pious Gifts

79

This man, a member of the lower aristocracy, takes the habit and brings to the monastic fraternity into which he is received a part of the allod he inherited. His next of kin have authorized its alienation. At his father's death a portion of the inheritance had passed to the women on the paternal side of the family, his aunts and his sisters; another portion went to his mother as her widow's jointure; the three sons kept the rest, probably jointly with the mother's dower. The gift here described therefore corresponds to a third of what ancient French law calls the frérèche, the joint inheritance enjoyed in common by brothers.

The land in question is a manse and its appurtenances in the neighbourhood of the ancient Roman road (which the local people called the Brunehaut Way) from Mâcon to Autun: the adjacent garden (the verchère); a dozen dispersed arable parcels, the largest bearing the name condemine, *synonymous in this region with the word* coûture *or* furlong; *woods and pastures with their own rights; finally rights of pasturage and usage in other woods and pastures.*

After division this part of a noble allod hardly appears to have exceeded the value of a large peasant farm. It was in any case similar in structure.

(1049-1109)

Let all present and future know that I, Josseran de Bérèzy, offer first of all myself to the Lord God, to serve him in the habit of a monk, in the monastery of Cluny directed by the venerable abbot Hugues. Of my hereditary property which was left me by my praents, I make a gift to the same monastery in order to obtain the remission of my sins and with the intention of persevering until my death. My mother and my brothers, Gauthier and Bernard, have approved and confirmed this deed.

I give therefore to God, to the Blessed Apostles, Peter and Paul and to the monastery of Cluny, half the wood of Monceau, the land which lies between the heath and Monceau, half of the meadow of the Aiguillon, the *manse* of Monceau, the garden of the same *manse*, from the old road up to the water and the pear tree; half the heaths which lie between the way called Brunehaut and the other road; half the land of Our Lady; a parcel on the *Sera Vela* above Lanque, another contiguous with the land which Hughes de Monceau holds; two parcels near the land of Our Lady above Lanque; another at *Orgivals* near the *condemine* of St Peter; a small parcel above Lanque near the *manse* of *Givirunt*; one other small parcel near the land of Our Lady, below the house of Oury Panperdut; another below the bridge of St Peter near my brothers' meadow; half the *condemine* near the plantation of the knight Pons de Sologny up to the fountain and up to the willow near the bridge of the Aiguillon; half of the land contiguous with that of Our Lady; a parcel which the Bérèzys possess at Perrone; pasturage in the woods *Fai* and *Breza* up to the old road for the use of the peasants who inhabit this land, for all that they need; similarly the pasturage on the heath which is between the protected part of Monceau and Lai; and all the lands of Monceau wherever they may be with the woods, fields, meadows and waters, save the meadows which Gauthier my father gave to his sisters and his daughters.

Recueil des chartes de l'abbaye de Cluny, Vol. IV, No. 3302.

This property, upon which a nobleman of middling rank had acquired certain rights through his wife, was also in the process of disintegration: a near relation had made a gift to the church of his portion; another portion was held as security by a creditor. But the gift to the neighbouring monastery of Cluny reassembled the property and protected it henceforth from any subsequent dismemberment.

The manse belongs to the master, flanked by a parish church and appurtenances, and spread over a carefully circumscribed territory, appears to have been an exceptionally well-preserved relic of a Roman villa. There were no tenures, only a single compact demesne in the middle of the woodland, cultivated for the profit of the lord by twelve dependent families. Some of these fulfilled certain tasks, the specialized occupations (like the oxherd who managed the farm). Three of them were 'formariés', i.e. their spouses did not belong to the master, who therefore owned only half the offspring of the marriages.

I, Josseran, knight, surnamed de Cipierre, with my wife Odile, desire that all . . . should know that . . . we give to God and to the Holy Apostles Peter and Paul, as well as to the monks of Cluny, under the direction of the venerable abbot Hugues, for our souls and for those of our ancestors, a demesne which is dependent on our rights, called Chaselle and situated in the territory of Mâcon, to wit the church and the grave-yard, the vineyards and the meadows, the clearings and the woods, the mills and waters, the watercourse, from the church of Ameugny as far as the *condemine* of les Plantes (and if they can acquire this *condemine*, either by themselves or by us, we grant it to them), as far as the forest of Bray, the meadow of Taizé, the forest of Chissé and all the cultivated and uncultivated land inside these limits which is recognized to belong to the *manse*; and if something outside these limits is established as dependent on the rights of the church of Our Lady of Chaselle, we give it to them. We have had all this approved and agreed by our sons, Letaud and Atton. We give also these serfs: the miller Guy and his sons; the forester Umbert, his spouse and his sons; and the sons of Joussaud the ploughman; similarly the other Joussaud and his sons; Umbert, son of Robert, with his mother and the sons of Mainbert; also the sons of the forester Giraud, the sons of Aleric; John the forester and half of his sons; Vincent the miller and half of his sons; Engeaume and half of his sons. As to the spouses of these last three, we do not keep for ourselves as long as they shall live, more than eight deniers for each as rent. We give also Marie and her sons. As for the part of this demesne which Amelie, aunt of my wife, has already previously given to the monks, a gift which she had had approved by her sons Richard and Geoffrey, we approve it. As for the tithe of the church which is held as security by a knight, we engage ourselves to give in exchange to this knight, if he will accept it, five sous of fixed rent on a land in the region of Mâcon. I have given approval to this gift, such as has been written by Umbert de Bourbon, Etienne de Casse, my nephew, being witness. Made in the year of the birth of Our Lord 1089, in the reign of Philip, king of France.

Recueil des chartes de Cluny, Vol. IV, No. 3636.

One great Lincolnshire lord donated only a small portion of his property. Namely, the land of a single tenant around the toft, with the possibility of expanding into the adjacent marsh; 10 acres of arable within each of two village 'fields'; a share in the common meadows which corresponded to the extent of this arable; lastly the right to drive a given number of sheep on to the collective pastures. The document gives the impression of an individual possession embedded within the village community.

(Before 1187)

To all the sons of the holy Church present and to come, Ralf, son of Stephen of Holland, greetings. Know ye that I have given and confirmed by this charter, to God and the Church of St Mary of Kirkstead and the monks of that place in perpetual alms a toft in the village of Snelland, upon which the monks may freely build if they wish. To wit between the toft of Richard Hariburn which is bounded by the ditch, and the toft of Ralf the clerk, between the road and the dyke. I give all that is dependent on my fief in the marsh, beyond the said dyke towards the south and east, so that they can extend the toft which I have given them and include in it all which is dependent on me on that side of the said dyke. Let them do with it what they wish for their profit and that of their convent. Furthermore, I have given them in the fields of the said village of Snelland a bovate of 20 acres of arable measured by the perch of 18 feet, that is, 10 acres in each part of the village with as much meadow as belongs to each 20 acres and with pasture for one hundred sheep (the great hundred, be it understood). In order that the said monks may possess these things freely, quit of all secular service, custom and exaction I and my heirs guarantee this property for the use of the monks from all things and services towards any man in perpetuity. And so that this may be firmly upheld, I, Ralf, have pledged my faith in the hand of Walter, chaplain of Holy Trinity. . . .

Documents illustrative of the Social and Economic History of the Danelaw,
F. M. Stenton (ed.), 1920, pp. 160–161.

3. Cistercian Demesnes

82

In the woods of Valois, the patrimony of the abbey of Chaalis was growing rapidly by gift and by purchase. It will be noticed how pastoral this patrimony was. It contained a few dispersed lands and assarts, but mostly woodlands (one of which was enclosed and entry to it prohibited), meadows, ponds, moors and above all rights of usage of pasture, herbage and the acorn crop. This extension worried the great lord, an officer of the royal household, who, in the forest region around his castle, held the justice, vicaria, and the gruerie, i.e. the oversight of the woodland area. He was 'guardian' of the monastery, but recognized its immunity by this agreement concluded before the royal court.

(1171)

Know ye all, present and to come, that Guy the Butler, our faithful follower, entered into a dispute with the church and brethren of Chaalis over diverse points, but that he ended by concluding with them a durable peace in our presence and in the following wise, with the consent of his wife Marguerite and his sons, Guy and William. He has given and granted to God and to the brethren and has abandoned to them in peace, the place where lies the monastery with its dependencies, the alder thicket, the wood round about the old pond with the meadows which are near by, the fishpool and the land, cultivated or not, contiguous with the pool, which is the gift of Ralf Potier; and also all the wood on the other side of the abbey with the assarts, enclosed on all sides by a ditch. He has given to the church and to the brethren the usage of all the forest of *Hespiognie*, of *Beeley* and of Trembleau with what is dependent on it, and the heath which is contiguous, to feed the flocks, the cattle and the swine, for construction of houses, for firewood, and for all which shall be necessary; and also Molton, Charlepont and the pool with its dependencies and all that the church of Chaalis owns at Commelle and in land, meadows, alder thickets, in wood and vineyards or in any other thing; and similarly the land of Longmont on the hill, the land of Néri which was at Milesende, the land of *Lombonne* and the furlong which lies between Fai and Henrivillers; and the herbage and acorns for the pasture of all their swine in all the woods of the manor of Dammartin, situated between Senlis and Paris in which he has the *gruerie*, save in the wood called *Lettum*. He has done the same for the grange of Fourcheret, with its lands and annexes, free of all justice and *voierie*, save that they may not cut nor shorten the public way without his consent. As for the lands of Ermenonville, which Joscelin and William, father of the Butler, have given to the church in alms, the church shall receive them in peace after the death of the Butler, with the exception of sixty *arpents*, which the Butler can as he pleases reserve for his descendants or leave to the church. He has also abandoned to the church the land which Pierre Bavin held for rent. All that the above mentioned church possesses under the guard of the Butler in meadows, lands, vineyards, woods, alder thickets, assarts, waters and pasturage, heath or any other thing, or that it can reasonably acquire from the fiefs of the patrimony of the Butler by the generosity of the faithful congregation, by purchase or by any other means, he grants it so that the church may hold it solidly in perpetuity, and confirms it with his seal.

A. Luchaire, *Études sur les actes de Louis VII*,
Paris, 1885, pp. 437-438.

83

When buying a village, rights in which were owned by lords and peasants, and the patronage of the parish church, this prelate gives the monks permission to transform the territory into a 'grange', a huge demesne cultivated by working lay brothers. In this case the extension of the Cistercian patrimony had as its aim the destruction of a peasant community by expelling the inhabitants and suppressing the rural parish.

(1159)

Gunther, Bishop of Speyer by the grace of God. . . . Apart from what I have already given through piety to the venerable monastery of Maulbronn and established by particular acts, I have bought the village of Eilfingen with all the free holdings and the tithe and I have made a present of it for the sake of my soul to the said establishment. The church of this village (situated in the provosty of St Vit which was then in my hands) being vacant, I acquired from the master of the land the right of investiture. I bought with my money from all the peasants and different lords who stated they had rights in the village all that belonged or seemed to belong to them, and what I received by rightful purchase I transferred according to custom, into the possession of the community at Maulbronn. The former inhabitants and cultivators of the whole village having been sent away, a grange was made there, and the lay brothers alone with their own ploughs cultivated all the fields. As these brethren ought to receive the holy sacraments only from priests of their order it was no longer necessary nor suitable to instal there anyone holding the office of parish priest, since there was no longer anyone whose cure he could have. After taking council with men who were both wise and holy, I have therefore caused the relics in the church of this village to be transferred to a more frequented spot. The remaining sacred things in these buildings, the church has been withdrawn from common use. . . . No priest or clerk of an inferior order may henceforth claim anything from it, but wholly with all its rights of tithe and other things, it shall depend on the said holy monastery. The threat of excommunication is held over whoever would desire to go against this donation.

G. Franz, *Deutsches Bauerntum*, pp. 124-126.

B. PEASANT TENURE IN THE TWELFTH CENTURY

84

The three following documents, which all come from the region of Mâcon, give us an idea of the status of land held 'in the peasant manner' in the twelfth century.

The first tenure – a manse of the old kind possessed by a single head of a family, a free peasant – was not bound by any labour service, only by different dues, spaced out on seven occasions during the year. There were small liveries of grain and wine, two items of smaller livestock, a meal, which was probably a 'right of shelter', but mostly money. It is permissible to see at least two of these levies in cash (at haymaking and at the grape harvest) as a substitute for former labour services.

(1096-1127)

May all the sons of the church at Mâcon, as well as all other faithful Christians, know that canon Etienne de Chaumont, in the presence of sire Bérard, bishop of Mâcon, and of his clerks, has given a *manse* situated in the region of Lyons, in the parish of la Chapelle, which belongs to the regular canons of St Peter, and in the village of

Brutoria, with its appurtenances. In this *manse* Guichard, a good peasant, lives, who owes service:

- at Easter, a lamb;
- at haymaking, six pieces of money;
- at harvest, a meal (with several associates) and a *setier* of oats;
- at the grape harvest, twelve deniers;
- at Christmas, twelve deniers, three loaves, and a half-*setier* of wine;
- at the beginning of Lent, a capon;
- at Mid-Lent, six pieces of money. . . .

Etienne has confirmed this charter and has had it confirmed.

Cartulaire de Saint-Vincent de Mâcon, p. 297.

85

This manse *situated in a suburb of the city was a winegrowing one. One of the tenant's chief obligations consisted in keeping the land in good heart and in seeing that it bore fruit. The former vinedresser, probably preferring to follow one of the specialized and more lucrative occupations of the urban economy, abandoned the vineyard; he had to be evicted. The text shows that the lord was helpless against his tenant who paid not the slightest attention to him. Finally the latter agreed to vacate the tenancy only by selling his rights at a very high price – nearly one thousand pieces of money. The size of this payment is evidence alike of the security of a peasant tenant's rights on his holding, the rise in the value of land near expanding towns, and the interest shown by the cathedral chapter in the production of wine.*

(1108-1139)

. . . Alard, called the Apostle, owned for many years a *manse* near the walls of the city of Mâcon, near the church of St John, in the peasant way and for an annual service, but by negligence he left the *manse* a wilderness open to animals, for he did not dig the vineyard nor cause it to be dug. Because of that Archdeacon Bernard from whom Alard held the *manse* became angered and addressed repeated and renewed reproaches to him and summoned him many times to render him his rights. Alard constantly refused to do so or to start working again, relying on vague replies, and holding to no account what Bernard said to him. Finally, through the good offices of Etienne Bourse and Pierre called Lemoine, agreeing of his own free will to what the archdeacon demanded, he claimed [a price] for giving up to the latter in peace all [that he had] in the manse.

The said Bernard, seeing the *manse* a wilderness and, further, wishing to establish something in favour of St Vincent for the profit of his soul, agreed and promised to give his acquiescence to this proposition. . . . Alard and his wife Grausa came [in the presence] of Sir Bernard the archdeacon and received from him four livres of deniers. They sold and granted all that they had and held in this *manse* and vineyard, they abandoned it in perpetuity and promised to maintain in peace this agreement. For her approval, the wife of Alard, Grausa, received five sous.

Cartulaire de Saint-Vincent de Mâcon, pp. 341-342.

In this statute of slightly later date, the tenure is no longer designated as a manse *and carries a single high rent in money. When they acquired this land the Cistercians of la Ferté (who no longer adhered to the rule forbidding them to levy a rent) made its status clear. It was granted to a family group who were to hold it from one generation to the next until the line died out, on three conditions; that the rent should be paid at the required time; that the property should not be sold nor in any way alienated (in particular by giving dowries to daughters who through marriage left the family community and became members of another family); and lastly that the right of justice on the land belonging to the lord should be respected and that his court should be the only one competent to deal with suits relating to the property.*

(*ca.* 1160)

May all those who profess the Christian faith, present and future, know that Robert Barbarot has abandoned to Notre-Dame and to the monks of la Ferté, withholding nothing, all that he claimed, justly or unjustly, in the land which Guichard Morel gave to the house of la Ferté at the time of his conversion. This land is cultivated by the Brutinanges of Laives who must give for it twenty sous of rent annually.

It shall be noted that they may not give this land as a dowry to the daughters, nor remove it in any manner from the right of la Ferté. They may cultivate it as long as they shall acquit the rent promptly. But if they do not wish to render the rent the land must revert to the house of la Ferté. If, by reason of this land, they suffer any wrong from their neighbours they must bring their case before the monks, exclusively.

For this, Robert has received four *bichets* of wheat and two cheeses, and he has sworn on the altar of St Martin, Julien, chaplain of Sennecé holding his hand, to keep the peace firmly. His sons have sworn the same thing. . . .

Recueil des pancartes de l'abbaye de la Ferté-sur-Grosne
(ed. G. Duby), 1953, No. 152.

87-88-89-90

In twelfth-century Italy and Provence the grant of a tenancy was made effective by a written agreement which bound the landlord and the man who farmed the holding by very precise conditions, and threatened both with a heavy money fine if the agreement were broken. There were no labour services, only rents. In Document No. 89 it can be seen that the lord preferred to receive his dues in kind, particularly in wine which he put on the market. No. 88 forbids tenants the right of alienation except to other tenants of the same lordship, or to the lord himself who had the right of repurchase.

In the name of God. The year of His birth 1103, the third of the nones of February, the twelfth of the proclamation. I, Martin, priest, rector of the church and monastery of the Blessed Mary, in the name of this church and according to the terms of our agreement, have decided to give in order to have, hold and work them, to enjoy and to improve them, to thee, Rainier, son of Bonand, all the parcels, lands, vineyards and property of which thou, Rainier, hast made a charter of gift in favour of the church and monastery of the Blessed Mary, which is situated in Campisitoli. The said properties are situated at Casi and other places. Giving and confirming these properties entirely with all the buildings which shall be found thereon to thee, Rainier, and to thy heirs. Thou, Rainier, and thy heirs must give for these lands and goods to us and to the said church and monastery, each year in the octave of Christmas, to us or to our envoy by you or your envoy for rent or customary dues, four good and shining deniers in money of Lucca, a shoulder of mutton and two peacocks, nothing more, and four sous for the renewal. And if, the agreement being kept by you, I, the prior, or my successors, either through the person we shall send or by a deed we shall have made previously, should come to oppose thee Rainier, or thy heirs and descendants on account of these lands and properties, lessening them in movables or immovables, taking them back or wishing to impose more than what has been read above, we must then pay you a fine of 20 sous in good Lucca deniers. And I, Rainier, declare that if I or my heirs and descendants, neglect to pay each year to the said church and monastery this fixed rent, as it has been read above, then we must pay to the church and monastery the said fine of twenty sous.

La Carte del Monastero di S. Maria di Montepiano, 1000-1200
(ed. R. Piattoli), *Regesta Chartarum Italiae*,
Rome, 1942, No. 19.

*   *   *

Quinto (Tuscany), May 1121

. . . Florent, son of the late Andrea Kyscio, and Martino Bastacaro, and Pietro, son of the late Guidolo de Runco, and Guidolo, son of the late Stefano, and Pietro de Rio and Giovanni de Colle, and Pietro and Florent, brothers, sons of the late Rustico, and Guiglielmo, son of the late Guinizo, and Guiducio de Gerard, and Azolino, son of the late Pietro Giovanni, and Giovanni, son of the late Pietro Fucola, and Giovanni Brittoli, by the staff which they held in their hands, have invested Giovanni, priest and archpriest of the chapter of Santa Reparata and Benedetto abbot of San Miniato. If in some way they or their heirs wished to alienate the lands or the vineyards which they hold from the said churches and their rectors, they shall give them to one of those who also hold lands and vineyards from the churches and their rectors if they wish and are able to take them, for the same price that they would have been able to obtain elsewhere without falsehood. And if such men cannot or do not wish to take them, they shall give them to the church of Santa Reparata and San Miniato, in a similar way, for the same price that they would have been able to obtain elsewhere without falsehood. And if one of them gives these lands to another and does not keep to what is read above, he shall lose this land and everything which he holds from these churches with all the rights which belong to them, and he shall pay besides to these churches sixty sous in good deniers of Lucca.

Le Carte della canonica della Cattedrale di Firenze, 723-1149
(ed. R. Piattoli), *Regesta Chartarum Italiae*, Rome, 1938, No. 164.

*   *   *

The year 1181, 14th October. . . . Marro, son of the late Guifredo, and Poisia, spouse, living under the Lombard law (and I, Poisia, with the consent of my husband Marro), in the presence of Jacopo, judge and representative of the lord Emperor Frederick, have together received from thee, the priest Uberto, in the name of lord Pietro, archpriest of Santa Maria di Monte Velate, eight livres in Milanese deniers for three pieces of land situated at Velate. The first is a vineyard and lies in the place called *a Croso* (in the morning, the land of Ambrogio, at noon, that of Lanfranco, son of Ugo de Pocheria, in the evening, the same, to the north, the road). The second is a field which is called *a Braria* (in the morning the land of Guiglielmo de Cosgiago, at noon and in the north, that of Botto Ramberto, of Velate, in the evening, the road). The third is a chestnut wood and lies in the place called *a Cassaria* (in the morning, the land of the heirs of Guidrado, at noon, that of the said Botto, to the north, the same, in the evening, that of Sant'Ambrogio). We promise to defend these lands. If we cannot do so then we promise to pay you double as a fine. Given at Velate. . . .

Marro and Pisa, spouses, have undertaken to defend these said parcels and they have given as surety Bertaroto, son of the late Girardo Ramberto of Velate, who has made a perpetual recognizance of all his goods to the value of the double fine. . . . And immediately, the said priest Uberto has invested the said Marro hereditarily with the said parcels for an annual fixed rent, payable to the said church at the wine harvest of Velate, of a waggon of unfermented wine; and if there is not enough unfermented wine, he will give what he has and will replace with cash, in the measure of eight Milanese sous for a waggon of unfermented wine. If it should happen that the tenant does not pay the rent during the year, he shall lose the said parcels. And there, the said Marro has bestowed on his wife Posia a field at *Braria* (in the morning the land of Botto, in the evening the road) and his field at Pisori (in the morning the land of the heirs of Lanfranco ser Girardo, in the evening that of Guifredo de Otino) and his wood of Crivi (in the morning and the evening the land of Santa Maria di Monte) and with his field of Traversiana (in the morning the land of the heirs of Viviano Garzolana, in the evening that of Guifredo de Otino) and the house in which he lives at Velate, for fifteen livres in Milanese deniers, which is her dowry. . . .

Regesto di S. Maria de Monto Velate sina all'anno 1200
(ed. C. Manaresi), *Regesta Chartarum Italiae*,
Rome, 1937, No. 244.

⋆　　⋆　　⋆

The year of the incarnation 1177, in the month of January. May all present and future know that I, Guillaume d'Alverny, master of the house of the Hospital of St Thomas, by the council and will of the brothers of the said house, give in *acapte* (lease) to thee, Pierre Geoffroy and R. thy brother, in good faith and without falsehood, a land on the river bank near Peron, bounded on the west by the vineyards of Verdeline and Collonges. And for the said *acapte* Pierre Geoffroy and R. his brother give us five sous. They promise always to render faithfully the fourth part and the tithe of the fruits of this land, seed deducted.

And I, the said Guillaume d'Alverny master of the said house of the Hospital, grant the said land to thee Pierre Geoffroy and R. thy brother and to your successors to do there what you will save the right of the Hospital, being agreed that you cannot sell nor pledge it without our council and will. The witnesses are Guillaume Armérier, Raimond Fourgon, Garnier, Bernard de Barbentane, Raimond de Lambesc, Josseran Pelerin. All these are brothers, but these are not: Pierre Roussin, Guillaume Roubaud.

Cartulaire de l'Hôpital de Trinquetaille, No. 70,
Archives des Bouches-du-Rhône, H(OM), 3217.

C. PERSONAL DEPENDENCE AND ITS EXPLOITATION

91

Out of piety, but also to avoid pressure by a neighbouring castellan who claimed the sub-mission of her allods to the authority of his ban, a well-born widow commended herself, her property and her offspring to the patron saint of a local monastery. She thus became a member of the 'household' and attached to the altar. Dependence was expressed by the payment of a very small annual due, which none the less maintained the bond which had been contracted. Only the male descendants had to pay it, and those female descendants who were 'foreigners'. In fact dependence in Lotharingia was transmitted by women; if they lived outside the land of their masters, they were compelled to return periodically to give evidence of their submission so that the memory of it could be preserved from one generation to the next.

(1024–1033)

. . . In the time of the lord Nantier, abbot of the church of Saint-Mihiel, and of the Duke Ferri, advocate of this church, at St Christopher near to Bonde and Marson, there was a matron called Gise, who, after the death of her husband, noble and free, whom she, noble and free herself, had married, began to suffer many outrages from other inhabitants of her village. Indeed the bailiffs of the lord Milon de Gondrecourt demanded dues and fixed rents from her for the lands which she held and which, until the death of her husband, she had owned as her own allod, absolutely free of all rent. Apprehending great anxiety on this subject and not suffering compulsion to such service to these men, she took a decision useful to herself and, afterwards, to her sons. For, having received council from her friends and relations, she came to the abbey of Saint-Mihiel in the diocese of Verdun, and there, on the day of the feast of Saint Mihiel, she delivered herself with all her posterity, born or to be born, to the holy Archangel, to his altar, as a member of his house, owing service to his altar and giving him a rent for the needs of the monastery. As a token she deposited there the bands of her headdress together with a coin with a hole in it and left them there. This is how the rents were constituted: her male issue, on reaching manhood, will pay, wherever they may be, for the needs of the monastery, on the day of the feast of St Mihiel, four deniers; female issue, if she should live in a village and under the authority of St Mihiel, will pay no rent; on the other hand if she wished to live outside the authority of St Mihiel, she shall pay on the day of the feast of St Mihiel a rent of one denier. . . .

Chronique et chartes de l'abbaye de Saint' Mihiel (ed. A. Lesort),
Mémoires et documents publiés par la Société nationale des Antiquaires,
Mettensia, VI, No. 33 (trans. M. Bloch).

A specialist in manorial administration drew up this description of the different personal statuses in English rural society at the time of Edward the Confessor. There are versions in Latin and Anglo-Saxon. Below the thegns, who were free men following a military calling, the author distinguished three categories of peasants, who all enjoyed liberty but were, however, dependent on a lord. The first constituted a sort of rustic aristocracy: they were horsemen, like the military men, but they had nevertheless to perform certain agricultural tasks for their masters, particularly in summer, since the need to bring the crops in speedily made it necessary to mobilize all available manpower.

Next, the kotsetla, *ancestor of the cottar and bordar of the Norman period, was attached to the domestic staff of the manor by regular weekly service – a 'week-work' of one day – except at harvest time, when he owed half his time to the master. A very small grant of land – five acres – was the reward for this work.*

The author then described the gebur, *the real peasant, who was more deeply involved in the cultivation of the manorial demesne than any other man. We see him as a domestic servant lodged under his own roof. His holding was much larger than that of the* kotsetla; *it supported him and his family and supplied him as well with enough to pay his dues in money and kind. But it compelled him to perform much heavier 'week-work' than was required of the* kotsetla, *and, in addition, periodic tasks, such as the cultivation of a fixed piece of land. Intimately connected with the lord's household which provided him with his working tools, his livestock, and the seed for at least a part of his fields, it was usual for all his possessions to revert after his death to his lord.*

(First half of the eleventh century)

Rectitudines singularum personarum

. . . The right of the *geneat* varies according to what is established in the manor. In some he pays a rent, and delivers each year a pig for the pasture, rides and performs a carting service and provides means of transport, works and shelters his lord, harvests and scythes, makes parks for deer and looks after the places where deer can be got, builds the lord's house and its enclosure, conducts strangers to the village, pays the church taxes and alms, guards his lord, looks after his horses and carries messages far and near according to orders.

The right of the *kotsetla* varies according to the custom of the manor. In some he must work for his lord every Monday throughout the year, and three days a week at harvest time. He does not pay for the land. He must have five acres or more if that is the custom of the manor; and if it is less, it is too little, for his labour is heavy. He must give St Peter's penny at Ascensiontide like every free man must and he must perform also the services on the demesne of his lord if he receives an order to do so, mounting guard by the sea, labouring on the enclosures of the king's deer and other things belonging to his station. He must pay church taxes at Martinmas.

The exactions of the *gebur* vary, here heavy, elsewhere light. In certain manors the custom is that he performs weekly labour on two days throughout the year and three days from Candlemas to Easter. If he performs cartage service he does not have to work while his horse is out. At Michaelmas he must pay six pennies in dues, at Martinmas 23 *setiers* of barley and two hens, at Easter a lamb or two pennies. He must in his turn sleep in the lord's sheepfold from Martinmas until Easter. From the beginning of ploughing until Martinmas he must plough an acre each week, and must take the seed himself to the manorial barn. He must also plough three acres in labour service and two on the pasture. . . . He must also plough three acres for his labour service, sowing them from his own barn; he must pay St Peter's penny. Each pair of *gebur* must keep a hunting dog and each *gebur* must give six loaves to the manorial swineherd when he takes the herd to be fattened.

On the land where this custom applies the tenant must receive two oxen, a cow, six sheep and seven sown acres. When he has performed all the duties which fall upon him, he must be given the tools which he has need of for his labour and the utensils for his household. At his death, the lord may enter into possession of what he leaves.

The law of the manor is fixed on each manor; in one place, as I have said, it is heavier, elsewhere it is lighter, for the customs are not the same in all manors. In some, the *gebur* must pay a rent in honey, elsewhere in food, elsewhere in beer. . . .

Liebermann, *Die Gesetze der Angelsach*,
Vol. I, 1898, pp. 444-449.

93

Exchange of female serfs who have married outside the manor

(1144)

Louis, by the grace of God, king of France and Acquitaine, to all and for ever. We make known to all, present and future, that we have granted to the church of the Holy Father at Chartres, Havissa daughter of Renaud de Dambron, wife of Gilon Lemaire, mayor of Germignonville, who was ours in servile status, and we have given her to be owned in person and perpetually, with all the fruit of her womb. The abbot and the monks of the said church have given us in exchange another woman of their *familia*, with the approval of Pierre Lemaire and Renaux de Rebrechien. . . .

A. Luchaire, *Études sur les actes de Louis VII*, p. 382.

94

The master of one dependant renounces all the rights, exactions and jurisdiction which he holds over him and his descendants.

(1153-1160)

Peter Boterel, to William, by the grace of God bishop of Norwich, to Goscelin, archdeacon, and to Earl Conan, his lord, greeting. Know ye that for the souls of my father, my mother, my ancestors, and for my own soul, I have given to the church of St Melaine at Rennes, Godwin, reeve of Nettlestead (Suffolk), and his heirs, with all that they hold of me. I have given it in perpetual alms, free and quit of all service, exaction and custom and released from all charge towards me, that he may leave my authority except for the service of the King and the Earl. I grant that the said Godwin and his heirs continue to enjoy in my village of Nettlestead the same rights in the commons that they held previously, in the woods, plains, pastures, waters, roads, paths and in all places. Furthermore, I give to the same church 12 acres of my demesne ... quit and free of everything due to me and to the King and the Earl. And if Godwin or one of his heirs is guilty of default for the service which he owes me, he shall be judged for this by the monks in the court of the said church. The same Godwin and his heirs shall not be forced by me or my bailiffs to go to the Hundred or the Shire, but after having paid the customary tax they may remain in peace. Furthermore I desire the said Church to hold this gift from me and my heirs, freely and in peace, for ever. The witnesses are: Maxilde, my wife, who joins me in this gift and agrees to it; Adam, the priest of the village ... Godric of the fountain, William, son of Lifrum ... and the whole village of Nettlestead.

D. C. Douglas, *The Social Structure of Medieval East Anglia*,
1927, p. 232.

95

In this case the system of farming on two great Rhineland demesnes had to be completely reorganized. Farmed by peasants who were both tenants of a manse and bondsmen, these two manors had to deliver to the monastery on which they depended, a fixed pension. But the tie which bound them did not prevent some members of the familia *from fleeing, probably to the new lands of the north and east, attracted by the great movement of agrarian conquest and by the advantages promised to the pioneers. Such an exodus overwhelmed those who remained behind. Because fewer in number they had to contribute a heavier quota to the payment of the annual fixed rent, which encouraged them too to run away.*

To avoid a complete desertion of these demesnes the lords first of all re-equipped them (regular investments were promised to keep them in order), then they were given as before to the peasants as a collective 'farm', but very likely with a small pension. Finally, whilst lightening them, they fixed in writing the charges due from them for body service: a small chevage, a marriage tax, and lastly mortmain on the best head of cattle (animal heriot). It should be noted that some dependants were registered as having no animals at all.

I, Frederick, second of the name, by the grace of God archbishop of Cologne, wish to uphold by the authority which God has given us the excellent intention ... of the servant of God Adelaide, abbess of the church of the Blessed Mary in Capitol at Cologne. ... Formerly the said church rejoiced in very great possessions, but today, because of the evil times and the negligence of the officials, some of the manors have almost fallen in ruins and devastation. Amongst these, Efferen and Fischenich would have gone to ruin and certain abandon if they had not received help from the said abbess and a better statute. The male and female dependants attached to these manors, who paid the entire rent, that is ten deniers of annual *chevage*, fled because of this excessive charge, and they became so few and so poor that the fixed rents of the church could not be levied in these manors and from this *familia*. The dependants having become too few on each demesne, the tenants who cultivated the *manses* there were forced in conformity with the rights of the advocate and the abbess to pay all the fixed rents of the church with their own dues. They decided to flee and to abandon their *manses*. Thus the injury to the church was double: on the dependent men and on the *manses*.

Before such a grave and injurious wrong Adelaide, the servant of God, on the counsel of the sisters and brothers of the same church, and also of Guillaume, the illustrious count of Juliers, and of the priors of Cologne, provosts as well as abbots, caused a return to their ancient status and profit in the following manner. To all dependants of each manor who formerly paid the entire rent, that is, ten deniers of *chevage*, she gave the right to be *censuales*, and to pay henceforth two deniers each per year. On the death of the man, the steward of the manor shall take the best of his animals, and if he has none, the best of his clothes and six deniers; the same on the death of the wife, the *Schultheiss* of the manor shall take her best garment and six deniers. For permission to marry, the man, like the woman shall pay six deniers.

In exchange for this improvement of their condition, the dependants attached to the said manor have sworn to help with their own labour and with their property the said servant of God to restore the manor of Efferen, in buildings as much as in agricultural work and in the firm establishment of her right: in such manner that each year this manor shall deliver eight marks of silver, thirty *muids* of wheat and seven *muids* of barley, for the maintenance of the sisters and brothers, and by the manor of Fischenich fifteen sous. Each hall shall receive complete equipment both in animals and tools and other necessities, according to the evidence given under oath by the *familia* of the hall. Furthermore so that the said manor of Fischenich can serve to the full, the abbess will allocate each year for purchases one mark of her own revenues.

Given in the year of the birth of Our Lord 1158. . . .

G. Franz, *Deutsches Bauerntum*, pp. 117-122.

D. PRIVILEGED MONOPOLIES (THE *BAN*)

1. The King

96

Here the monopolistic customs levied on the dependent village of an ecclesiastical manor over which the king extended his superior authority were regularized. All the exactions introduced by the king's officials were converted into a single annual payment, a rent proportionate to the number of plough animals in each peasant household.

In the name of the Holy and indivisible Trinity, I, Louis, king of France and duke of Aquitaine, make known to all present as well as future that the stewards of Janville have been in the habit of levying at Oinville-Saint-Liphard certain evil customs and exactions. To wit: protecting the wheat harvest, rights of shelter, meals, *tailles*, requisitions and other things of the same sort, which have led the said village to ruin. Considering that these acts were evil, for the soul of our father Louis of venerable memory and for the pardon of our sins, we have wholly enfranchised this village from these customs and from all the others which could be demanded in any way whatever. We have kept for ourselves this only in the village: for each complete plough the steward of Janville will have every year two *mines*[1] of wheat, for half of a plough one *mine*, and for a quarter of a plough, one-half. And the mayor of Oinville will arrange for this rent to be carried to the steward at Janville.

. . . Given publicly at Lorris, the year of the birth of Our Lord, 1143, the seventh year of our reign.

A. Luchaire, *Études sur les actes de Louis VII*, p. 370.

97

The king here takes a village under his particular protection at the request of its ecclesiastical lords who, probably threatened in some way, renounce their immunity. By this means a sort of pariage concerned with the profits of the superior rights of authority (ban) was instituted: an equal share in the profits of justice, the establishment of a fixed tax on the household of each inhabitant (a charge per hearth of one hen and one sou, the same for all), and livery of oats for the horsemen of the warden (the 'husbandman' had to provide twice as much). However, the king did not wish to offend a neighbouring castellan, who was his vassal, so he agrees neither to exploit nor to protect any of this lord's dependants who might come to settle there.

In the name of the holy and undivided Trinity, Amen. Louis by the grace of God, king of France. Know all present and future that, at the request of the dean Philippe, the treasurer Geoffroy, Mathieu of Beauvoir, provost of Léré, and the whole chapter of Saint-Martin of Tours, we have taken under our ward and protection their village called Aubigni with Ragis and all their dependencies on the following conditions: each male villein, today and in future, in these villages who works the land with an animal, will pay, every year at Michaelmas, to us and to the kings of France our successors, one *setier* of oats, twelve Parisian deniers, and a hen, and nothing more. The justice on this land which the provost of Léré owns . . . shall be in common to both us and the said provost. All the other things which the provost and the canons have there shall remain theirs free of all burden. We will not receive any of Gilon de Sulli's men. Our steward shall keep faith with the provost and in the chapter of Saint-Martin, and the provost's steward with us. We shall not alienate this from our hand, neither we nor our successors, kings of France, without the assent of the chapter of Saint-Martin. So that this shall never be in doubt but remain perpetually established, save for the rights of Gilon de Sulli and all others, we have provided the present charter with the authority of our seal and with the monogram of the royal name set above it.

Given at Vézelay, the year of the birth of Our Lord, 1178.

A. Luchaire, *Études sur les actes de Louis VII*, p. 460.

[1] A measure of capacity equivalent to half a *setier*.

Once again the royal protection is invoked, but this time it is at the request of a community of free peasants, probably threatened by lords who were nearer at hand and more grasping. The peasants agree to pay a rent in cereals fixed at a round figure.

Frederick, august emperor of the Romans. Know all faithful men of the Empire, present and to come. The villeins living at Bernheim have by a common agreement placed their village of Bernheim under our authority, which up to now they have possessed freely, in their own right, and exempt from all lordship, on the following conditions. They and their posterity shall deliver each year to the imperial authority 25 *muids* of wheat, and they shall remain henceforth under the protection of the imperial might, protected from all tyranny. If any man shall attempt to exercise violence of any kind on their bodies or their possessions, he shall be convicted of *lèse-majesté*. We have ordered this pact to be reinforced by the impression of our seal on this charter so that it shall not be broken by forgetfulness or other negligence. Given in the year 1172 of the birth of Our Lord, the fifth of the proclamation, under the reign of the glorious Emperor of the Romans Frederick, in the twenty-first year of his reign, the eighteenth of his succession to the Empire. At Würzburg, the thirteenth of the calends of May.

G. Franz, *Deutsches Bauerntum*, pp. 129-130.

99

The extensive rights of the English kings were vigorously re-enforced by Henry II after the troubles of the mid-twelfth century. These rights were particularly useful in establishing the strict royal monopoly over the forest regions and their products, such as game, timber, and pasture (Document No. 51 gives an indication of their vast extent). The following extracts from the 'Assize of the Forest' of 1184 show that these privileges, which were maintained by a collective oath required from all the male adults living in the neighbourhood, even encroached on the rights of individuals owning parcels of woodland adjacent to those of the king: their usage was carefully restricted, particularly around Michaelmas when the pigs were fattening on the acorn crop.

This is the assize of lord Henry, the king, son of Matilda, of the forest and its game in England; given at Woodstock with the counsel and assent of the archbishops, bishops, barons, earls and nobles of England. . . .

. . . 3. Item, he forbids any man to give or sell anything whatever which brings damage or destruction to his own woods lying within King Henry's forest; he graciously allows them to take what they need from their woods, but it must be done without damage and under the supervision of the king's forester. . . .

. . . 7. Item, the king has ordered that in every county where he has venison, twelve knights be charged with guarding his venison and his greensward as well as his forest, and that four knights be charged with pasturing beasts in his woods and with receiving and preserving his rights of pannage. The king has also forbidden any man to pasture beasts in his own wood if it is situated within the limits of the forest before the king's woods have been pastured. And the pasture of the lord king's woods begins fifteen days before Michaelmas and continues for fifteen days after Michaelmas.

8. And the king has commanded that if his forester has woods in his keeping in the lord king's domain and if these woods be destroyed and he can show no just cause, the person of the forester himself and no other shall be seized. . . .

. . . 10. And the king has commanded that his assarts, old and new, be inspected, as well as all purprestures and the damage of the forest and that all be written down. . . .

. . . 12. At Woodstock the king has commanded that sureties be taken from whomsoever shall be guilty of an offence against the forest, and similarly if he offends a second time; but if he offends a third time, for the third offence sureties shall not be taken nor anything else, but only the person of the culprit.

13. Item, the king has commanded that every male attaining the age of twelve years and living within the jurisdiction of the chase shall swear to keep the king's peace, and also clerks holding land in lay fief. . . .

. . . 15. Item, the king has forbidden any tanner or cleaner of skins to reside in his forest outside a borough. . . .

W. Stubbs, *Select Charters* . . . , 1913, pp. 186-188.

100

1. *There existed in England a corps of specialized officials who were in charge of the conservation of the royal forests: itinerant judges presiding over the special pleas (like this one which concerned Rockingham Forest in Northamptonshire), foresters and verderers, whose job was to protect the 'greensward' that is, the fodder upon which the chief game animal, the 'venison', fed.*

2. *The valuation of the security seized in the house of a poacher, who had not been able to find friends to act as his guarantors, enables us to have some idea of the very modest chattels of a country clerk. His stock of cereals (note particularly the relative importance of leguminous plants) in the middle of winter amounted to barely 2½ bushels.*

(19th January 1251)

It happened on Thursday the vigil of St Fabian and Sebastian in the 35th year that when Geoffrey Hog and John Ive, the walking foresters of the lord king of the park of Brigstock were on their way in the same park, they found a trap set in Aldenatheshawe; and they heard a man cutting wood by night in the park, and on account of the thickness of the wood and the darkness of the night they could not come to him. And on account of the suspicion which they had against Robert le Noble of Sudborough, chaplain, they left the wood for Sudborough to watch in concealment to see if anyone left the wood for the town; and so they met the said Robert the chaplain, who came from the wood and carried in his hand a branch of green oak and an axe. And the foresters demanded gage and pledge of him; and he could not find them pledges, so they took him to the town of Bridgstock to the house of Robert le N. . . .

In the morning the foresters and verderers went to his house at Sudborough to make search; and so they found in his house two barbed arrows with fletches and the woodwork of a certain trap with the string of the trap broken into two parts; and upon the string was hair from deer.

The chattels found there were appraised, to wit, a bushel of wheat of the price of 5d., a bushel of beans of the price of 3d., half a bushel of oats of the price of 2d.; a chest with dishes, cups and saucers of the price of 12d., and a mare of the price of 8d. A pelice was found there of the price of 12d.; and wood was found in his court of the price of 6d. Total 4s.

The aforesaid chattels, which were taken into the hands of the lord king, were given to four men of the town of Sudborough, to wit, William the son of Osmund, Robert Page, reeve, Henry the son of William Dolfyn and Jocelin of Deene, to answer for their price before the justices in eyre of the forest.

Select Pleas of the Forest, pp. 94-95.

2. Advocates and Castellans

We hardly know anything about the rights of exclusive privilege exercised by lay lords except through ecclesiastical documents. The only examples in existence are those exactions imposed from outside on territories or men subject to the immunity of a church which were on various occasions contested or limited by arbitration. But peasants were burdened by other customs which were never put in writing either because they were levied by ecclesiastical lords, or because they were not the object of litigation.

101

The king of Germania solemnly confirms and strengthens a privilege of immunity.

1. In the territory immediately surrounding the monastery (the banlieue*) the immunity was exclusive: all the villeins were subject to the abbot who held in particular the blood justice, the rights of marriage outside the franchise and mortmain.*

2. On the church lands situated outside this zone and on the men who lived on them, the 'advocates' extended a superior legal and military authority and levied the rights of shelter and tallage which were derived from them. Nevertheless, those villeins who were the personal dependants of the monastery and who were considered to belong to its household were exempt, unless the abbot should call on them in the execution of suits before his court. In such cases the 'advocate' appropriated one-third of the fines and confiscations.

3. The 'advocate' assumed, as a part of his fief, the military service required by the sovereign of the monastery.

4. The king levied an annual tribute in money which fell on the peasant cultivators of the monastic manor in the form of a fixed annual rent in 'current' deniers.

Conrad II, king of the Romans by the Grace of God. We make known to all faithful men of Christ and to ourselves, present and future, how our faithful and beloved Wibald, venerable abbot of Stavelot, who has long been distinguished in our service and in that of the kingdom by his activity and devotion, came before us in tears. He complains, amongst other difficulties which he encounters in restoring his church long decaying, of how the officials of his manors wish to hold their ministry in fief and hereditarily, that is, the functions of justice and stewardship. It has resulted in the orders of the abbot and his provosts remaining without effect and in the tenants of the church being reduced to indigence. This is why, by the common counsel of our nobles and of our general court held at Liège, with the consent of the same venerable abbot Wibald, we have decided that no judge commonly called *Schultheiss,* and no steward called mayor, may have or keep his ministry any longer, unless it is with the permission of the abbot. As soon as the order shall be given to him, let him give it back without opposition. After the death of the father, the son may not demand it as his inheritance. Furthermore, since the great rapacity of the advocates can hardly be restrained by so many judgments and privileges, in order that the church of Stavelot may be more firmly established, we concede and order that the advocate shall in the courts of this church neither over the officials nor over all the *familia,* have any right of justice, any right of plea, any right of shelter, tallage, and absolutely no exaction or service. All justice, all suits, all the profit from suits and pleas shall belong to the abbot. But if the abbot cannot himself or by his men punish, the advocate may on the invitation of the abbot come without delay or opposition, and receive the third of what he shall levy in the exercise of this justice. The advocate must, for the service of his fief, concern himself with the military service and the arms owing to us and to our successors, the abbot, the officials, the whole *familia* and all the possessions of this church being free of this and owing no aid to us nor to the advocate. That which our predecessor the Emperor Lothar III, decreed on the subject of the service of the church of Stavelot and which he confirmed by the Golden Bull, we establish without modification; nowhere else but at Aix shall he acquit his service, and after each harvest, if we come there, he must deliver twenty silver marks or a service worth twenty silver marks. Further, for the ministries or for the demesnes belonging to the monastery, he shall provide thirty marks or a service of thirty marks. When the abbot shall perform his service, each parish church which depends on his jurisdiction and his patronage shall pay five sous, and each *manse* twelve deniers, in the money current in the county where the possessions are situated; no church and no manse shall be exempt from this fixed rent, by any convention or fief or pledge, for the service of the kingdom may not and must not be pledged or delayed by any alienation whatever. The castle of Logne, with the fortifications which the same venerable abbot Wibald has caused to be constructed on the mount, we decide that it shall be in the hand and authority of the abbot for ever; the advocate shall have there no justice or authority or shelter. None of the abbots shall be able to concede it either in fief, or in exchange, or in *prestaria,* or in security to any mortal. We confirm the limits of the *banlieue* as they are contained in the ancient privileges: no duke or marquess, count or viscount, no secular or ecclesiastical person, great or small, shall exercise over these territories any authority, justice, or any power of jurisdiction; no person residing within these limits shall have any other lord but the abbot and no person shall depend on any other but the abbot for the marriage with a person of another status, for the letting of blood or for mortmain. The property which it has possessed in peace for ten years, we confirm it wholly for the use of the said church of Stavelot. And so that this may be immutable for always, we have caused this deed to be written and affixed with our seal and we have validated it with our own hand as it appears below. We have also caused the worthy witnesses whose names follow to participate in our confirmation. . . . The mark of the lord Conrad II, invincible king of the Romans . . . the year of the incarnation 1140, third of the proclamation, under the reign of Conrad II king of the Romans, the second year of his reign. Given at Worms, the 5th of the ides of February, in Christ. Amen.

G. Franz, *Deutsches Bauerntum*, pp. 99-104.

102

This deed, very solemn in form, which threatened a fine in gold so huge that the transgressor would hardly have been able to pay, or the king been capable of collecting, protected the immunity of the great royal monastery of St Médard at Soissons against the machinations of the Sire de Coucy, whose great castellany encompassed in part the estate of the abbey. The Sire claimed to be the advocate of the monastic domain, and demanded in consequence rights of shelter, usurped the judicial authority and requisitioned horses for his expeditions. There is a special mention here of merchants exporting wine from the valleys of the Aisne and the Oise to Flanders: the castellan had recently tried to profit from this increasing trade. It was a period when renewed commerce encouraged the creation of tolls.

In the name of the holy and undivided Trinity. I Philip, by the grace of God, king of France. Since, after the death of my father and during my infancy, under the tutelage of the Marquess Baudouin, there was a public discussion at Compiègne in which the said Marquess Baudouin, my tutor as I have said, and several bishops, amongst them Alard of Soissons, Guy of Amiens, another Guy of Beauvais, Baudoin of Noyon and Dreux of Thérouanne, took part. This assembly had been convoked mainly because of numerous complaints made not without cause by Renaud, abbot of St Médard, against Aubry de Coucy, who wished to own the advowson and an evil custom over the lands of St Médard. On the lands of St Médard he caused a repast to be provided where he wished and, from the monastery of St Médard and Vic-sur-Aisne, midway from his castle, he forced the peasants and inhabitants to come to his justice; when he went on military duties, he took with him, from these villages, as many horses as he wished and constrained their horsemen to come with him; he wished to judge on the territories of St Médard the merchants and carriers of wine coming from Flanders. Which is unheard of, and for him illegal, unless he had first carried a plea before the abbot and the provosts of the villages. None of his forebears had been allowed, as he had unjustly done until the day of this plea, to trouble on their comings and goings, the merchants of the four counties, to wit: Noyon, Vermandois, Amiens, Santerre, because these were under the patronage of a certain monk established to concern himself with these things and others of alike kind. Because he was not able to appropriate any of the things which we have recalled, neither by gift, nor by investiture nor by witness . . . on the condemnation of the whole assembly of bishops and laymen, he made amends for the injustice which, often without right, he had committed against the holy place. It was decided by the assembly of those present that if he continued to demand this and if there was a complaint from the abbot, unless he took care to make good within the fortnight what he had committed and to make restitution of the requisitioned goods, he must present himself on bail at Senlis, and that he should not be released without having rendered the capital and paid to the royal treasury ten golden livres for the injustice committed and for his audacity. This covenant he has given with his hand in that of Marquess Baudouin, my tutor, and he has promised to confirm it by oath when it shall be required of him. In order that the terms of this agreement shall remain always stable and inviolate, I, Philip, infant, king of France, the year of the birth of Our Lord 1066, fourth of the proclamation, fifth of my reign, have confirmed it in my own hand, ordered the confirmation by the impression of the royal seal, and instructed this act to be confirmed by the hand of many faithful men of the king of France who were present.

Recueil des actes de Philippe Ier (ed. Prou), 1908, No. 27.

103

The canons of Soissons were in conflict with the sire in two villages of his castellany.

1. *At Ambleny, the sire held the higher justice and the shelter (he requisitioned meat, the lord's food); he also demanded labour services with animals. The church obtained recognition of the exemption of those villeins who were its 'men', its personal dependants, or its settlers (hôtes), that is those who were installed on its lands. The immunity bore in fact a double aspect, personal and real.*

2. *At Chelle, a village wholly within the lordship of the church (at Ambleny it owned no more than some dispersed lands), the castellan was recognized as 'warden'. This function brought him the possession of two manses and the right to requisition draught animals from the village for certain labour services, which were however strictly limited.*

3. *It should be noted (a) that the sire, anxious to keep for the clearing of his woods all available manpower, obstructed the colonization of the church lands by the younger sons of peasant families who wished to set up on their own; (b) that only the animal labour services were of interest to the castellan and that the peasants of this region already owned draught horses; (c) that one of the labour services was earmarked specially for the carriage of wine (see Document No. 102); and (d) that the castellan regulated and exploited the activities of the rural artisans and that he controlled in particular the forge.*

. . . In order that between us and Nivelon de Pierrefonds, or his successors, there shall be no more discord, we have ordered to be written down below that which he has renounced, while confiding to writing and memory the things which are due to him in the villages. His stewards have the custom, while passing through Ambleny, to take pig meat, mutton or other, to eat according to the convenience of the moment. He has abandoned that, and also what he demanded for his provisioning on the day of the plea of the advowson from our settlers who were not his customary men. Nivelon's steward had also the custom of requisitioning for his labour our men's animals when and where he found them and without the consent of whoever they belonged to. When one of our men offended Nivelon in something, without bearing a complaint as they ought to have to us or to our officials, his officials left nothing to our dependants, pillaging their houses, and violating the sanctuary land. This also Nivelon renounced on this condition: the meat that he requires for provisions the day of his pleas from our settlers who owe the plea to him, he will take, but will buy it from them at the just price. It is also agreed not to pass over in silence if one of our men who has two sons or more and such a one, arrived at manhood, should wish to establish himself on our free holdings, over which Nivelon has nothing, and he forbids them to do so. This he has now admitted on condition that the cultivated lands of the advowson should not remain deserted. He has restored the portion of the area which he took from us. He has given back the site of the three houses situated at Darnel, those of Jean, son of Fulrad, of Grentin and of Aubrade, being proved by our oath that they were ours. He has left the pastures usurped by his officials, it being proved in the same manner that they belong to our domain. All this for Ambleny. We come now to what concerns Chelle. At Chelle, none of his forebears have ever had any right, save two *manses*, contiguous to this domain, and a labour service of half of the plough animals due for the ward of the village. But Nivelon burdened the village to such a point beyond his rights, that daily not only he but his horsemen and his serfs took horses, oxen and donkeys to perform all the labours. He forbade there to be, without his authorization, either smith, save for an annual due of twelve deniers per anvil, or baker, or shoemaker, or butcher, or tavern keeper. He caused several times a year our meadows and those of our tenants to be scythed and damaged by his grooms. Each year he claimed a labour service from the inhabitants of the village for the defence of his castle.

Excommunicated for all that he levied improperly and visited at last by the grace of God, by the council of his horsemen, and by the prayers of his upright wife, he abandoned to the Lord God and to us the unjust customs which he demanded at Chelle. But we, because he has the wardenship of Chelle, apart from the *manses* and the half labour service which he held from olden times, as has been said, for the wardenship of the village, in order that he henceforth performs better service and that he loves us more, we have granted him, to enlarge his fief in this same village, two labour services which he had not had until then, one at harvest time to carry the crops belonging to the demesne of the castle of Pierrefond, except the crops of Sermoise, Ciry and Autreches; the other, at the wine harvest to carry the wine, except that of the said villages. It has been agreed that the animals of the brothers' demesne and those of the provost, the mayor, the dean and the priest shall not go to perform these labour services, and that the officials of Nivelon shall not themselves take the animals for the labour services, but that they shall be requisitioned at the moments which have been said by our officials. If all the animals owing labour service cannot be provided on the same day, they shall be delivered within the fortnight without penalty. The labour service being performed, when the beasts shall be given back, if an animal has died during the labour service, we consider that its master shall be recompensed at the just price. This Nivelon has abandoned and has granted this to us. And by a common agreement we have caused these letters to be drawn up, in order that by them and by the witness underwritten by each party, all dispute shall be settled between us and him or his successors.

Given in the house of the Provost Lisiard, the year of the birth of Our Lord 1089.

Polyptyque de l'Abbé Irminon (ed. B. Guérard), Vol. II, 1844, Appendices, pp. 365-367.

104

1. *Here the* taille *levied by the advocate is moderated and regulated.*
2. *When people go to live in the woods and exploit them more intensively, limits have to be set to the forest zones in which the authority of the rival lords can be exercised.*

We make known to all present as well as future, that there has long been a dispute between our faithful Brunon, abbot of St Jean of Laon and Enguerran de Coucy, about the *tailles* of the villages on the edge of the forest which were under the advowson of the said Enguerran, and about the wood of Suzi, in which the same Enguerran claimed many things which the abbot did not recognize as being due to him. At last the two parties being come before us at Paris, Enguerran de Coucy admits before all his injustice and agrees that he will take no more than one *taille* per year from the men placed under his advowson in the villages along the woodland border, and that he will take it only to the extent that the church may not lose its revenues, that he will not burden the men too heavily nor force them to flee. Further, concerning the wood of Suzi, he has recognized and admitted before us that the wood of Vois situated between these limits (to wit from the Sébacourt way up to the great ditch which passes through the middle of the meadow called *Halumprez*, and from that ditch up to the dried-up stream, and from this stream up to the Tombelle, and from there along the way to the chapel and to the ditch of the lord bishop of Laon, which is the boundary of the forest of the church, and from there up the Vieule road), as well as the woods of Burseval and Moramont, belong to the church of St Jean of Laon, and must be free of all right of advowson and all exaction. We have, therefore, granted this thing in this manner and ordered that it should be kept. And in order that in the future it shall not be forgotten nor changed by the wickedness of any man, we have ordered it to be set down in writing and to be confirmed by the authority of our seal.

Given in the year 1164 of the Lord, at Paris. . . .

A. Luchaire, *Études sur les actes de Louis VII*, p. 424.

105

A sworn jury of the oldest men in the district who knew the most ancient customs, a pious gift on the part of the count who bought certain funerary observances, together with the presence of a royal expedition which had come to defend the rights of the church, resulted in the rights which the lord of the ban claimed over the immunity of the Cluniac community being limited.

1. *One of the monastic manors was completely exempt.*

455

2. *The count was warden of a second, which rendered him an annual rent in food (representing the right of shelter), the blood justice, punishment of the four principal crimes and the profits of the confiscations arising from them.*

3. *In three forest villages where the ecclesiastical property was more dispersed (note evidence of clearing 'tasks' levied on the assarts and four peasant farms deep in the forest), the count levies a due on the crops (double for husbandmen); this tax is the reward for policing the fields, as well as the public spaces, the roads and commons.*

Be it known to all, present and future, that a dispute has arisen between the noble count Gérard of Mâcon and the monks of Cluny concerning the unwarranted customs and unusual exactions with which the count and his agents burden beyond measure the lands of the church of Cluny situated in the diocese of Mâcon. Indeed the count claims in certain villages belonging to the monks, the advowson and the wardenship, the monks asserting that he owns nothing in these places. Elsewhere, where he really has the advowson, he appropriates unwarranted exactions and unusual customs. Proceedings having thus been instituted concerning this by the Cluny brothers, the disagreement was settled by the intervention of prudent and religious men in this wise: at St. Martin of Mâcon were met together Dom Thibaut, the venerable abbot of Cluny, with certain of the elders of Cluny, and the said count Gérard with many of his horsemen and stewards. They undertook to choose very old men, worthy of trust, accepting what they should say about the customs and status of this territory for the truth: what these witnesses should assert after having taken oath would be firmly kept by both these parties. The said witnesses, after swearing to seek the truth, deliberated for long between themselves and finally agreed on this evidence. It was stated by them that Count Guillaume, father of Count Gérard, had never had nor claimed any rights or customs in the household and village of Laisé, and Count Gérard willingly concurred with their evidence on this point. It was said that the Count had the levy of sheaves (*gerberie*) in the villages of Dommange and Igé, to wit one sheaf from the labourer and two from the husbandmen. At Aine the Count has the protection of the roads and pastures, which pastures are common to the count and the monks. In the wood called Jou, the count has half and the monks a quarter, and the count and the monks have here their 'tasks'. In the wood of Dommange the count has four *colongers*[1] upon which the monks levy nothing. At Dommange the count has half the 'tasks' and the monks the other. In these three villages the count and his agents have no other custom on the land of the monks. It must be said that in the obedientiary possession of Chevignes and its dependancies the count has robbery, adultery, homicide and usury, the guilt of which has been proved and legitimately recognized in the presence of the dean of Chevignes. He has also one hundred *miches* of rents, and the protection of roads and pastures. The right of shelter which, according to the said witnesses, he can have here at his pleasure, and certain other exactions and customs which he and his stewards claimed here, the said count, for the sake of his soul and for those of his ancestors and successors, abandons and gives entirely to the church of Cluny. In exchange for this gift, Abbot Thibaut and the community of Cluny have

[1] Tenants of a *colonge*

agreed that the meal he offered each year to the community of Cluny and the lepers of St Lazare shall be offered by the household of Chevignes; after his death this meal shall be transferred to the day of his birth. They have granted him a daily mass, for himself, his ancestors and his successors, and at his death the same ceremony shall be performed for him as for an abbot of Cluny (1180).

Recueil des chartes de l'abbaye de Cluny, Vol. V, No. 4279.

E. RENTALS AND CUSTUMALS

1. England

106

Rents in money, grain and livestock, obligations to cultivate pieces of land, haymaking tasks, liveries of split logs and unspecified week-works were services owed by the dependants of Hurstbourne Priory in Hampshire listed in a rental drawn up before the Conquest. All these things correspond very closely to the obligations of the gebur laid down in the Rectitudines (Document No. 92, p. 443), and differ little from the obligations of serfs living under their own roof on German manors in the Carolingian period.

(ca. 1050)

Here are inscribed the services due from the peasants of Hurstbourne.

For each hide they owe 40d. at the autumnal equinox and 6 measures of beer, and three measures of wheat for bread. They must plough three acres, sow them with their own seed and store the harvest. They owe 3 *li* of barley as rent, they must scythe half an acre of meadow and put the hay in ricks, provide four loads of split wood, stack them and provide sixteen perches of enclosure. At Easter they owe two sheep with two lambs (two young sheep count as one fully grown); they must wash the sheep and shear them, and work to order every week save three, at Christmas, Easter and Rogation Days.

Anglo-Saxon Charters, (A. J. Robertson, ed.).

107

1. On this manor of the abbey of Burton on Trent, nearly all holdings comprise two bovates, the equivalent of one virgate, a quarter of a hide, or a carucate, of about 30 acres of arable. When these holdings are in the possession of villeins they bear obligations for week-work, for the cultivation of a fixed amount of land and for boon works, some of which may be 'sold' if the lord so desires. Held for rent, they bear an annual charge of two or three shillings.

2. There are no more serfs or prebendary domestic servants on the manor. The ploughmen are rewarded by a small fief of 15 acres; the oxherd holds a villein holding but is exempt from almost all services. The miller is a 'farmer'; the priest received a fixed rent from his church and tithes from the parishioners and the demesne.

In Burton there is 'inland' for 2 ploughs. There are 2 ploughs with 16 oxen. Besides these there are 4 other oxen for carting lime and 4 for carting wood; and there is 1 brood mare in addition to the brood mares which were there in the time of Abbot Nigel: these between the mares and the foals then numbered 70. There are 3 Spanish asses; 19 cows; 1 bull; 8 calves; 2 beasts for food; 128 pigs –

The land of the men is assessed at 1½ hides. The villeins are Fredebert; Edward; Adelon; Alwin; Leviet; Uctebrand; Eluric; Edric. Each one of these holds 2 bovates and works [for the lord] for 2 days each week. He must find a horse each year for the journey to the abbot's court or pay 3 pence. He must go for salt once, and for fish once, or give 12 pence for each carrying service. He must cart 1 cartload of wood. He must pay 2 hens at Christmas and make 1 sester of malt and give pannage. He must plough twice in the year, and besides this half an acre in Lent. From Pentecost to the Feast of All Saints he must send his beasts into the lord's fold . . . he must find 1 man in August to reap. And anyone who between Pentecost and August goes to the wood for a cartload of timber must pay 2 pence.

Rauechetus holds 1 bovate and works for 1 day a week for the lord and goes where he is sent.

Alwin likewise. The monks' man likewise.

The cottars are Godric; Aluric; another Godric; Seietus; Leviet; Bristold; Ulviet; Lefldea; Alvena; Doune; William the Cobbler. Each has one croft, and works for one day. There are 2 monks' oxherds who each hold 1 bovate.

The rent-paying tenants are these:

William of 'Sobehalle' holds 2 bovates for 2 shillings, and must go wherever he is sent, either with the abbot or without the abbot.

The chief oxherd (?) holds 2 bovates for 2 shillings and 6 pence, and twice a year he must lend his plough, and thrice in August he must reap, twice with one man and the third time with all his household, with the lord providing their food; and the wife of Aldeon shall reap for 1 day.

Stevinulf holds 2 bovates for 3 shillings.

Uctebrand likewise must lend his cart for carting the demesne hay.

Aluric the Cook, Aluric the baker and Ulwin the mason, each hold 2 bovates for 2 shillings, and must perform the same customs. . . .

Wardbois holds 2 bovates and 3 acres of meadow for his rent, that is to say, for 2 shillings. . . .

Richard, son of Godit, holds 1 house.

Gilbert holds 1 dwelling for 16 pence.

Cacerel holds 1 house for 6 pence. . . .

Recelbert holds 4 acres of 'inland' and his dwelling on them, and he has half the revenue of the parish altar except the candles which he does not have, but which are found for him for his ministry; and he has 2 sheaves of the tithe of the demesne ploughs; and in Burton and Branston and in Stapenhill and in Winshill he has 1 thrave from everyone and a tithe of their cattle, and the ration of 1 monk in the Court. . . .

The mother of Steinulf 1 dwelling for 12 pence. . . .

Lepsi holds 2 mills for 50 shillings for 4 years from the Feast of All Saints in the first year of Abbot Geoffrey; and he must grind freely the corn and malt of the demesne and give such fishes as are caught; and he must restore the mills as well as they were when he took them and with new millstones if such be needed. . . .

Godwin holds 1 dwelling for the work of 4 weeks, to wit, 2 in the summer and 2 in Lent.

Durand holds a dwelling for 14 pence. . . .

English Historical Documents, 1042-1189, Vol. II
(D. C. Douglas & G. W. Greenaway, eds.), London, 1953, pp. 821-823.

108

The importance of dues in money, the differences in social structure and charges between the two manors, and the increasing weight of service laid upon the sokemen compared to what the Rectitudines *describe as typical of the* geneat *(Document No. 192, p. 443) should be noted in this document.*

This is the description of the manors of Peterborough Abbey as the archdeacon Walter received and held them in the king's hands.

At Kettering there are ten hides subject to royal geld. Of these 10 hides 40 villeins hold 40 virgates. These men plough in the spring four acres per virgate for the lord. Furthermore, they provide ploughs for the lord's work four times in the winter, three times in the spring and once in the summer. And these men have 22 ploughs with which they work. All these men work for the lord three days a week. Furthermore, they pay each year by custom 2s. 1½d. per virgate. Together they pay 50 hens and 640 eggs. Furthermore Aelric holds 13 acres, with two acres of meadow, and pays for this 16d. And there is a mill with a miller who pays 20s. And 8 'cotsets' who each have five acres, and they work one day a week, and make malt twice a year. And each one of them pays one penny for his goat, and if he has a she-goat a halfpenny. And there is a shepherd and a swineherd who holds eight acres. And in the ownership of the hall there are four ploughs with 32 oxen, 12 cows with 10 calves, two non-working animals, three draught horses, 300 sheep, 50 pigs, and as much additional meadow as would be worth 16s. The Church at Kettering depends on the altar of Peterborough Abbey, and for the charity of St Peter it owes 4 rams and two cows or 5s. . . .

At Collingham there are four carucates and a bovate, less the fiftieth part of a bovate, subject to royal geld. There are 20 villeins who hold one and a half carucates. Each one of them works one day a week for the lord throughout the year. And in August they perform three labour services. And all take 60 loads of wood to the lord's hall; they cut and carry 20 loads of peat and 20 loads of thatch (*coopertura*). And they must harrow the winter ploughing. Every year they pay rent of 4 *li*. And there are 50 sokemen who hold two and a half carucates of land. Each of them must work six days every year according to custom at the deer fence. And in August each must work three days. And all have fourteen ploughs and must plough with them four times for the lord in Lent. And the said sokemen plough 48 acres, and harrow them, and harvest them in August. And all these sokemen pay 12 *li.* each year. And in the ownership of the hall there are two ploughs with 16 oxen, four cows and calves, one non-working animal, 160 sheep and 12 pigs. . . .

Chronicon Petroburgense (Camden Society),
T. Stapleton (ed.), 1949, Appendix, pp. 157-159.

109

This description allows us to compare the manor about 1125 with its state soon after 1160. In the interval the number of ploughs has decreased, but that of draught horses has quadrupled. About a fifth of the villein holdings have been transformed into rent-paying holdings by commutation of the services into money dues. This change, and the consequent decrease in labour services, go hand in hand with the reduction of agricultural activity on the manorial demesne which is reflected in the decline in the number of ploughs. The monks of Ramsey drew a large sum of money every year from this manor, the whole of which, together with its stock and the services due from villeins, was farmed out.

(After 1160)

At Elton there was in the time of King Henry and there is now 10½ hides, each of 5 virgates. And it rendered at that time full farm in everything and 10 *li*, to the Abbot's chamber: this was its stock: 5 ploughs each of 8 oxen, each worth 40d., 10 cows and a bull at this price; 160 sheep, 2 horses for harrowing, 100 pigs.

Of the free tenements, Rainier, son of Aednoth, had in the time of King Henry, 3 free virgates, for which he followed the courts of the shire and the hundred.

Thuri, the priest, had 2 virgates and followed the shire and hundred courts. He also had 10 acres and a toft worth 8d. next to the church.

Edward, father of Jordan, had a virgate and a half; he followed the shire and hundred courts. He ploughed half an acre, every Friday he harrowed. He gave also 2s. each year in rent and 13d. This land, his son Jordan holds now for the same service, save that he pays 12d. more.

Blundel, grandfather of Gilbert, had a virgate and a half for the same service. Gilbert, his grandson, holds the same land in the same way. The aforesaid Blundel had also another virgate and a half for which he paid 7s. and it is his son Richard who now holds it in the same way.

Gilbert, the reeve, held then and holds now a virgate in the same way, paying 6s. and ploughing six acres. He holds another virgate 7s.

Thorold, the priest, held a virgate for 5s. and was free of all labour and service. And Reinald, brother of Robert the clerk, now holds this land in the same manner and is free.

Gisla the widow, had then and now a virgate for 6s. and for ploughing 6 acres.

The mill with one virgate and 6½ acres rendered in the old days 40s. And the farmer had from it then his food for the year.

Alan Rufus had 2 crofts for 4s. by gift of abbot William (1133-1160) and a virgate which had been held by a certain man called Dac for 4s.

In the time of King Henry there were in this village 35 virgates held for labour service; on the demesne there were lands of 8 ploughmen, one swineherd and one shepherd. Now there are no more than 28½ virgates held for labour services.

And this is the labour and service of one virgate.

From Michaelmas until the beginning of August, he works 2 days a week and ploughs a third, save at Christmas, Easter and Whitsuntide. From the beginning of August to the Nativity of Our Lady he works 3 days each week. From the Nativity of Our Lady until Michaelmas he works everyday but Saturday. In winter he ploughs half an acre, sows it with his own seed, he harrows and harvests it, as well as another half an acre in August. He performs carting services at his own expense. He makes 2 measures of malt with the lord's grain. . . . He also pays 4d. at Michaelmas and a halfpenny for wool. He carries messages. If he leaves the shire he is quit of his weekly service save ploughing. In August he gives a load of wood, an enclosure service, two loads of grain in August. Each group of 5 virgates gives 4d. for fish; each group of 2 virgates provides a load of straw and participates in works. When the thresher comes all must come to the 'hall' to beat the grain from day to day for the making of the farm. And if it has been so cold in winter that he could not plough, he must work Fridays instead. When the farmer demands labour service in August, he must come with all his household; he is then fed by the farmer.

After the death of King Henry, Ralf of Asekirk received from abbot Walter for 6s. a virgate which was formerly held for labour service.

Richard, son of Reinald, has 2 virgates which Thuri the priest held.

Francis holds a virgate for 6s. and ploughs 6 acres. . . .

The following is the stock of the 'hall' at Elton: 4 ploughs with 24 oxen and 8 horses and ten cows. Each ox and horse is worth 4s., each cow is worth 40d. 160 sheep; 26 pigs more than 1 year old, 24 hogs; 16 cocks. With this stock it must render the whole farm and 10 *li* in money; with the mill which gives 100s.

A certain William has half an acre for 2d.

Master Ralf holds one acre of the demesne.

The men of Elton give 17d. for a croft.

Cartularium monasterii de Rameseia
(W. H. Hart & P. A. Lyons, ed.), Vol. III, 1893, p. 257.

110

The bishop of Durham also farms out certain of his manors and delivers to the farmers their livestock and the seed grain (note the marked predominance of spring crops and the large investment, appropriate to the beginning of the agricultural season, for the purchase of 16 oxen to complete the plough-teams). Notice also the tax of 'cornage' on cattle, characteristic of northern England, and the presence of artisans – masons, carpenters and smiths – rewarded by fiefs and a share of the crops of the cultivated area where their services were employed. For certain boon works which the villeins were bound to perform, they received wages.

In Boldon there are 22 villeins, every one of whom holds two bovates of land of 30 acres and renders 2s. 6d. of scotpenny and the half of a scot-chalder of oats and 16d of averpenny and five waggon loads of wood and two hens and ten eggs, and works through the whole year three days in the week except Easter and Whitsunweek and 13 days at Christmastide and in the week except Easter and Whitsunweek and 13 days at Christmastide and in his works he does in the autumn four boon-days at reaping with his entire household except the housewife and they reap moreover three roods of the standing crop of oats and he ploughs three roods of oat stubble and harrows [it]. Every plough [team] of the villeins, also, ploughs two acres and harrows [them] and then they have once [only] a dole from the bishop and for that week they are quit of work, but when they make the great boon-days they have a dole and in their works they harrow when it is necessary and they carry loads, and when they have carried them every man has a loaf of bread; and they mow one day at Houghton in their work until the evening, and then they have a dole. And every two villeins build one booth for the fair of St Cuthbert. And when they are building lodges and carrying loads of wood they are quit of all other works.

There are 12 cottiers there, and every one of whom holds 12 acres, and they work through the whole year two days in the week, except at the three feasts aforenamed, and they render 12 hens and 60 eggs.

Robert holds two bovates of 36 acres and renders half a mark. The pinder holds 12 acres and he has a thrave of corn from every plough and he renders 40 hens and 500 eggs.

The mill renders 5½ marks.

The villeins in their work each year ought to make, if need be, a house 40 feet in length and 15 feet in breadth, and when they make it every man is quit of 4d. of averpenny.

The whole vill renders 17s. of cornage and one milch cow.

The demesne is at farm with stock of four ploughs and four harrows, and renders for two ploughs 16 chalders of wheat and 16 chalders of oats, and 8 chalders of barley, and for the other two ploughs ten marks. . . .

In Quarringtonshire, namely, in North Sherburn and Shadforth and Cassop there are 51 villeins, and every man holds, renders and works as they of Boldon. Also in North Sherburn, Ulkill holds two bovates for 40d. of rent and goes on the bishop's errands. And Thomas of Shadforth holds two bovates for 40d. of rent and goes on the bishop's errands. In Cassop William of Kent holds four bovates for half a mark and goes on the bishop's errands.

In South Sherburn, Christian, the mason, holds 40 acres, which the bishop gave him from the moor for 5s. and two bovates which used to belong to Arkill for 14d., but of these he shall be quit while he is in the service of the bishop for his work as mason. Watling, with Sama, his wife, holds four bovates and renders half a mark. Also five firmas hold there every man 12 acres and renders 2s. and one hen and 20 eggs, and does four boon-days in the autumn, and for every one of their ploughs they plough one acre. Also there are 10 cottiers there, every man of whom holds 6 acres, and they work from Lammas-day to Martinmas two days in the week and from Martinmas to Lammas-day one day on the week. The smith holds 12 acres there for making the iron gear of the ploughs. The pinder of Quarrington holds 20 acres and renders 120 hens and 1,000 eggs. The demesne of Sherburn is at farm with the stock of two ploughs and two harrows and renders 6 pounds. The demesne of 4 ploughs of Quarrington and the sheep, with the pasture are in the hand of the bishop. The reeve holds one bovate there for his service. The smith 12 acres for his service. Quarringtonshire renders 75s. of cornage and three milch cows.

Victoria County History of Durham, Page (ed.),
Vol. I, pp. 327-328 and 329-330.

III

This detailed assessment of the parish revenues conceded to the incumbent enables us to measure the weight of the charges of a religious origin borne by the peasants of the parish. The greater tithe, the grain tithe, was only partly assessed, since it went to the patron of the church. It is probable in this case that the priest did not levy the tithe directly; instead he enjoyed the output of a holding. The size of the 'oblations' required on each occasion, which was strictly laid down, should be noticed.

(End of the twelfth century)

The vicar of Chircham receives as grain tithes three-quarters of a virgate of land, and the tithe is estimated to be worth 13s. 4d. Item, he levies all the hay tithe of the men of the village, for which each year he levies at least 22s. Item, he levies tithes of wool, flax, calves, lambs, swine, geese, chickens, milk and eggs. Item, he levies 'oblations' on the four principal feasts in the year, which is worth 27s. He levies all other 'oblations' coming from nuptuals, confessions, funeral obsequies, and other sources, and every Sunday one penny, with the purification of women: 20s. Furthermore, he levies 2 marks every year and half an acre on which to build his house. He levies oblations on the chapel at Hyneham once a year on the Feast of St James: 4s. Item, at Bullgam, he levies on the demesne as well as on the tithes of the demesne on wool, flax, lambs, calves, swine, geese, chickens, milk, cheese, eggs, oblations and all other revenue; which is worth each year 6 *li* 2s. 6d. He has eight acres for the provision of lamps.

Total 11 *li* 6s. 10d.

Historia et cartularium Monasterii Sancti Petri Gloucestriae,
W. H. Hart (ed.), Vol. I, 1863, pp. 249-250.

2. *Eastern France*

112

A gang of servants, whom the scribe described by the word servientes *rather than* servus, *which seemed to him too strong a term, cultivated and kept up this demesne belonging to the bishop of Mâcon. They provided the lord's household with wood and with casks for the wine harvest. Groups of them went off to repair the cathedral and its adjoining buildings. Their occupation was domestic although they were housed on plots where their families lived and which produced enough to sell so that they could pay dues for the pannage of their swine.*

(ca. 1100)

The number of servants of Saint Vincent on the Manor of Romenay

First of all they must repair every year the roofs of St Vincent and St Gervais, the vault between St Jean and St Gervais, the hall and half the ceiling (*solier*). They must entirely repair the church of St Peter at Romenay, except the walls, and all the houses which depend upon this 'hall', and the barn and the stable and the kitchen. In this village they must cultivate two demesne furlongs, one for wheat and rye, the other for oats, by ploughing, sowing, harvesting, and carrying to the barn. They must scythe, toss, cart and stack the hay in two spinneys (*breuils*), one at St Romain and the other at Reyssouze. In May, each one owes a measure of oats, and twenty-two poles to make hoops. Every third year, all together they owe two loads of casks; they owe on St Andrew's Day two sous for the swine; between Martinmas and St Andrew's Day they owe the supply of wood; at Christmas a raft of wood.

Cartulaire de Saint-Vincent de Mâcon, No. 493.

113

In 1149, or more likely in 1155-1156, a complete inventory of the abbey of Cluny was undertaken for the abbot who wished to reorganize the system of provisioning the monastery. The commissioners' reports have been preserved for twelve of the manors, each managed by a monk appointed to the task as dean.

1. *The following fragment brings out how relatively small were the fixed dues and exactions, which were the only part of the patrimony directly to provide the lord with a money income: twelve livres, or hardly as much as was spent each year on renewing the footwear of the monks.*

2. *Tithes, bakehouses and mills brought in three times as much grain as was supplied by dues of the dependants.*

3. *Most other profits came from the demesne. This had little place for livestock, but its output was increased by planting vines, and even more by buying plough oxen, since it was basically a cereal farm growing wheat; the demesne produced eighteen times as much wheat as was received from dues.*

4. *There was in fact no labour service on this manor. Wage earners were only employed in the vineyards (their wages absorbed a third of the fixed money rents levied on the peasants, which thus found its way back into the hands of the local husbandmen). Métayage was used to a small extent to cultivate the fields: a small piece of land taken from the demesne (only a thirtieth part of the manorial arable) with half of a team and all the seed was entrusted to a peasant who had then to deliver half the crop. The manpower was almost exclusively domestic labour. The oxherds who drove the ploughs and tended the oxen were rewarded by an alloca-*

tion of grain; a score of servants were fed in the demesne 'hall' on the produce of the bakehouses and mills.

5. Only a quarter of the wheat harvested during the year of the inquest was kept for seed. The lord was able to sell a large surplus, one-eighth of the gross product.

The deanery of St Hippolyte. There nine livres and six sous are due at Martinmas, and on the nativity of St John the Baptist four livres. From each donkey going to take wood in the forest twelve deniers, which makes in all ten sous. And at Martinmas nineteen *setiers* of wheat by the Cluny measure, and twenty-one *setiers* of grain by the same measure, and sixty *setiers* and a half of wine, and fifteen capons, and five chickens.

At *Pugeos* there is a man who owns a plough and four oxen, two of which belong to the lord and the other two to this man, and the lord must have half of all the profit. For tithe and the 'task' eighteen *setiers* of grain by the Cluny measure are due, but this is in a barren year; when times are better, the number of *setiers* will increase. There are seven centres there, in which are double mill wheels, and when times are good, they render two *setiers* a week, and indeed with a bakehouse which is there they can maintain daily twenty men.

There are five ploughs, each of six oxen, and a seventh can be added. There are five yearling calves, and two of last year's, and seven oxen, and three donkeys, and nineteen pigs, big and small. There are vines, which, well maintained, can render six loads of wine. There is a new vineyard, from which, in the future, six loads of wine will be harvested, and this vineyard with the other vines can be easily cultivated for six livres. At St Hippolyte and at Chaselles sixty *setiers* of wheat are sown, and in the rented lands two *setiers* of wheat are sown, and the lord shall receive half of the produce.

At Martinmas at Chaselles 58 sous and six *setiers* of grain are due. On St Vincent's Day, 14 sous. On St John's Day twelve sous and more. Sixty loads of hay can be harvested here. There are two mills from which can be taken fifteen *setiers*, half in wheat and in barley.

Of the produce of sown lands this year . . . Cluny has received 150 *setiers* of wheat, the lord has sold 30 of them, and sixty are sown. In August 107 *setiers* of barley and oats have been received of the profit of the whole year. Each shepherd and oxherd has received 7 *setiers* of all grains.

The total of all this is: 18 livres, 26 *setiers* and a half of wheat, 169 *setiers* of grain, 7 and a half *setiers* of barley, three *muids* and twelve *setiers* and a half of wine, 15 hens and five chickens.

All this without counting the profit of the demesne. Besides this, twelve loads of wine and sixty loads of hay can be harvested on the demesne.

Recueil des chartes de l'abbaye de Cluny,
Vol. V, No. 4143, pp. 494-495.

114

This table gives all the items which can be extracted from the Cluniac inventory quoted in Document No. 113. In its entirety it confirms the lessons of the fragment analysed above.

DEANERIES	A. DUES[1] Cash (£ s. d.)	Kind (in setiers) Wheat	Rye	Oats	Wine	B. CHURCHES Number	Profit Cash	Kind (in setiers) of grain	B. MILLS Number	Profit	B. BAKEHOU... Number	Profi...
Cluny	90 0 0	20	–	7	–	–	–	–	1	20 setiers of grain	–	–
Laizé (ca. Mâcon-Nord)	16 17 0	17	–	25	1	1	50s.	50	5	–	1	–
Beaumont-sur-Grosne (ca. Sennecey)	7 19 0	37	–	81	180	4	55s.	40	4	maintenance of domestic staff	–	–
Malay (ca. Saint-Gengoux)	7 0 0	28	–	58	–	2	–	14	1	4 setiers of grain	–	–
Saint-Hyppolyte (ca. St Gengoux, co. Bonnay)	18 0 0	25	–	21	61	1	–	18	9	115 setiers of grain	1	–
Saint-Martin-des-Vignes (ca. and co. Mâcon-Nord)	12 4 3	14	–	2	79	5	70s.	40	1	3 setiers of grain	–	–
Berzé-la-Ville (ca. Mâcon-Nord)	2 16 0	24	–	18	100	1	8s.	20	1	1 setier of grain	–	–
Saint-Gengoux	3 16 2	25	–	30	3·5	4	4s.	36	9	52 setiers of grain	–	12 setiers of grain
Lourdon (ca. Cluny, co. Lournand)	47 16 8	23	–	60	10	5	–	162	2	24 setiers of grain	–	–
Arpayé (Rhône, ca. Beaujeu, co. Fleurie)	8 0 0	30	14	51	97	3	5s.	46	3	27 setiers of grain	–	–
Chaveyriat (Ain, ca. Châtillon-sur-Chalaronne)	18 16 5	53	7	44	130	4	20s.	70	1	4 setiers of grain	2	10 setiers of grain
Montberthoud (Ain, ca. Saint-Trivier-sur-Moignans, co. Savigneux.)	31 3 7	17	9	12	39	8	57s.	360	3	10s.; 2 setiers of grain; 2 setiers of wine; 2 pigs	1	5s.

[1] All quantities given in the inventory have been converted into *setiers* of the measure used at Cluny, accordi...
to equivalents between this *setier* and other measures of capacity set out in the inventory itself.

C. DEMESNE

liable to labour service	Labour		Horses	Donkeys	Oxen	Cows and calves	Pigs	Sheep	Wheat	Rye	Barley	Oats	Wine
	Ploughs liable to Labour Service								Production (in setiers)[3]				
	No.	Service							Wheat	Rye	Barley	Oats	Wine
–	–	–	–	–	–	–	–	–	–	–	–	–	–
–	–	–	–	–	–	–	–	–	–	–	–	–	–
–	20	3 ploughings	–	–	14(+28)	18	18	–	–	–	–	–	64
–	2	–	–	–	12	8(+1)	18	–	50	–	50	–	32
–	–	–	–	3	30(+6)	–	19	–	240	–	107	–	192
–	–	–	–	–	4(+2)	4	–	–	46	10	20	–	320
91	7	2 ploughings	1	3	12(+1)	5(+5)	18	40	52	–	–	–	320*
18	20	3 ploughings	–	–	5(+7)	0(+7)	–	–	–	–	–	–	160*
250	40	4 ploughings cartage	–	–	24(+6)	28	35	–	–	–	–	–	960*
–	40	1 ploughing	–	1	7(+7)	0(+10)	–	17(+200)	–	–	–	–	240*
–	12	2 ploughings	–	–	18	–	–	400	–	300*	–	–	320*
48	–	2 ploughings 3 cartage	–	2	19(+5)	5(+15)	1(+40)	110	50*	270	–	–	480*

[2] Beside the actual figure, preceded by the symbol +, is the figure for possible increase as given by the commissioners.

[3] The figures followed by the symbol ★ are those for the harvest in a good year as estimated by the commissioners, and not the actual harvest.

In one inventory of the possessions of the abbey of Bouzonville in Lorraine is a fragment containing a rental of the demesne at Loutzviller. Its general features are wholly Carolingian: services due from the manse; *cultivation of fixed pieces of land; enclosure and ploughing 'tasks'; unspecified labour on weeding, haymaking, harvesting, threshing. We see that the estate is in the charge of an 'oxherd'; that days of ploughing are not only required from tenants but also from villeins established within the* ban; *that the occasional labour services, much less oppressive than in the ninth century, are partly rewarded; that money dues replace certain tasks; that the proportion of money dues is very large (in particular the lord levies a heavy right of relief on heirs who succeed to a tenancy).*

A fragment of a custumal of the manor of Zissen follows. It fixes to begin with the recognized rights of the advocate who presides over the three annual general courts where crimes liable to corporal punishment were tried; apart from the third of the profits of justice, the advocate receives at each court a fixed rent in kind and in money which is the equivalent of the meal attached to the right of shelter. The exactions imposed on the men of the familia *are then described. These men are the personal dependants belonging to the immunity. The charges are* chevage, *animal heriot, and* formariage (*marriage outside the franchise*). *This applies to men only, and also takes the form of a funeral tax. The lord confiscates the whole inheritance except the widow's dowry; the children, who are not 'men' of the abbey, but of their mother's lord, have only the right to the share which comes to her from the paternal succession.*

(After 1163)

. . . Here are the dues which come to you from the under-mentioned *manses* each year.

The *manse* pays twenty deniers in two instalments, ten at Easter; at Martinmas ten and a chicken; at Easter six eggs. In April and May it must enclose six rods, each of 17 feet and a half. In spring, it shall plough two *arpents* and sow them with demesne seed. It shall plough the same area in June and in autumn. It shall weed these *arpents*, sow them, harvest them and store them in the demesne barn. Every villein, who is a hereditary tenant, shall plough two days, and whoever is within the *ban*, one day, three times a year; for ploughing shall be given in spring three loaves, two in June, and three in autumn. All that the demesne oxherd or the other peasants shall have ploughed in the demesne labour services, the tenants of that allod will weed, harvest and thresh. The *manse* owes two deniers for hay cutting; the peasants will collect it and stack it in the demesne barn. The man who shall take a *manse* by hereditary right shall give five sous. . . .

. . . When the abbot shall come, the steward shall give him food, also to his horses in the evening and the following day. He must leave for the abbot's use a quarter of the price of the common wood. If a man of the *familia* dies, his best animal shall be delivered to the abbot. If it is a woman, the abbot shall have the best object made with her hands. At Martinmas the miller shall give to the abbot two deniers of bread, two deniers of meat and a *setier* of wine; the forester and the dean shall give as much. The abbot must buy the millstones, which the *familia* must transport, but the abbot will pay the cost. Every man of the *familia* shall owe the abbot a *chevage* of six deniers, and the women as much, in money which is current where they live. If someone kills a man of the *familia* he shall give the abbot thirty sous and one obole.

If the movable and immovable goods of a man are confiscated by the abbot for some misdeed, the abbot shall have two-thirds and the advocate the third part. The miller shall give every year twelve *muids* of wheat and two others to make beer. It shall be known that in all the courts of the advocate no case may be argued except theft, debt, affray and the drawing of blood. The abbot shall owe three services to the advocate: at Christmas half a measure of wheat, twelve deniers for meat, two measures of wine and one of beer, a denier for pepper, an obole for salt, one measure of oats; two weeks later, he shall give the advocate twelve deniers so that he does not burden his men. The same things in all shall be delivered at Easter, as well as on St John's Day, but without the oats. Of what shall be paid at the courts, the abbot shall receive two-thirds, and the advocate the other third. If one of the abbot's men marries a wife from elsewhere, after his death his goods shall be confiscated by the abbot and a third part only shall be given to his children and his wife.

C. E. Perrin, *Recherches sur la seigneurie rurale en Lorraine
d'après les plus anciens censiers (IXe-XIIe siècles),*
Strasbourg, 1935, pp. 731-733.

3. Rhineland

116

In the course of the twelfth century, the canons of Strasbourg inserted in the middle of a deed of gift of the tenth century a rental-custumal of one of their demesne groups, in order no doubt to confer on it greater authority. The manse *remained, here too, the unit of taxation, but the labour services were very light. On the other hand, taxes on the transfer of property or on succession (joyeux avènement) allowed the lord to syphon off regularly the savings of the tenants, by levying either a large sum in cash, or by taking the best animal at the time of an inheritance.*

I, Odo, bishop, albeit unworthy, of the church of Strasbourg, by the grace of God, gave eighteen *manses* to Our Glorious Mary, Mother of God, patroness of this same church in Strasbourg, and to those who serve her, for the good of the soul of my parents and for the salvation of my soul, with access roads, meadows and fields, cultivated or uncultivated, and with all other usages. This property is situated in Ortenau, that is at Bohlsbach, Stadelhofen, Schwabhausen, Avenheim, Diersheim, Gamshurst. Volmersbach. Two *manses* are situated in Alsace at Schäffolsheim.

We have given this demesne on the following conditions: that each *manse*, except the demesne lands, pays five sous on St John's Day; four deniers, four chickens and ten eggs on St Adolphus's Day; and at Christmas twelve loaves one cubit in length and width, eight hams of full-grown pigs, a bucket of beer and twenty-four *emines* of oats. The same at Easter, twelve loaves and eight chickens. At the spring ploughing, two *arpents*; as much in autumn. Each *manse* shall provide four harvesters to harvest the winter grain, as much as for the summer corn. Each *manse* shall pay three times a year

469

at the three courts, four deniers. For the dues of the two *manses* situated at Schäffol-sheim, let them deliver for the use of the poor, on our birth day, two *muids* of bread and one of beans; for all the rest the full service to the Brothers. When the lord of this property shall change, the *manse* shall pay five sous to his successor; and if the tenant of the *manse* dies, the master shall take from it the best head of cattle. The man who shall acquire a *manse* shall give five sous to the lord.

It shall be known also that the advocate must have a half *manse* situated at Schwab-hausen in order to be protector and defender of the law. He shall exercise no other authority on this property, unless he shall be called on by the lord; Let him come then with six horses, and let the master offer him a sufficient meal.

We have prescribed this in the name of God and the Blessed Apostles Peter and Paul, and we have confirmed it under pain of anathema, in order that none dare appropriate this property nor alienate it, nor have the audacity to deflect its use from the brothers. . . .

. . . Given by us in the year of the birth of Our Lord Jesus Christ 961, fourth of the proclamation, under the reign of King Otto.

G. Franz, *Deutsches Bauerntum*, pp. 64-66.

117

This text of the Hofrecht, that is, manorial ordinances, of the 'hall' at Münchweier con-tains a codification of the advowson which is quite classical in form (the need to limit the claims of the advocate had most likely been the reasons for drawing up this document and fixing the usages (as in No. 115 above)). But it also registered the customs which the dependants ack-nowledged on the days when the court was in session three times a year. Because of this it makes use of a great many dialectical expressions, and is the precursor of the Weistümer *of the following centuries. Amongst the various clauses we can distinguish three categories of manorial prerogatives.*

1. Some taxes, connected with the grant of the tenure, were attached to the manses, *the services of which recalled those of the servile manses of Carolingian times. The tenants were, for most of their time, domestic servants; they owed an unspecified weekly service, and had to provide textiles woven at home by the women.*

2. Others issued from the territorial lordship and were borne by everyone who lived in the parish. All peasants who owned a house had to attend the pleas, thus placing themselves under the jurisdiction of the master, and had to perform some general labour services connected with ploughing and harvesting.

3. Finally, some of the inhabitants and tenants were the personal dependants of the lord as well, and he expected body rent and body service (Leibache) from them. From amongst these men he chose two prebendaries who managed the demesne and who received as a wage ('for the provision of vestments') a small piece of land about four acres in size, two animals which they reared, and some manure.

(Twelfth century)

1. Here are the laws recognized from the olden days at the monastery of Notre-

Dame by the oaths of nobles and people; they have been confirmed according to the statutes of the church of Strasbourg. . . .

5. The abbot of the monastery, or his envoy, shall judge the damage done to crops, vineyards and meadows, the pasture on these parcels and their ways across, the gathering of the crops, the cultivation of the fields, all that which is called in the common tongue *dratunge, azunge, bivangon, unde gulten.*

6. All the suits which must be judged here, the representative of the abbot and the monastery must judge them, except three, to wit, theft, and he who disobeys the abbot or his representative for whatever reason (what is commonly called *widershore*), and whoever commits a misdeed (what is called *fravile*).

7. Of the fine imposed for the theft and for the misdeed by the advocate, or by his representative, who must judge these three cases, two-thirds shall be given to the abbot, or to his representative, and one-third shall be for the advocate.

8. The court has the right of prizage, that is, *stoc.* The thief taken must be delivered to the court with all the goods found at his house, and the whole of his vesture shall be for the *webel* or the steward. The other accused men shall be guarded in the court, until they leave it legitimately. . . .

11. The abbot, by law, may constrain to come to his court all men of Notre-Dame who do not pay rent with their bodies.

12. To this man shall be given this provender: 120 handfuls of the best grain after wheat, as much oats, to him are granted three *arpents* in each field for the provision of vestments, what is commonly called *gewerland*; to him also shall be given a cow with her calf, and the dung from these two animals. All the refuse from the house shall be carried as manure to these *arpents*.

13. And there will be an oxherd to whom shall be given full provender.

14. . . . These two shall in turn cultivate their *arpents* in the following manner: the work of one shall take place one Saturday, that of the other on the following Saturday.

15. Furthermore, it has been established that the abbot has three pleas which are called *dinc*. These pleas must be announced the previous day and shall take place the day after. All those who have their house in this parish must assemble in the presence of the abbot in the acknowledgment of the established laws; and he shall first of all judge for himself, then for all those who shall have some suit; and the laws of the court shall be cited.

16. After these three *dinc* there have been laid down three *dingis tagedinc* where the cases still in abeyance should be adjudicated and where those who did not attend at the first plea shall be cited.

17. Whoever has a *manse* instituted in such a way that he must acquit all the rights shall provide the monastery on St Andrew's Day with a pig which is called *höbswin*, and the brothers and servants of Our Lady shall have the lard, and this pig shall be received under oath by the cook, the steward and the men of the monastery who, by sight and hearing, shall estimate the size and the price of it and will know what these ought to be.

18. His wife must come to the monastery and receive from the provost of the monastery a load of wool or prepared flax and a loaf, like that of the lords, and one *émine* of wine, that is *stoff*, and with this she shall prepare a linen or woollen cloth seven

ells in length and three in width; and this ready, she shall bring it to the monastery and shall again receive from the cellarer two loaves, like those which are given to the lords in the community.

19. By the same *manse* shall be given two *muids* of oats on St Thomas's Day; it gives *bannecins* and *maiecins*, that is chickens and eggs. Whoever has the *manse* shall work for two days a week.

20. All those who do *tagewane* (that is, *libache*) must cut hay according to the established law.

21. Every house of this parish, that is *hüsrochi*, shall perform one service of two days, that is two *ahche*, one when the wheat and rye is cut, the other when the oats are cut.

22. The man who has a plough with oxen shall perform four *ahche*, that is he will plough four times a year the 'hall' of Our Lady.

G. Franz, *Deutsches Bauerntum*, pp. 77–83.

F. THE MANORIAL STEWARDS

118

In this villeneuve (*see Document No. 37, p. 393*) *one of the co-lords instals the mayor, grants him, besides a small fief, the authority to levy certain additional taxes, and regulates his executive functions. But this official was himself a powerful man. He had dependants of his own and paid homage; in fact an agent fulfilled the office in his name. Thus did the hangers-on of power multiply to the detriment of both master and subject.*

(1113-1129)

I, Guillaume, abbot of St Père at Chartres, make known that I grant to Geoffroy d'Arrou the mayoralty of the land of Bois-Ruffin, which the lord Urson has given us in alms, and that I have invested him with this mayoralty in our chapter on the following conditions. I have bestowed on him in a suitable place on this same land, a piece of land for a plough, on condition however that he renders the half of the share of the crops (*terrage*) from the produce of this plough to the lord Urson. He shall have his profits and his rights (*droitures*) on this land, on condition, however, that his rights never exceed twenty deniers. He shall introduce before the monk who shall be appointed to this land all the pleas and the discussions of cases, and all the pleas shall be prorogued or remitted, discussed or terminated at the will of the monk and by his decision, save in all things his rights. As soon as the monk shall have established a house there, the pleas shall be held on the land; while waiting, at Arrou. If Geoffroy believes that the provost of the monks' land tries to annul pleas through over long delays, he may complain to the prior of Brou or to the lord abbot, and be recompensed by them. Should he have a wood on the land, he shall, as much for himself as for his men of Arrou, have the use of the wood only for the house, and the free pasture for his pigs but without pannage. If, while he has the wood, he takes a wild goat, fox, wild cat or a

472

hive of bees in the trees, they shall be his; if it is one of the settlers who takes them, he shall have a half. If one of the settlers conceals any one of the animals which have been caught, and if Geoffroy can seize any of them and prove it, he shall take it and confiscate it, without a fine.

According to these covenants, I, Guillaume, abbot have invested Geoffroy d'Arrou with the mayoralty of Bois-Ruffin; as for him, he has paid homage to me and lawful faith due to all our chapter. To be noted that Geoffroy shall have on this same land the steward whom he desires. For all offences that Geoffroy's steward shall commit, and after three summonses, if he does not pay the fine, the steward shall be removed from his office. . . .

Cartulaire de Saint-Père de Chartres, No. 484.

119

This judgment of the demesne court which punished an unfaithful steward with confiscation reveals him to have been not only endowed with a fief, the owner of a free-holding property which he had attempted to round off, and associated with knights who supported him during the case, but also as holding direct and personal powers over peasants who owed him shelter dues and gave him a share in their wine harvest. His sons were associated with him in his office which was a family possession.

(1103)

In the name of the Holy and undivided Trinity, may all know, present and future, that Duran, provost of Berzé, has given all his free holding and abandoned all the fief with all the lands which he has into the hand of the lord Hugues, abbot, and into our hands, to wit Josseran, Dom Seguin, Serge, Humbert the dean, and other brothers of ours, under the testimony also of these laymen, Guichard Nasu, Hugues de Meulin, Artaud de la Bruyère, Humbert, nephew of another Humbert, provost, Robert le Chauve, Guillaume, servant of Hardi, and many others. He has thus had to give up his possessions and our fief because he has not been able to deny that he and his relations have committed usurpations in divers things. But the lord abbot, wishing to remain within bounds, chooses to keep in demesne a *manse* with all the lands which depend on it and which Duran held because of this *manse*, that is, vineyards, fields and meadows. Furthermore he has held that land which was once belonging to the cook of Viscount Guigues, with a curtilage in another village, on which Hugues de Meulin had attempted to make a claim, although unjustly. Together with this all the meals which are due from the peasants for the wine harvest, with one measure of unfermented wine for each cutting, which measure is called *brazaige*. These things are transferred into our demesne rights in such a way that Duran has no subsequent claim there, nor anyone else on his behalf. Nevertheless, as long as he shall remain faithful to us, to him has been remitted, not as his due but by grace, half the income of all the rest, be it free holding or be it fief, and of all the resources which he claimed, be it in free holding, or be it in fief, for his, and which he assigns to himself. This share was given out of mercy to him who has lost all by the verdict of the law. But being said that it is on his behalf rather than on ours that are assigned all the goods which he had alienated of his possessions or of ours, and which he pledged to others. Taking for himself all the ill assured things, he left to us in our share the safest, until he had established the whole in an untroubled state. On each of the *manses* which Robert and Guigue held in their demesne when they gave them to us, had been granted to Duran two loaves with a *setier* of wine, and for four deniers of meat. And, the measure of mercy being filled to overflowing, in order that all occasion for recrimination or recantation should be removed, he has been given sixty sous by the dean of the said obedientiary of Berzé. The same Duran, with his sons, has taken an oath and has sworn on the holy altar in the tower that he would in good faith keep this agreement inviolate; if he violates it, within fourteen days after the dean's complaint he shall restore what he has taken, or else he shall go on bail where he shall be told and shall not leave. . . .

Recueil des chartes de l'abbaye de Cluny, Vol. V, No. 3666.

120

The lord here acts to restrain a forester who, clearing and encouraging clearances, is destroying little by little the woods which are under his care. There must be no more assarts, damaging usages, or clandestine appropriation of the acorn harvest, and no more hedges around meadows and fields already cleared, and which must fulfil their obligations.

(1096-1127)

Plea between the canons of Mâcon and Landry de Monceau on the subject of the wood of Chevignes and the assarts of this wood which is an allod of St Vincent.

The canons have granted to Landry the care of the wood on condition that henceforth it shall not be cleared neither to make a meadow nor to make arable. But when the wood contains acorns, Landry will faithfully perform his service in order that neither he nor any other harvests them until the canons give the order to introduce their pigs to eat the acorns; at this moment Landry shall introduce his herd. It has been agreed also here and there (the neighbours having, under pain of excommunication, borne witness that it was thus from ancient times) that the canons may take what they like in the wood for the use of the kitchen or refectory or for the work of their cloister. And the obedientiary of St Clement shall take in the same wood what he wishes for the work which he shall desire to do in the parish of St Clement. Similarly Landry shall take in this wood for the use of his own house and to make his *manses*; but he shall keep watch that, apart from the parishioners of St Clement, no man shall have access to the wood. He shall have for the guardianship one denier a year from each of the houses of the said parishioners having access to the wood. It has been decided on the subject of the meadow that Landry has made next to the wood that, each year, the hay being made, Laudry shall pay the *none* to the canons, that he shall not protect the meadow save against the depredations of the swine, until the other meadows which are in the neighbourhood are also protected. From the crops of the other assarts which he has or which others have for him, he shall render all the tithes and half the *nones* to the canons. In exchange for this benefaction, granted to him by the canons, Landry has paid homage and sworn fidelity to Sir Artaud, dean, and it is included in the agreement that whoever of his successors shall hold this benefaction from the canons shall pay homage and swear fidelity to the dean of the church of Mâcon. Given with the assent of the whole of the chapter, in the presence of Sir Béraud, venerable bishop.

Cartulaire de Saint-Vincent de Mâcon, p. 337.

121

The grant and regulation of the office of forester

To all members of holy Christianity, present as well as future, we make known that I, Hugues de Chilley, and Garin, my brother, and my sons, Oudin, Duran, Renaud, Guinebaud, give to God, to Our Lady of la Ferté and to the monks of this place what we possess or claim in the territory of Chilley, without anything held back, and the access which we claim in the wood of les Matheys.

This land which we give to the monks, we receive from them against a rent of three sous per year which we must pay at Martinmas for the lighting of the church at la Ferté, and as a token of investiture the monks have kept six parcels of this land with our will and permission. If one of us wishes to give or to sell to the monks some thing of the portion of this land which comes to him, we give him permission and we shall hold the monks in peace for this. If one of us wishes to pledge some things of his share, he must inform the monks and ask them if they wish to reserve it for themselves; if they do not wish to, he can pledge it on condition that whoever shall have the pledge gives the monks the rent corresponding to the share of the land and, when the monks shall desire it, they may buy it back and hold it until it shall be repurchased by the one who pledged it, or by one of his brothers. It shall be known that we need no longer live on this land, but at Mont or at Longepierre or in another village of the castellany of Navilly. . . . If we leave the country or if we go in any way whatever, the monks must protect our land like theirs, and if they cultivate it, they must render to us the 'tasks' and the land when we shall return. It shall be noted too that the monks of la Ferté have given me the office of forester in the wood of Chilley and les Matheys on the following conditions:

We shall take growing wood as much as we shall have need of for our own use. We may not sell or give this growing timber without the permission or wish of the monks. We may have, sell and give the dead timber. The monks may take, give and sell at their pleasure growing and dead timber. When there shall be acorns in the wood, we shall not let our pigs in before the pigs of the monks shall have entered. Never shall we place the pigs of other men under our hand and never shall we add them to ours. We may not sell or give acorns. When the monks shall admit the pigs of other men to pasture in the wood we shall have the tenth denier of the price paid until St Andrew's Day. When the monks put the pigs of others to fatten we shall have half the price. The pigs of the monks may graze at all times. If we take game in the wood with our snares, it shall be ours. If another takes it, the monks shall have the shoulder of the boar, the haunch of the stag. If we find bees there, they shall be ours. If another finds them, the honey, wax and half the bees shall belong to the forester and to the monks. It shall be noted that I may not leave the office of forester to several of my sons, but to one only, and he similarly to one only, and thus by succession from one to another. If the forester, on that which has been said, commits wrong or fraud against the monks, they may revoke his office and demand a fine and indemnity from him. If he refuses to pay the fine and indemnity, they may confide the office of forester to whom they shall wish. It shall be known too that the monks have promised my sons that if they can acquire the land which belonged to the children of my brother Lebaud, they will help them faithfully in this, and my children shall have it under the above mentioned rent. If they do not succeed and if the monks wish to acquire it, they will help them faithfully and they will hold them in peace. We have sworn, I, my four sons and Garin, my brother, to keep the peace and faith with the monks in all these things.

Recueil des pancartes de l'abbaye de la Ferté-sur-Grosne, pp. 211-213.

122

The Schultheiss holds the hereditary farm of this village. He is an official, but since he had risen but two generations earlier to the dignity of Ritter *he had become dangerous. A written deed had to be drawn up to make it absolutely clear that it was the abbey dignitary charged with the administration of the temporal power who alone possessed the authority of the* ban *and the power over these personal dependants* (lites), *with the rights over their bodies, marriage outside the manor, mortmain and the whole justice.*

(27th May 1176)

I, Conrad, abbot of the church of Corvey, to all my successors in perpetuity. . . .

A certain Bruno, official of our church, who has received the 'hall' of Haversford in the capacity of *Schultheiss* with the agreement and consent of our dear brother Henry, then prior and guardian, having died, Bernard, his son, having obtained the grant of the said 'hall' as a result of prayers, with the agreement and consent of the said brother Henry, prior and guardian, the same prior Henry requested that, by a deed established to us, we should take measures henceforth to ensure, in order that the rights of the guardian should not suffer prejudice, that this 'hall' should be administered by knights, for these kind of men are rarely satisfied with what they have, and have the habit of appropriating more than is granted to them. Herenfrid, in fact, father of the said Bruno, had been the first of the knightly condition to administer this 'hall', which up till then had always been administered by peasants. Which is why, in consideration of this request, pious and full of love towards St Vit, and for the sake also of our patron himself, for the possessions of his altar must be defended like the apple of our eye, we recognize, decide and decree that the whole village of Haversford with all its possessions, its dependencies and its limits and with all that is attached to it, that is the houses and other buildings, lands, meadows, woods, fields, waters, cultivated and waste places, must be within the *ban* of the guardian: to him are owed all the revenues of the village, the fixed rent of the village, the fixed rent of the 'hall', the fixed rent of the *manses*, the inheritance of deceased men, the rent of the *lites*, the marriage of the girls, which is commonly called *beddemunt*. The revenues also of the adjacent forest (which is commonly called *sundere*), as well as the dependencies of the village, belong to the guardian, although we have sometimes put our pigs to fatten in this village, what we have done is by grace of this same guardian. It is the guardian who, every time that it is necessary, shall judge with the *lites* concerning the village affairs since it is free of jurisdiction of the advocate. It is evident, then, from all this that the *villicus* of the 'hall' may not have any power over the *lites* and that he may not levy on them by prayers, any manorial right, he can only levy the profits of the 'hall' which is leased to him, but all the rest . . . remains in the hands of the guardian.

F. Franz, *Deutsches Bauerntum*, pp. 134-137.

123

The person convicted here is an official in a much higher walk of life, no less a person than the administrator of one of the king of England's forests. A man, however, who, like many officials, went too far in exploiting his power as intermediary between his master and the villagers.

(1269)

As yet of the extortions of Peter de Neville

It is presented by the same persons and proved that whereas the lord king had ordered that that place in which the sale was made in the park of Ridlington should be enclosed so that it could grow again, Peter de Neville agisted very many animals in that place after it was enclosed, which ate the shoots of the stumps of the oaks which had been sold and of the underwood which had been felled; and he caused a great part of those stumps to be uprooted and made into charcoal, so that it can never grow again, to the loss of the lord king and his heirs of one hundred pounds; for which let the same Peter answer, and to judgment with him for the aforesaid trespass.

The same Peter took for herbage in that place for the agistment aforesaid 35 pounds which belong to the lord king and not to the farm of the same Peter; for which let the same Peter answer, and to judgment with him for the unlawful taking.

The same Peter caused to be enclosed a certain place in the same park which is called la Dale, and he took as well for hay sold in the same place as for the escape of beasts and for herbage 16 pounds.

The same Peter appropriated to himself a certain parcel of land in Stoke which was taken into the hand of the lord king in the last eyre of justices itinerating for the pleas of the forest in the county aforesaid, and is called Esschelund; and he has taken, as the profit thereof, 4 marks up till now, for which let him answer, and let the land be taken into the hand of the lord king; and let it remain there; and to judgment with the aforesaid Peter for his unlawful appropriation.

The same Peter appropriated to himself the annual rent of 12d. of John of Uffington for one acre of land of the king's demesne in Depedale during his whole time as forester to the disinheritance of the king; wherefore let the same Peter answer for 20s. for 20 years, and to judgment with him for his unlawful appropriation.

The same Peter imputed to Master William de Martinvast that he was an evil doer with respect to the venison of the lord king in his bailiwick; and he imprisoned him at Allexton on two occasions, and afterwards he delivered him for a fine of one hundred shillings which he received from him; for which let him answer to the lord king, and to judgment with him because he delivered the aforesaid Master William without any warrant.

Select Pleas of the Forest, pp. 48-49.

IV   The XIII Century. Lords and Peasants

A. DESCRIPTIONS OF MANORS

1. Ecclesiastical Manors

124

This is a fragment of an inventory drawn up by commissioners in 1252 on the estate of Ramsey abbey describing the manor of Broughton in Huntingdonshire.

1. *The meadows occupied a large part of the farmland and it should be noted that some parts of the grassland were cultivated on a temporary basis.*

2. *The free tenants took part in the work of the demesne and particularly in the ploughing. Some rent-paying land originated in the purchase of fixed rents and the lordship of pieces of land formerly independent.*

3. *The services of the tenures in villeinage are described in great detail. The weight of the 'tasks', or week-works, should be noted. They absorbed the entire working hours of a man at harvest time and half of them for the rest of the year on all kinds of different activities which were carefully enumerated. The lord could sell the villein these week-works at will for very little (one day's work was worth hardly more than a loaf of bread). At haymaking time some of the 'tasks' were rewarded with a small wage. The workers had the right to a large ration of food when performing boon works which were mainly ploughing.*

4. *The villein holding was a large one (32 acres), and it should be noted that its incumbent had several plough animals and that he employed 'labourers', who were perhaps his sons, but may also have been paid workers.*

(1252)

The custom of the village is estimated at $2\frac{1}{2}$ ploughs per year.

These are the names of the meadows belonging to the manor. . . .

And if the abbot's demesne is sown in some part of these meadows, the said meadows may be prohibited; after the cutting and carrying of the hay nobody has the usage of these meadows with the lord, save 4 akermen who will have the right of pasture for 4 beasts with those of the master.

A wood belongs to the said manor, called Broughton wood; one part belongs to Little Raveley; all the men of Broughton and Little Raveley, free as well as villein, have common usage in this wood for their cattle, save goats and swine in the prohibited time; outside this wood on the Ripton side a green place remains in the demesne for reserved pasture. Nobody may take green or dry in this wood without permission.

In the marshes of Ramsey, Warboys and Wistow, the abbot may, because of his manor at Broughton, take peat, cut hay and graze his cattle at his pleasure, and give his men permission to cut hay and to graze. Freemen and villeins, however, give the manor of Warboys one goose per load for permission to enter the marshes.

The manor may keep two bulls, 20 cows with their progeny, 200 sheep, 100 pigs and 3 boars.

The sheep of cottars and strangers must be folded for the manure on the demesne land and not elsewhere. . . .

. . . In the village of Broughton there are 7 hides and half a virgate of land outside the abbot's demesne which are held by freemen and villeins.

6½ virgates make a hide and 32 acres make a virgate.

Ralf de Broughton holds a quarter of a virgate for which he does homage to the abbot and follows the court of Broughton, and he gives 12d. per annum and ploughs 2 roods per year. He gives hidage each time that service of the lord king is claimed from the abbey, pontage, sheriff's aid, and wodehac. He holds also a portion of land which belonged to Matthew, son of Nicolas, for which he gives 2d. to the lord abbot. This rent and the lordship of this land was bought by the lord abbot of Ramsey from the said Matthew. At the first autumn boon-work he comes with two men. . . .

. . . Thomas, son of Henry, holds one virgate of land for which he gives 12d., six on St Andrew's Day, and 6 on St Benedict's Day; for the sherriff's aid 2d. at Martinmas and 2d. on the Nativity of St John the Baptist; he makes one measure of malt or gives 6d. at the lord's will, to wit 2 at Martinmas, 2 at the Annunciation of the Blessed Virgin, and 2 on the Nativity of St John the Baptist. He shall give after Christmas one bushel of oats for foddercorn, at Christmas a hen and at Easter 10 eggs. He gives tallage, merchet, leyrwit, gersum, heriot, the view of frankpledge, hidage, pontage and wodehac, and also pannage, to wit 2d. for a pig per year, one penny for a six-month-old pig, a half-penny for a three-month-old pig, and he does it at the acorn harvest whether he sends them to the wood or not. After Michaelmas he may not sell his pig without having paid pannage. At the view of the frankpledge he gives a halfpenny of custom. He does the same thing for each male child of 12 years old who is in his keeping.

He shall mow rushes in the marsh at Warboys when it shall be required of him, 40 good sheaves in the view of the bailliff, the reeve and others for the day's task, but shall not cart them. For a task he shall mow, bind and carry 20 sheaves. And if the lord causes rushes to be mown for a task, he shall take a good cartload with 2 horses for two days task.

From Michaelmas until August he shall work three days a week, Monday, Tuesday and Wednesday; Friday he shall plough with all the beasts which he has in his plough half an acre, save at Christmas and Easter. If he must dig in the 'hall', dig a ditch, make a wall, cover or spread manure, he shall work from morning until evening. If he must dig a ditch outside the 'hall', he shall in open country do a perch of 16½ feet long with a depth of 2 'spadegraff' and a width of three feet. For putting old ditches in order he shall do two perches of the same length and width for a task. When he must thresh, he shall thresh 24 sheaves of wheat; 30 of barley, oats, beans and peas. He shall gather in Broughton wood 2 faggots of thorn or a faggot of sticks which he shall bring to the 'hall' for a task. In Wistow wood one faggot only for a task. He shall make an enclosure all day either inside or outside the 'hall'. In winter cultivation he shall harrow all day without stopping. In Lent, he shall harrow but with a halt for dinner but shall come back quickly afterwards. If he must cut or weed, he shall work all day. Each time that he mows in the village of Broughton he shall have a sheaf of hay in the evening, as much as he can lift on the handle of his scythe when it does not touch the ground; if it breaks or falls to the ground he shall lose the grass. The day when he shall mow the meadow at Houghton he shall with his companion have 18d. from the abbot's purse, according to custom, and one of the best cheeses in the 'hall' and a bowl of salt.

He shall make journeys in the hundred when he receives the order to do so, he shall do so alone for Elsworth; for Ellington, he and two other virgaters shall provide the horse. If it is for London, Shillington or other distant places, he and five virgaters shall make the journey with a horse, and they shall be free of all task until their return. And the load shall be a 'ringa' of wheat, barley or oats.

At each ploughing boon-work he shall come with his plough if he has a whole plough or if he is associated with another; and in that way each week he shall plough on the land of the master one day as on his own land. If the ploughing is put off because of bad weather or other reasonable cause he shall come the following week at the demand of the steward.

Every week from August to Michaelmas he shall work every day, except Saturday, from morning to night wherever the master wishes to assign him work for the task. At all the autumn boon-works he himself or his wife shall come, with all the manpower at his disposal; if he has less than three labourers one only shall work; if he has more he shall bring his labourers, but not his wife; if he is ill his wife shall stay at home to look after him, but he shall send all his labourers to the boon-work. At the first boon-work he shall have with his companion two loaves, one of which shall suffice for two; if bread is bought, he and his companion shall have a loaf worth three farthings; barley beer, soup, fresh or salt meat and a slice of cheese. At the second, fish. At the third, meat. At the fourth, if it should be necessary, fish. And at each boon-work he shall have bread, barley beer, soup and cheese, as at the first. The day after each boon-work, he shall provide two labourers whom he shall feed, for the days of boon-work are not counted as tasks.

He shall convoy a cart of corn when he shall receive the order, and this shall not be counted as a task. He shall convoy two carts of corn or straw for a day's task; he shall mow and gather straw all day.

If he wishes to sell a horse, an ox or a colt, he shall inform the bailiff so that the lord can exercise his right of pre-emption.

Every time he shall be ill, he shall be quit of all task, save the ploughing. And if his illness lasts a year and a day, he shall be quit during all this time of every task, save ploughing. After a year and a day he shall not be exempted of task for any illness.

If his wife survives him she shall give 5s. for heriot for which she shall be quit during 30 days of all task.

The lord may put all the tasks to rent if he wishes. They are valued in winter and in summer at one penny per day, and in autumn at 2d. save for the work which is put to task and which is valued at a halfpenny a day.

He shall gather a faggot of sticks in Warboys and Wistow woods or St Ives wood and shall carry them to St Ives, and shall make a trellis or a hurdle for a task; another day he shall make there another work which shall not be allowed for him as a task. He shall provide a man to mount guard for one night for a task. The day of his wedding the servants of the 'hall' shall receive bread, barley beer and meat according to his honour and his competence.

And if he becomes reeve, he shall have for two horses, 4 oxen and 2 cows, if he possesses them, the right of pasture with the beasts of the master, and he shall be quit of all task in exchange for his office for as long as he shall hold the reeveship. And he shall be fed at the 'hall' in the autumn.

Cartularium Monasterii de Rameseia, Vol. I (1884), pp. 332-338.

125-126-129

1. *Of these three extracts from inventories drawn up in 1265-1267 on the estate of the monastery of St Peter of Gloucester, the first provides a complete assessment of the little manor of Linkenholt. Here the arable (462 acres) probably exceeded the size of the holdings taken together. A three-year rotation was practised which left 'the third field' fallow. The value of an acre of arable varied a great deal from one field to another which shows that fertility was not the same in the different sectors. An acre of meadow was worth three times the best arable acre. The services of the villein tenures were much lighter than on the manor of Broughton (Document No. 124); and the money rents imposed on villein tenures were twice as valuable as the labour services. The lord left his villeins a much larger share of their own labour, but he took from them a share of their earnings in the form of cash.*

2. *Clifford, an example of tenure* per cartam, *was granted to a knight and it yielded a money rent of considerable value.*

3. *In the manor of Frocester two holdings of equal size, belonging to two widows, were treated very differently. The first did not owe any labour service, only rent, and the lord still enforced on this holding the restrictions on the sale of animals and rights of heriot characteristic of customary villein tenure. The other holding, on the contrary, provided mainly manpower. Note the surname of one of the tenants, which suggests a profession.*

125

(1250)

The inventory of the manor of Linkenholte made before Dominus R. de Sondhurst, cellarer, and Thomas de Tyringham, in the year 1250, how much and at what time the profits of the manor are worth per annum, made on the oath of the oldest and most reliable men of the manor.

They said on oath that in the field of Vaveham are 128 arable acres; the price per acre is 6d. The total value is 69s.

Item. In the field called Breitlonde are 202 arable acres, the price per acre is 8d. The total value is 6 *li* 14s. 8d.

Item. In the field called Roucombesdene are 72 arable acres, the price per acre is 6d. The total is 36s.

Item. In the field called Hydene are 50 arable acres; the price of an acre 3d. Total 12s. 6d.

The total acreage of arable land here is in all 462 acres, the total value in money is 12 *li* 12s. 2d., from which must be subtracted, for the third field in fallow 4 *li* 4s. o$\frac{1}{2}$d. Total 8 *li* 8s. 1$\frac{1}{2}$d.

Item. They said there are 8 acres of hay meadow; price per acre 2s. And the grazing on this meadow after cutting is worth in a normal year 4s. Total in a normal year 20s.

Item. They said that there is grazing in woodland, plain and pasture for 24 oxen which is worth 12s. And grazing for 12 cows which is worth 6s. And grazing for 500 sheep which is worth 62s. 6d. And grazing in woodland and elsewhere for 20 swine which is worth 6s. 8d.

They said that the lord has a wood and in a normal year without causing waste or damage 6s 8d. can be had from it.

Item, they said that the garden with curtilage is worth in a normal year 10s. Total 6 *li* 9s. 10d.

Robert le Fremon renders every year in free rent on the Annunciation of the Blessed Virgin 4s. and at Michaelmas 4s.

Item, the customary aid is 12s. per year.

Item, the windmill is worth 20s. and maintains itself.

Item, the pannage of swine and cattle is worth 4s. 6d. per annum.

Item, the pleas and inquests are worth every year 6s. 8d. Total 51s. 2d.

There are also 10$\frac{1}{2}$ virgates of land in villeinage of which each, apart from the services below renders 5s. each year. Total 52s. 6d.

Of these 10$\frac{1}{2}$ virgates of land Richard Coc holds one virgate of land. He must twice a year plough on the demesne, and he shall be fed by the master the day that he ploughs, and the ploughing service is worth 4d. He must harrow on the demesne between Christmas and Candlemas which is worth 4$\frac{1}{2}$d. He shall weed the lord's corn for 3 days, which is worth 1$\frac{1}{2}$d. He shall give a penny to mow the master's meadow and he shall be there throughout the haymaking which is worth 6d. And he must plant beans on one day which is worth $\frac{1}{2}$d. And he removes forage from the buildings of the hall for one day and it is worth $\frac{1}{2}$d. He shall wash and shear the master's sheep on 2 days which is worth 4d. And he carries on his back three times a year which is worth 3d. He shall harvest every week in autumn which is worth 3s. 2$\frac{1}{2}$d. And he shall do two boon works with one man and shall eat with the master which is worth 2d. He shall carry the master's corn in autumn which is worth 2s. 8d. He shall have a sheaf the day that he ploughs.

Total of these tasks, 8s. 1$\frac{1}{2}$d.

William in la Hasele holds a virgate of land and performs the same tasks, which is worth 8s. 1$\frac{1}{2}$d.

Richard of the Cross holds a virgate of land and performs the same tasks which is worth 8s. 1$\frac{1}{2}$d.

John of the Cross the same.

Henry Fray, the same.

Total of the five virgates of land, the value of the tasks per annum 40s. 7$\frac{1}{2}$d.

Simon and Herbert hold a virgate of land and plough on the demesne twice a year and shall eat with the master which is worth 4d. They shall harrow like the aforesaid virgate which is worth 4½d. They weed in like manner which is worth 1½d. And they shall give 2d. for mowing the master's meadow and shall be at haymaking which is worth 6d. They must harvest like the aforesaid tenants of virgates which is worth 3s. 2½d. They must make the grindstone for one day which is worth ½d. They shall wash and shear the master's sheep for two days with a man, which is worth 4d. And shall perform 2 boon-works with a man which is worth 2d. They must plant beans which is worth ½d. The day that they harvest they shall have 2 sheaves, and the day they perform boon-works they shall eat with the master and shall graze their animals at Lutleton which is worth 2d. And they shall have on that day a loaf and shall give 'chirshec', that is six hens and two cocks, which is worth 8d.

Total 6s. 1½d.

Elias and Henry Carter hold one virgate of land and perform the same tasks which are worth 6s. 1½d.

Walter Huwe and Edward the same.

Walter Wine and John Crol, the same.

Thomas Banz and Nicholas Carter, the same.

Richard the Messer holds half a virgate and Mondayman land and renders for all services 6s.

William Newman holds Mondayman land and renders 12d. per annum. And he must weed which is worth 1½d. And he shall wash and shear the sheep which is worth 2d. And he shall plant beans for one day which is worth ½d. He makes the grindstone as above, which is worth ½d. He shall lift the hay, which is worth 6d. And he must harvest every Monday in autumn which is worth 16d. And he shall give a hen and a cock for 'chirchec' which is worth 2d.

Total of these tasks 2s. 4½d.

Total 39s.

The total of the whole inventory, in certain value, is 24 *li* 15d.

Historia et cartularium Monasterii Sancti Petri Gloucestriae,
Vol. III, pp. 41-44.

126

From the Extent of the Manor of Clifford

(1266-1267)

Robert the Freeman holds 4 virgates of land and 2 acres of meadow by charter, each virgate being of 36 acres. And he holds by hereditary charter. And he renders each year 25s. 6d. in two annual payments. And if he dies, the master shall have his horse and his harness and his arms if he has any. And if his heir is under age, the master shall have the guardianship of him and his lands with the marriage. And if he is of age at the death of his father he shall do homage and shall give relief to his lord for his land and shall do the forensic services which appertain to his land.

Historia et Cartularium Monasterii Sancti Petri Gloucestriae,
Vol. III, p. 49.

127

Matilda, the reeve's widow, holds half a virgate of land containing 24 acres, and rendering every year 8s. in 2 terms, that is half at the Feast of the Annunciation and the other at Michaelmas. And she holds it until the death of the abbot. She gives 2s. 2¼d. as aid at Michaelmas. If she brews for sale, she shall give 16 measures of a gallon or their price and she shall have a white loaf and a black one. She may not sell an ox without permission. And if she sells a horse or a mare within the manor, the buyer and the seller shall give 4d.

She owes pannage for swine, to wit for a pig over one year old, one penny, for a young one a halfpenny, on condition that they are separated or in the process of being separated.

She must redeem her son and daughter at the lord's will.

And when she dies the lord shall have her best beast in the name of the lord and the other best beast in the name of the rector.

And to all the contributions for the lord king and the lord of the aforesaid manor and others she must contribute like the customary men mentioned below.

The same Matilda holds Monday land as it appears below amongst the customary men and she gives every year 4d. at the lord's will.

Kynemon holds a messuage with a curtilage at the lord's will and renders each year 16d. at the aforesaid terms. And he performs the other small customs like the aforesaid Matilda. He gives a hen which is worth one penny.

William the Weaver, holds a messuage with a curtilage and an acre of land, and renders 8d. every year at the aforesaid two terms; he gives 6d. for aid. He performs 3 boon-works which are worth 4½d. and he performs all the untaxed customs like the aforesaid Matilda. He gives a hen which is worth one penny.

Margery, the widow, holds half a virgate of land which contains 24 acres and she renders 3s. every year at two terms, 12d. at Christmas and 2s. at Michaelmas. And from Michaelmas to the Feast of St Peter in Chains she must plough half an acre every week, and one day's ploughing is worth 3d. And from the Feast of St John the Baptist until August she must perform manual service 3 days every week and the day is worth three farthings. The fourth day she carries on her back to Gloucester or elsewhere at the bailiff's will and that is worth three-halfpence. She shall mow the lord's meadow for at least 4 days and the day is worth 1½d, which is counted as manual service estimated above at three farthings. And she must lift the lord's hay for at least 4 days at her expense this not being counted as a task, and it is worth altogether 3d. She shall weed 2 days apart from the work due which is worth three-halfpence. And from the Feast of St Peter in Chains until Michaelmas she must perform manual service with a man 5 days a week and the day is worth three-halfpence.

And every second week during the same period she must perform carrying service for one day, this being counted as one day's task.

And furthermore she performs 8 boon-works with a man in autumn which is worth altogether 12d. And she gives 2s. 2¼d. for aid. She performs all the untaxed customs like the aforesaid Matilda. And she performs a harvest boon-work in autumn fed by the master which is worth, apart from the food, a halfpenny. And she must plough one day, fed by the master with half a plough.

And she shall give eggs at Easter at will.

William Brunge of Coveley, redeemed from servitude to the lord abbot gives annual rent of one pound of wax at Michaelmas.

Walter de Bykenovere holds an acre of land at the lord's will and renders 8d. a year at Michaelmas for all his service. . . .

Historia et Cartularium Monasterii Sancti Petri Gloucestriae,
Vol. III, pp. 88–90.

128

This fragment of an inventory of one of the manors of St Ouen of Rouen, reveals a close similarity between the structure of the Norman and the English villein holding. Manual services are, however, much lighter and usually rewarded by a small wage. In fact the land owed mainly a champart *or share in the fruits, but here it was fixed annually. It should be noted that on the death of the villein, the heir, if he was male, chose the best beast before the lord. Note also the service for the transport of timber* (mairien) *to the Seine, the waterway.*

(1291)

The villein messuage of Richard, son of Jehan contains 21½ acres of measured *champart* land; and yields 5 *deniers* of rent and 2 small *setiers* of oats, thinly measured, which he must take to the Seine landing-stage (port) between Villeboeuf and Criqueboeuf; and two hens at Christmas; and he owes 3 ploughing services every year – that is, to till and harrow half an acre with *trémois*, and to till and harrow half an acre with summer corn; and for the labour of each half-acre he must have a loaf (of the measure 13 to a *setier*); and he owes half an acre of fallow land and for this labour he shall receive bread to eat and stew once a day; and he owes a man and a horse for harrowing twice a year in the ploughlands of Saint Ouen, once with *trémois* and once with summer corn, and he shall have, for each day that he harrows, a quarter of bread of the said quantity in the morning, and in the evening half of one of the aforesaid loaves and a basin of oats, of which 3 basins make up a bushel of the Louviers oats; and he must also shear 4 sheep each year; and a man to sit for one day in the ploughlands at Saint Ouen and for this he shall be given bread 3 times a day to eat while seated, and a pennyworth of cheese, and a loaf in the evening when he leaves, of the aforesaid quantity; and he owes a man and a horse-drawn cart to carry the sheaves from the arable fields of Saint-Ouen to the barn, from the morning up to the hour of tierce (9 o'clock); and he should in his turn carry the ground corn on his horse to the mill from the demesne of Daubuef; and Saint Ouen should provide the sack, and it should be no more than the quantity of a small *setier*; and if he requires it, Saint Ouen must provide a boy to lead the horse, who must not ride on the horse because he who is on it might knock him to the ground with the sack; and when he comes to the mill, he must receive a pennyworth of bread from the servants of the abbess of Saint Sauveur d'Evreux, and some forage for his horse, or it may graze in the said abbess' meadow; and he may go into the abbess' woods to get kindling to warm him, at night, if he does not manage it by day; and he does not owe as much for the milling of the said corn; and the said Richard also owes his aid to transport timbers of the barn; and he should help to bring all the timber from Seine or as far as he can so that he can go home in the evening; and he owes 12 eggs at Easter, and 10 deniers at Rogation tide for revenue for a sheep and for a sumpter animal; and 2 deniers of rent on the Feast of Saint Gilles; and 2 3-day-old chicks (*dee de cavoe*), or 2 deniers in August to the officials who collect the *champart*; and 20 sheaves of corn and 20 sheaves of oats in September for *champart*; and the cart from Saint Ouen should go to fetch them in the town, and the eldest son should stack them in it; and he pays 3 bushels of wheat, thinly measured; and the right of relief is with an animal, and the male heir should have first choice and monseigneur the abbot the second choice; and if the heir is a woman, monseigneur the abbot should have first choice and the woman second; and if there is only one animal, monseigneur must have it.

> L. Delisle, *Études sur la Condition de la classe agricole en Normandie au Moyen Age*,
> Paris, 1851, p. 717.

129

The whole demesne owned by the cathedral chapter of Liège in these two localities is on short-term lease, except one demesne meadow for which some haymaking services are still required. The farmers deliver money, but mostly grain. It should be noted that at Roosbeck, the unit of manorial taxation is no longer the manse, *but its theoretical equivalent in arable land: twelve* bonniers. *The land is clearly granted in parcels of varying size (the 10 per cent tax on the transfer of property providing a very important casual income). The dissolution of the* manse *complicated the levying of mortmain: for example, which of the many tenants represented the 'principal person' whose death permitted the tax to be levied? Note (a) the maintenance of direct cultivation by the lay brethren of the Cistercian order who farmed out the land of St Lambert; (b) the continuing distinction between the* terre de mez (*the pieces of the ancient territory formerly comprising the appurtenances of the* manses) *and the* terre de sart, *more recently created by clearing the waste; (c) the acquisition of a perpetual rent on a peasant property, partly allodial, and partly rent-paying.*

(1280–1308)

Perpetual rent at Mons.

There is there for the *terres de sart* and *de mez* ten marks and nine sous of perpetual rent which are paid partly on St Lambert's Day and partly at the end of February.

Item, there are there 41 capons, 40 hens and 70 eggs.

Item, there are there 77 *muids* of spelt on the *terre de mez*.

Item, there are there 48 *muids* 7 *setiers* of oats.

Item, there are there 36 *bonniers* less three large roods of demesne furlong.

Item, there are six day-works and 17 little roods of the 'hall' where there is a neglected house and a barn worth 40 *muids* of spelt.

Item, there is there one *bonnier* and 24 little roods of meadow.

All this is held at farm by Hermann of Mons and Louis de Grotteux for twelve years for 42 Liège marks due, as they say, on St John's Day. Granted the year of Our Lord 1278.

Item, the high and low justice belongs to the church, at Hollogne as at Mons, and up to the places where the magistrates are accustomed to place the limits.

Item, there are there three general pleas in which the advocate may have eleven sous, the mayor and the magistrates 7 sous and the forester four, which must be levied on the first fines, notwithstanding the right of the advocate who has a third of all the fines. And if no fine is imposed, the deniers above mentioned shall be taken from the rent of the church, and the farmers above mentioned shall be held during all their time to deliver them to the church.

Item, there are there 16 *bonniers*, 18 large roods and 15 small from the endowment of the church of Hollogne which are worth every year 46 *muids* of *spelt*.

Item, there are there 15 *bonniers* and 16 large *roods* which are worth every year 22 *muids* and two *setiers* of spelt of which the lay brothers of the grange of Aulichamps cultivate 14 *bonniers* and six large roods for 12 *muids* and six *setiers* and a half (granted for 12 years in the year of Our Lord 1269). The rest is held by Louis and Parriot de Valroux.

This land and the above mentioned endowment are held at farm by Louis de Crotteux and Parriot de Valroux with the tithes large and small for six years for 365 *muids* of spelt. Granted the year of Our Lord 1278.

Item, there are there three *bonniers* and seven large roods which are called the land of the charcoal ditches, for which the lay brethren of Aulichamp pay to the barn for twelve years six *muids* and six *setiers* of spelt. Granted the year of Our Lord 1279.

Item, there are there 14 *bonniers* and 32 little roods of land which is called *de comines*, held at farm for twelve years by lady Yvette de Mons under an annual *trecens* of 20 *muids* of spelt, 19 for the church and one for the forester. Granted the year of Our Lord 1279.

Item, there are there four *bonniers* and 22 little roods of land which is called *de genore*, cultivated by those who pay seven *muids* and two *setiers*. Gilles de Rullier, nine days works and 15 little roods for four *muids* (and it is said that this land was granted hereditarily to Henri de Chenee, but we have not found it thus and it is worth more since I had from it five *muids*). Item, sir Rainier knight of Velroux, seven days works and seven little roods *en crotenvoz* for twelve years, for an annual *trecens* of three *muids* and three *setiers*, granted the year of Our Lord 1276.

Item, there are there seven *muids* of rye of perpetual rent on a mill which Rainier and his brother who have pledged it owe, or else their father, at the same time as the mill four *bonniers* of land for the above mentioned rent, of which three *bonniers* are situated at the side of Fontaine (two of allodial land held in corrody, the other of rented land quite close), the other at the edge of Souxhan.

Item, there is a meadow called *demenchepreit* that the *masuirs*[1] are bound to toss the

---

[1] Rent-paying tenants of a messuage.

hay, summoned for this by the forester, and it is two *bonniers*, 8 large roods and ten small, and the lord dean has it for his life.

Total of cash: 42 marks.

Total of spelt: 398 *muids* and 6 *setiers*.

*   *   *

At Roosbeck

At Roosbeck the church has three *manses* of land and each *manse* contains twelve *bonniers*. The *masuirs* have these *manses* hereditarily for 23 *muids* of rye and six *setiers* of Louvain measure and eleven *muids* six *setiers* of barley of the same measure. The rye is paid on St Denis's Day, the barley at Martinmas.

Item, on these lands, it has 23 sous 4 deniers of Liège and one of Louvain, with 38 capons and four hens due at Christmas.

Item, there is there a half-*bonnier* of land which belongs to the church for which two *muids* of rye of Tirlemont measure are at present paid.

Item, there is on three and a half *bonniers* of land in the territory of Butzel 26 sous eight deniers of Liège which Henri Paumier of Butzel must pay.

Item, the twelve *bonniers* of land of the said *manses* are held to take at their expense the capons to Liège for the nuncio of the church.

Item, the *manse* or the twelve *bonniers* are held to make to the lord of the place three payments during the year, on St Rémi's Day, St Denis's Day and at Martinmas.

Item, the twelve *bonniers* or the *manses* must pay *mortmain* when the principal person dies.

Item, at Butzel there are three 'halls' whose owners must pay *mortmain*.

Item, by custom and recognized right the church has, from every purchaser and seller of an inheritance, two sous of Louvain per livre.

Total of rye: 28 *muids* of the Liège measure.

Total of barley: eleven *muids*, six *setiers*.

Total of cash: 50 Louvain sous with 38 capons and four hens.

And nothing is counted of the other casual revenues.

All this is held for life by Sir Gilles de Wineham for twelve *muids* payable the half at Laetare and the half at Whitsuntide.

Le Polyptyque du 1280 de chapitre de la cathédrale Saint-Lambert à Liège
(ed. D. van Derveeghde), Brussels, 1958, pp. 68-69 and pp. 123-125.

2. Lay Manors

130

These fragments of the inventory of the possessions of the lord of Pamele-Audenarde illustrate several aspects of the structure of a very large Flemish estate. (1) There was no demesne properly speaking, except one wood, a fishpond (which was very productive), and a mill, the upkeep of which was very costly. Some lands were granted in métayage. (2) The holdings were composed of very scattered parcels of land each one burdened with a rent. (3) The memory of the clearing of

the wastes is preserved in the place-names. (4) The preponderance of dues in kind is most marked.
(5) When transfers of property took place the lord levied a double rent.

(*ca.* 1275)

LESSINES

These are the rights of the mills at Lessines.

Milling is to the 18th.

The lord of Audenarde has 19 of the 27 vessels[1] and the church of Notre-Dame of Cambrai has 8 others. Item, the division for milling and the corn is the same.

Item, the lord of Audenarde is miller, and installs a miller there as he likes.

And therefore he should provide, from his own property, hammers, pegs and spindles.

Item, eelpots; and, of the eels taken in them, the lord may have 5 and the church 4. And they should restock the eelpots according to how many eels they take out.

Item, the lord provides 5 of the 9 *deniers* for the mill, and the church the other 4.

Item, the lord pays a third of the cost for the mill cartage and the church pays two-thirds.

Item, the lord pays a third of the cost for the timber and the cartage as far as the piece of ground, and the church pays two-thirds.

Item, the lord should see to the working of the timber, and not the church.

Item, for iron-ware, such as reinforcing irons, hooks, nails and expenses (*despenses*) and for everything which saws wood, the lord pays a third, and the church two-thirds, of the cost.

Item, the lord pays a third of the cost for the iron posts and the fences, and the church pays two-thirds.

Item, each party pays half the cost for the big irons.

Item, for the houses.

(Total: 14 livres, 3 sous and 9 deniers, of rent.)

(Total: 546 capons.)

(Total: 18 *aues* (geese?).)

(Total: 20 hens.)

(Total of the oats at Lessines, estimated by Jehan Bokre: 87 *muids*, 1½ *rasières*,[2] and a third part. Out of this he has 19 *rasières* of oats from the Wood of Lessines. Dated September 1284.)

*   *   *

THE WOOD OF LESSINES

A large wood

These are the rents for the Wood of Lessines.

It is situated at Bronchines, on the left as one travels from Lessines to Oullenghien.

---

[1] Measure of capacity. For all these measures see Machabey, A., jnr., *La métrologie dans les musées de province*, doctoral thesis, Paris, 1959.

[2] Measure of capacity (for fruit, grain, etc.).

Ysabel of Bronchines owes 3½ *rasières* of oats and 3½ capons from her tenement at Bronchines, adjacent to the manor of Walter of Bronchines.

Item, 2 *sous* for beechwood, in the month of May.

Item, 34 *deniers* for the third part of a small *bonnier* taken out of 6 *bonniers* of ground, which lies between the lands of Walter of Bronchines and those of Little Walter.

Item, 6 *deniers* and 1 *obole* for a little more than a *bonnier* of land, adjacent to Ronde Haie of Watrelos and the land of Sébile, the burgess of Lessines.

Item, 3 *oboles* for a day-work of land, which lies next to the lands of Colart de Watrelos and Sébile the Bourgeoise, on the one hand, and next to the lands of Crétin's wife and Bernart Fainient, on the other.

The heir of Huon Mairel owes 3 *oboles*, for a day-work adjacent to the aforesaid daywork.

The heir of Walter of Bronchines [owes] 6 *rasières* of oats and 6 capons, from his tenement close behind the tenement of Ysabel of Bronchines, before Oullenghien, and adjacent to the land of Hémeri the Burgess, who is from the Lessines.

Item, 2 sous for beechwood.

Item, beyond the road in front of his door, half a *rasière* of oats and half a capon from a little land close to the Oullenghien road, and close to a little land belonging to the said dame Ysabel, which is with her site.

Item, 9 *deniers* for a field, 1½ *bonniers* of land, next to the hedge of Watrelos and the land of the aforesaid dame Ysabel.

Item, 23 *deniers*, for a little less than 4 *bonniers* of land adjacent to the land of Colin Enghelrat.

The church of the Wood of Lessines (owes) 3 *oboles*, for a day-work of land next to a day-work belonging to the hospital of Lessines.

★   ★   ★

THE WOOD OF LESSINES

There are woods, in the Wood of Lessines: in the wood of Notre-Dame, where the church of Cambrai owns half of it (there are 28 *bonniers* and more; for which Monseigneur must pay 35 livres).

The fish pond of Foubert Sart, when quite full, covers about 28 *bonniers*: 100 livres (50 *li*).

The leases and the *métayage* are worth 50 *muids* of corn and 80 *muids* of oats a year. (Of this, the priest receives 3½ *muids* of corn and the same amount of oats. Total: 112 *sous*.) Revenue from oats: 70 *muids* and 1 *rasière* (42 *li*). The capons: 435 capons. Item 4 *awes* (geese?) (18 *deniers*). The fields: (14 livres *blancs*) among the assarts. The beeches: (14 livres *blancs*: out of this the hospital of Lessines gets 9 *li* 6s. and 8d. *blancs*; there remains 4 *li* and 13 sous and 4 *deniers blancs*).

(The beeches: 40 t.)

(The house and the site that Medame bought: 4 *li*.)

(The Wood of Lessines has, on account of all these agreements, each year: 422 capons; and it was estimated as such in the year 1291 (?); and 70 *muids* and 2 *rasières* of oats.)

(70 *muids* and 1 *rasière* of oats.)

(35 *muids* and 5 *rasières* of corn, from the land of which my lord has given in *métayage*.)

It should be known that a double rent is levied in the Wood of Lessines in the following case: if a man or a woman sell their lands and inheritance, he owes double the rent that the land or inheritance owes; and if a married man dies, his wife owes a double rent on such land or inheritance as may remain to the wife, which she may sell or pledge; but if the wife should die, the husband owes nothing on it, nor do their children owe anything, when their father or mother dies, on the inheritance that falls to them.

Le polyptyque illustré dit 'Veil Rentier' de Messire Jehan de Pamele-Audenarde, vers 1275 (ed. L. Verriest), Brussels, 1950, p. 117 r⁰; p. 118 r⁰; p. 144 r⁰ and v⁰.

131

Recognitions of title to property often contain detailed descriptions of the lands and rights which constitute the fief. This one, apart from a small estate which is mentioned at the end of the text, lists rent-paying holdings most of which were centred round the curtilage, a small inhabited enclosure.

We, B., official of the court of Lyons, make known to all those who shall see these letters that Hugues Raimond, esquire, in our presence, spontaneously and in full knowledge of the case, by an oath sworn bodily on the Holy Evangelists of God, has recognized before us and confessed to have paid homage to the church of St Just of Lyons the properties named below:

The curtilage which Brun de Montferran held of the said Hugues for which are due twelve deniers and a hen as rent; the land of Monsec and the land of la Combe, for which are due 22 deniers and a hen; the house and the garden of Jean Croset, for which twelve deniers and one hen, and six deniers, which are due for the sluice of a meadow; the hemp field for which are due six deniers and a hen; the curtilage of Etienne Bret and the meadow situated near the sluice of Sir Audin, and the curtilage which Jean Ribaud holds, situated near the house of Costrable, for which are due five strong sous, two deniers and two hens; the curtilage of Jean Oulard and of Pierre his brother for which are due three strong sous and three hens; two meadows which the same Jean holds, situated at la Combe de Crueis for which are due nine deniers; the curtilage of the Mont and the meadow situated near the meadow Berout, for which are due seven sous and one hen; the curtilage which le Blanc holds, for which are due six deniers and a hen; the curtilage of Nevel, for which are due 18 deniers and a hen; the curtilage which belongs to Joffrey, for which are due three sous and one hen; the meadow situated near Sir Audin's mill, for which are due two sous; the meadow of Perasant for which are due six deniers; the grange of la Combe and the 'task' of Leyse, the piece of land situated near Bernard Reinaud's house, the field of the Madman of Paisseley, the Narbonnan field, a hemp field, a garden, and a house, which is in the village of Vauxonne, and for all the appurtenances of these said properties. For all these above mentioned things, the said Hugues has confessed before us, under oath, to owe homage to the said church. . . . Given this year of Our Lord 1241, in August.

Cartulaire Lyonnais, Vol. I, pp. 452–453.

Burgesses of a little town sell their share of a joint possession in a modest manor, made up of a demesne (arable, vineyard and meadow), of a manse, of a bondsman, of dues in kind and of ploughing services.

We, master James, clerk of the bailiff of Mâcon, holding the castellany of St Gengoux, and master Stephen of Vergisson, canon of Mâcon and curé of the church of St Gengoux, make known to all those who will see the present letters that Guy Pelars, of St Gengoux, and Huguette, his wife, and Peronelle, sister to Guy, in our presence acting freely and with full knowledge, have sold, delivered, ceded and granted to the venerable and holy men, Yves, by the grace of God abbot of Cluny and the convent of the said place, and to their successors in perpetuity, the property and rights below:

Six day-works of land, situated at Collonge-sous-St-Boil; one *bichet* of annual wheat dues, which the sons of Ruf and their associates owe them, a third of a *setier* of wine dues, a third of a quarter of 18 *ouvrées*[1] of vineyard; a third of seven poultry dues, their right to one waggon of hay in the meadow of la Fontaine, a third of the *manse* of Vincent Juif; a third of Aimon de Collonge; a bushel of oats service, and all that the said vendors have in common with Bernard and Robert de Flay and Duran Magnin.

For the price of twelve livres of Vienne which the said vendors have acknowledged before us as having received in full from the monks, the purchasers, in hard cash.

Given the year of Our Lord 1277, in January.

Recueil de Chartes de l'Abbaye de Cluny,
Vol. VI, No. 5232, pp. 665-666.

133

A widow gave to the community of women with which she was associated for the foundation of an anniversary all the scattered property which she possessed in a Saxon village. These came to her from her allod, from land investments which she had made, and from a donation from her husband. The demesne was an important one, and the tenants collaborated in a small way in the ploughing and in the harvesting of the fields; money dues constituted their main burden. Repeated evidence of recent colonization and mention of rural artisans should be noted.

(1298)

Let all present and to come know that this is the total of the properties situated at Strassberg which I Cunegonde, advocate of Plauen, have given to the sisters of Cronschwitz. Of my allod, are dependent 72 fields, an orchard, and a kitchen garden, item two little meadows opposite Kloschwitz, near the stream which is called Rosenbach; item, the meadow where Hermann Schutelok's forge was; item, a large meadow contiguous with the allod which I have bought from Hartmann the dog for six marks, which I have paid him for completely, and all his children have renounced their rights for always; item, a meadow situated at the foot of the Kupferberg. In all these meadows

---

[1] A measurement used in vineyards; ⅕ of a day-work.

shall be each year 22 waggons of hay. Item, Bezoldus, of Aupres du lac, and Conrad, his brother, give each year two marks. Item, Cunegonde, daughter of Hovemann, gives half a *ferton*[1] for a curtilage in the village of Trachans. Item, Walter the miller, gives two marks for his mill and the same gives one *ferton* for some fields and meadows contiguous to the forge of Phannensmith; item, the same for his mill two hens, two cheeses and two harvesters; item, the same for this meadow has promised to help me one day in its cultivation. Item, Gozo, for half a meadow and fields gives a *ferton* and helps me one day in its cultivation. Item, the same Gozo, for his house and his fields, the half a mark; item, the *Schultheiss* Siboto, for all his property, one and a half marks; item, Bezold de Kemnitz, three *fertons*, two chickens, two cheeses, and two harvesters; item Th., son of Wolfram, three *fertons* and a half for all his property, two chickens, two cheeses, and four harvesters; item Henry Charles, three *fertons* less one *loton*,[2] two chickens, two cheeses and two harvesters; item, Hermann Scutelok, half a mark for his 'hall'; item, Henri le Chaufournier for his 'hall' and his fields one and a half *ferton*, two chickens, two cheeses and two harvesters; item, the same one and a half *loton* for his fields newly cleared. Item, the wife of Conrad Sorgelin, half a mark; item, the same, half a *ferton* for the fields newly cleared; item, the same, nine sous in deniers; item, three chickens, three cheeses, three harvesters. Item, Lupold, half a *ferton* for his fields newly cleared, and one sou for his hotel, a chicken, a cheese, two harvesters. . . . Item, Henri Zideler has bought the curtilage of Hildebold and his property; all this, he has had from me and from the sisters of Cronschwitz, and he must serve to the value of half a *ferton*; for the patronage of this curtilage and of all its property, I have given two marks and Hildebold, his wife and all their children have renounced their rights for ever. Item, for this half *ferton* which Zideler pays I have also given two marks to this woman. Item, from the stream which descends from the new village and which runs in the valley which is called Kampanthal and descends towards Elster, and from this part of Strassberg right up to the village of Strassberg, there are hills, some fields which belong to me and to my men. Item, from the part of Strassberg on the side of Kurbitz up to the stream which is called Jossnitz and some fields beyond, all the fields, lands and hills belong to me and to my peasants.

Item, let all know that the stream of Elster from the valley which is called Kampanthal up to the bridge of Kurbitz belongs to me, as well as to the sisters of Cronschwitz after my death, for every use, to place mill or other according to my wish and those of the sisters, save the right of fishing which I have exchanged for other property with the lords of Plauen. Item, H. son of Eberbard, who married the daughter of Phannensmith, gives a *ferton* for his field which is situated in the wood which is called Forst (this *ferton* was given me by my husband and his son called Bohem and that in good faith so that he was responsible with full rights for property situated at Strassberg). Item, I have bought from sister Jutte of Strassberg and from Jordan, the son of her brother, certain fields situated at Strassberg, a rent of 12 sous on two parcels of built-upon land, four cheeses, four chickens, four harvesters, two skinned lambs at Easter, for 27 marks. All this I give and assign, as well as all that which is in this letter, in perpetual possession to the sisters of Cronschwitz. From the fields and from the last rent bought for 27 marks I wish and dispose from henceforth that a solemn service and abundant repast should be

[1] Quarter of a mark.   [2] Quarter of a *ferton*.

made for the sisters at the time of my anniversary, and devotedly and faithfully celebrated each year.

G. Franz, *Deutsches Bauerntum*, pp. 226-231.

B. THE MANAGEMENT OF THE DEMESNE

1. *Direct Cultivation*

134

On English manors which were directly cultivated, the management of the demesne was in the hands of the reeve. The position of this official is explained in these two fragments of 'A Writ on the Ordering of the Household and its Staff', drawn up on the estate of the abbey of St Peter of Gloucester. Amongst other hints on good agrarian practice, the importance of the quality of the seed, of the preparation of the land by three successive ploughings, and of the use of straw in order to economise firewood, should be noted. Domestic servants were recruited from the villein tenants; these were reviewed after harvest time and the most efficient were selected and engaged for the year.

(1266-1285)

Rules concerning the Management of Manors

The reeve shall, at least once a month, cause to be clearly and openly recited before his companion the messer, the articles of this writ, and he shall strictly observe, according to his authority, the form of the rules which are contained therein, with great diligence and solicitude, taking care to restore that which has been omitted, unless he is prevented by an obvious need, an urgent necessity or any other reasonable cause that he must prove before his superior when it shall be required of him.

First of all, one month before Michaelmas all the serfs of the manor shall be called to the manor where they were born, and there before the steward of the place and by his authority it shall be strictly established which of them shall be kept in the lord's service, for what occupation, in what place, in what form, for what livery and for what wage. It being understood that when it shall please the bailiff of the place, they shall be transferred from one place to another to the lord's advantage, their liveries, and their wages being determined beforehand. And no one shall be received in the lord's service without pledge to serve faithfully and to make good the loss in case of omission. Those who must remain shall be warned to prepare to stay. Those who must return home shall merely be warned not to cheat over their service. It shall not be forgotten that if one of those who are kept back owe to his lord services or labour by reason of personal status these must not be omitted on account of his engagement as the latter carries with it a full wage.

Item, let the demesne servants care for the horses and the other offices which shall be assigned to them, holidays as well as other days; let them not be absent from the hall without special permission in order that the whole village community should at all times be subject to the judicial authority of the court which could not be done by the demesne officers in cases when they happen to be absent from the court. . . .

. . . These things are enjoined on reeves, but not however on oath.

Firstly, let them not change the division of lands, acres, meadows, woods, pasture or anything else, in whatever place it has been done, between the lord and his neighbours, or between tenants except in a certain and reasonable case, because this customary division must, in law, remain in the exact and customary state; and let them not plant trees nor erect new banks to the detriment of the lord or one of his tenants.

Item, let, as far as it shall be possible at the appropriate season, the lord's land be ploughed the first time and the second time after the fallow, and be ploughed and sown, taking care that no seed be sown of whatever kind, if it be not of the first quality, or at least perfectly threshed. Let nothing be sown except by skilled hands. And the seed remaining in the grange should be faithfully delivered to the bailiff but not against a tally but converting into certain quantities.

Item, let not customary men be allowed to make exchanges of land, meadows or other tenements without permission obtained before the Hallmoot.

Item, let the meadows and the corn be examined by prominent men before haymowing and harvesting, in order that if anything shall be damaged by the harvesters' negligence, it shall be fully restored to the lord.

Item, let the barren and uncultivated places within the enclosure of the hall be restored to cultivation, in order that no unused space may be found.

Item, let care be taken of the stubble in the fields, that it may be cut and brought in to thatch the houses, or be used to heat the oven or the household whichever is most convenient. . . .

Historia et Cartularium monasterii Sancti Petri Gloucestriae,
Vol. III, 1867, pp. 213-217.

135

The following inventory, which is of one of the demesne centres exploited by Thierry d'Hireçon, reveals the dual connection between arable and pastoral agriculture. The household was well equipped with plough horses and its barns contained enormous quantities of grain which was in the process of being threshed (a part of the wheat had been already taken to market). There were many sheep in the stables and a great many bales of wool. The number of iron tools is also remarkable.

(1328)

Inventory made by Huon de Dourier, clerk of the bailiff's court of Arras, and Jacquemon de Larbre, mounted sergeant of the court, on the Tuesday night after Saint Martin's day, in the winter of the year 1328, those present being Mahieu the coffee-maker, Jehan his brother, and magistrates Pierrot Ghellent, Gosson de Hanons, Willaume Lebleu, Baudin le Valin, and several others, of all the possessions of the house of Sailli in Ostrevaus, which belonged to Monseigneur the bishop of Arras.

PLATE VIII

Document 136
Tithe barn at the abbey of Ter Doest in Flanders

First, about 11 *muids* of threshed corn, with 9 *muids* taken to Douay. And about 16,200 sheaves of corn, and 11,220 sheaves of oats. And about 3,000 bundles of vetch. And 300 bundles of pease. And 3 arches[1] full of hay from the new barn.

Item, 13 harness horses, provided with traces and harness.

Item, a large mare and her 2 foals.

It., 156 sheep.

It., 155 ewes in lamb.

It., 118 lambs.

It., 40 pigs, young and full grown.

It., 13 milch-cows and 2 large oxen.

It., 9 calves, 1 little bull, 4 small sucking calves.

It., 78 *pierres* and 7 pounds of wool.

It., 6 *pierres* and 2 pounds of lambskins.

It., 8 bad feather-beds.

It., 5 fur cover called carpets.

It., 17 pairs of bad household sheets for the domestic staff.

It., 2 old tablecloths and an old towel.

It., 3 copper pots: the biggest holds about 8 *los*.

It., 4 brass basins and 2 old cauldrons.

It., 2 half-*los* measures and 1 tin vessel.

It., 4 tripods, 3 pails and 1 white cauldron.

It., 4 old bins, 2 old baskets.

It., 1 kneading-trough with lid.

It., 3 stall planks.

It., 1 fishing net.

It., 1 skiff and 1 small boat for fishing.

It., 2 scythes.

It., 2 bushels for measuring corn and *rasière*.

It., 4 iron-mounted carts, in current use.

It., 2 hampers and one box without wheels.

It., 5 pairs of plough-irons.

It., 5 hoes, in current use.

It., 4 harrows and 4 ploughs.

It., 3 pack-saddles and 5 sacks.

136

Constructed about 1200, more than 160 feet long, nearly 100 feet wide and 78 feet high, this tithe barn (Plate VIII) at the Flemish abbey of Ter Doest is striking evidence of the vast quantity of grain receipts, mostly collected from the demesne.

1 'Arch' here obviously implies the measurement still used in country districts to measure the quantity contained in a section of the barn between an 'arch' of wood.

A great inquest, undertaken in 1338 in all the Provençal houses of the Order of Hospitalers, was the basis for budgetary estimates for each commandery as laid down by the visitors. The following tables of anticipated receipts and payments (below & opposite) show the tremendous diversity in the economy of these manors. At Bras (below) the largest profits came from the demesne; most of the expenditure went towards paying the hired labour; the manorial household spent much more money in the neighbourhood than it received (we can see the figures presented in another way in the individual details of the budget of this house). St Jean de Trièves, a little mountain manor, was not able to support the twenty-four persons who made up the 'family' of the masters. The manorial farm at Poët-Laval was also in deficit and had hardly any demesne revenue at all, properly speaking. On the other hand, the prosperity of Puimoisson came from demesnes and tithes, while Sallier's prosperity was founded on a very large use of métayage.

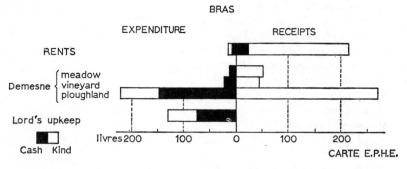

2. *Farm Leases*

138-139

The archbishop of Rouen begins by leasing 'at farm' (to a priest, probably a member of his domestic staff) the individual arable fields of his demesne at Alihermont, keeping for himself half the crop. Two years later, well before the expiration of the lease, he grants the same 'farmer' the whole of the demesne, with the livestock, the woods, the levying of tithes and the control of a tile-kiln, but only for three years and in return for a large money payment. The lord keeps the right of shelter for himself and his retainers, all the rents and the justice. He obtains a guarantee against a deterioration of the property. The colonization of this region by settlement (abergements) is completed at this period; traces of the characteristic long-street village are preserved in the present landscape.

Brother Odo, by the grace of God unworthy minister of the church of Rouen, to all those who shall see these letters, eternal salvation in Our Lord Jesus Christ. Know then that we have leased at farm to our beloved and trusty Reginald, clerk, our lands at Alihermont, assarted as well as to be assarted, with the settlements of Croixdalle for six

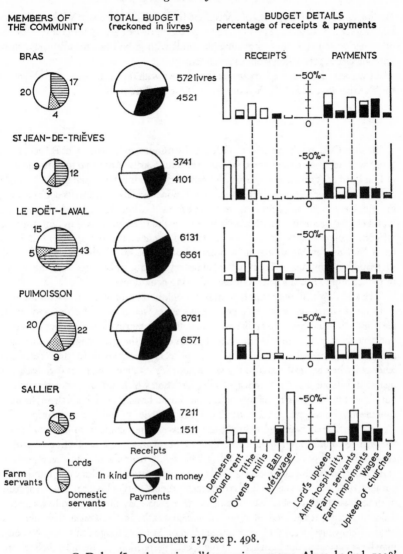

MEMBERS OF THE COMMUNITY

TOTAL BUDGET (reckoned in livres)

BUDGET DETAILS percentage of receipts & payments

BRAS — 20, 17, 4 — 572 livres / 4521

ST JEAN-DE-TRIÈVES — 9, 12, 3 — 3741 / 4101

LE POËT-LAVAL — 15, 5, 43 — 6131 / 6561

PUIMOISSON — 20, 22, 9 — 8761 / 6571

SALLIER — 3, 5, 6 — 7211 / 1511

RECEIPTS   PAYMENTS

Farm servants — Lords — In kind — In money — Domestic servants — Receipts — Payments

Demesne, Ground rent, Tithe, Ovens & mills, Ban, Métayage, Lord's upkeep, Alms hospitality, Farm servants, Farm implements, Wages, Upkeep of churches

Document 137 see p. 498.

G. Duby, 'La seigneurie et l'économie paysanne, Alpes du Sud, 1338' in *Études rurales*, 2, 1961.

years, from Assumption Day in the year 1253. In order that he holds our said lands for six harvests on the following conditions:

That the said Reginald has the land ploughed and sown at his expense; the crops shall be a common expense; he shall bring them in with his own, shall have half of them, shall faithfully reserve for us the other half, and for the division of these fruits shall await our order. As for the assarted lands, they shall be at our expense, and we shall pay the marling and the necessary costs of upkeep and the repair of the houses. We keep the tile-kiln wholly for ourselves. He is bound to use the straw of the said corn for fertilizer or other necessary usages and to fertilize the lands with it, and not to take it elsewhere without special permission from us or our envoy.

In witness of which we have sealed these letters with our seal. Given at Alihermont the Tuesday after St Luke's Day, the year of Our Lord, 1253.

*　　*　　*

Brother Odo, by the grace of God unworthy minister of the church of Rouen, to all those who shall see these letters, salvation in Jesus Christ. Know ye that, in the year of Our Lord 1255, in August, we have leased at farm to our beloved and trusty Reginald du Tremblay, clerk, our manor of Alihermont and Croixdalle, with all its dependencies, in demesne as well as in tithe, tile-kiln and forest (except the charcoal burning and wood cutting according to what he is accustomed until now: he will not introduce it without our consent) and all the other rights dependent on the manor, except the rents from land due at Martinmas in winter and at Pentecost which we keep, for one thousand livres minted at Tours, to be paid every year for three years from the octave of the assumption of this year. On the following conditions:

The said Reginald must supply us or our people in the said manor straw for the beds and for the horses, hay and vetches for the horses, as well as wood for fire, and water. He must grind and bake the grain and prepare the bread, provide us with hens, capons, pork, chickens, geese and other household provisions, on the reckoning of our manciple and cook, and we shall reply to him with the price. He shall provide for the costs of our seneschal when he shall come to the said manor for its affairs; he must give back the manor and all our barns in the village in the condition which they are, or better roofed; but if they tumble down by decay or if they are burnt, he need not rebuild them; he shall roof the new houses which we shall make; he shall provide us with tiles at the price at the tile-kiln; in case of war, bad weather, fire (if this does not come from his own house) we shall be bound to relieve him according to the calamity; in case of a fine exceeding 18 sous, we shall pay the excess, as well as what results from the high justice, above the said 18 sous; at the end of the lease he shall restore the livestock value for value, number for number, on a fair estimate; he shall collect their produce during his farm, but of the fruit of these beasts nothing shall leave our demesne. He shall pay the thousand livres on the following terms: three hundred livres at Candlemas at the gate of Rouen, three hundred on the following Ascension Day, four hundred on St Mary Magdalen's Day. Nobody may be associated in this farm without our special permission. . . . Item, he shall restore to us the lands in the state in which he received them, that is, ploughed the first and the second time, and he may not cultivate them in the wrong season; but he shall harvest them just as if the end of his farm did not come in the middle of the harvest. If his men are not subject to the justice of the knights, according to what is agreed between us, he may exploit the forest up to a value of two hundred livres minted at Tours, taking account of the revenue and grain from the forest. It shall be known that if, for an offence, the land of one of our men is assigned to us, we shall be bound to give him back the tithes which he has a right to collect on the said land. Item, during the entire year in which he shall give up the farm, he shall be bound to provide us with straw, vetches and hay. It shall be known that of the straw of St Nicholas's tithe and from the demesne, he may not at the end of the farm take away or sell anything save grain. The number and value of the animals which are handed over to him are thus: 173 sheep and 46 ewes at four sous six deniers each; 60 ewes and 50 others aged one year, at three sous each; eleven yearling calves worth 330 sous; two cows and three yearling calves worth 55 sous; seven cows, worth eight livres 15 sous; one bull worth 35 sous; two cows, two heifers and one young bullock worth seven livres ten sous; four bullocks, worth 64 sous; three heifers worth 36 sous. Reginald for the faith which he owes us, is bound to keep faithfully and to defend all our rights in the demesne as in the forest, in men, rents and warren as in all other things. He has further promised on oath to hold firmly and inviolably these agreements and to do nothing against them, giving us as guarantee for this all his movable goods and property, present as well as future wherever they may be.

In witness of which we have sealed these present letters with our seal.

Given at Alihermont, the year of Our Lord, 1255, in the month of August.

Regestrum visitationum archiepiscopi Rhotomagensis,
Journal des visites pastorales d'Eudes Rigaud, archévêque de Rouen, (1248-1269)
(ed. T. Bonnin), Rouen, 1852, pp. 769-771.

140

In this métayage lease of a Rhineland manor the importance of the yield in cash for the wages of the harvesters, winter purchase of additional fodder and the costliness of marling operations should be noted. Also the cultivation stolen from the fallow course.

Thierry, called the Dean, has received the manor of Lagheim on half shares for six years from the Holy See in the year of Our Lord 1277. The lords of St Géréon will give to the said husbandman every year 15 *muids* of rye and 18 *muids* of oats for seed, and eleven sous to cut the grain and harvest it. Besides, the said lords have given the said husbandman four marks which shall be devoted to marling during the next three years at three sous the day-work. Item, the lords and the husbandman shall have an equal number of oxen, pigs, ewes and other animals in the manor; and the husbandman shall not have any other animal for himself alone, save chickens and geese; and when it shall be necessary in the winter, their feed, like that of the other animals, shall be bought at joint expense. Item, the lords and the husbandman shall share equally the apples, nuts and other fruits of the manor. Item, the husbandman every year may sow for himself two day-works in the fallow field; and all that he shall sow over and above this in the fallow field shall be shared between the lords and the husbandman. Item, the husbandman shall himself transport at his own expense the grain which he shall have sown for the lords to their barn at Cologne. Item, the lords shall give nothing nor make any payment for guarding the ewes, the oxen, the pigs or other animals.

G. Franz, *Deutsches Bauerntum*, pp. 210-211.

Here it is the village community which receives the 'farm' of the entire manor.

(1279)

To all the faithful in Christ who shall see and hear this writ, William, by the grace of God, abbot of Ramsey, greeting in the Lord.

Know ye, that we have granted to our men of Hemingford our manor of Hemingford from Michaelmas of the eighth year of the reign of King Edward, son of King Henry, for the seven years following for 40 *li* to be paid to us every year in four instalments, to wit 10 *li* on the Feast of St Andrew, 10 *li* on the day of the Annunciation and 10 *li* on the Nativity of St John the Baptist.

Our men aforesaid shall hold the manor with all its dependencies save the benefice of the church when it shall be vacant, our fishery and the mill which we have kept in our own hand.

They shall also have all the profits of the village save our tallage, the aid of the sheriff and of the Hundred, and the wardpennies, and the scutage of the lord king, and save the profits of those cases which cannot be adjudicated without us or our bailiffs, of which issue they should have half, and save the view of the frankpledge, and save the ploughman's land (*acremanland*) and the acres of the reeve of Ramsey.

It shall be known that if a customary tenant dies without heir of his body we shall grant his land and house to whomsoever we shall wish and we shall keep the *gersum*. . . .

The said farmers may not concede land or house to any stranger or to anyone owing homage to another lord without our special permission. . . .

Furthermore, the said farmers have received the following stock.

The grange full of wheat on either side of the door up to the doorposts and up to the beams behind the door and rising nine feet and from beside the door the length of the wall up to the ceiling of the barn.

They have also received the oat grange full of oats on the East side of the door.

The width of the grange is 28 feet, its length 39 feet, and the grange is round on the east side. The true height in the middle is 19 feet.

The true width from (*hostio*) to the far end of the round wall is 30 feet long. The height 5½ feet.

They have received also a heap of barley 36 feet long, 11 feet wide, 11 feet high and 18 feet wide in the middle.

They shall be free of the sergeant every autumn save the last year, when they shall have a steward who, according to the abbey custom, shall view the stock.

They shall also be free of our annual hospitality, save that every time we shall come, they shall bring us salt, straw and hay.

At the end of seven years they shall give back the manor and the stock that they received at the beginning.

They shall give back the land well tilled by two ploughings.

Cartularium Monasterii de Ramseia
(W. H. Hart & P. A. Lyons, eds.), Vol. II, pp. 244-245.

★   ★   ★

The dean of the chapter of the church of Lübeck, to all, greetings in the Lord. . . .

Between us and our peasants of our village of Hansfelde, situated in Holstein near the city of Lübeck, was made this agreement at a common assembly. The said peasants and their legitimate heirs shall have in perpetuity, in this village and in all the dependencies such as are contained within its limits, the usage and usufruct as they have done up till now. They shall pay to us and our church for the village every year in rent and tithe twenty marks in deniers of Lübeck, to be sent to Lübeck to our collector at Martinmas. We and our successors are content with this rent and we shall not demand more from the said farmers. The said farmers shall have with the farmers of our village of Hamberge joint pastures and the right to cut all save oaks within the said limits of the said Hamberge, like the farmers of this village who have the usage to cut wood for their requirements for firewood. It should be also added that, in conformity with the right and general custom of the country, if one of the husbandmen wishes to sell his property, his right, his inheritance or his movables, the object of sale shall first be offered to our chapter. If our chapter does not wish to buy, he may sell freely, but not to a burgess or a citizen, or to a man of the manor, but to someone who lives as a husbandman on his property. The husbandmen shall not have the power to modify the village *manses*; they may not share or divide the *manses* otherwise than they are now, nor draw boundaries in a different way. Furthermore, they shall not build new cabins, which are vulgarly called cot, without special permission of the chapter. The husbandmen shall not claim any right on the mill and the adjoining yard, nor on the meadow called Herschewisch, on the hill adjacent to this meadow, nor on the great meadow called Hudewisch, which we keep entirely for ourselves with the lordship of the village of Hansfelde. In order that this writ may remain stable, we have caused our seal to be affixed. The witnesses are the canons of the church of Lübeck and other clerks and laymen worthy of trust.

Given in the year of Our Lord 1296, on the eve of St James, apostle.

G. Franz, *Deutsches Bauerntum*, pp. 221-224.

C. THE CONDITION OF THE PEASANTS

1. Tenancies

143

The superior lord lays down punishments for recalcitrant tenants and for peasants who neglect to pay the fixed rents on their land.

It is established that the peasant who shares the produce with his landlord, if he does not give back the land which was rented out to him, to the man who rented it out or to the proprietor, at the end of the period of the rental, shall be punished with a fine of forty sous and forced to restore the rented thing to the renter.

It is ordered that if the rent-paying tenant, or whoever pays the rent, interrogated by the *podesta* or his vicar before the law suit, denies owing the rent or the pension to the master or to the mistress, and then is belied, he shall be punished with a fine of twenty sous and shall be bound to pay the rent. . . .

. . . It is ordered that the rent-paying tenant who has not paid the rent in wheat or in other grain in the month of August to the master or to the mistress shall be punished by a fine of twelve sous per bushel and shall be forced to pay the rent late or its equivalent at the choice of the master or mistress.

It is ordered that any man being bound to pay a rent in cash or by another means of payment, who shall not have done so before the end of the month of June to the master or to the mistress, shall be punished by a fine of five sous and shall be forced to pay the rent improperly in arrears.

> *Statuto della val d'Ambra 1208 del Comte Guido Guerra III*
> (ed. F. Bonaini), Pisa, 1851, p. 57.

144

Because cultivation had been abandoned in wartime, strips were carved out of the three 'fields' which composed this Bavarian territory and were assigned to each manse (Hof).

The demesne of Isarhofen and all the other demesnes in all the county of Bogen, by the acts of count Albert and of his enemies had come to the point where no one knew any longer which were the fields and the meadows of the demesne, because they had been for long without cultivators, and because the knights and the powerful men used to cultivate only the fields near the village, the more remote ones being left to scrub and waste. Peace having returned on the death of the count, the peasants of the church and the feudal knights disputed the areas and boundaries. Which is why I, Hermann, abbot, by reason of supplications and prayers to the lord duke Otto, have induced certain knights to swear on the relics of the saints to speak the truth about what each ought justly to own. It was done in the following manner:

It was thus agreed that the largest field, the one on the Ahalmingen side, shall be measured with cords, and to each *Hof* shall be assigned twelve arpents, each of twelve furrows. These parts being distributed to the feudatories, all the rest shall remain for the church. In as many parts as the largest field shall be divided, the second and the third shall also be divided, although in these two fields twelve arpents cannot be assigned to each *Hof* as in the first field.

This division of the fields was begun by the monk Alvinus, who drew it up, the provost, brother Berthold, and the official, Rudolf, who have measured with cords in the presence of the abbot Hermann and the people. The year of Our Lord 1247.

> G. Franz, *Deutsches Bauerntum*, pp. 190-191.

145

In the thirteenth century the practice of granting tenancies by written contract spread to the North of France. The object of this rent-paying lease concerning the right of 'entry' is a mill which was also used for fulling woollen cloth.

We, brother Philip, dean of Cluny, make known to all those who shall see these letters that Jacques, son of the late Duran, provost of Blanot ... has acknowledged having leased on behalf of himself and Jean, the clerk his brother, two mills at Merzé with the old sluice, the flail and the fullery. Item, his pasture before the said mill; item, the water flowing from the old sluice as far as Merzé. To Benoît de Lancharre, for 14 *panneaux* of barley and 13 level *panneaux* of wheat to be delivered every year to the said brothers; item, for an annual rent of 18 sous three deniers of money minted at Cluny and ten sous of Cluny as entry fine, paid in cash to the said Jacques, for himself and for his brother. Item, the said Jacques has agreed to give for the use of the mills and the appurtenances of these mills, every year to the said Benoît and to his heirs, timber which can be found in his own woods and to transport it, it being understood that the cost of construction shall fall on the said Benoît for the rebuilding of the mills and their appurtenances. And the said Jacques and his heirs, when they shall wish to grind, shall have the power to do so, as soon as grain shall have been introduced into the mill hopper, save that they shall pay flour dues like others. But in order to full their serge once a year, the said Jacques and his heirs shall pay nothing to the said Benoît save that bread and wine shall be provided for the labour. Jacques has promised Benoît in good faith to hold this arrangement in peace according to his ability against claims from no matter whom. . . .

Given the year of Our Lord 1251, in May.

Archives de Saône-et-Loire, H.1. No. 7.

146

It was as frustrating in thirteenth-century, as it had been in twelfth-century France to deal with a recalcitrant tenant (see Document No. 85, p. 438).

(November 1263)

We, P., prior of Lagnieu, and Etienne, rector of the church of this place, make it known ... that a lawsuit existed between brother G., prior of the Charterhouse of Portes, of the one part, and Jean Malian of Lagnieu, of the other part, concerning a vineyard held by the said Jean of the said prior and of the brothers of the said house, near the house of Gerveil, for a quarter of the crop and a rent, situated near the vineyard of Girard Malian, and the land which the said brothers have bought from the said Girard, and the road which leads from Gerveil to Noyandes, because the said prior and brothers claimed that the said vineyard ought to revert to them because he did not cultivate it as he ought to have done, and because he had not paid the service for more than thirty years. The said Jean, acknowledging these facts, asked the prior and the brothers to approve the concession of the said vineyard to Jeanne his daughter as a dowry. The said prior and brothers, not wishing to give this approval, the said Jean and Jeanne his daughter with the approval of her husband Jean have delivered the said vineyard to the said prior and brothers and have vacated it for ever; they have divested themselves of the said vineyard and have vested it in the prior, who has received it in the name of the said house . . . for this act of renouncement and for the investiture of the said vineyard, the prior has given the said Jeanne 45 sous minted in Vienne.

Cartulaire lyonnais (ed. M. Guigue),
Vol. II, Lyons, 1893, pp. 178-179.

147-148

At the end of the thirteenth century, Bresse was a region of dispersed colonization. The Templars organized settlement and exploited peasants in search of land. For permission to settle on a manse the young man in the following document had, with his father's consent, to give up to the lord a parcel of the family's allod. In the second document the four brothers who took up the joint cultivation of a group of dispersed meadows and lands paid a very heavy entry fine. All these men had, in addition, to make an avowal of bodily dependence which subjected their movable goods to assessment for taille and to confiscation in the event of their giving up the holdings.

(December 1287)

We, Ainard de Bardonnèche, bailiff and judge in the territory of Bâgé for the illustrious lord Amédée, count of Savoy and sire of Bâgé, make known that . . . before our representative, master Hugues de Bey, sworn clerk to the court of the lord count . . . Aimonnet Robelet, parishioner of Polliat, has acknowledged that brother Jean Castelour, preceptor of the house of the Temple at Laumusse and Belleville, has given and conceded in perpetual settlement to him and to his, a *manse* with its appurtenances which formerly Perraud de Polliat owned, situated in the parish of Polliat, for three *bichets* of wheat and two *bichets* of rye in annual service, as it is said in the letters given on this *abergement*. For this the said Aimonnet has given and granted himself from henceforward as liege man subject to *taille* and exploitable by the house of the Temple, by the authority and order of his father. Item, Aimonnet has acknowledged . . . to have given and conceded by irrevocable gift, given between living persons, by the wish and order of his father . . . from the time of the contract of the said settlement, to God, to Our Lady and to the house of the Temple a parcel situated at Confrançon, in the middle of the road which goes to Bourg, adjoining the land of Etienne Cordier on one side, and that of Bernard Rseverchia on the other. The said Aimonnet, by an oath sworn on the Holy Evange-list, . . . has promised . . . not to go against this acknowledgment, gift and oath of homage. . . .

Cartulaire lyonnais, Vol. II, pp. 535-536.

*   *   *

We, brother Jean Castelour, humble preceptor of the house of Laumusse . . . estab-lish and cede in perpetual emphyteutic lease to Jean Martin, Aimon, Guillaume and Guigue his brothers, the lands arable or not, which Jean son of the late Girard, provost of Replonges, has given and bequeathed . . . to wit the field of Guitet, the meadow of Lugunyre and the contiguous land, the meadow Hugunnier, the meadow of la Barrière, a parcel situated by the side of the road which is adjacent to the tithe barn of St Peter of

Mâcon which Messier Jean Bruyère, priest, holds, the meadow Boyon, the end piece of ground situated beside the demesne furlong, two measures of land (*coupées*) situated at Laubespin, a parcel situated beside the meadow of la Barrière, a parcel of land situated beside the land of Jean Lenor's son, and what the said Jean has near to Laiserablet, which properties are situated in the parish of Replonges ... for an annual service of 20 sous minted in Paris and a *meitier* of wheat to be paid every year at Christmas. ... Item, we cede ... all the appurtenances of the said properties which are ... from the lordships of other lords in such a way that the said lessees must pay services and rents to those lords on whom the appurtenances depend. We place in bodily ownership ... the said lessees and in perpetuity those of their family who shall reside there. For which agreements we have had entry fines ... twelve livres and forty sous minted in Vienne. On the other part, the said Jean Martin, Aimon, Guillaume and Guigue have wished and acknowledged to be, they and theirs, men of Laumusse, to the use and customs of this house in perpetuity.

Archives du Rhône, 48 H., 1921, No. 19.

149

The lord's court (in this case Ramsey Abbey) adjudicates between contending parties over the status of a holding and its burdens. Here we should note the periodic money tallage which burdened all villein holdings, and, even from time to time, the whole village community.

(Early thirteenth century)

They say that in the time of the late Abbot Richard, when Walter de Styvecle was steward of Ramsey, a certain John, son of Pagan de Wystowe, brought a complaint before the itinerant judges against Simon the Brewer about this virgate of land which now Richard the clerk holds. And because it was in the banlieue of Ramsey, the said steward had jurisdiction there as far as Smithscroft. There it was established that the land owed servile custom. To wit, at Easter, tallage of 12d. At Michaelmas according to the importance of the livestock; for the sheriff's aid, 6d. per year. For 'warthsilver' one farthing; for 'wethersilver' one penny; and each week one ploughing service like others in the village. And at each precaria of ploughs with its plough like others in the village. And when barley is sown, it owes the ploughing of a furrow of 'loveboon', like the others. And in any case where the village community is at mercy, it must be associated with it. Simon the Brewer performed all these services when he lived. And Thomas his son did the same after the death of his father. And he is in the hide like the villeins.

Cartularium monasterii de Ramseia, Vol. III,
pp. 315-316.

2. Justice

150-151-152-153

English manorial court rolls contain a wealth of detail about the daily life of villagers. When the lord exercised the privilege of the 'view of the frank pledge' all the inhabitants had to present themselves periodically at his court grouped in associations for mutual responsibility known as 'tithings', to which all male peasants had to belong as soon as they reached manhood. They had then to denounce all misdemeanours of which members of the tithing might have been guilty, and to answer for those who were absent. The ordinary courts recognized all infractions of manorial custom (such as being late with labour services, or surreptitious marriages, or sales), transfers of property between tenants were presented to them, and they recorded promises of payment (in Document No. 151 a new tenant obtained a postponement of three instalments of a heavy entry fine). Villagers brought their complaints about disputed boundaries and dowries which had not been delivered. Every judgment permitted the holder of justice to levy a small fine.

Amongst other things to be noted are surnames indicating craft specialization, the presence of a domestic servant on the tenancy of a widow (151) and the system of guarantees ('pledges') required for each personal engagement. The pension paid by a son to his parents who had sold him their tenancy provides a little evidence about dietary habits (151).

*   *   *

The whole tithing of Hartley comes as it ought to come and presents that all is well.

The tithingman of Brightwaltham with his whole tithing present that all is well, save that William of Westwood has made default. They say also that John son of Richard at Cross dwells at Bromham and is not in a tithing. Therefore his father is ordered to produce him at the next court. They say also that Harry Smith struck Sir Robert the chaplain and drew blood and then to conceal his fault raised the hue. Therefore he is in mercy; pledges, John Atgreen, Richard Young and Thomas Smith. They also present that Christine widow of Ralf Smith has received [a guest] contrary to the assize. Therefore she is in mercy; pledge Richard Smoker.

*   *   *

Court of Brightwaltham holden on the Wednesday next before the feast of St Peter in Chains in the twenty-second year of King Edward (A.D. 1294).

*   *   *

Prohibition is made that none of the lord's tenants upon pain of a half mark do in any wise give any sheaves in the fields to anyone of the township or to any stranger.

Inquest is made by the steward on Tuesday the morrow of St Matthew as to the abduction of sheep and other trespasses committed in the manor of Brightwaltham in the said year: by which inquest it is found that John Sket bought from the reeve three sheep and when particulars had been agreed on between them the said John pastured the said sheep in the lord's pasture. Therefore he is in mercy. Pledges, John Parlefrens and Richard Young; [amercement] 40d.

Select Pleas in Manorial and other Seignorial Courts, F. W. Maitland (ed.),
Vol. I, 1889, pp. 166-167.

*   *   *

(1294)

Viewed at Cranfield, Monday, the day after St Valentine's Day, the 22nd year of the reign of King Edward and the 8th year of Abbot J, before William Wassingle.

508

John Cross	William Ingeram
Thomas Godwin	Richard of the Field
Geoffrey of the Meadow	Laurence the Clerk
Ralf de Pyro	John le Falcon
John Wyking	Robert son of John Beneyt
Richard the Shepherd	William the Smith

They give the lord 13s. 4d. in *capitagium.*

From Elias de Bretingdon and William Curtis because they could not reply for John de Bretingdon, his son, who had taken a hare in the lord's warren, they gave pledges for each other. . . .

. . . From Geoffrey of the Meadow for not having come to the lord's corn harvest in autumn, 3d.

From Geoffrey of the Meadow for his ploughing of 4 furrows which is overdue from Lent 6d.; pledge, Thomas atte Hache. It is said he will pay the said ploughing.

From Emma of the mount because her servant threshed the lord's corn badly, 3d.; pledge, Simon Beadle.

Thomas atte Hache, John Robert, William Curtis and William de Barton complain of William, miller of Salford, because they were his pledges when he took the mill at Cranfield at farm, and William has caused them to incur damages up to 4s. Afterwards they were in agreement and William the miller was in mercy, 12d.; pledges: Roger son of Sarre.

John Cnap carried plaint against Thomas atte Hache, John Robert, William Curtis and William de Barton, pledges for William the miller, who have not paid 6 bushels of 'tollcorn' for the said William. It has been said that they would pay the corn, and for unjustly withholding it they are in mercy, 12d.; pledges, for each other.

From Robert of the Mill because he carried the lord's plough out of the hall badly, 12d.; pledge: the beadle.

William Robert was pledge to Nicholas de Crawele for coming to show the charter of the tenement he had bought to the said William, and nothing was done, William, in mercy, 3d.; pledge: the beadle, and it is said that he shows the charter. . . .

. . . Richard the Shepherd has given as pledges Simon of the Meadow, the elder, Geoffrey of the Meadow, Thomas Alfred and Roger le Sweyn to pay William de Wassingle between now and Whitsuntide 42s. for wool bought from the said William. . . .

The autumn wardens reveal that Roger le Falcon received two strange women who did damage in the autumn fields. For this he is in mercy, 3d.; pledge John le Falcon.[1]

And they said that Ralf, Robert le Franc's man crossed the hedge of Hokes while looking for firewood. For this, he is in mercy, 2s.; pledges, Thomas Hethewy and Robert of the Mill.

And they said Cecilia of Southwood was married at Merston without permission. For this in mercy, 3s.; she then came and proved that she had paid 'gersum' of 3s. in the time of William of Stowe. And Richard of the Field swore that he was then reeve and had received the money. . . .

---

[1] 15 others are fined for the same.

. . . Elias de Bretendon has sold before the whole court a messuage and half a virgate of rent-paying land at Cranfield with the adjacent woodland and all its other appurtenances and 3 acres of 'forlond' in favour of his son John. Which John came, presented by William le Moyne of Barnwell, his attorney, and recognized that he owed the lord abbot 3 silver marks to have his land. Of this money he will pay one mark at the Translation of St Bene't in the 8th year of Abbot J, one mark at Michaelmas in the 9th year of Abbot J, and the 3rd on the following Christmas. His pledges are Thomas Hache, Simon of the Meadow, the younger, William the Smith, John Falconer and Thomas Godwin. The said Elias will, until next Michaelmas, suitably cultivate and sow the said land at his expense, and from this land he and Christine, his wife, will receive next autumn half of all the fruit. And the said John from the remainder shall provide for the honourable maintenance of Elias and Christine, his wife, in food and drink as long as they shall live and they shall reside with the said John in the dwelling in the principal messuage. And if by ill fortune it happens that disputes arise in the future between the two parties, such as prevent them from remaining in peace in the same house, the said John shall provide Elias and Christine or the survivor a house in the hall with a curtilage where they can live honourably and shall give them every year 6 quarters of corn at Michaelmas, to wit 3 quarters of wheat, $1\frac{1}{2}$ quarters of barley, and half a quarter of peas and beans and one quarter of oats. Furthermore the said Elias and Christine by agreement established between the two parties shall have for themselves all the chattels of the said house movable and immovable which were there when the said Elias gave up the said land of his into the lord's hands.

Court Rolls of the Abbey of Ramsey and of the Honour of Clare (ed. W. O. Ault), Newhaven, Conn., 1928, pp. 233-236.

*   *   *

(1296)

Walter Mile complains of John Brockhole and says that he has raised a wall and hedge between their tenements to his damage and prays an inquest. And John freely grants that an inquest be made. The inquest says that the wall is not raised wrongfully but that the hedge is raised wrongfully and to Walter's damage. Therefore it is considered that John be in mercy for the hedge which is wrongfully raised and that amends be made and that Walter be in mercy for his false complaint (fine 8d.).

Walter Mile demands against John Parson 35s. 11d. wherein he is bound to him (so he says) for things promised and due to him as part of the marriage portion of John's daughter etc. And John says that in no respect is he bound to (Walter) as regards the said marriage portion, save as to a mantle, price 5s.; and this he offers to verify by his law. . . . Therefore is Walter in mercy (fine 4d.) and John also is in mercy for the wrongful detainer of the mantle, etc. (fine 4d.).

Select Pleas in Manorial and other Seignorial Courts, pp. 46-47.

*   *   *

(25th March 1307)

. . . Because Elias, beadle, bondsman of the lord, did sell all his chattels and also all his corn crop on the half-virgate that he holds of the lord to a certain merchant of Erhyth, the bailiff is required to seize all the aforesaid goods into the hand of the lord until etc. He then pays a fine of 2s. by pledge of the reeve.

From Stephen Plumbe, because he has exchanged his land with John le Porter without the lord's permission, 6d.: pledge, the reeve.

From John, son of Alan, because he pulled grass in the lord's corn, 3d. From Hugh, son of Alan, for the same thing, 3d. From little John, for the same thing, 6d. From Emma de Warboys, for the same thing, 6d.

From Richard le Porter, William Ode, John le Porter and Reginald, son of Reginald, for having badly ploughed the lord's land, a share; pledges, every man for the others.

Court Rolls of the Abbey of Ramsey and the Honour of Clare, pp. 242-243.

154

Registers of rural courts of justice are also to be found in French records, but they are much less frequent and of later date. The one which follows is dated 1371-1373. Note the payment in grain by several instalments for a plough horse.

527. Amy du Port has declared to Pierre le Cordinnier that by process of law he should confirm the sale of his house by the Great Charterhouse, or else he must withdraw from the deal and the said Pierre will have to restore what he had from him. The said Pierre has replied that he will not break the law.

528. This day Jehan le Mercier was sentenced to pay Jehan Chascevent 3 *sous* and 2 *deniers*, as wages for threshing in the barn and expenses, etc.

529. Perrin Jourdin, living at Ferroles, undertakes to pay 14 *setiers* of maslin, without barley or oats, to Jehan Roussel for the sale of a horse, leaving the sum of 17 *setiers* to pay, which he must pay 3 *mines* in measures of Villeneuve monthly: to begin with 3 *mines* a week from today, then 3 *mines* the following week and for the remainder 3 *mines* to be paid each month until the completion of the agreement.

530. On Tuesday the 15th day of February, Pasquier Bigot was forbidden in court to draw wine in his tavern out of the permitted hours under pain of a fine.

531. This day Jehan Ansel was placed in our safekeeping, and Simonet Ollive was notified of the arraignment. . . .

540. The fine incurred by Odin Cordier for the game of dice has been fixed at 40 *sous parisis* and the fine for his disobedience towards Foillet has been fixed at 40 *sous parisis* from all of which he has appealed to Monseigneur the abbot at the next assizes, those present being master Martin Double, G. de la***, P. le Maistre and others.

541. The fine incurred by Jeannin le Charron for having struck Jeannin le Picquart has been fixed at 20 *sous parisis*, against which he has appealed to the next assize in the presence of the aforementioned.

542. The fine incurred by Jean le Picquart for having contradicted Jeannin le Charron with bloody injuries has been fixed at 10 *sous parisis*, against which he has appealed, in the presence of the aforementioned.

543. The fine incurred by Guillemin de Gomez for the game of dice has been fixed at 40 *sous* of Tours.

544. The fine incurred by Thomas Bigot for the game of dice has been fixed at 40 *sous* of Tours.

> *Registre civil de la Seigneurie de Villeneuve-Saint-Georges (1371-1373),*
> L. Tanon (ed.) in *Nouvelle Revue Historique de*
> *Droit français et étranger,* 1886.

3. *Franchises*

155

This Rhineland deed is interesting from two aspects.

1. The deed lays down the personal status of the inhabitants of a manor and lightens it. The men pay light chevage, heriot and marriage taxes.

2. The system which German historians call Villikation *applies to this manor. A* Meyer *or 'farmer' (see Documents No. 175 and 176), chosen or elected from amongst the dependants, is charged with its management during the year, and with delivering to the monastery the farm which it owes. The* Meyer *is responsible for the 'pension' but the men of the manor must help him.*

(1207)

Bruno, abbot of Deutz by the grace of God, greeting in the Lord to all those to whom these letters shall come. Regarding certain men, serfs of our monastery and belonging to our manor of Rhade, it has been agreed between them and us with the council of the whole community of our men, and also of Count Everhard of Altena, advocate of this place, that these men and their descendants shall be liberated from this condition and shall enjoy the common right of the *cerocensuales*. Each one of them of both sexes, every year on Ascension Day, shall pay for his head twopence in Cologne money in the chapel of the said manor for the needs of the *Meyer*, but the rent and the whole service of this 'hall' shall not be lessened by the act of this covenant.

And if the position of *Meyer* of the manor should become vacant for any reason, the abbot of the monastery of Deutz shall name whoever he wishes as *Meyer*. And if he does not wish to name the *Meyer*, the aforesaid men holding property in this manor shall elect as *Meyer*, on the abbot's order, one of themselves, chosen for his means, zeal and faithfulness. This man shall be held to exercise the office of *Meyer* for a year and shall pay whatever rent had to be paid before our covenant. And if he refuses, he shall renounce the property which he holds in the manor, and the men shall elect once more from amongst themselves a worthy person.

Moreover, it has been decided that if one of them, of either sex, wishes to marry, he shall do so with a person of his own status, or else, if he does so with a person of different status, the latter shall take the status of the spouse, otherwise he and their offspring shall never come into possession of property dependent on the manor. It has been added and accepted by them that they may change status, but the right of the manor must not be lessened where it concerns the powers of the office of the *Meyer* or the renting of the *manses*. All these things, the aforesaid men have promised and accepted for themselves and for their successors. If they violate in any way the said covenant, they shall return to their old status. It was added for the security of the monastery, and under the aforesaid punishment, that if the *Meyer* says that he cannot pay the customary rent for some reason, the men holding property in the aforesaid manor shall lend him from their goods aid by which the *Meyer* may render the whole service in the expected time, or else they shall lawfully establish that he can fully serve without their aid. If a dispute arises amongst them about this, they must pay the travel and living expenses of the abbot of Deutz or of his envoy until they obtain satisfaction of the usual rent. In all these things the right of the abbot shall be safeguarded. From the forests which are called Camervorst and Sunder the men named above shall levy nothing, save 4s. The right of *cerocensuales* of which there is mention is this: none of the men may marry without the permission of the *Meyer*. When permission is obtained, he shall pay 6d. If he marries without permission, the *Meyer* shall obtain from him 5 *sous*. Furthermore, if the husband dies, he shall have the best of the four-footed animals and two deniers. If he has no animals, the *Meyer* shall receive two deniers and the best garment in use. If it is the wife who dies, the best garment she made with her own hands shall be assigned to the *Meyer* with two deniers.

This has been given in the year 1207 of the birth of Our Lord, the tenth of the convocation.

G. Franz, Deutsches Bauerntum, pp. 145-149.

156

The peasants of these villages near Paris purchased (and purchased dearly, for the sum paid is a measure either of their reserves of cash or their ability to borrow) their liberty, i.e. the abolition of the characteristic dues of servitude. Nevertheless they were personally to lose their freedom if they married one of the lord's dependants; this was how he protected the rights he still held over part of the peasant population in neighbouring localities. The danger of incest which their low legal status might force upon these men if they wished to avoid marrying outside their group, was one of the reasons invoked by the abbot for enfranchisement.

(1248)

To all those who shall see these present letters, William, abbot of St Denis in France and the convent of the said place, greetings in the Lord. We make known that which follows. Having regard to the danger which the souls of certain of our bondsmen run, as much by marriages contracted by them as by excommunications which bind and could in the future bind many of them (for it is not only the annual rent due by reason of their servitude towards us, it is also their own persons, which, are seen and may in the future be seen furtively removed from our church). Moreover having taken counsel of good men we have liberated and liberate by piety our bondsmen of the warren villages, that is, of Villeneuve, Gennevilliers, Asnières, Colombes, Courbevoie and Puteaux, labourers in these villages at the time of the grant of this liberty, with their wives and their heirs issued or to issue in the future from their bodies. We have delivered them in perpetuity from all the burdens of servitude by which they were formerly held to us, that is, from *formariage*, *chevage*, mortmain and all other kind of servitude by whatever name it shall be called, and we give them their liberty.

However, we do not hold them free of the respect and other duties which by reason of patronage the law demands of the liberated towards the authors of that liberation. Moreover, it shall be known that if one of these aforesaid men, after the liberty granted to them, marries a woman of our household, according to the ancient custom of that church he shall be judged to be subject to his wife's condition, notwithstanding the privilege of liberty granted. We preserve also over the individuals of both sexes the justice of every kind that we have over our other freed men, according them nevertheless exemption in the town of St Denis from all dues on wine sold in the cask, all collection of dues, and of river tolls only that which is customary to pay for the sale of eggs and cheese. This while they shall be labourers in the aforesaid warren villages, we meanwhile retaining the other river tolls (*tonlieux*) and customs of the town of St Denis, reserved and due by them, as the other freed men in our other villages pay us in the said town of St Denis. We desire, moreover, with their assent, that in the said villages of the warren we shall be paid dues on the retailing of wine (*forages*) by tavernkeepers, in such a way however that they shall not be held to pay more than 6 deniers per cask. On the other hand we have not granted the said liberty except to the aforesaid men, their wives and their heirs of both sexes, our other men and women being completely excluded.

It shall be known finally that the aforesaid men have given to us and to our church one thousand seven hundred Parisian *livres* for this liberty so as to buy our church revenue.

In witness of which, and for the memory of future times, we have given the present parchment confirmed by the force of our seals to these same men and their heirs.

Given the year of Our Lord 1248 in the month of November.

Thirteenth century copy; Archives Nationales, LL 1157, fol. 493
(transcribed by M. Bloch).

157

This franchise, granted only to those living in three localities and which forbade the transfer of the lord's lands to persons whom he could not exploit, such as nobles, priests or members of a free town, was accompanied by a reduction of customs. Note the importance of monopolies and their many applications: an obligation to buy wine for a certain sum, to grind, press and the monopoly of the wine harvest. The money aid imposed by the king on the lord was passed on to the peasants.

(February 1249)

To all those who shall see these letters, Brother Thomas, by the grace of God, humble minister of St Germain-des-Prés of Paris, and the whole community of the place, eternal greetings in God. We make known that our church was from immemorial time in peaceful possession of the right to levy mortmain, *formariage, taille à merci* every year on the men of Villeneuve St Georges, of Valenton and of Crosne, and on all the other labourers within the parish limits of these said villages. After diverse negotiations, the men of these said villages for their redemption and in order that they and their heirs should be henceforth liberated from the said mortmain, *formariage* and annual *taille à merci* had indeed wished to pay 1,400 Parisian livres, which we have been paid in full. It has been established between us of the one part and the men of the said villages of the other part that they may not do anything in common in these villages . . . without licence obtained from us or from our successors, nor belong to any free community as long as they live in these villages. Item, that they may not by gift, sale, exchange or otherwise, alienate the tenements situated in these villages in favour of any church or monastery, of any ecclesiastic (save if he is the descendant of a man of the village), of a free town or a member of a free town, nor of a knight. And if it should happen to one of them to enter a free town or if any part of a tenement situated in the territory of these villages passes by inheritance, legacy or otherwise into the possession of a member of a free town, they may not claim the privileged liberties and usages of the free town in connection with the burdens and usages of these tenements. Item, every adult man of these villages is bound at the request of us or of our prior of Villeneuve to help us and to defend personally like a good man defends his lord against the violences directed against our person or our property in the territory of these villages. . . . All this, the men have approved and have promised to keep in good faith; binding specially and perpetually themselves and their descendants. Save all rights and lordship of ourselves and our church in these villages and all other revenues, rents and customs.

These are the customs:

All the men of Villeneuve St Georges and of Valenton are bound to lead all their animals drawing a plough to work five days in the year on our lands; that is one day in the first ploughing, two in the second, one to cover the seed in autumn, and one in the march ploughing. Save the settlers of the abbey of St Maur and the enfeoffed men who are only bound for four days (one day at each ploughing) when they are required. Save the settlers of our community at Villeneuve who are not compelled to these services. At the first ploughing, at the second and at the covering of the seed in autumn, each plough receives two loaves at twopence and a quart of wine; in March our prior gives three-pence to the ploughmen of each plough. Item, we have at Villeneuve St Georges the monopoly (*ban*) for a month from Easter Day and during all that month we may sell in our house or elsewhere in one or more places in the village through our servants or by others, the wine which we wish and as much as we can. Each messuage is bound to take and receive one *setier* of wine, by the monopoly, up to the value of eight pence at least, and as long as our monopoly lasts none of our settlers may sell wine in the village. Item, all our settlers at Villeneuve St Georges and at Valenton must grind at our mill by the monopoly; all the men of Villeneuve must by the monopoly bake in our ovens, and pay a heaped bushel for five *mineaux* of corn through the whole year and the baking due. . . . Item, whoever holds for rent vines or land planted as vineyard, must take his vats and his wine harvest to our manor in the said villages of Villeneuve and Valenton, and deliver two *setiers* of must per *muid* as tithe, and the third of all the pressing; save for the vines of the press called Emery which owe as tithe only one *setier* per *muid* and the third of the pressing remaining, and save for the fief vines which only pay us one *setier* per *muid* for tithe. None may harvest grapes without permission from the prior. The day when the vines of our enclosure of Villeneuve shall be harvested, the said men shall cease to harvest all other vines. Every year at the wine harvest the men are bound . . . to [pay] us an annual rent of 75 *muids* of wine, a rent called 'good'. . . . Item, the men of Villeneuve St Georges shall provide sheets and a mattress for the abbot every time he shall sleep in the village and shall assure the maintenance of those of his household who shall pass the night in the village. Item, our settlers of Villeneuve, residing on the land of the late Odo Rigaud, knight, free of all monopoly at the mill, ovens and of wine, are compelled to pay an annual rent at St Denis of 24 *sous* for their messuage, with *chevage*. . . . The year when the lord king shall levy *sous* on us, we may levy on the men the sum which we shall fix in good faith in relation to our burden and our taxable land. They have consented that this sum . . . shall be assessed and levied by twelve men elected by the community of these villages who shall swear before us or our prior before marking the assize to do it in good faith without adding or lightening more than his due. . . . They shall bring the collected sum to our church two months after the sum required from these villages shall have been established and shall pay it fully. If any man does not play his part our prior shall be bound to send the sergeant to seize his property, and by this seizure constrain somebody to pay. . . .

We desire that the men named above shall enjoy these franchises and liberties, with their wives and their heirs who shall be in their guardianship at the moment of establishing these letters and those people, whatever their origin, at that time residing within the limits of the parishes of Villeneuve St Georges, Valenton and Crosne, and the natives of these parishes who are on journeys or in the service of others, but who have not yet contracted marriages elsewhere. . . .

Polyptyque de l'abbé Irminon (Guérard, ed.), Vol. II,
Appendices, pp. 383-387.

158

Liberating settlers and fixing services due from the manse *are accomplished here by collective purchase of seigneurial rights by the village community.*

(1268)

Conrad, Bishop by the grace of God, Gottschalf, Dean, and all the chapter of the church of Meissen, to all the faithful in Christ who shall see these present letters, greeting in the Lord. Let it be known to all that, by the common council of our chapter, we have sold all the property of our church at Mischwitz, save our allodial land, to the peasants of the village and to their heirs to possess for always by hereditary right, for forty marks of fine silver, this sum being devoted to the needs of our church. The said peasants and their heirs who are vulgarly called *Gast*, are henceforth liberated of this kind of servitude, but they shall each year be bound to me by the following services. To pay for each *manse* at Martinmas a rent of half a mark in money of Freiberg. Item, to feed one of us who shall then be lord of the said village three times a year, once after Easter, the second time after Michaelmas and the third time after Christmas, when he shall come to visit them. Item, three times a year to plough for each *manse*. At harvest time each *manse* shall work three days for us, one day to bind the sheaves, and two days to harvest with the scythe. Item, they must give us these services three times a year, at Easter 30 eggs from each *manse*, at Michaelmas two chickens from each *manse*; the same in Lent, two chickens from each *manse*.

Given the year of Our Lord 1268, the 6th of the nones of May.

G. Franz, *Deutsches Bauerntum*, pp. 201-203.

In the English countryside there were no collective charters of 'liberty', but individual grants of franchises were made to peasants who had become rich.

(1277)

To all the faithful of Christ to whom this writ shall come, Reginald by the grace of God, abbot of St Peter's Gloucester, greeting in the everlasting Lord.

Let it be known to all that we have manumitted and given freedom to Henry Bitele, our serf of Berton; desiring and granting, we and our successors, that the said Henry, with all his descendants, can freely come and go on our land, without impediment on our part or on that of our bailiffs, and to take his livestock from our land at his pleasure. Neither we, nor our successors, nor any one in our name may henceforth demand anything nor claim anything from him, from all his succession, or from his livestock by reason of servitude, and we shall be for ever wholly excluded from all rights over him, his inheritance and his property. Save for us an annual due of a pair of spurs to be paid at Easter for all service which belongs to us from the act of servitude.

Given at Gloucester in the octave of Trinity, the fifth year of the reign of Edward [I].

Historia et Cartularium Monasterii Sancti Petri Gloucestriae,
Vol. II, p. 265.

(1296)

Court of Brightwaltham holden on Wednesday next before the feast of St Margaret the virgin in the 24th year of King Edward. To this court came John Bolter and in full court confessed himself the born bondman of the lord abbot of Battle, and he gives his lord two marks of silver that he may freely depart from his lord's franchise without any claim of naifty[1] being made against his body at any time hereafter. Pledges of the said John with the said fine of two marks will be paid before Michaelmas next, Robert Osmund and Ralph Tailor.

Select Pleas in Manorial and other Seignorial Courts, F. W. Maitland (ed.),
Vol. I, 1189, p. 175.

4. Individual Wealth

161

There are very few opportunities to find out anything about peasant wealth, but here the property of two villagers of Champagne is valued in the accounts of a royal agent.

1. The official known as the estraière remits to the lord the property of bastards or strangers who died without heirs. In the first case the man was a vinegrower, husbandman and timber merchant, and he owned fairly valuable 'chattels', but it should be noted that he had no livestock. As the king's men had to harvest the grain and grapes, the accounts provide extremely valuable

[1] The action of naifty is that by which a lord reclaims a runaway bondman (*nativus*).

evidence about farming costs (harvesting and threshing absorbed 12 per cent of the value of the corn). The dead man held a field against rent in kind, but also possessed land in the form of an allod. This had been pledged to a Lombard, who sold it, but its value was not as much as the movables.

2. In the second case the abbot of Molesme was a partner in pariage with the king and together they owned a bondswoman, a domestic servant, who died without heir. The king levied heriot according to the custom of the region which entitled the lord to seize the dead woman's entire property. This consisted of grain, a little cash, a few sums owed by one or two debtors, and a small debt which she owed to her employer.

Inventory of the possessions of Walter Veluaut de Seiles, executed at Troyes, and compiled by the said Pierre, Nicholas de Voues, Michelet Gauchier, provost of this place, sire Martin de Seiles, Collin, his brother, Viart the labourer and others, on Sunday, feast day of the Holy Cross, in September. Chattels. Two tuns for trampling grapes; three empty casks for containing wine; three puncheons; two small vats; one bread-bin; two small old kneading-troughs; one bucket; one mortar; an old pan with no handle; two old feather beds; two old cushions; two old bed sheets; two hoes; about 40 pieces of timber; a round tub; an old bench; two trestles; 36 hanks of hemp for retting; a few faggots of vine-shoots and wood; a mound of wheat and a mound of barley in the barn of the said Walter, ready for threshing, about 6 *setiers* in all, honestly estimated, and as much wheat as barley; item, two cart-loads of wheat sheaves for threshing which were put in the barn of Jehan son of Sire Martin by the sergeant of Seiles at the request of Jehan d'Aigniey because they had grown on his land, which land the said Walter held on lease from the said Jehan for a crop of nine bushels of wheat and nine bushels of barley; item, a piece of land with growing hemp; item, the harvest from Walter's vines which yield an estimated four *muids* of wine.

The said corn for threshing contained in the inventory has been threshed by the hand of Sire Collin de Seiles, and the said Jehan d'Aigniey has paid him from the crops from his land, as contained in the said inventory, the king's share being 2¼ *setiers* of wheat, and three *mines* 1½ bushels of barley.

The grapes were gathered by the said Pierre and Viart the labourer of Seiles, and the king's share of the wine was 2½ *muids*.

Expenses and costs of the work mentioned above

First, to have the said corn reaped by the labourer, Raymond, son of Hehannet by Martin Vidaignel and by two women, the king's share, 8s.

To have it brought to town in Jehan Plasnel's cart and Perrin le Milleron's cart, the king's share, 22d.

To have it threshed by the hand of the said sire Collin, the king's share, 8s. 2d.

To have the hemp brought to town in Jehan Plasnel's cart and Perrin le Milleron's cart, the king's share, 5d.

To have the said grapes gathered, trampled and barrelled by the said Pierre and the labourer, and brought to town in Jehan d'Aigniey's cart and sire Collin's cart, for all this, the king's share, 3d.

For Jehan d'Aigniey's cart, which took the said wheat to Bar, the king's share, 2s.

Total of all these expenses on behalf of the king: 27s 11d.

Landed property nothing, since Testes the Lombard has sold it according to the custom of the fairs for 6 *li* which the said Walter owed him on a recognizance of the fairs.

Sale of the chattels listed above

First, all the chattels contained in the said inventory, except for the timber, the hemp to be gathered, the corn to be threshed and the grapes to be harvested, sold to Jehan d'Aigniey as *remasance* (residence due) on behalf of the king: 30s.

The hemp to be gathered sold to Mercant as *remasance*, the king's share of it 2s. 6d.

The timber sold to Jacquet le Bouchart, by auction, as *remasance*, on behalf of the king; 16s. 10d.

The 2¼ *setiers* of wheat, the king's share, sold in open market at Bar-sur-Seine, by the wife of Jehan d'Aigniey: 36s.

Monetary total from the sale of all the chattels of the said inventory, for the king's share, 7 *li* 9s. 5½d.

Total expenses for the king's share comes to 27s. 11d.

Monetary total of the value of confiscated property, with expenses subtracted, for the king's share, 6 *li* 18½d.

* * *

Fraiguignes, Inventory of the property in heriot of Anne, daughter of Biau Regart, of Poligny, living at Fraiguignes, bondswoman of the said partnership, made in the presence of Monseigneur Jehan de Marroles, Michelet Gaucher, provost of the partnership, Monseigneur Pierre, curé of Marroles, Jehan Marant de Vandes and others, on the Wednesday after Saint Vincent's day.

First, 14 bushels of wheat which Jehan Quarrez, with whom she lived, owed her, and one *setier* of barley, three *setiers* and 5 bushels of oats which the said Jehan owed her. All this sold to the said Jehan Quarré as *remasance*; the wheat at the price of 15d. the bushel, the *setier* of barley at the price of 12s., the oats at the price of 10s. the *setier*, all of which comes to 62s. 7½d.

Item, found in the purse of the said deceased in *esterlins* (sterling), in Parisian *doubles* and in money of Tours, 13s.

Item, 3s. 3d. which Estienne le Louvers owed her.

Item, 4s. which Perrars l'Ecorcier owed her.

Besides this she owed the said Jehan Quarré her master 6d.

Comptes Royaux, 1314-1328, Maillard & Fawtier (eds.),
Vol. I, Paris, 1961, pp. 492-495.

V XIV-XV Centuries

A. DEPOPULATION AND ITS EFFECTS

162

Number of hearths enumerated in the bailiwick of Puget-Théniers, in the Nice district.

	1297	1313	1315	1343	1364	
					Suffi-cient hearths to assess	Insuffi-cient hearths
Ascros	80	70	70	43	20	
Beuil		200	200			
Bairols	34	46	51	35		
Châteauneuf-d'Entraunes		64	64	38	26	28
Entraunes		147	147	66	50	21
Ilonse		109	119			
Isola		182	178			
Lieuche		42	42			
Malaussène	40	44	44		18	
Massoins (Bas-)	80	70	70		30	
Peone		75	75			
Pierlas		35	60			
Pierrefeu	20	25	25		9	
Puget-Théniers	280	249	247	195		
Rigaud		111	111	60		
Rimplas		41	41			
Roure		86	90			
Roubion		36	47			
Saint-Delmas-le-Selvage		129	154			
Saint-Étienne-de-Tinée		360	360			
Saint-Martin-d'Entraunes		120	122	58	28	6
Saint-Sauveur		68	68			
Sauze-et-la-Bastide		46	47		11	3
Thiéry		40	47			
Touet-de-Beuil	66	68	68	19	13	

	1297	1313	1315	1343	1364 Suffi-cient hearths to assess	Insuffi-cient hearths
Tournefort	28	27	34		18	
Villars-du-Var	110	129	134		38	
Villeneuve-d'Entraunes		64	64	42	17	3

After E. Baratier in *Provence Historique*, section 14, pp. 60-61.

163

Nicholas Campion was the sole survivor of a large family after the two plagues and he thus came into the possession of a very large group of holdings. It should be noted that he was able to obtain grants of parcels of woodland and moorland, and that in this Midland county uncultivated land was still being brought into use at the end of the fourteenth century.

(1392)

Nicholas Campioun holds hereditarily of the ancient blood Sokemanry of the manor after the death of John his father, a messuage and half a virgate and a quarter of land. And two acres and a half and one rood of land with appurtenances formerly belonging to John Michael, sokeman. Rendering each year 2s. 2¾d., suit of three men in three courts and a boon work with a stick, heriot, relief and other customary dues. Which tenement the said John had acquired with the permission of the abbot from the said John Michael.

Item Nicholas Campioun holds for himself and his heirs by a grant of the abbot given under the great seal to Alice, wife of Thomas Campioun and her heirs, a meadow in Westwode called Ruysschemedewe with two parcels of new land of two acres between the said meadow and the same road. Rendering each year for all services 12d.

Item he holds thirteen and a half acres and half a rood and three small pieces of waste at Wythybed. And half a rood at Schutehok. And half an acre and one rood in front of his door near the land of the Temple called le Mor. And at Flaggemor one acre of enclosure in Westwode by a charter of abbot John given to Thomas Campioun and his heirs. Rendering each year 7s. 9d. and two suits of the court for all services.

Item, he holds hereditarily six acres in Westwode of which five lie at Haytele and the sixth lies opposite [the land of] John Michael, by charter of Abbot John given to John Campioun and his heirs the fifteenth year of the reign of King Edward (1286-1287). Rendering every year 4s. for all services.

Item, he holds hereditarily one messuage with a curtilage which makes two cottages with appurtenances with four acres of land rendering each year 16d., suit of three men in three courts, heriot, relief, one boon-work with a stick, which tenements were formerly Richard Almayn's. The rents and services of these tenements were given by the said Richard Almayn to the abbot and his successors in perpetuity as is given in the court roll of the twelfth year of Edward, son of King Edward (1318-1319).

Item, he holds hereditarily one croft called Michelescroft rendering 12d. each year for all services.

Item, he holds hereditarily two and a half acres acquired from William Moys. Rendering 2½d. each year for all services.

Item, he holds hereditarily two acres of grazing in Westwode called Seriauntescroft, rendering 16d. each year for all services.

Item, he holds eight butts which count as one acre next to his messuage rendering 6d. each year acquired from the abbot.

Item, he holds one moor called Fyntesmor for one acre and two acres of land of the deceased Isolde Campioun rendering each year 4d.

Item, he holds one moor in exchange for an acre of his tenement and a portion of meadow in exchange for other land by charter of the time of Thomas Pype, abbot, as is contained in the charter.

Total of acres of waste that the said Nicholas holds, 24.

Total of his rent in money, 20s. 2¼d.

It should be remembered that John Campioun, father of the said Nicholas, had four sons: namely, John who died without heirs before the said John his father in the first pestilence and Thomas who had a son John which Thomas also died before his said father in the first pestilence leaving the said John his son alive in London who died, as it is reported, in the second plague without heirs of his body. He had a third son, the said Nicholas, who holds the aforesaid tenements, to whom his father left all the lands and tenements with appurtenances which he had in Flechamstede by charter . . . (1350). And it was discovered by the court that the said Nicholas had the said tenements as appears from the enquiry without permission of the lord against the custom of the manor and not by hereditary descent. Abbot Thomas then seized the tenements into his hand at the court held on the Thursday before the feast of St Barnabas the Apostle (1377) the first year of the reign of King Richard II after the conquest as tenements forfeited to him. And subsequently the second year of the reign of King Richard on the Thursday next before the feast of the Nativity of St John the Baptist in the same court the said Nicholas showed sufficiently before the abbot and his bailiffs that he had acquired the said tenements for himself and his heirs with the permission of the lord Abbot Robert after having paid a tax for a payment of a fixed fine. And thus by the decision of the said court, abbot Thomas caused them to be delivered to him to have and to hold according to the custom of the said manor. Therefore after the death of John, son of his brother, as heir of the said John, he holds the said tenements in the aforesaid form. John Campioun, the father of the said Nicholas, had also a fourth son Thomas who also died without heirs of his own in the first pestilence.

The Stoneleigh Leger Book,
R. H. Hilton (ed.), 1960, pp. 184-186.

Here depopulation led to liberation and lightening of seigneurial rights.

(1361)

We make known to all, now and hereafter, that the inhabitants of our town of Buxeaul in Burgundy have declared to us that they owe us tax, from all alike, and willingly, twice a year, that is, at Saint Rémy and at the beginning of Lent, and they owe us ploughing, certain *corvées* and other dues. It happens that the said inhabitants are for the most part diminished in numbers because of the plague caused by the massacre, which has occurred in parts of this area; for before this massacre, there were 50-60 households and more in the said town, while now there are no more than about 10. Nevertheless they have paid, and would like to pay, as large a tax as they did before the said massacre; which thing they could neither do nor support, but would have to flee and leave the place, and become poor beggars. They have thus humbly begged us to spare them these things, especially as through wars they have been pillaged and ruined by our enemies, in such a way that little or nothing remains to them, wherefore some of the said inhabitants have left the place and are still leaving from day to day. And thus those who have remained would not be able to pay the said taxes and other dues, unless they are spared by our favour. We, in consideration and regard to the above-mentioned things, and because the said town is much damaged, and a great part of its buildings ruined by inhabitants or beggars leaving them, and also so that those from the said place who have left on account of the heavy burden of the taxes and other above-mentioned dues, may return to live there, we, in our joyful accession in Burgundy, have granted and grant to the said inhabitants, for them, their heirs, and the succeeding inhabitants of the said town, in certain knowledge, full power and special favour, by these present, that the said 2 taxes, paid each year at the time of Saint-Rémy and the beginning of Lent, should be made into one tax, which will in future be paid at the time of Saint-Rémy only, and that the said inhabitants shall not be taxed except according to their means which they have or will have at the time they are taxed, and not in accordance with previous taxes if their means do not run to it. And moreover, in addition to our said favour, we have freed them and do free them forever, and their heirs and succeeding inhabitants of the said town, from the heriot we have over them and their possessions, in case of heriot of inheritance when it is due to us, by nevertheless paying the rents and dues that they owe us each year. We issue a mandate by these letters, to our castellan of Aisy, and to all the Justiciaries and officers of our Duchy of Burgundy, present and hereafter, or to their Lieutenants, and to each of those as it is fitting, which our present Ordinance, grant and favour accomplish and maintain: to allow and suffer the said inhabitants, their heirs and succeeding inhabitants henceforth to enjoy and use in peace these rights; and may the terms of our said Ordinance, favour and grant, not hinder, molest or constrain them; nor cause them to be hindered, molested or constrained in any way; but if anything be done to the contrary, they should report or cause it to be reported in a proper statement without any delay. And so this may be a firm and fixed thing for ever, we have had our seal appended to these letters. This was done in the said town of Buxeaul, the year of grace 1361, in the month of February.

Ordonnances des Rois de France de la troisième race, Secousse (ed.),
Vol. IV, Paris, 1734, pp. 402-403.

165

For more than twenty years a hamlet was completely depopulated and remained uncultivated. The lord had to wait for the rights of any possible owners or their heirs to be extinguished before granting the land anew.

(3rd February 1365)

Let it be known that the honourable lord official of Bordeaux has received the instance, supplication and request of the procuror and syndic of the honourable and discreet lords, dean and chapter of the Church of St Andrew of Bordeaux, who have reported the following facts. There were tenants who had, and held in fief, at the time they were living certain houses in the place called 'St Julian's', near Bordeaux, for which they were bound to pay annually certain rents, at certain times, contained and specified in the rolls and registers of St Andrew's church, and furthermore certain fines for recognition of transfer. The tenants are dead and none of their heirs nor any other person, to whom the houses belonged or ought to belong, has come or presented themselves before the lords, dean and chapter, have informed them of their rights, or paid the rents due for these properties, and this during the space of twenty years and more; and the houses have been reduced to – and are still – in the state of deserted and abandoned sites, to the great prejudice and damage of the said church and the lords of the chapter. And the latter have not known the heirs nor the property holders of these tenements, nor known if there were any or not.

And upon this, the procuror and syndic of the lords has prayed, required and supplicated the lord official of Bordeaux to be so good as to award the rents and the arrears of these sites, and this in order that the lords dean and chapter may dispose of them. The official has made proclamations, announcements and public and peremptory callings in the largest church and in the fifteen parochial chapels of Bordeaux, once, twice, thrice and a fourth time additionally, and after three defaults, announcing what follows: if any person or persons exist to whom these sites belong or ought to belong in whole or in part as heirs of the deceased, or who believe themselves to have a right to them through succession, purchase, infeodation, gift, obligation, mortgage, or for any other cause, let them come and appear, at the days and hours fixed by the said public proclamation before the lord official of Bordeaux, at the instance of the procuror and syndic above mentioned, to inform him of their rights, pay to the lords, dean and chapter the rents and relief, arrears, and other rights due for the sites and recognition of them; if not the lord official of Bordeaux will award these sites by default to the lords, dean and chapter and to their church, as being their lords of fief, will authorize them to dispose of them, and will impose a perpetual silence on these suits to the non-appearers despite their absence.

At the days and hours contained and set out in the public announcements, nobody has appeared except the procuror and syndic; and the lord official of Bordeaux has awarded these sites to the lords, dean and chapter and has given to them and drawn up licence and authority to dispose of them to the profit and utility of their church. All these clauses, at the same time as several others, I, the notary below named, have seen and read that they were fully contained in the public announcements given by the lord official on these questions, and especially in a memorandum of the last judgment by default, containing the award of the sites and the sentence, of which the date is as follows: given at Bordeaux, the Wednesday after the feast of the conversion of St Paul, 29th January of the year of Our Lord indicated below.

Thus, let it be known that the lords of the chapter of St Andrew's church at Bordeaux – the dean of the said church being absent – has given in fief feudally and by new title of fief, according to the tribunals and customs of the Bordeaux district, and to Arnold de Longueville, of the parish of St Eulalie of Bordeaux, and to Aliande, his wife, absent, all that piece of ground where there is a site and a half, which is outside the gate of St Julian. Arnold de Longueville has been invested by the honourable and discreet lord, Master Bertrand Bonaffos, canon of the said St Andrew's church, and the same Master Bertrand Bonaffos has feudally invested him against 5s. of the current money at Bordeaux as fine for recognition of transfer and 22s. 6d. of the said current money of Bordeaux of annual rent brought to Bordeaux the day of the feast of the Purification of Our Lady, the Virgin.

> R. Boutruche, *La crise d'une société. Seigneurs et paysans du Bordelais pendant la Guerre de Cent Ans*, Paris, 1947, pp. 524-527.

166-167

In spite of the intervention of authority, mortalities caused a rise in wages which continued in England right up to the end of the fourteenth century.

A. *The Statute of Corn, proclaimed in 1348 by the commune of Florence.*

The peasants and tillers of the soil, all those who by indigence work and cultivate the land for a wage and by the day, may not ask, demand or have a salary or wage higher than below mentioned, i.e. from the calends of November to the calends of February of each year, three sous and six deniers of small florin per day, or per task, providing themselves with all their expenses; from the calends of February to the calends of June, four sous of small florin per day or per task, providing themselves with all their expenses; from the calends of June to the calends of November they may not demand more than three sous of small florin per day or per task, under pain of one hundred sous each time for the contravener. And if the contravener cannot pay the fine he shall remain one month in the prison of the commune of Florence, and the punishment shall be executed thus. In this matter the oath of him who would have wished to perform the work or he who would have paid the price shall be held.

> *Statutum bladi reipublicae fiorentinae*
> (1348) (G. Masi, ed.), 1943, p. 182.

*   *   *

B. *Indices of wheat prices and money wages in England.*

Period	Index of wheat prices	Index of wages	Ratio of wages to prices
1320–1339	100	100	100
1340–1359	88	94	107
1360–1379	99	105	106
1380–1399	72	122	169
1400–1419	76	116	153
1420–1439	71	105	148
1440–1459	59	101	171
1460–1479	52	82	158

B. H. Slicher van Bath, *The Influence of Economic Conditions on the Development of Agricultural Tools and Machines in History*, in *Mechanization In Agriculture*, Meij (ed.), p. 23 (after data in M. Postan, 'Some Economic Evidence of Declining Population in the Later Middle Ages' in *Economic History Review*, 2nd ser., II, 1950).

168-169

The transfer in the modern era of vast areas of cultivated land into grazing has spread a blanket of turf over a large part of the English countryside in which the topographical features of pre-fourteenth-century agrarian life have been fossilized. Aerial photographs taken in a slanting light have revealed these remains and enable us to see the sites and structure of these 'lost villages'.

1. The existence of the manor of Grenstein in Norfolk is proved by documents dated 1250 and 1266, and its simple ground plan can be seen beneath the meadowland. Two roads encompass a central pasture shaped like an elongated triangle: close to the lower road lie several enclosures, and in two of them depressions can be distinguished which we may assume were the foundations of medieval buildings. Later all trace of this little community disappears, and it must have declined at an early period, before the end of the thirteenth century. Its territory was completely absorbed in to that of the neighbouring village. See Plate IX.

2. The decline of Cublington in Buckinghamshire did not begin until about the year 1300 and then gathered speed, aggravated perhaps by a sudden impoverishment of the arable soil. In 1283 the village contained at least 39 peasant households, who cultivated about 400 acres. A manorial inventory of 1304 records only 300 acres of arable, which was reduced to 160 acres in 1346. In 1341 an inquest conducted to assess a royal aid makes known that 'there are two carucates of land in the said parish of Cublington which lie fallow and uncultivated, and thirteen houses stand empty. Their tenants have gone away because of their poverty. Sheep

PLATE IX

Document 168
Grenstein. A Norfolk village deserted in the early fourteenth century

PLATE X

Document 169
Cublington. A village in Buckinghamshire, deserted soon after 1341 and later rebuilt
on a new site.

and lambs are few, and there is no one in the parish substantial enough to be taxed to the fifteenth'. It seems that the Black Death dealt this community a final blow, and it became completely deserted. Sixty years later the village was rebuilt a short distance away. See Plate X.

These two examples show that villages began to be deserted well before 1348.

Aerial photographs taken from M. W. Beresford & J. K. S. St. Joseph, *Medieval England. An Aerial Survey,* 1958, figs. 42A, p. 112, and 38B, p. 102.

170

In this district intersected by the Weser and the Diemel woodland encroached considerably between the end of the thirteenth century and approximately 1430, and the number of villages in the area covered by the two maps fell from 140 to 27. But this was at least partly a result of demographic concentration: at the end of the Middle Ages six urbanized areas can be seen where there were only two in the thirteenth century.

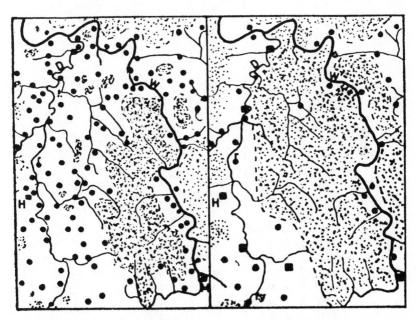

End of thirteenth century   About 1430

■ town
● village
⠿ woodland

From H. Jager, 'Die Ausdehnung der Wälder in Mitteleuropa über offenes Siedlungsland', in *Géographie et histoire agraires,* Nancy, 1959, p. 305.

B. MANORIAL FARMING

1. The Demesne

171

The periodical enumeration of draught animals maintained in the manorial stables at Houghton, a dependent manor of Ramsey Abbey, gives proof of the contraction of the cereal farming practised by the lords during the fourteenth and fifteenth centuries (horses were not used to draw the plough).

Year	Bullocks	Oxen	Horses	− Ploughs +	
1307	14	28	6		5 (2)
1319	16	3	6		2 (3)
1326	10	16	6		3 (2)
1336	7	21	5		3 (4)
1365	6	13	6		2 (3)
1369	6	14	5	(4)	3
1371	6	14	5	(4)	3
1372	6	13	6		2 (3)
1380	5	12	5		2 (1)
1383	4	9	5	(3)	2
1387	4	12	5		2
1388	5	16	6	(3)	3
1389	4	15	5		2 (3)
1392	5	10	6	(1)	2
1393	5	10	6	(1)	2
1395	4	10	5	(2)	2
1403	6	6	6	(4)	2
1404	4	4	6		1
1405	4	6	5		1 (2)
1406	4	6	5		1 (2)
1407	4	6	5		1 (2)
1410	4	6	5		1 (2)
1419	4	5	6		1 (2)
1445	0	0	12		
1449	0	0	12		
1450	0	0	12		
1451	0	0	12		
1453	0	0	12		
1454	0	0	12		
1460	0	0	4		

J. A. Raftis, *The Estates of Ramsey Abbey*, Toronto, 1957, p. 135.

In the manor of Wistow, also dependent on Ramsey Abbey, the decline in direct cultivation showed itself as a progressive reduction in the quantity of grain sown and harvested. We see that the reduction affected first of all oats, then wheat. The yield of both these two cereals fell in the fourteenth century. That of wheat, which was about 6:1 in the second half of the thirteenth century, fell to 3.3 in 1318 and 1325, then to 2.7 in 1346. The ratio of seed to oats, already very low in the mid-thirteenth century (2.7), had fallen almost to nothing one hundred years later. On the other hand sowings of barley increased (its yield was maintained above 7:1) and also of leguminous plants.

SEED

Year	Wheat	Barley	Oats	Legumi-nous	Mixture	Total
1247	38. 4	16	99	0	0	153. 4
1250	36. 4	14. 4	86. 4	3· 6	6. 5	147. 7
1252	37. 4	19	84	4. 4	7. 6	152. 6
1297	30	11	62. 4	10. 4	15. 4	129. 4
1298	34. 4	—	—	—	—	—
1307	32	19. 4	28. 4	10. 4	19. 4	110
1311	41. 4	32. 4	39	17	27	157
1315	31. 4	16	—	—	—	—
1318	41	15. 4	54. 4	18. 4	15. 4	145
1335	32	27	23	29	16	127
1346	37	18	7	34	13	109
1351	—	18	18	35	21	—
1352	39	18	7	34	13	109
1368	37	—	5	31	0	—
1379	17	31	3	39	0	90
1388	19	46	4	37	0	106
1389	19	44	4	36	0	103
1393	16	49	4	33	0	102
1394	18	40	4	25	0	87
1403	19	50	4	31	0	104
1419	7	—	0	30	0	—
1422	—	—	0	17	0	—
1423	5	60	0	30	0	95

Reckoned in quarters and bushels.

HARVEST

Year	Wheat	Barley	Oats	Legumi-nous	Mixture	Total
1247	236. 2	125	267. 6	0	0	656
1250	158	104	301	28	57	648
1252	220	133	264	17	0	634
1297	196	50	93	37	49	415
1298	—	—	—	—	—	—
1307	181	140	101	59	85	566
1311	211	91	68	47	72	489
1315	—	—	—	—	—	—
1318	137	66	90	61	52	406
1335	106	108	23	135	105	477
1346	91	121	8	147	84	451
1351	—	127	7	54	65	253?
1352	—	—	—	—	—	—
1368	—	227. 4	—	104. 2	0	332?
1379						
1388						
1389						
1393						
1394						
1403						
1419						
1422						
1423						

J. A. Raftis, *The Estates of Ramsey Abbey*, Toronto, 1957, p. 165.

173

These three parcels of land, taken from the demesne of a Cistercian grange, had been granted on perpetual rent a few years previously, in return for a money rent proportionate to the area. The lord repurchases his rights from the tenant, which he holds against a loan of cereals.

(1323)

To all those who shall see and hear these letters. . . . I, Philip, called li Sauraz. . . . John, called li Sauraz, my late father, had taken on perpetual rent or received on perpetual long lease from . . . Dom Peter, of good memory, abbot of la Ferté-sur-Grosne . . . and the whole community . . . two pieces of arable land, to wit the land or field vulgarly called 'Cham Calot' and 'dou Fraigne', situated in the territory of the grange of

St Nicolas, near the road which goes from this grange to St Gengoux of the one part, and the land held by Philip called Chival for Margaret, his wife, daughter of the late Lambelin du Bois, of the other part. . . . Item, near the field of Perreau Lambelin, clerk, of the one part, and the field of the said Philip Chival of the other. Item, one other parcel situated in the said territory in the place called 'ou Corcham', near the land of the said Perreau of the one part, and that of the said Philip Saurat of the other, each day-work of the said lands for 18 deniers in the current money of Burgundy, to pay on the Feast of the Annunciation . . . with the tithe of all the fruits. . . . I, the said Philip . . . considering that the renting of the said lands was of no profit to me, but rather injurious . . . and because the said monks have remitted nine *livres* of a debt of thirteen *li* 15s. of money of Tours which I owed them for the purchase of corn, I have abandoned to them the said renting or long lease, in all rights and action . . . on these lands . . . desiring and granting . . . that if settled letters shall be found between my father or any of my ancestors and the said monks concerned with this renting . . . they shall be null and without value. . . . Promising thus in addition not to have either alienated or engaged or placed under any servitude the said lands and the said property since the time of the above mentioned renting. . . . In faith of which, I, Philip, have requested that the seal of the court of Chalon shall be affixed on these letters and we, official of the court of Chalon . . . affix our seal, by Perreau Lambelin, Clerk, juror of our court, specially deputed by us for this, and in whom we place complete faith in these things and in others.

Given the year of Our Lord 1323, the Monday after the Feast of St Luke.

Arch. de Saône-et-Loire, H. 32 No. 44.

174

The lord had in this case attempted himself to exploit a vineyard formerly rented out against a proportionate share of the crop. He decides to give up direct management and lets out the vineyard again, but this time for a fixed money rent.

(20th December 1423)

Let it be known that the honourable and discreet lords, dean and chapter of the church of St Seurin of Bordeaux, hold and possess in their hands, in the name of their church, all that piece of waste vineyard which is in the Graves of Bordeaux, in the place called 'à Pradères', from which they have the custom of taking and gathering annually the quarter and the tithe of the fruit of the vine and the grape harvest.[1] And they have seen and taken note that it is of no profit or utility to them to hold in their hand this piece of vineyard, in view of the great cost and expense which they must enter into in order to work it annually.

This is why the honourable and discreet lords, canons of the church of St Seurin (the dean being, as is known to all, absent and outside the diocese of Bordeaux) assembled to hold their chapter, as is customary, within the sound of the bell in the refectory adjoining the cloisters of the church, and sitting there for them, for all the other absent

[1] When it was rented out.

lords of the chapter, and for all their successors, deliver feudally in fief, and by title of new fief, to Arnold Costau, dresser of vines of the parish of St Paul and burgess of Bordeaux, all this piece of waste vineyard against two deniers of the current money of Bordeaux (as a fine in recognition of the transfer, and five sous of the said money or annual rent to be paid each year on Christmas Day and to be brought, on the order of the rent clerk of the church, to the sanctuary of the church of St Seurin.

This piece of deserted vineyard, Arnold Costau has promised to till, and to perform there all the work and skill required by the Graves vines, following the tribunals and customs of the Bordeaux district.

R. Boutruche, *La crise d'une société.*
Seigneurs et paysans du Bordelais pendant la guerre de Cent Ans,
Paris, 1947, pp. 531-532.

175

The system of Villikation succeeded that of direct management. This was the grant of the whole manor, previously exploited by the lay brothers, to two Meyern or 'farmers', in return for a share in the crops and 'farm'.

(1324)

We, Otto, by the grace of God bishop of Hildesheim, to those present. The goodman Ernst, provost of the monastery of Escher, has up till now caused the manor of Edding-hausen to be cultivated by his lay brothers. The method being very disadvantageous and desiring, as a faithful administrator, the prosperity and greatest profit of his monastery, he has let the said manor, with the property belonging to it, to two *Meyern*, Dietrich Siberingh and Ludolf called Langheben, for three years to be counted from the next Chair of St Peter, before us and on the following conditions. The provost, in the name of the said monastery, shall levy each year the tithe of the fruits and the animals in the said manor and in its possessions. With this the said *Meyern* shall give to the monastery a third part of all the fruits of these possessions; furthermore each year, they shall deliver to the monastery for these possessions twelve pigs, each of half a *fertou*, item a mark of pure silver, 62 chickens, twelve geese, twenty *soixantaines* (1200) of sheep at Michaelmas. At the end of the three years, the said *Meyern* shall return the said manor with its possessions to the monastery, not in worse state than at present, but at least equal in value, or, if it can be arranged, rather improved. So that there is no doubt about this, we have given them in witness the said letter sealed with our seal.

Given the year of Our Lord 1324, 3rd of the ides of September.

G. Franz, *Deutsches Bauerntum*, pp. 239-240.

176

Here the Cistercian monastery of Bebenhausen in Swabia has divided its demesne between 'mayors' (the word Meyer means in this part of Germany 'farmer', see Documents No. 155 and

174) who deliver a part of the crop. This document fixes the ordinances of cultivation (Meyer-recht). *Note the limitation of leguminous plants.*

(1356)

It shall be noted that we have let our manors of Plieningen and possessions which belong to it on the following conditions.

At the harvest time we must give to each of them a servant, who can do the work of a wage earner, to supervise and gather our share, and they shall be bound to give him to eat and drink on working and feast days, and the above-mentioned 'mayors' must conduct the share of corn which comes to us from the village over a distance of one mile where it shall please us without any damage to us and at their own labour and expense. If the servant supervising our share does not work or cannot do the work of a wage earner, then we shall be bound to give him to eat and to drink.

It shall be noted that none of our 'mayors' may sow more than one arpent with vetches which shall be common between us and him. He who has fields for a whole plough may sow one arpent and not more; he who has fields for half a plough, half an arpent. . . .

G. Franz, Deutsches Bauerntum, pp. 259-260.

2. *Farming Contracts*

177

This is a lease for 'two lives' in place of a succession of very short-term grants. The old system had encouraged incumbents to exhaust the land by too intensive cultivation and this, together with the absence of investment, had lowered the lord's return.

(1332)

John, son of the illustrious king of England, earl of Cornwall, to all and singular who shall see or hear the present writing indented, greeting in the Lord. Know ye that, having regard to the no small decrease and decay of rents and farms pertaining to our manor of Kirton in Lindsey in times past, for that tenants of escheated tenements in the same manor, having no estate of the same tenements save from year to year or at least to the will of the lords, our predecessors there, have made no outlay or the least which they could on the maintenance of the buildings on the same tenements; and wishing to raise again the aforesaid rents and farms as much as we can have advantage; we have granted for us and our heirs and by our present writing have demised to John of Westminster, Emma his wife and Thomas their son, those two parts of all those tenements with the appurtenances in the town of Kirton aforesaid which the same John before the making of this writing held of us during our pleasure, as of an escheat formerly in our hand of the tenements which were sometime of Thomas of Bromholm; to have and to hold to the same John and Emma his wife and Thomas son of the same John and Emma, and which of them that lives the longer, for their whole life, of us and our heirs, rendering therefrom yearly to us and our heirs 100s. sterling at the feasts of Easter and Michaelmas by equal portions.

English Economic History, Select Documents,
Bland, Brown & Tawney (eds.), London (1914), p. 83.

178

Grant of a life lease.

(1397)

To all Christ's faithful to whom the present writing shall come, Morgan Gogh, greeting in the lord. Know ye that I have demised, granted and by this my present writing indented confirmed to John Druwere a cottage with a curtilage situate in Modbury between the cottage of John Janekyns on the east side and the tenement of Thomas Cobbe on the west side, and three acres, one rood of arable land lying in the fields of Modbury, whereof one acre lies in Brokeryg between the lord's land on either side, one acre in Totecombe between the lord's land and the land of William Cockes, a half acre there between the land of Thomas Cobbe and the land of Ralph Smale, and a half acre of meadow lies in Sturtilmede between the meadow of Gilbert Scolemaystre on either side, with pasture for one plough-beast and two draught beasts in common; which land, meadow and pasture John Pipere lately held for term of his life; to have and to hold of the aforesaid cottage with the curtilage, land, meadow, and pasture, to the aforesaid John for term of his life, of me and my heirs or my assigns freely, quietly, well and in peace, rendering therefore yearly to the aforesaid Morgan and his heirs or his assigns 3s. 4d. sterling at the four principal terms of the year by equal portions for all services, saving the royal service, and doing suit to my court yearly upon reasonable summons. ... Nor shall it be lawful for the aforesaid John to demise to any man the said cottage, with the curtilage, land, meadow and pasture, as well in parcels as in whole, during his life, under the penalty of loss of the aforesaid cottage with all its appurtenances. ...

English Economic History, Select Documents,
Bland, Brown & Tawney (eds.), p. 76.

179-180

A formulary, drawn up at Namur towards the end of the fourteenth century, transcribed as models a number of deeds regulating the relations of lords and peasants in the surrounding country-side. By one of these, a farmer who cultivated other land elsewhere took over a gagnage for twelve years on a share-cropping lease. The deed contains certain requirements concerning agricultural practice, particularly in connection with manuring.

The second contract grants the lease, for the same period of twelve years, of the whole of a manor belonging to a Cistercian monastery. The master lets the farm completely fitted out with cattle and equipment but keeps for himself the right of shelter (gîte) (see Document No. 139, p. 500). The area of the different courses of 'corn', 'spring sowing' and fallow, the number of ploughings (four on the ploughlands and two on the spring sowing), the stocking of the pond with fish, of great importance to the estate, were fixed in great detail.

(3rd May 1382)

To all those who will see and hear these present letters, we, Jehan de Ham and Margrite de Namur, his wife and faithful spouse, on the one hand, and Thiri, called Hanar, son of the former Evrard du Piroit from Rinez, near Namur, on the other hand, greetings and knowledge of the truth. We make known that we have made and do make, together and mutually, such agreements and accords as follow hereafter. This is to declare that we, the aforesaid Jehan and Margrite, have given and do give by these present letters, to the aforesaid Thiri Hanar, who takes and accepts it, cattle pasture and ox pasture which we have and hold in the said town of Rinez and in its territory, on half-share in the lease, for a term of 12 years to follow, beginning the day of the date of these present letters and ending on the same day when the 12 years are up, without deceit, so that the aforesaid Thiri should have and will have during the said lease so that he may maintain our said pasture, the profit and the income of our meadows which we have and hold at Rinez, at Centinez and in the territory, together with all our holding of Rinez, and the dwelling house, hall, meadows, hedged gardens, gardens and pasture lands, with nothing excluded save only that we should have half the revenue of the dovecote on condition that we provide each year to the said Hanar for feeding the doves 1 *muid* of fine corn called *drawe*. And we should receive from year to year during the said lease one quarter of seed at the beginning of Lent. And we should receive half the fruits which grow in the said holding which he should bring us from year to year at our house in Namur. And we should also receive in our said dwelling the profit to put to our share. He should have the first cut. And therewithal he should deliver our grain every year to our granary at Namur. The said Hanar should from year to year put 500 *walz*(?) of wood on our manor at his expense and cost, where there is the greatest need for it, without deceit. And if new buildings are needed, we have to deliver timber to him at Namur or near to the work, and he should transport it to our said dwelling without deceit, after which we must provide the workmen who do the construction, and pay their day-work, while the said Hanar should give them their eating expenses, without deceit. And therewithall, we should every year deliver to the said Hanar or else pay him a *muid* of spelt to our barn at Rinez, without deceit. The said Thiri Hanar found on his entry the corn sown at the most favourable time on the assarts, and the spring sown fields ('*maisage*') between Rinez and Le Chenoit. We have lent him half of the land sown with grain to put on one side for the last year, since he got nothing from the *maisage* because Jehan Vinchin, our previous husbandman, cultivated it and took half of it away. The said Hanar should, in the last year, receive half of the March grain, and we the other half. The said Hanar entered into our said holding at the beginning of May, the year of the birth of our Lord Jesus Christ 1378. He found all our lands at the most favourable moment, ordered in sovereign cultivation, and 2 *bonniers* ploughed by spring ploughing and he should leave them in such a condition at his departure, without deceit. And as the said Hanar possessed several lands, which he ploughed and worked, and wanted to plough together with ours, it was agreed that he should have the right to throw up fences made at our place around his land and ours, with a free conscience.

Moreover the said Hanar found on his entry a palisade in the courtyard with which he enclosed about half a *bonnier* of land, and he should leave as much on his departure, without being obliged to put it back into a proper state. The said Thiri Hanar should have, furthermore, all the revenue of our woods and all that is cut from our willows, poplars and birches, to warm him and to fence in meadows, lands and curtilages without deceit. We declare furthermore that we should every year at the time of harvest, put a watchman in our fields, at our expense, and the said Thiri Hanar should give him lodging and food. We have lent nothing else to the said Hanar beyond what is stated above and he has nothing to return to us in the last year. The aforesaid Hanar should, moreover, possess the revenue during the whole lease, without giving anything back to us, of all our lands and meadows which we have and hold in the territory of Saint-Denis near Bovech.

We promise and have made an agreement with the aforesaid Thiri Hanar, by obligation of us and all our possessions, that we will let him have in peace our said holding for the whole of our said lease, and our heirs and successors, without deceit. And I, the said Hanar, acknowledge that I have taken the holding from my said masters and that I should well and faithfully cultivate, manure and sow it, just as the other neighbours above and below me do theirs, without deceit. I have, on the other hand, undertaken for me and mine towards my co-contractors to keep the said lease. In witness of which, we, the afore named Jehan de Ham, for myself and my said wife, and the said Hanar, for his part, have put and appended our own seals to these present letters, which were made and given the day of the Holy Cross, in May, the year from the birth of Our Lord Jesus Christ 1382.

Formulaire namurois du XIVe Siècle,
introduced and edited by L. Genicot & J. Balon, Brussels (1955), pp. 79-81.

★ ★ ★

(*ca.* 1384)

To all those who will see and hear these present letters, greetings and knowledge of the truth. Be it known that the holy, venerable and prudent man, Monsieur the abbot and the monastery of Villier in Brabant, of the order of Cîteaux in the diocese of Liège, have given, in faithful rental to the ways and customs of the churches of Liège, their manor and all the houses of Ostin with all the appertaining lands, meadows, woods, fish pools, hedgerows and pastures, to T., for 12 consecutive years, beginning on St John the Baptist's Day in the year 1383 and ending on the same day at the close of the said 12 years, according to the conditions and agreements which follow hereafter; for the which rent the said T. will give, and has agreed to give, to the said monks every year 100 florins, 2 old *écus* reckoned as 4 florins of good quality gold and of proper weight, or the equivalent in money, half to be paid between Christmas and Candlemas, and the other half on St John the Baptist's Day, on condition that 10 florins are deducted from the first payment, and that for these 10 florins he must maintain the buildings. And we make known that the said T. should prune the woods of the said holding once within the period of 12 years, that is, each time that the copse shall be 12 years old, and for the older trees he has nothing to do. And he can prune the hedgerows once and no more within the said term, each year a 12th part. And he should not prune woods or hedgerows nor any tree more than 12 years old in any other place on the said property, but if there is a dead one he may cut it down, and replant 2 green trees of the same kind as the dead one, in the same place. And the said T. should immediately restore and re-dig the ditches of the woods and hedgerows he prunes or has pruned, well and sufficiently so that neither his, nor others', animals do any damage to them. And the said T. should not let his animals roam among copses that are not 6 years old or more. And the said T., within the duration of the lease should maintain and has agreed to maintain the roofs of the houses in the said courtyard with pitch, straw and anything else that is needed, without deceit. And if much timber is needed, the monks of Villier will give it to him from their nearest wood and the said T. will take it and have it put to use at his expense and cost. And in such a way he should leave and deliver it on his departure. Furthermore, the said T. should maintain and endure military duties, tempest, riding services, all expenses and costs, and any other accident which could befall the holding without any deduction to be made from the said monks, no matter what may happen. Furthermore, the said T. is subject to the right of shelter towards the order, and must receive Monseigneur the abbot of Villier and his company, as is required of a good and honest tenant, once a year or twice if it pleases the abbot to come, and without any deduction, and also receive the monks, lay-brothers and persons of the household of Villier whenever they should chance to come by, with such fare as they find there. Furthermore we make known that the said monks of Villiers have furnished the said T. with animals, carts and harness to the value of 275 and a half *moutons* (gold coins), 3 francs counting as 4 *moutons*. Furthermore the said monks have lent the said T., on his entry, the same quantity to be given back at his departure, without valuation, the whole building of the said holding that is, first etc. Then we make known that the said T. cannot nor should not sub-let the said holding nor the possessions belonging to the said property, in whole or in part, nor put it in other hands if it is not by the will and consent of the monks of Villier. And he must leave on his departure all the meadows of the said holding, intact, without his or others' animals having pastured on them, and unscythed except for 5 day-works of meadow. Furthermore the said monks may, if they like, employ a sower, in the last year, to sow all the arable and border lands, and the said Louis should well and faithfully deliver grain to them, with sieve, winnow and flail at their leisure, without any deduction. And within the lease the said T. should plough the lands well and faithfully and the fallow with 4 crop rotations and the marshland with 2 rotations, and the fallow well cut and reduced, always at the right time and season. And the said T., in the last year, should leave at his departure 40 *bonniers* of sown corn, ploughed on 4 rotations at the right time and season, and 30 *bonniers* of corn ploughed on 5 rotations; item, 40 *bonniers* of marshland well ploughed on 2 rotations and 40 *bonniers* on 1 rotation; item, he should leave 80 *bonniers* of fallow well ploughed at the right time and season, of which there will be 12 *bonniers* to be cut again; item, he must leave the beet, sown as he found it. And the said T. must not change the use of the lands, nor sell or give away any straw. And he must bring everything that grows on the lands of the said holding into the barn on the holding and then pasture his animals there and not elsewhere, and perform the work necessary and enclosures, and lead them from time to time on the lands of the said holding for a moment and at his departure all the fences should be brought back to the said lands. Furthermore the said T. must raise dues, rents and tithe owed by the said holding on the income of the said holding, without making any deduction to the said owners of the said rent-paying holding, whether in dues, rents, tithes or in any manner whatsoever. Furthermore the said T. should at his departure leave the fish pool of the said holding restocked, firstly, with 450 year-old fish, item, with 4,000 roach, 600 perch or thereabouts, and with 2 female carp, at the right time and season, and in the presence of the said monks or their representative, and not otherwise. And all the said restocking should be suitably checked by a fisherman, without deceit. Furthermore the said T. should leave at his departure 26 *setiers* of peas sown on 2 rotations, 1 *muid* of large barley on 3 rotations, and 2 *muids* of barley on 2 rotations. And if the said T. or his successors should at any future time fail to pay and fulfil the payments and the above-mentioned agreements, in whole or in part, the said monks can take as a pledge what is contained in certain letters and their said holding peaceably, at whatever time and occasion, and all the possessions found within and without the said holding, and they can handle the said possessions and pledge according to their will and advantage, without argument, until payment in full. And if he has taken anything from the said holding, the said monks may pursue him under any lord as their serf, at his expense and cost, without him being able to deduct anything from what he may owe them, and may give to whatever lord they require to constrain him to meet his obligations, a gift of 2 *livres* in old weight. And if there are costs or damages to pay for neglecting any of the aforesaid agreements, they must cause them to be paid to the said T., with no reduction from the main sum, and they are believed on their word alone. And the said T. renounces, without deceit, during the period of the lease all franchises, agreements, burgess rights, and other rights and privileges in general and in particular which could permit him to contravene the above-mentioned agreements and harm or distress the said monks. And the said parties have agreed and accepted to all these above-mentioned agreements, and have agreed to keep and maintain them mutually, not departing therefrom. In witness of which things, we etc. . . .

Formulaire namurois du XIVe siècle, pp. 311–313.

181

In this métayage *contract drawn up in a village of Upper Provence, the lessor undertakes to share half the expenses of the different agricultural tasks which necessitate the recruitment of paid workers. It proves that small cultivators themselves employed day labourers.*

ca. 1330

. . . To Raymond Béraud, of the said place, present and receiving these things for the next six years or for four seasons. For which *facherie* of the said lands, the said Raymond has promised and agreed for himself and his, to give and deliver to the said William or to his, half of all the corn, the straw remaining for the plough-oxen, and to plough well and loyally these lands and to sow them at the desired time. It has been established between these parties aforesaid that the said William must place at the services of the said lands every year the half share, and perform half of the weeding, the cutting, the harvest and the treading out of the said corn. Given at Cipierres in the first chamber of the Court.

Archives des Bouches-du-Rhône, 396 E 17, fo. 86.

182–183

Here are two Italian contracts of mezzadria. *In the second the cultivator employs paid workers, and the two plough oxen represent considerable capital.*

(2nd September 1342)

In the name of God, Amen. Bernardo, son of the late Vannello Asquini, citizen of Lucca, of the quarter of SS Simon and Jude, has let and granted to Dino of the late Collucio, called Ortica, of the commune of Capella San Bartolomeo, of the parish of Massa Pisana, a piece of land with vines, with a house with an attic with olive and fig and other fruit trees, and with a 'hall' and a well, situated in the confines of the territory of the said commune of San Bartolomeo . . . at the place called 'by the chestnut trees' bounded on one side by the land of Lemmo de Portico of Lucca, on the other by the land and house of Bartolomeo, son of the late Ugolino, of the late Master Bartolomeo of Lucca, on the other by the public way and on the other by the land of the Asquini sons. Item another piece of land partly olive grove, partly woodland, situated within the confines and the territory of the commune San Giovanni de Scheto, in the same parish, bounded on the one side by the land of the Asquini sons, on the other by the land of Pietro Paganelli of Lucca, on the other side by the working land of San Giovanni Maggiore of Lucca, on the other by the land of the monastery of San Giorgio of Lucca, on the other by the public way, and the place 'by the quarry' or 'by the chestnut trees'. Item, he has let and granted to the said Dino, with the said lands, the following equipment: a jar containing about 104 *setiers* of wine, a cask containing about 36 *setiers* of wine, a small jar containing about 12 *setiers* of wine, a wicker basket containing about 24 *setiers* of corn, all of which are in the said house. For these lands and pieces of land to plough well, to improve and not wittingly to allow to deteriorate, and these things and equipment to use in good faith without their deteriorating, after the next calends of October, for the next ten years.

And the said Dino, cultivator, has promised in exchange faithfully to plough, manure and sow the said pieces of land which are arable, at the desired time and at his expense. To plough, hoe, dress and tie that which is vineyard, while providing expense, labour, ties, props and to renew and layer this vineyard every time it shall be useful. To keep the hedges and ditches in good condition. Not to cut the chestnut, olive and fruit trees without the permission of Bernardo, the lessor or his heirs. . . . To harvest the corn, gather and press the grapes, pick the olives, chestnuts and fruit at the desired time. To give, deliver and carry the half of all these fruits, corn, wine, oil, chestnuts, figs and other fruits of the said lands . . . in good faith and at his expense to the said Bernardo and his heirs. . . . And to resign the said things and equipment in the said house, in the state in which they were to the said Bernardo and his heirs at the end of the aforementioned term.

I. Imberciadori, *Mezzadria classica toscana*
con documentazione inedita dal IX al XIV sec.,
Florence, 1951, pp. 137-138.

★　　★　　★

In the name of God, Amen, of the 18th of November 1384.

Let it be manifest to whoever shall read this writ that I Recho di Mugnaio have granted to Andrea di Braccio my property of Poggio, with all its possessions and confines, situated in the parish of Santo Cervagio at Pelagho, with the vineyards and all the pieces of land which belong to this farm. With this covenant: I, Recho, must put half of all the seed which shall be sown on the said property, and Andrea the other half. And he must give me half of that which is harvested on the said property, corn, oats, oil and wine. The said Andrea must keep two pigs on the said property, and he must pay half their pannage, and I, Recho, the other. And he must give me half the meat. The said Andrea must also put two workers each year in the vineyard of Recho. And I, Recho di Mugnaio, must lend him for the oxen fifteen gold florins and the said Andrea must keep a pair of oxen at his expense and for all injury, from which God protect him, and for all the cultivation. And we desire that the concession shall be made for the four years to come. And the said Andrea must give me each year a pair of good capons and ten dozen eggs. And the said Andrea must still make oil from the olives which shall be on the said farm.

D. Catellacci, *Tre Scritte di mezzeria in volgare*
del secolo decimo quarto, in Archivio storico Italiano, 1893.

184

This fragment of an account kept by a Florentine citizen shows that to be master of a méta-*yage necessitated very close supervision over the farmer and active participation in management.*

The farm of Macia Lunga, To have:

. . . On the 10th June 1410 for two and a half jars of oil which come to me for our share, to wit two jars which we have had of the crop and which Chele has sent me, and half a jar of profit which he sent me for the press. The jar is worth 5 lire 10 sous. In all 13 lire 15 sous.

On 16 July Chele sent me for our share from the crop 14½ bushels of corn, the bushel was then worth 25 sous; in all 18 lire 15 sous.

And then, that which I have had from him in restitution of the things which he took from me so often. To wit, my share of a pig which he sold without telling me, and which was for half shares, and the reeds which he sold for two years and the wood which he sold without telling me. Furthermore, for the grain: he did not sow his share for two years, which went for half shares, and he did not sow what I gave him for my share, or hardly. And furthermore, for the share of a pig he kept: my share was not sent.

Then, for the acorns harvested which were given to the pig and sheep kept by him and nothing to me. And afterwards, for the straw which he carried off to his house. And in addition, for two pieces of plough timber which he took from me, and a trunk of a nut tree of three spans. Further, for many stakes which he made at home, and then sold to others. Further, for many stakes which he carried away and which he bought at Cerracchio. And then for the beans which he sowed and which he ate and harvested without giving me any. Then, for much of my iron which he took away from the house. And then, as reparation for the grain which he stole from me when he harvested and hid the sheaves in the wood, here and there, and we found it in various places, as Fruosino di Donato and Monna Nanna, his wife, who I found going by the wood pasturing his oxen saw him. There was also the sister of Agnolo di Nanni di Castruccio. We were aware the first time that Chele and Monna Bella, his wife and all his family came there late one night; and Martino and Andrea, who went by the fields, saw them leaving that place and, they calling me, we caught them; and then suspecting a greater injury we searched and we found it hidden there in several different places. Realizing this wickedness, I chased him. Wishing to bring me to reason, he begged ser Payolo, our priest, Lolo and Marcoccio, and other neighbours, after having heard more of this wickedness, to be so kind as to arrange the matter. About all of which in the end I satisfied myself, and, after much talking, they learnt from the same Chele, how he has taken all the things aforementioned, of which things he made restitution to me. And I gave him his half share of the crops which was seven bushels three quarters, and the value of the grain rose to 31 sous for this quality. Thus this made in all 12 *li* 3d. I have made this memorandum in order to have always in mind what this rogue Chele did to me, and also his family, me who treated him like a brother or a father. I have in all 12 *li* 3d.

185

This métayage *contract from the region of Toulouse was possibly combined with a* gasaille *(livestock lease). Notice the requirement to grow woad and the attention devoted to manure which was economized, divided into equal shares and concentrated on a very small portion of the cultivated ground.*

(29th April 1430)

Item ... Peter Bernard and Bernard Bernard, brothers, inhabitants of Gardube ... both together ... have accepted to hold in *gasaille* ... of the noble lady, dame Humberte de Gavaret, co-dame of Gardube ... all the *borde* situated in the appurtenances of Gardube, in the place called 'à Laval' with all its buildings, lands, fields, meadows and other possessions belonging to the said *métairie*. Item, one vineyard which she says she has in the said appurtenances in the said place 'à Laval' and the lands which belonged to Peter Cabosse of the said Gardube, in the place called 'al Gavelli', containing six *sétérées* of land or thereabouts, bounded on the North by the cart-track, on the south by John de Lontar, with all their rights, ways in and out, etc., to have them from the present day for the next four harvests for which time the said noble lady Humberte has promised to be a good guarantor etc. .... under mortgage and obligation of all her goods etc. **And** the said share-cropping brothers have promised to plough and cultivate the said lands and to deliver from it to the said lady a quarter of the fruits on the threshing floor where they have been trodden out. Furthermore the said share-croppers have promised to dig and hoe the said vineyard at the required time and to give to the said lady a quarter of the wine harvest, carried to Gardube to the house of the said noble lady. Item, it has been agreed that the said share-croppers may each year during this time take for themselves the hay of the meadows belonging to the said *borde*, except from the meadow in the place called 'a las Correias', bounded on the north by Hugh de Feron, of St Roman, and a parcel in the place called 'a la Perge'. Item, it has been agreed that the said share-croppers must pay to the said noble lady at Christmas six hens every year during this time, and at Pentecost six chickens every year during this time. Item, the two parties have agreed that each party, the said lady as well as the said share-croppers, must devote to the repair of the embankments of the said possessions eight days each. Item, it has been agreed that the said share-croppers must at the end of the term replace in the said lands 17 *sétérées*, properly ploughed, in which corn may be sown, or else give to the said lady ten livres of Tours in the case where they do not wish to plough the said 17 *sétérées*, at the choice of the said share-croppers, and they must say so at the last All Saints Day in the aforesaid term.

Item, it has been agreed that the said share-croppers may take the wood of the said *borde* and use it for their heating, during the term. Item, it has been agreed between the parties that the said share-croppers must give to the said lady half of all the nuts from the nut-trees of the farm in the case where the said share-croppers crack the said nuts, otherwise the lady shall take the nuts for herself. Item, it has been agreed that at the end of the term the said share-croppers must render the *borde* empty and the key, etc. .... The said share-croppers must manure one *éminée* of land for their profit, and another for the profit of the lady, and put the rest of the manure on the lands of the said *borde*. Item, the said share-croppers must cultivate one *sétérée* of land and sow there woad and render to the said lady a quarter of the husks of the woad. Item, it has been agreed that in the case where the said share-croppers wish to keep animals on their own account on the said *borde*, they may do so, but must keep in the same way animals belonging to the said lady on *gasaille*, for half the profit and half the loss. These rules each party has promised to keep in the aforementioned form under mortgage and obligation of all their possessions, etc. They have wholly renounced and have wished to be constrained in all rigour without arrest of their person. They have made the notaries ordinary procurers and have sworn. Witnesses: noble Stephen of Castillon, messire Stephen Truchand, priest, Peter Charbonnier and John de Vaure, of Gardube.

> G. Sicard, *Le métayage dans le Midi toulousain, à la fin du Moyen Age*,
> in *Memoires de l'Académie de législation*, II, Toulouse (1958), p. 88.

186

The partnership of métayage *on this estate in Sologne lays down the costs of farming, not only for the wages of the harvesters and threshers, but also for the renewal of the tools, particularly 'ironmongery'. Apart from the common contributions, the lessor places the large and small livestock on a livestock lease, for the cultivators took sheep belonging to third parties in* 'gasaille'. *It should also be noticed that the food provided for the harvesters is not so plentiful as in the stipulations of some thirteenth-century documents.*

(1468)

The nobleman Jehan de Voisines, squire, lord of Voisines, who, etc. . . . has acknowledged, etc. . . . truly, rented and given in *métayage*, by name and title of annual rent, to Martin, Avonnet and Pierre, his children, present and accepting, who have taken, received and retained from the said squire the place, the manor of Poillevillain, located and situated in the parish of the said Nançay, for the term of 5 consecutive years, to be reckoned and to begin from the last All Saints Day 1468 and finishing on the said day 1473. This is to make known that all corn, large and small, will belong to and remain with the said squire and the said *métayers*, each receiving half; the pigs will also be shared. Item, the harvests will be divided in half and the threshing will be shared, that is, they will provide half the reapers and threshers. Item, the carts, ploughs, forks, harrows, yokes and straps will all be paid for by half shares; and all ironware by half share. Item, the said *métayers* will mow the meadows of the said farm at their expense, and the said squire will give them the sum of half an *écu* each year. Item, the said squire, lessor, will be obliged to hand over half the seed, and the said *métayers* will be obliged to give to the reapers cheese and butter and to provide them with it during the harvesting. Item, the said *métayers* will take wood to warm themselves from wherever the said squire shall show them. Item, the said squire leaves to the said *métayers* all the meadows appertaining to the said place, except for the meadows of Collonnet and the meadow of La Fontaine, and the said *métayers* will take a cartload of hay into the middle of the said squire's meadows to feed the lambs.

Item, the said farmers will, on the appointed day, leave the hay and straw enclosed in the barn, and all the bales will remain with the said squire at the end of the said term.

Item, it has been said and agreed between the said parties that if the said squire wants to dismiss the said *métayers* within 2 years from the said *métairie*, he will let them know at the next St John's Day, and also if the said *métayers* want to leave the said *métairie* within the said 2 years, they will let the squire know at the said term of the next St John's Day. Item, the said farmers have brought to the said farm 4 oxen, and the said squire gives them 4 more, to match them, and 2 bulls, and the said squire gives them 2 more, to match them, and 2 cows against 2 more cows. Item, 14 head of horned cattle, that is, 1 ox, 6 cows and the rest heifers and calves, which the said squire has given to the said farmers so that he can take the income for the sum of 18½ francs. Item, the said *métayers* have brought to the said *métairie* 35 head of sheep, and the said squire gives them as much again, half of which will belong to the said squire and half to the said *métayers*. Item, the said farmers acknowledge they hold '*à cras et chatel*'[1] from the said squire 140 head of sheep. Item, 80 head of sheep which the said *métayers* hold from Brossart d'Aubigny, in which the said squire of Voisines will have

[1] A farming term; where the income in kind belongs to the farmer who pays the owner in money. The word 'cras' means a percentage; in this case the 'majority', i.e. half and a little more.

no share; and the said squire keeps 80 of his sheep and lambs in which the said *métayers* have no share; and if the *métayers* cannot provide the said sheep and lambs, he will take the income up to the total amount of the 80 head of sheep, and if the said ewes bear lambs, the said *métayers* will have no share in them.

For thus, etc. . . . Promising, etc. . . . Obliging, etc. . . . Renouncing, etc. . . .

I. Guérin, *La vie rurale en Sologne aux XIVe et XVe siècles,*
Paris, 1960, pp. 309-310.

C. PEASANT BONDAGE

187

Gift of a bondman.

(1358)

To all who shall see or hear this writing, Geoffrey, by divine permission abbot of Selby, and the convent of the same place, greeting in the Lord. Know ye that we, with the unanimous consent of our chapter, have given, granted and by this our present charter confirmed to John de Petreburgh, John son of William de Stormsworth, our bondman, with all his brood and chattels, so that the aforesaid John with his brood and all his chattels, as is aforesaid, remain, henceforth for ever, in respect of us and our successors, free, and quit of all bond of serfdom, so that neither we nor our successors nor any man in our name shall be able henceforth to demand, claim or have any right or claim or any action in the aforesaid John, his brood or his chattels, by reason of serfdom, villeinage, or bondage. . . .

English Economic History, Select Documents,
Bland, Brown & Tawney (eds.), 1914, p. 98.

188

The bodily dependence of which these two brothers made avowal entailed an obligation to reside in a certain place and to pay the master an arbitrary tallage.

(23rd June 1343)

Let it be known that Peter Desclaus the elder and Peter Desclaus the younger, full brothers of the parish of la Tresne in Entre-Deux-Mers, and sons of the late John Desclaus, of the parish of la Tresne in Entre-Deux-Mers, under no force or constraint, but of their own good will and in full knowledge of the case, as they have said and admitted in the presence of me, notary public, and of the witnesses below inscribed – for them and for all their heirs in direct line, in perpetuity – have admitted and confessed that they all, and each of them, were and ought to be men subject to *taille* at the

will of the honourable and holy lords abbot and the convent of the monastery of St
Croix of Bordeaux and their successors, for that which follows: their bodies, their
goods and all that third of 'manse', with the lands and vineyards which it encloses,
which they have and hold of the lords abbot and convent of the monastery of St Croix
of Bordeaux, in hommage and tallage, situated in the parish of la Tresne, at the place
called 'au Claus' between the common way on one side and the fief of the lady Joan of
Pardaillan, wife of the noble messire Gaillard de Grésignac, knight, deceased, on the
other side and at both ends.

Peter and Peter Desclaus, brothers, have desired and drawn up, for themselves,
for all their heirs and for all theirs having rights, that the lords abbot and convent of
the said monastery, and their successors, may demand *taille* from them each year at
their mercy, and demand of them and their heirs descending from their body for all
time in perpetuity and from all their goods and things, all their own will following
the manner in which all lords may require *taille* from their men subject to *taille* at
will according to the tribunals and customs of the Bordeaux region.

Furthermore, if it should happen that the same Peter and Peter Desclaus, their heirs,
theirs having rights and the heirs of heirs descending from them in direct line, in
perpetuity, wish to depart and leave the third of 'manse' and the other things above-
mentioned, and go to settle and live in another place: city, town, castle, new or old
bastide, within or outside a sanctuary, or elsewhere, wherever it is or could be, Peter
and Peter Desclaus have desired that the same lords abbot and convent of the monastery, for themselves and for their successors, may take them.

And they have required the lord, the bailiff or their lieutenants of authority or
lordship where they themselves shall be, to take them, bail them and deliver them to
the lord abbot and convent men like their subject to *taille* at will. . . .

R. Boutruche, *La crise d'une société.*
Seigneurs et paysans du Bordelais pendant la guerre de Cent Ans,
Paris, 1947, pp. 457-458.

189

*These Lancashire peasants who take up villein lands on short-term lease accept for the
duration of the grant the imposition of specific dues of personal bondage such as heriot or
'leyrewite'.*

(1386)

Warkington. At the view of the frank pledge holden there on 20th October, 10
Richard II, it was granted to all the lord's tenants in the presence of John Mulso,
Nicolas Lovet, Edmund Bifeld, Stephen Walker of Keteryng and others there
present, that after it pleased the lord they might hold certain bond lands and tenements at a certain rent and service, as follows, during a term of six years next after
the date above written, the term beginning at Michaelmas last past; to wit, that each
tenant of a messuage and a virgate of bond land shall render to the lord 18s. yearly at
four terms, to wit, at the feasts of St Edmund the King and Martyr, Palm Sunday,

the Nativity of St John the Baptist, and Michaelmas, of equal portions, and shall do two ploughings a year at what times of the year he shall be forewarned by the bailiff of the manor for the time being, and shall work in 'le keormode' as he used before, save that the lord shall find him food and drink for the ancient customs, that is for half a sheep and for each scythe ½d. and so he shall reap in autumn for two days, to wit, one day with two men and another day with one man, at the lord's dinner[1]; he shall give 4d. for a colt if he sell it, he shall pay heriot if he die within the term, and he shall make fine for marrying his daughters and for his sons attending school, and for 'leyrewite' as he used before.

English Economic History, Select Documents,
Bland, Brown & Tawney (eds.), 1914, p. 84.

D. THE CONTRIBUTION OF URBAN CAPITAL AND THE MOVEMENT OF EXCHANGE

190

Rural property of the inhabitants of one of the quarters of Toulouse in 1335 (taken from tax registers containing 'estimates' of their wealth). See pp. 547, 548 and 549.

191

A contract of partnership for livestock rearing concluded between a citizen of Genoa and a farmer in the neighbourhood.

The 28th April.
John called Ravagliano di Bernardini, of Biascia, of the river of Genoa, living at Massa de Luni, has from me, Miliadusso, in *soccida* a sow with black hair, the left shoulder of white hair and the forefeet white, bought with my money ten livres of money of Lucca. He must keep her for the next three years to come. The half of the produce which the said sow shall have in this period shall belong to the said John, the other to me. Death without cause shall be at my risk, bad care at the said John's risk. At the end of the said period, half of the said sow shall belong to the said John, the other to me. And she shall be divided at auction, and I owe him no help when the said sow shall have piglets. But I must pay half when he takes her to the boar. . . .

Given the charter of the said *soccida* by ser Stefano di ser Guido notary of Massa, the year of the nativity of Our Lord 1355, 28th April. . . .

Ricordi di cose familiari di Meliadus Baldiccione de' Casalbati, pisano, del 1339 al 1382
(F. Bonaini, ed.) in *Archivio storico italiano,* 1850, pp. 28-29.

[1] The lord providing the dinner.

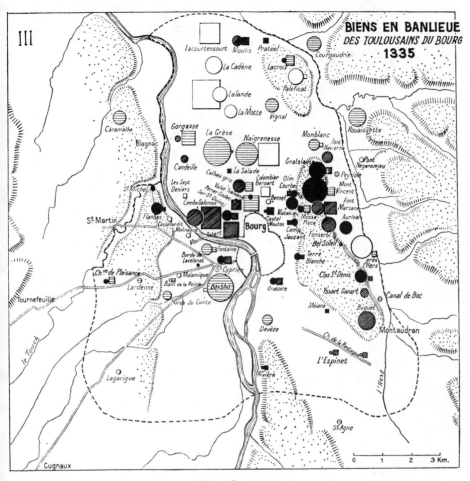

Value of an arpent

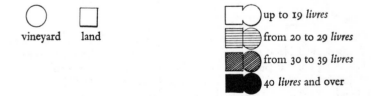

vineyard   land

up to 19 *livres*

from 20 to 29 *livres*

from 30 to 39 *livres*

40 *livres* and over

Document 190, (see p. 546)
Rural property of the inhabitants of Toulouse

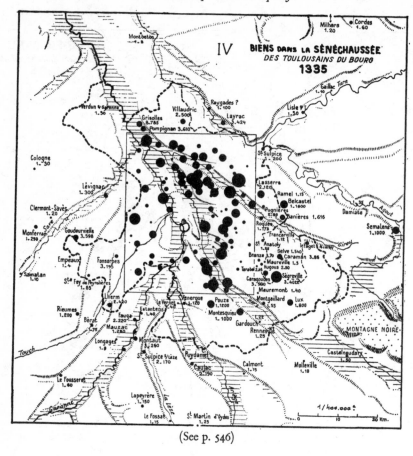

(See p. 546)

192

An extract from a late fourteenth-century formulary of Namur (see Documents Nos. 179-180). This sale, with possibility of re-purchase and re-letting on livestock lease for a year, is a legal fiction; the animals actually guarantee a loan of money contracted by the cultivator.

(1384)

We, T., squire, make known to all that we have bought from T. 5 head of cows, that is, 3 red and 2 black, among which there is a 2-year-old heifer, for the sum of 5 golden *doubles* of the coin of Brabant, which we have paid to the said T., and we have handed these animals over to him to feed, from the next St Martin's Day until the following St Martin's Day, for the sum of 5 *muids* of oats which he should pay us for the manure of the said animals on the said St Martin's Day, which will be in the year of grace 1384, and if by chance the said Servaix in the meanwhile, or on the said St Martin's Day and not before, would like to return the said sum of florins, as it is

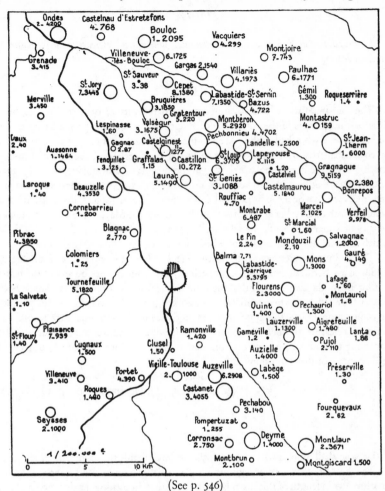

(See p. 546)

(Ph. Wolff, *Les 'estimes' toulousaines des XIVe et XVe siècles*
(Bibliothèque de l'Association Marc Bloch), Toulouse, 1956, maps III and IV

described, we have agreed with him to break the contract without impediment, on condition that we have agreed to return and pay the 5 *muids* of aforesaid oats for the manure of the said cows. And we have also agreed that if any or all of the said animals should die before the said day, the said T. should deduct from the said sum of florins one *double* for each one dead before time, as it is agreed, and we can ask nothing else from the said T., nor the said T. from us, on account of the said animals, except the manure, in proportion to the time and their hides. And so that all the above said things may be better established and remembered, we have given T. these present letters, sealed with our own seal, made and given, etc. . . . .

Formulaire namurois du XIVe siècle, p. 140.

Statutes drawn up by Italian rural communities, with special reference to the regulation of livestock rearing.

(1411)

The said magistrates have instituted and ordered further that, considering how little pasture there is in the commune of Bucino, every man or person living in the said commune who shall wish to keep in the said commune sheep, ewes, goats, sows or cows, shall pay by reason of pasture to the chamberlain of the said commune, levying it for the commune, every year in the calends of November, for every goat or billy-goat that he wishes to keep 10s. and for every sow, 5s., and for every cow 5s., and for every ewe or sheep or ram, 8d. in the time aforementioned, that is 4d. for the whole month of October and 4d. for the whole month of May, of the said year, under penalty of a quarter more for he who shall not pay in the said time and for each animal which is found not to have paid, of which fine the podesta shall have the quarter. . . .

The said magistrates have also instituted and ordered that no person shall dare to saddle an ass, harness oxen, plough, or perform any manual work on any of the feasts of Our Lady, the twelve Apostles, the four Evangelists, St Apollinarius, Sundays or Easter Day, without the permission of his excellency the podesta, under penalty of 5s. per animal. Save that it is permitted on these said days for each man to pile the grain in a heap in the field, to go to the mill with a load, to carry fodder to the house for the animals, except that on Easter Sunday, Our Lady's Day and Good Friday, none of these said things may be done.

Statuto volgare del Buccine dell'anno 1411
(J. Cicchierai, ed.), Florence, 1886, pp. 16 and 136.

*   *   *

(1427)

He who shall plough with oxen or other animals beside the sown land of another, where wheat or other corn or leguminous plants shall be sown, must leave at the side four furrows in length of this sown land, in order that, in turning, he does no damage, and who shall go against this, shall be condemned on each occasion to [pay] 10s. and the repair of the damage to whoever has suffered it.

If a person from Montepescali takes animals from a stranger in *soccida*, on whatever condition, he must inform the vicar and the priors in the eight days following the establishment of the said *soccida*; the vicar must write it down and make a note of it, with the number of animals and also the time, in the memorandum book, on penalty of 100s. in money, and notwithstanding the right of pasture, it shall be paid to the commune.

Every husbandman must and shall be bound to plough on the land of the commune twelve bushels per equipped plough, according to the custom of the country and whoever shall not have more than a pair of oxen . . . shall be bound to plough six bushels of land, and to deliver to the commune the customary tithe payment or the customary part which has been given him, under penalty of 5s. per bushel which must be given to the commune for tithe or share of the fruit. . . .

Statuti del commune di Montepescali (*1427*),

I. Imberciadori (ed.), Siena, (1938), pp. 116, 120, 135.

195

Stockraising in eastern Provence. Numbers of animals kept by peasants, which were recorded in an inquest made for taxation purposes in 1471, (see p. 552).

196

The tariff of the tolls levied in a village in Sologne show which were the principal goods circulating in this rural area: they were primarily cattle, leather and wood; then cloth, sea fish (salted) and fresh-water fish (produce of the fishponds of the region); wine, corn, timber and milling equipment.

(23rd April 1448)

. . . Item, the toll and crossing of the said lands and lordship of Sallebris, which is on the following condition: that all produce, and the merchants conducting and leading it through the country, if they pass through the said lands, must pay the said toll in the following manner, that is: for a live ox, one Tours denier, for a cow, one *maille* (small coin); for 3 sheep or ewes, one Tours denier; for a boar, one denier; and for the sow, one *maille*; for a feather bed and a cushion, 20 deniers; for a 4-legged fish-tank 4 deniers; out of a 100 fleeces or pelts, the 3 fleeces not scoured, or skins with all the wool, are charged one denier; for an ox's hide, with hair, one denier, and a cow's, one *maille*; for a horse to be sold, if he is shod, 4 Parisian deniers, and for a shod donkey, 4 Tours deniers; for a shod mare, 2 Tours deniers; for a shod female donkey, 2 Tours deniers; for an unshod colt, one Tours denier; for a filly, one denier; a horse loaded with corded cloth, will pay 4 Parisian deniers; for a cartload of the same, 4 Tours deniers; and if the cloth in the cart is corded, 4 Parisian deniers the piece; for a waggon-load of uncorded cloth, 8 deniers; for a bale of madder, 4 Parisian deniers; for a horse loaded with peas, 2 Tours deniers; for a cartload of the same, 4 Tours deniers; for a waggonload of peas, 8 deniers; for a horse loaded with whale blubber, one *livre*; for a cartload of the same, 2 *livres*, and a waggon-load, 4 *livres*; for a horse or donkey loaded with salmon, one salmon out of every 5; for a quarter of lampreys, one lamprey; for 100 shad, 1 shad; for 100 cuttlefish or herring, a cuttlefish or a herring, from each; for 1,000 seadogs (? sprats) 4 Tours deniers, and if not as much as 1,000, a charge for the horse, 2 Tours deniers; for a cartload of fresh-water fish, 4 Tours deniers; for a lump of wax or tallow, whether carried by cart or on horseback, each lump 1 denier and 16 deniers per 100; for a cartload of wine or corn, timber hoops for wine-casks in squared wood, 2 Tours deniers; for a hogshead of oil, 2 Tours deniers; for a millstone, 2 Tours deniers; for the wooden mill conduit, 2 deniers; for

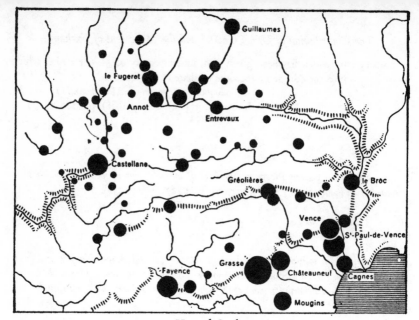

Horned Cattle

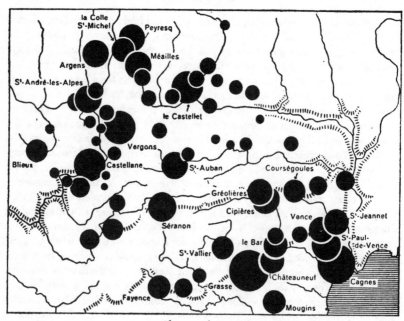

Sheep and Goats

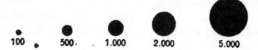

100   500   1.000   2.000   5.000

(see p. 551)   Th. Sclafert, *Cultures en haute Provence*,
Paris (1959), pp. 146-147.

the cartload, 4 deniers, and the waggon-load, 8 Tours deniers; salted bacon, 1 denier; and all the other commodities passing through the said lands owe full toll, which can easily bring in 40 Tours *livres* each year.

J. Guérin, *La vie rurale en Sologne aux XIVe et XVe siècles*, Paris (1959), pp. 304-305.

Glossary

Abergement, the right of settlement

Abonnée, regularizing the *taille*

Affictum, short-term lease (Italian)

a fitto, land leased out for a fixed payment (Italy)

Agrier, a levy of 4th, 9th or 12th sheaf of harvest (S. France)

Ansange, plot of land to be cultivated by compulsory service of the tenant for the benefit of the master. See also *lot-corvée*

Arpent, 1 acre

Ban, power originally wielded by the king, but later assumed by counts and castellans to exploit men and levy dues and services in return for protection. Hence *ban inférieur*, *seigneurie banale*, etc.

Banvin, Monopoly of wine sales at end of season

Baronnie, Supplementary profits arising from the exploitation of men

Bastide, see *Gagnage*

Bauding, tenants' assembly (Bavaria)

Bonnier, between 2·2 and 3·5 acres

Borde, peasant holding in Toulouse region

Brandes arces, heathlands of the Sologne district

Brassier, all-but landless peasant

Buteil, lord's right to a third or half share of his man's estate (Germany)

Casal, measured parcel of settlers' land attached to house (Aquitaine)

Casés, domestic servants housed in their own cabins

Censives, rent-paying lands, hence *terre censales*

Champart, levy of 4th, 9th or 12th sheaf of the harvest (N. France)

Chevage, poll tax, or personal charge due from dependants

Complant, contract between lord and tenant to create a new vineyard, also *Méplant*

Condemine, demesne furlong, arable (Burgundy). Also *coûture*

Couchants et levants, Burgundian peasants bound to the soil

Coûture, demesne furlong, arable

Coutumier, seigneurial inventory recording rents and customs. Also *censier-coutumier*. See *Weistum*

Crouée, demesne furlong, arable

Défens, land from which peasants' grazing animals were temporarily or permanently excluded

Dimanche-prés, demesne furlong

Entrage, entry fine

Entsiedlung, contraction in the occupation of the soil

Facherie, share-cropping agreement (Provence)

Familia, group of dependants attached to lord's household

Ferrage, homestead garden (Provence)

Feu serf, habitation conferring servile status on the occupant

Formariage, fine on marriage to an individual not dependent on the same lord (English = merchet)

Freistift, revokable tenancy (Bavaria)

Gagnage, enclosed farm on the outskirts of arable area, particularly in the Metz region. Also *Bastide*

Gärtner, all-but landless peasant

Gasaille, livestock lease (France). See also *Soccida*

Garrigue, heathland in Provence

Gesindedienst, service from children of the domestic *familia*

Gîte, right of shelter or maintenance for the lord or his agents

Gite de chevaux, due levied by lord for stabling horses (Mâconnais)

Grangier, Meyer, 'farmer'

Hommes de maisnie, men of the household

Hommes de queste, see *Questaux*

Hôtise, measured parcel of settler's land attached to the house (Ile de France)

Hufe, measured parcel of settler's land attached to house (Germany)

Leibeigene, term used in Swabia for men of servile status

Livello, emphyteutic lease inherited from Roman antiquity (Italy)

Lot-corvée, see *Ansange*

Mainferme, Life lease (France)

Malservi, term used in Provence for men of servile status

Maréchaussée, due levied by lord for protecting harvest (Mâconnais)

Mas, isolated farm in certain regions of France

Medietates, métayage, share-cropping agreement

Meilleur catel, lord's right to one head of cattle from dependant's estate after death

Meix taillable, land which conferred servile status on the occupant

Mégerie, see *Facherie*

Méplant, see *Complant*

Mesnie, household, see also *Homme de Maisnie*

Métayage, share-cropping agreement; hence *métayer*, share-cropper; *métairie*, share-cropping holding

Meyer, 'farmer'. See *Grangier*

Mezzadria, share-cropping agreement (Italy)

Ministérial, domestic official

Moissonage, levy on crops (Mâconnais)

Mainmorte, mortmain. The lord's right to a share of his men's personal estate after death. See also *Buteil, meilleur catel*

Muid, measure of capacity

Novale, tithe on newly assarted land

Questaux, term used in Aquitaine for men of servile status

Pariage, partnership between equals to colonize land or establish a new town

Parier, partner, associate

Sainteur, dependant of religious foundation of too high a status to perform manual labour (Germany and N. France)

Sauvement, levy for protection of village communities

Sauvetés, settlements founded by Templars near Toulouse as sanctuaries from ill-treatment and exactions

Schultheiss, office of minor judge (Germany)

Setier, measure of capacity

Soccida, livestock lease (Italy)

Socherie, manufacture of ploughshares. Hence *Sochier*, maker of ploughshares

Söldner, all-but landless peasant

Tâche, levy of 4th, 9th or 12th sheaf of the harvest (S. France)

Taille à merci, arbitrary tallage

Tasque, levy of 4th, 9th or 12th sheaf of the harvest (S. France)

Terrage, the same (N. France)

Terre de sarte, new lands around *terre de mes*, the ancient portion attached to the *manse* (Lotharingia)

Terre gaste, Outfield, waste

Terrier, record of boundaries of parcels within village territory (Central and S.W. France)

Tonlieux, river toll

Vendange, grape harvest

Villefranche, town with a charter of franchise

Villeneuve, new towns established by franchise

Weistum, record of customs made at assembly of manorial inhabitants (Germany). See *coutumier*

Wüstungen, deserted holdings and settlements reverted to waste (Germany)

Bibliography

I GENERAL

A. General Surveys and Statements of Method

1. ABEL, W., *Agrarkrisen und Agrarkonjonktur. Ein Geschichte der Land- und Ernährungswirtschaft Mitteleuropas seit dem hohen Mittelalter*, 2nd ed., Hamburg/Berlin, 1966.
2. BELOW, G. VON, *Geschichte der deutschen Landwirtschaft des Mittelalters in ihren Grundzügen*, Jena, 1937.
3. BLOCH, M., *French Rural History; an essay on its basic characteristics* (Trans. J. Sondheimer), London, 1966. Also *Les caractères ouginaux* ... Vol. II supplement from M. Bloch's notes, Paris, 1956.
4. BOUTRUCHE, R., 'Histoire des institutions: Moyen Age'. *IXe Congrès international des sciences historiques, I: Rapports*, Paris, 1950.
5. *Cambridge Economic History, The*, Vol. I, *The Agrarian Life of the Middle Ages*, CLAPHAM, J. H., & POWER, E. E. (eds.), Cambridge, 1941.
6. —— Vol. II, *Trade and Industry in the Middle Ages*, POSTAN, M. M. & RICH, E. E. (eds.) Cambridge, 1952.
7. CAROSELLI, R., 'Saggio di una bibliografia di storia economica italiana' in *Economia e Storia*, 1958.
8. CARSTEN, F. L., *The Origins of Prussia*, Oxford, 1954.
9. DOREN, A., *Italienische Wirtschaftsgeschichte*, Jena, 1934.
10. FOREVILLE, R., & MOLLAT, M., 'Bibliographie pour servir à l'histoire de la société féodale et du régime seigneurial en France, du IXe au XIIIe siècle', in *Revue d'histoire de la philosophie et d'histoire générale de la civilisation* (Faculté des Lettres de Lille), 1946.
11. FOURASTIÉ, J., 'Histoire, Science et Action', in *Hommage à Lucien Febvre*, I, Paris, 1953.
12. FRANZ, G., *Bücherkunde zur Geschichte des deutschen Bauerntums Neudamm*, 1938.
13. GEORLETTE, R., 'Apports français à l'histoire rurale et aux questions agraires' in *Annales de Gembloux*, 1955.
14. —— 'L'agriculture et la vie rurale en France au Moyen Age' in *Annales de Gembloux*, 1956.

N.B. This list makes no pretence to be exhaustive. It contains no more than the most essential studies which have appeared during the last twenty years. Of works published before then, only the most fundamental books on rural history have been retained, as well as some whose use is indispensable in the absence of more recent research.

15. —— 'Les sources de l'histoire de l'agriculture et des campagnes françaises au Moyen Age' in *Annales de Gembloux*, 1956.
16. HILTON, R. H., 'The Content and Sources of English Agrarian History before 1500' in *Agricultural History Review*, III, 1955.
17. KRZYMOWSKI, R., *Geschichte der deutschen Landwirtschaft*, 2nd ed., Stuttgart, 1951.
18. KULA, W., 'Histoire et économie: la longue durée' in *Annales E.S.C.*, 1960.
19. KULISHER, I. M., *Allgemeine Wirtschaftsgeschichte des Mittelalters, und der Neuzeit*, latest edition, Berlin, 1954.
20. LAMPRECHT, K., *Deutsches Wirtschaftsleben im Mittelalter*. *Untersuchungen über die Entwicklung der materiellen Kultur des platten Landes auf Grund der Quellen, zunächst des Mosellandes*, 3 vols., Leipzig, 1885-1886.
21. LÜTGE, F., *Deutsche Sozial- und Wirtschaftsgeschichte*, Berlin, 3rd ed., 1966.
22. LUZZATTO, G., *Storia economica d'Italia, I. L'antichità e il Medio Evo*, Rome, 1949.
23. —— *Breve storia economica d'Italia dalla caduta dell'Impero romano al principio del cinquecento*, Turin, 1958.
24. PIRENNE, H., *Histoire économique de l'Occident médiéval*, Bruges, 1951.
25. POSTAN, M., 'Histoire économique: Moyen Age', *IXe Congrès international des sciences historiques*, Vol. I: *Rapports*, Paris, 1950.
26. —— Die wirtschaftlichen Grundlagen der mittelalterlichen Gesellschaft' in *Jahrbuch für Nationalökonomie und Statistik*, 1954.
27. ROUPNEL, G., *Histoire de la campagne française*, Paris, 1932.
28. SAALFELD, D., *Bauernwirtschaft und Gutsbetrieb in der vorindustrielle Zeit (Quellen und Forschungen zur Agrargeschichte*, VI), Stuttgart, 1960.
29. SAPORI, A., 'Problemi di Storia economica e sociale' in *Nuova Rivista Storica*, 1958.
30. —— *Le condizione giuridiche e soziale in cui si e sviluppata l'agricultura italiana*, Rome, 1955.
31. SLICHER VAN BATH, B. H., *The Agrarian History of Western Europe (A.D. 500-1850)* (trans. O. Ordish), London, 1963.
32. TROW-SMITH, R., *A History of British Livestock Husbandry*, Vol. I, *to 1700*, London, 1957.
33. TYMIENIECKI, K., 'Quelques parallèles de l'histoire agraire au moyen âge' in *Acta Poloniae Historica*, 1958.
34. WOLFF, PH., 'Le moyen âge' in *Histoire générale du travail*, Vol. II, *L'Age de l'artisanat (Ve-XVIIIe siècles)*, by Ph. Wolff & F. Mauro, Paris, 1960.
35. —— 'L'étude des économies et des sociétés avant l'ère statistique' in *L'histoire et ses méthodes (Encyclopédie de la Pléiade)*, Paris, 1961.

B. *Natural Conditions and the Agrarian Structure*

36. ALLIX, A., *L'Oisans au Moyen Age. Étude de géographie historique en haute montagne* Paris, 1929.
37. AMERIJCKX, J. & VERHULST, A, *Enkele historisch-geographische Problemen in verband met de oudste geschiedenis van de vlaamse kustvlakte*, Ghent, 1958.
38. BADER, K., 'Gartenrecht' in *Zeitschrift der Savigny Stiftung. Germanische Abteilung*, 1958.
39. BAUJOUAN, G., 'Le temps historique' in *L'histoire et ses méthodes (Encyclopédie de la Pléiade)*, Paris, 1961.
40. BERESFORD, M. W. & ST JOSEPH, J. K. S., *Medieval England. An Aerial Survey*, Cambridge, 1958.
41. BLOCH, M., 'Champs et villages' in *Annales d'histoire économique et sociale*, 1934.

42. BONENFANT, P., 'A propos des limites médiévales' in *Hommage à Lucien Febvre*, Vol. I, Paris, 1953.

43. BRUNET, P., 'Problèmes relatifs aux structures agraires de la Basse Normandie' in *Annales de Normandie*, 1955.

44. —— *Structure agraire et économie rurale des plateaux tertiaires entre la Seine et l'Oise*, Caen, 1960.

45. CHAMPIER, L., 'La structure des terroirs bourguignons' in *Annales de Bourgogne*, 1955.

46. CHAUMEIL, L., 'L'origine du bocage en Bretagne' in *Hommage à Lucien Febvre*, Vol. I, Paris, 1953.

47. DARBY, H. C. (ed.), *An Historical Geography of England*, Cambridge, 1936.

48. —— *The Domesday Geography of Eastern England*, Cambridge, 1952.

49. —— & TERRETT, B., *The Domesday Geography of Midland England*, Cambridge, 1954.

50. DEFFONTAINES, P., *Les hommes et leurs travaux dans les pays de la moyenne Garonne*, Lille, 1932.

51. DERRUAU, M., *La grande Limagne auvergnate et bourbonnaise*, Paris, 1949.

52. DION, R., *Le Val de Loire: Étude de géographie régionale*, Tours, 1934.

53. —— 'La part de la géographie et celle de l'histoire dans l'explication de l'habitat rural du Bassin Parisien' in *Publications de la société de géographie de Lille*, 1946.

54. FEL, A., 'Réflexions sur les paysages agraires des hautes terres du Massif Central' in *Annales de l'Est*, *Mémoire No. 21*, Nancy, 1959.

55. FÉNELON, P., 'Structure des finages périgourdins' in *Annales de l'Est*, *Mémoire No. 21*, Nancy, 1959.

56. FIRBAS, F., *Spät- und nacheiszeitliche Waldgeschichte Mitteleuropas nördlich der Alpen*, 2 vols. Jena, 1949-1952.

57. FLATRÉS, P., 'La structure agraire ancienne du Devon et du Cornwall et les enclôtures des XIIIe et XIVe siècles' in *Annales de Bretagne*, 1949.

58. FOUGÈRES, M., 'Les régimes agraires: recherches convergentes' in *Annales d'histoire sociale*, 1941.

59. *Géographie et Histoire agraire*, *Annales de l'Est* (publiées par la Faculté des Lettres et des Sciences humaines de l'Université de Nancy), *Mémoire No. 21*, 1959.

60. HIGOUNET, C., 'Observations sur la seigneurie rurale et l'habitat en Rouergue, du IXe au XIVe siècle' in *Annales du Midi*, 1950.

61. —— 'L'occupation du sol du pays entre Tarn et Garonne' in *Annales du Midi*, 1953.

62. —— 'La géohistoire' in *L'histoire et ses méthodes* (*Encyclopédie de la Pléiade*), Paris, 1961.

63. HÖMBERG, A., *Siedlungsgeschichte des oberen Sauerlandes*, Berlin, 1938.

64. HOSKINS, W. G., 'The English Landscape' in *Medieval England*, Oxford, 1958.

65. JUILLARD, E., 'La genèse des paysages agraires' in *Annales E.S.C.*, 1951.

66. —— & MEYNIER A., 'Die Agrarlandschaft in Frankreich. Forschungsergebnisse der letzten zwanzig Jahre' in *Münchner Geographiphische Hefte*, IX, 1955.

67. ——, ——, DE PLANHOL, X., & SAUTER G., *Structures agraires et paysages ruraux. Un quart de siècle de recherches françaises. Annales de l'Est*, *Mémoire No. 17*, Nancy, 1957.

68. KEUNING, H. I., 'Siedlungsform und Siedlungsvorgang. Einige Gedanken über die Entwicklung der ländlichen Siedlungen in den niederländischen Sandgebieten' in *Zeitschrift für Agrargeschichte und Agrarsoziologie*, 1961.

Bibliography

69. KÖTSZSCHKE, R., *Salhofund Siedelh of in älteren deutschen Agrarwesen*, Berlin, 1953.
70. LE ROY LADURIE, E., 'Histoire et climat' in *Annales E.S.C.*, 1959.
71. —— 'Aspects historiques de la nouvelle climatologie' in *Revue Historique*, 1961.
72. LIZERAND, G., *Le régime rural de l'ancienne France*, Paris, 1942.
73. MAAS, W., *Les moines défricheurs. Études sur les transformations du paysage au Moyen Age aux confins de la Champagne et de la Lorraine*, Moulins, 1954.
74. MEYNIER, A., 'La commune rurale française' in *Annales de Géographie*, 1945.
75. —— 'Problèmes de structure agraire' in *Annales E.S.C.*, 1955.
76. MORTENSEN, H., 'Zur Entstehung der Gewannflur', in *Zeitschrift für Agrargeschichte und Agrarsoziologie*, 1955.
77. —— 'Die mittelalterliche deutsche Kulturlandschaft und ihr Verhältnis zur Gegenwart' in *Vierteljahrschrift für Sozial- und Wirtschaftsgeschichte*, 1958.
78. PÉDELABORDE, P., *Le climat du Bassin Parisien; essai d'une méthode rationnelle de climatologie physique*, Paris, 1957.
79. PLANHOL, X. DE, 'Essai sur la genèse du paysage rural en champs ouverts' in *Annales de l'Est, Mémoire No. 21*, Nancy, 1959.
80. RODERICK, A. J., 'Openfield Agriculture in Herefordshire in the Middle Ages' in *Trans. Woolhope Natural Field Club*, XXXIII, 1949.
81. SAINT-JACOB, P. DE, 'Les enclosures anglaises' in *Information historique*, 1955.
82. SCHOVE, J. & LOWTHER, A. W. G., 'Tree rings and Medieval Archaeology' in *Medieval Archaeology*, 1958.
83. SCLAFERT, T., *Cultures en Haute-Provence. Déboisements et pâturages au moyen âge*, Paris, 1959.
84. SERENI, E., *Storia del paesaggio agrario italiano*, Bari, 1961.
85. STEENSBERG, A., 'Plough and Field Shape' in *Selected papers of the fifth International Congress of Anthropological and Ethnological Sciences*, Philadelphia, 1956.
86. TITOW, J., 'Evidence of Weather in the Account Rolls of the Bishopric of Winchester, 1206-1350' in *Economic History Review*, 2nd ser., XII, 1960.
87. TIMM, A., *Studien zur Siedlungs- und Agrargeschichte Mitteldeutschlands*, Cologne, 1956.
88. TULIPPE, O., *L'habitat rural en Seine-et-Oise. Essai de géographie du peuplement*, Liège, 1934.
89. UTTERSTRÖM, G., 'Climatic fluctuations and population problems in early modern history' in *The Scandinavian Economic History Review*, 1955.
90. VERHULST, A., 'Probleme der mittelalterlichen Agrarlandschaft in Flandern' in *Zeitschrift für Agrargeschichte und Agrarsoziologie*, 1961.
91. WREDE, G., 'Die mittelalterliche Ausbausiedlung in Nordwestdeutschland' in *Blätter für deutsche Landesgeschichte*, 1956.

C. Demography

92. BARATIER, E., *La démographie provençale du XIIIe au XVIe siècle, avec chiffres de comparaison pour le XVIIIe siècle*, Paris, 1961.
93. BOUTRUCHE, R., 'Les courants de peuplement dans l'Entre-Deux-Mers' in *Annale d'Histoire économique et sociale*, 1935.
94. CIPOLLA, C., DHONDT, J., POSTAN, M., & WOLFF, PH., 'Anthropologie et démographie. Moyen Age', *IXe Congrès international des sciences historiques*: Vol. I, *Rapports*, Paris, 1950.
95. DELATOUCHE, R., 'Agriculture médiévale et population in *Les Études sociales*, 1955.

96. REINHARD, M., & ARMENGAUD, A., *Histoire générale de la population mondiale*, Paris, 1961.

97. ROBINSON, W. C., 'Money, Population and Economic Change in late Medieval Europe' in *Economic History Review*, 2nd ser., XII, 1959 (followed by a note by M. POSTAN).

98. RUSSELL, J. C., *British Medieval Population*, Albuquerque, 1948.

99. —— *Late Ancient and Medieval Population*, Trans. American Historical Philosophical Society, New series, Vol, 48, Philadelphia, 1958.

D. *Labour and Technique*

100. BARATIER, E., 'Production et exportation du vin du terroir de Marseille du XIIIe au XVIe siècle' in *Bulletin Philologique et Historique*, 1959.

101. BENOIT, F., *Histoire de l'outillage rural et artisanal*, Paris, 1947.

102. BOUVIER-AJAM, M., *Histoire du travail en France des origines à la Révolution*, Paris, 1957.

103. BRENTJES, J., 'Der Pflug. Ein Forschungsbericht' in *Zeitschrift für Agrargeschichte und Agrarsoziologie*, 1955.

104. DELATOUCHE, R., 'Élites intellectuelles et agriculture au moyen âge' in *Recueil d'études sociales à la mémoire de Frédéric Le Play*, Paris, 1956.

105. DION, R., *Histoire de la vigne et du vin en France, des origines au XIXe siècle*, Paris, 1959.

106. FAUCHER, D., 'A propos de l'araire' in *Pallas*, IV.

107. FRANKLIN, T. B., *History of Agriculture*, London, 1948.

108. GABOTTO, F., *L'agricoltura nella regione saluzzese dal secolo XI al XV*, Pinerolo, 1901.

109. GEORLETTE, R., 'Les coutumes et les usages agricoles des pays de l'Ancienne France' in *Revue des Sciences économiques*, 1956.

110. GILLE, B., 'Le moulin à eau, une révolution technique médiévale' in *Technique et civilisation*, 1954.

111. —— 'Les développements technologiques en Europe, de 1150 à 1400' in *Cahiers d'histoire mondiale*, III, 1956.

112. GRAND, R., & DELATOUCHE, R., *L'agriculture au Moyen Age, de la fin de l'Empire romain au XVIe siècle*, Paris, 1950.

113. GRAS, N. S. B., *A History of Agriculture in Europe and America*, New York, 1925.

114. HARVEY, W., 'Walter of Henley and the Old Farming' in *Agriculture*, LIX, 1952-1953.

115. HAUDRICOURT, A. G., 'Contribution à la géographie humaine et à l'ethnologie de la voiture' in *Revue de géographie et d'ethnologie*, 1948.

116. —— & HÉDIN, L., *L'homme et les plantes cultivées*, Paris, 1943.

117. —— & JEAN BRUNHES-DELAMARRE, M., *L'homme et la charrue à travers le monde*, Paris, 1955.

118. *Historia Agriculturae*, 2 vols., Groningen, 1954-1955.

119. HODGEN, M. T., *Change and History. A Study of the dated Distribution of Technological Innovations in England*, New York, 1952.

120. LEE, N. E., *Harvests and Harvesting through the Ages*, Cambridge, 1960.

121. LENNARD, R., 'Statistics of corn-yields in Medieval England' in *Economic History Review*, 2nd ser., III, 1937.

122. LESER, P., *Entstehung und Verbreitung des Pfluges*, Münster, 1931.

123. LINDEMANS, P., *Geschiedenis van de Landbouw in België*, 2 vols., Antwerp, 1952.

124. MEUVRET, J., 'Agronomie et jardinage aux XVIe et XVIIe siècles' in *Hommage à Lucien Febvre*, Vol. II, Paris, 1953.

125. OLSON, L., 'Pietro de Crescenzi: the Founder of Modern Agronomy' in *Agricultural History*, XVIII, 1944.

126. OSCHINSKY, D., 'Medieval Treatises on Estate Accounting' in *Economic History Review*, XVII, 1947.

127. —— 'Medieval Treatises on Estate Management' in *Economic History Review*, 2nd ser., VIII, 1956.

128. PAYNE, F. G., 'The British Plough: some stages in its development' in *Agricultural History Review*, 1957.

129. SAMARAN, C., 'L'agriculture Française au Moyen Age' in *Journal des Savants*, 1951.

130. SCHRÖDER-LEMBKE, G., 'Entstehung und Verbreitung der Mehrfeldwirtschaft im nordöstlichen Deutschland' in *Zeitschrift für Agrargeschichte und Agrarsoziologie*, 1954.

131. SCLAFERT, T., 'Usages agraires dans les régions provençales avant le XVIIIe siècle. Les assolements' in *Revue de Géographie Alpine*, 1941.

132. SINGER, C., *A History of Technology*, Vol. II, Oxford, 1956.

133. SÜDHOF, S., 'Das deutsche Pilzbuch des Mittelalters und seine Einflüsse auf die europäische Gartenliteratur der Neuzeit' in *Zeitschrift für Agrargeschichte und Agrarsoziologie*, 1954.

134. —— 'Die Stellung der Landwirtschaft im System der mittelalterlichen Künste' in *Zeitschrift für Agrargeschichte und Agrarsoziologie*, 1956.

135. TIMM, A., 'Zur Geschichte der Erntegeräte' in *Zeitschrift für Agrargeschichte und Agrarsoziologie*, 1956.

136. USHER, A. P., *A History of Mechanical Inventions*, 2nd ed., Cambridge (Mass.), 1954.

137. VERHULST, A., 'Bijdragen tot de studie van de agrarische structuur in het Vlaamse land. Het probleem van de verdwijning van de braak in de Vlaamse landbouw (XIIIe-XVIIe eeuw)' in *Natuurwetenschappelijk Tijdschrift*, 1956.

138. WHITE, L., 'Technology and Invention in the Middle Ages', in *Speculum*, 1940.

E. *Prices and Exchange*

139. BEVERIDGE. W., *Prices and Wages in England from the twelfth to the nineteenth century* London, 1965.

140. DUPRÉ DE SAINT-MAUR, N. F., *Recherches sur la valeur des monnoies et sur le prix des grains avant et après le Concile de Francfort*, Paris, 1762.

141. FIUMI, E., 'Fioritura e decadenza dell'economia fiorentina' in *Archivio storico italiano*, 1958.

142. POWER, E. E., *The Medieval English Wool Trade*, Oxford, 1941.

143. RENOUARD, Y., 'Le grand commerce du vin au Moyen Age' in *Information historique*, 1958.

144. —— 'Le grand commerce des vins de Gascogne au Moyen Age' in *Revue historique*, CCXXI, 1959.

145. SUHLE, A., *Deutsche Münz- und Geldgeschichte von den Anfängen bis zum 15. Jahrhundert*, Berlin, 1955.

146. THOROLD-ROGERS, J. E., *A History of Agriculture and Prices in England*, 7 vols., Oxford, 1866.

147. USHER, A. P., *A History of the Grain Trade in France*, Cambridge (Mass.), 1913.

148. VIGNERON, B., 'La vente dans le Mâconnais du IXe au XIIIe siècles' in *Revue historique de droit français et étranger*, 1959.

F. Social Structure

149. BENNETT, H. S., *Life on the English Manor. A Study of Peasant Conditions, 1150-1400*, Cambridge, 1937.

150. BLOCH, M., 'Village et Seigneurie: quelques observations de méthode à propos d'une étude sur la Bourgogne' in *Annales d'Histoire économique et sociale*, 1937.

151. —— 'L'esclavage dans l'Europe médiévale' in *Annales d'Histoire économique et sociale*, 1939.

152. —— *Feudal Society* (trans. L. A. Manyon), London, 1961.

153. BOEREN, P. C., *Étude sur les tributaires d'Église dans le comté de Flandre du IXe au XIVe siècle*, Amsterdam, 1936.

154. BOGNETTI, G. P., 'Sulle origini dei communi rurali nel medio evo' in *Studi nelle scienze giuridiche e sociali*, XI, Pavia, 1927.

155. BOUTRUCHE, R., *Seigneurie et féodalité: I. Le premier âge des liens d'homme à homme*, Paris, 1959.

156. CAGGESE, R., *Classi e communi rurali nel medio evo italiano*, Florence, 1903.

157. CAM, H. M., *Liberties and Communities in Medieval England*, Cambridge, 1944.

158. COULTON, G. C., *The Medieval Village*, Cambridge, 1925.

159. DOLLINGER, P., *L'évolution des classes rurales en Bavière depuis la fin de l'époque carolingienne jusqu'au milieu du XIIIe siècle*, Strasbourg, 1949.

160. GIBBS, M., *Feudal Order, a study of the Origins and Development of English Feudal Society*, London, 1949.

161. HILTON, R. H., *The Social Structure of Rural Warwickshire in the Middle Ages*. Oxford, 1950.

162. HOMANS, G. C., 'The Rural Sociology of Medieval England' in *Past and Present*, 1953.

163. JOUON DES LONGRAIS, F., 'Le vilainage anglais et le servage réel et personnel. Quelques remarques sur la période 1066-1485' in *Recueil de la Société Jean Bodin*, II. *Le servage*, Brussels, 1937.

164. LEICHT, P. S., *Operai, artigiani, agricoltori in Italia dal secolo VI al XVI*, Milan, 1946.

165. LUZZATTO, G., *I servi nelle grande proprietà ecclesiastiche italiane, nel secolo IXe X*, Senigallia, 1910.

166. —— 'La servitù in Italia nell'età feudale in confronto ai paesi d'oltralpo' Xe *Congresso Internazionale di Scienze storiche*, Roma, 1955, III, Florence, 1955.

167. LYON, B., 'Medieval real estate developments and freedom' in *American Historical Review*, 1957-1958.

168. MAITLAND, E. W., *Domesday Book and Beyond. Three Essays in the Early History of England*, Cambridge, 1897.

169. MARTINI, F., 'Das Bauerntum im deutschen Schriftum von den Anfängen bis zum 16. Jahrhundert' in *Vierteljahrschrift für Litteraturwissenschaft und Geistesgeschichte*, 1944.

170. MAYER, T., 'Bemerkungen und Nachträge zum Problem der freien Bauern' in *Zeitschrift für Württemberg. Landesgeschichte*, 1954.

171. PERRIN, C. E., 'Le servage en France et en Allemagne' Xo *Congresso Internazionale di Scienze storiche*, Roma, 1955, *Relazioni*, III, Florence, 1955.

172. —— 'Les classes rurales en Bavière au Moyen Age (à propos du livre de Ph. Dollinger)' in *Revue historique*, 1952.

173. SAINT-JACOB, P.DE, 'Études sur l'ancienne communauté rurale en Bourgogne' in *Annales de Bourgogne*, 1941, 1943, 1946, 1953.

174. STEPHENSON, C., 'The Problem of the Common Man in Early Medieval Europe' in *American Historical Review*, 1946.

175. VERLINDEN, C., *L'esclavage dans l'Europe médiévale, I. Péninsule Ibérique-France*, Bruges, 1955.

176. VERRIEST, L., 'Les faits et la terminologie en matière de condition juridique des personnes au Moyen Age: serfs, nobles, vilains, sainteurs' in *Revue du Nord*, 1939.

177. WINMILL, J. M., 'The Story of an Essex Village from the Confessor to the Reformation' in *Essex Review*, 1952.

G. *The Manor*

178. ASTON, T. H., 'The English Manor' in *Past and Present*, 1956.

179. BALON, J., 'La structure du domaine' in *Tijdschrift voor Rechtsgeschiedenis*, 1958.

180. —— *Jus medii aevi. I. La structure et la gestion du domaine de l'Église au Moyen Age dans l'Europe des Francs. II. Lex juridictio. Recherches sur les assemblées judiciaires et législatives, sur les droits et sur les obligations communautaires dans l'Europe des Francs*, Namur, 1959-1960.

181. BLOCH, M., 'La genèse de la seigneurie: idée d'une recherche comparée' in *Annales d'histoire économique et sociale*, 1937.

182. —— 'La seigneurie anglaise du Moyen Age' in *Annales d'histoire économique et sociale*, 1938.

183. —— *Seigneurie française et manoir anglais (Cahiers des Annales 16)*, Paris, 1960.

184. BOUTRUCHE, R., *Une société provinciale en lutte contre le régime féodal: l'alleu en Bordelais et en Bazadais, du XIe au XVIIIe siècle*, Rodez, 1947.

185. BRUNNER, O., *Land und Herrschaft, Grundfragen der territorialen Verfassungsgeschichte Österreichs im Mittelalter*, Vienna, 1959.

186. DAVENPORT, F. G., *The Economic Development of a Norfolk Manor, 1086-1565*, Cambridge, 1906.

187. FINBERG, H. P. R., *Tavistock Abbey. A Study in the Social and Economic History of Devon*, Cambridge, 1951.

188. FLEMING, L., *History of Pagham in Sussex, illustrating the Administration of an Archiepiscopal Hundred, the Decay of Manorial Organization and the Rise of a Seaside Resort*, 3 vols., Ditchling, 1949-1950.

189. GÉNICOT, L., *L'économie rurale namuroise au bas Moyen Age (1199-1429). I. La seigneurie foncière*, Namur, 1943.

190. —— *L'économie rurale namuroise au bas Moyen Age. II. Les hommes; la noblesse*, Louvain, 1960.

191. JONES, P. J., 'An Italian Estate, 400-1200' in *Economic History Review*, 2nd ser., VII, 1956-1957.

192. KONOPKINE, A. V., 'Some features of the landowning system in medieval France' (in Russian) in *Ucenye Zapiski Ivanovskoyo pedagogicesko istituta*, II, 1957.

193. LEICHT, P. S., *Studi sulla proprietà fondiaria in Italia nel medio evo, I. Curtis e feudo*, Padua, 1903.

194. *Les dîmes en Forez (Chartes du Forez, XV)*, Mâcon, 1957.

195. LOT, F., 'L'alleu en Bordelais et en Bazadais (à propos de la thèse de R. Boutruche)' in *Journal des savants*, 1947.

196. —— & FAWTIER, R., *Histoire des institutions françaises au Moyen Age. I. Les institutions seigneuriales*, Paris, 1957.

197. LUZZATTO, G., 'Contributo alla storia della mezzadria nel medio evo' in *Nuova rivista storica*, 1948.
198. MILLER, E., *The Abbey and Bishopric of Ely. The Social History of an Ecclesiastical Estate from the 10th century to the early 14th Century*, Cambridge, 1951.
199. OURLIAC, P., 'Tenures et contrats agraires' in *Atti del primo Convegno internazionale di diritto agrario di Firenze*, Milan, 1954.
200. PERRIN, C. E., *Recherches sur la seigneurie rurale en Lorraine d'après les plus anciens censiers (IXe-XIIe siècles)*, Strasbourg, 1935.
201. RAFTIS, J. A., *The Estates of Ramsey Abbey. A Study in Economic Growth and Organization*, Toronto, 1957.
202. *Recueils de la société Jean Bodin, III. La tenure*, Brussels, 1938.
203. —— *IV. Le domaine*, Brussels, 1949.
204. RICHTERING, H. W., *Bauerliche Leistungen im mittelalterlichen Westfalen mit besonderer Berücksichtigung der Naturalabgeben und ihrer Verbreitung*, Münster, 1949.
205. SLOET, L., *Oorkondenboek van Gelre en Zutfen*. 3 vols. 1872-76
206. TABACCO, G., 'La dissoluzione medievale dello stato nella recente storiografia' in *Studi Medievali*, 1960.
207. TENANT DE LA TOUR, G., *L'homme et le terre, de Charlemagne à Saint Louis*, Paris, 1943.
208. VERHULST, A. E., *De sint-Baafs-abdij te Gent – haar grondbezit (VIIe-XIVe eeuw)*, Brussels, 1958.
209. VERRIEST, L., *Institutions médiévales, Introduction au Corpus des records de coutumes et des lois de chefs-lieux de l'ancien comté de Hainaut*, Mons, I, 1946.
210. WITTICH, W., *Die Grundherrschaft in Nordwest Deutschland*, Leipzig, 1896.

II IX-X CENTURIES

A. General Conditions

211. BERGENGRUEN, A., 'Adel und Grundherrschaft im Merowingerreich' in *Vierteljahrschrift für Sozial- und Wirtschafsgeschichte*, Beiheft 41, 1958.
212. BLOCH, M., 'The Rise of Dependent Cultivation and Seignorial Institutions' in *The Cambridge Economic History*, I, 2nd ed., Cambridge, 1966.
213. —— 'Les invasions: (A) Deux structures économiques; (B) Occupation du sol et peuplement' in *Annales d'histoire sociale*, 1945.
214. —— 'Comment et pourquoi finit l'esclavage antique' in *Annales E.S.C.*, 1947.
215. CIPOLLA, C. M., 'Encore Mahomet et Charlemagne' in *Annales E.S.C.*, 1949.
216. —— 'Questioni aperte sul sistema economico dell'alto medio evo' in *Rivista storica italiana*, 1951.
217. DAVID, M., 'Les *laboratores* jusqu'au renouveau économique des XIe et XIIe siècles' in *Études d'histoire du Droit privé offertes à Pierre Petot*, Paris, 1959.
218. DÉLÉAGE, A., *La vie rurale en Bourgogne jusqu'au début du XIe siècle*, 2 vols., Mâcon, 1941.
219. DOEHARD, R., 'Ce qu'on vendait et comment on le vendait dans le Bassin Parisien au temps de Charlemagne et des Normands' in *Annales E.S.C.*, 1947.
220. DUBLED, H., '*Allodium* dans les textes latins du Moyen Age' in *Le Moyen Age*, 1951.

Bibliography

221. DUPONT, A., 'Quelques aspects de la vie rurale en Septimanie carolingienne (fin VIIIe-IXe siècles) in *Annales de l'Institut d'Études Occitanes*, 1954.

222. —— 'Considérations sur la colonisation et la vie rurale dans le Roussillon et la Marche d'Espagne au IXe siècle' in *Annales du Midi*, 1955.

223. FOUGÈRES, M., 'Aux origines de notre société rurale (à propos de la thèse de A. Déléage)' in *Mélanges d'histoire sociale*, 1942.

224. FOURNIER, G., 'Les transformations du parcellaire en Basse Auvergne au cours du haut moyen âge' in *Annales de l'Est, Mémoire No. 21*, Nancy, 1959.

225. HARTMANN, L. M., *Zur Wirtschaftsgeschichte Italiens in frühen Mittelalter*, Gotha, 1904.

226. HERLIHY, D., 'The Agrarian Revolution in Southern France and Italy, 801-1150' in *Speculum*, 1958.

227. LATOUCHE, R., *Les origines de l'économie occidentale, IVe-XIe siècles*, Paris, 1956.

228. LENTACKER, F., 'Débats entre historiens et géographes à propos de l'évolution de la plaine maritime flamande au cours du haut moyen âge' in *Revue de Nord*, 1960.

229. LUZZATTO, G., 'Mutamenti nell'economia agraria italiana dalla caduta dei carolingi al principio del secolo XI' in *Settimane di studio sull'alto medio evo*, II, Spoleto, 1955.

230. SAINT-JACOB, P. DE, 'La Bourgogne rurale au haut Moyen Age. A propos d'un ouvrage récent (la thèse de A. Déléage)' in *Revue historique*, 195, 1945.

231. SCHRÖDER-LEMBKE, G., 'Zur Flurform der Karolingerzeit' in *Zeitschrift für Agrargeschichte und Agrarsoziologie*, 1961.

232. STENTON, F. M., *The Oxford History of England, II. Anglo-Saxon England*, 2nd ed., Oxford, 1963.

233. VERHULST, A., 'Différents types de structure domaniale et agraire en Basse et Moyenne Belgique au haut moyen âge: un essai d'explication' in *Annales E.S.C.*, 1958.

234. WERVEKE, H. VAN, 'La densité de la population du IXe siècle. Essai d'une estimation' in *Annales du XXXe Congrès de la Fédération archéologique et historique de Belgique*, 1936.

B. *The Manor*

235. CONSTABLE, G., '*Nona et Decima*. An Aspect of Carolingian Economy' in *Speculum*, 1960.

236. DUBLED, H., 'Encore la question du manse' in *Revue du Moyen Age latin*, 1949.

237. —— '*Mancipium*' in *Revue du Moyen Age latin*, 1949.

238. —— 'Quelques observations sur le sens du mot *villa*' in *Le Moyen Age*, 1953.

239. ENDRES, R., 'Das Kirchengut im Bistum Lucca vom VIII. bis X. Jahrhundert' in *Vierteljahrschrift für Sozial- und Wirtschaftsgeschichte*, 1916-1918.

240. FOURNIER, G., 'La propriété foncière en Basse Auvergne aux époques mérovingiennes et carolingiennes' in *Bulletin historique et scientifique de l'Auvergne*, 1957.

241. GANSHOF, F. L., 'Le domaine gantois de l'abbaye de Saint Pierre-au-Mont-Blandin à l'époque carolingienne' in *Revue belge de philologie et d'histoire*, 1948.

242. —— 'Manorial Organization in the Low Countries in the 7th, 8th and 9th centuries' in *Trans. of the Royal Historical Society*, 4th ser., XXXI, 1949.

243. —— 'Les avatars d'un domaine de l'église de Marseille à la fin du VIIe siècle' in *Studi in onore di Gino Luzzatto*, Milan, 1949.

244. —— 'Grondbezit en Gronduitbating tijdens de vroege Middeleeuwen' in *Brabants Heem*, 1954.

245. —— 'Observations sur le manse à l'époque mérovingienne' in *Revue historique de droit français et étranger*, 1955.

246. GRAND, R., 'Note d'économie agraire médiévale: *mansus vestitus* et *mansus absus*' in *Études d'histoire du Droit privé offertes à Pierre Petot*, Paris, 1959.

247. GRIERSON, P., 'The Identity of the Unnamed Fiscs in the *Brevium exempla ad describendas res ecclesiasticas et fiscales*' in *Revue belge de philologie et d'histoire*, 1939.

248. HERLIHY, D., 'The Carolingian *mansus*' in *Economic History Review*, 2nd ser., XIII, 1960.

249. —— 'Church Property on the European Continent, 701-1208' in *Speculum*, 1961.

250. LATOUCHE, R., 'L'exploitation agricole dans le Maine' in *Annales de Bretagne*, 1944.

251. METZ, W., *Das Karolingische Reichsgut, Eine Verfassungs- und Verwaltungsgeschichtliche Untersuchung*, Berlin, 1960.

252. MOTTE-COLAS, M. DE LA, 'Les possessions territoriales de l'abbaye de Saint-Germain-des-Prés du début du IXe au début du XIIe siècle' in *Mémorial du XIVe centenaire de l'abbaye de Saint-Germain-des-Prés*, Paris, 1960.

253. MUSSET, L., 'Notes pour servir d'introduction à l'histoire foncière de la Normandie. Les grands domaines de l'époque franque et les destinées du régime domanial, du IXe au XIe siècle' in *Bulletin de la Société des Antiquaires de Normandie*, 1942-1945.

254. PERRIN, C. E., 'Observations sur le manse dans la région parisienne au début du IXe siècle' in *Annales d'Histoire sociale*, 1945.

255. —— 'A propos d'une redevance en *fossoirs* inscrite au polyptyque d'Irminon' in *Études d'Histoire du Droit privé offertes à Pierre Petot*, Paris, 1959.

256. —— 'Le manse dans le polyptyque de l'abbaye de Prüm à la fin du IXe siècle' in *Études historiques à la mémoire de Noël Didier*, Paris, 1960.

257. PIVANO, S., *I contratti agrari in Italia nell'alto medio evo*, Turin, 1904.

258. SAINT-JACOB, P. DE, 'Recherches sur la structure terrienne de la seigneurie' in *Annales de l'Est*, Mémoire No. 21, Nancy, 1959.

259. VERHEIN, K., 'Studien zu den Quellen zum Reichsgut der Karolingerzeit' in *Deutsches Archiv für Erforschung des Mittelalters*, 1953-1955.

III XI-XIII CENTURIES

A. *General*

260. DANNENBAUER, H., 'Politik und Wirtschaft in der altdeutschen Kaiserzeit' in *Grundlagen der mittelalterlichen Welt*, Stuttgart, 1958.

261. DUBY, G., *La société aux XIe et XIIe siècles dans la région mâconnaise*, Paris, 1953.

262. —— 'Thoughts on the rural economy of France in the mid-XIIIth century (in Polish) in *Kwartalnik Historyczny*, 1960.

263. HALPERIN, J., 'Les transformations économiques aux XIIe et XIIIe siècles', in *Revue d'Histoire économique et sociale*, 1950.

264. GANSHOF, F. L., 'Medieval Agrarian Society in its Prime: France, the Low Countries, and Western Germany' in *Cambridge Economic History*, I, 2nd ed., 1966.

265. GRATSIANSKI, F., *The Burgundian Countryside from the X to the XII Centuries* (in Russian), Moscow-Leningrad, 1935.
266. HILTON, R. H., 'Life in the Medieval Manor (with a short glossary of manorial terms)' in *Amateur Historian*, I, 1952-1953.
267. HOSKINS, W. G. (ed.), *Studies in Leicestershire Agrarian History* (Leicestershire Archaeological Society), 1949.
268. LENNARD, R., *Rural England, 1086-1135. A Study of Social and Agrarian Conditions*, Oxford, 1959.
269. PERROY, E., *La terre et les paysans en France aux XIIe et XIIIe siècles. Explications de texte* (les cours de Sorbonne), Paris, 1953.
270. POOLE, A. L. *Obligations of Society in the Twelfth and Thirteenth Centuries*, London, 1946.
271. POSTAN, M. M., 'Medieval Agrarian Society in its Prime: England' in *Cambridge Economic History*, I, 2nd ed., Cambridge, 1966.
272. SABATA, T., 'On the Formation of Feudal Society in Western Europe' (in Japanese) in *Rekishigakukenju*, 1960.
273. —— 'Lord and Village in Feudal Society' (in Japanese) in *Shirin*, 1960.
274. SABBE, F., 'De Cistercianser economie' in *Cîteaux in de Nederlanden*, 1952.
275. STENTON, D. M., *English Society in the Early Middle Ages, 1066-1307*, London, 1952.
276. STRAYER, J. R., 'Economic Conditions in the County of Beaumont-le-Roger, 1261-1313' in *Speculum*, 1951.
277. VINOGRADOFF, P., *English Society in the XIth Century. Essays in English Medieval History*, Oxford, 1908.

B. *The Growth of Rural Production*

278. BISHOP, T. A. M., 'The Rotation of Crops at Westerham, 1297-1350' in *Economic History Review*, 2nd ser., IX, 1958.
279. BOUSSARD, J., 'Hypothèses sur la formation des bourgs et des communes de Normandie' in *Annales de Normandie*, 1958.
280. CHÉDEVILLE, A., 'Mise en valeur et peuplement du Maine au XIe siècle, d'après les chartes de l'abbaye Saint-Vincent du Mans' in *Annales de Normandie*, 1958.
281. DARBY, H. C., 'Domesday Woodland' in *Economic History Review*, 2nd ser., III, 1950.
282. DE SMET, A., 'De l'utilité de recueillir les mentions d'arpenteurs cités dans les documents d'archives du Moyen Age' in *Fédération archéologique et historique de Belgique, 33e Congrès*, III, 1951.
283. DONKIN, R. A., 'The Marshland Holdings of the English Cistercians before c.1350' in *Cîteaux in de Nederland*, 1958.
284. —— 'Bercaria and Landria', in *Yorkshire Archeological Journal*, 1958.
285. —— 'Settlement and depopulation on Cistercian estates during the twelfth and thirteenth centuries, especially in Yorkshire' in *Bulletin of the Institute of Historical Research*, 1960.
286. DUBY, G., 'Techniques et rendements agricoles dans les Alpes du Sud en 1338' in *Annales du Midi*, 1958.
287. FEUCHÈRE, L., 'Le défrichement des forêts en Artois du IXe au XIIIe siècle' in *Revue d'Histoire économique et sociale*, 1950.
288. FINBERG, H. P. R., 'The Domesday Plough-team' in *English Historical Review*, 1951.

289. —— *Gloucestershire Studies*, Leicester, 1957.

290. FOCKEMA ANDREAE, J. S., 'Embanking and drainage authorities in the Netherlands during the Middle Ages' in *Speculum*, 1952.

291. —— 'L'eau et les hommes dans la Flandre maritime' in *Tijdschrift voor Rechtsgeschiedenis*, 1960.

292. FOURNIER, G., 'La vie pastorale au Moyen Age dans les monts Dore' in *Mélanges Philippe Arbos*, Clermont-Ferrand, 1953.

293. GAUSSIN, P., 'La terre de Saint-Oyen et le peuplement du Haut-Jura' in *Cahiers d'histoire*, 1957.

294. GÉNICOT, L., 'Sur les témoignages d'accroissement de la population en Occident, du XIe au XIIIe siècle' in *Cahiers d'histoire mondiale*, I, 1953.

295. GRIMM, P., *Hohenrode, eine mittelalterliche Siedlung im Südharz*, Halle, 1939.

296. GSTIRNER, A., 'Die Schwaighöfe im ehemaligen Herzogtum Steiermark' in *Zeitschrift des historischen Vereins für Steiermark*, 1937.

297. HALLAM, H. E., *The New Lands of Elloe: a Study of Early Reclamation in Lincolnshire* (Department of English Local History, Occasional Papers, No. 6). Leicester, 1954.

298. —— 'Some thirteenth-century Censuses' in *Economic History Review*, 2nd ser., X, 1958.

299. —— 'Population Density in Medieval Fenland' in *Economic History Review*, 2nd ser. XIV, 1961.

300. HARLEY, J. B., 'Population Trends and Agricultural Developments from the Warwickshire Hundred Rolls of 1279' in *Economic History Review*, 2nd ser., XI, 1958.

301. HAUSMANN, O., 'Die bergbäuerliche Produktion im Raum von Staffler im 13-14. und im 20. Jahrhundert' in *Zeitschrift für Agrargeschichte und Agrarsoziologie*, 1957.

302. HIGOUNET, C., 'Chemins de Saint-Jacques et Sauvetés de Gascogne' in *Annales du Midi*, 1951.

303. —— 'L'expansion de la vie rurale au XIIe et au XIIIe siècle' in *Information historique*, 1953.

304. —— 'L'assolement triennal dans la plaine de France au XIIIe siècle in *Comptes rendus des séances de l'Académie des Inscriptions et Belles-Lettres*, 1956.

305. —— 'La plus ancienne sauveté de l'abbaye de Moissac: La Salvetat de Belmont' in *Xe Congrès de la Fédération Languedoc-Pyrénées-Gascogne*, Montauban, 1956.

306. —— 'Le Moyen Age derrière la géographie. Un village d'hôtes royaux du XIIe siècle. Toufou' in *Information historique*, 1957.

307. —— 'Une carte agricole de l'Albigeois vers 1260' in *Annales du Midi*, 1958.

308. —— 'Les types d'exploitations cisterciennes et prémontrées du XIIIe siècle, et leur rôle dans la formation de l'habitat et des paysages ruraux' in *Annales de l'Est*, Mémoire No. 21, 1959.

309. HUBERT, J., 'La frontière du comté de Champagne du XIe au XIIIe siècle' in *Mélanges Clovis Brunel*, II, Paris, 1955.

310. ILG, K., 'Die Walser und die Bedeutung ihrer Wirtschaft in den Alpen' in *Vierteljahrschrift für Sozial- und Wirtschaftsgeschichte*, 1950.

311. LATOUCHE, R., 'Un aspect de la vie rurale dans le Maine au XIe et au XIIe siècle: l'établissement des bourgs' in *Le Moyen Age*, 1937.

312. —— 'Défrichement et peuplement rural dans le Maine, du IXe au XIIe siècle' in *Le Moyen Age*, 1958.

Bibliography

313. LENNARD, R., 'Domesday Plough-teams: the South-Western Evidence' in *English Historical Review*, 1945.

314. —— 'The Composition of Demesne Plough Teams in XIII century England' in *English Historical Review*, 1959.

315. —— 'Statistics of Sheep in Medieval England' in *Agricultural History Review*, 1959.

316. MARTEL, H., 'Le défrichement en Artois du IXe au XIIIe siècle' in *Bulletin de la Société des Antiquaires de Morinie*, 1956.

317. MARTIN DEMEZIL, J., 'Recherches sur les origines et la formation de l'aireau blésois' in *Recueil de travaux offert à Clovis Brunel*, II, Paris, 1955.

318. MOLITOR, E., *Die Pfleghaften des Sachsenspiegels und das Siedlungsrecht im Sächsischen Stammesgebiet*, Weimar, 1941.

319. MOLLAT, M., 'Les hôtes de l'abbaye de Bourbourg' in *Mélanges Louis Halphen*, Paris, 1951.

320. OURLIAC, P., 'Les sauvetés de Comminges. Étude et documents sur les villages fondés par les Hospitaliers dans la région des coteaux commingeois' in *Revue de l'Académie de législation*, 1947.

321. —— 'Les villages de la région toulousaine au XIIe siècle' in *Annales E.S.C.*, 1949.

322. QUIRIN, K. H., *Herrschaftsbildung und Kolonisation im mitteldeutschen Osten*, Göttingen, 1949.

323. RICHARDSON, H. G., 'The Medieval Plough team', in *History*, 1941-1942.

324. SCLAFERT, T., 'A propos du déboisement dans les Alpes du Sud' in *Annales de Géographie*, 1933.

325. STOLZ, O., 'Die Schwaighöfe in Tirol' in *Wissenschaftliche Veröffentlichung des deutschen und österreichischen Alpenvereins*, 5, 1930.

326. —— 'Beiträge zur Geschichte der alpinen Schwaighöfe' in *Vierteljahrschrift für Sozial- und Wirtschaftsgeschichte*, 1932.

327. TUCOO-CHALA, P., 'Forêts et landes en Béarn' in *Annales du Midi*, 1955.

328. VAN DER LINDEN, H., *De Cope*, Assen, 1955.

329. VERHULST, A., 'Historische geografie van de Vlaamse Kustvlakte tot omstreeks 1200' in *Bijdragen voor de geschiedenis der Nederlanden*, 1959.

330. WINTER, J. M. VAN, 'Vlaams en Hollands recht bij de Kolonisatie van Duitsland in de XIIe en XIIIe eeuw' in *Tijdschrift voor rechtsgeschiedenis*, 1953.

C. Trade

331. AUBENAS, R., 'Commerce du drap et vie économique à Grasse en 1308-1309' in *Provence Historique*, 1959.

332. CAGGESE, R., 'La Repubblica di Siena e il suo contado nel secolo XIII' in *Bolletino senese di storia patria*, 1906.

333. DONKIN, R. A., 'The Disposal of Cistercian Wool in England and Wales during the XIIth and XIIIth centuries' in *Cîteaux in de Nederland*, 1957.

334. —— 'Cistercian sheep-farming and wool-sales in the thirteenth century' in *Agricultural History Review*, 1948.

335. EMERY, R. W., *The Jews of Perpignan in the thirteenth Century*, New York, 1959.

336. ENGELMANN, E., *Zur städtischen Volksbewegung in Südfrankreich. Kommunefreiheit und Gesellschaft. Arles 1200-1250*, Berlin, 1959.

337. FARMER, D. L., 'Some Price Fluctuations in Angevin England' in *Economic History Review*, 2nd ser., IX, 1956.

338. —— 'Some Grain Price Movements in Thirteenth-Century England' in *Economic History Review*, 2nd ser., X, 1957.

339. FONTETTE, F., *Recherches sur la pratique de la vente immobilière dans la région parisienne au Moyen Age (fin Xe - début XIVe siècle)*, Paris, 1957.

340. —— 'La vie économique dans la région parisienne d'après les actes de vente immobilière au XIIIe siècle' in *Revue historique de droit français et étranger*, 1959.

341. HERLIHY, D., 'Treasure Hoards in the Italian Economy, 960-1139' in *Economic History Review*, 2nd ser., X, 1957.

342. HIGOUNET, C., 'L'arrière pays de Bordeaux au XIIIe siècle (esquisse cartographique)' in *Revue historique de Bordeaux et du département de la Gironde*, 1955.

343. —— 'Les Alaman, seigneurs bastidors et péagers du XIIIe siècle' in *Annales du Midi*, 1956.

344. JORIS, A., 'Les moulins à guède dans le comté de Namur pendant la seconde moitié du XIIIe siècle' in *Le Moyen Age*, 1959.

345. MIRA, G., 'Il fabbisogno di cereali in Perugia nei secoli XIII-XIV' in *Studi in onore di Armando Sapori*, I, Milan, 1957.

346. MUNDY, J. H., 'Un usurier malheureux' in *Annales du Midi*, 1956.

347. MUSSET, L., 'A-t-il existé en Normandie au XIe siècle une aristocratie d'argent?' in *Annales de Normandie*, 1959.

348. PERROY, E., 'Les Chambon, bouchers à Montbrison, circa 1220-1314' in *Annales du Midi*, 1955.

349. —— 'Le décrochage des monnaies en temps de mutation. Le cas du viennois faible 1304-1308' in *Le Moyen Age*, 1958.

350. POSTAN, M., 'The Rise of a Money Economy' in *Economic History Review*, XIV, 1944.

351. SCHNEIDER, J., *La ville de Metz aux XIIIe et XIVe siècles*, Nancy, 1950.

352. TIHON, C., 'Aperçus sur l'établissement des Lombards dans les Pays-Bas aux XIIIe et XIVe siècles' in *Revue belge de philologie et d'histoire*, 1961.

353. ZANONI, L., *Gli Umiliati nei loro rapporti con l'eresia, l'industria della lana ed i communi nei secoli XII e XIII*, Milan, 1911.

D. The Manor

I. GERMANY

354. DARAPSKY, E., *Die ländliche Grundbesitzverhältnisse des Kölnischen Stifts St. Gereon bis zum Jahre 1500*, Cologne, 1943.

355. DOLLINGER, P., 'Les transformations du régime domanial en Bavière au XIIIe siècle d'après deux censiers de l'abbaye de Baumburg' in *Le Moyen Age*, 1950.

356. DOPSCH, A., *Herrschaft und Bauer in der deutschen Kaiserzeit*, Jena, 1939.

357. GENSICKE, H., *Landesgeschichte des Westerwaldes*, Wiesbaden, 1958.

358. HILLEBRAND, W., *Besitz- und Standesverhältnisse des Osnabrücker Adels, 800 bis 1300*, Göttingen, 1962.

359. KUUJO, E. O., *Das Zehntwesen in der Erzdiozese Hamburg-Bremen bis zu seiner Privatisierung*, Helsinki, 1949.

360. LÜTGE, F., *Die mitteldeutsche Grundherrschaft*, Jena, 1934.

361. —— *Die Agrarverfassung des frühen Mittelalters im mitteldeutschen Raum vornehmlich in der Karolingerzeit*, Jena, 1937.

362. MAGER, F., *Geschichte des Bauerntums und der Bodenkultur im Lande Mecklemburg*, Berlin, 1955.

Bibliography

363. MAYER, T., *Adel und Bauer im deutschen Staat des Mittelalters*, Leipzig, 1943.
364. MOEREN, E., *Zur sozialen und wirtschaftlichen Lage des Bauerntums vom 12. bis 14. Jahrhundert. Studien über die Ländlichen Lehen auf Grund von Mainzer und Xantoner Quellen*, Frankfort, 1939.
365. PERRIN, C. E., 'La société rurale allemande du Xe au XIIIe siècle d'après un ouvrage récent' in *Revue historique de droit français et étranger*, 1945.
366. RODEN, C. VON, 'Wirtschaftliche Entwicklung und bäuerliches Recht des Stiftes Frondenberg an der Ruhr' in *Münstersche Beiträge zur Geschichtsforschung*, 1936.
367. RULAND, H., *Die Entwicklung des Grundeigentums der Abtei Camp am Niederrhein im Bezirk des jetzigen Kreises Bergheim*, Emsdetten, 1936.
368. SCHÄFER, A., 'Zur Besitzsgeschichte des Klosters Hirsau von 11. bis 16. Jahrhundert' in *Zeitschrift für Württembergische Landesgeschichte*, 1960.
369. SCHOEMBERGER, F., *Geschichte des Kurkolnischen Amtes und der Dörfer Zeltingen und Rachtig an der Mosel*, Bonn, 1940.
370. SCHÖNING, A., *Der Grundbesitz des Klosters Corvey im ehemaligen Landes Lippe*, Detmold, 1958-1959.
371. STOLZ, O., *Rechtsgeschichte des Bauernstandes und der Landwirtschaft in Tirol und Vorarlberg*, Bolzano, 1949.
372. WEIBELS, F., *Die Grossgrundherrschaft Xanten im Mittelalter. Studien und Quellen zur Verhaltungeines mittelalterlichen Stift am unteren Niederrhein*, Neustadt, Aisch, 1959.
373. WIESSNER, H., *Sachinhalt und wirtschaftliche Bedeutung der Weistümer im deutschen Kulturgebiet*, Vienna, 1934.
374. WITTE, B., *Herrschaft und Land im Rheingau*, Meisenheim, 1959.
375. WITTICH, W., 'Die Entstehung des Meierrechts und die Auflösung der Villikationsverfassung in Niedersachsen und Westfalen' in *Zeitschrift für Sozial- und Wirtschaftsgeschichte*, 1904.

2. ENGLAND

376. ASTON, T. H., 'The Origins of the Manor in England' in *Trans. of the Royal Historical Society*, 5th ser., VIII, 1958.
377. BARG, M. A., 'The Norman Conquest and the Organisation of the Dependent Peasant in England' (in Russian) in *Voprosii Istorii*, VII, 1957.
378. BEVERIDGE, W., 'Wages in the Winchester Manors' in *Economic History Review*, 2nd ser., VII, 1956.
379. —— 'Westminster Wages in the Manorial Era' in *Economic History Review*, 2nd ser., VIII, 1956.
380. BLAKE, P., 'Norfolk Manorial Lords in 1316' in *Norfolk Archeological Papers*, 1952.
381. DALE, M. K. (ed), *Court Roll of Chalgrove Manor, 1272-1312*, Streatley, 1950.
382. DAVIS, R. H., *The Kalendar of Abbot Samson of Bury St Edmunds and Related Documents*, London, 1954.
383. DENHOLM-YOUNG, N., *Seignorial Administration in England*, Oxford, 1937.
384. DREW, J. S., 'Early Account Rolls of Portland, Wyke and Elewell' in *Proceedings of Dorset Natural History and Archeological Society*, LXVII, 1947.
385. FAULKNER, P. A., 'Domestic Planning from the Twelfth to the Fourteenth Century' in *Archeological Journal*, 1958.
386. FENN, R. M., 'The Assessment of Wiltshire in 1083 and 1086' in *Wiltshire Archeology and Natural History Magazine*, 1944.
387. GRAVES, C. V., 'The Economic Activities of the Cistercians in Medieval England, 1128-1307' in *Analecta sancti ordinis Cisterciensis*, 1957.

388. GRIFFITHS, W. A., 'Some Notes on the Earlier Records of the Manor of Deythur in *Montgomeryshire Collects*, LI, 1949.
389. GUTNOVA, E. G., 'The Problem of the Immunity in thirteenth-century England' (in Russian) in *Srednie Veka*, III, 1951.
390. HALCROW, E. M., 'The Decline of Demesne Farming on the Estates of Durham Cathedral Priory' in *Economic History Review*, 2nd ser., VII, 1955.
391. HILTON, R. H., 'Gloucester Abbey Leases of Late Thirteenth Century' in *Univ. of Birmingham Historical Journal*, IV, 1953.
392. —— 'Winchcombe Abbey and the Manor of Sherborne' in *Univ. of Birmingham Historical Journal*, III, 1949.
393. HOLLINGS, M. (ed), *The Red Book of Worcester*, IV, London, 1950.
394. HOMANS, G. C., 'The Frisians in East Anglia' in *Economic History Review*, 2nd ser., IX, 1957.
395. HOYT, R. S., 'The Nature and Origins of the Ancient Demesne' in *English Historical Review*, 1950.
396. JOHN, E., *Land Tenure in Early England*, Leicester, 1960.
397. JONES-PIERCE, R., 'A Caernarvonshire Manorial Borough' in *Trans. of Caernarvon Historical Society*, 1941.
398. —— 'Growth of Commutation in Gwynedd during the Thirteenth Century' in *Bulletin of Celtic Studies*, X.
399. KOSMINSKY, E. A., 'Services and Money Rents in the XIIIth Century' in *Economic History Review*, V., 1935.
400. —— 'The Small Manor in Medieval England' in *Izvestiia Akademiia Nauk*, Ser. 1st, I. *Philos-Philol*, I, No. 4, 1944.
401. —— 'Labour on English Manors in the Thirteenth Century' (in Russian) in *Voprosii Istorii*, 1945.
402. —— 'The Evolution of Feudal Rent in England from the XIth to the XVth Centuries' in *Past and Present*, 1955.
403. —— *Studies in the Agrarian History of England in the XIIIth Century*, Oxford, 1956.
404. LAWSON-TANCRED, T., *Records of a Yorkshire Manor (Aldborough)*, London, 1937.
405. LENNARD, R., 'The Hidations of "demesne" in some Domesday entries' in *Economic History Review*, 2nd ser., VIII, 1956.
406. —— 'The Demesne of Glastonbury Abbey in the XIth and XIIth Centuries' in *Economic History Review*, 2nd ser., VIII, 1956, [See No. 415 below.]
407. LEVETT, A. E., *Studies in Manorial History*, Oxford, 1938.
408. MORGAN, M., *The English Lands of the Abbey of Bec*, London, 1946.
409. OSCHINSKY, D., 'Notes on the Lancaster Estates in the Thirteenth and Fourteenth Centuries' in *Trans. of Lancashire and Cheshire Historical Society*, 1949.
410. PAGE, F. M. (ed.), *Wellingborough Manorial Accounts, 1258-1323*, Northamptonshire Record Society, 1936.
411. PLUCKNETT, T. F. T., *The Medieval Bailiff*, London, 1954.
412. POSTAN, M. M., 'Chronology of Labour Services' in *Trans. of the Royal Historical Society*, 4th ser., XX, 1937.
413. —— 'The Manor in the Hundred Rolls' in *Economic History Review*, 2nd ser., III, 1950.
414. —— *The 'Famulus', the Estate Labourer in the XIIth and XIIIth Centuries*, Cambridge, 1954.
415. —— 'Glastonbury Estates in the Twelfth Century: a Reply' [to No. 407] in *Economic History Review*, 2nd ser., IX, 1956.

416. PUGH, R. B., 'The Early History of the Manors in Amesbury' in *Wiltshire Archaeology and Natural History Magazine*, 1947.

417. SAWYER, P. H., 'The "Original Returns" and Domesday Book' in *English Historical Review*, LXX, 1955.

418. SIMPSON, J. W., *The History of South Warnborough in Hampshire, Church, Manor and Plough*, I. Winchester, 1946.

419. TAYLOR, E. G. R., 'The Surveyor' in *Economic History Review*, XVII, 1947.

3. FRANCE

420. BARATIER, E., 'Maillane et ses seigneurs à l'époque médiévale' in *Provence historique*, 1956.

421. BERTHET, B., 'Abbayes et exploitations' in *Annales E.S.C.*, 1950.

422. BLOCH, M., 'Sous saint Louis: le roi, ses seigneuries et ses champs' in *Annales d'histoire économique et sociale*, 1938.

423. BOUSSARD, J., 'La seigneurie de Bellême aux Xe et XIe siècles' in *Mélanges Louis Halphen*, Paris, 1951.

424. —— *Le comté d'Anjou sous Henri Plantagenet et ses fils, 1151-1204*, Paris, 1938.

425. CAILLET, L., 'Le contrat dit de facherie' in *Nouvelle revue historique de droit*, 1911.

426. CARABIE, R., *La propriété foncière dans le très ancien droit normand (XIe-XIIIe siècles)*. I. *La propriété domaniale*, Caen, 1943.

427. CASTAING-SICARD, M., 'Contrat de travail et louage d'ouvrage dans la vie toulousaine des XIIe et XIIIe siècles' in *Recueil de la société d'histoire du droit écrit*, 1958.

428. CHANTEUX, H., 'Quelques notes sur les vavasseurs' in *Revue historique de droit français et étranger*, 1958.

429. CHÉDEVILLE, A., 'Les restitutions d'églises en faveur de l'abbaye de Saint-Vincent du Mans' in *Cahiers de civilisation médiévale*, 1960.

430. CONSTABLE, G., 'Cluniac tithe and the Controversy between Gigny and Le Miroir' in *Revue Bénédictine*, 1960.

431. COOPLAND, G. W., *The Abbey of S. Bertin and its Neighbourhood, 900-1350*, Oxford, 1914.

432. DAVID, M., *Le patrimoine foncier de l'église de Lyon de 984 à 1267. Contribution à l'étude de la féodalité dans le Lyonnais*, Lyon, 1942.

433 DIDIER, N., 'Les censiers du prieuré de Domène' in *Cahiers d'histoire*, 1957-1958.

434. DUBAR, L., *Recherches sur les offices du monastère de Corbie jusqu'à la fin du XIIIe siècle*, Paris, 1951.

435. DUBLED, H., 'Seigneurs et paysans en Languedoc' in *Mémoire de la Société d'histoire du droit écrit*, 1958.

436. —— 'Aspects de l'économie cistercienne en Alsace au XIIe siècle' in *Revue d'histoire ecclésiastique*, 1959.

437. —— 'La justice au sein de la seigneurie foncière en Alsace du XIe au XIIIe siècle' in *Le Moyen Age*, 1960.

438. —— 'Administration et exploitation des terres de la seigneurie rurale en Alsace aux XIe et XIIe siècles' in *Vierteljahrschrift für Sozial- und Wirtschaftsgeschichte*, 1960.

439. —— 'Taille et "Umgeld" en Alsace au XIIIe siècle' in *Vierteljahrschrift für Sozial- und Wirtschaftsgeschichte*, 1960.

440. —— 'La notion de ban en Alsace au Moyen Age' in *Revue historique de droit français et étranger*, 1961.

441. DUBY, G., 'Économie domaniale et économie monétaire; le budget de l'abbaye de Cluny entre 1080 et 1155' in *Annales E.S.C.*, 1952.

442. ——— 'Un inventaire des profits de la seigneurie clunisienne à la mort de Pierre le Vénérable' in *Studia Anselmiana, 40, Petrus Venerabilis*, 1956.

443. ——— 'La structure d'une grande seigneurie flamande à la fin du XIIIe siècle' in *Bibliothèque de l'École des Chartes*, 1956.

444. ——— 'Note sur les corvées dans les Alpes du Sud en 1338' in *Études d'histoire du droit privé offertes à Pierre Petot*, Paris, 1959.

445. ——— 'La seigneurie et l'économie paysanne. Alpes du Sud, 1338' in *Études rurales*, 1961.

446. EPINOIS, H. DE L', 'Comptes relatifs à la fondation de l'abbaye de Maubuisson' in *Bibliothèque de l'École de Chartes*, 1857-1858.

447. FEBVRE, L., 'Deux contributions à l'histoire seigneuriale; I: la seigneurie au pays de Namur; II: alleu contre féodalité' in *Annales E.S.C.*, 1948.

448. FEUCHÈRE, P., 'Un obstacle au réseau de subordination: alleux et alleutiers en Artois, Boulonnais et Flandre wallonne' in *Études publiées par la section belge de la Comm. intern. pour l'Hist. des assemblées d'États*, IX, 1955.

449. FOSSIER, R., 'Les granges de Clairvaux et la règle cistercienne' in *Citeaux in de Nederlanden*, 1955.

450. FOURNIER, G., 'La création de la grange de Gergovie, par les Prémontrés de Saint-André' in *Le Moyen Age*, 1950.

451. ——— 'La seigneurie en Basse-Auvergne aux XIe et XIIe siècles, d'après les censiers du cartulaire de Sauxillanges' in *Mélanges Louis Halphen*, Paris, 1951.

452. ——— 'Cartulaire de Saint-Martin-des-Aloches' in *Revue d'Auvergne*, 1951.

453. ——— 'Les origines du terrier en Basse-Auvergne, XIe-XIVe siècles' in *Revue d'Auvergne*, 1955.

454. GAUSSIN, R., 'De la seigneurie rurale à la baronnie: l'abbaye de Savigny en Lyonnais' in *Le Moyen Age*, 1955.

455. GRAND, R., 'Une curieuse appellation de certaines corvées au Moyen Age: le "biau", "biain" ou "bien". Son origine, sa nature' in *Mélanges dédiés à la mémoire de Félix Gret*, I, Paris, 1946.

456. HIGOUNET, C., 'Cartulaires des Templiers de Montsaunés' in *Bulletin philologique et historique*, 1957.

457. HIGOUNET, C. & NADAL, A., 'L'inventaire des biens de la Commanderie du Temple de Sainte-Eulalie du Larzac en 1308' in *Annales du Midi*, 1956.

458. KIEFT, C., VAN DE *Étude sur le chartrier et la seigneurie du prieuré de la Chapelle-Aude (XIe-XIIIe siècles)*, Amsterdam, 1960.

459. LAPORTE, DOM J., 'L'état des biens de l'abbaye de Jumièges en 1338' in *Annales de Normandie*, 1959.

460. LAURENT, H., 'Deux documents d'un type unique pour servir à l'histoire du régime seigneurial et de la vie rurale: le Terrier de l'évêque de Cambrai et le Rentier du seigneur d'Audenarde' in *Bulletin de la Commission royale d'histoire de Belgique*, 1939.

461. LEMARIGNIER, J. F., 'La dislocation du *Pagus* et la problème des *consuetudines*, Xe-XIe siècles' in *Mélanges Louis Halphen*, Paris, 1951.

462. ——— 'Le domaine de Villeberfol et le patrimoine de Marmoutier (XIe siècle)' in *Études d'histoire du droit privé offertes à Pierre Petot*, Paris, 1959.

463. MUSSET, L., 'Autour de l'abbaye de Saint-André-en-Gouffern (Calvados), Notes d'histoire sociale' in *Bulletin de la Société des antiquaires de Normandie*, 1946.

Bibliography

464. —— 'Un type de tenure rurale d'origine scandinave en Normandie. Le man-sloth' in *Mémoires de l'Académie des Sciences et Belles-Lettres de Caen*, 1952.

465. —— 'La vie économique de l'abbaye de Fécamp sous l'abbatiat de Jean de Ravenne, 1028-1078' in *L'abbaye bénédictine de Fécamp. XIIIe centenaire*, Fécamp, 1958.

466. —— 'Les censiers du Mont-Saint-Michel. Essai de restitution d'une source perdue' in *Revue du département de la Manche*, 1960.

467. PERRIN, C. E., 'Essai sur la fortune immobilière de l'abbaye alsacienne de Marmoutier aux Xe et XIe siècles' in *Histoire du droit et des institutions de l'Alsace*, fasc. 10, Strasbourg, 1935.

468. —— 'Esquisse d'une histoire de la tenure en Lorraine au Moyen Age' in *Recueils de la Société Jean Bodin, III. La tenure*, Brussels, 1938.

469. PETOT, P., 'La constitution de rente aux XIIe et XIIIe siècles dans les pays coutumiers' in *Publications de l'Université de Dijon*, 1928.

470. PICOT, J., *La Seigneurie de l'abbaye de l'Ile-Barbe des origines à 1312*, Lyons, 1952.

471. PIERRENET, P., 'Les droits de seigneurie en Bourgogne' in *Mémoires de la Société pour l'histoire du droit et des institutions des anciens pays bourguignons . . .*, VII, 1940-1941.

472. REYNAUD, F., 'L'organisation et le domaine de la commanderie de Manosque' in *Provence historique*, 1957.

473. RICHARD, J. M., 'Thierry d'Hireçon, agriculteur artésien' in *Bibliothèque de l'École des chartes*, 1892.

474. SCHNAPPER, B., 'Les baux à vie' in *Revue historique de droit français et étranger*, 1957.

475. STRAYER, J. R., *The Royal Domain in the Bailliage of Rouen*, Princeton, 1936.

476. VIARD, P., 'La dîme ecclésiastique dans le royaume d'Arles et de Vienne aux XIIe et XIIIe siècles' in *Zeitschrift der Savigny Stiftung, Germanische Abteilung*, 1911.

4. ITALY

477. GUKOVSKIJ, M. A., *Italianskoe Vozrozhdenie*, I, Leningrad, 1947.

478. IMBERCIADORI, I., *Mezzadria classica toscana. Con documentazione inedita dal IX al XIV secolo*, Florence, 1951.

479. JONES, P. J., 'Medieval Agrarian Society in its Prime. Italy' in *Cambridge Economic History*, I, 2nd ed., Cambridge, 1966.

480. NASALI-ROCCA, E., 'La gestione dei beni del monastero cistercense di Chiaravalle della Colomba' in *Economia e storia*, 1956.

481. ROMEO, R., 'La signoria dell'abate di sant'Ambrogio di Milano sul commune rurale di Origgio nel secolo XIII' in *Rivista storica italiana*, 1957.

5. THE LOW COUNTRIES

482. BRUWIER, M., 'Note sur l'exploitation des bois de Mirwart par le comte de Hainaut en 1333' in *Mélanges Félix Rousseau*, Liège, 1958.

483. DERVEEGHDE, D. VAN, *Le domaine du Val Saint-Lambert de 1202 à 1387. Contribution à l'histoire rurale et industrielle du pays de Liège*, Paris, 1955.

484. GODDING, P. & GANSHOF, F. L., 'Le prieuré de Grand-Bigard depuis sa fondation jusqu'en 1381' in *Annales de la société royale d'Archéologie de Bruxelles*, 1948-1955.

485. MULLER, S. (ed)., *Oorkondenboek van het sticht Utrecht tot 1301*, 4 vols., 1920-1954.

486. SMET, J. DE, *Het memoriaal van Simon de Rikelike, Vrijlaat te St Pieters-op-den-Dijk, 1323-1336*, Brussels, 1933.
487. STIENSON, J., *Étude sur le chartier et le domaine de l'abbaye Saint-Jacques à Liège, 1015-1209*, Paris, 1951.

E. *Personal Dependence and Domestic Officials*

488. BORNE, L., 'Notes pour servir à l'histoire de la mainmorte dans le comté de Bourgogne' in *Mémoires de la société pour l'histoire du droit . . . des anciens pays bourguignons . . .* , 1950-1951.
489. BOSL, K., 'Freiheit und Unfreiheit' in *Vierteljahrschrift für Sozial- und Wirtschaftsgeschichte*, 1957.
490. BOUSSARD, J., 'Serfs et *colliberti* (XIe-XIIe siècles)' in *Bibliothèque de l'école des Chartes*, 1947-1948.
491. BRELOT, J., 'La mainmorte dans la région de Dole' in *Mémoires de la Société pour l'histoire du droit . . . des anciens pays bourguignons . . .* , 1950-1951.
492. DIDIER, N., 'Les plus anciens textes sur le servage dans la région dauphinoise' in *Études d'histoire du droit privé offertes à Pierre Petot*, Paris, 1959.
493. DODWELL, B., 'The Sokeman of the Southern Danelaw in the Eleventh Century' in *Bulletin of the Institute of Historical Research*, 1938.
494. DUBAR, L., 'Les mairies rurales du monastère de Saint-Riquier' in *Revue du Nord*, 1958.
495. DUBY, G., 'Géographie ou chronologie du servage. Note sur les *servi* en Forez et en Mâconnais du Xe au XIIe siècle' in *Hommage à Lucien Febvre*, I, Paris, 1953.
496. GÉNICOT, L., '*Nobiles, milites, villici* au XIe siècle' in *Namurcum*, 1957.
497. IMBERT, J., 'Quelques aspects juridiques de la mainmorte seigneuriale en Lorraine' in *Mémoires de la Société pour l'histoire du droit . . . des pays bourguignons . . .* , 1950-1951.
498. LEBON, M., 'Textes sur le formariage en Lorraine, des origines au début du XIIIe siècle' in *Annales de l'Est*, 1951.
499. OURLIAC, P., 'L'hommage servile dans la région toulousaine' in *Mélanges Louis Halphen*, Paris, 1951.
500. —— 'Le servage dans la région toulousaine' *Xo Congresso Internazionale di Scienza storiche, Roma, 1955, Relazioni, III*, Florence, 1955.
501. PETOT, P., 'L'évolution du servage dans la France coutumière du XIe au XIVe siècle' in *Recueils de la Société Jean Bodin, II. Le servage*, Brussels, 1937.
502. —— 'L'origine de la mainmorte servile' in *Revue historique de droit français et étranger*, 1940-1941.
503. —— 'Licence de mariage et formariage des serfs dans les coutumes françaises du Moyen Age' in *Czasopismo Prawno Historyczny*, II, 1949.
504. —— 'Servage et tonsure cléricale dans la pratique française du Moyen Age' in *Revue d'histoire de l'Église de France*, 1954.
505. TITS-DIEUAIDE, M. J., 'Un exemple de passage de la ministérialité à la noblesse: la famille de Wesemael (1166-1250)' in *Revue belge de philosophie et d'histoire*, 1958.
506. VACCARI, P., *L'affrancazione dei servi della gleba nell'Emilia e nella Toscana*, Bologna, 1926.
507. —— *L'affrancazioni collettive dei servi della gleba*, Milan, 1939.
508. VINOGRADOV, P., *Villainage in England*, Oxford, 1892.

Bibliography

F. Peasants and the Village Community

509. AUBENAS, R., *Chartes de franchises et actes d'habitation (Documents, textes et mémoires pour servir à l'histoire de Cannes et de sa région)*, I, fasc. I, Cannes, 1943.

510. AULT, W. O., 'Village By-Laws by Common Consent' in *Speculum*, 1954.

511. —— *The Self-Directing Activities of Village Communities in Medieval England*, Boston, 1952.

512. BADER, K. S., *Das mittelalterliche Dorf als Friedens- und Rechtsbereich*, I, Weimar, 1957.

513. BERNI, G., '*Cives e rusticii* alla fine del 12. secolo ed all'inizio del 13. secondo il *Liber consuetudinum mediolani*' in *Rivista storica italiana*, 1957.

514. BOG, I., *Dorfgemeinde, Freiheit und Unfreiheit in Franken*, Stuttgart, 1956.

515. BOGNETTI, G. P., *Sulle origini dei communi rurali del medioevo con speziali osservazioni dei territorii milanese e comasco*, Pavia, 1927.

516. BOSL, K., 'Eine Geschichte der Deutschen Landgemeinde' in *Zeitschrift für Agrargeschichte und Agrarsoziologie*, 1961.

517. BRELOT, J., 'Caractères originaux du mouvement communal dans le comté de Bourgogne' in *Mémoires de la société pour l'histoire du droit . . . bourguignon, comtois et romand*, 1954.

518. CIPOLLA, C. M., 'Populazione e proprietari delle campagne attraverso un ruolo di contribuenti del secolo XII' in *Bolletino della societa pavese di storia patria*, 1946.

519. DAVID, M., 'Les *laboratores* du renouveau économique du XIIe siècle à la fin du XIVe' in *Revue historique de droit français et étranger*, 1959.

520. DODWELL, B., 'The Free Peasantry of East Anglia in Domesday' in *Norfolk Archaeology*, XLVI, 1940.

521. —— 'The Free Tenantry of the Hundred Rolls' in *Economic History Review*, XIV, 1944.

522. DOPSCH, A., *Die ältere Wirtschafts- und Sozialgeschichte der Bauern in den Alpenländern Österreichs*, Oslo, 1930.

523. DOUGLAS, D. C., *The Social Structure of Medieval East Anglia*, Oxford, 1927.

524. DOVRING, F., 'Contribution à l'étude de l'organisation des villages normands au Moyen Age' in *Annales de Normandie*, 1952.

525. ENNEN, E., 'Ein Teilungsvertrag des Trierer Simeonstiftes, der Herren von Berg, von Lister und des Ritters von Südlingen' in *Rheinische Vierteljahrsblätter*, 1956.

526. EPPERLEIN, S., *Bauernbedrückung und Bauernwiderstand im hohen Mittelalter*, Berlin, 1960.

527. HOMANS, G. C., 'Partible Inheritance of Villagers' Holdings' in *Economic History Review*, VIII, 1937.

528. —— *English Villagers in the Thirteenth Century*, Harvard, 1942.

529. HOYT, R. S., 'Farm of the Manor and Community of the Vill in Domesday Book' in *Speculum*, 1955.

530. KONOTKINE, A. V., 'The struggle of peasants towards autonomy and free association in northern France in the XIIth-XIVth centuries' (in Russian) in *Voprosy Istorii*, 1948.

531. KOSMINSKY, E. A., *The English Village in the Thirteenth Century* (in Russian), Leningrad, 1935.

532. LENNARD, R., 'The Economic Position of the Bordars and Cottars of Domesday Book' in *Economic Journal*, 1946, and 1947.

533. —— 'Peasant Tithe Collectors in Norman England' in *English Historical Review*, LXIX, 1954.

534. LUZZATTO, G., 'L'inurbamento delle popolazioni rurali in Italia nei secoli XII and XIII' in *Studi di storia e di diritto in onore di E. Besta*, Milan, 1938.

535. MAAS, W., 'Loi de Beaumont und Jus Theutonicum' in *Vierteljahrschrift für Sozial- und Wirtschaftsgeschichte*, 1939.

536. MARTIN-LORBER, O., 'Une communauté d'habitants dans une seigneurie de Cîteaux aux XIIIe et XIVe siècles' in *Annales de Bourgogne*, 1958.

537. PERRIN, C. E., 'Chartes de franchise et rapports de droit en Lorraine' in *Le Moyen Age*, 1946.

538. PLESNER, J., *L'émigration de la campagne à la ville libre de Florence au XIIIe siècle*, Copenhagen, 1934.

539. POSTAN, M., & TITOW, J., 'Heriots and Prices on Winchester Manors' in *Economic History Review*, 2nd ser., XI, 1959, followed by LONGDEN, G., 'Statistical Notes on Winchester Heriots'.

540. SCHNEIDER, F. H. G. H., *Die Entstehung von Burg- und Landgemeinde in Italien*, Berlin, 1946.

541. STEINBACH, F., *Ursprung und Wesen der Landgemeinde nach Rheinischen Quellen*, Cologne, 1960.

542. STEPHENSON, C., 'Commendation and Related Problems in Domesday' in *English Historical Review*, LIX, 1944.

543. WALREAT, M., 'Les chartes-lois de Prisches (1158) et de Beaumont-en-Argonne (1282). Contribution à l'étude de l'affranchissement des classes rurales au XIIe siècle' in *Revue belge de philologie et d'histoire*, 1944.

544. WIESNER, H., *Beiträge zur Geschichte des Dorfes und der Dorfgemeinde in Österreich*, Klagenfurt, 1946.

IV   XIV–XV CENTURIES

A.   *The Economic Climate*

I.   GENERAL CONSIDERATIONS

545. ABEL, W., *Die Wüstungen des ausgehenden Mittelalters. Ein Beitrag zur Siedlungs- und Agrargeschichte Deutschlands*, 2nd ed., Stuttgart, 1955.

546. BOUTRUCHE, R., 'Aux origines d'une crise nobiliaire: donations pieuses et pratiques successorales en Bordelais, du XIIIe au XIVe siècle' in *Annales d'histoire sociale*, 1939.

547. —— *La crise d'une société: seigneurs et paysans du Bordelais pendant la guerre de Cent Ans*, Paris, 1947.

548. CIPOLLA, C. M., 'Revisions in Economic History: The Trends in Italian Economic History in the later Middle Ages' in *Economic History Review*, 2nd ser., II, 1949.

549. —— 'L'economia milanese. I movimenti economici generali 1350–1500' in *Storia di Milano*, Milan, 1957.

550. FAWTIER, R., 'La crise d'une société durant la guerre de Cent Ans: à propos d'un livre récent' in *Revue historique*, CCIII, 1950.

551. FOURQUIN, G., *Les campagnes de la région parisienne à la fin du Moyen Age* (*du milieu du XIIIe siècle au début du XVIe*), Paris, 1962.

552. GRAUS, F., *Die erste Krise des Feudalismus. 14. Jahrhundert* (Ceskoslovenska Akademie Ved-Historicky Ustav), Prague, 1955.

553. GUÉRIN, I., *La vie rurale en Sologne aux XIVe et XVe siècles*, Paris, 1960.

554. HILTON, R. H., 'Y eut-il une crise générale de la féodalité?' in *Annales E.S.C.*, 1951.

555. —— 'L'Angleterre économique et sociale des XIVe et XVe siècles' in *Annales E.S.C.*, 1958.

556. JONES-PIERCE, T., 'Some tendencies in the Agrarian History of Caernarvonshire during the later Middle Ages' in *Trans. Caernarvon Historical Society*, 1939.

557. KOSMINSKY, E. A., 'Peut-on considérer le XIVe et le XVe siècle comme l'époque de la décadence de l'économie européenne?' in *Studi in onore di Armando Sapori*, I, Milan, 1957.

558. —— 'Les problèmes de base du féodalisme d'Europe occidentale dans la recherche historique soviétique' *Xo Congresso internazionale di scienze storiche*, *Roma, 1955, Atti*, Florence, 1955.

559. LÜTGE, F., 'Das 14. und 15. Jahrhundert in der Sozial- und Wirtschafts-Geschichte' in *Jahrbuch für Nationalökonomie und Statistik*, 1950.

560. LUZZATTO, G., 'Per la storia dell'economia rurale in Italia nel secolo XIV' in *Hommage à Lucien Febvre*, II, Paris. 1953.

561. MAŁOWIST, M., 'Crisis of the Feudal System in the XIV and XV centuries' (in Polish) in *Kwartalnik Historiczny*, 1953.

562. MOLLAT, M., JOHANSEN, P., POSTAN, M., SAPORI, A., & VERLINDEN, C., 'L'économie européenne aux deux derniers siècles du Moyen Age' *Xo Congresso internazionale di scienze storiche, Roma, 1955, Relazioni, VI*, Florence, 1955.

563. PERROY, E., 'La crise économique du XIVe siècle d'après les terriers foréziens' in *Bulletin de la Diana*, 1945-1946.

564. —— 'A l'origine d'une économie contractée: les crises du XIVe siècle' in *Annales E.S.C.*, 1949.

565. POSTAN, M., 'The Fifteenth Century' in *Economic History Review*, IX, 1939.

566. SALTMARSH, J., 'Plague and Economic Decline in England in the Later Middle Ages' in *Cambridge Historical Journal*, 1941.

567. SCHREINER, J., *Pest og prisfall i sen middel alderen*, Oslo, 1948.

568. —— 'Wages and Prices in England in the Later Middle Ages' in *Scandinavian Economic History Review*, 1954.

569. STEENSBERG, A., 'Archeological dating of the Climatic Change in North Europe about A.D. 1300' in *Natura*, 1951.

570. TIMM, A., *Die Waldnützung in Nordwestdeutschland im Spiegel der Weistümer. Einleitende Untersuchungen über die Umgestaltung des Stadt-Land-Verhältnisses im Spätmittelalter*, Cologne, 1960.

2. POPULATION

571. ARNOULD, M. A., *Les dénombrements de foyers dans le comté de Hainaut* (*XIVe-XVe siècles*) (Comm. roy. d'Hist.), Brussels, 1956.

572. DUBLED, H., 'Conséquences économiques et sociales des mortalités du XIV siècle, essentiellement en Alsace' in *Revue d'histoire économique et sociale*, 1959.

573. FÉVRIER, P. A., 'La population de la Provence à la fin du XVe siècle d'après l'enquête de 1471' in *Provence historique*, 1956.

574. FOURQUIN, G., 'La population dans la région parisienne aux environs de 1328' in *Le Moyen Age*, 1956.

575. FUJIWARA, H., 'Population and the manors in England in the XIV century' (in Japanese) in *Shigaku Zasshi*, LIX, 1950.

576. GEREMEK, B., 'The Problem of Labour in Prussia in the First Half of the XV century' (in Polish) in *Przeglad Historyczny*, 1957.

577. GLENISSON, J., 'Essai de recensement et d'interprétation des sources de l'histoire démographique en France au XIVe siècle', *XIe Congrès international des sciences historiques, Stockholm, 1960. Résumés des communications*, Stockholm, 1960.

578. GUENÉE, B., 'La géographie administrative de la France à la fin du moyen age: élections et bailliages' in *Le Moyen Age*, 1951.

579. HELLEINER, K., 'Europas Bevölkerung und Wirtschaft im späteren Mittelalter' in *Mitteilungen des Instituts für Österreichische Geschichtsforschung*, 1954.

580. —— 'Population Movements and Agrarian Depression in the Later Middle Ages' in *Canadian Journal of Economic and Political Sciences*, XV, 1959.

581. MEINSMA, K. O., *De Zwarte Dood, 1347-1352*, Zutphen, 1924.

582. POSTAN, M., 'Some Economic Evidence of Declining Population in the later Middle Ages' in *Economic History Review*, 2nd ser., II, 1950.

583. RENOUARD, Y., 'Conséquences et intérêt démographique de la peste noire de 1348' in *Population*, 1948.

584. WERVEKE, H. VAN, 'De Zwarte Dood in de Zuidelijke Nederlanden, 1349-1351' in *Mededelingen Koniklike Vlaamse Akademie voor Wetensch (Lettres)*, 1950.

3. THE RETREAT OF CULTIVATION

585. ABEL, W., 'Wüstungen und Preisfall im spätmittelalterlichen Europa' in *Jahrbuch für Nationalökonomie und Statistik*, 1953.

586. BERESFORD, M. W., 'The Lost Villages of Medieval England' in *Geographical Journal*, 1951.

587. —— *The Lost Villages of England*, London, 1954.

588. BOUTRUCHE, R., *La dévastation des campagnes pendant la guerre de Cent Ans et la reconstruction agricole de la France* (publ. de la Faculté des Lettres de l'Université de Strasbourg, Vol. 106: Mélanges, II), Strasbourg, 1945.

589. FRÖLICH, K., 'Rechtsgeschichte und Wüstungskunde' in *Zeitschrift für Rechtsgeschichte*, 1944.

590. HILTON, R. H., 'Old Enclosure in the West Midlands: a hypothesis about their Late Medieval Developments' in *Annales de l'Est, Mémoire No. 21*, Nancy, 1959.

591. HURST, J. G., 'Deserted Medieval Villages' in *Amateur Historian*, II, 1955.

592. JAEGER, H., 'Zur Entstehung der heutigen Forsten in Deutschland' in *Bericht zur Deutschen Landeskunde*, 1954.

593. —— 'Die Ausdehnung der Wälder in Mitteleuropa über offenes Siedlungsland' in *Annales de l'Est, Mémoire No. 21*, Nancy, 1959.

594. KELTER, E., 'Das Deutsche Wirtschaftsleben des 14. und 15. Jahrhunderts im Schatten der Pestepidemie' in *Jahrbuch für Nationalökonomie und Statistik*, 1953.

595. KLEIN, H., 'Das Grosse Sterben von 1348-1349 und seine Auswirkung auf die Besiedlung der Ostalpenländer' in *Mitteilungen der Gesellschaft für Salzburger Landeskunde*, 1960.

596. KRENZLIN, A., 'Das Wüstungsproblem im Lichte Ostdeutscher Siedlungsforschung' in *Zeitschrift für Agrargeschichte und Agrarsoziologie*, 1959.

Bibliography

597. MORTENSEN, H., *Zur Deutschen Wüstungsforschung*, Göttingen. 1944.
598. —— 'Neue Beobachtungen über Wüstungsbannfluren und ihre Bedeutung für die Mittelalterliche Kulturlandschaft' in *Berichte zur Deutschen Landeskunde*, 1951.
599. —— 'Die Mittelalterliche Deutsche Kulturlandschaft und ihre Verhältnis zur Gegenwart' in *Vierteljahrschrift für Sozial- und Wirtschaftsgeschichte*, 1958.
600. —— 'Probleme der Mittelalterlichen Kulturlandschaft' in *Berichte zur Deutschen Landeskunde*, 1958.
601. POHLENDT, H., *Die Verbreitung der Mittelalterlichen Wüstungen in Deutschland*, Göttingen, 1950.
602. RICHTER, G., 'Klimaschwangungen und Wüstungsvorgange in Mittelalter' in *Petermanns Mitteilungen*, 1952.
603. SCHARLAU, K., 'Neue Probleme der Wüstungsforschung' in *Berichte zur Deutschen Landeskunde*, 1956.
604. ZIENTARA, B., *Agrarian Crisis in Uckermark in the XIVth Century* (in Polish), Warsaw, 1961.

4. FAMINES

605. CAPRA, P., 'Au sujet des famines en Aquitaine au XIVe siècle' in *Revue historique de Bordeaux*, 1955.
606. CURSCHMANN, F., *Hungersnöte im Mittelalter*, Leipzig, 1900.
607. FOSSIER, R. & L., 'Aspects de la crise frumentaire en Artois et en Flandre gallicante au XIVe siècle' in *Recueil de travaux offert à Cl. Brunel*, I, Paris, 1955.
608. LARENAUDIE, M.-J., 'Les famines en Languedoc aux XIVe et XVe siècles' in *Annales du Midi*, 1952.
609. LUCAS, H. S., 'The Great European Famine of 1315, 1316 and 1317' in *Speculum*, 1930.
610. WERVEKE, H. VAN, 'La famine de l'an 1316 en Flandre et dans les régions voisines' in *Revue du Nord*, 1959.

5. RURAL PRODUCTION

611. CIPOLLA, C. M., 'Per la storia delle terre della "bassa" Lombarda' in *Studi in onore di Armando Sapori*, I, Milan, 1957.
612. DEBIEN, G., *En Haut-Poitou, Défricheurs au travail, XVe-XVIIIe siècles* (Cahiers des Annales, No. 7), Paris, 1952.
613. FÉVRIER, P.-A., 'Quelques aspects de la vie agricole en Basse-Provence à la fin du Moyen Age' in *Bulletin philologique et historique*, 1959.
614. —— 'La basse vallée de l'Argens, Quelques aspects de la vie économique de la Provence orientale aux XVe et XVIe siècles' in *Provence historique*, 1959.
615. LATOUCHE, R., *La vie en Bas-Quercy du quatorzième au dixhuitième siècle*, Toulouse, 1923.
616. PAYNE, R. C., 'Agrarian conditions on the Wiltshire Estates of the Duchy of Lancaster, the Lords Hungerford and Bishopric of Winchester in the Thirteenth, Fourteenth and Fifteenth Centuries' in *Bulletin of the Institute of Historical Research*, XVIII, 1940.
617. SICARD, G., 'Les techniques rurales en pays toulousain aux XIVe et XVe siècles d'après les contrats de métayage' in *Annales du Midi*, 1959.

618. SLICHER VAN BATH, B. H., 'The Rise of Intensive Husbandry in the Low Countries in *Britain and the Netherlands*, 1960.

619. TUCOO-CHALA, P., 'Productions et commerce en Béarn au XIVe siècle' in *Annales du Midi*, 1955.

620. —— 'Une charte sur la basse vallée d'Ossau au bas Moyen Age' in *Annales du Midi*, 1959.

B. Social Movements and the Condition of the Peasantry

621. ASTON, M. E., 'Lollardy and Sedition, 1381-1431' in *Past and Present*, 1960.

622. AUBENAS, R., 'Le servage à castellane au XIVe siècle' in *Revue historique de droit français et étranger*, 1937.

623. BAVOUX, R., 'Les particularités de la mainmorte dans la terre de Luxeuil' in *Mémoire de la Société pour l'histoire du droit . . . des anciens pays bourguignons . . .*, 13, 1950-1951.

624. BOSSUAT, A., 'Le servage en Nivernais au XVe siècle, d'après les registres du Parlement' in *Bibliothèque de l'École des Chartes*, 1959.

625. BOUYSSON, L., 'La condition juridique du foyer rural en Haute-Auvergne au XVe siècle' in *Revue historique de droit français et étranger*, 1942.

626. CELLIER, L., 'Les mœurs rurales au XVe siècle d'après les lettres de rémission' in *Bulletin philologique et historique*, 1959.

627. CHOMEL, V., 'Communautés rurales et *casanae* lombardes en Dauphiné (1346)' in *Bulletin philologique et historique*, 1953.

628. DUNKEN, G., 'Der Aufstand des Fra Dolcino zu Beginn des 14. Jahrhundert' in *Wissenschaftliche Annalen*, VI, 1957.

629. FALLETI, L., 'Le contraste juridique entre Bourgogne et Savoie au sujet de la mainmorte seigneuriale' in *Mémoires de la Société pour l'histoire du droit . . . des anciens pays bourguignons . . .*, 13, 1950-1951; 14, 1952.

630. FLAMMERMONT, J., 'La Jacquerie en Beauvaisis' in *Revue historique*, 1879.

631. GÉNICOT, L., 'Le servage dans les chartes-lois de Guillaume II, comte de Namur: 1391-1418' in *Revue belge de philologie et d'histoire*, 1945.

632. GONON, M., *Les institutions et la société en Forez au XIVe siècle d'après les testaments*, Paris, 1960.

633. —— *La vie familiale en Forez au XIVe siècle et son vocabulaire d'après les testaments*, Paris, 1960.

634. GRAUS, F., 'Au bas moyen âge: pauvres des villes et pauvres des campagnes' in *Annales E.S.C.*, 1961.

635. HILTON, R. H., 'Peasant Movements in England before 1381' in *Economic History Review*, 2nd ser., II, 1949.

636. —— & FAGAN, H., *The English Rising of 1381*, London, 1954.

637. HUBRECHT, G., 'Le servage dans le Sud-Ouest de la France, plus particulièrement à la fin du Moyen Age' in *Études d'histoire du droit privé offertes à Pierre Petot*, Paris, 1959.

638. HUGENHOLZ, F., *Drie boerenopstanden uit de vertionde eeuw*, Haarlem, 1949.

639. JUGLAS, J., 'La vie rurale dans le village de Jonquières, 1308-1418' in *Provence historique*, 1958.

640. LINDSAY, P., & GROVES, R., *The Peasants' Revolt of 1381*, London, 1950.

641. LUC, P., *Vie rurale et pratique juridique en Béarn aux XIVe et XVe siècles*, Toulouse, 1943.

642. MERCIER, H., 'Étude sur la mainmorte dans le pays de Montbéliard' in *Mémoire de la Société pour l'histoire du droit . . . des anciens pays bourguigons . . .*, 13, 1950-1951.

643. PATRONE, A. M., *Le casane astigiane in Savoia*, Turin, 1959.

644. PIRENNE, H., *Le soulèvement de la Flandre maritime de 1323-1328*, Brussels, 1900.

645. PROST, B., *Inventaires mobiliers et extrait des comptes des ducs de Bourgogne de la maison de Valois, 1363-1477*, 2 vols., Paris, 1912-1913.

646. RICHARDOT, H., 'Note sur les roturiers possesseurs de fiefs nobles' in *Mélanges A. Dumas* (Annales de la faculté de Droit d'Aix), 1950.

647. SAMARAN, C., 'Note sur la dépendance personnelle en Haute-Provence au XIVe siècle' in *Annales du Midi*, 1957.

648. SAPRYKIN, J. M., 'The Levellers and the Class Struggle for Land' (in Russian) in *Vestnik Mosk. Univ.*, 1951.

649. SKASKIN, S. D., *Le condizioni storiche della rivolta di Dolcino* (Rapporti della delegazione sovietica al Xe Congresso Internazionale di scienze storiche a Roma), Moscow, 1955.

650. TESSIER, G., 'Vente d'hommes de corps et aveu consécutif de servitude (16 juillet 1340)' in *Études d'histoire du droit privé offertes à Pierre Petot*, Paris, 1959.

651. TOUBERT, P., 'Les statuts communaux et l'histoire des campagnes lombardes au XIVe siècle' in *Bulletin d'archéologie et d'histoire publié par l'École française de Rome*, 1960.

652. VIGNIER, F., 'L'exercice de la mainmorte par les ducs de Bourgogne dans le nord du bailliage de la Montagne au XIVe siècle' in *Mémoire de la société pour l'histoire du droit . . . des anciens pays bourguignons . . .*, 16, 1954.

653. WILKINSON, B., 'The Peasants' Revolt of 1381' in *Speculum*, 1940.

C. The Manor

654. BEAN, J. M. W., *The Estates of the Percy Family, 1416-1537*, Oxford, 1958.

655. CHOMEL, V., 'La perception des cens en argent dans les seigneuries du Haut-Dauphiné aux XIVe et XVe siècles' in *Recueil de Travaux offerts à Cl. Brunel*, Paris, 1955.

656. DAVISO DI CHARVENSOD, M., 'Coltivazione e reddito della vigna a Rivoli nel secolo 14' in *Bolletino storico-bibliografico subalpino*, 1950.

657. DELATOUCHE, R., 'Le rouleau de la Dame d'Olivet' in *Bulletin de la Commission historique de la Mayenne*, 1956.

658. DONNELLY, J. S., 'Changes in the Grange Economy of English and Welsh Cistercian Abbeys (1300-1540)' in *Traditio*, 1954.

659. DU BOULAY, F. R. H., 'The Pagham Estates of the Archbishops of Canterbury during the Fifteenth Century' in *History*, 1953.

660. DUBY, G., 'Le grand domaine de la fin du Moyen Age en France' in *Première conférence internationale d'histoire économique, Stockholm, 1960*, Paris, 1960.

661. FILHOL, R., 'Chartes poitevines relatives aux droits seigneuriaux' in *Études d'histoire du droit privé offertes à Pierre Petot*, Paris, 1959.

662. GARRIGOUX, A., 'Chasse et pêche en Haute-Auvergne au XIVe siècle. Transaction entre le seigneur Louis de Dieuse et ses tenanciers au sujet de la chasse et de la pêche' in *Revue historique de droit français et étranger*, 1939.

663. HAENENS, A. D', 'La crise des abbayes bénédictines au bas Moyen Age. Saint-Martin de Tournai, 1290-1350' in *Le Moyen Age*, 1959.

664. —— 'Le budget de Saint-Martin de Tournai, 1331-1348' in *Revue belge de philologie et d'histoire*, 1959.

665. —— 'Les gardiens de Saint-Martin de Tournai de 1309 à 1348' in *Revue d'histoire ecclésiastique*, 1959.

666. —— *L'abbaye de Saint-Martin de Tournai de 1290 à 1350. Origines, évolution et dénouement d'une crise*, Louvain, 1961.

667. HILTON, R. H., *The Economic Development of some Leicestershire Estates in the 14th and 15th Centuries* (Oxford Historical Series), London, 1947.

668. —— 'A Study in the Pre-history of English Enclosure in the Fifteenth Century' in *Studi in onore di Armando Sapori*, I, Milan, 1957.

669. —— (ed.), *The Stoneleigh Leger Book*, Oxford, 1860.

670. HOLMES, G. A., *The Estates of the Higher Nobility in Fourteenth Century England* (Cambridge Studies in Economic History), Cambridge, 1957.

671. JANSEN, H. P., *Landbouw pacht in Brabant in de veertiende en vijftiende eeuw*, Assen, 1955.

672. JEANCARD, R., *Les seigneuries d'outre'Siagne du XIVe au XVIe siècle*, Cannes, 1952.

673. JONES, P. J., 'Le finanze della badia cisterciense di Settimo nel 14. secolo' in *Rivista di storia della chiesa in Italia*, 1956.

674. LEWIS, E. A., 'The Court Rolls of the Manor of Broniarth, 1429-1464' in *Bulletin of Celtic Studies*, XI, I.

675. MARTENS, M., 'L'administration du domaine ducal en Brabant au Moyen Age (1250-1406)' in *Mémoires de l'Académie Royale*, Brussels, 1954.

676. MARTIN-LORBER, O., 'L'exploitation d'une grange cistercienne à la fin du XIVe siècle et au début du XVe' in *Annales de Bourgogne*, 1957.

677. MERLE, L., *La métairie et l'évolution agraire de la Gâtine poitevine, de la fin du Moyen Age à la Révolution*, Paris, 1958.

678. MIROT, L. & A., *La seigneurie de Saint-Vérain-des-Bois, des origines à sa réunion au comté de Nevers, 1480*, La Charité-sur-Loire, 1943.

679. MOREL, P., 'Les baux à cens avec réduction des redevances en Limousin après la guerre de Cent Ans' in *Revue historique de droit français et étranger*, 1939.

680. PERROY, E., 'Wage Labour in France in the Later Middle Ages' in *Economic History Review*, 2nd ser., VIII, 1955.

681. PLAISSE, A., *La baronnie du Neufbourg, Essai d'histoire agraire, économique et sociale*, Paris, 1961.

682. PUTNAM, B., 'Records of the Courts of Common Law, especially of the Sessions of the Justices of Peace. Sources for the economic history of England in the XIVth and XVth Centuries' in *Proceedings of the American Philosophical Society*, XCI, 3, 1947.

683. ROSS, C. D. N. & PUGH, T. B., 'Materials for the Study of Baronial Income in Fifteenth-Century England' In *Economic History Review*, 2nd ser., VI, 1953.

684. SALZMAN, L. F., 'The Property of the Earl of Arundel, 1397' in *Sussex Archeological Collection*, 1953.

685. SICARD, G., *Le métayage dans le Midi toulousain à la fin du Moyen Age*, Toulouse, 1956.

686. THIELEN, P. G. (ed), *Das Grosse Zinsbuch des Deutschen Ritterordens, 1414-1438*, Marburg, 1958.

687. TOMS, E., 'The Manors of Chertsey Abbey under Abbot John de Rutherwy (1307-1347)' in *Bulletin of the Institute of Historical Research*, XIV, 1937.

688. TUCOO-CHALA, P., *Gaston Fébus et la vicomté de Béarn, 1343-1391*, Bordeaux, 1959.

689. WOLFE, B. P., 'The Management of English Royal Estates under the Yorkist Kings' in *English Historical Review*, 1955.
690. WOLFF, P. H., 'La fortune foncière d'un seigneur toulousain au milieu du XVe siècle' in *Annales du Midi*, 1958.

D. *Towns and Countryside*

691. BARATIER, E., 'Le notaire Jean Barral, marchand de Riez au début du XVe siècle' in *Provence historique*, 1957.
692. BORLANDI, F., 'Futainiers et futaines dans l'Italie du Moyen Age' in *Hommage à Lucien Febvre*, II, Paris, 1953.
693. BOSSUAT, A., *Le bailliage royal de Montferrand (1425-1556)*, Paris, 1957.
694. CARUS-WILSON, E., 'Trends of the export of English Woollens in the XIVth Century' in *Economic History Review*, 1950.
695. —— 'Evidence of Industrial Growth on some Fifteenth-Century Manors' in *Economic History Review*, 2nd ser., XII, 1959.
696. COORNAERT, E., 'Draperies rurales, draperies urbaines' in *Revue belge de philologie et d'histoire*, 1950.
697. CRAEYBECKX, J., *Un grand commerce d'importation. Les vins de France aux ancient Pays-Bas (XIIIe-XVIe siècle)*, Paris, 1958.
698. FÉDOU, R., 'Une famille aux XIVe et XVe siècles, les Jossard de Lyon' in *Annales E.S.C.*, 1958.
699. GEREMEK, B., 'Problems concerning the relations between town and country in Teutonic Prussia during the first half of the XVth century' (in Polish) in *Przeglad Historyczny*, 1956.
700. HEERS, J. (ed.), *Le livre de comptes de Giovanni Piccamiglio, homme d'affaires génois (1456-1459)*, Paris, 1959.
701. HOUTTE, H. VAN, *Documents pour servir à l'histoire des prix de 1381 à 1794*, Brussels, 1902.
702. KERLING, N. J. M., *Commercial Relations of Holland and Zeeland with England from the late 13th century to the close of the Middle Ages*, Leyden, 1954.
703. MAŁOWIST, M., 'Les produits des pays de la Baltique dans le commerce international au XVIe siècle' in *Revue du Nord*, 1960.
704. —— 'A Certain Trade Technique in the Baltic Countries in the XVth-XVIIth Centuries' in *Poland at the XIth International Congress of Historical Sciences at Stockholm*, 1960.
705. NUBLING, E., *Ulms Baumwollweberei im Mittelalter*, Leipzig, 1890.
706. PETTINO, A., *Lo zafferano nell'economia del medio evo* (Pubblicazione della Facoltà di economia e commercio dell'Universita di Catania, Seria I, vol. I), Catania, 1950-1951.
707. REY, M., 'Un témoignage inédit sur l'hôtel du roi: le journal de la dépense du premier semestre 1417' in *Annales Littéraires de l'Université de Besançon*, 1955.
708. VERRIEST, L., 'Étude d'un contrat privé de droit médiéval: le bail à cheptel vif à Tournai (1297-1334) in *Revue du Nord*, 1946.
709. WOLFF, P., *Commerces et marchands de Toulouse (vers 1350 - vers 1450)*, Paris, 1954.
710. —— *Les 'estimes' toulousaines des XIVe et XVe siècles*, Toulouse, 1956.
711. YVER, J., 'Évolution de quelques prix en Normandie aux XIVe et XVe siècles' in *Revue historique de droit français et étranger*, 1958.

Index

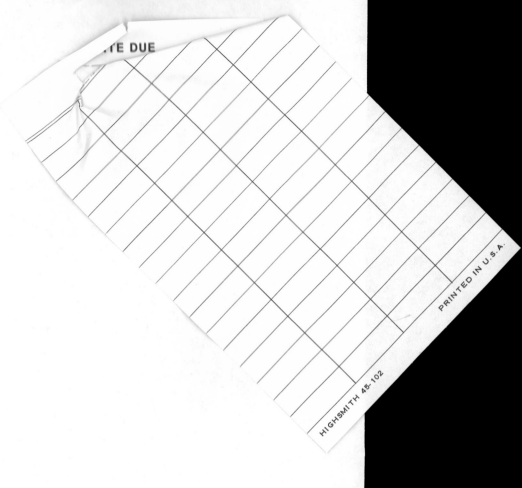